Cutlip & Center's

Effective Public Relations

TENTH EDITION

Glen M. Broom, Ph.D.

Professor Emeritus, School of Journalism and Media Studies

San Diego State University

Adjunct Professor, Queensland University of Technology

Brisbane, Australia

Prentice Hall
Upper Saddle River, NJ 07458

Library of Congress Cataloging-in-Publication Data

Broom, Glen M.

  Effective public relations / Glen M. Broom, Scott M. Cutlip, Allen H. Center.—10th ed.
    p. cm.
  Includes bibliographical references and index.
  Prev. eds. entered under 2nd named author.
  ISBN-13: 978-0-13-602969-4 (casebound)
  ISBN-10: 0-13-602969-8 (casebound)
  1. Public relations. I. Cutlip, Scott M. II. Center, Allen H. III. Cutlip, Scott M.
  Effective public relations. IV. Title.
  HM1221.C88 2009   2008028579

AVP/Executive Editor: Melissa Sabella
Editorial Director: Sally Yagan
Editorial Assistant: Karin Williams
Product Development Manager: Ashley Santora
Senior Marketing Manager: Anne Fahlgren
Marketing Assistant: Susan Osterlitz
Permissions Project Manager: Charles Morris
Senior Managing Editor: Judy Leale
Production Project Manager: Clara Bartunek
Senior Operations Specialist: Arnold Vila
Creative Director: Christy Mahon
Senior Art Director: Janet Slowik
Art Director: Steven Frim
Designer: Ilze Lemesis
Cover Designer: Ray Cruz
Cover Photos: Aircraft Carrier—courtesy of Glen M. Broom; Woman writing on clear
board—courtesy of Tracey Jones; "You can help" poster—courtesy of Library of Congress, Washington DC;
Chef—courtesy of Debra Lynn Ross.
Manager, Rights and Permissions: Zina Arabia
Manager, Visual Research: Beth Brenzel
Image Permission Coordinator: Vickie Menanteaux
Manager, Cover Visual Research & Permissions: Karen Sanatar
Composition: Aptara
Full-Service Project Management: Thistle Hill Publishing Services, LLC
Printer/Binder: Edwards Brothers
Typeface: 10/12, Times Ten Roman

Credits and acknowledgments borrowed from other sources and reproduced, with permission, in this textbook
appear on appropriate page within text. All photos supplied by Glen M. Broom, unless otherwise indicated.

Pearson Education Ltd., London
Pearson Education Singapore, Pte. Ltd
Pearson Education, Canada, Inc.
Pearson Education–Japan
Pearson Education Australia PTY, Limited

Pearson Education North Asia, Ltd., Hong Kong
Pearson Educación de Mexico, S.A. de C.V.
Pearson Education Malaysia, Pte. Ltd
Pearson Education Upper Saddle River, New Jersey

Prentice Hall
is an imprint of

10 9 8 7 6 5 4 3 2 1
ISBN-13: 978-0-13-602969-4
ISBN-10:   0-13-602969-8

In memory

of

Allen H. Center,

APR, Fellow (1912–2005)

A true benefactor, pathfinder,
and leader of public relations practice
and education.

Brief Contents

Contents

Preface

After all, it was Cutlip and Center, as much as anyone, who gave those of us who strayed or wandered into the profession from journalism and other professional pursuits, a sense of substance and legitimacy about practicing our adopted craft.

—Stephen H. Baer

"Cutlip, Center, and Broom" . . . [is] the standard against which all basic public relations textbooks are measured.

—Donald K. Wright

Beginning with the first edition in 1952, *Effective Public Relations* (*EPR*) has introduced the theory and principles of public relations, schooled its practitioners, and served as a reference for those in the calling worldwide. This tenth edition completes **six decades** of advancing public relations toward professional status.

Effective Public Relations is the book most frequently used by those preparing for accreditation exams, most frequently cited in public relations literature, most widely used worldwide in English, and most translated for study. You are in good company when you use this book in preparation for an exciting and rewarding career.

Cutlip and Center

Students and practitioners alike often refer to *Effective Public Relations* simply as "Cutlip and Center," using the original authors' names instead of the actual title. **Scott M. Cutlip** and **Allen H. Center** created the book that made public relations education an academic area of study on university and college campuses. Many of their ideas and ambitions in the early editions still serve as beacons leading public relations education and practice.

EPR is known to this day as "the bible of public relations." "After all," as one long-time counselor and consultant said, "it was Cutlip and Center, as much as anyone, who gave those of us who strayed or wandered into the profession from journalism and other professional pursuits, a sense of substance and legitimacy about practicing our adopted craft."[i]

Because the body of knowledge in public relations has outgrown the bounds of a single textbook, no longer can *EPR* serve as a comprehensive encyclopedia of public relations. Public relations education and professional practice extend well beyond the limits of a single book or course. Yet *EPR* remains the basic reference for the field worldwide and it will serve you well in your career. As one reviewer said, "'Cutlip, Center, and Broom' . . . [is] the standard against which all basic public relations textbooks are measured."[ii]

This tenth edition has Cutlip's and Center's names above the title for the first time. Their contribution to the field and this work led Pearson and me to honor them in this way. Scott Cutlip died in 2000 and Allen Center in 2005, but their influence and contributions remain intact in *Cutlip and Center's Effective Public Relations*, Tenth Edition. Learn more about Cutlip and Center's contribution to the field of public relations in Chapter 4, pages 109 and 110.)

Contents

What will you learn from the tenth edition of *EPR?*

- You will learn basic concepts necessary to understand what public relations is and is not, and how it evolved to today's practice.
- You will learn the values, theory, principles, and management process that guide the practice.
- You will learn updated information and read key examples to help you understand contemporary public relations practice in a variety of settings.

Each chapter begins with a study guide that outlines specific learning objectives to help you focus your reading and master the material.

The tenth edition comprises four parts:

- Part I (Chapters 1–4)—Concept, Practitioners, Context, and Historical Origins
- Part II (Chapters 5–10)—Foundations
- Part III (Chapters 11–14)—Management Process
- Part IV (Chapters 15–17)—The Practice

In short, the book covers a broad range of public relations theory and practice. However, *EPR* does not trivialize public relations by presenting brief, oversimplified case studies. Rather, *EPR* gives you a foundation for subsequent courses and books devoted to developing, implementing, and evaluating programs.

Following is an annotated description of each of the chapters:

Chapter 1, "Introduction to Contemporary Public Relations," introduces the concept of contemporary public relations and defines terms often confused with the practice. Most importantly, the chapter introduces for the first time "core axioms" that spell out the principles and values central to contemporary practice (Exhibit 1.4, page 26).

Chapter 2, "Practitioners of Public Relations," presents recent data on employment, salary, diversity, population demographic changes, and the feminization of the field. Three new "Day in the Life of . . ." exhibits introduce you to what practitioners do at work in nonprofits, corporate departments, and public relations firms.

Chapter 3, "Organizational Settings," gives public relations work context by explaining how organizational settings and other factors affect the role of practitioners and outlines how public relations often begins and is integrated into organizations. The chapter also outlines the pluses and minuses of internal departments and outside counsel, and and presents data on major national and international firms and their councils.

Chapter 4, "Historical Origins," describes how the practice evolved, identifies historical leaders who led the evolution, and traces the origins of current practice. This edition features Harold Burson, Rachel Carson, Allen Center, Scott Cutlip, Daniel Edelman, Tim Traverse-Healy, Inez Kaiser, Dr. Martin Luther King Jr., Ralph Nader, and Betsy Plank in discussions of recent public relations history.

Chapter 5, "Professionalism and Ethics," introduces the professional and ethical principles that underpin the practice. Chapter exhibits document the development of public relations internationally, particularly in Australia, Sweden, and China, as well as with the Global Alliance for Public Relations and Communication Management.

Chapter 6, "Legal Considerations," summarizes the legal considerations so vital to public relations practice. Included in this chapter are guidelines for copyright law and permission requirements, and exhibits explaining the hierarchy of the law and campaign finance reform. In response to a series of corporate scandals and bank-ruptcies, the chapter discusses new federal legislation (the Sarbanes–Oxley Act of 2002) and Securities and Exchange Commission and New York Stock Exchange rules that increase transparency and timeliness, hold top management accountable for financial reports, and reduce insiders' power to set their own compensation and to take unfair advantage when trading stock.

Chapter 7, "Theoretical Underpinnings: Adjustment and Adaptation," outlines a theoretical foundation for the practice—systems theory. The chapter distinguishes between an open system approach and the reactive, closed system approach that all too often characterizes the practice. The ink-squirting cuttlefish serves as a memo-rable metaphor for the routine, publicity-dominated practice.

Chapter 8, "Communication and Public Opinion," presents communication and public opinion theories and models essential to understanding the function of pub-lic relations in organizations and society. Within a systems theory framework, the chapter also focuses on the changes in what people inside and outside the organiza-tion know, feel, and do that affect organization-public relationships and the public opinion climate.

Chapter 9, "Internal Relations and Employee Communication," discusses orga-nizational culture and the application of systems theory to employee communica-tion programs. The chapter also covers traditional and new media used in internal communication.

Chapter 10, "External Media and Media Relations," discusses the workhorse medium in public relations—newspapers—and the other traditional and new media for communicating program messages to external publics. The chapter also covers new uses of old media and how new media—blogs, e-mail, social media, and so on—have changed organization-public interaction in the digital virtual world.

Chapter 11, "Step One: Defining Public Relations Problems," introduces the benchmark model for applying theory to practice in the "four-step public relations process." The model demonstrates the logic of using research to "benchmark" the beginning of the program by defining problems and setting program goals. (The model is repeated in Chapter 14 to illustrate the three phases of evaluation and to close the loop on benchmarking.) Chapter 11 also describes new technology used to gather data for detecting, exploring, and describing public relations problems.

Chapter 12, "Step Two: Planning and Programming," builds a rationale for strategic planning, using many examples to illustrate key concepts. The chapter ex-pands the traditional four-step public relations process presented in Chapter 11 into a detailed 10-step strategic planning outline. The steps include how to identify publics and how to write objectives for each target public, and how to apply working theory to developing program strategy.

Chapter 13, "Step Three: Taking Action and Communicating," illustrates major tactics for implementing program strategy. The chapter emphasizes the necessity of taking action, particularly corrective action, in addition to communication. Actual examples from practice illustrate the challenges and barriers to framing and dissem-inating effective messages.

Chapter 14, "Step Four: Evaluating the Program," outlines how to track program progress and assess impact. The discussion of the three phases of program evaluation—preparation, implementation, and impact—includes numerous models and examples to illustrate and clarify evaluation steps. The chapter also covers practical research methods used in program evaluation, including a discussion of how to use content analysis for tracking media placement effectiveness in program implementation.

Chapter 15, "Business and Industry Public Relations," outlines the role of public relations in corporate social responsibility, corporate philanthropy, and corporate finance. The chapter reflects the growing interest in corporate governance following almost two decades of corporate scandals and financial malfeasance exposés. The discussion also addresses globalization and its impact on the practice in corporations and global public relations firms.

Chapter 16, "Government and Public Affairs," covers the role of media and media relations in governmental public affairs, including the journalist embed program implemented during Operation Iraqi Freedom. The chapter discusses public relations practice in local, regional, and national governments in the United States and other nations. Additionally, the chapter explains how technology is changing public relations in government.

Chapter 17, "Nonprofits, Trade Associations, and Nongovernmental Organizations," covers public relations practice in a broad range of "Third Sector" and other not-for-profit organizations. The chapter discusses how tight government budgets have forced private groups to take on many formerly public tasks, thus creating greater need for volunteerism and philanthropy, and an expanded role for public relations in securing both. Of particular importance is a discussion of the role of public relations in and the impact of global nongovernmental organizations (NGOs).

Contributors

My former students formed a pipeline of new information and examples for the tenth edition, for which I am grateful and in their debt. **Ronald Anderson**, Associate Professor, College of Communication, University of Texas at Austin, suggested changes in the four-step process chapters, but those contributions are not credited in the chapters. However, the following former students are identified with their contributions: **Erin Barrier**, Senior Account Executive, GolinHarris, Los Angeles; **Mark S. Cox**, APR, Director of Public Communications, City of Chesapeake, Va.; **Greg Davy**, Communications Specialist, Williamsburg–James City County Public Schools, Williamsburg, Va.; **Yelena Durmashkin**, Senior Coordinator, Corporate Communications, Qualcomm, Inc., San Diego; **Rachel Kay**, Principal, Rachel Kay Public Relations, San Diego; **MaryLee Sachs**, Chairman, Hill & Knowlton USA, New York; **Jim McBride**, president of McBride Communications and lecturer, School of Journalism and Media Studies, San Diego State University; and **Lieutenant Commander Wendy L. Snyder**, APR, Public Affairs Officer, U.S. Navy Region Europe, Naples, Italy.

Other colleagues in the practice contributed important new material to the tenth edition. **Bill Furlow**, Partner, Furlow Communications, Natchez, Miss.; **Tracy Jones**, FPRIA, Managing Director Creative Territory Pty. Ltd., Darwin, Australia; **George Lennon**, Director for Public Affairs, National Science Foundation, Arlington, Va.; **Debra Lynn Ross**, Director, Corporate Communications, Consorta, Inc., Schaumburg, Ill.; and **Susan D. Simmons**, Development Associate, Dress for Success Worldwide, New York.

Colleagues in the academy once again made significant contributions new to the tenth edition and are credited in the text. **Rochelle L. Ford**, Ph.D., APR, Associate Dean, Research and Academic Affairs, John H. Johnson School of Communications, Howard University, Washington, D.C.; **Martin Kruming**, J.D., private practice lawyer and lecturer, School of Journalism and Media Studies, San Diego State University; **Larsåke Larsson**, Professor, Örebro University, Sweden; **Suman Lee**, Ph.D., Assistant Professor, Greenlee School of Journalism and Communication, Iowa State University, Ames; **Jim Macnamara**, Ph.D., FPRIA, Professor, Public Communication, and Director, Australian Centre for Public Communication, University of Technology Sydney; **Ming Anxiang**, Professor, Institute of Journalism & Communication, Chinese Academy of Social Sciences, Beijing; **Juan-Carlos Molleda**, Ph.D., Associate Professor, College of Journalism and Communications, University of Florida, Gainesville; **Bey-Ling Sha**, Ph.D., APR, Associate Professor, School of Journalism and Media Studies, San Diego State University. In addition, two colleagues gave me useful feedback and guidance, but their contributions were embedded in the revision without specific attribution: **David Dozier**, Ph.D., Professor, and **Kenn Ulrich**, APR, PRSA Fellow, Lecturer, School of Journalism and Media Studies, San Diego State University.

Alas, I cannot list all the former students and colleagues in education and in the practice who contributed to this edition. They will recognize how their feedback changed and improved the book. Many responded to my requests for help, while others cited in the book contributed through their own publications. I could not have revised the book for the tenth edition without the support, suggestions, and critical analysis of such friends and colleagues. I thank them all and hope that you will be as generous with your feedback and suggestions as you study this tenth edition.

Pearson Prentice Hall editors provided able assistance and firm direction in getting the tenth edition produced: **Ashley Santora**, Product Development Manager, Business and Economic Publishing, and **Clara Bartunek**, Project Manager, guided the process from manuscript to an actual book. **Angela Williams Urquhart**, Editorial Director, Thistle Hill Publishing Services, LLC, Fort Worth, Texas, made sure that the words you are reading made sense and were spelled correctly. I appreciated their help in producing the tenth edition and relieve them of any responsibility for typos and wording problems created by yours truly.

I am also grateful for the love and support of my wife, **Betty**, professor emerita of nursing at San Diego State University, who taught students how to help families bring healthy babies into the world. As I worked on this revision, she was teaching her last semester before retiring. We look forward to more travel and house remodeling projects before I start work on the eleventh edition.

I hope this book helps you prepare for the challenging and rewarding calling of building organization-public relationships in the digital age. Best wishes for success in that mission.

Glen M. Broom, Ph.D.

Notes

[i]Stephen H. Baer, Fellow, PRSA, writing in a book review published in *Public Relations Review* 18, No. 4 (Winter 1992): 392.

[ii]Donald K. Wright, "Review of Public Relations Literature: Basic Textbooks," *Public Relations Review* 22, no. 4 (Winter 1996): 380.

Student Supplements

Companion Website

This text's Companion Website at **www.pearsonhighered.com/broom** contains valuable resources for students including access to an online Study Guide.

CourseSmart eTextbooks Online

Developed for students looking to save money on required or recommended textbooks, CourseSmart eTextbooks Online saves students money compared to the suggested list price of the print text. Students simply select their eText by title or author and purchase immediate access to the content for the duration of the course using any major credit card. With a CourseSmart eText, students can search for specific keywords or page numbers, make notes online, print out reading assignments that incorporate lecture notes, and bookmark important passages for later review. For more information, or to purchase a CourseSmart eTextbook, visit **www.coursesmart.com.**

Cutlip & Center's

Effective
Public Relations

Part 1

Concept, Practitioners, Context, and Origins

chapters

Introduction to Contemporary Public Relations

STUDY GUIDE   After studying Chapter 1, you should be able to:

▶ Define public relations as the management function that emphasizes, builds, and maintains relationships between organizations and their publics.

▶ Distinguish between public relations and marketing, identifying the exchange between provider and customer as the distinguishing characteristic of marketing relationships.

▶ Define and differentiate among related concepts—publicity, advertising, press agentry, employee relations, public affairs, issues management, lobbying, investor relations, and development.

▶ Outline how public relations helps improve organizations and society.

Individuals and groups have always entered into relationships with others to satisfy mutual wants and needs. In the interconnected global community, however, increasing interdependence requires even more complex social, political, and economic interaction. As a result, establishing and maintaining relationships at all levels of social systems have become important areas of scholarly study and professional practice.

For example, *human relations, marital relations,* and *interpersonal relations* describe the study and management of relationships between individuals. At the other extreme, *international relations* deals with relationships among nations in the largest social system. Courses and books are devoted to the study of all these relationships, as well as relationships in families, work teams, groups, organizations, and other social entities.

This book is about *relationships between organizations and their stakeholder publics*—people who are somehow mutually involved or interdependent with particular organizations. The term *public relations* refers to the management of organization–public relationships and is one of the fastest-growing fields of professional employment worldwide.

In everyday conversation and in the media, however, people use "public relations" to refer to many things, and often their definition is not positive. For example, some say "it's just public relations" as a pejorative description for what they consider to be an insincere public gesture. Public relations, according to critics, is "an industry designed to alter perceptions, reshape reality and manufacture consent."[1] Others say it is "good public relations" or "great PR" if something appears in the media, equating public relations with anything that attracts media coverage. As one publicist said, "We encourage that feeling because that's what we do."[2] Critics see public relations as an attempt to hide the truth or to put a positive "spin" on bad news. One author suggested that "the terms PR and public relations have become widely accepted shorthand

Public relations is the management function that establishes and maintains mutually beneficial relationships between an organization and the publics on whom its success or failure depends.

for subterfuge and deception."[3] Even more extreme is a long-held view that public relations people "pull the wires which (sic) control the public mind, who harness old forces and contrive new ways to bind and guide the world."[4]

This book is **not** *about the kind of public relations represented in those views.* Rather, this chapter introduces public relations as the management, art, and science of building and maintaining relationships between organizations and their stakeholder publics. The pages that follow define public relations as an organizational management function, discuss its parts and specializations, and distinguish it from other management functions and activities. The analysis begins with a review of how the concept of public relations has changed over the years.

Evolution of the Concept

Changes in the concept and practice of public relations reflect the evolving roles of organizations in society, the increasing interest in applying the findings of the social sciences, and the never-ending march of social and cultural change, to name but a few of the forces. Highlights of the evolution illustrate how the function became a part of organizational management and portray an emerging profession seeking its own identity and recognition. (Chapter 4 outlines a more detailed historical analysis.)

Powerful business interests in the early 1900s employed public relations to defend themselves and their monopolies against muckraking journalists and a growing interest in government regulation. The strategy was to tell their side of the story and to counterattack to influence public opinion. The goal was to prevent increased governmental regulation of business.

As the United States prepared for World War I, President Woodrow Wilson created the "Committee on Public Information." George Creel headed a staff of young propagandists, some of whom would later establish public relations firms. The committee's goal was to unite public opinion behind the war through a nationwide campaign. During those early years, public relations took the form of one-way persuasive communication designed to influence others—often referred to simply as "propaganda."

Many still define public relations as merely persuasion. For example, one dictionary defined public relations as "*inducing* the public to have understanding for and goodwill" (emphasis added). This definition reflects the writings of Edward L. Bernays—one of the founders of public relations and a member of Creel's staff—in his influential book, *The Engineering of Consent* (1955). Even today, many practitioners work with managers and clients who think public relations is simply one-way communication to persuade others.

During the decades following World War II, however, knowledge of media effects became more sophisticated. Consequently, definitions evolved to include notions of two-way communication and relationships. Definitions of public relations included words such as **reciprocal, mutual,** and **between,** indicating a maturing view. This interactive concept appeared in *Webster's Third New International Dictionary*'s definition: "The art or science of developing reciprocal understanding and goodwill." The British Institute of Public Relations defined the practice as an effort to establish and maintain "mutual understanding between an organization and its publics."

Early editions of this text also defined public relations as an interactive concept—"the planned effort to influence opinion through good character and responsible performance, based on mutually satisfactory two-way communications."

FIGURE 1.1

"Old School 'PR'"

Courtesy Carmichael Lynch Spong, Minneapolis.

Similarly, another influential text published in 1984 presented another version of the interactive concept—"the management of communication between an organization and its publics."[5]

Yale professor and *Public Opinion Quarterly* founder Harwood L. Childs had introduced an even more advanced concept in the late 1930s. Going against conventional wisdom, Childs concluded that the essence of public relations "is not the presentation of a point of view, not the art of tempering mental attitudes, nor the development of cordial and profitable relations." Instead, he said, the basic function "is to reconcile or adjust in the public interest those aspects of our personal and corporate behavior which have a social significance."[6] Childs saw the function of public relations as helping organizations *adjust* to their social environments, a concept that reemerged many decades later in contemporary public relations. The adjustment concept of public relations suggests a management-level, policy-influencing role that calls for corrective action in addition to communication. The International Public Relations Association (IPRA) adopted such a concept by including "counseling organization leaders" and implementing "planned programs of action" in its definition of public relations.

In summary, the one-way concept of public relations relies almost entirely on propaganda and persuasive communication, typically in the form of publicity. The two-way concept emphasizes communication exchange, reciprocity, and mutual understanding. Additionally, the two-way concept includes counseling management on **changes** needed within the organization. Although the one-way concept still dominates in many settings, contemporary practice increasingly includes management-level status and participation in corrective action, as well as two-way communication.

Defining the Concept in Contemporary Practice

Hundreds have written definitions attempting to capture the essence of public relations by listing the major operations that make up the practice—what public relations does. A longtime public relations scholar and professional leader, the late Rex F. Harlow, collected almost 500 definitions. He then identified major common elements in an attempt to define public relations. His definition includes both conceptual and operational elements:

> Public Relations is the distinctive management function which helps establish and maintain mutual lines of communication, understanding, acceptance and cooperation between an organization and its publics; involves the management of problems or issues; helps management to keep informed on and responsive to public opinion; defines and emphasizes the responsibility of management to serve the public interest; helps management keep abreast of and effectively utilize change, serving as an early warning system to help anticipate trends; and uses research and sound and ethical communication as its principal tools.[7]

The Public Relations Society of America (PRSA) adopted an even longer definition—"Official Statement on Public Relations." A blue-ribbon panel of PRSA leaders attempted to provide society members a definition of the field that stressed public relations' contributions to society. In addition to this conceptual aspect of the definition, the panel included activities, results, and knowledge requirements of public relations practice. (See Exhibit 1.1.)

In summary, the many definitions suggest that public relations:

1. Conducts a planned and sustained program as part of an organization's management.
2. Deals with the relationships between an organization and its stakeholder publics.
3. Monitors awareness, opinions, attitudes, and behavior inside and outside the organization.
4. Analyzes the impact of policies, procedures, and actions on stakeholder publics.
5. Identifies policies, procedures, and actions that conflict with the public interest and organizational survival.
6. Counsels management on the establishment of new policies, procedures, and actions that are beneficial to both the organization and its publics.
7. Establishes and maintains two-way communication between the organization and its publics.

EXHIBIT 1.1

Public Relations Society of America's "Official Statement of Public Relations"

Public relations helps our complex, pluralistic society to reach decisions and function more effectively by contributing to mutual understanding among groups and institutions. It serves to bring private and public policies into harmony.

Public relations serves a wide variety of institutions in society such as businesses, trade unions, government agencies, voluntary associations, foundations, hospitals, schools, colleges, and religious institutions. To achieve their goals, these institutions must develop effective relationships with many different audiences or publics such as employees, members, customers, local communities, shareholders, and other institutions, and with society at large.

The management of institutions needs to understand the attitudes and values of their publics in order to achieve institutional goals. The goals themselves are shaped by the external environment. The public relations practitioner acts as a counselor to management and as a mediator, helping to translate private aims into reasonable, publicly acceptable policy and action.

As a management function, public relations encompasses the following:

- Anticipating, analyzing, and interpreting public opinion, attitudes, and issues that might impact, for good or ill, the operations and plans of the organization.
- Counseling management at all levels in the organization with regard to policy decisions, courses of action, and communication, taking into account their public ramifications and the organization's social or citizenship responsibilities.

- Researching, conducting, and evaluating, on a continuing basis, programs of action and communication to achieve the informed public understanding necessary to the success of an organization's aims. These may include marketing, financial, fund raising, employee, community or government relations, and other programs.
- Planning and implementing the organization's efforts to influence or change public policy.
- Setting objectives, planning, budgeting, recruiting and training staff, developing facilities—in short, managing the resources needed to perform all of the above.
- Examples of the knowledge that may be required in the professional practice of public relations include communication arts, psychology, social psychology, sociology, political science, economics, and the principles of management and ethics. Technical knowledge and skills are required for opinion research, public-issues analysis, media relations, direct mail, institutional advertising, publications, film/video productions, special events, speeches, and presentations.

In helping to define and implement policy, the public relations practitioner uses a variety of professional communication skills and plays an integrative role both within the organization and between the organization and the external environment.

—Courtesy of Public Relations Society of America.

8. Produces measurable changes in awareness, opinion, attitude, and behavior inside and outside the organization.

9. Results in new and/or maintained relationships between an organization and its publics.

Public Relations Defined

As one scholar observed, definitions serve at least two purposes: to help us understand the world around us and to argue for a particular worldview of how one concept relates to other concepts.[8] Consequently, the definition of **public relations** describes what public relations is and does, as well as how it relates to other organizational activities:

This definition of public relations positions the practice of public relations as a **management function,** meaning that management in all organizations must attend to public relations. It also identifies building and maintaining **mutually beneficial**

Public relations is the management function that establishes and maintains mutually beneficial relationships between an organization and the publics on whom its success or failure depends.

relationships between organizations and publics as the moral and ethical basis of the profession. At the same time, it suggests criteria for determining **what is** and **what is not** public relations. And finally, it defines the concept of public relations that is the subject of this book.

Confusion with Marketing

Many people confuse public relations with another management function—**marketing.** Job openings for "public relations representatives" turn out to be positions as door-to-door sales representatives or telephone solicitors. In some organizations, the same person does both public relations and marketing, often without distinguishing between the two. Because of such confusion, some mistakenly conclude that there is no difference.

Confusion also occurs in nonprofit organizations and government agencies in which "nonprofit marketing" and "social marketing" often refer to building and maintaining relationships with members, patients, donors, and other constituencies. In one such case, a practitioner at a large hospital arrived on a Monday morning to find a new sign on her office door—"Marketing Communication Department." Much to her surprise, management had changed the title of the "Public Relations Department" without telling her! Hospital administration apparently saw no problem with putting a marketing title on the public relations department. After all, in their view, they were not changing anything but the title.

Those in the practice also add to the confusion. Some public relations practitioners' business cards say that they do "marketing communications" (often referred to simply as "marcom") or "integrated marketing communications." Some public relations firms have "marketing communications" or "marketing public relations" in their titles and on their letterheads. A former principal of one such firm wrote a book describing "marketing public relations" as "programs that encourage purchase and consumer satisfaction through credible communication of information and impressions. . . ."[9]

In fact, many hired into "public relations" jobs spend much of their time supporting marketing, introducing new products and services, publicizing their uses, and generally supporting the marketing strategy. For many firms, marketing support pays the bills. As one firm owner said, "Take away our work in marketing and you take away more than half our business." After considering the distinction between public relations and marketing, the CEO of another public relations firm concluded, "Seventy-five percent of public relations people are really in marketing." Even the president of the Council of Public Relations Firms added to the confusion, stating that public relations works ". . . better and more cost-effectively than other marketing disciplines."[10]

Paul Holmes, president of The Holmes Group, described the confusion:

> Someone once told me he was changing his firm's name from XYZ Public Relations to XYZ Marketing Communications because "we've broadened our portfolio of services." But marketing (managing the relationship between a company and its customers) is a much narrower discipline than PR (managing the relationship between a company and all stakeholders), though it's not narrower than publicity, which is probably what the firm was doing.[11]

Some marketing authors add to the confusion by suggesting that public relations (read "publicity") is really just a tactic used in marketing: "No exciting product to talk about? Get one. This is the job of the PR strategist today. Find an idea that will generate publicity. And not any kind of publicity either. Publicity that will build a brand."[12] Another wrote that public relations "is the marketing of an organization . . . to relay information about that organization's products and practices."[13]

If not always clearly defined in practice, public relations and marketing can be distinguished conceptually and their relationship clarified. First, people's wants and needs are fundamental to the concept of marketing. What people want or need gets translated into consumer demand. Marketers offer products and services to satisfy the demand. Consumers select the products and services that provide the most utility, value, and satisfaction. Finally, the marketer delivers the product or service to the consumer in *exchange* for something of value. According to marketing scholars Philip Kotler and Gary Armstrong:

> Exchange is the act of obtaining a desired object from someone by offering something in return. . . . Marketing consists of actions taken to build and maintain desirable exchange *relationships* with target audiences involving a product service, idea, or other object.[14]

This special relationship distinguishes the marketing function—two parties *exchanging* something of value to each other. In short, marketing creates quid pro quo relationships in which ownership—title—changes hands. The definition uses the exchange to distinguish marketing from public relations.

The goal of marketing is to attract and satisfy customers on a sustained basis in order to secure "market share" and to achieve an organization's economic objectives. To that end, product publicity and media relations are used to support marketing. Because public relations specialists typically know how to write for the news media, how to work with journalists, and how to plan and implement internal communication programs for sales staff, marketers call on them to help in the marketing effort.

For example, Apple Computer uses publicity to launch new models, new products, and updated versions of its operating systems—even getting Steve Jobs on the covers of *Time* magazine and in the lead stories of television news programs. WD-40 uses publicity and its Web site to discover and promote new uses of its major product. The dairy industry uses media events and publicity—in addition to its "Got Milk?" advertising campaign—to promote the health benefits of drinking milk. Mattel used press conferences and other publicity to defend the company and to announce product recalls during the marketing crisis associated with lead paint on toys made in China as toy sales plummeted during the holiday shopping season.

A few organizations see the marketing relationship with customers as only one of many organizational relationships. On their organization charts, marketing is part of the larger public relations function. Many other organizations view marketing as the major function, viewing all noncustomer relationships (with employees, investors, neighbors, government, media, etc.) as necessary only in the context of supporting marketing. In these organizations, typically, the top public relations officer reports to marketing. A few organizations identify "consumer relations" as part of public relations, making the public relations department responsible for communications with customers and other consumers regarding instructions for using products, safety, complaints, and repair services. In the majority of organizations, however, marketing and public relations are separate management functions with different but overlapping and complementary goals.

In summary, effective public relations contributes to the marketing effort by maintaining a hospitable social and political environment. For example, a hospital

Marketing is the management function that identifies human needs and wants, offers products and services to satisfy those demands, and causes transactions that deliver products and services in *exchange* for something of value to the provider.

that maintains good relationships with volunteers, nurses, physicians, local employ- ers, local government, and community groups will likely enjoy success in the mar- keting effort to attract patients, physicians, and referrals. Likewise, successful marketing and satisfied customers help build and maintain good relations with em- ployees, investors, government regulatory agencies, and community leaders.

On the other hand, misguided marketing strategies and gimmicks illustrate how these efforts can backfire and create public relations problems. The classic—"Joe Camel"—may have been an effective marketing tactic for reaching children and teenagers, but it may have been the straw that broke the camel's back for the to- bacco industry as it defended itself in numerous court cases. Nestlé's successful mar- keting of Nan™ baby formula—apparently ignoring the intent of the World Health Organization's Code of Marketing Milk Substitutes—prompted the National Al- liance for Breastfeeding Advocacy to charge Nestlé with "using a vulnerable popu- lation for a grab at market share . . ." as quoted in the *Wall Street Journal*.[15]

These examples illustrate that organizations must attend to both public rela- tions and marketing in order to achieve organizational goals. Each makes unique but complementary contributions to building and maintaining the many relation- ships essential for organizational survival and growth. To ignore one is to risk failure in the other.

Parts of the Function

Some confuse public relations with its activities and parts. For example, many think that "publicity" is simply another way of saying "public relations." Publicity is often the most visible part, but seldom the only program tactic. Similarly, "lobbying" may be the most noticeable public relations activity in Washington, D.C., and in state capitals, but it usually is only one part of an overall public relations strategy and may not be viewed as part of the organization's larger public relations function. Another part, employee communication, may dominate in some organizations, but it repre- sents the internal public relations effort that is necessary before dealing with rela- tionships outside the organization.

The contemporary concept and practice of public relations includes all the fol- lowing activities and specialties.

Internal Relations

Critical to the success of any organization, of course, are its employees. Before any relationships can be maintained with customers, consumers, neighbors, investors, and others outside the organization, management must attend to those who do the work—the employees. Hence, CEOs in organizations talk about employees as their "number one public" or as "the organization's most important asset," and they try to create an "organizational culture" that attracts and retains productive workers. This part of public relations practice is **internal relations.**

Internal relations is the specialized part of public relations that builds and maintains a mutually beneficial relationship between managers and the employees on whom an organization's success depends.

Internal relations specialists work in departments called "employee communi- cation," "employee relations," or "internal relations." They plan and implement communication programs to keep employees informed and motivated, and to pro- mote the organization's culture. According to Jon Iwata, senior vice president of communications at IBM, "When we talk about employee communications, we really think of it in terms of corporate culture—how work gets done in our company, how we view things here." He points out that the CEO plays a critical role: "The CEO has to get his or her business to perform, and that is down to the workforce. The realization is that in order to drive any business results, the employees have to be with you . . . ."[16]

According to Alvie Smith, former director of corporate communications at General Motors, two factors explain management's respect for this part of the public relations function:

1. The value of understanding, teamwork, and commitment by employees in achieving bottom-line results. These positive aspects of worker behavior are strongly influenced by effective, way-of-life interactive communications throughout the organization.

2. The need to build a strong manager–communication network, one that makes every supervisor at every level accountable for communicating effectively with his or her employees. This needs to be more than just job-related information and should include key business and public issues affecting the total organization.[17]

Internal relations staff work closely with the human resources department to communicate about benefits, training, safety, and other topics important to employees. They work with the legal department in communication related to labor relations during contract negotiations and work stoppages. And internal relations staff work with external relations staff to coordinate messages so the organization speaks with "one voice." (Chapter 9 discusses internal relations and employee communication in greater detail.)

Publicity

Much of the news and information in the media originates from public relations sources. Because the sources do not pay for the placement, however, they have little or no control over *if* the information is used, *when* it is used, and *how* it is used, or misused, by the media. Public relations sources provide what they judge to be newsworthy information—**publicity**—with the expectation that editors and reporters will use the information. Media decision makers may or may not use the information, based on their judgment of its news value and interest to their audiences. They may use the information as provided, change the original information, or change how it is presented, usually without identifying the original source. In the eyes of readers, listeners, or viewers, the medium carrying the information is the source.

Examples of publicity include a story in a newspaper's financial section about increased earnings for a corporation, a photo and caption on the business page announcing a new product launch, a columnist's item on the progress of a charity fund-raising campaign, a feature story in the city magazine outlining the latest scientific findings from a cancer research center, an entertainment tabloid listing of the local concert of your favorite music group, and television news coverage of a new civic center dedication ceremony. Typically, such stories came from the corporation's public relations department, the charitable organization's director of donor relations and development, the university medical school's news bureau, the music group's publicist, and the mayor's director of media relations (sometimes called "press secretary").

Print media usually receive a press release, feature story with photographs, or press kit including detailed background information. Broadcast media typically receive a broadcast-style news script, recorded interview or "sound bites," video news release (VNR), or press kit including material suitable for broadcast (see Figure 1.2). To generate publicity, the source must know what information will attract media

Publicity is information provided by an outside source that is used by the media because the information has news value. This is an *uncontrolled* method of placing messages in the media because the source does not pay the media for placement.

FIGURE 1.2

Publicity Materials

Courtesy Nuffer, Smith, Tucker, Inc., San Diego.

attention, identify a newsworthy angle and lead, and write and package the information appropriately for each medium. It also helps to have journalists think of you as a trustworthy news source.

Newsworthy *events* also generate publicity by attracting media coverage. Groundbreaking ceremonies, ribbon cuttings, open houses, reunions, dedications, telethons, marathons, ceremonial appointments, honorary degrees, contract and legislation signings, protest demonstrations, press conferences, and other "media events" are designed to be "news." An amusement park makes news, for example, when the 500-millionth "guest" enters the park. Network news crews cover the president signing health care reform legislation as leaders of health care groups pose alongside on the White House lawn. Those staging such events hope to attract media coverage and to gain some control over what is reported. Successful publicity events have real news value; appeal to media gatekeepers; offer photo, video, or sound opportunities; and communicate the source's intended message.

The publicity model of practice often operates under the "public information" title. "Telling our story" remains one of the most frequently practiced models of public relations. Many top managers and clients hire public relations specialists to secure media coverage that will put the organization in a favorable light. Those operating under the publicity model typically began their careers as journalists and use their understanding of the media to craft newsworthy messages and events that will attract media coverage.

In its infancy, public relations practice comprised publicity produced by former journalists, so it is not surprising that some still confuse publicity with the broader concept of public relations. There is much more to public relations than publicity, however.

Advertising

Unlike when using publicity, advertisers control content, placement, and timing by paying for media advertising time and space. Although both publicity and

advertising are mediated communication, advertising gives the source *control* over content and placement.

Many associate advertising with marketing goods and services, but it is not limited to that purpose. Other parts of the organization also use this controlled means of placing messages in the mass media for nonmarketing purposes. For example, human resources departments place advertisements in newspaper classifieds and Sunday business sections to announce job openings. Legal departments place advertisements in "newspapers of record" to conform with public notification requirements when corporations issue new bonds or sell shares, when recalling a defective product, or when complying with a court settlement.

Public relations uses advertising to reach audiences other than the customers targeted by marketing. When Andersen Consulting changed its name to Accenture, the company placed advertisements in business publications announcing the new name. Investor relations at another company placed advertisements to assure stockholders and financial analysts that the corporation had thwarted a hostile takeover attempt. Nordstrom advertisements in store communities announced that applications are being accepted for four-year Nordstrom Scholarships to be awarded to high school juniors who plan to go to college. The Embassy of Kuwait purchased full-page advertisements in major U.S. newspapers to announce that "America is our ally" and support for "the international effort to eradicate terrorism" following the 9/11 World Trade Center catastrophe. An aerospace company's community relations department placed an advertisement announcing its gift to the local symphony, yet not a single member of the intended audience buys the wing assemblies and air frames manufactured by the company. A local charity's public relations committee bought a full-page advertisement to thank contributors who funded a new center for the homeless. Merck & Company used advertising to announce its withdrawal of VIOXX™ from the market (see Figure 1.3).

Mobil Oil (now ExxonMobil) began the practice of using "advertorials" on op-ed pages and in magazines in 1970 "to speak out on a variety of issues designed to reach opinion makers."[18] According to Mobil's then–public relations vice president, Mobil's chairman wanted to make the company's positions on economic and political issues part of public debate. The advertisement did not sell Mobil products. The *Minnesota Law Review* described such corporate advertising as "a hybrid creature designed to use the means of paid advertising to accomplish the goals of PR."

Similarly, some charities also use advertising for public education. For example, the American Cancer Society has long relied on advertising to achieve its public awareness goals:

> The society was the first traditional health charity to engage in paid advertising and, to be sure, for years our ad budget, which is less than 2% of our revenues, was spent raising awareness of things such as colorectal cancer and breast cancer screenings and tobacco prevention.[19]

Organizations also use advertising for public relations purposes when they want to address criticism in the media—over which they have no control, when they feel that their point of view is not being reported fairly, when they feel that their publics do not understand the issues or are apathetic, or when they are trying to add their voices to a cause. For example, Nike ran full-page newspaper advertisements denying that the company used unfair labor practices in its Asian factories. Advertising messages attempted to counter the critical news coverage of "Asian sweatshops" and to deflect attention from editorial criticism and ridicule by editorial cartoonists,

Advertising is information placed in the media by an identified sponsor that pays for the time or space. It is a *controlled* method of placing messages in the media.

FIGURE 1.3

VIOXX Recall
Advertisement

Courtesy Merck & Company,
Inc.

IMPORTANT INFORMATION
FOR PATIENTS TAKING VIOXX® (rofecoxib)

 MERCK

September 30, 2004

Merck Voluntarily Withdraws VIOXX

Dear VIOXX Patient:

Merck & Co., Inc. announced today a voluntary withdrawal of VIOXX®.

This decision is based on new data from a three-year clinical study. In this study, there was an increased risk for cardiovascular (CV) events, such as heart attack and stroke, in patients taking VIOXX 25 mg compared to those taking placebo (sugar pill). While the incidence of CV events was low, there was an increased risk beginning after 18 months of treatment. The cause of the clinical study result is uncertain, but our commitment to our patients is clear.

Patients who are currently taking VIOXX should contact their health care providers to discuss discontinuing use of VIOXX and possible alternative treatments. In addition, patients and health care professionals may obtain information from merck.com and vioxx.com or may call 1-888-368-4699.

Merck will reimburse all patients for their unused VIOXX. All dosage strengths and formulations of VIOXX are affected by this voluntary withdrawal. Information can be found at vioxx.com or at 1-888-368-4699.

Merck is notifying physicians and pharmacists and has informed the Food and Drug Administration of this decision.

We are taking this action because we believe it best serves the interests of patients. That is why we undertook this clinical trial to better understand the safety profile of VIOXX. And it's why we instituted this voluntary withdrawal upon learning about these data.

Be assured that Merck will continue to do everything we can to maintain the safety of our medicines.

Raymond V. Gilmartin,
Chairman, President & CEO

Please read the Patient Prescribing Information for VIOXX.

Where patients come first ✸ MERCK

including the *Doonesbury* comic strip. Subsequent advertisements reported the results of Ambassador Andrew Young's six-month investigation of Nike labor practices overseas.

In the final analysis, given an adequate budget, *organizations use advertising to control content, placement, and timing for placing public relations messages in the media.*

Press Agentry

In *Walking the Tightrope*, the late Hollywood publicist Henry Rogers summarized the essence of press agentry, "When I first started, I was in the publicity business. I was a press agent. Very simply, my job was to get the client's name in the paper."[20] He candidly reported that he had lied to the West Coast editor of *Look* magazine about Rita Hayworth's "fabulous" wardrobe. The magazine devoted its cover and 10 pages of photographs to the then-relatively unknown actress and her hastily borrowed clothes. Following such attention in a major national magazine, she became the talk of Hollywood, and Columbia Pictures extended her contract. To the extent that mass media coverage confers status, Rita Hayworth's early stardom can be attributed in part to her press agent's lies about the size and worth of her wardrobe.

Press agents attract public notice more than build public understanding. Publicity is their major strategy. They base their approach on agenda-setting theory, which says that the amount of mass media coverage subsequently determines public perception of the relative importance of topics and people (see Chapter 8 for more on agenda setting). In other words, the goal of **press agentry** is to create the perception that the subject of the publicity is a newsworthy subject deserving public attention.

And the press coverage does not have to be positive, according to some. For example, the *New York Times* quoted a spokesperson for Bruno Magli shoes— featured as evidence in the O. J. Simpson murder trial—putting a positive spin on what many considered to be negative publicity, "It's certainly not the best way to get the name out there, but it's effective. Now we have a bigger audience of people who know about our shoes."[21] Most would agree, however, that the impact of negative publicity seldom has positive outcomes. Press coverage featuring the antics of Britney Spears, Lindsey Lohan, and Michael Vick may bring notoriety—even celebrity, but surely will not positively impact their respective careers.

Press agentry plays a major role in the music recording industry, professional sports, tourist attractions, motion picture studios, television, concert and theater performances, and business enterprises headed by celebrities. For example, press agents gave us the legends of Davy Crockett and Courtney Love; promoted the Indianapolis 500 Memorial Day auto race and the Super Bowl into national events; turned Fort Lauderdale and Cabo San Lucas into internationally known spring break destinations; positioned Disneyland Resort Paris and Hong Kong Disneyland as vacation destinations even before opening days; and made the *Harry Potter* movies and each new Disney-Pixar animated release must-see movies even before the final edit. Press agentry also is an important factor in political campaigns and national political party conventions attempting to build name recognition and attract voters through media exposure.

> **Press agentry** is creating newsworthy stories and events to attract media attention in order to gain public notice.

FIGURE 1.4

Nest Heads "Publicity" Comic Strip

Courtesy Copley News Service.

In the candid words of a veteran press agent, "We stoop to anything, but our stuff gets printed." And it can pay off. A musical group's earning power may be as much a tribute to the skill of its press agent to get publicity as to its musical abilities. A career-launching appearance on a popular talk show may reflect the work of a press agent more than the talent of the guest. Likewise, a good press agent can make a new club or restaurant the "in place" even before a single customer experiences the ambiance, food, or entertainment of the place itself. A favorable review by a restaurant reviewer or entertainment critic may jump-start a new bistro or band. For example, the young press agent who worked for a struggling band later admitted that he reported that the band "sold 50,000 albums this week when I knew it was 5,000, but it made a better story."[22] By the way, the "struggling band" was the Beatles.

There are full-time press agents, or celebrity publicists, but many public relations practitioners have used press agentry tactics at some time or another to attract media attention to their clients, causes, or organizations. This was the case when College Tonight, Inc. hired the Rogers & Cowan firm "to create and implement a comprehensive publicity campaign to publicize" the national roll-out of its social networking service for college students—collegetonight.com. There is more to public relations than press agentry, however.

Confusion results when press agents describe what they do as "public relations" or use that term to give their agencies more prestigious, but less accurate, titles. Hence, many journalists mistakenly refer to all public relations practitioners as "flacks," even though the *Associated Press Stylebook* defines "flack" as "slang for press agent." In fact, consumer press writers often use "flak" or "flack" when referring to public relations people (30 percent of 1,350 articles in one study). Only "spin doctor" was used more often—in 56 percent of the stories.[23]

Public Affairs

The armed services, many governmental agencies, and some corporations use the title "public affairs" as a substitute for public relations. In the military and government, this title is part of a name game dating back to the 1913 Gillett Amendment to an appropriation bill in the U.S. House of Representatives. The amendment stipulates that federal agencies cannot spend money for publicity unless specifically authorized by Congress. This legislative hostility was reaffirmed in Public Law 93–50, Section 305, enacted July 1, 1973. This law expressly prohibits government spending on "publicity or propaganda purposes designed to support or defeat legislation pending before the Congress." Historian J. A. R. Pimlott concluded that limitations imposed on government public relations "springs from the fear lest programs undertaken in the name of administrative efficiency should result in an excessive concentration of power in the Executive."[24]

Neither the 1913 amendment nor the 1973 law actually refers to public relations. Nevertheless, many federal, state, and local governmental officials apparently confuse publicity with the larger concept of public relations. As a result, governmental agencies typically use other terms to describe building and maintaining relationships with their constituents. It is nothing more than a label switch, however, as thousands of public relations specialists work in local, state, and federal government under titles such as "public affairs," "public information," "communications," "constituent relations," and "liaison."

Recognizing the obvious need for building and maintaining relations with citizens, beginning in the Johnson administration, the federal government created Federal Information Centers (now Federal Citizen Information Centers) to give citizens a single place to get information about federal programs and services. As summarized by Mordecai Lee:

> First, they perform a marketing function, helping increase the utilization of public-sector services and products. Second, as a medium for answering questions about the federal government that aren't related to obtaining a service, FICs accomplish democratic accountability to the public. They contribute to an informed citizenry, the sine qua non of democracy.[25]

In corporations, "public affairs" typically refers to public relations efforts related to public policy and "corporate citizenship." Corporate public affairs specialists serve as liaisons with governmental units; implement community improvement programs; encourage political activism, campaign contributions, and voting; and volunteer their services in charitable and community development organizations. Hewlett-Packard's public affairs department states its mission as to "shape public policy to foster an environment that allows HP to achieve its business objectives."[26]

Likewise, public relations counseling firms use the public affairs label for their lobbying and governmental relations services designed to help clients understand and address regulatory and legislative processes. As Ruder Finn-D.C. managing director Neil Dhillon says, "The real value in what we do is knowing how to navigate the process and understanding how to work with the appropriate people." Steve Behm, vice president of public affairs, Edelman Worldwide in Atlanta, adds, "Particularly in public affairs, what has become so important is that those relationships are done through honest and transparent communications."[27]

A public affairs specialist described the relationship between public relations and public affairs as follows: "**Public affairs** is the public relations practice that addresses public policy and the publics who influence such policy."[28] An association executive based in Washington, D.C., defined public affairs as "PR tactics applied to GR (government relations) strategies to produce 'excellent public policy.'"[29] A survey of public affairs officers identified major public affairs responsibilities as including (in descending order) federal government affairs, state government affairs, local government affairs, community relations, political action committees, contributions, grassroots support, and issues management. Forty-three percent of their departments use the title "public affairs." Other public affairs specialists operate in departments called "corporate affairs," "corporate relations," "government relations," and "external affairs."[30]

For example, when the San Diego Chargers National Football League team embarked on campaign to build a new football stadium, team owners hired former Clinton administration special counsel Mark Fabiani to work with local governments and citizen groups to build "grassroots" support for a new stadium. The primary stumbling block for replacing the current stadium—public financing for part or all of the new stadium—called for public affairs expertise not usually found in sports public relations departments.

Growing interest in public affairs parallels high turnover in government, changes in communication, increasing importance of state and local governments, and a more complex regulatory environment. For example, term limits imposed on elected officials and voter dissatisfaction with those in office produced unprecedented levels of turnover in all levels of government. Turnover increases the power of staff members, who often outlast the elected officials they serve, and increases the need to provide information to newly elected officials. In short, public affairs work

Public affairs is that specialized part of public relations that builds and maintains relationships with governmental agencies and community stakeholder groups in order to influence public policy.

FIGURE 1.5

Public Affairs Job
Description

PUBLIC AFFAIRS MANAGER

We seek a public-policy oriented individual holding a B.A. degree combining public relations and political science, and at least five years full-time experience in corporate–government relations. Graduate work or a law degree would be a definite plus.

Basic requirements include strong oral and written communication skills, as well as knowledge of local government and/or public sector regulatory processes. Some media experience also desired.

The successful candidate, reporting to the vice president of Corporate Relations, will work with district managers to develop and implement broad-based public affairs programs related to cable television policy. Other responsibilities include monitoring franchise compliance, leading media relations and producing press materials, and conducting district community relations programs.

If you are a talented writer, assertive and skilled professional, and experienced in working with top management to achieve corporate goals, we want you to apply for this high-profile, well-compensated position in our rapidly growing cable distribution and production company.

FIGURE 1.5

Public Affairs Job Description

occurs in an increasingly complex and democratic environment, leading to a major role for public relations in the formulation of public policy.

Lobbying

Lobbying is a specialized part of public relations that builds and maintains relations with government primarily to influence legislation and regulation.

An even more specialized and criticized part of public affairs—**lobbying**—attempts to influence legislative and regulatory decisions in government. The United States Senate defines lobbying as "the practice of trying to persuade legislators to propose, pass, or defeat legislation or to change existing laws."[31]

Even though the U.S. Constitution protects the right to petition the government, some view lobbying as an attempt to manipulate government for selfish ends. Movies and television programs depicting smoke-filled rooms and payoffs by lobbyists working for powerful corporate and special interests perpetuate this cynical view of lobbying. News stories sometimes report illegal or questionable cash contributions to legislators, lavish fundraising parties, and hosted weekends at exotic golf resorts. However, lobbying more often takes the form of open advocacy and discussion on matters of public policy.

Registration laws and their enforcement vary from state to state, but all who engage in lobbying the U.S. Congress must register with the Clerk of the House and Secretary of the Senate. Failure to register carries a fine of up to $50,000 under the Federal Regulation of Lobbying Act (see Chapter 6). Twice a year, lobbyists also are required to report their clients, expenditures, and issue-related activities.

Despite occasional abuse and public rebuke, lobbying remains a legal and accepted way for citizen groups, associations, labor unions, corporations, and other special-interest groups to influence government decision-making. Although clearly labeled and monitored at national and state levels, similar lobbying efforts on county and municipal issues often are part of and undifferentiated from public affairs, community relations, or other public relations efforts. Many large cities, however, have or are developing regulations to make lobbying more transparent in making local public policy.

Lobbyists at all levels of government must understand the legislative process, know how government functions, and be acquainted with individual lawmakers and officials. Because this knowledge may not be part of many public relations practitioners' educational preparation and professional experience, lobbyists often have backgrounds as well-connected lawyers, governmental administrators, elected officials' important staff members, or other insiders with good relationships with governmental decision makers. In fact, critics of "the public–private revolving door" say that lobbyists working for special interests "cash in" on the access and credibility they earned while working in government.

The number of lobbyists has increased dramatically. According to the U.S. House of Representatives Legislative Resource Center, there were 5,045 "registrants" (lobbying firms and other organizations) and 22,972 "active lobbyists" (individuals) registered with the federal government in January 2008.[32] A Washington watchdog group estimates that lobbyists spent $2.45 billion in 2006 lobbying the U.S. Congress, averaging more than $4.5 million per legislator. Lobbyists spent more than $1.3 billion to lobby state governments, with an average of five lobbyists for every legislator spending more than $200,000 for each state legislator.[33]

In practice, lobbying must be closely coordinated with other public relations efforts directed toward nongovernmental publics. Sophisticated lobbyists mobilize like-minded constituents to get their voices heard by lawmakers and officials in government. Targeted mailing lists, high-speed printers, and software for individualizing letters can produce a flood of mail, phone calls, faxes, and personal visits from constituents. Customized e-mail address lists and "blast" broadcast faxing, as well as online news groups, social media, podcasts, and blogs provide even faster ways to mobilize constituents.

Getting the folks "back home" to take up the cause is referred to as "grassroots lobbying" and is part of many coordinated public relations efforts to influence public policy. In some cases, however, responses actually come from "front" groups created to deceive or mislead policy makers about public sentiment. Some refer to these pseudo-grassroots movements as "Astroturf lobbying." Examples of such front groups include "Citizens for Riverboat Gambling," funded by a gambling organization trying to pass a local referendum, and numerous pro-gun ownership "grassroots networks" formed by National Rifle Association of America (NRA) members at the encouragement of the NRA's lobbying arm, the Institute for Legislative Action. Such front organizations are designed to give the appearance of widespread citizen support, when in reality they often are created by sponsors to promote narrow interests.

In its primary roles as credible advocate and reliable source of information, however, lobbying takes the form of information designed to educate and persuade (see Exhibit 1.2). Lobbyists succeed or fail in part based on their traditional public relations skills—researching legislators' positions on issues and information needs, and communicating persuasive information to government officials, to grassroots constituencies, and to their clients. In addition to those abilities, lobbyists need sophisticated knowledge of government, legislative process, public policy, and public opinion. Stereotypical images of the cigar-chomping insider dispensing stacks of cash no longer apply to most lobbyists and their work:

> Indeed, lobbyists spend substantially more time collecting information from government than they do communicating to it, since sound lobbying strategies, tactics, and positions are highly dependent on a strong base of information.[34]

EXHIBIT 1.2

Lobbying

"Lobbying involves much more than persuading legislators. Its principal elements include researching and analyzing legislation or regulatory proposals; monitoring and reporting on developments; attending congressional or regulatory hearings; working with coalitions interested in the same issues; and then educating not only government officials but also employees and corporate officers as to the implications of various changes. What most lay people regard as lobbying—the actual communication with government officials—represents the smallest portion of a lobbyist's time; a far greater proportion is devoted to the other aspects of preparation, information and communication."

—Courtesy American League of Lobbyists, Alexandria, VA (www.alldc.org/resources.htm).

E-mail has changed lobbying, according to researcher Kurt Wise. He called the explosion of e-mail the " 'Blackberrization' of Capitol Hill." As one lobbyist told him, "Now, I can get so much more done sitting right here [at his desk] than I can walking the hall [on Capitol Hill] and invading their space. I can get quicker information without taking them away from what they are doing." However, lobbyists still see face-to-face communication as necessary for maintaining relationships with their contacts: "On the Hill, it is better to be seen and known than to just be an anonymous voice on the phone or e-mail."[35]

Lobbying is an outgrowth of our democratic system in a pluralistic society, keeping government open to those affected by proposed legislation and government regulation. In Washington, D.C., and state capitals, the role of lobbying and other public affairs efforts play increasingly important roles in formulating and implementing public policy. More effective regulation of campaign finance and lobbying remains a challenge, however. In the end, *the role of lobbyists is to ethically advocate the interests of their clients in the public policy debate.*

Issues Management

Issues management is the proactive process of anticipating, identifying, evaluating, and responding to public policy issues that affect an organization's relationships with its publics.

Two points capture the essence of **issues management:** (1) early identification of issues with potential impact on an organization, and (2) a strategic response designed to mitigate or capitalize on their consequences. For example, in the context of public opinion, issues management "attempts to discern trends in public opinion so that an organization can respond to them before they amplify into serious conflict."[36]

As originally conceived by the late public relations consultant W. Howard Chase in 1976, issues management includes identifying issues, analyzing issues, setting priorities, selecting program strategies, implementing programs of action and communication, and evaluating effectiveness. He said the process "aligns corporate principles, policies and practices to the realities of a politicized economy."[37] More recently, Chase defined issues management as the process of closing the "gap between corporate action and stakeholder expectation."[38] A panel of experts expanded the definition to include:

> . . . anticipating, researching and prioritizing issues; assessing the impact of issues on the organization; recommending policies and strategies to minimize risk and seize opportunities; participating and implementing strategy; evaluating program impact."[39]

Even though issues management was originally touted as a new approach that would give practitioners elevated status, many do not see it as anything different from what they already do. Others express concern that the term suggests something unlikely and unacceptable because it sets up visions of manipulation—that an organization can "manage" major public issues. Many major corporations, however, have created issues management departments or "task forces," either by establishing specialized sections or by renaming existing issues tracking and research units. They focus on how to respond to public concerns such as terrorism, global warming, deregulation, offshore "outsourcing," globalization, biotechnology (genetic engineering), toxic waste disposal, managed care, an aging population, and corporate influence in politics.

Conceptually, if not always administratively, issues management is part of the public relations function. When viewed merely as persuasive communication, however, it becomes a tactic to influence public policy, not part of an organization's strategic planning. When concerned with adjusting the organization and building relationships with stakeholders to achieve mutual goals, "public relations and issues management are quite similar and result in similar outcomes."[40]

Investor Relations

Also referred to as "IR" and "financial relations," **investor relations** is another specialized part of public relations in publicly held corporations. Investor relations specialists work to enhance the value of a company's stock. This reduces the cost of capital by increasing shareholder confidence and by making the stock attractive to individual investors, financial analysts, and institutional investors.

Investor relations specialists keep shareholders informed and loyal to a company in order to maintain a fair valuation of a company's stock. Their work involves tracking market trends, providing information to financial publics, counseling management, and responding to requests for financial information. Annual and quarterly reports, SEC-required 10-K forms, e-mailed earnings reports, press releases distributed by newswire services, and home page links to "material" financial information are methods used to disseminate timely information to analysts, investors, and the financial press. An example illustrates how it works to benefit both a company and its investors:

A new biotechnology company has 10 million shares outstanding, with each share selling for $20. This means the company has a "market capitalization" of $200 million. Assume that the stock becomes more attractive to institutional investors, financial analysts, and individual investors as they learn more about the company's products, its management, "financials," and plans. If the share price increases to $25, the market value of the company increases to $250 million! Now assume that the company needs $10 million to pursue research on promising new products. At $25 a share, it needs to sell only 400,000 company-held shares, versus 500,000 shares at $20, to raise the $10 million to finance the research. Not only are investors' holdings worth more, but the company must sell fewer shares to raise additional capital.

On the other hand, consider what happens to the value of stockholder investments and the cost of new capital when a corporation loses shareholder confidence, fails to respond to analysts' concern about the latest quarterly earnings report, or receives negative coverage in the financial press. For example, when Compaq Computer merged with Hewlett-Packard, HP stock lost almost one fifth of its

Investor relations is a specialized part of corporate public relations that builds and maintains mutually beneficial relationships with shareholders and others in the financial community to maximize market value.

pre-merger value and Compaq stock fell about 10 percent. Some specialists criticized how the investor relations staffs had failed to address investors' concerns that had been extensively reported in the financial press before the rumored merger.

Investor relations specialists must know corporate finance, accounting, Wall Street, international equities trading (the Tokyo Stock Exchange is the world's largest), international business trends, business journalism, and much more. Most of all, however, they must know Securities and Exchange Commission and stock exchange financial reporting requirements. These requirements became much more rigorous in 2002 with the passage of the Sarbanes-Oxley Act. Passed on the heels of corporate scandals (Enron, WorldCom, Tyco, HealthSouth, and Martha Stewart Living Omnimedia, to name just a few), this act requires disclosure "on a rapid and current basis" of "material information" that might be useful to investors and others. "Public relations practitioners who do not have solid training and experience in business, management, and law will apparently be unable to fill even entry level positions in investor relations," according to researchers who studied CEO perceptions of investor relations.[41]

As a result, those aspiring to careers in investor relations should combine studies in public relations with coursework in finance and business law. An MBA degree is often necessary preparation (see Figure 1.6). It also helps to know more than one language, to study economics, to be widely traveled, and to follow the rapidly changing international political scene. Corporations and investor relations specialists increasingly deal in a global economy. Because few practitioners have the required combination of corporate finance and public relations, and the competition for those who do is great, investor relations practitioners are among the highest paid in public relations.

FIGURE 1.6

Investor Relations Job Description

Courtesy Titan Corporation (now L-3 Communications Titan Group), San Diego.

Finance

INVESTOR RELATIONS

The Titan Corporation, a high-tech San Diego-based NYSE company, is currently seeking a seasoned professional to manage the company's investor relations programs. Reporting to the CEO, the successful candidate must be able to effectively communicate company information to all audiences, including shareholders, brokers, analysts, media and employees. Responsibilities include: liaison to the financial community; preparation of financial press releases; assisting CEO with shareholder and road show meetings; development and distribution of investor materials and company story; review of SEC filings; and maintenance of current shareholder, mailing and fax lists.

The ideal candidate will possess 10 years' direct experience in investor relations and corporate communications, excellent verbal/written communication skills, ability to deal with Board of Directors and Executive Staff, computer skills, and the highest standards of ethics and integrity. MBA preferred.

In return for your expertise, we offer an excellent salary and benefits package, including bonus and stock option programs. To take advantage of this excellent opportunity, please submit resume, including salary history in confidence to: The Titan Corporation, 3033 Science Park Rd., San Diego, CA 92121. Fax (619) 552-9745, Via E-mail to: resumes@titan.com We are an equal opportunity employer.

http://www.titan.com

TITAN
Technology for Changing Times

Development

Just as investor relations helps finance publicly held corporations, fund-raising and membership drives provide the financial support needed to operate charitable and nonprofit organizations. These organizations typically use the title "development" or "advancement" for this aspect of public relations. Nonprofit hospitals, social welfare groups, disease research foundations, service charities, and universities have directors of development. Organizations that rely on membership fees for some or all of their revenues—museums, zoos, theaters, symphony orchestras, professional societies, unions, trade associations, and citizen-action groups—often have a "director of member services and development."

> **Development** is a specialized part of public relations in nonprofit organizations that builds and maintains relationships with donors and members to secure financial and volunteer support.

Development specialists work for charities, public broadcasting stations, disease research foundations, hospitals, community arts groups, museums, zoos, youth clubs, universities, and religious organizations. Because these organizations depend on donations, membership fees, volunteers, or all three, they rely heavily on annual campaigns and special events to call attention to their needs and to solicit public support and contributions.

An annual telethon, 10K run, open house, homecoming, and celebrity auction, however, represent only a few of the activities in a yearlong program to establish and maintain relationships with volunteers, alumni, members, and donors, as well as prospective members, volunteers, and donors. Fund-raising activities and membership services make up a major part of the overall program. Because development deals with the lifeblood of nonprofit organizations, it often plays a major role in the larger public relations function in such organizations.

Confusion of Terms

The preceding sections discuss terms that are all parts of the broader organizational management function known as public relations. They all deal with organizations' relationships with specific groups or publics. Some organizations divide the function into *internal* and *external* departments. Internal relations deals with publics involved in the internal workings of organizations, such as employees, families of employees, and volunteers. Relations with publics outside organizations—neighbors, consumers, environmentalists, investors, and so forth—are the responsibility of external relations.

Title confusion is further complicated when the total function is given one of many other labels such as corporate relations, corporate communication, university advancement, hospital relations, public affairs, and public information. Whatever name is used, the basic concept and motivation of public relations are similar from one organization to the next—large or small, local or global. *All effective organizations strive to establish and maintain relationships with those identified as important to survival and growth.*

In practice, however, too often employers and clients define public relations narrowly or wrongly based on the various goals and tasks they assign to it. In one organization, public relations takes the form of candid, open communication with many publics. In another, it attempts to maintain a silent, low profile. For one organization the purpose can be to provoke controversy and to maintain adversarial relationships that motivate and activate its members, as in the case of an organization engaged in the gun-control debate. In yet another, public relations tries to reconcile and compromise with an important public; for example, management may attempt to reconcile differences with a labor union in order to avoid a work stoppage.

Likewise, practitioners define public relations every day by what they do and by what they call "public relations." For example, many do product publicity because that is what they are paid to do under the rubric of public relations. Others see it as "getting ink" or "hits" (exposure in the mass media or on the Web site), because that is their experience as former journalists now working in public relations.

Concerned citizens see frequent references to "PR," "public relations," and "flacks" in press coverage of scandals, oil spills, industrial pollution, political campaign shenanigans, city hall corruption, and other breaches of the public trust. Movies and television programs featuring public relations practitioners often do not present accurate portrayals. Media coverage seldom associates public relations with positive stories of organizations and their accomplishments. Books such as *PR! A Social History of Spin* and *Toxic Sludge Is Good for You* sensationalize accounts of press agentry and advocacy on behalf of clients and causes later proven to be of dubious merit. There is little news value or market for reports about the good work done by public relations on behalf of clients and causes judged worthy of public support. Who outside a hospital's stakeholder publics pays attention to a successful development campaign that funded a new pediatric wing? Other than investors and employees, what other groups care if the investor relations staff successfully debunked press reports of impending bankruptcy? In other words, it depends on who values what and who has a stake in the organization's success or failure.

In short, most people know public relations by what they see organizations and practitioners do under the banner of "public relations" and by what media report as "public relations." Few study the concept itself or the roles public relations plays in organizations and society. The challenge for practitioners is to define and perform public relations in ways consistent with the contemporary meaning of this necessary organizational and social function.

Toward Recognition and Maturity

Some scholars credit public relations for the heightened attention to public accountability and social responsibility among government administrators and business executives (see Exhibit 1.3 on page 25). Others emphasize the function's role in making organizations more responsive to public interests and more accepting of their corporate social responsibility (CSR):

> The new era of transparency is part of an offshoot movement in CSR that's been dubbed "sustainability." Sustainability proponents argue that companies that are consistently indifferent to their impact on the environment and its various stakeholders—such as employees and customers—are threatening their own long-term sustainability.[42]

As the dust jacket of *The Naked Corporation: How the Age of Transparency Will Revolutionize Business* says, "If you have to be naked, you had better be buff."[43] One business leader long ago said:

> We know perfectly well that business does not function by divine right, but, like any other part of society, exists with the sanction of the community as a whole. . . . Today's public opinion, though it may appear as light as air, may become tomorrow's legislation for better or worse.[44]

Public relations also helps organizations anticipate and respond to public perceptions and opinions, to new values and lifestyles, to power shifts among the

EXHIBIT 1.3

Public Relations in the Tylenol Crises

Lawrence G. Foster,
Corporate Vice President—
Public Relations (retired),
Johnson & Johnson

A different form of terrorism was unleashed on America in 1982 with the grim news of cyanide-laced Tylenol poisonings in the Chicago area. Seven people died. Because the extent of the contamination was not immediately known, there was grave concern for the safety of the estimated 100 million Americans who were using Tylenol.

The first critical public relations decision, taken immediately and with total support from company management, was to cooperate fully with the news media. The press was key to warning the public of the danger. The poisonings also called for immediate action to protect the consumer, so the decision was made to recall two batches of the product and later to withdraw it from store shelves nationally.

During the crisis phase of the Tylenol tragedy, virtually every public relations decision was based on sound, socially responsible business principles, which is when public relations is most effective.

Johnson & Johnson's corporate Credo strongly influenced many of the key decisions. Robert Wood Johnson, son of the company founder and, at the time, chairman of the company, wrote the one-page Credo in 1943. The Credo lists four responsibilities. The customer is placed first and foremost, followed by responsibility to employees, to the communities where they work and live, and finally, responsibility to the stockholders. (See the complete Credo in Chapter 12.)

At Johnson & Johnson, Lawrence G. Foster, corporate vice president of public relations, reported directly to chairman and CEO James E. Burke, who promptly formed a seven-member strategy committee to deal with the crisis. Foster and five other senior executives on the committee met with Burke twice daily for the next six weeks to make key decisions, ranging from advertising strategy and network television interviews to planning Tylenol's comeback in tamper-resistant packaging.

In the weeks following the murders, Foster and his three senior staff members, all former journalists, responded to more than 2,500 calls from the press. They were helped by the smaller public relations staff at McNeil Consumer Products (manufacturers of Tylenol). While the corporate staff was dealing with the press, Burson-Marsteller, which had the product publicity account for Tylenol, began planning a unique 30-city video press conference via satellite to reintroduce the product. Polls showed that 90 percent of Americans did not fault the company, and 79 percent said they would again purchase Tylenol. The satellite relaunch took place in just six weeks. Later, sales of Tylenol began soaring to new highs.

The *Washington Post* wrote: "Johnson & Johnson has effectively demonstrated **how** a major business ought to handle a disaster."

The unthinkable happened four years later. A woman in Westchester County, New York, died after ingesting a Tylenol capsule that contained cyanide. A second contaminated bottle was found in a nearby store a few days later. Chairman Burke reconvened the strategy committee, and the Credo was at the center of the discussions. The next day, Johnson & Johnson announced that, henceforth, no J&J company worldwide would market any over-the-counter capsule product because the safety of customers could no longer be assured, even when the capsules were in the new safety packaging. The public made Tylenol caplets a best seller soon after, and to this day Johnson & Johnson has kept its pledge not to market an over-the-counter capsule product anywhere in the world.

Once again, Robert Wood Johnson's Credo had shown the way. The Tylenol tragedies demonstrated that public relations is a business of basics and that the best public relations decisions are closely linked to sound business practices and a socially responsible corporate philosophy.*

---

*For more detailed discussion of the Tylenol crises, see Lawrence G. Foster, "Tylenol: 20 Years Later," *The Public Relations Strategist* 8, Issue 4 (Fall 2002), 16–20; and Foster's *Robert Wood Johnson: The Gentleman Rebel* (Ashland, OH: Lillian Press, 1999).

—Courtesy Lawrence G. Foster, Corporate Vice President—Public Relations (retired), Johnson & Johnson. Used with permission.

electorate and within legislative bodies, and to other changes in the social and political environment. This dialogue contributes to making the democratic process more effective in meeting social needs. Without effective public relations, organizations tend to become insensitive to changes occurring around them and to become dysfunctional as they grow increasingly out of step with their environments.

Public relations also makes information available through the public information system that is essential to both democratic society and organizational survival. Practitioners increase public knowledge and understanding by promoting expression and debate in the competitive marketplace of ideas regarding, for example, the need for health care and immigration reform, the causes and cures of global warming, the value of a new public transportation system, the impact of international trade barriers, or the need for blood and organ donations. Public relations serves the public interest by providing organizations and interest groups voices in the public forum for alternative points of view, including the views of those—such as the homeless and powerless—who would not otherwise be heard because of limited media attention.

The practice serves society by mediating conflict and by building the consensus needed to maintain social order. Its social function—its mission—is accomplished when it replaces ignorance, coercion, and intransigence with knowledge, compromise, and adjustment. In other words, *public relations facilitates adjustment and maintenance in the social systems that provide us with our physical and social needs.*

In the final analysis, an organization's relationships are the responsibility of top management. As public relations counselor Henry DeVries rephrased our definition of public relations, "Public relations is the boss's job to build and keep strong bonds with key groups that the organization needs to grow and thrive." Once this concept of public relations is embraced at the top, it spreads and becomes part of an organization's culture. The axioms outlined in Exhibit 1.4 spell out the principles and values central to this concept of contemporary practice.

Public relations professionals who help organizations establish and maintain mutually beneficial relationships perform an essential management function that

EXHIBIT 1.4

Core Axioms of Public Relations

1. Public relations takes a broad view of an organization's environment by attending to a wide range of issues and relationships with stakeholders.

2. Public relations is part of strategic management, seeking to avoid or solve problems through a goal-directed process.

3. Public relations outcomes must be quantified and measured. This requires a detailed understanding and assessment of what's happening now and of desired future states.

4. Strategic planning begins by identifying the current conditions motivating the process, the contributing forces and actors in the situation, the objectives to be achieved with each target public, and the overall program goal.

5. Public relations programs outline how the organization will get from where it is to where it wants to be.

6. Public relations initiatives must have senior management's support and cooperation, and cannot be isolated from other operations.

7. Success or failure depends more on what the organization *does* than on what it *says*, unless the communication itself becomes a problem. Success, however, requires a coordinated program of deeds and words.

8. Success also requires that all actions, communication, and outcomes are ethical, legal, and consistent with the organization's social responsibility.

9. Ultimately, success will be judged by the organization's impact on society and culture—as will the character and professional careers of the public relations practitioners who helped plan and implement its programs.

has an impact on the larger society. They encourage social responsibility in organizations and promote public relations' essential role in maintaining social order. Inherent in this concept of public relations is a moral commitment to mutual adjustment among interdependent elements of society. That calling motivates the chapters that follow.

Notes

1 John Stauber and Sheldon Rampton, *Toxic Sludge Is Good for You! Lies, Damn Lies and the Public Relations Industry* (Monroe, ME: Common Courage Press, 1995), 2.

2 Thomas J. Madden, *Spin Man: The Topsy-Turvy World of Public Relations . . . a Tell-All Tale* (Boca Raton, FL: TransMedia Publishing, Inc., 1997), 1.

3 Stuart Ewen, *PR! A Social History of Spin* (New York: Basic Books, 1996), viii.

4 Edward L. Bernays, *Propaganda* (New York: Horace Liveright, 1928), 9–10, as quoted by Larry Tye in *The Father of Spin: Edward L. Bernays & the Birth of Public Relations* (New York: Crown Publishers, Inc., 1998), 92.

5 James E. Grunig and Todd Hunt, *Managing Public Relations* (New York: Holt, Rinehart and Winston, 1984), 6.

6 Harwood L. Childs, *An Introduction to Public Opinion* (New York: John Wiley and Sons, 1940), 3, 13.

7 Rex F. Harlow, "Building a Public Relations Definition," *Public Relations Review* 2, no. 4 (Winter 1976): 36.

8 Joye C. Gordon, "Interpreting Definitions of Public Relations: Self Assessment and a Symbolic Interactionism-Based Alternative," *Public Relations Review* 23, no. 1 (Spring 1997): 57–66.

9 Thomas L. Harris, *The Marketer's Guide to Public Relations* (New York: John Wiley and Sons, 1991), 12. This book is not about public relations. Rather, it describes how public relations practitioners apply their knowledge and skills to support marketing.

10 Kathy H. Cripps, "Wanted: More of the Best Examples of the Best in PR," *PRWeek* (January 9, 2007), 5.

11 Paul Holmes, "To Overcome Its Identity Crisis, the Industry Has to Define and Defend 'Public Relations'." *PRWeek*, 17 March 2003, 9.

12 Al Ries and Laura Ries, *The Fall of Advertising & the Rise of PR* (New York: HarperCollins Publishers, Inc., 2002), 129.

13 Fraser P. Seitel, "What Is the Difference Between Marketing, Advertising and PR?" *O'Dwyer's PR Report* (May 2006), 39.

14 Philip Kotler and Gary Armstrong, *Principles of Marketing,* 12th ed. (Upper Saddle River, NJ: Pearson/Prentice Hall, 2008), 7.

15 Miriam Jordan, "Nestlé Markets Baby Formula to Hispanic Mothers in U.S.," *Wall Street Journal,* 4 March 2004, www.breastfeedingtaskforla.org/media/WSJ%2003%2004%2004%20Nestle%20Formula.pdf.

16 "Employee Comms Vital to How IBM's Work Gets Done," *PRWeek*, 17 May 2004, 7.

17 Alvie L. Smith in letter to authors, March 28, 1993.

18 Gerri L. Smith and Robert L. Heath, "Moral Appeals in Mobil Oil's Op-Ed Campaign," *Public Relations Review* 16, no. 4 (Winter 1990): 49.

19 Richard C. Wender, M.D., "Cancer Society Was First to Issue Awareness Ads," *Wall Street Journal* (September 24, 2007), A17.

20 Henry C. Rogers, *Walking the Tightrope: The Private Confessions of a Public Relations Man* (New York: William Morrow, 1980), 14.

21 "A Shoe-In for Product Publicity," *Public Relations Tactics* 4, no. 1 (January 1997), 3.

22 Robert Barr (Associated Press), "King of the Tabloid Publicists Usually Holds the Smoking Gun," *San Diego Union-Tribune*, 1 January 2000, A-33.

23 "Preach What We Practice," *PRWeek*, 18 February 2002, 21.

24 J. A. R. Pimlott, *Public Relations and American Democracy* (Princeton, NJ: Princeton University Press, 1951/1972), 76.

25 Mordecai Lee, "A Public Relations Program Even Congress Could Love: Federal Information Centers," *Public Relations Review* 30, no. 1 (March 2004): 62.

26 Raymond L. Hoewing, "The State of Public Affairs: A Profession Reinventing Itself," in *Practical Public Affairs in an Era of Change*, ed. Lloyd B. Dennis (Lanham, MD: University Press of America, 1996), 45.

27 Marc Longpre, "Public Affairs Pros Must be Open to New Relationships," *PRWeek* (April 30, 2007), 6.

28 John L. Paluszek, "Editorial Note: Defining Terms," in *Practical Public Affairs*, xviii.

29 Rich Long, "PR and GR: So Happy Together?" *The Public Relations Strategist* 8, no. 3 (Summer 2002), 17.

30 Hoewing, "The State of Public Affairs," 34.

31 United States Senate, Virtual Reference Desk (February 6, 2008) at http://www.senate.gov/reference/reference_index_subjects/Lobbying_vrd.htm

32 U.S. House of Representatives Legislative Resource Center, author's interview with clerk in the Office of Records and Registration, January 29, 2008. Similar data are published in *Washington Representatives 2008 Package*

(Bethesda, MD: Columbia Books & Information Services, 2008). Available at http://www.columbiabooks.com/servlet/the-Directories/Categories. (Note: Some commercial publications list larger numbers of lobbyists, because the lists include both active and inactive lobbyists who have registered in the last decade.)

[33] "Influence: A Booming Business," The Center for Public Integrity, Washington, D.C. Downloaded from http://www.publicintegrity.org/hiredguns/report.aspx?aid=957, January 28, 2008.

[34] Charles S. Mack, "Lobbying and Political Action," in *Practical Public Affairs*, 105.

[35] Kurt Wise, "Lobbying and Relationship Management: The K Street Connection," *Journal of Public Relations Research* 19, no. 4 (2007): 368.

[36] Priscilla Murphy, "Chaos Theory as a Model for Managing Issues and Crises," *Public Relations Review* 22, no. 2 (Summer 1996): 103.

[37] W. Howard Chase, "Public Issue Management: The New Science," *Public Relations Journal* 33, no. 10 (October 1977): 25–26.

[38] W. Howard Chase and Teresa Yancey Crane, "Issue Management: Dissolving the Archaic Division between Line and Staff," in *Practical Public Affairs*, 130–31.

[39] Kerry Tucker and Glen Broom, "Managing Issues Acts as Bridge to Strategic Planning," *Public Relations Journal* 49, no. 11 (November 1993): 38–40.

[40] Martha M. Lauzen, "Understanding the Relation between Public Relations and Issues Management," *Journal of Public Relations Research* 9, no. 1 (1997): 80. For a theoretical basis of issues management, see Robert L. Heath, *Strategic Issues Management: Organizations and Public Policy Challenges* (Thousand Oaks, CA: Sage Publications, Inc., 1997).

[41] Barbara K. Petersen and Hugh J. Martin, "CEO Perceptions of Investor Relations as a Public Relations Function: An Exploratory Study," *Journal of Public Relations Research* 8, no. 3 (1996): 205–6.

[42] "CSR: Beyond Lip Service," *PRWeek*, 6 January 2003, 17.

[43] Don Tapscott and David Ticoll, *The Naked Corporation: How the Age of Transparency Will Revolutionize Business* (New York: The Free Press, 2003).

[44] Ibid.

Additional Sources

Cameron, Glen T., Dennis L. Wilcox, Bryan H. Reber, and Jae-Hwa Shin. *Public Relations Today: Managing Competition and Conflict.* Boston, MA: Pearson/Allyn & Bacon, 2008. An alternative take on the basic concept of public relations—"managing competition and conflict"—as if organizations have such power.

Center, Allen H., Patrick Jackson, Stacey Smith, and Frank R. Stansberry. *Public Relations Practices: Managerial Case Studies and Problems*, 7th ed. Upper Saddle River, NJ: Pearson Prentice Hall, 2008. Collection of classic and recent case studies illustrating management problems and opportunities in public relations.

Clarke, Torie. *Lipstick on a Pig: Winning in the No-Spin Era by Someone Who Knows the Game.* (New York: Free Press/Simon & Schuster, 2006). Former Pentagon spokeswoman and Assistant Secretary of Defense for Public Affairs outlines why the concept of "spin" is both not possible and irrelevant in the Internet age.

Grunig, Larissa A., James E. Grunig, and David M. Dozier. *Excellent Public Relations and Effective Organizations: A Study of Communication Management in Three Countries.* Mahwah, NJ: Lawrence Erlbaum Associates, 2002. The third volume of "excellence study" reports that document the relationship-building concept of public relations.

Heath, Robert L., and W. Timothy Coombs. *Today's Public Relations: An Introduction.* Thousand Oaks, CA: Sage Publications, 2006. Another recent addition to the list of useful introductory texts.

Kelly, Kathleen S. *Effective Fund-Raising Management.* Mahwah, NJ: Lawrence Erlbaum Associates, 1997. Introduces history, theory, ethics, legal issues, and techniques of expanding practice of fund-raising and development in not-for-profit settings from a public relations perspective.

Kotler, Philip. *Marketing Management*, 11th ed. Upper Saddle River, NJ: Prentice Hall, 2003. A marketing expert's view of public relations as one of "four promotional tools" in the marketing "tool box."

Lattimore, Dan, Otis Baskin, Suzette T. Heiman, and Elizabeth L. Toth. *Public Relations: The Profession and the Practice,* 2nd ed. New York: McGraw-Hill, 2007. Yet another useful introductory textbook for the field.

Schultz, Don, and Heidi Schultz. *IMC: The Next Generation* (New York: McGraw-Hill, 2003). Updates and expands concept of integrated marketing communication (IMC), but reaffirms IMC's focus on *customers* and *prospects* (pp. 48 and 69) and "a customer-centric organization" (p. 52)—in other words, *marketing.*

Wilcox, Dennis L., and Glen T. Cameron. *Public Relations: Strategies and Tactics*, 8th ed. Boston: Pearson Allyn & Bacon, 2007. Yet another useful introductory text.

Practitioners of Public Relations

STUDY GUIDE After studying Chapter 2, you should be able to:

▶ Describe practitioners' characteristics and work assignments.

▶ Define the four major roles played by practitioners, discuss the major differences among the roles, and distinguish among them in practice.

▶ List the five criteria for evaluating the professional status of public relations and discuss the extent

to which public relations measures up on each of the criteria.

▶ Outline the major requirements for success in public relations, identifying writing as the primary requirement for entry to the field and success in the practice.

This chapter discusses public relations practitioners—who they are, what they do, the roles they play, and their professional aspirations. Compared to accounting, law, and medicine, the relatively young practice of public relations is an *emerging profession*. Unlike the more established professions, public relations does not require a prescribed educational preparation, government-sanctioned qualifying exams, and peer review to ensure competent and ethical practice. Nor do its practitioners operate in clearly defined roles recognized as essential for the common good. And because there are no complete official lists, estimates of how many practice public relations are based on membership data from the major professional societies worldwide and statistics from the U.S. Department of Labor.

Number and Distribution

Little agreement on the underlying concept and inconsistent use of titles complicate attempts to count the number of public relations practitioners, even in the United States, let alone worldwide. As noted in Chapter 1, what one organization calls "marketing communication" may actually describe a public relations position. What another organization calls a "public relations representative" would be more accurately titled "sales" or "customer service representative."

The U.S. Department of Labor reports public relations employment statistics in its monthly Employment and Earnings for "public relations specialists" under the occupational heading "professional and related occupations." Unfortunately, these categories do not include all who work in the field. Artists, graphic designers, photographers, videographers, lobbyists, receptionists, researchers, and other specialists who work in public relations departments and firms may be counted in other categories. As a result, the Labor Department's figures probably include fewer than half of all those working in public relations. Even though the data are incomplete, magazines like *Fortune* and *U.S.*

The way to gain a good reputation is to endeavor to be what you desire to appear.
—Socrates

To be credible and effective as a communicator both inside and outside, truth, trust and transparency must be your modus operandi.[1]
—Rear Admiral (ret.) T. L. McCreary

News & World Report typically rate public relations among the most rapidly growing and "best jobs."

For example, the Labor Department reported 129,000 employed in public relations in 2000. By 2006, however, the reported total of almost 210,000 indicated continued growth in public relations employment.[2] The Bureau of Labor Statistics put the 2006 employment total at 243,000 and projected an 18 percent increase to 286,000 by 2016.[3] No doubt, the actual totals are much larger, but there is little agreement on the actual numbers.

Growth is worldwide. For example, the data from China indicate rapid development of public relations in all manner of public affairs in just a matter of two or three decades. The leading public relations expert in China, Ming Anxiang, estimates that there are more than 100,000 practitioners; 10,000 public relations firms; public relations courses offered at 10,000 universities and colleges; and professional societies at the national, provincial, and municipal levels.[4] Similarly, public relations is a growing profession throughout the rest of Asia, Africa, Australia and New Zealand, Europe, and Latin America.

Even as the number of people engaged in public relations work continues to increase worldwide, so do where they work and who they are.

Where They Work

Employment opportunities for public relations specialists exist in almost every community but are concentrated in major population centers. For example, in the United States, the greatest numbers of Public Relations Society of America (PRSA) members are in California, New York, Texas, Ohio, Michigan, Pennsylvania, and Illinois. Washington, D.C., however, has the largest PRSA chapter, with more than 1,300 members in the National Capital chapter. The Atlanta, Georgia, chapter is second with 900; the New York chapter has 730 members (a sharp decline from 920 in 2004); the Philadelphia chapter has 600 members; the Detroit chapter, 550; the Chicago, Denver, and Los Angeles chapters, about 500 each; and Dallas and Houston, more than 400 each. The Chicago chapter celebrated its 60th anniversary and the Denver chapter celebrated its 50th anniversary in 2008. One third of members in the Detroit chapter, founded in 1947, are "APR"—Accredited Public Relations (see section on "Accreditation" in Chapter 5).

The largest employers of practitioners are business and commercial corporations followed by public relations firms and advertising agencies. Many also work as individual consultants ("sole practitioners"), often after being released from positions in downsizing internal departments (see Table 2.1).

The single largest employer for public relations is the federal government. According to the latest available data from the U.S. Office of Personnel Management, about 4,400 "public affairs" specialists work under various titles. The total jumps to more than 18,000 in the "Information and Arts" category, which includes photographers, writers and editors, visual information specialists, and others working in internal and external communication for the government.[5] However, because the function is often camouflaged to hide it from Congress and the press, reliable figures on the number of public relations specialists in government are not available.

The growing number of public relations firms range in size from an individual counselor (who may use "and Associates") to a large national and international firm with a staff of several hundred. For example, the four largest international firms—New York–based Weber Shandwick, Hill & Knowlton, and Burson-Marsteller, and St. Louis–based Fleishman-Hillard—each employ between 2,500 and 3,000. The

TABLE 2.1

Public Relations
Employers

Organization Type	Estimated Percentage of Practitioners[1]
Corporations: manufacturing, industrial, consumer goods, financial, insurance, media, and entertainment	35
Public relations firms, advertising agencies, marketing communication firms, and individual practitioners	25
Associations, foundations, and educational institutions	15
Health care: hospitals, health promotion organizations, clinics, home health-care agencies, and mental health centers	9
Government: local, state, and federal	8
Charitable, religious, and social welfare organizations	8

[1]Estimates based on PRSA and IABC membership profiles, and descriptive statistics from *PRWeek* and other surveys of practitioners.

largest independently owned firm—Edelman Public Relations Worldwide (with headquarters offices in New York and Chicago)—employs almost 2,900. Seattle-based high-tech firm Waggener Edstrom Worldwide has more than 800 employees and New York–based Ruder Finn more than 600.[6]

Several major corporations have 100 or more public relations specialists in headquarters and branch offices. Downsizing during the 1990s and 2000s greatly reduced the number of large staffs and shifted work (outsourcing) to a growing number of increasingly specialized external firms and individual practitioners. For example, *Fortune* 500 company Goodrich Corporation has about 24,000 employees worldwide, but only seven in its public relations function—vice president Lisa Bottle and staffs of five in the United States and one in the United Kingdom.[7] Similarly, when Elise Eberwein was vice president of corporate communication at America West Airlines, she supervised a staff of seven for a company with 13,000 U.S. employees, most of whom "work at 30,000 feet." When the airline merged with U.S. Airways in 2005, she became senior vice president of people, communications, and culture, supervising a staff of nine. Her team now does media relations, employee communication, and investor relations for the new U.S. Airways Group with 36,000 employees worldwide.[8]

The New Majority: Women

According to 1968 U.S. Department of Labor statistics for the "public relations specialists" occupational category, only 25 percent were women. By the end of 1983, women held more than 50 percent of public relations jobs. In 2006, more than 68 percent were women.[9]

When the late Rea Smith wrote "Women in Public Relations: What They Have Achieved" in 1968, only one in ten members of PRSA was female.[10] The ratio was one in seven in 1975 when Sondra Gorney concluded that "the walls of the traditional 'man's world' have not tumbled yet."[11] Apparently the walls had tumbled by 1990, when PRSA membership was 54 percent female, and International Association of Business Communicators (IABC) membership was 60 percent female.[12]

Current professional society membership profiles show that 65 to 75 percent are female, and data from colleges and universities indicate that at least 64 percent and, in some schools, more than 80 percent of public relations majors are female.[13] *In 2006, 80 percent of public relations graduates were female.*[14] Simply put, public relations is a female-dominated profession.

Education and Preparation

More than 90 percent of practitioners are college graduates, including almost 30 percent with some postgraduate studies without a graduate degree completed, 28 percent with master's degrees, and 2 percent with doctoral degrees. Surveys historically show that practitioners entered the field from many academic majors and work experiences. Historically, the majority of practitioners majored in journalism, with news-editorial graduates outnumbering public relations graduates two to one. English, speech, communication, and business followed journalism as college majors of those entering public relations. But that has changed in the last two decades. For example, nearly 40 percent of the respondents to *PRWeek*'s annual salary survey in 2008 reported public relations as their college major, with fewer than 20 percent marking journalism as their major.[15]

Increasingly, employers look for specialized public relations degrees and advanced degrees emphasizing research and social science. The Commission on Public Relations Education quoted the former University of California at Berkeley chancellor, Clark Kerr, who suggested that requiring such specialized education indicates progress as a profession:

> Some new professions are being born; others are becoming more professional. . . . The university becomes the chief port of entry for these professions. In fact a profession gains its identity by making the university the port of entry.[16]

In addition to the more than 350 colleges and universities offering public relations undergraduate and graduate programs, PRSA, IABC, Institute for Public Relations, Arthur W. Page Society, and other professional and commercial groups offer continuing education courses, institutes, seminars, and conferences. These professional development programs—now seen as essential for maintaining cutting-edge skills and knowledge—attract increasing numbers of working practitioners.

Public relations employment no longer requires journalism experience. On the other hand, journalistic media experience gives practitioners an understanding of media gatekeepers' values and ways of working. If that experience leads to a "journalist-in-residence" approach, however, public relations will be limited to news dissemination and media relations. Older and more experienced practitioners have typically worked in the media prior to their career in public relations. Fewer than one out of five younger practitioners have worked for newspapers, magazines, radio stations, or television stations before being hired in public relations. More and more employers and public relations managers consider public relations education desirable preparation, making it easier to move directly into the field after graduation. Given the choice, however, employers still value media experience, even if only with the college newspaper or radio station.

Many employers also look for education or experience in a specialized field in addition to public relations. The most difficult positions to fill are those that require specialized preparation and backgrounds such as computer technology, corporate finance, health care, and agriculture. For example, students who combine public relations education with a minor in health care promotion or hospital administration have a clear advantage when applying for hospital public relations openings. Likewise, graduates who minored in computer science while completing their public relations education have a competitive advantage in the world of high-tech public relations.

Salaries

Salary survey reports typically show that the highest salaries are paid to practitioners working for corporations, particularly those in industry and manufacturing, followed closely by those in high-tech and power utilities. The highest paid specialties are financial/investor relations and crisis management, followed by issue/reputation management.[17]

Many experienced practitioners earn $300,000–$500,000, or more. These practitioners typically work for multibillion-dollar corporations in which the top public relations executives often are corporate officers, either elected or appointed. Officers typically receive stock options, bonus or profit-sharing checks, and lucrative retirement programs in addition to their six-figure salaries. Fringe benefits and perquisites add considerable value to their positions. Employers do not frivolously dispense high salaries or extra benefits, however. Just as when recruiting other top executives, employers must compete for top public relations professionals and managers. As a result, compensation packages for the top public relations post at major corporations often are in the $1–$2 million range. For example, when Wal-Mart lured Edelman Public Relations vice chairman Leslie A. Dach from Washington, D.C., to Bentonville, Arkansas, as executive vice president of corporate affairs and government relations, his compensation package became big news. *The New Yorker* magazine reported:

> He was given three million dollars in stock and a hundred and sixty-eight thousand stock options, in addition to an undisclosed base salary. He and his wife, a nutritionist, recently bought a $2.7-million house in the Cleveland Park neighborhood of Washington. He commutes to Bentonville during the week, to an apartment furnished out of a Wal-Mart store.[18]

Competition for management-level talent is so intense that executive search firms (sometimes called "headhunters") are retained to identify, screen, and recruit finalists for top public relations positions. Executive recruiters report that senior corporate public relations posts are now paying more than $500,000, and companies have a hard time filling them. Searches may last a year.

Salaries tend to be highest in the Northeast and Middle Atlantic states, led by New York and Washington, D.C. The West also pays relatively high salaries, with the Seattle area, San Francisco, and California's Silicon Valley leading that part of the country. Salaries in the Midwest and South are below the national median. Recent Department of Labor data indicate that for all "public relations specialists" the *mean* salary for 2006 was $53,760, and for "public relations managers," $99,250.[19] A more recent survey of PRSA members found that the average salary was $75,400.[20]

PRWeek's "Salary Survey 2008" of 994 self-selected online respondents found an overall *median* salary of $82,400. Corporate practitioners made a median salary of $97,500, while those working in public relations firms made $75,400. As is usually the case, financial and investor relations was the highest paid specialty with a median salary of $158,300, followed by reputation management ($145,600), and crisis management ($137,500). Also, not surprisingly, salaries increase with years of experience—rising from a median of $40,300 for those with two or less years of experience, to a median of $171,400 for those with 21 or more years of experience.[21]

Salary survey results show a pay difference in public relations that deserves special attention: Surveys consistently find that salaries paid to women are below those paid to men. Department of Labor statistics, however, show that the trend shows a narrowing gap. For example, in 1979, the youngest women entering the workforce made 79 percent of what their male counterparts made. By 2005, they were making 93 percent of male counterparts' salaries.[22] Comparisons of salaries in public relations over time indicate "gaps" in the range of $10,000 to $20,000 between men's and women's salaries.[23]

One series of studies tracked practitioner salaries from 1979 to 1985 to 1991. Between 1979 and 1985, the salary gap between men and women increased. The results showed that women earned less than men even when they had equal education, professional experience, and tenure in their jobs.[24] The disparity diminished, however, when researchers later compared 1979 salaries with 1991 salaries. When they controlled for years of professional experience, role in management, and participation in decision making, the salary differences between men and women were not statistically significant.

> The relation between gender and salary is not statistically significant . . . after controlling for the influences of professional experience, manager role enactment, and decision-making participation . . . [which] suggests that patterns of gender salary discrimination and gender role segregation may be breaking down in public relations work.[25]

The researchers cautioned, however, that although this one study indicates progress toward gender equity, it does not mean that the glass ceiling has been removed. Further analyses discovered that the income discrepancy was associated with the middle years of their careers, but was not statistically significant when comparing the salaries of men and women with 0 to 6 years of experience and with 19-plus years of experience.[26]

Hutton, who has long questioned the gender salary gap, reanalyzed salary data from a *PRWeek* annual salary survey that had a *self-selected* e-mail sample of almost 5,000. He concluded:

> In line with the very limited number of serious studies that have been conducted in the past 10–15 years (and contrary to popular belief and many unfounded assertions), a sophisticated analysis of the *PRWeek* salary data demonstrates that gender plays little or no role in PR salaries. Clearly, factors such as experience and hard work are far more important than gender.[27]

There also are other positive signs. Newsletters and publications covering public relations in the United States increasingly reflect the pattern of women being promoted to the top public relations positions in all types of organizations. Of course, this not surprising, given the gender makeup of the students in the major and those entering the practice. This may not be the case worldwide, however.

Work Assignments

Some describe public relations work by listing the specialized parts of the function: media relations, investor relations, community relations, employee relations, government relations, and so forth. Such labels do not describe the many activities and diverse assignments in the day-to-day practice, however. The following ten categories summarize what public relations specialists do at work:

1. *Writing and Editing:* Composing print and broadcast news releases, feature stories, newsletters to employees and external stakeholders, correspondence, Web site and other online media messages, shareholder and annual reports, speeches, brochures, video and slide-show scripts, trade publication articles, institutional advertisements, and product and technical collateral materials.

2. *Media Relations and Placement:* Contacting news media, magazines, Sunday supplements, freelance writers, and trade publications with the intent of getting them to publish or broadcast news and features about or originated by an organization. Responding to media requests for information, verification of stories, and access to authoritative sources.

3. *Research:* Gathering information about public opinion, trends, emerging issues, political climate and legislation, media coverage, special-interest groups, and other concerns related to an organization's stakeholders. Searching the Internet, online services, and electronic government databases. Designing program research, conducting surveys, and hiring research firms.

4. *Management and Administration:* Programming and planning in collaboration with other managers; determining needs, establishing priorities, defining publics, setting goals and objectives, and developing strategy and tactics. Administering personnel, budget, and program schedules.

5. *Counseling:* Advising top management on the social, political, and regulatory environments; consulting with the management team on how to avoid or respond to crises; and working with key decision makers to devise strategies for managing or responding to critical and sensitive issues.

6. *Special Events:* Arranging and managing news conferences, 10K runs, conventions, open houses, ribbon cuttings and grand openings, anniversary celebrations, fund-raising events, visiting dignitaries, contests, award programs, and other special observances.

7. *Speaking:* Appearing before groups, coaching others for speaking assignments, and managing a speakers' bureau to provide platforms for the organization before important audiences.

8. *Production:* Creating communications using multimedia knowledge and skills, including art, typography, photography, layout, and computer desktop publishing; audio and video recording and editing; and preparing audiovisual presentations.

9. *Training:* Preparing executives and other designated spokespersons to deal with media and to make other public appearances. Instructing others in the organization to improve writing and communication skills. Helping introduce changes in organizational culture, policy, structure, and process.

10. *Contact:* Serving as liaison with media, community, and other internal and external groups. Communicating, negotiating, and managing conflict with stakeholders. Meeting and hosting visitors.

Although last on this list, being "good with people" is often the first thing many attribute to public relations. True enough, public relations people often find themselves dealing with people problems and sensitive relationships, but it would be misleading to limit one's view of public relations work to this commonly held stereotype.

FIGURE 2.1

Job Descriptions

Director–University Relations
Director will report directly to university president and lead program of media relations, publications, electronic media and issues management. Responsible for researching, writing and editing news releases, feature stories, fact sheets and other materials about the university to national news media. Must be hands-on leader with knowledge of strategic management, publication production and new media design.

VICE PRESIDENT
INVESTOR RELATIONS
International pharmaceutical company seeks experienced investor/financial relations executive. New VP reports directly to CEO/president and serves on the exec. committee. VP manages IR web site; maintains institutional, broker and retail investor contacts; coordinates financial reporting; and produces annual reports. Corp./IR communication exp.; and strong analytical, writing and management skills; and working knowledge of SEC disclosure requirements. MBA preferred and prior exp. in pharm./health care necessary.

PUBLIC RELATIONS
Software company seeks PR
writin
article
ade
s
nd
ce dir
her
or

COORDINATOR—INTERNAL
COMMUNICATIONS
Medical center Communications Division opportunity for leader with 8-10 years significant supervisory experience in organizational communication. Coordinator will supervise internal publications, staff communications and recruiting outreach support. Must have extensive writing, planning, consulting and project management experience. Experience and knowledge of new communication technology required. Master's degree preferred.

public relations account executive
Requires minimum five years experience in tourism / hospitality industry account service, travel writing background and strong media contacts. Fluency in Spanish helpful. Portfolio of results-oriented work and strong reference letters from previous clients required for interview.

COMMUNICATION DIRECTOR
Laser systems company seeks accomplished professional to direct government/community relations and public affairs. You also will direct institutional advertising, environmental communications, customer relations, employee and plant tours.

Public Relations Director
Health care provider seeks senior manager to plan strategic public relations activities and collaborate with other departments heads to maintain relationships with payors, physicians, area consumers, and employees. Must have top-level media and community contacts.

Director of Campaign Communications
Major charitable foundation seeks pro to direct media relations, special events, donor relations and campaign communications. Requires significant experience in fund raising; proven record of establishing program goals, identifying target publics, and setting specific communication objectives; significant experience managing multi-media communications program; and strong presentation skills. Successful candidate will plan, manage and direct implementation of a $5-million capital campaign. Position reports directly to Executive Director.

The mix of assignments and responsibilities varies greatly from organization to organization, but one task is the common denominator: writing. (Study the job descriptions in Figure 2.1.) Writing skills remain a requirement throughout one's career. Daily logs in Exhibits 2.1, 2.2, and 2.3 illustrate the central role of writing in public relations work. To manage their jobs, individual practitioners devise and apply similar strategies and approaches day in and day out. In other words, they develop and play roles.

EXHIBIT 2.1

Day in the Life of a Nonprofit Development Associate

Susan D. Simmons*
Development Associate
Dress for Success Worldwide
New York

8:30 a.m.   Coordinated "DFS 101" open house, introducing potential donors and volunteers to Dress for Success. Those attending learned how to volunteer with the organization, how to organize clothing drives to benefit the organization, and how to encourage their friends and companies to donate funds to the organization.

10:00   Sat in on conference call with a new gala sponsor to discuss deadlines and specifics of their sponsorship—how many seats they will have at their table, what benefits accompany their sponsorship, etc. (Annual gala is our main fundraiser. The goal is to raise at least $1.1 million this year.)

10:30   Sent sponsorship request letters to our gala honorees' contacts, asking them to sponsor the honoree as well as the organization with a contribution.

11:25   Contacted potential donors for our silent auction, one of the other main fundraising components of the gala.

12:15 p.m.   Researched foundations to verify changes in eligibility requirements and deadlines.

1:00   Attended America's Charities event to build brand awareness for DFS and to make direct contact with participating donor organizations. America's Charities is an organization that allows donors to designate an amount of money each pay period to the charity of their choice.

2:30   Brainstormed potential silent auction packages with our director of special events and our corporate contributions manager. Our goal is to create exciting auction packages that will motivate high bids by those attending the gala.

2:55   Followed up with current gala sponsors to confirm their gift bag items and journal ads.

3:10   E-mailed and called gala planning committee members to learn what items each of them secured for the silent auction. (Note: A big part of my job is recruiting and working with DFS volunteers who do much of the behind-the-scenes work related to the gala—sending invitations, entering gala-related data, and working on the silent auction.)

3:35   Wrote bio on a recent Dress for Success client for a NASCAR event. NASCAR is one of our gala sponsors and is hosting two of our clients for a weekend in Los Angeles to celebrate their journey through the DFS program.

3:50   Researched community organizations that might be interested in purchasing a journal ad for the gala.

4:15   Updated donor and event database.

4:45   Wrote first draft of a "Thank You" letter to individual donors and auction donors.

5:15   Compiled weekly revenue report—a recap of the money raised so far for the gala.

---

*Served as president of the D. Parke Gibson chapter of the Public Relations Student Society of America (PRSSA) while a student at Howard University.

Roles

Over time, practitioners adopt patterns of behavior to deal with recurring situations in their work and to accommodate others' expectations of what they should do in their jobs. Four major public relations roles describe much of the practice. At one

EXHIBIT 2.2

Day in the Life of a Corporate Communications Coordinator

Yelena Durmashkin,
Senior Coordinator
Corporate Communications
Qualcomm, Incorporated
San Diego, CA

7:30–8:30	Make bi-weekly conference call to India office and public relations firm to discuss their public relations activities, status of interviews, and market situation updates.
8:30–9:10	Check e-mail and respond to requests.
9:10–10:15	Review public relations plans from international offices to ensure consistency with corporate messaging. Make edits to messaging, objectives, tactics, and media list before sending to senior manager and director for approval.
10:15–11:00	Draft public relations plan for the Company's community outreach project in Indonesia next month and forward to senior manager and director's additional approval.
11:00–11:40	Review press releases from the international offices and edit for AP style, corporate style, as well as content and messaging. Route edited releases for approval through corporate review cycle.
11:40–12:00	Meet with intern to discuss weekly activities and make new assignments, including first drafts of two press releases, a media alert, and an internal communication announcing a new press release policy.
12:00–1:00	Lunch with colleague from the government affairs department to discuss the community outreach project in Indonesia.
1:00–2:00	Attend bi-weekly meeting with internal company clients to discuss public relations support for upcoming projects.
2:00–3:00	Review interview information to be given to executives for media interviews next week.
3:00–3:30	Hold meeting with supervisor to discuss weekly activities and status of projects.
3:30–4:00	Review international office media proposals and Q&A documents before routing to senior manager and director for approval.
4:00–4:45	Finalize logistics of next week's media interviews and press conference.
4:45–5:45	Place bi-weekly public relations strategy call with Southeast Asia offices and agencies to discuss public relations activities in the regions, status of interviews, and public relations plan for the next fiscal year. (Yes, these calls actually happen on the same day due to time zone differences, so I get up early and stay late like this once every two weeks.)

time or another, however, practitioners play all these and other roles to varying degrees, even though a dominant role emerges as they go about their day-to-day work and dealings with others.

Communication Technician

Most practitioners enter the field as communication technicians. Entry-level job descriptions typically list communication and journalistic skills as requirements. Communication technicians are hired to write and edit employee newsletters, to write news releases and feature stories, to develop Web site content, and to deal with media contacts. Practitioners in this role usually are not present when management defines problems and selects solutions. They are brought in later to produce the

EXHIBIT 2.3

Day in the Life of a Senior Account Executive

Erin Barrier
Senior Account Executive
GolinHarris,
Los Angeles, CA

9:00 a.m. Get to my desk, start my computer, and review to-do list. Check messages and e-mails, responding to the most urgent messages.

9:30 Quickly scan the *Los Angeles Times, USA Today, New York Times,* and LAist.com for articles of interest to clients. Forward articles to associate account executive for inclusion in daily coverage report.

9:50 Meet with a colleague to brainstorm ideas for the next issue of a hotel client's e-newsletter to meeting planners.

10:00 Respond to museum exhibition client's e-mail requesting meeting next week. Notify team and write quick to-do list to prepare for meeting.

10:10 Make follow-up calls to trade magazines regarding recent news announcement for hotel client. Send requested press materials and images, as needed. Input call notes into media follow-up status grid and route to team for their additions.

11:00 Review daily coverage report for entertainment client and give approval to send to client.

11:10 Receive call from museum exhibition client regarding upcoming press conference. Discuss pros and cons of current location and review additional venue options. Revise current to-do list to accommodate new client request and research other potential venues. Recommend new venue and send to supervisor for review.

12:30 p.m. Grab quick lunch and head back to desk. Peruse various Web sites and blogs while eating, tagging anything that might be of interest to clients.

1:00 Receive call from hotel client who wants us to immediately distribute a press release announcing the company's new executive team. Call an impromptu team meeting and delegate tasks so the release can be sent out promptly. Update client on target distribution list. (Revise to-do list, again, based on new deadlines for the day.)

2:00 Participate in office-wide brainstorm to generate ideas for a new project for electronic game client.

2:45 Return call to sports reporter who wants to interview my entertainment client tomorrow regarding an upcoming cycling event. Take notes about interview request and send e-mail to the client regarding opportunity.

3:15 Review press release drafted by an account executive regarding a new museum exhibition; meet with her to provide edits and feedback.

3:30 Receive e-mail from entertainment client with his availability for interview. Call reporter to schedule time of interview. (Set a reminder in my calendar to confirm interview time with client tomorrow morning.)

3:45 Review weekly hour reports to determine if we are on track to meet, exceed, or under deliver on projected monthly billings. Meet with team to re-delegate some tasks.

4:15 Participate in conference call with toy manufacturer client to discuss upcoming anniversary road tour. Review conference call recap drafted by an account executive and send to client. Call road tour vendor to discuss changes to schedule and pass along to client for review.

5:00 Work on slides for new business presentation, thinking through all the elements needed in order to deliver against our strategies and objectives.

5:30 Review media outreach notes from team regarding earlier press release distribution announcing hotel client's new executive team; make edits and send to client.

5:45 Review to-do list for the day, checking off completed tasks and adding new duties (with deadlines noted) for tomorrow's to-do list.

6:00 Enter my time log for the day, cataloging tasks by account and amount of time spent on each task.

6:15 Tidy my desk area and leave the office!

communications and implement the program, sometimes without full knowledge of either the original motivation or the intended results. Even though they were not present during the discussions about a new policy or management decision, they are the ones given the job of explaining it to employees and to the press.

Practitioners not only begin their careers in this role but also spend much of their time in the technical aspects of communication, as illustrated by the list of work assignments presented in the preceding section and by the job descriptions in Figure 2.1. When limited to this role, however, practitioners typically do not participate significantly in management decision making and strategic planning. They complain that they are not part of the management team and that they are "the last to know."

Expert Prescriber

When practitioners take on the expert role, others see them as the authority on public relations problems and solutions. Top management leaves public relations in the hands of the expert and assumes a relatively passive role. Practitioners operating as expert practitioners define the problem, develop the program, and take full responsibility for its implementation. Other managers may want to keep public relations as the sole responsibility of practitioners so they can get back to business as usual, content that things will be handled by the "PR experts."

The expert prescriber role seduces *practitioners* because it is personally gratifying to be viewed as the authority on what needs to be done and how it should be done. It seduces *employers* and *clients* because they want to feel sure that public relations is being handled by an expert. They also erroneously assume that they will no longer have to be involved once the expert is on the job. Limited participation by key top managers, however, means that their relevant knowledge does not get factored into the problem-solving process. Public relations becomes compartmentalized and isolated from the mainstream of the enterprise.

By not participating themselves, managers become dependent on the practitioner any time public relations issues arise. Managers also develop little or no commitment to public relations efforts and do not take responsibility for the success or failure of programs. In effect, other managers in the organization assume an it's-not-my-job stance on public relations matters. They see public relations as a sometimes-necessary job handled by support staff not directly involved in the organization's main line of business.

Whereas the expert prescriber role is called for in crisis situations and periodically throughout any program, in the long run it hinders the diffusion of public relations thinking throughout the organization. It also leads to the greatest dissatisfaction with practitioners, because they are held solely accountable for program results even though they had little or no control over critical parts of the situation and the factors that led to public relations problems in the first place. Top management often responds by simply replacing one expert with another, endlessly searching for someone who can make public relations problems go away without having to make needed changes in organizational policy, products, or procedures.

Communication Facilitator

The communication facilitator role casts practitioners as sensitive listeners and information brokers. Communication facilitators serve as liaisons, interpreters, and mediators between an organization and its publics. They maintain two-way communication and facilitate exchange by removing barriers in relationships and by keeping channels of communication open. The goal is to provide both management and publics the information they need for making decisions of mutual interest.

Practitioners in the communication facilitator role find themselves acting as information sources and the official contacts between organizations and their publics. They referee interactions, establish discussion agendas, summarize and restate views, call for reactions, and help participants diagnose and correct conditions interfering with communication relationships. Communication facilitators occupy boundary-spanning roles and serve as links between organizations and publics. They operate under the assumption that effective two-way communication improves the quality of decisions that organizations and publics make about policies, procedures, and actions of mutual interest.

Problem-Solving Facilitator

When practitioners assume the role of problem-solving facilitator, they collaborate with other managers to define and solve problems. They become part of the strategic planning team. Collaboration and consultation begin with the first question and continue until the final program evaluation. Problem-solving practitioners help other managers and the organization apply to public relations the same management step-by-step process used for solving other organizational problems.

Line managers play an essential part in analyzing problem situations, as they are the ones most knowledgeable of and most intimately involved with the organization's policies, products, procedures, and actions. They are also the ones with the power to make needed changes. As a result, they must participate in the evolutionary thinking and strategic planning behind public relations programs. When line managers participate in the public relations strategic planning process, they understand program motivations and objectives, they support strategic and tactical decisions, and they are committed to making the changes and providing the resources needed to achieve program goals.

Problem-solving facilitators get invited to the management team because they have demonstrated their skill and value in helping other managers avoid and solve problems. As a result, public relations thinking is factored into management decision making.[28]

What Roles Research Tells Us

Researchers have studied what leads practitioners to play different roles, as well as what happens when they enact different roles in their organizations. Their findings have isolated factors that influence role selection and enactment, salary and career advancement, and participation in organizational decision making. Other scholars have used the role models to describe similarities and differences in the practice internationally.

Technicians Versus Managers

Research findings show that practitioners play several roles, but that over time one emerges as the dominant role. For example, in a study of PRSA and IABC members in the United States, 37 percent rated themselves dominant in the expert prescriber role and 37 percent scored communication technician as their dominant role. Another 21 percent scored the problem-solving facilitator role as dominant, and only 5 percent put themselves in the dominant role of communication facilitator.[29] In the same study, researchers found that the percentage of men enacting the manager role remained constant over the six years between surveys—about 57 percent—while the percentage of women increased from 28 percent to 39 percent.[30] Given the major changing demographic of the field, no doubt that gap has continued to diminish.

In a similar study of Canadian Public Relations Society and Canadian IABC members, 42 percent rated themselves in the dominant role of communication technicians, 16 percent as expert prescribers, 15 percent as problem-solving facilitators, and 12 percent as communication facilitators. Fifteen percent weighted two or three roles equally.[31]

High scores on the communication technician role are not correlated with high scores on other roles. For the other three roles, however, high scores on one tend to go with high scores on the other two. In other words, practitioners who play the dominant role of expert prescriber, communication facilitator, or problem-solving process facilitator also tend to play the other two roles. High correlations among the three roles suggest that they go together to form a single, complex role that is distinct from the communication technician role. As a result, *two major dominant roles occur in practice: public relations technician and public relations manager.*

Public relations technicians are primarily concerned with writing, producing, and disseminating communications, such as press releases, speeches, Web sites, feature stories, and annual reports. They tend to be creative, artistic, and technically proficient; see themselves as their organization's "wordsmith"; and exhibit little inclination or aptitude for strategic planning and research. For the most part they focus on communications and other activities in the process. Those in this dominant role typically make less and are not part of the management inner circle, but enjoy high levels of job satisfaction if they remain in the technician role by choice. This role constitutes the traditional core of public relations work—writing mediated communications and doing media relations.

The public relations manager role casts practitioners as part of organizational management. This role calls for research skills, an aptitude for strategic thinking, and a tendency to think in terms of the *outcomes* or *impact* of public relations activities. Practitioners in the public relations manager role do not limit their tactics to communications. They use environmental scanning and organizational intelligence, negotiation and coalition building, issues management, program evaluation, and management counseling as public relations tools. Accountability and participation in organizational management earn these practitioners high salaries, as well as high stress and responsibility. Researchers who studied 321 organizations in the United States, Canada, and the United Kingdom, however, found that the major predictor of public relations excellence was the extent to which the organization's top public relations executive was able to enact the manager role versus the technician role.[32]

Environmental Influences

Important distinctions are lost when the three managerial roles are combined. For example, as Table 2.2 illustrates, a practitioner's dominant role is a function of an organization's environment. Communication technicians tend to work in organizations with relatively stable, low-threat environments, such as many nonprofit organizations and charities. Communication facilitators predominate in organizations with relatively turbulent settings that pose little threat, such as school districts and some governmental agencies. Problem-solving process facilitators and expert prescribers work in organizations with threatening environments. In relatively stable settings, including some utilities and associations, the problem-solving process

TABLE 2.2

Organizational
Environments and
Roles

	Low Threat	High Threat
Little Change	Communication technician	Problem-solving facilitator
Much Change	Communication facilitator	Expert prescriber

facilitator role dominates. Expert prescribers dominate in rapidly changing environments, particularly in public relations firms that specialize in crisis communication and in consumer products companies subject to high levels of competition and government regulation. [33]

In short, the expert prescriber role appears when immediate action is imperative, whereas the problem-solving process facilitator dominant role is preferred when there is time to go through a process of collaboration and joint problem solving. Highly paid problem-solving process facilitators and expert prescribers tend to work for organizations most threatened by competition, government regulation, labor conflicts, and public scrutiny, such as financial and insurance companies, utilities, and the public relations firms who work for these companies. By contrast, lower-paid communication technicians and communication facilitators typically work as promotional publicists for media and advertising agencies or for educational and religious organizations and charities.

Scanning and Evaluation

The various studies of public relations roles have consistently demonstrated the impact of using research to manage the function. In the three-phase study of roles reported previously, practitioners who use all types of research and information gathering were the ones most likely to operate in the management roles. The relationship between research and managerial roles also appears in the findings of an international sample of IABC members.[34] Operating in the manager role correlates with the use of scientific, informal, and mixed approaches to research, whereas operating in the technician role does not. Canadian researchers found a similar pattern when they surveyed members of the Canadian Public Relations Society (CPRS) and Canadian members of IABC, but the highest correlations were for communication facilitators. The researchers concluded, "Perhaps communication facilitators require more objective information than the others in order to keep channels of communication open between various parties."[35]

Research shows that all types of information gathering help practitioners move into management roles. The obvious conclusion is that practitioners must be actively gathering information useful in decision making before they are invited to the management table. Furthermore, becoming part of the management team does not happen simply because of years on the job. Rather, the amount of research practitioners do determines the likelihood of their having a seat at the management decision-making table.[36] Moving into the management role, however, "does not immediately ensure that practitioners have the knowledge or expertise to enact the manager role," according to Lauzen and Dozier.[37] Simply put, practitioners long accustomed to operating in the technician role may find moving into the strategic manager role a difficult adjustment.

Many factors influence practitioner roles, including education, professional experience, personality, supervision, and organizational culture and environment. Practitioners who understand the causes and consequences of playing different roles can develop strategies for dealing with a variety of situations and with others' views of practitioner roles. This understanding may be particularly important for women because role differences are associated with both salary and participation in management decision making.

The Glass Ceiling

Studies of women in public relations historically have found both a salary gap and a "glass ceiling" on promotions to management positions. As one researcher put it, there is a "million-dollar penalty for being a woman," noting the effects of male–female salary differences and limited advancement opportunities over the course of a career.[38]

Those who study the glass-ceiling problem suggest the following strategies:

1. Women aiming for top management must develop career plans and select employers with care and not plan on "being in the right place at the right time." "Women have to get into the game and be as aggressive and determined as any male counterpart."

2. Women must develop management skills: goal setting, analysis, planning, research, program execution, measurement, and evaluation. They must also know how to communicate with managers. As one female manager put it, "I think as time goes on, and this is especially critical for women, communicators are going to have to think like managers, talk like managers, and communicate with other managers."

3. Women must aim higher. One study found that when women are asked to estimate what salary they will be making in 10 years, they project only 60 percent of what men project. Rather than undervaluing themselves, they should research salaries in the area and in comparable organizations before accepting an offer. Researchers also found that women may forget to negotiate perks: professional dues, conference expenses, and other benefits in addition to salary.[39]

As the feminization of public relations expands worldwide, even these strategies may not overcome stereotypes embedded in some cultures. For example, in Germany, where more than half of all practitioners are female, researchers Fröhlich and Peters found that women working in public relations firms often stereotyped *themselves* and other female practitioners as "PR bunnies." They caution that there is a "thin line between a successful use of 'typical female' attributes and becoming a victim of the stereotype."[40] Pointing out the interconnectedness of "self-selection," women judging other women, and structural aspects of organizations, they conclude:

> The existence of a "PR bunny" stereotype among female public relations professionals . . . as "natural born communicators" is accompanied by a recoding process of female attributes as deficiencies in managerial tasks, professionalism, and public relations competence and, therefore, fundamentally threatens women's ability to overcome the glass ceiling effect.[41]

Much of the credit for progress goes to women in public relations who struggled to break through the managerial glass ceiling, and to feminist scholars who documented the process and effects of gender discrimination. Although the glass ceiling and gender discrimination may not have been eliminated, as one group of researchers put it, "Watch for falling glass."[42]

Minorities

Surveys of public relations workforces and professional society memberships show that people of color are severely underrepresented in public relations practice. Yet 2006 enrollment in undergraduate journalism and mass communication programs—where public relations is often one of the majors—was 13.6 percent Black, 6.8 percent Hispanic, 3.4 percent Asian, and .6 percent Native American.[43] The U.S. Census Bureau projects the nation's population in 2010 will be 15 percent Hispanic, 13 percent Black, 5 percent Asian, and 3 percent other non-White races. By 2020, the percentages increase particularly for the Hispanic population to 18 percent and to more than 24 percent by 2050 (see Table 2.3).[44] Yet, when it comes to reflecting current demographics in the public relations practice, U.S. chairman of Hill & Knowlton, MaryLee Sachs, says, "We're not anywhere close to the tipping point."[45]

Recognition of the importance of building and maintaining relationships with all racial and ethnic segments of the community has increased opportunities for individual practitioners as well as for minority-owned firms. Globalization has also increased demand for skilled practitioners able to bridge cultural and communication gaps.[46] For example, Sachs made diversity a priority at Hill & Knowlton: "We should be reflective of the cities in which we operate, and reflective of our clients, our clients' businesses, what they're trying to do, and the types of audiences they're trying to reach."[47]

However, surveys continue to show that minorities are underrepresented in corporate departments, firms, and other major organizations' public relations staffs. Educational programs in public relations continue to recruit minority students, scholarships and internship programs encourage participation, and employment opportunities reward those who take advantage of them. Minority practitioners with public relations training and skills will continue to be in demand because all organizations need to communicate with the many publics in an increasingly pluralistic society (see Exhibit 2.4). Ketchum's Raymond Kotcher succinctly summarized the challenge: "The public relations profession should aspire to be representative of the communities served by our companies, clients and organizations across the nation."[48]

	2010	2030	2050
Population Total	308,936,000	363,584,000	419,854,000
Percent of Total Population			
White alone, not Hispanic	65.1	57.5	50.1
Hispanic (of any race)	15.5	20.1	24.4
Black alone	13.1	13.9	14.6
Asian Alone	4.6	6.2	8.0
All other races[a]	3.0	4.1	5.3

TABLE 2.3

Projected Population of the United States, by Race and Hispanic Origin

[a] Includes American Indian and Alaska Native alone, Native Hawaiian and Other Pacific Islander alone, and Two or More Races.

Source: Adapted from U.S. Census Bureau, 2004, "U.S. Interim Projections by Age, Sex, Race, and Hispanic Origin," www.census.gov/ipc/www/usinterimproj/. Internet Release Date: March 18, 2004.

EXHIBIT 2.4

Diversity Dimensions

Rochelle L. Ford, Ph.D., APR
Associate Dean, Research
and Academic Affairs
John H. Johnson School
of Communications
Howard University

Diversity, multiculturalism, and inclusiveness are becoming common concerns in public relations, yet at times their meanings and application within the practice of public relations can be challenging. Diversity is so essential to public relations practice that the Commission on Public Relations Education infused the concept throughout its 2006 report and addressed it as a foundational concept.

Common definitions of diversity typically address all the differences that exist between and among people. Primary diversity characteristics are innate and cannot be changed, such as gender, age, nationality, sexual orientation, ethnicity, and race. Secondary diversity characteristics—religion, geographics, and marital and military service status—can change over time.

Likewise, culture is often defined as the sum of ways of living, including behavioral norms, linguistic expression, styles of communication, patterns of thinking, and beliefs and values of a group large enough to be self-sustaining, and transmitted over the course of generations. Groups defined on the basis of an element of diversity may have a unique culture or co-culture, but it may not persist.

According to Stephen P. Banks, Ph.D., author of *Multicultural Public Relations: A Social-Interpretive Approach,* public relations is at its heart cultural communication, whether it's intra-cultural communication occurring within one culture, intercultural addressing two cultures, or multicultural communicating between more than two cultures.

When communicating across cultures, it is important to ensure that publics feel respected and valued even if differences exist. Such respect and value are achieved through the spirit of inclusion or inclusiveness—recognizing different groups, listening to them, taking into account what they have to say, and communicating with them.

Therefore, a public relations practitioner must conduct research in order to understand both the culture(s) of the organization and the public(s) of the organization. Likewise, modern public relations professionals must understand whom they are, what cultures they represent, and the power or privilege held or perceived because of roles or diversity characteristics.

Communicating with different groups requires an understanding of the situational nature of identity. In other words, although a practitioner may be a Black Latina mother from South Texas doesn't mean that she is thinking about those diversity characteristics in every communication situation. Only through research will a practitioner know which aspect of her identity is likely to be important in a particular situation. The key is approaching public relations with sensitivity, informed by research.

Diversity, multiculturalism and inclusion are also important to the staffing of the public relations function. Indeed, the Excellence Theory in Public Relations explains that support for women and minorities are important, but the term "minorities" is becoming outdated as Hispanics and Blacks outnumber Caucasian and non-Hispanics in many communities, and the U.S. Census Bureau projects continued population growth of Hispanics and Blacks in the U.S. (see Table 2.3). When an organization has a diverse team, it will be able to monitor and address issues more effectively because of the diversity of ideas and perspectives that the team members bring to the issue.

Here are five trends to consider regarding diversity in public relations:

1. Growth of Hispanic population in the United States

2. Growing recognition of gay, lesbian, bi-sexual, and transgender communities and culture

3. The consistent power of Black and Spanish-language radio to mobilize communities on issues

4. Internet and other digital communities expand the reach and connections among people, particularly along diversity dimensions.

5. Immigration changes the culture and workforce of all nations.

Note: More information on diversity is available online at www.commpred .org, and in my past "Diversity Dimensions" *PRTactics* columns posted on PRSA's Web site, www.prsa.org.

Professionalism

When practitioners assemble at professional meetings, discussions typically turn to the extent to which public relations qualifies as a profession. The topic of professionalism dominates many conferences. The many publications and newsletters serving the field all address the professionalization of public relations. Concern about professionalism prompted PRSA to require accredited members to complete continuing education in order to maintain their accredited status.

Criteria used to assess the professional status of a field date back to preindustrial England. Sons of wealthy landowners went to either Cambridge or Oxford to receive a liberal arts education before taking exams to enter the practices of law and medicine. Wealth was a prerequisite because professional practice provided little, if any, remuneration.

By the late 1800s the "status professionalism" of England began to give way to "occupational professionalism." Specialized skills and knowledge became the basis for entry, opening the way for the growing middle class. Although being challenged in some fields, many of the values associated with the origins of professions persist today: "personal service, a dislike of competition, advertising and profit, a belief in the principle of payment in order to work rather than working for pay and the superiority of the motive of service."[49]

Many have attempted to define contemporary professions, but no single definition fits all fields. Typically, disagreement results when an occupational group argues for a specific and unique characteristic designed to exclude others. There is general agreement, however, that the following criteria apply to all professions:

1. Requires specialized education to acquire a body of knowledge and skills based on theory developed through research. The practice is based more on unique knowledge than on performance skills.

2. Provides a unique and essential service recognized as such by the community. Practitioners are identified with their profession: "She's a lawyer" or "He's the accountant."

3. Emphasizes public service and social responsibility over private interests. Private economic gain and special interests are subordinate to the public good. There is "nobility of purpose."

4. Gives autonomy to and places responsibility on practitioners. Freedom to decide and act means individuals are held accountable.

5. Enforces codes of ethics and standards of performance through self-governing associations of colleagues. Values are interpreted and enforced by disciplining those who deviate from accepted norms and prescribed behaviors. Professional societies set standards for specialized educational preparation, determine who is admitted into practice, monitor practitioner performance against agreed-upon standards, and confer different levels of status on practitioners.

Any discussion of practitioners' educational backgrounds makes it clear that entry into public relations does not require specialized educational preparation. A small percentage of practitioners belong to the major professional associations. An even smaller number are "accredited" or "certified," meaning that they have passed a battery of tests and been judged to be competent practitioners by a panel of their professional peers. No state requires a license to practice public relations or requires enforcement of a code of ethics or standards of practice. Not only are there varied and often bizarre perceptions about what constitutes public relations, there is also disagreement within the field.

Frequent examples of self-serving behavior and advocacy on behalf of special interests bring into question the extent to which public service and social responsibility guide the practice. News reports expose "public relations spin doctors" or "damage control specialists" retained by clients charged with unethical or illegal activities. Only a small percentage of practitioners work as truly independent counselors. In fact, most function in staff positions accountable to line management, so autonomy and personal responsibility are not commonly associated with their roles. And because only a small proportion of practitioners belongs to strong professional associations, the vast majority is not subject to enforced codes of conduct.

These issues are discussed more fully in Chapter 5, but it is obvious that a strict interpretation of the criteria precludes qualifying public relations as a profession. In fact, if required to completely adhere to the standards, few, if any, fields could pass the test. Many practicing public relations, on the other hand, qualify as "professionals" on the basis of their commitment to meeting professional and ethical standards. Widespread efforts in education and the professional associations advance the calling and professionalize the field. Professionalism is an important concern and goal for those entering the emerging profession of public relations.

Requirements for Success

Surveys of top public relations executives show that they think communication skills, knowledge of media and management, problem-solving abilities, motivation, and intellectual curiosity are needed for success. The late public relations executive and professor Richard Long listed five qualities of those on the career "fast track":

1. *Results.* The single most important key to success is a reputation for getting results, being goal oriented. Employers and clients pay for results, not hard work and effort.

2. *Conceptualizing.* Those on the fast track have an ability to focus on the employer or client's needs. The strong conceptualizer is a "quick study" who is a good listener and thorough note taker.

3. *Human Relations.* Persons on the fast track are team players who balance personal goals with those of the organization. These persons also know how to deal with management, including when they do not agree with the boss.

4. *Style.* The most important style-related trait is a "can-do" attitude. (See Figure 2.2 for a humorous take on this quality.) Another is constructive competitiveness. Those on the fast track translate confidence into persuasive advocacy and substantive public relations contributions.

5. *Intangibles.* This quality almost defies description, but charisma, presence, and moxie affect the way other managers evaluate people in public relations. Go to school on the boss. The bottom line with bosses, however, is to find ways to make their jobs easier. Know what your boss expects of you.[50]

Among other traits sought by employers are an understanding of how the business works (whatever a particular organization's business is), possessing skills with computer software and new media technology, being well read and informed on current events, having an ability to deal with frustration and stress, and being able to

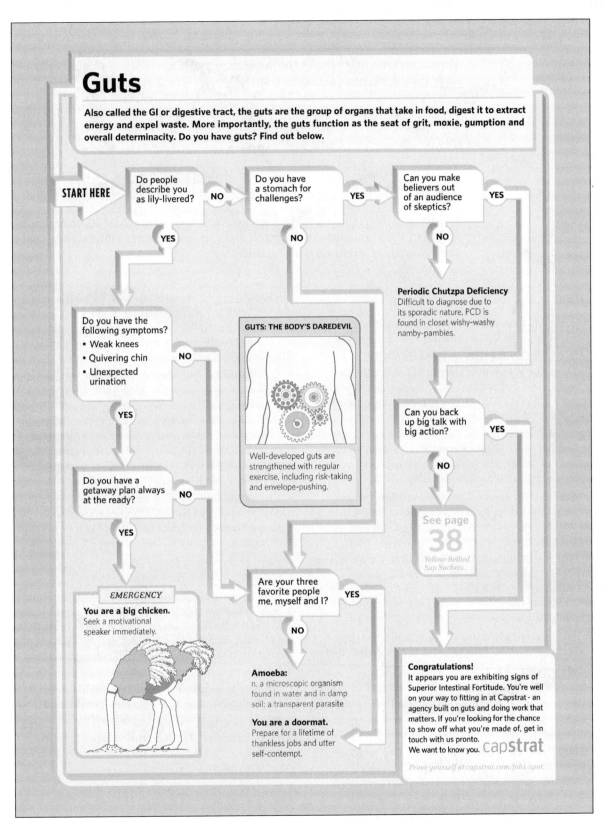

FIGURE 2.2

Capstrat "Guts" Advertisement

improvise. One trait tops every list, however. Ability to write is number one by a wide margin. As one executive put it:

> Too often, clear writing is not stressed sufficiently and the public relations professional goes through his or her career with one hand tied behind. Learn how to write before you start to climb the public relations ladder.[51]

Another said, "If our experience is typical, writing is one of the very weakest areas of most new graduates. That's probably being kind . . . 'appalling' is what's really crossing my mind."[52]

In short, both entry-level employment and long-term career success require the ability to write grammatically correct, easy-to-read, forceful, informative, and persuasive copy for publication and speech.

Notes

[1] Address to military public affairs officers in graduate program at the School of Journalism and Media Studies, San Diego State University, February 20, 2008.

[2] U.S. Department of Labor, Bureau of Labor Statistics, February 7, 2008. For updated data, check under Specific Occupational Code 27-3031 ("Public Relations Specialists") at www.bls.gov/oes/current/oes273031.

[3] Bureau of Labor Statistics, U.S. Department of Labor, *Occupational Outlook Handbook, 2008–09 Edition, Public Relations Specialists*, online at www.bls.gov/oco/ocos086.htm (visited February 13, 2008).

[4] Personal communication from Professor Ming Anxiang, Institute of Journalism & Communication, Chinese Academy of Social Sciences, February 14, 2008. See Exhibit 5.7 for more about public relations in China.

[5] U.S. Office of Personnel Management, Office of Workforce Information, *Federal Civilian Workforce Statistics: Occupations of Federal White-Collar and Blue-Collar Workers* (Washington, DC: Government Printing Office, September 30, 1995), 34.

[6] For data on employee numbers for independent firms, see current editions of "Jack O'Dwyer's Newsletter" and *O'Dwyer's Directory of Public Relations Firms*.

[7] Personal communication with author, February 14, 2008.

[8] "America West's Turnaround Is Down to Its Employees," *PRWeek* (June 14, 2004): 8. Updated by personal communication with author, February 18, 2008.

[9] U.S. Department of Labor, Bureau of Labor Statistics, *Employment and Earnings* (Washington, DC: U.S. Government Printing Office) Various reports available online at www.bls.gov/oes/current/oes273031.

[10] Rea W. Smith, "Women in Public Relations," *Public Relations Journal* 24 (October 1968): 26, 27, and 29.

[11] Sondra K. Gorney, "Status of Women in Public Relations," *Public Relations Journal* 31 (May 1975): 10–13.

[12] David Y. Jacobson and Nicholas J. Tortorello, "Salary Survey," *Public Relations Journal* 46, no. 6 (June 1990): 18–25; and *Profile '89* (San Francisco: International Association of Business Communicators and IABC Research Foundation, 1989).

[13] See Tamara L. Gillis, "Dollars and Sense," *Communication World*, September–October, 2007, 35–37 (online at www.iabc.com/rf), and Lee B. Becker, Tudor Vlad and Joel D. McLean, "Enrollments Level Off; Online Instruction Now Routine," *Journalism & Mass Communication Educator*, 2006, 62 (3), 263–288. The latter and updated reports available online at www.grady.uga.edu/ANNUALSURVEYS.

[14] Lee B. Becker, "The Feminization of Broadcasting: Good News or Bad News?" Paper presented to the 2007 Association for Journalism and Mass Communication Convention, Washington, D.C., August 12, 2007.

[15] Aarti Shah, "Salary Survey 2008: A Cautious Optimism," *PRWeek* (February 25, 2008): 24.

[16] John L. Paluszek, "Public Relations Students: Today Good, Tomorrow Better," *The Public Relations Strategist* 5, no. 4 (Winter 2000): 29. See also "A Port of Entry: Public Relations Education for the 21st Century" (Report of the Commission on Public Relations Education, October 1999): 2.

[17] For current salary figures, see the "Annual Salary Survey" published by *PRWeek* (www.prweek.com).

[18] Jeffrey Goldberg, "Selling Wal-Mart: Can the Company Co-Opt Liberals?" *The New Yorker,* April 2, 2007. Downloaded February 15, 2008, at www.newyorker.com/reporting/current/oes273031.htm.

[19] U.S. Department of Labor, Bureau of Labor Statistics (www.bls.gov/oes/2003.may/oes273031.htm). Downloaded February 15, 2008.

[20] Bey-Ling Sha and Elizabeth Toth, "2006 PRSA Work-Life Survey: Overview of Key Findings." Paper presented to 2006 Public Relations Society of America International

Conference, Educators Academy, Salt Lake City, UT, November 14, 2006.

[21] Shah, "Salary Survey 2008," pp. 17–24.

[22] Bureau of Labor Statistics, "Women's Weekly Earnings as a Percent of Men's . . . 1979–2005." 7 February 2008 www.bls.gov/opub/ted/2006/oct/wk1/art02.txt.

[23] Larissa A. Grunig, Elizabeth L. Toth, and Linda C. Hon, *Women in Public Relations: How Gender Influences Practice* (New York: The Guilford Press, 2001), 206–208.

[24] Glen M. Broom and David M. Dozier, "Advancement for Public Relations Role Models," *Public Relations Review* 12, no. 1 (Spring 1986): 37–56.

[25] David M. Dozier and Glen M. Broom, "Evolution of the Managerial Role in Public Relations Practice," *Journal of Public Relations Research* 7, no. 1 (1995): 17–18.

[26] David M. Dozier and Glen M. Broom, "The Centrality of Practitioner Roles to Public Relations Theory," in Public Relations Theory II, ed. Carl H. Botan and Vincent Hazleton (Mahwah, NJ: Lawrence Erlbaum Associates, 2006): 157.

[27] James G. Hutton, "The Myth of Salary Discrimination in Public Relations," *Public Relations Review* 31, no. 1 (March 2005), 82.

[28] For the original conceptual definitions of the roles, see Glen M. Broom and George D. Smith, "Testing the Practitioner's Impact on Clients," *Public Relations Review* 5, no. 3 (Fall 1979): 47–59.

[29] These previously unreported data were gathered as part of the 1991 role study cited in note 23.

[30] Dozier and Broom, "Evolution of the Managerial Role," 16.

[31] Jennie M. Piekos and Edna F. Einsiedel, "Roles and Program Evaluation Techniques Among Canadian Public Relations Practitioners," *Public Relations Research Annual* 2 (1990): 95–113.

[32] David M. Dozier (with Larissa A. Grunig and James E. Grunig), *Manager's Guide to Excellence in Public Relations and Communication Management* (Mahwah, NJ: Lawrence Erlbaum Associates, 1995): 23–37.

[33] Lalit Acharya, "Public Relations Environments," *Journalism Quarterly* 62, no. 3 (Autumn 1985): 577–84.

[34] David M. Dozier, "The Innovation of Research in Public Relations: Review of a Program of Research," *Public Relations Research Annual* 2 (1990): 24.

[35] Piekos and Einsiedel, "Roles and Program Evaluation Techniques," 109.

[36] Glen M. Broom and David M. Dozier, "Advancement for Public Relations Role Models," *Public Relations Review* 12, no. 1 (Spring 1986): 37–56.

[37] Martha M. Lauzen and David M. Dozier, "Issues Management Mediation of Linkages Between Environmental Complexity and Management of the Public Relations Function," *Journal of Public Relations Research* 6, no. 3 (1994): 180.

[38] Carolyn Garret Cline, "Public Relations: The $1 Million Penalty for Being a Woman," in *Women in Mass Communication: Challenging Gender Values*, ed. Pamela J. Creedon (Newbury Park, CA: Sage Publications, 1989), 263–75.

[39] Adapted and quoted from Cline, "The $1 Million Penalty for Being a Woman," 272–74.

[40] Romy Fröhlich and Sonja B. Peters, "PR Bunnies Caught in the Agency Ghetto? Gender Stereotypes, Organizational Factors, and Women's Careers in PR Agencies," *Journal of Public Relations Research* 19, no. 3 (2007), 243.

[41] Ibid., 247.

[42] Shirley A. Serini, Elizabeth Toth, Donald K. Wright, and Arthur G. Emig, "Watch for Falling Glass . . . Women, Men, and Job Satisfaction in Public Relations: A Preliminary Analysis," *Journal of Public Relations Research* 9, no. 2 (1997): 99–118.

[43] Lee B. Becker, Tudor Vlad, and Joeal D. McLean, "Annual Survey of Journalism & Mass Communication Graduates," *AEJMC News* 41, no. 1 (November 2007), 1, 6–9. Data downloaded online from www.grady.uga.edu/ANNUALSURVEYS, February 15, 2008.

[44] U.S. Census Bureau, "U.S. Interim Projections by Age, Race, and Hispanic Origin"; published March 2004; www.census.gov/ipc/www/usinterimproj/. Downloaded February 18, 2008.

[45] Randi Schmelzer, "The Diversity Riddle," *PRWeek* (December 17, 2007): 16.

[46] Raymond L. Kotcher, "Diversity in Today's Workplace and Marketplace," *Public Relations Quarterly* 40, no. 1 (Spring 1995): 7.

[47] "Diversity Survey 2003—Wanted: A More Diverse Workforce," *PRWeek* (December 1, 2003): 19.

[48] Kotcher, "Diversity in Today's Workplace," p. 8.

[49] Philip Elliott, *The Sociology of Professions* (London: Macmillan, 1972), 52–3. Useful reference on the origins and evolution of professions.

[50] Adapted from a speech by the late Richard K. Long, "LONG-term Solutions," Federal Way, WA. Long formerly served as public relations executive at Dow Chemical Company, Midland, MI, and Weyerhaeuser, Tacoma, WA. Used with permission of the author.

[51] From speech to Black Public Relations Society of Greater New York by Kenneth R. Lightcap, managing director, Manning Selvage and Lee, New York, April 17, 1991.

[52] James E. Lukaszewski, Chairman, The Lukaszewski Group, Inc., as quoted in Jack Haberstroh, "PR Graduates Don't Measure Up as Writers," *Public Relations Quarterly* 39, no. 4 (Winter 1994–95): 22.

Additional Sources

Bowen, Shannon A. "I Thought It Would Be More Glamorous: Preconceptions and Misconceptions of Public Relations among Students in the Principles Course." *Public Relations Review* 29 (2003): 199–214.

Carstarphen, Meta G., and Richard A. Wells. *Writing PR: A Multimedia Approach*. Boston, MA: Pearson/Allyn and Bacon, 2004. Introduces a wide range of writing assignments in public relations practice.

Creedon, Pamela J., ed. *Women in Mass Communication*, 2nd ed. Newbury Park, CA: Sage, 1993. Essays explore feminist theory and the women's movement in mass communication.

Grunig, Larissa A., Elizabeth L. Toth, and Linda C. Hon. *Women in Public Relations: How Gender Influences Practice*. New York: The Guilford Press, 2001. Authoritative synthesis of almost two decades of scholarly inquiry on gender issues in public relations.

Hon, Linda Childers, Larissa A. Grunig, and David M. Dozier. "Women in Public Relations: Problems and Opportunities." In *Excellence in Public Relations and Communication Management*, edited by James E. Grunig, 419–38. Mahwah, NJ: Lawrence Erlbaum Associates, 1992.

Organizational Settings

3

Years of acquisitions, divestitures, downsizing, globalization, reengineering, and mergers have produced great changes in the structure of organizations. Budget cuts and deficits, taxpayer revolts, and deregulation have led to reorganization, decentralization, and staff cuts in all levels of government. Nationally publicized scandals, embarrassing revelations about executive salaries and benefits, increasing demand for social services, and vigorous competition for funds have forced changes in the missions and fund-raising methods in many nonprofit organizations. Employees at all levels have learned to live and work with sometimes contradictory rhetoric saying that their organization was trying to become "lean and mean," that reorganization and retraining meant "empowerment," that layoffs and plant closings were aimed at "right-sizing," and that high overhead and budget cuts had forced "outsourcing." Technology revolutionized how organizations manage and communicate. In short, organizational changes have transformed much in public relations practice.

Many, if not most, organizations reorganized the public relations function, reduced department staff size, and tried to do more with fewer people. Many shifted part or all of the workload to outside counseling firms and agencies, producing dramatic increases in cash flow and profitability. Small public relations firms merged, acquired others, or affiliated to form regional, national, and international networks. Large national public relations firms became international by opening or acquiring branches outside their headquarters country or by merging with firms in other countries.

In other words, practitioners work in turbulent organizational settings, dealing with both internal and external change. Many work at the highest levels of management, helping chief executive officers (CEOs) and others manage change. This chapter discusses the origins and place of public relations in organizations, its responsibilities, and its working relationships with other departments.

Public relations people, if they are to be truly respected by management colleagues, must merit "a seat at the management table."
—*The Public Relations Strategist*[1]

Origins within Organizations

Public relations in organizations often can be traced back to unintended and humble beginnings. It can begin with someone simply answering letters from customers or members; with someone writing copy for direct mail, institutional advertising, or the annual report; with someone handling visitors, conducting tours, or arranging the annual meeting; or with someone serving as an organization's ombudsman for employees or neighbors. In other organizations, public relations starts as product publicity, as news support for a national advertising campaign, or as a fund-raising or membership drive.

Public relations' creation, however, does not always spring from a welcome opportunity. For example, an emergency product recall, a plant fire or explosion that threatens neighbors, or a plant closing or massive layoff will attract public and media attention. If no one on the staff is qualified to deal with the media and to handle public information during such crises, then the organization must retain outside public relations counsel. After the emergency or crisis subsides, those brought in on a short-term basis may be hired or retained on a continuing basis. Over time, public relations will be defined and redefined to fit changing missions, new problems and opportunities, and the values and views of a succession of CEOs.

Because so many factors influence how public relations begins in organizations, even some large organizations have small public relations departments. Conversely, some relatively small enterprises employ many practitioners, in some cases supplemented by outside counsel. Many top public relations executives report directly to the CEO, whereas others report to the top human resources, marketing, or legal officer. Some organizations retain outside counselors, even though setting up their own internal staff would be logically the more appropriate choice. In others, internal staffers are assigned tasks that could be better handled by outside counsel.

Such mismatches often represent nothing more than delays in adapting to change. But even practitioners disagree about what is the best structure and place for the function in various types of organizations. As a consequence, each internal public relations department is tailor-made to suit a particular organization and its unique circumstances, particularly the expectations of the CEO.

Establishing a Public Relations Department

The position of public relations on the organization chart and its relationship to top management often can be explained by how the function came into being. For example, top managers in a rapidly growing corporation discover that they have lost touch with employees, and their former face-to-face communications with all employees are no longer possible. The CEO then directs the human resources department to hire a writer-editor to create a weekly news update for the company's intranet and to publish a quarterly newsletter for employees and their families. On the basis of the success of these employee communication efforts, top managers soon ask the energetic and ambitious communication specialist to write occasional news releases about employee achievements and corporate successes. Shortly after, the job expands to include duties such as speechwriter for the CEO and as media contact. The communication specialist hires an assistant to handle a growing number of internal and external communication needs.

Because the function expanded beyond its original employee communication origins, top management moves it out of the human resources department and gives it a new title—"Public Relations Department." The new department manager reports directly to the CEO. Its missions are to improve communication and to build better relationships with all the corporation's major internal and external stakeholders.

As the corporation grows, the public relations department takes on responsibilities for maintaining relationships with investors and financial analysts, government agencies at all levels, community groups, environmental and other special-interest groups, and an increasingly diverse workforce. The public relations manager gets promoted to vice president and appoints managers for each of the specialized areas. In some instances, the new vice president is elected to the executive committee and participates in corporate decision making at the highest level.

From its origin as a low-level communication support function in the human resources department, the role evolved to become an integral part of the management team. To stay on the management team, however, it must contribute to achieving organizational goals and demonstrate accountability through measurable results.

Retaining Outside Counsel

Client relationships with outside counseling firms also can begin in simple and unexpected ways. For example, an organization retains an outside firm (sometimes called an "agency") to conduct a survey of community public opinion regarding a proposed trash-to-energy recycling plant. After receiving the survey results, client management asks the firm to help interpret the findings "from an outsider's perspective" and to help solve a public opinion problem identified by the survey. Success in the follow-up project leads to a continuing and expanding relationship as the client draws on the full range of the firm's public relations capabilities.

The client pays the firm a monthly retainer fee, ensuring access to outside counsel and covering a set number of hours of service each month. Above and beyond regular counsel and services, the firm takes on special projects such as producing the annual report, designing and creating the organization's Web site, and special-event planning for the grand opening of a new facility. The firm bills the client an agreed-upon hourly fee or a fixed fee to cover all costs associated with the additional projects.

The firm's account executive and the internal department's management work as a team to plan and carry out the public relations program. The firm's account executive meets periodically with the client's senior management and public relations staff to discuss plans and to assess progress. The client–firm relationship becomes so close that the firm's account executive sits in on many of the client's internal planning meetings.

Friction sometimes develops, however, when the account executive is not available because of travel and work demands from other clients or, more commonly, when the firm bills for more hours than the client's management anticipated. A hastily called meeting to discuss the invoice reminds both the account executive and internal public relations management that outside counsel is a variable cost and that the outside firm has its own economic goals. The relationship continues but with frequent reminders that the client's staff and the outside counselors work from different perspectives. That outsider's perspective was, after all, why the client retained the counseling firm in the first place.

Public Relations Starts with Top Management

One of the few safe generalizations in public relations is that an organization's public reputation derives in substantial part from the behavior of its senior officials. As those in top management act and speak, so go the interpretations and echoes created by the public relations function. Thus, public relations is inescapably tied, by nature and by necessity, to top management, with public relations staff providing counsel and communication support.

For example, when traces of benzene were found in its bottled water, Source Perrier's top management first suggested that it resulted from a single, isolated cleaning accident and that contaminated bottles were limited to only the few being recalled in North America. The next installment of top management's story came when scientists found benzene-tainted products in Europe. This time, management attributed the benzene to a simple problem with the filter system. Finally, red-faced Perrier management announced a worldwide recall. Tests showed that consumers around the world had been drinking contaminated products for months. The media blasted Perrier, questioning management's integrity and raising concern for public safety. Perrier lost and has not regained its former share of the bottled water market.

Likewise, Exxon's CEO did not go to Alaska after the tanker *Exxon Valdez* spilled millions of gallons of crude oil into the environmentally sensitive Prince William Sound. TWA's (airline now merged into American Airlines) CEO resigned three months after 230 people lost their lives in the crash of Flight 800. He had been criticized for delaying 13 hours before leaving London to go to the crash site and for not immediately expressing concern about crash victims and their families. Both companies struggled to regain public confidence and respect.

Johnson & Johnson's handling of the Tylenol tampering crisis, however, stands in stark contrast. Top management put customer safety first, immediately pulling the product off retail shelves and recalling capsules in the United States and abroad. Management took these dramatic steps even though the only known tampering cases were limited to the Chicago area. Media coverage praised the company's socially responsible actions, reported the company's cooperation with federal agencies, and gave full coverage to later announcements of new tamper-resistant packaging.

Similarly, then-Texaco's CEO quickly apologized when taped recordings were released that exposed a group of senior managers discussing past racial discrimination and the planned destruction of evidence for a civil rights case. He then announced the formation of an independent task force to help the company implement its plan to increase diversity in its employees and management and among the outside firms hired by Texaco.

Unlike the crises at Perrier, Exxon, and TWA, Johnson & Johnson's crisis became a classic case study in crisis communication management and Texaco's embarrassing revelation motivated long-overdue change. In both cases, the CEOs set the course and became the public face in responding to the crises.

Crises potentially involve and affect many stakeholder groups: customers, employees, wholesalers and retailers, consumer action groups, government agencies, stockholders and investment analysts, international media, and concerned citizens around the world. The Perrier case probably contributed to the subsequent series of investigations and media disclosures about the quality and purity of all bottled waters, so even competing brands were affected. Exxon credit card holders cut up and returned their cards, quit buying Exxon products, and even protested the use of single-hull tankers. TWA lost its CEO and media relations director, suffered a major setback in consumer confidence, and had to play down rumors of impending bankruptcy. A few years later, the airline went bankrupt and was acquired by American Airlines.

By contrast, Johnson & Johnson's response positioned it as a leader in safe packaging, forcing competing brands to follow suit; led to Johnson & Johnson's annual ranking among the most respected corporations; and helped the company retain market share for Tylenol. Texaco's quick apology, immediate corrective actions, and announced long-term strategy for organizational change cut short public criticism and made the company's responses part of the story. Each crisis provides an example of top management's key role in an organization's public relations.

These cases illustrate that public relations credibility starts with management's integrity and socially responsible actions. In addition, long-term success in public relations calls for the following from top management:

1. Commitment to and participation in public relations
2. Retention of competent public relations counsel
3. Incorporation of public relations perspectives in policy making
4. Two-way communication with both internal and external publics
5. Coordination of what is done with what is said
6. Clearly defined goals and objectives

The first and continuing task for public relations is to earn and hold support from top management. Johnson & Johnson's former public relations head reports that such support is not easily earned and requires mutual respect:

> Perhaps in more than any other relationship among senior executives in a company, the chemistry that exists between the CEO and the senior public relations executive is most critical. If things are working as they should, the public relations person is given the unique opportunity to become the CEO's "loyal opposition," the one who, behind closed doors, can say, "If you do this, you are making a huge mistake."[2]

Staff Role

Public relations is one of several staff functions, meaning that it advises and supports line managers who have responsibility and authority to run the organization. Practitioners therefore need to understand the staff role.

The line–staff management model originated in the military but now is used in most large organizations. For example, *line functions* in industry include the product- and profit-producing functions: engineering, production, and marketing. *Staff functions* include those that advise and assist line executives: finance, legal, human resources, and public relations. Iowa-based publisher and broadcaster Meredith Corporation makes the staff role explicit in the position title—"Staff Vice President/Director of Public Relations." (Notice how the legal and public relations vice presidents' reporting lines differ from those of the other vice presidents in Figure 3.1.)

Staff support becomes increasingly necessary as an organization increases in size and complexity. Line executives have the authority and responsibility to set policy and to oversee the operations. To do their jobs, however, they need assistance in the form of research, advice, and support services from staff. Many years ago, a management expert made the distinction between line and staff managers rather bluntly: "Specialists are necessary, but 'they should be on tap—not on top.'"[3]

Line management and public relations staff should be able to count on each other for support. Management reasonably expects the following from the public relations staff:

1. Loyalty
2. Counsel on the public relations aspects of decisions

FIGURE 3.1

Line and Staff
Organization Chart

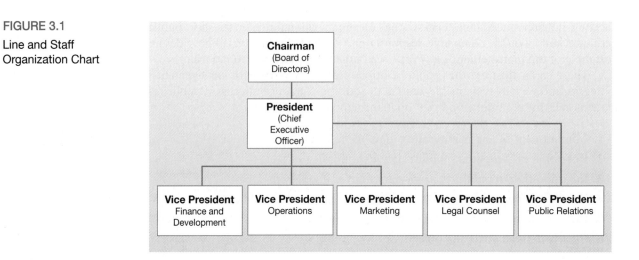

3. Skill in articulating principles and in enhancing public understanding of the organization

4. Inspiration to help all members do their best

5. Influence in restraining other members from saying or doing anything detrimental to the organization's welfare

6. Character—honesty, trustworthiness, and discretion

One CEO defines the ideal public relations officer as:

Honest, trustworthy, discreet, with solid analytical skills, and a total comprehension and understanding of the core business and the key publics. He or she will have the ability to listen, the ability to counsel, and the ability to help the CEO manage competing priorities. The most important qualities, however, are chemistry, trust, and respect. Without them, it's impossible for the CEO and chief communication officer to establish a productive long-term relationship.[4]

Public relations staff expect the following from line management:

1. Positive public relations leadership

2. Support of approved communication policy

3. Strategic plans embracing all policies and programs

4. Adequate budget to do the job, including funds for adequate public opinion research, analysis, and program evaluation

5. Reasonable availability for consultation and for public appearances

Each also has the right to expect the other to demonstrate the character and performance that will withstand public scrutiny and fulfill the organization's social responsibility.

Public relations practitioners typically applaud when public relations executives move into line management but view the reverse with alarm. In a bit of semantic tyranny, they label the movement of "nonpublic relations professionals" from other staff or line units into public relations management as "encroachment," identifying it as a threat. When the senior public relations manager enacts the manager role, "Public relations will be seen as a powerful organizational function, making the assignment of nonpublic relations professionals to manage the public relations function unnecessary and undesirable."[5] On the other hand, some argue that when executives gain public relations experience, they move on to other assignments with a greater understanding of the function.

Line managers often rotate through a variety of assignments before reaching the top. Not many, however, include public relations in their regular rotation of assignments. Public relations experience would add to the credibility of public relations as a management function, demystify the function for other managers, and expand career opportunities for those now viewed as communication technicians with no role in management.[6] In most organizations, however, the demarcation between line and staff management continues to guide decision making.

Role in Decision Making

Traditional and somewhat rigid distinctions between line and staff managers—giving orders versus giving advice—do not always represent their respective roles in decision making. For example, practitioners operating in the expert prescriber role often have the power to choose among public relations program alternatives, with line management later endorsing the selections or exercising veto power. Practitioners, when in a problem-solving process facilitator role, often collaborate with line managers to make decisions. Increasingly, practitioners are assuming positions in the policy-setting and decision-making processes, but those positions are earned, not automatically awarded.

Proximity and *access* are important factors influencing the role of public relations in management. For example, when faced with bankruptcy, Federated Department Stores expanded its dominant coalition to include the vice president of corporate communication:

> They moved the corporate communications function to the 20th floor; the 20th floor is where the senior management offices are located. So we were literally right in the midst of things. . . . It's a very informal communications process. There was an amazing amount of contact that occurred in the hallway. The president would just walk down the hall and come in my office. It is casual in that respect, but really is an important component of the access to the thought process, access to the person, access to judgment calls when they need to be made.[7]

The term "dominant coalition"—generally five to eight senior executives—describes those who hold power in organizations.[8] Although many members of the dominant coalition hold formal power through their offices—such as a CEO, or COO—a person holding informal power may also be included in the dominant coalition. Such is the case with major donors, figure heads, or influential members of a board of directors who have influence over decisions.

Power comes to the public relations function in an organization when the members of the dominant coalition value it as a vital management function, rather than relegate it to simply a technical role implementing the communication strategy decided by others.[9] If public relations has a "seat at the table" of the dominant coalition, then public relations plays a greater role in determining and achieving organizational outcomes.[10]

Fulfilling this strategic role, however, requires that public relations profession-als have strategic management skills not typically associated with many practition-ers, according to the Excellence Project researchers:

> These strategic functions are evaluation research, environmental scanning, and research to segment publics. In short, the data suggest that communication managers are more likely to be technical supervisors than strategic managers.[11]

Organizational changes also can enhance or diminish the role of public rela-tions in management. For example, Volvo's CEO, upon appointment at the Sweden-based manufacturer, elevated the senior communication and government relations officers to the top management team. At United Airlines, establishment of an em-ployee stock option plan led to an expanded role for public relations in corporate management. Then-vice president of corporate communication John Kiker said that since that change, United's CEO and other managers increasingly seek public rela-tions input and counsel before making decisions, rather than "make decisions first, and communicate the decisions afterwards."[12] When Boeing Company acquired McDonnell Douglas Aircraft Company, it restructured its management team, form-ing an executive council that reports to the chairman's office. The vice president of communications and investor relations and the vice president of ethics report to the council, placing these staff management executives in positions to influence.[13]

On the other hand, when Germany-based Daimler AG (makers of Mercedes-Benz cars) sold the Chrysler division to Cerberus Capital Management LP, new CEO Robert Nardelli restructured the company, making corporate communications re-port to the senior vice president of human resources. Jason Vines, who as vice presi-dent of corporate communications had been reporting directly to the CEO, resigned.[14]

In addition, *characteristics of the practitioners* themselves—particularly *personal credibility*—contribute to their inclusion or exclusion from the dominant coalition. Researchers have identified practitioners' lack of broad business experi-ence, passivity, naïveté about organization politics, technical education, gender, and tenure in their organizations as factors contributing to the relatively limited power of public relations in organizations.[15]

Public relations participation in management also depends on *the extent to which the function conducts various kinds of research.* Researchers have called such research "organizational intelligence," "environmental scanning," "scanning for planning," and simply "metrics." Regardless of labels, survey results consistently show that when the function does research, there is a greater likelihood that public relations staff will participate in decision making and other management planning activities.[16]

The major determinant of public relations' role in organizational decision making, however, is the degree to which line managers and practitioners them-selves view the function as part of the management team. When top manage-ment views the function as marginal and outside the main line of business, it remains outside the dominant decision-making coalition. The Excellence Study researchers discovered that CEOs in the top 10 percent of organizations were almost three times more supportive of the public relations function than were CEOs in other or-ganizations. Likewise, top public relations executives in the top 10 percent of organ-izations in the study rated the dominant coalition as more than three times more supportive than did public relations executives in other organizations.[17]

When public relations operates in the realm of *programmed* decisions, it is seen as part of organizational routine and overhead. When it participates in *nonprogrammed* decision making, on the other hand, it is seen as playing an important strategic role in achieving organizational goals and contributing to the bottom line. When public relations employs management by objectives (MBO), management by results (MOR), or management by key results to guide program planning and management, then the focus shifts from producing communications (process) to results and consequences (impact). It also makes public relations part of the management team held accountable for achieving organizational goals.

According to Robert Dilenschneider, former president and CEO of Hill & Knowlton and now chairman of the Dileschneider Group of New York and Chicago, "seven deadly sins in this business" threaten progress in integrating the function:

1. Overpromising—making commitments for things they know they cannot deliver.
2. Overmarketing—overselling the client on the capabilities or expertise of public relations.
3. Underservicing (sometimes referred to as "bait-and-switch")—listing senior people as part of the account team but using junior staff to do the work.
4. Putting the public relations firm's profits ahead of the client's performance and results.
5. Using public relations quick fixes—shortsighted responses to complex problems that require long-lasting solutions. (An example would be yielding to client or management expectations that public relations has the power to fix problems without having to make changes in the organization.)
6. Treating public relations as simply a support function charged with implementing strategies formulated by lawyers, financial officers, and top-line managers.
7. Violating ethical standards, thereby damaging public relations' reputation for ethical conduct and concern for social responsibility.[18]

As a management function, public relations is part of an organization's structure and process for adapting to change. Its responsibilities include helping organizations identify, assess, and adjust to their turbulent economic, political, social, and technological environments. In the words of one corporate CEO,

> I believe the public relations field will continue to be pressed by the dynamics of public media and special interest group scrutiny, and the acceleration of global telecommunications technologies. The public relations profession needs to anticipate social, political, and economic issues that have the potential of impacting business plans, instead of being only reactive.[19]

In the final analysis, however, as Pacific Gas and Electric's former CEO Richard A. Clarke said, "The only way CEOs can get what they need from their public relations advisers is to have them at the table when the policies, strategies, and programs are being hammered out."[20]

Determinants of Excellence

The landmark "Excellence Study," funded by the International Association of Business Communicators (IABC) Research Foundation, identified the major factors that make public relations an effective management function in organizations. A summary of the major research findings provides a guide for how to structure and manage public relations.

1. **Empowerment of the Public Relations Function**
   - The senior public relations executive participates in the organization's strategic management, and communication programs are developed for strategic publics identified as a part of strategic management.
   - The senior public relations executive is a member of the dominant coalition of the organization, or has a direct reporting relationship to senior managers who are part of the dominant coalition.
   - Diversity is embodied in all public relations roles.

2. **Roles**
   - The public relations unit is headed by a manager rather than a technician.
   - The senior public relations executive or others in the public relations unit must have the knowledge needed for the manager role (review Chapter 2's section on roles), or the communication function will not become a managerial function.
   - Both men and women must have equal opportunity to occupy the managerial role.

3. **Organization, Relationship to Other Functions, and Use of Consulting Firms**
   - An excellent public relations function integrates all public relations programs into a single department or provides a mechanism for coordinating programs managed by different departments.
   - Public relations should be a management function separate from other functions.

4. **Models of Public Relations**
   - The public relations department and the dominant coalition share the worldview that the department should reflect the two-way symmetrical model of public relations.
   - Communication programs developed for specific publics (including employees) are based on the two-way symmetrical model.
   - The senior public relations executive or others in the public relations unit must have the knowledge and skill needed to implement the two-way symmetrical model.[21]

The Excellence theory provides guidelines for how public relations should be conducted, structured, and implemented in order to contribute to overall organizational excellence. The Excellence Study also produced evidence demonstrating how the organizational context nurtures or impedes the effectiveness of public relations departments.

The Internal Department

The internal department is the most common structure for serving the public relations needs of organizations. The department may consist of only one person, as in a small hospital, or a staff of of hundreds, as in a major corporation. A public relations department may be concentrated in the organization's headquarters or scattered among many locations. For example, of the 175 working at Johnson & Johnson, only about 30 make up the central corporate communication team, whereas the remainder are decentralized among the many specialized "franchises" in the three major business units—consumer, pharmaceutical, and medical devises and diagnostics.[22] The department's size, role, and place in the organization chart vary from one organization to the next. (See Figure 3.2 for a typical department organization chart.)

The Department's Advantages

An internal department has at least four factors working in its favor:

1. Team membership
2. Knowledge of the organization
3. Economy to the organization for many ongoing programs
4. Availability to associates

Team membership is the department's greatest advantage over outside counsel. In some organizations the top public relations executive's office is next door to the chief executive's office. As an example of the close working relationship, for years the top public relations executive at Eastman Kodak began most workdays by meeting with the CEO. Federated Department Stores moved the public relations function to the 20th floor where other senior management offices are located because "it's a more complicated, complex, interrelated . . . involvement than ever before."[23]

Frequent contact between the public relations department and top-line management is the rule rather than the exception. Surveys typically show that at least 60 percent of public relations executives meet with their CEOs at least once each week. Many meet or talk at the beginning of every day. Such a close working relationship between the public relations department and the CEO builds confidence, trust, and support. It can also position public relations as a key player on the management team. (See Figure 3.3 for an example of a department's mission.)

Knowledge of the organization means an intimate, current knowledge that comes from being an insider. Staff members know the relationships among individuals and departments, and are fully aware of the undercurrents of influence and internal politics. They can call on key people to make decisions and avoid those who put personal ambition and expedience above organizational and public interests. They are aware of who can serve as able and articulate spokespersons as opposed to those who become tongue-tied or who do not perform well on camera.

Occasionally a trusted outside counselor is able to acquire such knowledge, but insiders are in a better position to do so and to apply their knowledge on a continuous basis. Because they are part of the organization, internal departmental staff are able to advise, conciliate, and provide services while taking into account intimate details of organizational history, culture, and people.

Economy can occur from typically lower overhead costs and efficient integration in an organization. When the need for public relations is continuous—and in most organizations it is—then a full-time, permanent staff is typically more cost effective than outside counsel and services. For example, the marginal costs of an internal department are typically a small portion of overhead costs in a large organization. The outside firm's overhead might be higher than that of an internal department simply because outside firms are typically smaller than the client organizations they serve, so economies of scale on overhead—such as the costs of facilities, employee benefits programs, and supplies—are lost.

Start-up costs for projects can be less, because internal staff members already have the necessary background and access to managers and files. Routine work, such as weekly news releases, monthly publications, quarterly reports, and so forth,

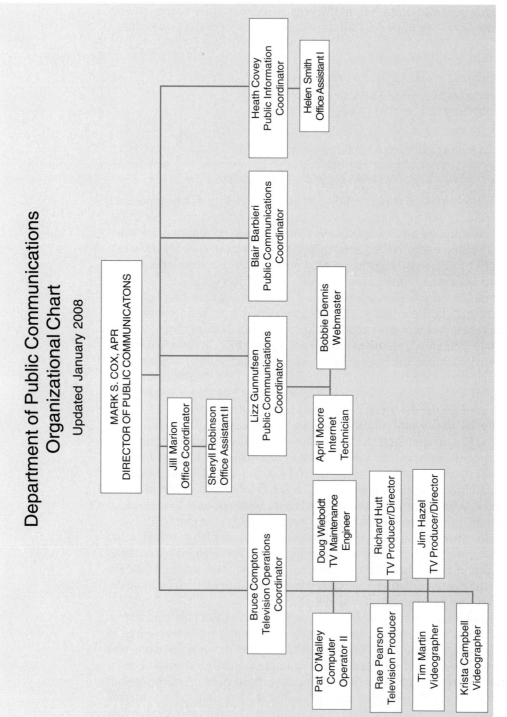

Department of Public Communications Organizational Chart

Updated January 2008

MARK S. COX, APR
DIRECTOR OF PUBLIC COMMUNICATONS

- Jill Marion
  Office Coordinator
- Sheryll Robinson
  Office Assistant II

Lizz Gunnufsen
Public Communications
Coordinator

- Bobbie Dennis
  Webmaster
- April Moore
  Internet
  Technician

Blair Barbieri
Public Communications
Coordinator

Heath Covey
Public Information
Coordinator

- Helen Smith
  Office Assistant I

Bruce Compton
Television Operations
Coordinator

- Doug Wieboldt
  TV Maintenance
  Engineer
- Pat O'Malley
  Computer
  Operator II
- Richard Hutt
  TV Producer/Director
- Rae Pearson
  Television Producer
- Jim Hazel
  TV Producer/Director
- Tim Martin
  Videographer
- Krista Campbell
  Videographer

FIGURE 3.2

Dept. of Public Communications Department Organization Chart

Courtesy City of Chesapeake, Virginia.

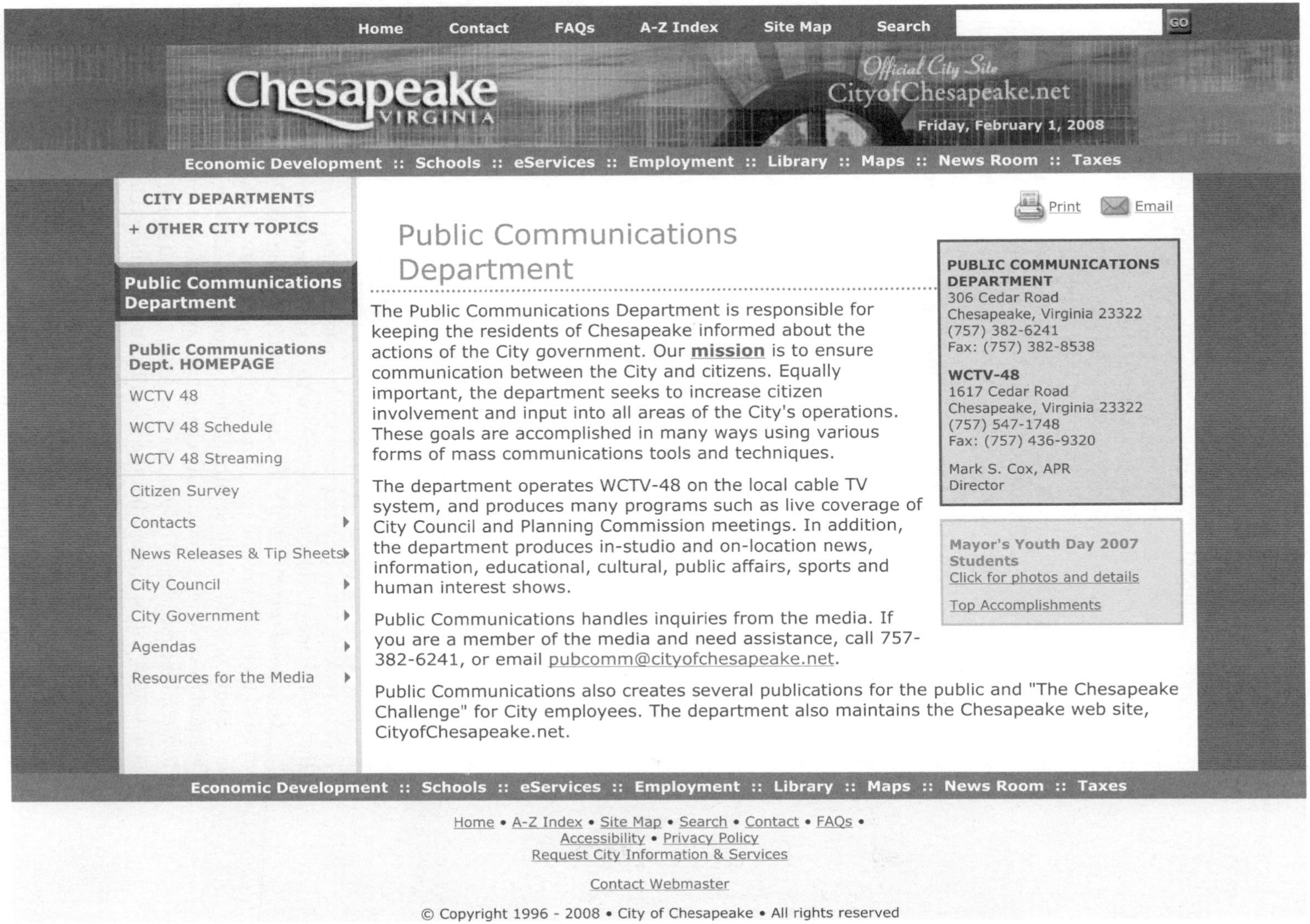

Home
Contact
FAQs
A-Z Index
Site Map
Search
GO
Chesapeake
VIRGINIA
Official City Site
CityofChesapeake.net
Friday, February 1, 2008
Economic Development :: Schools :: eServices :: Employment :: Library :: Maps :: News Room :: Taxes
CITY DEPARTMENTS
+ OTHER CITY TOPICS
Public Communications Department
Public Communications Dept. HOMEPAGE
WCTV 48
WCTV 48 Schedule
WCTV 48 Streaming
Citizen Survey
Contacts
News Releases & Tip Sheets
City Council
City Government
Agendas
Resources for the Media
Print
Email
Public Communications Department
The Public Communications Department is responsible for keeping the residents of Chesapeake informed about the actions of the City government. Our mission is to ensure communication between the City and citizens. Equally important, the department seeks to increase citizen involvement and input into all areas of the City's operations. These goals are accomplished in many ways using various forms of mass communications tools and techniques.
The department operates WCTV-48 on the local cable TV system, and produces many programs such as live coverage of City Council and Planning Commission meetings. In addition, the department produces in-studio and on-location news, information, educational, cultural, public affairs, sports and human interest shows.
Public Communications handles inquiries from the media. If you are a member of the media and need assistance, call 757-382-6241, or email pubcomm@cityofchesapeake.net.
Public Communications also creates several publications for the public and "The Chesapeake Challenge" for City employees. The department also maintains the Chesapeake web site, CityofChesapeake.net.
PUBLIC COMMUNICATIONS DEPARTMENT
306 Cedar Road
Chesapeake, Virginia 23322
(757) 382-6241
Fax: (757) 382-8538
WCTV-48
1617 Cedar Road
Chesapeake, Virginia 23322
(757) 547-1748
Fax: (757) 436-9320
Mark S. Cox, APR
Director
Mayor's Youth Day 2007 Students
Click for photos and details
Top Accomplishments
Economic Development :: Schools :: eServices :: Employment :: Library :: Maps :: News Room :: Taxes
Home • A-Z Index • Site Map • Search • Contact • FAQs •
Accessibility • Privacy Policy
Request City Information & Services
Contact Webmaster
© Copyright 1996 - 2008 • City of Chesapeake • All rights reserved

FIGURE 3.3

Chesapeake, VA, Public Communications Dept.

Courtesy City of Chesapeake, Virginia.

are efficiently handled by those closest to the sources and other departments in the organization. Efficiency contributes to cost effectiveness.

Availability of staff practitioners has several advantages. When things go wrong, practitioners are only a minute away from a face-to-face meeting with the organization's officers. And as deputies, they can be entrusted with delicate matters. For example, if a senior executive defects in a huff to a competitor, the CEO wants a public relations specialist on the spot who knows the background, understands the dangers of mishandling the news, and has credibility with the news media and other key players.

Availability also means being on call for all other departments, divisions, and operating units. Staff members can be called into meetings on short notice. In some organizations—such as Johnson & Johnson—where public relations is largely decentralized, the on-site internal staff members are relatively handy for consultation in each operating unit. In others, a centralized function operates from headquarters much in the fashion of an outside firm, treating operating units and other departments as "clients."

The Department's Disadvantages

Team membership can be a problem when a person sacrifices objectivity and perspective in order to be a team player. If people are too loyal, they may be exploited when friendships and collegiality lead to subservience. Availability can cast the function as a catchall if it does not have a clearly defined mission and specified roles.

A *loss of objectivity* can happen ever so slowly and unwittingly as practitioners are subjected to day-to-day pressure and politics in the workplace. In supporting and being supported, they tend to be absorbed and compromised by group views. Their ability to see other points of view gives way to the subjectivity that afflicts those they were hired to counsel. They lose their ability to do the boundary spanning needed to avoid or solve problems in the organization's relationships with others. In effect, practitioners run the risk of becoming part of the problem. After all, they work hard to be a member of the management team.

Domination and *subservience* result when the function becomes co-opted, resulting in a group of yes-men and -women. Being team players and helping others is one thing; being diverted from goals, planning, and strategy to run errands for others is another. Practitioners walk a narrow line between providing professional services that are valuable, helpful, and appreciated and rendering low-level technical support that is easily replaced. Also, practitioners must guard against inaction based on fear of making what they perceive to be a career-threatening move or decision, as that undermines their role as counselor to top management.

Confused mission and roles can result from being readily available. Practitioners find themselves serving as stand-ins for top executives who make commitments but do not or cannot follow through themselves. For example, a CEO accepts an invitation to serve on a community charitable organization board but finds it difficult to attend the meetings. The practitioner gets a call to attend in the CEO's place. One could argue this indicates that the CEO trusts the public relations officer to effectively represent the organization. External constituencies are seldom pleased, however, to have a public relations representative instead of the CEO. They accept the switch in order to maintain the organization's support and permission to use the CEO's name on the letterhead.

The dilemma of a state bar association public relations director illustrates confusion about mission and roles. Among many miscellaneous duties, he was put in charge of the housekeeping staff and was directed to deal with the homeless population who entered the main reception area to use restroom facilities and to seek refuge from the cold and rain. How did the practitioner get such duties? Being the only nonlawyer at the director level probably did not help, but a vague and open-ended job description made the function vulnerable. The public relations director also was the most available, because other directors were often out of the office conducting programs and providing direct services to members. It became a vicious cycle: The more miscellaneous assignments the director accumulated, the less time he had for the association's public relations efforts and publications. Not surprisingly, the executive director eventually questioned the public relations director's effectiveness and criticized him for missing publication deadlines.

Titles and Reporting Relationships

Titles and positions of departments vary greatly, but across all organizations, "public relations" remains the most commonly used title. "Public information" remains a frequently used title in nonprofit organizations and government agencies. Military branches use "public affairs" almost exclusively. Many corporations use "corporate relations," "corporate communications," or "communications," with about one in ten using "public affairs." Among *Fortune* 500 companies, however, only about one in five use "public relations" titles (alone or in combination with other names).

There is no compelling reason to conclude that some other title will replace "public relations." To the contrary, "public relations" has survived almost a century despite the many attempts by practitioners themselves to find an alternative, despite the occasional taint of malpractice by individual practitioners, and despite public relations bashing by the media. Both news media and publics worldwide have come to understand the term and to use it to describe this function in organizations. Switching labels does not change more than 100 years of history.

More significant than the department's title, however, is the top public relations executive's place on the organizational chart and reporting relationship to the CEO. Too often, public relations is not included in the CEO's decision-making circle, the executive committee—sometimes referred to as "the C-suite." In a corporation, for example, that group typically brings together the CEO, the president (if someone other than the CEO), and the heads of manufacturing, finance, marketing, engineering, research and development (R&D), and legal. If public relations is not included, then implications of decisions on the organization's relationships with key stakeholders and communication needs may not be part of the discussion when decisions are made.[24] Even if not included in the decision circle meetings, however, the top public relations executive typically reports directly to the CEO.

Reporting relationships and job functions are included in organization charts and job descriptions. These lay the groundwork for division and specialization of work, communication up and down the chain of command, and acceptance of various functions throughout the organization. Some practitioners, however, become preoccupied with trying to change the charts and edit their job descriptions, as though these, with no other changes, will elevate the public relations function or somehow change how it functions. As one long-standing opponent of organization charts—the late Clarence Randall, a management innovator when he headed Inland Steel—pointed out,

> To know who is to do what and to establish authority and responsibility within an institution are the basic first principles of a good administration, but this is a far cry from handing down immutable tablets of stone from the mountaintop. . . . It is not the preparation of the organization chart that I condemn, but its abuse: this blowing up its significance to a point where guidance ceases and inhibition sets in.[25]

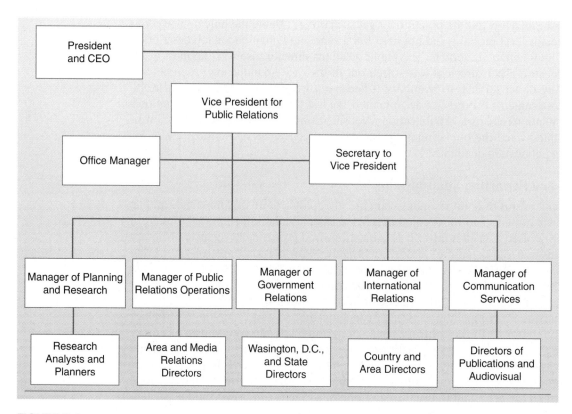

FIGURE 3.4

Corporate Public Relations Department

Organization charts are, at best, approximations, but they do help clarify the role and relationships of various functions. Figure 3.4, for example, details reporting relationships within a corporate public relations department.

Working with Other Departments

Public relations staff typically work most closely with the marketing and finance units. They also collaborate with the human resources, industrial or employee relations, and legal departments. These functions overlap with public relations in varying degrees, occasionally leading to unavoidable confusion or even outright conflict over their respective roles. To achieve organizational goals, however, each function needs the support and cooperation of the others.

Marketing

As discussed in Chapter 1, public relations is most often confused with marketing. These two major communication and outreach functions must work in harmony in dealing with an organization's many publics—sometimes referred to as "integrated communication." Conflict can arise over which function should be responsible for institutional advertising and product publicity. Confusion results if marketing specialists define "public relations" as simply publicity or media relations, or even more mistakenly, as "journalism." Some think that any goal-driven strategic plan is "marketing" and define public relations as simply media relations.

Some hold the mistaken notion that advertising is the sole province of marketing. Advertising designed to establish, change, or maintain relationships with key publics other than customers (usually by influencing public opinion) should, by its objectives and strategic nature, be implemented as part of public relations strategy. Advertisements addressing public policy issues, corporate reputation, financial news, or special events may require the advertising department's expertise to produce and place. The outcomes sought by such advertising, however, have more to do with public relations than with selling goods or services—marketing.

Conversely, publicity about products and services designed to increase sales is clearly directed to achieving marketing outcomes. Because public relations staff members are typically more skilled at writing and placing publicity, they often are enlisted to help publicize new products, product changes, price changes, product recalls, and special promotional activities as part of the marketing effort. For example, Microsoft uses national publicity efforts, along with advertising, to help introduce each edition of Windows. Even though it may have had an impact on publics other than customers—such as investors, competitors, and government regulators—the publicity was designed primarily to support the marketing effort.

Advertising and publicity produced by either public relations or marketing should be coordinated with the other's communications. For example, public relations should not be communicating about the company's commitment to protecting the environment and reducing the company's carbon footprint when marketing is advertising a nationwide sale of "non-green" products sold in non-biodegradable packaging. The growth of articulate protest and consumer groups, widespread use of the Internet globally, investigative and consumer reporting, and government scrutiny all make cooperation between public relations and marketing essential.

Competition, even conflict, between these two functions is understandable. Practitioners often compete on parallel career tracks for recognition, job advancement, and budgets. For example, a public relations author published an article with the subtitle "How to Steal Budget from Those Folks in Advertising." In some organizations, marketing and public relations report to the same executive, who is charged with coordinating efforts. Usually, however, they are separate departments, with public relations in a staff relationship to the chief executive officer and marketing in the line management chain of command.

Legal Counsel

The conflict between public relations and legal staffs is an old one. In the days of the muckrakers, corporate executives turned first to their lawyers to fix things. Some still do. One of the founders of public relations, Ivy Lee, felt strongly about this in 1925:

> I have seen more situations which the public ought to understand and which the public would sympathize with, spoiled by the intervention of the lawyer than in any other way. Whenever a lawyer starts to talk to the public, he shuts out the light.[26]

Traditionally, legal and public relations counselors approach situations from different perspectives. Lawyers tend to favor "no comment," pointing out that what you say may come back to haunt you (be used as evidence in court) and reminding that you are not legally obliged to say anything. Public relations practitioners, on the other hand, espouse the virtues of transparency and openness, of sharing information as soon as possible, of cooperating with the media, and of responding to people's claims to a right to know. Lawyers are accustomed to getting extensions, to protracting the process in private, and to delaying responses as long as possible. Public relations specialists routinely meet deadlines, recognize media time constraints as real, and respond immediately to media requests.

Public relations practitioners work to build and maintain mutuality and harmony in relationships. If public relations succeeds, then top management assumes that things are going smoothly and that there is no need for counsel. Lawyers, on the other hand, are called on when conflict and discord dominate an organization's relationships. Under conditions of threatened or actual legal action, top management turns to legal counsel for advice and protection. Hence lawyers gain power when organizations face conflict and discord with publics that turn to the courts for redress.

Cooperation between these two functions can protect the organization legally while at the same time serving the public interest, as when Sentry Insurance led the way in the insurance industry by rewriting policies and literature in plain English. The new policy descriptions meet the test of legal counsel and greatly increase information value to policyholders and prospective customers.

Cooperation also is critical during labor contract negotiations, product recalls, layoffs or other sensitive personnel matters, consumer protests or boycotts, and other situations that could lead to litigation. In such cases, "litigation public relations" involves "managing the communications process during the course of any legal dispute or adjudicatory proceeding so as to affect the outcome or its impact on the client's overall reputation."[27] Additionally, legal and public relations counsel must be coordinated on such matters as booklets explaining benefits to employees, the legality of advertising or publicity claims, plant security, and disclosure of financial information.[28]

Examples from various settings illustrate the need: Universities defend themselves both in the courts of justice and public opinion when fraternity hazing deaths, shootings, date rapes, or discrimination charges in tenure decisions become news. The presidents of Stanford, MIT, and other major universities called in both lawyers and public relations specialists when excessive overhead charges on federally funded research projects made headline news.

Increasingly, legal and public relations specialists collaborate when counseling CEOs and coordinate their responses in courts of law and in courts of public opinion. Additionally, one survey of CEOs found that almost one-third had law degrees.[29] As one lawyer advised fellow legal counselors, however, "Make sure you are the lawyer and that public relations is handled by a public relations professional."

Human Resources

Potential problems between public relations and human resources include (1) whether human resources strategic planning during downsizing (read "layoffs"), reengineering, mergers, and acquisitions extends to areas outside employee relations; (2) the extent to which communication efforts within the community constitute an extension of the organization–employee relationship; and (3) whether programs directed to the employees draw more on public relations concepts than on those from human resources. Compromise comes when practitioners and human resource specialists realize that internal relationships inevitably reverberate externally.

Employee communications (not the whole of employee relations) is the most frequent source of conflict and requires the greatest cooperation between these two functions. Addressing concerns about employee loyalty and mobility, quality-of-life and work-life balance, health care and security, and employee education and training affects the bottom line. Recognizing that the workforce has changed and continues to change, many organizations have increased efforts to develop their major resource, people.

> Change is now probably the only corporate constant. And if employees are expected to go along with the new programs, who better to collaborate and strategize about workforce changes than human resources and public relations?[30]

Strategic management of human resources, organizational culture, and organizational change requires close cooperation and collaboration between public relations and human resources specialists. Recognizing this need, chocolate maker Hershey Company named Charlene Binder senior vice president and "chief people officer" to oversee both public relations and human resources. Absent such coordination, some organizations created new units to conceive and implement internal and external communication strategy to support organizational restructuring and cultural change.

The Outside Counseling Firm

Beginning in the 1980s, many "public relations agencies" changed their titles to "public relations firms." The change reflects an increased emphasis on counseling and strategic planning services, viewed as more professional than the communication tactics produced by press agents and publicity agencies. Another reason for the switch is to position the firm as something different from advertising agencies working on commissions and low-cost vendors of communication services. Rather, most in the field prefer to be associated with law firms, management consulting firms, certified public accounting firms, architectural firms, and consulting engineering firms. However, some still refer to their "agency" in unguarded moments and proudly announce that a client has chosen their firm as "agency of record" (AOR).

Public Relations Firms

Public relations counseling firms range widely in size and scope. *O'Dwyer's Directory of Public Relations Firms* lists more than 2,000 firms by location and specialty in the United States and abroad, cross-indexed with their 8,500 clients. New York and London lead all cities in the number of firms, followed closely by Chicago and Washington, D.C. The world's largest firm, New York–based Weber Shandwick, has 83 offices in 41 countries. St. Louis–based Fleischman Hillard has 72 offices, but only 21 are abroad. Hill & Knowlton has a total of 70 offices, with 54 of those outside the United States. Burson-Marsteller's 57 wholly owned offices, when combined with 45 partially owned firms, give the firm a presence in more than 100 cities worldwide. Olgilvy PR Worldwide wholly owns 8 U.S. offices and 46 in other countries, and has partial interest in 20 other firms.[31]

In contrast, worldwide there are uncounted thousands working as independent self-employed counselors or consultants. Many work as "_____ and Associates," meaning, "If I can't handle the project myself, I know other practitioners I can bring in to assist."

With the growing recognition of the global economy and expansion of the European Union, the public relations capital has shifted from New York to London. For example, Hill & Knowlton's London office is bigger than its New York headquarters in both size and billings. Business in Europe increased dramatically with the introduction of a common currency (the euro) and removal of many international barriers to commerce. In the meantime, the business boom in China and the rest of Asia is drawing global firms and inspiring local start-ups. Hill & Knowlton now employs more than 120 in their China offices.

Phone directories in every major city list firms under "Public Relations" and "Publicity." For example, the London yellow pages directory contains listings under "Public Relations Consultancies" (outside the United States, "consultancy" is typically used instead of "firm" or "agency") and "Publicity Consultants."

Public relations and every other aspect of corporate business became global enterprises when markets and economies became global, as global alliances formed, and as global media delivered messages around the world within seconds. Today, public relations firms in most major cities operate internationally, either through affiliates or by subcontracting with local firms in other countries. For example, Kellen Communications, based in New York, used local firms in Germany, Japan, Mexico, and Italy for a program directed to the automotive industries in those countries. According to president Peter Rush,

> We demand the same things of firms in other countries that we demand of ourselves—credibility, accountability, expertise, experience, ethics, and, most important, results—although we fully understand that we have to allow them to execute the work in keeping with their cultural norms, especially as they relate to media relations.[32]

Networks of independent firms offer yet another approach when clients need global reach but do not want to be confined to a single brand firm. For example, software firm Mindset management evaluated options as the company's contract with a large global public relations firm was about to end. Instead of retaining the firm, management chose GlobalFluency (GF), a network of 34 independent firms operating in 40 countries. Mindset cut its public relations costs by 40 percent without cutting back on programming. When working on GF contracts, member firms operate under the GF name, not their own names. Other large networks include Worldcom, the largest with 86 member firms in 39 countries; Pinnacle Worldwide, with 60 firms in 30 countries; and IPREX, with 58 firms in 25 countries.[33] Whatever the approach, public relations firms now serve clients with new approaches to communication and counsel in a global village.

Standards of practice for public relations firms are more closely monitored and enforced in Europe than in the United States and Asia. More than 125 firms belong to the United Kingdom's Public Relations Consultants Association (PRCA), founded in 1969 (www.prca.or.uk). The trade association requires member consultancies to follow specific guidelines for dealing with the media, clients, and competitors; for conducting investor relations for publicly traded companies; and for enforcing the "Professional Charter" through arbitration and settlement. Strict enforcement forced then–Ogilvy Adams & Rinehart to withdraw from PRCA when it refused to list all of its clients in the association's confidential "Annual Register" as required in the PRCA Professional Charter.

PRCA belongs to the International Communications Consultancy Organisation (ICCO), which represents public relations consultancies across the globe. ICCO members are the national associations that represent more than 1,000 individual firms or consultancies in Africa, America, Asia, Australia, Europe, and the Middle East. The goals are to raise standards, address ethical issues, standardize practice, and share knowledge. ICCO promotes standards of practice through its professional code—*The Stockholm Charter*, guidelines for media relations—*Charter on Media Transparency*, and its quality guarantee—*Consultancy Management Standard*—which has been adopted by more than 200 consultancies worldwide. (See www.iccopr.com.)

The first such association of firms in the United States was formed in 1998 after 38 founding firms, representing most of the major national and international firms, contributed $200,000 to establish the American Association of Public Relations Firms (AAPRF). Renamed the Council of Public Relations Firms (CPRF), it now serves more than 100 members with education, standards of practice, and a code of ethics. Its mission is "To advance the business of public relations firms by building the market and firms' value as strategic business partners." CPRF is a member of the ICCO and subscribes to its charters and standards (see www.prfirms.org).

Advertising Agency Ownership

Many of the largest firms are subsidiaries of large advertising agencies. Many were acquired as advertising agencies bought out retiring founders and principals of closely held public relations firms. The trend began in 1978, when Foote, Cone and Belding purchased Carl Byoir and Associates. The largest U.S.–based firms are now owned by advertising agency conglomerates: Burson-Marsteller, Cohn & Wolfe, Ogilvy PR Worldwide, and Hill & Knowlton, Inc., by London-based WPP Group PLC; Ketchum Public Relations, Porter Novelli International, and Fleishman-Hillard by Omnicom Group Inc.; and Weber Shandwick and GolinHarris by Interpublic Group. In contrast, Edelman Public Relations Worldwide, with an international network of more than 45 offices, remains the largest independently owned firm.

Problems arise when two strong institutions—advertising agencies and public relations firms—with different traditions and cultures try to perform as a team, especially when historically they were competitors. Though under the umbrella of common ownership, each unit is rewarded on the basis of how much business it generates and how much it contributes to the conglomerate's bottom line. In effect advertising and public relations units compete for the clients' business and budgets. Moreover, few clients use the conglomerates as communication supermarkets. Rather, some large clients prefer to spread their business over several agencies and firms, expanding the range of perspectives and client experiences. As a result, large public relations firms typically compete for new business and clients, even though in some cases they are owned by the same conglomerate.

Specialization

Most firms claim to be "full-service" firms, but some carve out specialized client–service market niches. Although there are many specialties, the most dramatic growth has occurred in Washington, D.C., firms that specialize in government relations—lobbying, public affairs, and legislative affairs. Clients retain these firms primarily to participate in the public policy process and to have influence on those who formulate and implement public policy.

Client lists at many such firms also include foreign governments and foreign corporations who follow developments in the U.S. capital and who want their points of view to be considered in the White House, Congress, or federal agencies. The service can be nothing more than putting out news releases about a visiting dignitary or providing updates on legislation of interest to a foreign client. Regardless of the assignment, individuals who represent foreign interests must register with the U.S. Department of Justice, as required under the Foreign Agents Registration Act of 1938 (see Chapter 6). Globalization and increased international commerce of all kinds suggest that this will continue as a growth area for public relations firms specializing in government relations.

Unfortunately, the "Beltway Set" and "K Street" (Washington, D.C.) also include influence peddling operations that rise and fall with administrations and as the public-service–private-sector revolving door produces more and more insiders with connections with their former government employers. Commenting on the antics of those who turned government service into profitable public relations and lobbying practices, one editorial writer asked, "Has the murky 'profession' of public relations turned to sleaze?" In fact, for some who abused their positions of public trust, it meant prison time and hefty fines for illegal lobbying. Those exceptions aside, there remains a large and growing need for legitimate public relations counsel on legislative affairs and lobbying in the nation's capital, as well as in every state capital and major city.

Other specialties include agriculture, financial public relations and investor relations, health care, high tech, sports, and travel and tourism, to name only a few. In agriculture, for example, Morgan & Myers, with offices in Waukesha, Wisconsin; Waterloo, Iowa; and Minneapolis, Minnesota, serves clients such as the Iowa Corn Growers Association, The Soybean Council, Cargill, and Monsanto (see Figure 3.5). Sloane & Company (New York), specializing in investor relations, serves clients such as AIG Financial Products, Gaylord Entertainment, and TiVo, Inc. The client list at Dorland Global Health Communications (Philadelphia) includes American Diabetes Association, Baxter BioPharma Solutions, and Procter & Gamble Pharmaceuticals. In the entertainment capital, Los Angeles, California, Bender/Helper Impact serves clients such as 20th Century Fox Home Entertainment, DreamWorks Home Entertainment, NBC/Universal, and Sony Pictures Mobile.

In addition to industry specialization, a few firms provide specialized services to help clients target particular communities. For example, when retailer Eddie Bauer was threatened with a national boycott after a nationally publicized security guard's questionable accusation that a Black customer had shoplifted, the company retained the Black- and woman-owned firm Robinson Associates, LLC (Washington, D.C.) for counsel on crisis media relations and community relations.

Reasons for Retaining Outside Counsel

Chester Burger, longtime consultant to the public relations industry, lists six reasons why organizations retain firms.

1. Management has not previously conducted a formal public relations program and lacks experience in organizing one.

2. Headquarters may be located far from communications and financial centers.

3. The firm has a wide range of up-to-date contacts.

4. An outside firm can provide the services of experienced executives and creative specialists who would be unwilling to move to other cities or whose salaries a single organization could not afford.

5. An organization with its own public relations department may need highly specialized services that it cannot afford or does not need on a full-time, continuous basis.

6. Crucial policy matters require the independent judgment of an outsider.

As an example, GTE Diversified Products retained Hill & Knowlton to help plan and conduct the global public relations program for its joint venture with Siemens A.G., Germany. Charged with coordinating internal and external communication

FIGURE 3.5
Morgan & Myers

**Moving from one end of the food market
to the other requires skillful navigation.**

Whether your target is at the helm of a tractor
or the head of the kitchen table,
we'll help steer you in the right direction.

Morgan
&Myers   *Public
                Relations
                Counselors*

Phone: 414-674-4026 · **Fax:** 414-674-6670 · **E-mail:** *gmyers@morganmyers.com*

Member
The
WORLDCOM
Group, Inc.

JEFFERSON, WISCONSIN · MILWAUKEE · MINNEAPOLIS · WATERLOO, IOWA operations in the United States and 22 other countries, the vice president of public affairs enlisted experienced outside help:

> By retaining their (Hill & Knowlton) services, we benefited from an existing network of media contacts, saving us some of the trouble of tracking down outlets we needed to contact with news of the joint venture. We also used their capabilities in resolving problems in translating, designing, and delivering documents in a manner appropriate to each of our markets.
>
> If you don't have a structure in place, you should consider hiring the services of an outside firm that can provide you with the necessary expertise. . . . In a global setting, doing all this requires more effort, more forethought, and more skills than ever. There are simply more variables to contend with. And this puts even greater demands on public affairs staff.[34]

Client–Firm Relationships

Sometimes counseling firms initiate contact with clients they think need help. More commonly, clients call counseling firms (see Figure 3.6 for how they select a firm). For instance, an oil company may have a persistent problem with government regulation of offshore drilling, a long-planned enterprise in which millions of dollars have been invested. However, plans are held up because of opposition to exploration by environmental groups, investor concern that stock value will drop because of unfavorable reports in the business press, and public skepticism that the oil com-

FIGURE 3.6

Checklist for Selecting a Firm

Courtesy Harland W. Warner, Bill Rolle & Associates, Inc. Washington, D.C., and *Public Relations Journal.*

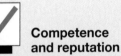

Competence and reputation

- Years in business
- Size—people and billings
- Full service—specialties
- Reach—local, regional, national, international
- Growth pattern/financial stability
- Types of accounts
- Experience with accounts similar to yours—any conflicts
- Samples of work
- Sample list of suppliers used

Staff

- List and qualifications of staff— full time, project clients, freelance/ consultants
- Names of several former employees
- Staff to be assigned to your account—qualifications and longevity with firm
- Percent of their time to be devoted to your account—other accounts they will handle
- Staff or personnel backup available
- Staff turnover in the past two years

Clients

- Existing client list
- Past clients
- Average number of clients during past three years—retainer clients, project clients
- Oldest clients and length of service
- Average length of client–firm relationships
- Clients lost in last year

Results and measurement

- Does firm understand your objectives/needs?
- How will progress be reported?
- How will results be measured?
- What will it cost—billing process, hourly rate, expenses billed, approval process?

pany will protect fragile ocean ecosystems. All this is framed by memories of the *Exxon Valdez* oil spill in Alaska's Prince William Sound. The internal department convinces the chairman and CEO that it is time to seek the best outside help available to help design and manage a strategic plan to address these public relations problems. Unfortunately, it too often takes a *Valdez* oil spill, stock sell-off, or some other crisis to get top management's attention.

It is not uncommon for the client–firm relationship to begin with an emergency, as was the case when Arizona Economic Council officials called on Hill & Knowlton. After Arizona voters defeated a ballot initiative establishing a state holiday honoring Martin Luther King Jr., the National Football League announced that it would move the Super Bowl game from Tempe, Arizona. In such emergencies, counsel provides advice and helps the client manage the crisis. Depending on the outcome, the firm may be retained on a long-term basis to prevent such crises in the future. In the Arizona situation, however, the Super Bowl game was moved to the Rose Bowl in Pasadena, and Hill & Knowlton lost the Arizona Economic Council as a client. (Arizona did host the 2008 Super Bowl.)

Under more typical circumstances, a counseling firm begins its service after being invited to present a proposal. It begins by researching the client's problem situation and its relationships with the publics affected by or involved in the situation. Called a "public relations audit," this initial exploration can take several days or even weeks. The counsel then arranges to make a presentation—"new business pitch"—outlining the following:

1. Research findings and situation analysis of the problem or opportunity
2. Threats and gains to the organization, given various courses of action or nonaction
3. Immediate action and communication responses, if needed to meet a crisis
4. Overall strategy and program goals, as well as objectives for various publics
5. Highlights of the communication and action program for achieving the goals and objectives
6. Evaluation research plan for monitoring the program and assessing impact
7. Staffing, budget, and timetable

Typically, competing firms make presentations (see Figure 3.7), and one is selected on the basis of its demonstrated capabilities and the presentation. Once retained, the counselor usually functions in one of three ways:

1. Provides advice and strategic plan, leaving execution to the client's internal staff
2. Provides advice and works with the client's staff to execute the program
3. Provides advice and undertakes full execution of the program

Occasionally, client–firm relationships take a turn the client does not anticipate. To get the business (win the account), usually a team of experienced professionals makes the new business pitch. The client is duly impressed by the talent and depth of experience that they assume will be devoted to their problem. In some instances, however, that may be the last they see of many of the team. Instead, the account is assigned to account coordinators and assistant account executives who do not have the same range of experience as the new business development team. Critics justifiably refer to this practice as a "bait-and-switch" tactic. The firm's senior executives

FIGURE 3.7

Counselor's Presentation

Courtesy Mary Correia-Moreno, Vice President and COO, Nuffer, Smith, Tucker, Inc., San Diego.

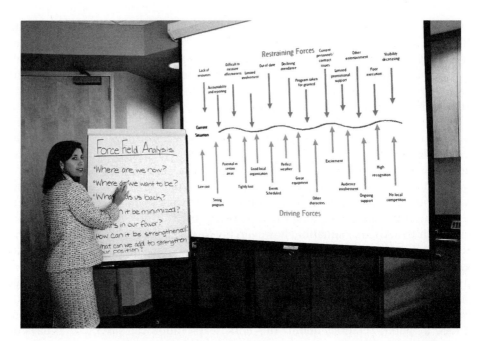

show up just often enough to reassure the client, but in fact the work is done by junior staff. Firms employ such a strategy at the risk of losing clients.

Clients occasionally call for a review of the firm's work or even reopen the selection process by requesting proposals from competing firms. A review may simply be a cover for having already decided to change firms. To soften the blow, the incumbent firm is given the "courtesy" of making the "short list" of finalists before another firm gets the account. In some cases, clients call for reviews and entertain proposals from competing firms simply to remind the incumbent firm that the client's business should not be taken for granted or given anything less than prime attention.

Some counselors suggest yet another reason why some clients conduct reviews and call for proposals: to get new ideas—free. The suspicion is that there is no real intention to replace the incumbent firm or to award the business to a firm. The published request for proposals (RFP) or the invitation to selected firms represents an unethical search for new ideas without having to pay for the counsel. Consequently, some firms will not do speculative pitches unless the client pays a fee that covers the cost of preparing the presentation. Critics of the RFP selection process say that quality is often sacrificed when price considerations lead to choosing the low bidder.

For the most part, however, trust and respect characterize many client–firm relationships that are built on a foundation of cooperation, collaboration, and collegiality developed while working together through both the worst and best of times.

Counselors' Advantages

Most large corporations retain external counsel at corporate headquarters and also hire local and regional counseling firms to supplement corporate-wide efforts and to handle local problems and issues. A Public Relations Society of America Counselors Academy survey found that almost three out of four corporations use outside counsel even though they have their own internal departments. Survey results from a wide range of organizations, including government and nonprofit settings, show increased use of outside counsel. The trend has been to cut in-house staff and outsource work to external firms.[35] Clearly, external counsel provides valuable services not readily available internally.

Counselors rank *variety of talents and skills* as their greatest advantage over internal staffing. *Objectivity,* relatively untrammeled by the politics within an organization, ranks second. *Range of prior experience* is third; *geographical scope of their operations,* fourth; and the *ability to reinforce and upgrade a client's internal staff,* fifth.

Counseling firms with large staffs emphasize the *flexibility* of their personnel and operations as a prime advantage. In their offices, or on call, are skilled researchers, artists, models, new media specialists, copy editors, magazine feature writers, media coaches, talk show experts, photographers, videographers, and legislative experts. A client can request a highly technical and specialized service, and an account executive can attend to the need immediately.

Flexibility is also tied to scope of operations and to range of experience. A firm based in New York, Washington, or Chicago can serve clients in Colorado, West Virginia, and California through its branches or affiliates. A global firm is as likely to have a network of branch offices or affiliated firms in London, Beijing, and Sydney as in Denver, Dallas, and Seattle.

In the course of a year, counselors work on many different problems for several different clients. In effect, a public relations firm is a repository of living case histories. Each project adds to its fund of knowledge. Experience and versatility of staff make this synergy possible. The counselor approaches each situation bolstered by experience with similar situations and knowledge of the success or failure that attended previous encounters.

The counselor's *reputation* can be a major advantage. Externally, a counselor's reputation among the press and government officials can work to the advantage of clients. Internally, outside experts often can introduce ideas that internal staffers have struggled unsuccessfully to place on the agenda. Apparently, paying a hefty fee increases top management's attention to public relations counsel. And from the client's point of view, knowing that the counselor's reputation and subsequent referrals are on the line also helps ensure performance.

Counselors' Handicaps

With rare exceptions, intervention by outside counsel—and this applies to almost all consultants—meets with *internal opposition* ranging from nonacceptance to outright rejection. This is, at least in theory, the counselor's most serious handicap. Antagonism toward and resistance to outsiders and their recommendations are natural human traits. The old guard resists change—the new idea, new approach, new look—and sees it as a threat to security and established ways of doing business. Their realm is being invaded; their judgment is being criticized. The offended ask, "What does this outsider know about our organization, our way of doing things?" Then, under the guise of scrutiny and concern, they raise questions about cost, return on investment, or qualifications. Dealing with the internal staff and others in the client organization calls for special consulting skills.

Counselors, however, overwhelmingly cite *questions of cost* as their most frequent problem with clients. They list *threat to old guard and set ways* as the second most persistent handicap. *Resistance to outside advice* comes in third, and *unforeseen conflicts of personality or conviction* is fourth. Some counselors include *clients' lack of understanding of public relations and unavailability of client managers* at times when counselors need approvals, clearance, or other decisions before the work can proceed.

Counseling Firm Costs

Clients retain counseling firms for specific projects or for indefinite periods of continuing service, reviewable and renewable at agreed upon intervals. Fees for services typically are established in one of four ways:

1. A monthly retainer covering a fixed number of hours and services
2. A minimum retainer plus monthly billing for actual staff time at hourly rates or on a per diem basis
3. Straight hourly charges for staff time, using fees based on the range of staff experience and expertise
4. Fixed project fee, typically resulting from competitive bidding in response to a request for proposal (RFP)

The recent trend toward fixed project fees has changed the nature of business. Instead of having a stable client list and steady cash flow from retainers and hourly fees, firms have to compete for contracts to do specific and limited projects. As one firm's principal put it, instead of having 30 clients, the firm has to have 300 clients because so much of the work is piecemeal. One of the costs to clients of such an approach can be loss of continuity and an uncoordinated series of tactics that are not part of an overall strategy.

Out-of-pocket expenses are generally billed at cost and are exclusive of the retainer fee. In some cases, the client deposits an advance with the firm to cover such expenses. Some firms, however, mark up actual costs of certain expenses by 15 to 20 percent to cover overhead costs. One firm, for example, marks up advertising placements, photography, and printing by 20 percent, but bills actual cost for entertainment, clipping services, and postage.

Fees vary widely. Counseling firms have minimum retainer fees, usually in the range of $1,000 to $10,000, but up to $100,000 and more per month for major accounts. For example, a large wood products company might retain a large national firm for $125,000 per month, plus expenses, to lead the company's national media relations and lobbying in Washington, D.C. At the other end of the scale, a small client might pay as little as a $500 monthly retainer to write an occasional news release or as little as $100 for a single news release.

Hourly fees range from a low of about $60 for account coordinators or other junior staff to several hundred dollars for every hour worked by senior counselors and firm principals. Large firms retained by large clients typically charge $100 to $500 hourly for professional project staff. These rates typically reflect salary markups in the range of three to six times actual hourly staff costs. Figures differ from city to city, but five elements are reflected in counseling fees and charges:

1. Actual cost of staff time devoted to the project
2. Executive time and supervision
3. Administrative and other nonproject time, such as clerical and accounting
4. Overhead costs, such as space, benefits, and utilities
5. Reasonable profit for doing the work, based on what the market will bear

Results of benchmarking surveys of public relations firms indicate a 25 percent pretax profit is the target, and that revenue per professional should range from $150,000 to $160,000 in smaller firms and $185,000 to $200,000 per professional in larger firms. Regardless of the size and management of the firm, three external factors influence a firm's profitability—market size and share, competition, and overall market trends.[36] In practice, however, many firms operate at levels below the target benchmarks and would celebrate mightily if they achieved 25 percent pretax profit.

The most common threat to client–firm relationships is conflict over the costs and hours billed. As a result, most firms use sophisticated accounting methods to record and track staff hours and project expenses. "Billable hours" often becomes a criterion for assessing employee productiveness. Some firms, formally or informally, expect each practitioner to "bill out" a minimum of 30 hours each week, just as in most accounting and law firms. In other words, the employee's time log—recorded in tenth- or quarter-hour units—documents 30 or more hours of work charged each week to specific client projects. Each client's monthly bill, then, reflects the total hours recorded on all staff time logs designated to that account or project. The account executive monitors these time records and detailed expenses to keep costs in line with the client–firm agreement. (Figure 3.8 shows a typical paper time sheet for recording hours, but most firms use software programs to enter and manage time and expense reports.)

New Approaches

Increasingly, organizations are using a combination of internal departments and outside counsel to fulfill the public relations function. Moreover, top management increasingly recognizes how essential public relations is to organizational success. More and more high-level practitioners have joined the executive decision-making group or at least are consulted on major decisions. Practitioners in firms increasingly serve as counselors and strategic planners, rather than mere press agents and communication technicians. In short, public relations is an integral part of most organizations' management structure.

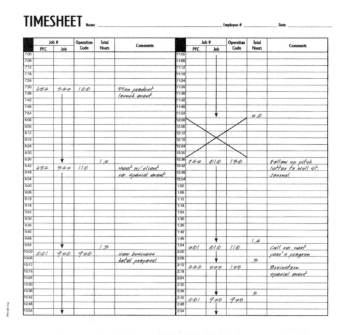

FIGURE 3.8

Time Sheet

Reprinted with permission from *The New PR Client Service Manual,* 4th ed. (San Diego, CA: PRSA Counselors Academy and GablePR, 2001), chapter 12, p. 7.

The president of one public relations firm predicts these changes will affect both internal departments and the firms serving them:

> Traditional, large, central PR departments will almost certainly become relics. Very tight, small and expert departments are likely to become the norm and outsourcing may be the word most commonly used. In many cases, the PR chief will use a broad array of consulting firms, rather than just one. He or she may conclude that it is far more effective to use a small, expert local company in a Third World country, rather than the local office of a U.S. multinational agency. The agencies, for their part, will need to find ways to demonstrate that they have significant comparative advantage relative to these small, local rivals.[37]

Former AT&T public relations executive Edward M. Block, who oversaw what was at the time the largest public relations department (before the 1984 breakup of AT&T), agrees that the smaller departments will increasingly work with outside firms:

> Given the choice, I would never have built anything so large. . . . Rather than build huge staffs it (the firm) can be a cost-effective way to out-source noncritical functions. But the high priority, core responsibilities must remain in-house. A firm may even be a counselor, but not a substitute or surrogate for handling the vital PR roles.[38]

Global markets, strategic planning, and the convergence of communication and technology have attracted other types of consulting firms to public relations. Management consulting firms have added "communications specialists" to their staffs. Job descriptions read much like position descriptions in traditional public relations firms. Some large law firms also have started offering "public relations counsel" (read "media relations advice") to complement legal counsel and services in high-profile cases that attract media coverage.

Regardless of the source of counsel and services, public relations has an impact in an organization when people begin to tell each other that candor in communication is the best policy and that socially responsible actions are in the best interest of the organization. This means that public relations consciousness is gaining ground and there is growing confidence in the internal staff and outside counselors.

Exposing a clean organization to public gaze and operating in the mutual interests of itself and its publics does not mean that everything about the organization should be made public. In business there are competitors to consider. In the military there are security considerations. In health institutions there are ethical limitations on disclosure of patient information. In government agencies there are political and regulatory factors. Everywhere there are legal pros and cons. Common sense helps, but organizations must have specialized staff or counsel to perform the public relations function in an ethical and professional manner. That is a lesson from public relations' history, the topic of the next chapter.

Notes

[1] Quoted from introduction to David R. Drobis, "Stop Whining and Take a Seat!" *The Public Relations Strategist* 2, no. 1 (Spring 1996): 37.

[2] Lawrence G. Foster, "10 CEOs Send a Message to Public Relations," *The Public Relations Strategist* 1, no. 1 (Spring 1995): 8.

[3] Henry H. Farquhar, "The Anomaly of Functional Authority at the Top," *Advanced Management* 7, no. 2 (April–June 1942): 51.

[4] Gary F. Grates, "Why the Coveted Top Spot Is Losing Its Allure," *Communication World* 14, no. 3 (February 1997): 26.

[5] Martha M. Lauzen, "Public Relations Roles, Intraorganizational Power, and Encroachment," *Journal of Public Relations Research* 4, no. 2 (1992): 61–80.

[6] Bruce R. Barstow, "An Insider's Outside View of Public Relations," in *Precision Public Relations,* ed. Ray Eldon Hiebert (New York: Longman, 1988), 65. First published in *Public Relations Review* 10, no. 1 (Spring 1984): 10–17.

[7] Adam Shell interview with Carol Sanger, vice president of corporate communications, Federated Department Stores, "Talk from the Top: Communicating in Tumultuous Times," *Public Relations Tactics* 3, no. 4 (April 1996): 30–31.

[8] James E. Grunig, ed., *Excellence in Public Relations and Communication Management* (Hillsdale, NJ: Lawrence Erlbaum Associates, 1992). The term "dominant coalition" is introduced on p. 24 and used throughout the book.

[9] Ibid., 299.

[10] Larissa A. Grunig, James E. Grunig, and David M. Dozier, *Excellent Public Relations and Effective Organizations: A Study of Communication Management in Three Countries* (Mahwah, NJ: Lawrence Erlbaum Associates, 2002), 535.

[11] Ibid., 61.

[12] *Jack O'Dwyer's Newsletter* 29, no. 42 (October 23, 1996): 7.

[13] Jeff Cole, "Boeing Names New Managers, Alters Structure," *Wall Street Journal,* August 5, 1997, p. B7.

[14] Jeff Bennett and Neal E. Boudette, "Chrysler's Top Spokesman Resigns," *Wall Street Journal* (December 11, 2007): B8.

[15] Larissa A. Grunig, "Power in the Public Relations Department," *Public Relations Research Annual* 2 (1990): 115–55.

[16] For a detailed analysis, see David M. Dozier, "The Innovation of Research in Public Relations Practice: Review of a Program of Studies," *Public Relations Research Annual* 2 (1990): 3–28.

[17] David M. Dozier, with Larissa A. Grunig and James E. Grunig, *Manager's Guide to Excellence in Public Relations and Communication Management* (Mahwah, NJ: Lawrence Erlbaum Associates, 1995), 78–80.

[18] Robert L. Dilenschneider, "The Seven Deadly Sins," *PRWeek* (November 14–20, 1988): 11. For a similar perspective with extensive case examples, see Dilenschneider's edited book, *Dartnell's Public Relations Handbook,* 4th ed. (Chicago: Dartnell Corporation, 1997).

[19] Foster, "10 CEOs Send a Message," p. 11.

[20] Ibid., p. 9.

[21] Adapted from Larissa A. Grunig, James E. Grunig, and David M. Dozier, *Excellent Public Relations and Effective Organizations: A Study of Communication Management in Three Countries* (Mahwah, NJ: Lawrence Erlbaum Associates, 2002), 12–16.

[22] Hamilton Nolan, "J&J Divides to Conquer Comms," *PRWeek* (May 21, 2007): 12.

[23] Shell interview with Carol Sanger, "Talk from the Top," p. 31.

[24] Roy T. Cottier, "Communication: A Management Strategy, Not a Professional Technique," *Vital Speeches* 53, no. 18 (July 1, 1987): 556–59. Speech to International Association of Business Communicators, Toronto. Cottier is former senior vice president of corporate relations at Northern Telecom Limited.

[25] Clarence Randall, *The Folklore of Management* (Boston: Little, Brown, 1959), 24.

[26] Ivy Lee, *Publicity: Some of the Things It Is and Is Not* (New York: Industries Publishing Company, 1925), 58–59.

[27] James F. Haggerty, Esq., *In the Court of Public Opinion: Winning Your Case with Public Relations* (Hoboken, NJ: Wiley & Sons, 2003): 2. Written by the CEO of the PR Consulting Group, New York—a lawyer by training—chapter 6 discusses "Lawyers, Clients, and Public Relations Professionals: How We Can Work Together": 143–172.

[28] See Chapter 6 for a more detailed discussion of legal considerations.

[29] Ellen Joan Pollock, "Order in the Boardroom: Lawyers Rise to CEO," *Wall Street Journal,* September 11, 1996, p. B1.

[30] Jean Cardwell, "Learning to Waltz with Human Resources," *The Public Relations Strategist* 2, no. 1 (Spring 1996): 44.

[31] Office totals are from the *PRWeek Agency Business Report 2007* (undated) and the Web sites of the firms listed.

[32] As quoted by Lee Levitt, "U.S. Firms Tap Foreign Shops for Client Work," *O'Dwyer's PR Services Report* 11, no. 6 (June 1997): 34.

[33] Tanya Lewis, "Networks Foster a Collaborative Spirit," *PRWeek* (April 16, 2007): 13.

[34] Geoffrey L. Pickard, "Bridging the Gap in Joint Venture Communications: Global Public Affairs," *Vital Speeches* 53, no. 5 (December 15, 1986): 145–48.

[35] Thomas L. Harris & Co., Highland Park, IL, conducts an annual survey of clients using the largest public relations firms.

[36] Richard Goldstein, "Managing for Prosperity in '08," *O'Dwyer's PR Report* 22, no. 2 (February 2008): 32.

[37] Frank Vogl, "Expectations of the Chief Corporate Public Relations Officer in 2001," speech presented to Arthur W. Page Society, Annual Spring Seminar, New York, March 28, 1996.

[38] As reported in "John Budd's Plain Talk" (a supplement to *PR Reporter*), no. 14 (December 1, 1997): 3. (Unfortunately, *PR Reporter* is no longer published.)

Additional Sources

Dozier, David M., with Larissa A. Grunig and James E. Grunig. *Manager's Guide to Excellence in Public Relations and Communication Management.* Mahwah, NJ: Lawrence Erlbaum Associates, 1995. Deals with power and change in organizations, building linkages to and working with top management, and qualities of public relations excellence.

Grunig, Larissa A., James E. Grunig, and David M. Dozier, *Excellent Public Relations and Effective Organizations: A Study of Communication Management in Three Countries.* Mahwah, NJ: Lawrence Erlbaum Associates, 2002. Final report in the Excellence series, summarizing the findings and updating the theory.

Hammer, Michael, and James Champy. *Reengineering the Corporation: A Manifesto for Business Revolution.* New York: HarperCollins, 1993. The book that drove the reengineering craze that led to changes in processes, structures, and cultures in all types of organizations in the 1990s.

Lukaszewski, James E. *Why Should the Boss Listen to You? The Seven Disciplines of the Trusted Strategic Advisor.* San Francisco, CA: Jossey-Bass, 2008. Outlines the skills and disciplines needed to gain influence and to become a trusted advisor to senior managers.

Maister, David H. *Managing the Professional Service Firm.* New York: Free Press, 1993. Widely read guide for maximizing service, satisfaction, and success (profitability) in firms.

Miller, Katherine. *Organizational Communication: Approaches and Process,* 3rd ed. Belmont, CA: Wadsworth, 2005.

O'Dwyer, Jack, ed. *O'Dwyer's Directory of Public Relations Firms.* New York: J. R. O'Dwyer Co. Annual listings and descriptions of more than 2,000 public relations firms and their clients.

Historical Origins

4

STUDY GUIDE   After studying Chapter 4, you should be able to:

▶ Use examples to illustrate how the development of public relations occurred during attempts to mobilize public opinion in struggles for power and to promote change.

▶ Name major historical leaders in public relations and describe their respective contributions to the development of public relations and to current practice.

▶ Trace the evolution of public relations from its American beginnings to modern practice.

▶ Cite the origins of some of the principles and techniques of contemporary public relations.

Studying how public relations evolved provides insight into its functions, its strengths, and its weaknesses. Unfortunately, many practitioners do not have a sense of their calling's history and thus do not fully understand its place and purpose in society. Nor do they realize how history and the development of public relations are intertwined. Published histories typically oversimplify what is a complex and dramatic story by emphasizing novelty and a few colorful personalities. But understanding public relations' historical context is vital to the professionalization of today's practice.

Efforts to communicate with others and to deal with the force of public opinion go back to antiquity; only the tools, degree of specialization, breadth of knowledge, and intensity of effort are relatively new. This chapter traces the evolution of public relations.[1]

Those who cannot remember the past are doomed to repeat it.
—George Santayana, American philosopher, poet, and cultural critic

Ancient Genesis

Communicating to influence viewpoints and actions can be traced from the earliest civilizations. Archaeologists found a farm bulletin in Iraq that told farmers of 1800 B.C. how to sow their crops, how to irrigate, how to deal with field mice, and how to harvest their crops. Rudimentary elements of public relations also appear in descriptions of the king's spies in ancient India. Besides espionage, the spies' duties included keeping the king in touch with public opinion, championing the king in public, and spreading rumors favorable to the government.[2]

Greek theorists wrote about the importance of the public will, even though they did not specifically use the term "public opinion." Certain phrases and ideas in the political vocabulary of the Romans and in writings of the medieval period relate to modern concepts of public opinion. The Romans coined the expression *vox populi, vox Dei*—"the voice of the people is the voice of God." Machiavelli wrote in his *Discoursi,* "Not without reason is the voice of the people compared to the voice of God," and he held that the people must be either "caressed or annihilated."

Public relations was used many centuries ago in England, where the kings maintained Lords Chancellor as "Keepers of the King's Conscience." Even kings acknowledged the need for a third party to facilitate communication and adjustment between the government and the people. So it was with the church, traders, and artisans. The word *propaganda* appeared in the seventeenth century, when the Catholic Church set up its *Congregatio de Propaganda Fide*—"Congregation for Propagating the Faith."

American Beginnings: Born in Adversity and Change

The American beginnings of public relations appear in the American Revolution's struggle for power between the patriots' grassroots movement and the commercial, propertied Tories. Later efforts to gain public support included the conflict between the trade and property interests led by Alexander Hamilton and the planter-and-farmer bloc led by Thomas Jefferson, the struggle between Andrew Jackson's agrarian pioneers and the financial forces of Nicholas Biddle, and the bloody Civil War.

Before the Revolution

Using publicity to raise funds, promote causes, boost commercial ventures, sell land, and build box-office personalities in the United States, however, is older than the nation itself. The American talent for promotion can be traced back to the first settlements on the East Coast in the seventeenth century. Probably the first systematic effort on this continent to raise funds was that sponsored by Harvard College in 1641, when that infant institution sent a trio of preachers to England on a "begging mission." Once in England, they notified Harvard that they needed a fund-raising brochure, now a standard item in a fund drive. In response to this request came *New England's First Fruits,* written largely in Massachusetts but printed in London in 1643, the first of countless public relations pamphlets and brochures.[3]

Pushing for Independence

The tools and techniques of public relations have long been an important part of political weaponry. Sustained campaigns to shape and move public opinion go back to the Revolutionary War and the work of Samuel Adams and his cohorts. These revolutionaries understood the importance of public support and knew intuitively how to arouse and channel it. They used pen, platform, pulpit, staged events, symbols, news tips, and political organization in an imaginative, unrelenting way. Adams worked tirelessly to arouse and then organize public opinion, proceeding always on the assumption that "the bulk of mankind are more led by their senses than by their reason." Early on, he discerned that public opinion results from the march of events and the way these events are seen by those active in public affairs. Adams would create events to meet a need if none were at hand to serve his purpose.[4]

Far more than most realize, today's patterns of public relations practice were shaped by innovations in mobilizing public opinion developed by Adams and his fellow revolutionaries. In fomenting revolt against England, these propagandists, operating largely from the shadows, developed and demonstrated the power of these techniques:

1. The necessity of an organization to implement actions made possible by a public relations campaign: the Sons of Liberty, organized in Boston in January 1766, and the Committees of Correspondence, also born in Boston in 1775

2. The use of symbols that are easily identifiable and arouse emotion: the Liberty Tree

3. The use of slogans that compress complex issues into easy-to-quote, easy-to-remember stereotypes: "Taxation without representation is tyranny"

4. Staged events that catch public attention, provoke discussion, and thus crystallize unstructured public opinion: the Boston Tea Party[5]

5. The importance of getting your side of a story to the public first, so that your interpretation of events becomes the accepted one: the Boston Massacre

6. The necessity for a sustained saturation campaign using these techniques through all available channels of communication to penetrate the public mind with a new idea or a new conviction

The revolutionaries recognized the enormous difficulty of mobilizing public opinion to fight a war and to form a government:

> They knew that there was a wide gap between their public professions and American reality. They knew that there was bitter opposition to Independence and that the mass of the people were [*sic*] mostly indifferent. They knew, too, that there were deep rivalries and serious differences among the colonies.[6]

But neither the revolutionaries nor the anti-independents

> . . . could have anticipated . . . the stunning effect of *Common Sense*. The little pamphlet had become a clarion call, rousing spirits within Congress and without as nothing else had. The first edition, attributed to an unnamed "Englishman" [Thomas Paine] . . . appeared January 9, 1776. By the time Adams had resumed his place in Congress a month later, *Common Sense* had gone into a third edition and was sweeping the colonies. In little time more than 100,000 copies were in circulation.[7]

One history buff called Paine's *Common Sense* "the greatest PR act of the Revolution" and traced three additional principles of modern practice to tactics used by revolutionaries:

> Swaying Early Adopters: Samuel Adams and "The Committees of Correspondence"
>
> The White Paper: Thomas Paine and "Common Sense"
>
> The Product Launch Press Release: Thomas Jefferson and the "Declaration of Independence"[8]

In weak contrast to the revolutionists' effective communication, the Tories, supporters of King George and the British Empire, relied not so much on propaganda as on legal and military pressures, to no avail. It is little wonder that an exuberant Sam Adams would exult when he heard the firing at Lexington, "Oh, what a glorious morning is this!" He and his fellow propagandists had done their work well.[9] The emotion-laden revolutionary campaign set patterns for the nation's political battles that were to follow.[10]

The next public relations landmark in the new nation came with publication of *The Federalist Papers*, 85 letters written to newspapers in 1787 and 1788 by Alexander Hamilton, James Madison, and John Jay. The letters urged ratification of the Constitution, in what one historian called the new nation's "first national political campaign":

> The political ordeal that produced the Constitution in 1787 and brought about its ratification in 1788 was unique in human history. Never before had the representatives of a whole nation discussed, planned, and implemented a new form of government in such a manner and in such a short time.[11]

Another historian, Broadus Mitchell, wrote,

> In parrying blows against and enlisting support for the Constitution, the authors of the *Federalist* did the best job of public relations known to history. Objectors were not so much repulsed as refuted. Honest fears were removed. Ignorance was supplied with information and illustration. The manner was earnest rather than passionate, was persuasive by a candor that avoided the cocksure. He [Hamilton] addressed his readers' judgment in a spirit of moderation.[12]

Historian Allan Nevins credited Alexander Hamilton with "history's finest public relations job":

> Obtaining national acceptance of the Constitution was essentially a public relations exercise, and Hamilton, with his keen instinct for public relations, took thought not only to the product but to the ready acquiescence of thoughtful people; and he imparted his views to others. . . . Once the Constitution came before the country, the rapidity with which Hamilton moved was a striking exemplification of good public relations. He knew that if a vacuum develops in popular opinion, ignorant and foolish views will fill it. No time must be lost in providing accurate facts and sound ideas.[13]

Promoting Growth and Change

Early developments in public relations are directly tied to the *power struggles evoked by political reform movements*. These movements, reflecting strong tides of protest against entrenched power groups, were the catalytic agents for much of the growth of public relations practice, because the jockeying of political and economic groups for dominance created the need to muster public support.

The first clear beginnings of presidential campaigns and of the presidential press secretary's function came in the era of President Andrew Jackson. In the late 1820s and early 1830s, the common man won the ballot and the free public school was started. Literacy increased greatly, and a burgeoning, strident party press stimulated political interest. As the people gained political power, it became necessary to campaign for their support. No longer was government the exclusive concern of the patrician few. With the rise of democracy in America came increasing rights for, and power of, the individual.[14] The ensuing power struggle produced an unsung pioneer in public relations—Amos Kendall.

As a key member of President Jackson's "Kitchen Cabinet," Kendall served as pollster, counselor, ghostwriter, and publicist. The Kitchen Cabinet was unexcelled at creating events to mold opinion. On all vital issues that arose, Jackson consulted these key advisers, most of whom, like Kendall, were former newspapermen.

Jackson, unlettered in political or social philosophy, had difficulty getting his ideas across. Like many of today's executives, he needed a specialist to convey his ideas to Congress and the country. Jackson's political campaigns and his government policies clearly reveal the influence of Kendall's strategy, sense of public opinion, and skill as a communicator.[15]

Likewise, Bank of the United States president Nicholas Biddle and his associates were fully alert to the methods of influencing public opinion in their political battles with Jackson and Kendall. In fact, banks were the first businesses to use the press for this purpose; by loans to editors and placement of advertisements, they influenced many newspapers and silenced others. In March 1831, the bank's board authorized Biddle's publicist, Mathew St. Clair Clarke, to saturate the nation's press with press releases, reports, and pamphlets pushing the bank's case. But the pamphlets, the many articles planted in the press, and the lobbying efforts by Biddle and his associates did not prevail over the forces of Jackson and Kendall.[16]

The evolution of public relations also is tied to attempts to *gain public acceptance and utilization of innovation.* Early efforts promoted adoption of electricity, telegraph, telephone, and automobile—"the horseless carriage." Public information and persuasion campaigns to promote change have long been mainstays in the public relations arsenal. For example, when the Bell Telephone System switched to all-number telephone dialing, it ran into a storm of public opposition on the West Coast from the Anti-Digit Dialing League, organized by Carl May against what he called the "cult of technology."[17] Similarly, the U.S. Postal Service had to implement a public education campaign to overcome resistance when it introduced zip codes.

The evolution of public relations makes sense only when viewed in the historical context of crises of power conflicts and change. It is not mere coincidence that in the past, business interests took public relations most seriously when their positions of power were challenged or threatened. Nor is it a coincidence that labor's programs intensified when waning public support led to regulatory legislation, or when trade agreements led to well-paid union jobs being lost to countries with cheap labor. Similarly, the most intense developments in public relations within government came in periods of crisis: World War I, the Great Depression and New Deal, World War II, the uneasy Cold War years with the Soviet Union, the Vietnam War, the Persian Gulf War, the attack and the removal of Iraq's Saddam Hussein that led to America's longest war, and the continuing global effort against terrorism. Threats to public health spawned development of sophisticated campaign strategy and tactics designed to gain public adoption of safe food canning and storage methods, hybrid seed and fertilizers in agriculture, smoking cessation, not drinking and driving, and vaccinations to prevent disease, to name but a few public safety and health promotion topics.

Press Agentry Origins

To say that public relations evolved from press agentry, although a gross oversimplification, contains a kernel of truth. Systematic efforts to attract or divert public attention are as old as efforts to inform and persuade. Much of what we define as public relations was labeled "press agentry" when it was being used to promote land settlement in the unsettled U.S. West or to build up political heroes.

Biddle and the Bank of United States effectively demonstrated the power of press agentry when Jackson's opponents created the myth of Davy Crockett. Biddle's press agent, Mathew St. Clair Clarke, decided to build up "a brash, loud-talking Tennessee Congressman, the colorful Colonel Davy Crockett and to build him up as a frontier hero to counter Old Hickory's [President Andrew Jackson] appeal to the frontiersmen."[18] As Scott Cutlip reported, "The transmogrification of Davy Crockett from a boorish, backwoods boob into a colorful frontier statesman was the work of several ghostwriters and press agents," when in fact Crocket "spent four years loafing and boasting at the Congressional bar."[19]

The ghostwritten Crockett campaign included books, widely distributed printed speeches (which were not the words he actually spoke when he stood up!), theatrical

FIGURE 4.1

P. T. Barnum and Tom Thumb

plays, and letters to editors. Reality has a way of catching up, however, so the Crockett strategy failed to keep Jackson from winning a second term as president or to prevent the election of Jackson's choice as his successor, Martin Van Buren, in 1836. Crockett failed in his own reelection bid and headed to Texas, where he was killed by Santa Ana's troops in the Siege of the Alamo. It was Walt Disney, however, who revived the legend of Davy Crockett, further embellished the myth, and cashed in on the creative work done by press agents more than 100 years earlier.

But the master of embellishment was P. T. Barnum, and he knew it. Barnum lived from 1810 until 1891, a period of great importance in the evolution of public relations. His influence continues.

> Today's patterns of promotion and press agentry in the world of show business were drawn, cut, and stitched by the greatest showman and press agent of all time—that "Prince of Humbug," that mightiest of mountebanks, Phineas Taylor Barnum.[20]

Barnum's circus, now know as the Ringling Bros. and Barnum and Bailey Circus, put on display such oddities as the alleged 160-year-old nurse of George Washington, fake mermaids, the midget Tom Thumb (see Figure 4.1), and so many large oddities that he introduced the word "jumbo" to our language. Promoter Barnum even employed his own press agent, Richard F. "Tody" Hamilton, whom he credited with much of the success of the circus.[21]

Railroad publicists played an important role in settling our nation and in creating the romantic aura that still surrounds the West. Beginning in the 1850s, railroads and land developers used publicity and advertising to lure people westward. Charles Russell Lowell, who directed the Burlington Railroad's publicity campaign that was launched in 1858, wrote, "We are beginning to find that he who buildeth a railroad west must also find a population and build up business." He had good advice for today's practitioner: "We must blow as loud a trumpet as the merits of our position warrants."[22]

Success begot imitators. Barnum led the way, and others followed in ever-increasing numbers. For example, Colonel William F. Cody ("Buffalo Bill") used similar techniques to promote his "Wild West Show" (see Figure 4.2). During the

FIGURE 4.2

Buffalo Bill Poster

Dorling Kindersley

two decades before 1900, press agentry spread from show business to closely related enterprises. But as press agents grew in number and their exploits became more outrageous—although successful, more often than not—it was natural that they would arouse the hostility and suspicion of editors and inevitable that the practice and its practitioners would become tainted.

Business Practices

The last two decades of the nineteenth century brought other discernible beginnings of today's practice. Frenzied and bold development of industry, railroads, and utilities in America's post–Civil War era set the stage for public relations in the twentieth century.

Between 1875 and 1900, America doubled its population and jammed its people into cities, went into mass production and enthroned the machine, spanned the nation with rail and wire communications, developed the mass media of press and magazines, and replaced the plantation owner with the head of industry and the versatile pioneer with the specialized factory hand. These 25 years laid the foundation for a mighty industrial machine.

The rise of powerful monopolies, the concentration of wealth and power, and the roughshod tactics of the robber barons brought a wave of protest and reform in the early 1900s. Contemporary public relations emerged from the melee of the opposing forces in this period of the nation's rapid growth. In this "the public be damned" era, exploitation of people and of natural resources was bound to bring protest and reform once people became aroused.

The then-prevailing hard-bitten attitude of businesspeople toward the public— be they employees, customers, or voters—was epitomized in the brutal methods used by Henry Clay Frick to crush a labor union in the Carnegie-Frick Steel Company's Homestead, Pennsylvania, plant in 1892. The Pennsylvania state militia helped break the employees' strike, and the union was destroyed. Cold-blooded power won this battle, but the employees eventually won the war.[23] Historian Merle Curti observed, "Corporations gradually began to realize the importance of combating hostility and courting public favor. The expert in public relations was an inevitable phenomenon in view of the need for the services he could provide."[24]

Beginning in 1897, the term "public relations" appeared with increasing frequency in railroad literature and in speeches of railroad tycoons. In the American Association of Railroads' 1897 *Year Book of Railway Literature,* the stated objective was "to put annually in permanent form all papers or addresses on the public relations of railways, appearing or being delivered during the year, which seem to have enduring value."[25] *The Railway Age Gazette* pleaded for "better public relations" in a 1909 editorial entitled, "Wanted: A Diplomatic Corps."

First Corporate Department

The first corporate public relations department was established in 1889 by George Westinghouse for his new electric corporation. Westinghouse had organized his company in 1886 to promote his revolutionary alternating-current system of electricity. Thomas A. Edison had earlier established Edison General Electric Company, which used direct current. The infamous "battle of the currents" ensued.

Edison, aided by the astute Samuel Insull, launched a scare campaign against the Westinghouse alternating-current system. As Forrest McDonald recorded,

Edison General Electric attempted to prevent the development of alternating current by unscrupulous political action and by even less savory promotional tactics. . . . The promotional activity was a series of spectacular stunts aimed at dramatizing the deadliness of high voltage alternating current, the most sensational being the development and promotion of the electric chair as a means of executing criminals.[26]

When the state of New York adopted electrocution in 1888, Westinghouse hired Pittsburgh journalist Ernest H. Heinrichs to get his story to the public. When Westinghouse's AC system won public acceptance despite the Edison–Insull propaganda scare campaign, it demonstrated "that performance and merit are the foundation stones of effective public relations."[27]

Professional groups also were paying attention to public opinion in the mid-1800s. In 1855, the American Medical Association (AMA) passed a resolution "urging the secretary of the Association to offer every facility possible to the reports of the public press to enable them to furnish full and accurate reports of the transactions."[28] And in 1884, the AMA launched the first of its many programs to counter antivivisectionists' attacks, a problem that persists to this day as animal rights groups protest using animals in research.

Evolution to Maturity

Although the roots of today's practice lie far in the past, its definite beginnings date from the early 1900s, when the world entered the twentieth century, which spanned from the horse and buggy to the international space station. The dividing lines blur a bit, but the growth can be traced through seven main periods (see Figure 4.3) of development:

1. *Seedbed Era* (1900–1916)   of muckraking journalism countered by defensive publicity and of far-reaching political reforms promoted by Theodore Roosevelt and Woodrow Wilson through the use of public relations skills.

FIGURE 4.3

Time Line of Defining Events and People in Public Relations

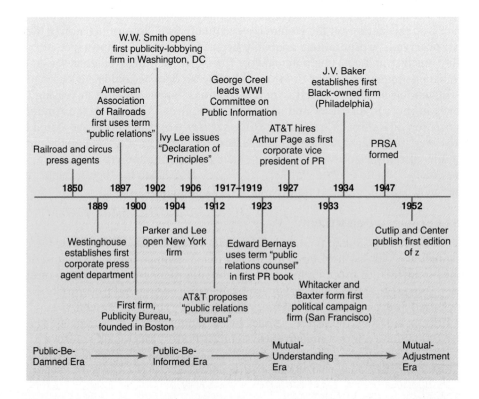

2. *World War I Period* (1917–1918)   of dramatic demonstrations of the power of organized promotion to kindle a fervent patriotism: to sell war bonds, enlist soldiers, and raise millions of dollars for welfare.

3. *Booming Twenties Era* (1919–1929),   when the principles and practices of publicity learned in the war were put to use promoting products, earning acceptance for changes wrought by the war-accelerated technology, winning political battles, and raising millions of dollars for charitable causes.

4. *Roosevelt Era and World War II* (1930–1945),   an era dominated by Franklin D. Roosevelt and his counselor, Louis McHenry Howe; the Great Depression; and World War II—events profound and far reaching in their impact on the practice of public relations.

5. *Postwar Era* (1946–1964)   of adjustment as the nation moved from a war-oriented economy to a postindustrial, service-oriented economy, shouldered leadership of the "Free World," brought widespread acceptance of public relations—strong professional associations, the beginnings of public relations education, and the emergence of television as a powerful communications medium.

6. *Period of Protest and Empowerment* (1965–1985)   of student and activist protests against environmental pollution, racial and gender discrimination, concentration of special interest wealth and power, the Vietnam War, governmental abuse of the public trust, and consequently, an increasing recognition of social responsibility and more responsive organizations.

7. *Digital Age and Globalization (1986–present),*   with accelerating technology; multiplying communication channels; and a world economy that features global competition, interdependence, instantaneous interaction, and terrorism.

These periods of development followed what Edward Bernays called the *"public-be-damned"* period of American enterprise, coming after the Civil War and lasting until about 1900. During public relations' seedbed era, Bernays suggested that the country had entered the *"public-be-informed"* period. He labeled the period following World War I as the time of *"mutual understanding,"* when the lessons of the behavioral sciences were being applied to public relations practice. Beginning in the late 1960s things changed.

Antiwar protests, the consumer movement, environmental activism, civil rights, and other demonstrations of the increasing power of citizens—including aroused minorities—challenged the status quo. Mutual understanding no longer satisfied those demanding *change*. Corrective *action* became the requirement, leading to the era of *"mutual adjustment."* This paradigm shift in society dramatically changed how public relations would be practiced in the latter part of the twentieth century and in the twenty-first century. The following sections outline the key actors and events in that evolution.

Seedbed Era: 1900–1916

Muckraking journalists—David Graham Phillips, Lincoln Steffens, Charles Edward Russell, Upton Sinclair, Ida Tarbell, and others—effectively exploited the newly developed national forums made possible by popular magazines, national wire services, and feature syndicates. Regier says, "Muckraking . . . was the inevitable

FIGURE 4.4

"A Nauseating Job" for
President Theodore
Roosevelt

Culver Pictures, Inc.

result of decades of indifference to the illegalities and immoralities attendant upon the industrial development of America."[29]

The exposé and reform period extended roughly from 1900 to 1912. The muckrakers took their case to the people and got action. The agitation before 1900 had been primarily among farmers and laborers; now the urban middle class took up the cry against government corruption and the abuses of big business. President Theodore Roosevelt joined the movement as the "trustbuster" president (see Figure 4.4).

The muckrakers thundered out their denunciations in boldface in the popular magazines and metropolitan newspapers, which now had huge circulations. By 1900, there were at least 50 well-known national magazines, several with circulations of 100,000 or more. *The Ladies Home Journal,* founded only 17 years before, was approaching a circulation of one million. The impact of the mass media was growing.[30]

The work was begun dramatically by Thomas W. Lawson's "Frenzied Finance" series of articles in *McClure's* magazine in 1903. Ida Tarbell's *History of the Standard Oil Company,* described at the time as "a fearless unmasking of moral criminality masquerading under the robes of respectability and Christianity," and Upton Sinclair's book, *The Jungle,* which exposed the foul conditions in the meatpacking industry, both produced a violent public reaction. Public protest and reform brought regulatory legislation and a wave of trust busting. Businesses were forced to go on the defense.

Long accustomed to a veil of secrecy, business leaders felt the urge to speak out in self-defense but did not know how. Their first instinct was to turn to their advertising planners and lawyers. In the first stages of the muckraking era, many great corporations sought to silence the attacks from the press by the calculated placement and withdrawal of advertising. The strategy produced limited success.

Early Firms

The Publicity Bureau.   The nation's first publicity agency and forerunner of today's public relations firm was founded in Boston in mid-1900. George V. S. Michaelis, Herbert Small, and Thomas O. Marvin organized the Publicity Bureau "to do a general press agent business for as many clients as possible for as good pay as the traffic would bear." Michaelis, a Boston journalist once described by an associate as "a young man of many expedients," took the lead in organizing this new enterprise and was with it until 1909. One of the first people hired was James Drummond Ellsworth, who would later work with Theodore N. Vail in building the public relations program of American Telephone and Telegraph Company.[31]

Harvard University was the Publicity Bureau's first client. Michaelis, the firm's president, wrote to the president of Harvard boasting about the success of an early publicity effort: "We have met with very satisfactory success in publication of the articles, and I shall be glad to show you the clippings upon your return." And in a subsequent letter, he outlined what was surely the first fixed-fee plus expenses arrangement:

> In the matter of payment, we understand that you are to pay the Bureau $200 a month for our professional services, and those of an artist where drawings seem to be required. That this sum is to include everything except the payment of mechanical work, such as printings and the making of cuts, and the postage necessary to send out the articles themselves to the various papers, which items are to be charged to the University.[32]

The reorganized Publicity Bureau came into national prominence in 1906, when it was employed by the nation's railroads to head off adverse regulatory legislation then being pushed in Congress by President Roosevelt. Journalist Ray Stannard Baker reported,

> The fountainhead of public information is the newspaper. The first concern, then, of the railroad organization was to reach the newspaper. For this purpose a firm of publicity agents, with headquarters in Boston, was chosen. . . . Immediately the firm expanded. It increased its Boston staff; it opened offices in New York, Chicago, Washington, St. Louis, Topeka, Kansas, . . . and it employed agents in South Dakota, California, and elsewhere.[33]

According to Baker, the Publicity Bureau operated secretly, "careful not to advertise the fact that they are in any way connected with the railroads." This firm effectively used the tools of fact-finding, publicity, and personal contact to saturate the nation's press, particularly weeklies, with the railroads' propaganda. The campaign was to little avail, however, because the Hepburn Act, a moderately tough regulatory measure, passed in 1906 after President Roosevelt used the nation's press and the platform to publicize a more persuasive case. Failure of their nationwide publicity effort caused railroad executives to reassess their public relations methods. Within a few years, many set up their own public relations departments. The Publicity Bureau faded into oblivion in 1911.[34]

Smith & Walmer. The second firm also was the first to be based in Washington, D.C. William Wolff Smith quit his job as correspondent for the *New York Sun* and the *Cincinnati Enquirer* in 1902 to open a "publicity business" with a partner named Walmer in the capital. (Walmer's role and tenure with the firm are not known.) A *New York Times* reporter later recalled that the Smith & Walmer firm solicited "press-agent employment from anybody who had business before Congress."[35]

Smith closed the firm in 1916 and returned to law school, which he had quit in 1893 to take his first newspaper job. His "law practice," primarily devoted to lobbying the new regulatory agencies that resulted from the muckraking exposés, was the forerunner of the many law firms and public relations firms in Washington, D.C., and state capitals engaged in lobbying.

Parker & Lee. Also during the seedbed era, former Buffalo reporter and veteran political publicist George F. Parker and young publicist Ivy Ledbetter Lee established the third firm in New York, Parker & Lee. They formed their partnership in 1904 after working together in the Democratic Party headquarters handling publicity for Judge Alton Parker's unsuccessful presidential race against Theodore Roosevelt. The firm lasted less than four years, but the junior partner—Lee—was to become one of the most influential pioneers in the emerging craft of public relations (see pages 97–98).

Hamilton Wright Organization, Inc.   The fourth firm—The Hamilton Wright Organization—was founded in 1908 when Hamilton Mercer Wright, a freelance journalist and publicist, opened a "publicity office" in San Francisco. Wright's first publicity work was for the California Promotion Committee, but he was also known for his promotion of Miami using publicity photographs. His agency's first account, however, was to promote the Philippine Islands on behalf of U.S. business interests, making his the first international firm.

He moved to New York City in 1917, after World War I cut short his work promoting tourism in Central America for the United Fruit Company. His son and grandson, both carrying the same name, followed in the founder's footsteps by specializing in promotion of foreign countries in the United States. The Wrights closed the firm in 1969.

Pendleton Dudley and Associates.   The fifth agency, started during the first decade of this century, lasted until 1988. Pendleton Dudley, who was to become an influential figure in public relations for half a century, took his friend Ivy Lee's advice and opened a publicity office in New York's Wall Street district in 1909. His first business client, AT&T, retained Dudley until his death at the age of 90 in 1966. He was among the few then in practice who saw the value of research and the need to measure program effectiveness. For all those 57 years, Dudley remained the active head of his firm, which in 1946 had become Dudley-Anderson-Yutzy Public Relations when Thomas D. Yutzy and George Anderson joined the firm. In 1970, sisters Barbara Hunter and Jean Schoonover acquired the firm and changed the name to D-A-Y. The firm became a subsidiary of Ogilvy & Mather in 1983, which dropped the separate D-A-Y identity and operation in 1988.[36]

Thomas R. Shipp and Co.   In 1914, Thomas R. Shipp organized the nation's sixth firm and the second located in Washington, D.C. Shipp, like William Wolff Smith, was a native of Indiana and a former reporter. He spent six years learning publicity and politics from two experts, Theodore Roosevelt and Gifford Pinchot. In 1909 they gave Shipp administrative and publicity responsibilities for the newly formed National Conservation Association (NCA)—"the center of a great propaganda for conservation" (see Figure 4.5). Historians credit the NCA with making "conservation" and "natural resources" powerful terms in the public vocabulary. Shipp opened his own "publicity company" when Smith closed his to return to law school. When the United States entered World War I, Shipp headed the first American Red Cross fund drive, raising an unprecedented $100 million (see Figure 4.7). After the war, such corporations as General Motors, Standard Oil Company of New York, Swift & Company, and International Harvester retained Shipp as Washington public relations counsel.[37]

Early Pioneers

The period of 1900–1916 saw an intensive development of public relations skills by the railroads and the public utilities. These businesses, particularly the local transit companies, were the first to feel the heat of public anger and to be brought under public regulation. The Interstate Commerce Act set the pattern. In a 5-year period, 1908–1913, more than 2,000 laws affecting railroads were enacted by state legislatures and by Congress.

For the most part, big businesses hired former reporters to counter the muckrakers with whitewashing press agentry, demonstrating little grasp of the fundamen-

FIGURE 4.5
Theodore Roosevelt and
naturalist John Muir at
Yosemite 1903
Corbis/Bettman

tal problems in the conflict. But there were exceptions. One was Georgia native Ivy Lee, credited by many as the "father of public relations."

Ivy Ledbetter Lee.   Lee, a Princeton graduate and New York newspaper reporter covering business, saw the possibility of earning more money in the service of private organizations that were seeking a voice. After five years as a reporter, in 1903 Lee quit his low-paying job on the *World* to work in Seth Low's campaign for mayor of New York. This led to a job working with George F. Parker in the press bureau of the Democratic National Committee (DNC) during the 1904 presidential campaign.

Ivy Ledbetter Lee

Parker also had started working for the DNC in 1904 after not being appointed as the nation's first press secretary by President Grover Cleveland, for whom he had worked during three presidential campaigns. When Democrat presidential candidate Judge Alton B. Parker failed to unseat President Theodore Roosevelt in 1904, Lee and Parker started their agency.[38] The agency dissolved in 1908 when Lee went to work full time for one of the firm's clients, the Pennsylvania Railroad. He became director of the railroad's publicity bureau, which he had organized while the company was a client of Parker and Lee.[39]

When the anthracite coal mine operators hired Parker & Lee to tell management's side in the 1906 strike, Lee issued a "Declaration of Principles." Lee's statement of philosophy profoundly influenced the evolution of press agentry and publicity into public relations. Going against the prevailing feeling on Wall Street that "the public be damned," Lee's declaration made it clear that the public was no longer to be ignored, in the traditional manner of business, nor fooled, in the continuing manner of the press agent. It was to be informed. Lee mailed his newsworthy declaration to all city editors:

> This is not a secret press bureau. All our work is done in the open. We aim to supply news. This is not an advertising agency; if you think any of our matter ought properly to go to your business office, do not use it. Our matter is accurate. Further details on any subject treated will be supplied promptly, and any editor will be assisted most cheerfully in verifying directly any statement of fact. . . . In brief, our plan is, frankly and openly, on behalf of business concerns and public institutions, to supply to the press and public of the United States prompt and accurate information concerning subjects which it is of value and interest to the public to know about.[40]

Lee's new approach greatly simplified the work of reporters assigned to cover the strike. Although reporters were not permitted to attend strike conferences, Lee provided reports after each meeting in the form of a "handout" (now called "press release" or "news release"). His success in generating favorable press coverage for the coal operators prompted the Pennsylvania Railroad to retain Parker and Lee in the summer of 1906. Lee handled the account.[41]

John D. Rockefeller

During this period, Lee used the term "publicity" to describe what is now public relations; the concept and Lee's success grew steadily. In December 1914, Lee was appointed as a personal adviser to John D. Rockefeller Jr. The Rockefellers were being savagely attacked for the strikebreaking activities of their Colorado Fuel and Iron Company. Newspapers and other critics referred to the tragic event as "Bloody Ludlow" and "the Ludlow Massacre." Cartoonists and editorial writers called Rockefeller "the biggest criminal of the time." Lee served the Rockefellers until John D. died in 1934, eulogized by the press as the "great benefactor of society." Obviously, Lee had done his job.

Ivy Lee did much to lay the groundwork for contemporary practice. Even though he did not use the term "public relations" until at least 1919, Lee contributed many of the techniques and principles that practitioners follow today. *He was among the first to realize the fallacy of publicity unsupported by good works and to reason that performance determines the publicity a client gets.*

In his 31 years in public relations, Lee changed the scope of what he did from publicity to counseling clients. For example, he said, "If you issue an untruth in a public statement, it is going to be challenged just as soon as it sees the light."[42] His counsel extended beyond publicity, telling his audience at the 1916 Annual Convention of the American Electric Railway Association that "the actual relationship of a company to the people . . . involves far more than *saying*—it involves *doing*."[43]

Lee's record, although substantial, is not free from criticism. When he died, he was under fire for his representation of the German Dye Trust, controlled by I. G. Farben. Lee advised the cartel after Adolf Hitler came to power in Germany and the Nazis had taken control. Headlines at the time sensationalized his work—LEE GIVES ADVICE TO THE NAZIS and LEE EXPOSED AS HITLER PRESS AGENT. Although he never received pay directly from the Nazi government, Lee was paid an annual fee of $25,000 and expenses (a large sum at the time) by the Farben firm from the time he was retained in 1933 until his firm resigned the account shortly after his death in 1934.[44]

One of the craft's most forceful representatives, his practice and preachments made public relations an occupation. Ironically, however, as Lee biographer Ray Hiebert concluded, he was not able to do for himself what he had done so effectively for others:

> He was rarely able to explain his work adequately or to gain understanding for the underlying principles by which he operated. He often admitted that he did not know what to call himself, and that what he did was an art that he could not explain.
>
> When reporters reached him in Baden [Germany] after the news of his I. G. Farben work had been made public, he pulled within his shell and refused to make a statement.[45]

Theodore Vail

Theodore N. Vail. The former American Telephone and Telegraph Company pioneered in public relations as well as in telephonic communications. Although public relations got short shrift when Theodore N. Vail was forced out in 1887 until he returned to power in 1902, the company did organize a "literary bureau" in Boston around 1890 and was one of the first clients of the Publicity Bureau. After Vail returned as a director, the policies that became identified with AT&T began to take shape, and they were brought to the fore when Vail became president in 1907. Vail hired James Drummond Ellsworth to begin a publicity and advertising program.

The company tried to eliminate public criticism through efficient operation and consideration for the needs of subscribers. A systematic method of answering complaints was put into effect. Unlike other utilities, Bell did not fight public regulation but accepted it as a price of monopoly. Vail and Ellsworth, in collaboration with the N. W. Ayer advertising agency, began an institutional advertising campaign that continued for decades[46] (see Exhibit 4.1).

Theodore Roosevelt. Theodore Roosevelt has received little credit for the part he played in spurring the evolution of public relations. The colorful president was a master in the art and power of publicity, and he used his knowledge and skill to achieve his political goals. Observers claimed that Roosevelt ruled the country from the newspapers' front pages.

One of his first acts upon assuming the presidency was to seek an understanding with the press. Veteran reporter David S. Barry later observed that Roosevelt "knew the value and potent influence of a news paragraph written as he wanted it written and disseminated through the proper influential channels." Roosevelt's successful and well-publicized antitrust suit against the Northern Securities Company turned the tide against the concentration of economic power. His conservation policies, effectively promoted by Gifford Pinchot in the government's first large-scale publicity program, saved much of America's resources from gross exploitation.

As one historian observed, "Roosevelt's colorful, outgoing personality and shrewd sense of publicity had his name constantly in the papers, and in ways to make him a national hero."[47] He saw the White House as a "bully pulpit."

EXHIBIT 4.1

Proposal for a Public Relations Bureau at AT&T in 1912

The establishment of a Public Relations Bureau in the American Telephone and Telegraph Company, in which all information concerning the relations of the telephone companies to the public should be concentrated and made available for use, would serve to coordinate much of the work now done independently by various departments of that company and the operating companies.

The bureau could bring together a large sum of material at present scattered, and a proper arrangement and collation of this would make it readily available and eliminate a considerable amount of duplication.

It would also be able to give its attention to the trend of public opinion and the drift of legislation, and by a study of these, bring to the attention of executive officers in a condensed form the broader lines of public sentiment in time to enable the telephone company to meet new phases of legislation and in many cases to forestall legislation by remedying conditions which have been the cause of trouble.

By employing a central organization to collect, analyze, and distribute material relating to these questions there will be a distinct saving in times of those actually engaged in work in the field and a broader and more efficient treatment of the problems.

All the available material can be brought together and everyone dealing with these questions be kept in touch with the trend of public opinion and action throughout the country . . .

With the growth of mass-circulation newspapers, Roosevelt's ability to dominate the front pages demonstrated a newly found power for those with causes to promote. He had a keen sense of news and knew how to stage a story so that it would get maximum attention. His skill forced those he fought to develop similar means. Roosevelt fully exploited the news media as a new and powerful tool of presidential leadership, and remade the laws and the presidency in the process.

Rex Harlow

Rex F. Harlow.   Others recognized the need for publicity services in other parts of the country. Rex F. Harlow began a lifetime career in 1912 in Oklahoma City when he was hired by an older brother to promote *Harlow's Weekly.* Harlow's career spanned the evolution of this young, uncertain calling to its maturity in the 1980s and helped shape today's practice. While teaching at Stanford University in 1939, he began teaching public relations courses and founded the American Council on Public Relations (ACPR). In 1945 he started the monthly *Public Relations Journal,* published until 1995 by the Public Relations Society of America and reactivated in 2007 as an online journal (www.prsa.org/prjournal/). Harlow died April 16, 1993, at 100 years of age.

Growth in Other Areas

Equally important public relations developments were taking place outside the business community. After Harvard retained the Publicity Bureau in 1900, the seedbed years brought innovative publicity programs to colleges and universities. The University of Pennsylvania's public relations program dates from 1904, when it set up the University Bureau of Publicity. That same year, pioneer journalism educator Willard G. Bleyer organized a press bureau at the University of Wisconsin at the direction of public relations–minded President Charles R. Van Hise. But it was William Rainey Harper, the dynamic builder of the University of Chicago, who did more than any other educator to harness the power of publicity to the cause of higher education. His methods and his resulting success were observed and copied by many others.[48]

The whirlwind high-pressure campaign to raise money for charitable causes was first fabricated in 1905 in Washington, D.C., by YMCA fund-raisers Charles Sumner Ward and Lyman L. Pierce. They were the first to use full-time publicists in a fund drive. The Y's successful techniques were soon used in the annual appeals of churches, colleges, civic centers, and health and welfare agencies.[49] The Ward–Pierce campaign format has endured the test of time and can be easily recognized in today's annual United Way drives.

World War I Period: 1917–1918

The contemporary practice of public relations first emerged as a defensive measure, but World War I gave it great offensive impetus. President Woodrow Wilson, who was keenly aware of the importance of public opinion, established The Committee on Public Information (CPI)—often referred to as the "Creel Committee." The CPI was charged with mobilizing public opinion in support of the war effort and Wilson's peace aims in a country in which opinion was divided when war was declared. Wilson appointed George Creel chairman.

George Creel

George Creel.   George Creel and his CPI demonstrated as never before the power of publicity to mobilize opinion. Without a campaign manual to guide him, Creel improvised as he went along. For example, he had no national radio or television to reach the nation quickly, so he created the Four Minutemen, a network of 75,000 civic leaders covering the nation's some 3,000 counties. These volunteers, alerted by telegrams from Washington, would fan out to speak to schools, churches, service clubs, and other gatherings. By the war's end nearly 800,000 of these four-minute messages had been delivered.

Creel assembled as brilliant and talented a group of journalists, scholars, press agents, editors, artists, and other manipulators of the symbols of public opinion as America had ever seen united for a single purpose. The breathtaking scope of the huge agency and its activities were not to be equaled until the rise of the totalitarian dictatorships after the war. Creel, Carl Byoir, and their associates were public relations counselors to the U.S. government, carrying first to the citizens and then to those in distant lands the idea that gave motive power to the wartime undertaking of 1917–1918 (see Figure 4.6).[50]

Analyzing the influence of the Creel Committee, the *New York Times* commented in 1920:

FIGURE 4.6
"Under Four Flags" Poster

> Not only did he have a staff of press agents working immediately under him in a central office, but Creel decentralized the system so that every type of industry in the country had its special group of publicity workers. In this manner, more than in any other, were the heads and directors of movements of every type introduced to and made cognizant of the value of concentrating on publicity in so-called "drives."[51]

To illustrate the *Times*'s point, when America entered the war, the American Red Cross had a membership of fewer than 500,000 in 372 chapters scattered across the nation and $200,000 in working funds. In September 1918, as the war neared its end, the Red Cross had 20 million members in 3,864 chapters and had raised more than $400 million in gifts and membership dues (see Figure 4.7). Another example: On May 1, 1917, there were only some 350,000 holders of U.S. bonds; six months later, after two organized publicity and sales drives for "Liberty Bonds," there were 10 million bondholders.

After the war, many held an overly optimistic belief in the power of mass communication. A noted political scientist, Harold D. Lasswell, observed, "When all allowances have been made, and all extravagant estimates pared to the bone, the fact remains that propaganda is one of the most powerful instrumentalities in the modern world."[52]

FIGURE 4.7
"You Can Help— American Red Cross"

Carl Byoir. The Creel Committee trained a host of practitioners who took their wartime experiences and fashioned a profitable calling. Among these was Carl Byoir, who at age 28 had been associate chairman of the CPI. After a decade's tour into other endeavors, Byoir founded a publicity firm in 1930 to promote tourism in Cuba. The firm would become one of the country's largest public relations firms, Carl Byoir & Associates (CB&A). Some of the nation's largest corporations retained CB&A, including B. F. Goodrich, Honeywell, Kimberly Clark, John Deere, The Atlantic & Pacific Tea Company (A&P), Woolworth, and Swift. Long-term clients included Hughes Aircraft, a client for 40 years; Hallmark, 37 years; RCA, 34 years; and Borg Warner, 20 years.

Carl Byoir

Noted for its high standards of client service, Byoir and his associates are credited with introducing grassroots advocacy groups and the third-party endorsement, popularizing the Jeep, helping make the tubeless tire acceptable to consumers, and using the full-page editorial advertisement.[53] Byoir also devoted his own time and

CB&A resources to social causes, such as raising money for the March of Dimes to fund research that ultimately eliminated the feared infantile paralysis—polio. Byoir died in 1957 at 68.[54]

Booming Twenties Era: 1919–1929

Vigorously nourished by wartime developments, the public relations specialty quickly spread. It showed up in government, business, education, churches, social work—now burgeoning in the war's aftermath, the labor movement, and social movements. The victory of the Anti-Saloon League in achieving national prohibition and the triumph of the women's suffrage movement, both in 1920, provided fresh evidence of the newly found power of public relations.

This period also saw increased use of public relations advertising as a tool. Illinois Central Railroad started a campaign in 1920 that sought "promotion of a better understanding and closer relationship with the patrons of our lines." In 1922, Metropolitan Life Insurance Company started a good-health campaign. In 1923, General Motors (GM) began to use advertising to sell itself as an institution.

Doris Fleischman

Edward Bernays

Edward L. Bernays and Doris E. Fleischman.   Among those vying with Ivy Lee for prominence and for business in the 1920s was Edward L. Bernays. Prior to World War I, Bernays had worked as a press agent. While he worked for the Creel Committee during the war, his busy mind envisioned the possibility of making a life's work of what he called "engineering public consent." Many have credited Bernays with introducing the term *public relations counsel* in *Crystallizing Public Opinion* (1923), the first book on public relations. In fact, Bernays said that he and his wife and business partner, Doris E. Fleischman, came up with the term after opening his first office in 1919.[55]

Bernays married Fleischman in 1922. Together they ran their firm—Edward L. Bernays, Counsel on Public Relations—until formally retiring from active practice in 1962. She died in 1980. They counseled major corporations, government agencies, and U.S. presidents from Calvin Coolidge through Dwight Eisenhower, with Bernays taking the spotlight for most assignments. Although credited with being an equal partner with Bernays in the firm, with creating the first public relations newsletter, and with collaborating with Bernays to develop the term *public relations counsel*, Fleischman struggled for professional equality because of her gender.[56] For example, in one of her two books she wrote,

> Many men resented having women tell them what to do in their business. They resented having men tell them, too, but advice from a woman was somewhat demeaning. I learned to withdraw from situations where the gender of public relations counsel was a factor or where suggestions had to be disassociated from gender. If ideas were considered first in terms of my sex, they might never get around to being judged on their own merits.[57]

Fleischman was an early feminist, who, after marrying Bernays, retained her birth name long before it was socially acceptable:

> During the next three decades, Fleischman continued to sign into hotels—and twice into maternity hospitals—as "Miss Doris E. Fleischman," and in 1925 she received the first U.S. passport granted to a married woman under her birth name. That was her name on the 1928 book she edited on careers for women and on the seven magazine articles and book chapters she published between 1930 and 1946.[58]

Bernays's first book on public relations followed Walter Lippmann's 1922 *Public Opinion,* a book that reflected the growing interest in power and nature of public opinion. In all the years prior to 1917, only 18 books on public opinion and publicity were printed. At least 28 titles appeared between 1917 and 1925.

Scholarly interest also dates from this period. Social scientists began to explore the nature of public opinion and the role of mass communication in its formation. Although sophisticated opinion-measurement methods did not appear until the 1930s, the postwar work of social scientists contributed much to the development of market research, public opinion polls, and communication science. Bernays broke more new ground in 1923 when he taught the first public relations course at New York University.

Bernays continued in his roles as author, lecturer, advocate, and critic into the 1990s. Many refer to Bernays as the other father of public relations. *Life* magazine included Bernays in its 1990 special issue, "The 100 Most Important Americans of the 20th Century." He died March 9, 1995, at age 103.

John W. Hill.   Despite a booming economy and rapidly growing media, there were only six public relations firms listed in the Manhattan telephone directory in 1926. In 1927, John W. Hill, a Cleveland journalist, started a firm in that city. In 1933, he formed a partnership with Don Knowlton and shortly thereafter moved to New York to found Hill & Knowlton, Inc. (H&K). Knowlton remained to run the Cleveland office. The two firms, connected only by overlapping ownership, operated independently until 1964, when Knowlton retired and the Cleveland office was sold to a successor firm. Hill died in 1977. In 1980, JWT Group, the holding company that owned the J. Walter Thompson Company advertising agency, acquired H&K for $28 million. The British conglomerate WPP Group acquired the JWT Group of companies in 1989 (see www.hillandknowlton.com).

John Hill

Long viewed as an ethical and respected leader of public relations counseling, Hill's role in helping the major tobacco companies form the Tobacco Industry Research Committee (TIRC) threatens his legacy. On his recommendation, the presidents of the major tobacco companies agreed to fund the TIRC, which allegedly funded research projects that challenged others' findings that smoking posed health threats. Hill fought the tobacco wars on behalf of the cigarette industry until he retired from H&K in 1962.[59] Throughout his professional life, however, Hill saw himself as a man of integrity and principle, committing his views to paper:

> Should an existing client company adopt policies which the counsel believes are not in the public interest, he would advise against such policies—and, if he has integrity, be prepared to resign the account in case the client persisted.[60]

When asked directly about his role in the formation of the TIRC and in tobacco public relations, in 1966 Hill responded, "I decline to comment on this matter on the basis that this is an active, highly sensitive account," and he did not cover H&K's tobacco account in his 1963 memoir, *The Making of a Public Relations Man.*[61] Long after Hill's death in 1977, however, there is little doubt about his role in creating a public relations front for the tobacco industry:

> Though John Hill had long since passed from such earthly battles, the fact remains that he was the guiding force in the formation of the Tobacco Industry Research Committee and later the Tobacco Institute. Thus, Hill must bear responsibility for that "brilliantly conceived and executed plan" that served the selfish interests of the tobacco industry at the expense of millions of Americans' good health.[62]

Two years before Hill set up shop in Cleveland, **Edward D. Howard II** had also organized a public relations agency there that celebrated its 80th anniversary in 2005. Edward Howard & Company is Ohio's oldest public relations firm and the nation's longest surviving independently owned firm. It also has offices in Columbus and Dayton and is a member of the Pinnacle Worldwide network of independent public relations firms.

Arthur Page

Arthur W. Page.   Among the pioneers shaping today's practice, Arthur W. Page stands at the summit. Page built three successful business careers, yet found time to contribute his talent to many public service endeavors. He was a writer and editor of *World's Work* magazine and other periodicals of Doubleday, Page and Company from 1905 until 1927. Then he accepted Walter Gifford's offer to succeed James D. Ellsworth as vice president of American Telephone and Telegraph Co.

At the outset Page made it clear that he would accept only on the conditions that he was not to serve as a publicity man, that he would have a voice in policy, and that the company's performance would be the determinant of its public reputation. Page's philosophy is summed up in this statement:

> All business in a democratic country begins with public permission and exists by public approval. If that be true, it follows that business should be cheerfully willing to tell the public what its policies are, what it is doing, and what it hopes to do. This seems practically a duty.[63]

Although he continued nominally as vice president of AT&T during World War II, he devoted most of his time to the war effort. As Page biographer Noel Griese reported, surely Page's most widely distributed news release, written for President Harry S. Truman, was issued in Washington, D.C., at 11:00 a.m., Monday, August 6, 1945:

> Sixteen hours ago an American airplane dropped one bomb on Hiroshima, an important Japanese Army base. That bomb had more power than 20,000 tons of TNT. It had more than two thousand times the blast power of the British "Grand Slam" which is the largest bomb ever yet used in the history of warfare.
>
> The Japanese began the war from the air at Pearl Harbor. They have been repaid manyfold. . . . It is an atomic bomb. It is a harnessing of the basic power of the universe. The force from which the sun draws its powers has been loosed against those who brought war to the Far East.[64]

After the war, Page stayed on at AT&T to mentor his replacement. Page retired January 1, 1947, after integrating public relations concepts and practices into the Bell System. From then until his death in 1960 at age 77, he served as a consultant to many large corporations and gave much of his time to the service of government, higher education, and other causes. However, it was Page's work for AT&T that left his lasting imprint on public relations. His precepts and principles not only endure in the companies that used to be part of AT&T (broken up in 1984 by court order to foster competition), but also are renewed and promoted by the Arthur W. Page Society. (Page's principles are listed in Chapter 5.)

Paul Garrett

Paul Garrett.   Although General Motors had started using institutional advertising in 1923, it did not set up its own public relations department until 1931. GM president and management innovator Alfred P. Sloan Jr. brought in Paul Garrett, another influential pioneer, to head the department. Garrett was the second corporate public relations practitioner to hold the office of vice president. He and AT&T's Page were among the first to use the new science of public opinion polling as the basis for planning and evaluating public relations programs. At GM Garrett built an innovative corporate program, which was widely copied by other corporations. He retired from GM in 1957 and was retained to counsel the then-new Xerox Corporation.[65]

Alice L. Beeman.   It was also during this period that a sense of identification and professionalism began to emerge in this new craft. For example, the Association of American College News Bureaus had been organized in April 1917, but had lapsed into inactivity during World War I. It came alive again in the 1920s.

Alice Beeman

At the 1925 convention, the organization took on new strength, reflecting the growth of the practice in higher education. Symbolic of its growth in ensuing years, the organization's name was changed in 1930 to the American College Publicity Association, in 1964 to the American College Public Relations Association, and in 1974—after a merger with the American Alumni Council—to the Council for the Advancement and Support of Education (CASE). This merger reflected a shift in emphasis in college public relations from publicity to development and fund-raising.

CASE reinvented itself under the leadership of its first president, Alice L. Beeman. In her new position as president of CASE, Beeman was the first woman to head a national public relations association.

Roosevelt Era and World War II: 1930–1945

Propelled by wartime lessons and a changing America, the practice of public relations moved full speed ahead until the stock market crash in 1929. Events flowing from the Depression and the New Deal brought home to every group the need to build informed public support. New Dealers soon found that this was essential to pave the way for their radical reforms, and government public relations had its greatest expansion under President Franklin Roosevelt. The Depression brought a tremendous expansion in social welfare needs and agencies, whose administrators also came to realize the need for better public understanding. Military leaders, looking apprehensively at the buildup of the Nazi and Fascist war machines, began to promote support for more adequate armed forces. Colleges and universities, caught in the web of financial woes, turned more and more to public relations to raise funds.

Business leaders increasingly used public relations specialists to counter Roosevelt's biting criticisms and his legislative reforms. There was a marked trend away from occasional and defensive efforts and toward more positive and continuous programs administered by newly established departments. A growing labor movement, too, found that it had problems and needed guidance. School administrators, recognizing the need for bigger and better schools, also were made to realize the dangers of an uninformed public. This period also brought the tool that promised more precise, more scientific measurement and assessment of public opinion. The Roper and Gallup polls, begun in the mid-1930s, won wide respect in the presidential election of 1936. Perceptive practitioners began using this new tool to advise management and to formulate programs. The public opinion poll, with the application of new sampling methods, has steadily improved in reliability and in utility.

Louis McHenry Howe.   FDR combined strong leadership with consummate skill to harness the forces of protest into an effective political coalition. He won his battles on front pages and over the radio, a new medium he used with matchless skill. Roosevelt's adroit moves in the public arena can be credited in large part to his public relations mentor, Louis McHenry Howe. The astute, tough-minded Howe served FDR faithfully and effectively from 1912 until Howe's death in 1936.[66]

Joseph Varney Baker.   In 1934, the first minority-owned firm opened in Philadelphia. Joseph Varney Baker left his position as city editor of the *Philadelphia Tribune* to provide counsel to the Pennsylvania Railroad Company. Baker was the first African American to serve as president of a PRSA chapter and the first to be accredited by PRSA. His firm's list of clients included Chrysler, Gillette, Procter & Gamble, NBC, RCA, and Scott Paper Company. One authority on minorities in public relations concluded that during the 40 years that Baker's firm existed, it "was hired to communicate only with the black consumer market, and the practice has continued to this day."[67]

Leone Baxter

Leone Baxter and Clem Whitaker.   This era also produced the forerunner of a major segment of today's practice: the political-campaign specialist. In 1933, husband and wife Clem Whitaker and Leone Baxter formed the first agency specializing in political campaigns, headquartered in San Francisco. California, with its heavy reliance on the initiative and referendum and its weak political party organizations, provided fertile ground for the growth of political firms. From 1935 through 1958, the firm managed 80 major campaigns and won all but six. This agency brought a new approach to politics, including the "media blitz" in the final days of the campaign. Today it has countless imitators.

Whitaker and Baxter met in 1933 at a Sacramento, California, gathering of supporters who had proposed that the Central Valley Project sell electrical power to public agencies. Not surprisingly, private utilities—led by Pacific Gas & Electric—got a proposition put on the ballot to defeat the proposal. Even with a small budget, the Whitaker–Baxter campaign defeated the referendum funded by powerful corporate interests. *Time* magazine called them "the acknowledged originals in the field of political public relations."[68]

World War II produced more violent changes in the environment, accelerating the development of public relations. Once more the government led the way, demonstrating the power of an organized informational campaign. This time the instrument was the Office of War Information (OWI).

In the opinion of two public relations scholars, the OWI's greatest contributions derived from its work as the predecessor of the U.S. Information Agency (USIA). OWI was the agency that pointed out the danger in not countering distorted ideas about the United States throughout the world.[69]

Military public relations makes up a major segment of modern practice. Prior to the outbreak of World War II, however, it had been given scant support by military leaders. In 1935, General Douglas MacArthur, then Army chief of staff, appointed a young major, Alexander Surles, to head a public relations branch with the "dual job of getting before the public the War Department's anxiety over things to come in Europe and to help newsmen pry stories out of the War Department."[70]

With the advent of war, the "bureau of public relations" staff quickly grew from 3 to 3,000 officers and civilians. Concurrently, the Navy Department moved to expand and strengthen its public relations. The Army Air Corps, under the imaginative leadership of General H. H. "Hap" Arnold, a former information officer, quickly recruited a host of skilled public relations and advertising specialists. Their task was to sell air power in an age of trench-minded generals. The work was largely a matter of publicity, censorship, and assistance to war correspondents. In the process they trained countless practitioners for this work after the war and built a solid foundation for practice in the postwar boom.

World War II brought paid advertising to the fore as a major tool of public relations, now in its many forms: public relations advertising, public service advertising, issue or advocacy advertising, and institutional advertising. Beginning in 1942, the War Advertising Council worked with industry and the government to make advertising a major tool in getting citizens to produce for the war, to recycle, to ration scarce resources, to buy war bonds, and to serve in the armed forces.

Postwar Boom: 1946–1964

World War II brought new opportunities; new demonstrations of the utility of public relations in motivating war production, military morale, and civilian support; and new techniques and channels of communication. The war also schooled about 75,000 persons in the practice. The uneasy years of conversion from a wartime to a peacetime economy and from an industrial to a postindustrial, service-oriented society accentuated and extended these developments. For example, in the late 1940s, industry was wracked by a series of bitter, prolonged strikes as organized labor fought to redress grievances built up in the no-strike war period and to keep wartime gains in pay. These struggles and increased public criticism of big business placed heavy demands on public relations in business and industry.[71]

Similarly, the postwar baby boom and the enrollment bulge of soldiers returning from World War II brought new and heavy demands on the nation's schools and colleges. Administrators recognized the need for public relations counsel. School districts had to promote one bond issue after another to build additional schools, and the nation's institutions of higher education had to scramble for funds for more teachers and buildings to meet the exploding demand for higher education and research.

Tim Traverse-Healy.   In Europe, a leader emerged whom some called the "Edward Bernays of Europe"—a World War II British officer who formed a public relations firm, Traverse-Healy Limited, in 1947. As a Royal Marine Commando attached to Special Forces, Tim Traverse-Healy had parachuted into rural France during the German occupation to work with the French resistance. He and the locals reactivated an abandoned bakery to bake bread, in which they could encase messages to be distributed to resistance forces. After the war, young Traverse-Healy and his bride converted the bakery into a vacation residence.

Tim Traverse-Healy

During his illustrious career, he counseled major international corporations, lectured around the world, and cofounded both the British Institute of Public Relations and the International Public Relations Association. He was awarded two of England's highest honors—Fellowship of the Royal Society of Arts and Officer of the Order of the British Empire (OBE). The latter is second only to knighthood and was awarded by the Queen of England for "services to the profession of public relations." He was the first public relations practitioner from outside the United States to address the Public Relations Society of America conference (1957 in Philadelphia), and is the only "foreigner" [his word] inducted into the Arthur W. Page Society "Hall of Fame" (1990).[72] His long career as a practitioner included serving clients such as Airbus Industrie, General Motors, Lockheed, Hilton Hotels, National Westminster Bank (1952–1993), AT&T, and Johnson & Johnson. He sold his firm in

1993 and turned his attention to lecturing and writing standards for public relations practice for the European Union.

Daniel Edelman

Daniel J. Edelman.   Many of the major public relations firms that dominate the practice today were established in the postwar years. In Chicago, following World War II service in the U.S. Army Psychological Warfare and Information Control divisions and four years as public relations director of Toni Company (Gillette), former CBS reporter Daniel J. Edelman started his firm in 1952. Within eight years, expansion began with a branch office in New York, followed by openings in Los Angeles, London, Washington, D.C., and Frankfurt, Germany. Edelman Public Relations Worldwide is now the world's largest independent firm (not owned by a communication conglomerate), with more than 1,800 employees in 40 offices worldwide. Edelman's son, Richard, is now CEO, operating out of coheadquarters in New York and Chicago (see www.edelman.com).

Harold Burson

Harold Burson.   Harold Burson had operated his own firm for six years before teaming up with advertising executive Bill Marsteller in 1953 to form Burson-Marsteller. Burson worked as a newspaper journalist before serving with combat engineers in Europe during the last two years of World War II. After the war, he covered the Nuremberg Trials for the American Forces Network. Burson served as chairman and CEO of the firm until 1987. By 1983, Burson-Marsteller was the world's largest public relations firm, with more than 2,400 employees in 58 offices in 27 countries. Unlike firms that grow by acquiring other smaller firms, Burson-Marsteller has expanded by opening its own offices. Today, the firm's 57 wholly owned offices and 45 affiliated firms are in 60 countries, making it a truly global firm. Communication conglomerate Young & Rubicam purchased the firm in 1979 and was in turn purchased in 2000 by the even larger British conglomerate, WPP Group. In conjunction with its 50th anniversary in 2003, the firm and a number of Burson's clients funded the Harold Burson Chair in Public Relations at Boston University (see www.bm.com).

Inez Kaiser

Inez Y. Kaiser.   In Kansas City, Missouri, Inez Yeargan Kaiser established in 1961 the first public relations firm owned by an African-American female to serve national accounts. Inez Y. Kaiser & Associates, Inc., worked for 7-Up, Sears, Sterling Drug, Sperry Hutchinson, Continental Baking Company, and Pillsbury, among others. During her 33-year business career, Kaiser was the first Black woman to join the Public Relations Society of America and helped form the National Association of Minority Women in Business. Public relations educators in the Association for Education in Journalism and Mass Communication created the Inez Kaiser Award in 1993, providing one-year memberships to minority graduate students pursuing advanced degrees in public relations education.

Betsy Ann Plank.   After working for a Pittsburgh radio station, Betsy Ann Plank began her career in public relations in 1947. She was executive vice president and treasurer for Daniel Edelman's Chicago firm before joining AT&T in New York as director of public relations planning. She transferred to Illinois Bell Telephone Company in 1974, where she was the first woman to head a department. She directed external affairs until she retired in 1990.

In 1973, Plank became the first woman to serve as president of the Public Relations Society of America. Since then, PRSA has awarded her the Gold Anvil, recognizing her as the nation's outstanding professional (1977); the Lund Award for civic

Betsy Plank

and community service (1989); and the first Jackson Award for distinguished service to PRSA (2001). The Arthur W. Page Society awarded her its first Distinguished Service Award (2000). When she accepted the Institute for Public Relations' Alexander Hamilton Award, also in 2000, Plank summarized her concept of public relations:

> Public relations is fundamental to a democratic society where people make decisions in the workplace, the marketplace, the community and in the voting booth. Its primary mission is to forge responsible relationships of understanding, trust and respect among groups and individuals—even though they often disagree.[73]

As PRSSA's most enthusiastic supporter and benefactor, along with the late Jon A. Riffel, she co-founded the Champions for the Public Relations Student Society of America in 1981. An alumna of the University of Alabama, Plank endowed the "Plank Center for Leadership in Public Relations" in the university's College of Communications and Information Sciences. The university inducted her into its Communication Hall of Fame in 2001.

The 1946–1964 boom period also produced a tremendous spurt in the number of books, articles, and journals devoted to the practice and its principles, problems, and techniques. As the body of knowledge grew, so did the number of college courses and programs specifically designed to prepare practitioners. Academic preparation in public relations led to greater acceptance of young graduates in the job market. Much of the impetus in education can be attributed to the original co-authors of this book—*Effective Public Relations*—first published in 1952, and referred to for many years as simply "Cutlip and Center."

Scott M. Cutlip.   West Virginian Cutlip began his career as a journalist in Morgantown, West Virginia. He earned a bachelor's degree in journalism and political science at Syracuse University in 1939 and a master's degree from the University of Wisconsin in 1941. After a short stay as public relations director for the West Virginia State Road Commission, he enlisted in the U.S. Army Air Force in 1942, advancing from private to major in three years while with the Fifth Air Force from Australia to the occupation of Japan.

Scott Cutlip

After World War II, Cutlip returned to the University of Wisconsin in 1946 as the president's assistant for public relations and to introduce public relations courses in the then-School of Journalism. He is widely credited with establishing public relations as a legitimate field of academic study. He also served as professor and mentor to many military public relations officers who came to Wisconsin to earn master's degrees as part of the Department of Defense effort to professionalize the function. He left Wisconsin in 1975 to become dean at what is now Grady College of Journalism and Mass Communication at the University of Georgia. He retired in 1985 and returned to his beloved Madison, Wisconsin, and the Wisconsin Historical Society.

His long and illustrious career garnered the major lifetime achievement awards of major public relations, journalism, and mass communication associations and societies, including PRSA's first national Outstanding Educator Award in 1970 and the Gold Anvil in 1995. He was invited to speak, conduct seminars, and counsel corporations and governments worldwide. In addition, he was awarded an honorary doctorate from West Virginia Wesleyan College, which he had attended as a youth. He died August 18, 2000, at the age of 85.

His legacy, however, is tied to his books about public relations history cited in this chapter, including *Fund Raising in the United States: Its Role in America's*

Philanthropy, Public Relations History from the 17th to the 20th Century, and *The Unseen Power: Public Relations—A History.* But it was the book that came from his collaboration with Allen H. Center that defined them both.

Allen Center

Allen H. Center.   Center's public relations career began during World War II in the Southwest Pacific. For three years in Guadalcanal, New Guinea and the Philippines, Corporal Center edited a daily newspaper for the 13th Army Air Force Fighter Command Headquarters. As Tom Brokaw said in his book, *The Greatest Generation,* Center's generation learned lessons in the war that served them throughout their lives. In his unpublished family history, *The Center Line,* he wrote:

> Looking back, the main lesson or benefit from my three years of military service was the conviction never to relinquish or delegate control of my own destiny . . . no matter what the gain in money, brownie points, or recognition. I, alone, must be in charge of my life. My time would be for sale, but not my character, standards, or convictions.

After the war, Center returned to his prewar employment with the American Chicle Company in New York, while he searched for a job in his newfound calling—public relations. His search led to the position as publications editor, then public relations director, at Parker Pen Company in Janesville, Wisconsin. In Wisconsin, he met Professor Scott Cutlip, who shared his interest in writing an authoritative text for the growing field of public relations. Referred to for years as "the bible of public relations," their book has introduced students and practitioners worldwide to the theory and practice of public relations for almost six decades.

He left Parker Pen after seven years to join Motorola as public relations director to help the Consumer Products Division introduce color television. Then the large Chicago advertising agency—Leo Burnett—lured him from Motorola, making him vice president of public relations. While holding this position for two years, he also served as the president of the Chicago chapter of PRSA.

He returned to Motorola in 1961, serving as corporate vice president for public relations until he took early retirement in 1973 to write the first edition of the advanced public relations case studies textbook, *Public Relations Practices,* now in its seventh edition with co-authors.[74] When he retired to the San Diego area in 1976, San Diego State University invited Center to teach part-time as the first and only person to hold the title "Distinguished Resident Lecturer." He taught there until 1987.

In 1981, he received the PRSA's highest national honor—the Gold Anvil—for his contributions to advancing the field. In 1986, he was the second person to be inducted into the Arthur W. Page Society's Hall of Fame. (Page's son John was the first and Scott Cutlip third.)

In a lifetime of achievement, Center was a true pathfinder who set the standards and aspirations for the emerging profession. He also served as a role model for generations of students and practitioners who share his vision of the social value and nobility of purpose in building harmonious relationships. Center died November 13, 2005, at the age of 93.

Additional impetus for the growth of professionalism came with the establishment of one strong general organization and the emergence of a number serving specialized fields of practice. Public Relations Society of America was born August 4, 1947, when representatives of the West Coast American Council on Public Relations and the East Coast National Association of Public Relations Counsel met in Chicago. Members of the Washington-based American Public Relations Association voted not to come in at that time but merged in 1961. Dr. Rex F. Harlow was the moving force in bringing about this merger.

Period of Protest and Empowerment: 1965–1985

This era put "consumerism," "environmentalism," "racism," and "sexism" at the top of the public agenda. Add to those "isms," "peace." A new breed of investigative muckrakers and powerful new advocacy groups pushed for social change, new social safety nets, and increased government oversight of business and industry. Through public demonstrations and "Great Society" legislative initiatives, as well as good-faith negotiation, power was redistributed, and organizations became more responsive to public concerns and values. Protecting the environment and securing civil rights became the flagship causes of this era.

Activist Leaders

Rachel Carson.   Reminiscent of the early part of the twentieth century, "big business" again became the target of protest movements and media criticism. Also repeating that earlier era, books led the charge. For example, many credit Rachel Carson's *Silent Spring* (1962) with beginning the environmental movement.[75] President John F. Kennedy directed his science advisory committee to study the book's documented charges that DDT indiscriminately killed all manner of insects and animals when applied to crops as a pesticide, and that DDT had contaminated the entire food chain. The big pesticide manufacturers responded by threatening that without DDT the Dark Ages would return, and that insects and disease would go unchecked. (Surely, this was not public relations' finest hour.) Public apathy changed to public demands to regulate the pesticide industry and to protect the environment.

FIGURE 4.8
Rachel Carson Testifying Before Senate Committee

Legislators' responses were immediate and long lasting (see Figure 4.8). Congress passed the Clean Air Act of 1963, the National Environmental Policy Act of 1969 (making the protection of the environment national policy), and the Water Quality Improvement Act of 1970. The first "Earth Day" was celebrated in April 1970, and the Environmental Protection Agency (EPA) was created in October 1970. Carson had taken on corporate America . . . and won, setting the stage for an era of protest and change.

Ralph Nader.   General Motors was another target of protest and public scrutiny, opening the door to greater corporate accountability. Ralph Nader gave birth to the consumer movement when he wrote *Unsafe at Any Speed: The Designed-In Dangers of the American Automobile* (1965).[76] Nader charged that the Chevrolet Corvair's suspension system made the car subject to rolling over. GM's legal department responded by investigating Nader's private life. Subsequently, the company's president had to appear before a Senate subcommittee and apologize to Nader for resorting to intimidation. In addition, the company settled lawsuits out of court for invading Nader's privacy and agreed to change the Corvair suspension system. The National Traffic and Motor Vehicle Safety Act that spelled out safety standards on all vehicles passed in 1966. (Congress also mandated safety in the workplace when it passed the Occupational Safety and Health Act [OSHA] in 1970.)

FIGURE 4.9
Ralph Nader

Nader used the cash settlement and his book royalties to establish the Project on Corporate Responsibility, staffed by young lawyers and investigators. Nader became the "consumer crusader" media darling for the fledgling consumer movement (see Figure 4.9). Corporate secrecy and arrogance suffered many setbacks as "Nader's Raiders" continued to press for corporate accountability over the next four decades. One tactic was to ask shareholders to give their vote proxies to Nader so he could challenge corporate policy and board elections.

Saul Alinsky, a self-described "radical," used similar tactics to take power from corporate America and others in the "establishment." He made his intentions clear in the first paragraphs of his book:

> *The Prince* was written by Machiavelli for the Haves on how to hold power. *Rules for Radicals* is written for the Have-Nots on how to take it away.
>   In this book we are concerned with how to create mass organizations to seize power and give it to the people. . . .[77]

Even his book title—*Rules for Radicals*—captures the tenor of that era. And he succeeded in creating widespread participation in his movement, as volunteers offered their proxy votes and active participation:

> "Enclosed find my proxies. I wonder whether you have heard from anyone else in my suburb? If you have, I would appreciate receiving their names and addresses so that I can call a housemeeting and organize a San Fernando Valley Chapter of Proxies for People." The second letter said, " . . . *we don't know why you should go to the board meetings with our proxies—why can't we go with our proxies, of course all organized and knowing what we want, but we would like to go ourselves."* [Emphasis added by Alinsky.][78]

FIGURE 4.10

Dr. Martin Luther King Jr.

Dr. Martin Luther King Jr.   Without a doubt, Dr. Martin Luther King Jr. is the icon of this era of social change and empowerment. His rise to national leadership began in 1955 when he stood up for Rosa Parks, who was arrested for refusing to give up her seat on a Montgomery, Alabama, bus to a white passenger. He gave his famous "I Have a Dream" speech August 28, 1963, to an estimated 250,000 at the Lincoln Memorial in Washington, D.C. Dr. King gave his prophetic last speech, "I've Been to the Mountain Top," in Memphis, Tennessee, the day before he was assassinated on April 4, 1968. He became the martyr and symbol of the civil rights movement that produced, among many other changes, the 1965 Voting Rights Act and the Open Housing Law (1968). In short, Martin Luther King Jr. and the civil rights movement helped define this era of change and empowerment, affecting both internal and external relationships for all organizations.

Successes of the civil rights movement energized the equal rights movement spearheaded by Gloria Steinem, Bella Abzug, Shirley Chisholm, and Betty Friedan. They formed the National Women's Political Caucus in 1971 to help women run for political office. In addition, the organization endorses candidates supportive of women's issues. The organization continues to call for passage of an amendment to the Constitution mandating equal rights for women, first passed by the Congress in 1972 but never ratified by the states. Regardless, women have entered all phases of work—becoming the majority in public relations, for example—because of the doors opened during this era.

Surely the Vietnam War protests were the most divisive of this era, contributing to the "generation gap," "hippies," the "sexual revolution," and—ultimately—Watergate and the impeachment of President Richard Nixon. Students staged antiwar protests on campuses nationwide, but none with more disastrous results than the 1970 demonstrations against the U.S. incursion into Cambodia. National Guard troops shot to death four students on the Kent State University (Ohio) campus, and Mississippi State Police killed two students on the campus of Jackson State College. Seven months later, Congress repealed the 1964 Tonkin Gulf Resolution, which had authorized U.S. action in Vietnam. On January 27, 1973, the United States, North Vietnam, South Vietnam, and the Viet Cong Provisional Revolutionary Government signed the agreement "Restoring Peace in Vietnam." The genie was out of the bottle, however, as citizen action had changed public policy and removed a president. A popular saying was "Power to the People," which also captured the essence of this era.

Corporate Campaigns

Power to the people took yet another turn during this era in the form of organized attacks on corporations' profits and reputations. Referred to as "corporate campaigns," strategy and tactics originally developed by radicals to oppose the Vietnam War were soon adopted by churches, labor unions, and other organized protest groups to force change on corporations. For example, men's clothing maker Farah Manufacturing opened a new, nonunion plant in El Paso, Texas, in 1970. By 1972, the Amalgamated Clothing Workers Union (ACWU) had organized consumer boycotts and pressured Farah to recognize the ACWU as the bargaining agent for all 9,000 employees.[79]

As media and political science scholar Jarol Manheim points out, the corporate campaign is designed to systematically exploit key stakeholders' relationships with the corporate target:

> If a union or some other advocacy group pursuing a grievance against a company can turn the company's customers, suppliers, shareholders, or some other group on whose goodwill it depends against it, that stakeholder group becomes a *de facto* supporter of the campaign. If enough such supporters can be mobilized in this manner, the pressure on the company may well be irresistible. Management may be willing to do almost anything to make the pain disappear. That is, at least, the theory of the corporate campaign.[80]

In other words, this era's early activists pioneered a powerful combination of communication and action now systematically employed to empower those trying to force change on the part of corporations, government, churches, universities, charities, and all other types of organizations.

Public relations textbooks written near the end of this era also reflected a major change in public relations practice: No longer was the journalist-in-residence model of "telling our story" going to fulfill the new role of public relations in organizations responding to the new balance of power in society. For example, the sixth edition of this book introduced "adjustment and adaptation" as the basis of contemporary practice (see Chapter 7). Research courses were added to the public relations curriculum on many campuses, and practitioners who engaged in information gathering were invited to join the management decision-making team in many organizations.

Emerging from the era of protest and empowerment, public relations could no longer focus simply on domestic relations. Technology and global commerce required new approaches to communication and international relations.

Digital Age and Globalization: 1986–Present

In the digital age, computers became affordable for home use. Information became "0s" and "1s" distributed over—in sequence—copper, fiber-optic, and wireless networks, and stored on ever-smaller devices—first on "floppies," then hard drives, then

CDs and DVDs, and then "thumb drives." DVDs replaced videotapes. Blu-ray Discs replaced HD-DVD. The Internet changed everything—introducing e-mail, online searches, and nearly unrestricted access to a powerful and instantaneous distribution system. Access made "self-publishing" a reality, leading to less control over the public information system by traditional media, to greater diversity in points of view, to increased interest in organizational transparency, and to precisely targeted communication with stakeholders.

This chapter began with a quotation from George Santayana about people who do not remember the past being doomed to repeat it. The "inconvenient truth" is that another unpopular war in Iraq and concern about global environmental damage are again at the top of the public agenda . . . worldwide.

Of course, we live in this era and it prescribes the concept and practice of public relations described in the chapters of this book. Readers of this book will play a role in writing this part of public relations history.

Notes

[1] The authoritative references on public relations history are by Scott M. Cutlip: *The Unseen Power: Public Relations— A History* (Hillsdale, NJ: Lawrence Erlbaum Associates, 1994), and *Public Relations History: From the 17th to the 20th Century* (Hillsdale, NJ: Lawrence Erlbaum Associates, 1995).

[2] A. L. Basham, *The Wonder That Was India* (London: Sidgwick and Jackson, 1954), 122.

[3] Samuel Eliot Morison, *The Founding of Harvard College* (Cambridge: Harvard University Press, 1935), 303. Also see Hugh T. Lefler, "Promotional Literature of the Southern Colonies," *Journal of Southern History* 33 (1967): 3–25.

[4] Philip Davidson, *Propaganda and the American Revolution, 1763–1783* (Chapel Hill: University of North Carolina Press, 1941), 3.

[5] For the patriots' version of this historical event, see James Bowdoin, Dr. Joseph Warren, and Samuel Pemberton, "Short Narrative of the Horrid Massacre in Boston," in *Tracts of the American Revolution, 1763–1776*, ed. Merrill Jensen (New York: Bobbs Merrill, 1967). Also available at www.bostonmassacre.net/trial/acct-anonymous1.htm.

[6] Merrill Jensen, "The Sovereign States: Their Antagonisms and Rivalries and Some Consequences," in *Sovereign States in an Age of Uncertainty*, 226–50, ed. Ronald Hoffman and Peter J. Albert (Charlottesville: University of Virginia Press, 1981).

[7] David McCullouch, *John Adams* (New York: Simon & Schuster, 2001), 96.

[8] Jason Karpf, "Adams, Paine and Jefferson: A PR Firm," *Public Relations Tactics* (January 2002): 12.

[9] For the Tory side of the propaganda battle, see Carol Berkin and Jonathan Sewall, *Odyssey of an American Loyalist* (New York: Columbia University Press, 1974).

[10] William Baldwin Jr., "Bicentenary of a Classic Campaign," *Public Relations Quarterly* 10 (Spring 1965).

[11] Robert A. Rutland, *The Ordeal of the Constitution: The Antifederalists and the Ratification Struggle of 1787–88* (Boston: Northeastern University Press, 1983), 3.

[12] Broadus Mitchell, *Alexander Hamilton: Youth to Maturity, 1755–1788* (New York: Macmillan, 1957), 422–23.

[13] Allan Nevins, *The Constitution Makers and the Public, 1785–1790* (New York: Foundation for Public Relations Research and Education, 1962), 10. Also in *Public Relations Review* 4, no. 3 (Fall 1978): 5–16.

[14] T. Swann Harding, "Genesis of One 'Government Propaganda Mill,'" *Public Opinion Quarterly* 11 (Summer 1947): 227–35. (A history of public relations in the U.S. Department of Agriculture.)

[15] Cutlip, *Public Relations History*, 68–120. For an extended source about Kendall's work, see Lynn Marshall, "The Authorship of Jackson's Bank Veto Message," *Mississippi Valley Historical Review*, vol. L (December 1963). For an estimate of Kendall's influence, see Arthur M. Schlesinger Jr., *The Age of Jackson* (Boston: Little, Brown, 1945).

[16] Cutlip, *Public Relations History*, 88–105. For earlier accounts of this epic public relations battle, see Bray Hammond, *Banks and Politics in America* (Princeton, NJ: Princeton University Press, 1957).

[17] John Brooks, *Telephone: The First Hundred Years* (New York: Harper and Row, 1976), 270–71.

[18] Cutlip, *Public Relations History*, 100.

[19] Ibid., 101.

[20] Ibid., 171. For accounts of Davy Crockett's buildup, see Dixon Wecter, *The Hero in America: A Chronicle of Hero-Worship* (New York: Charles Scribner's Sons, 1941/1972), 189–193; Michael Lofaro, ed., *Davy Crockett: The Man, the Legend, the Legacy, 1786–1986* (Knoxville: University of

Tennessee Press, 1985); and Michael Lofaro and Joe Cummings, eds., *Crockett at Two Hundred: New Perspectives on the Man and the Myth* (Knoxville: University of Tennessee Press, 1989).

[21] Ibid., 175. See also Irving Wallace, *The Fabulous Showman: Life and Times of P. T. Barnum* (New York: Alfred A. Knopf, 1959); and Phineas Taylor Barnum, *The Life of P. T. Barnum Written by Himself* (New York: Redfield, 1855), 154–74.

[22] Richard C. Overton, *Burlington West* (Cambridge, MA: Harvard University Press, 1941), 158–159.

[23] For a concise account, see Leon Wolff, *Lockout* (New York: Harper and Row, 1965).

[24] Merle Curti, *The Growth of American Thought,* 3rd ed. (New York: Harper and Row, 1964), 634.

[25] Cutlip, *Public Relations History,* 208.

[26] Forrest McDonald, *Insull* (Chicago: University of Chicago Press, 1962), 44–45. (Biography of the utility magnate who blazed many public relations trails before he crashed in ruin.)

[27] Cutlip, *Public Relations History,* 203.

[28] Morris Fishbein, *History of the American Medical Association, 1847–1947* (Philadelphia: W. B. Saunders, 1947), 61.

[29] C. C. Regier, *The Era of the Muckrakers* (Chapel Hill: University of North Carolina Press, 1932). For a generous sampling of newspaper articles, see Arthur Weinberg and Lila Weinberg, eds., *The Muckrakers* (New York: Simon and Schuster, 1961). For a discussion of the most prolific, if lesser known, muckraker, see Robert Miraldi, "Charles Edward Russell: 'Chief of the Muckrakers,'" *Journalism & Mass Communication Monographs* 150 (April 1995).

[30] Vernon Parrington, *Main Currents in American Thought,* vol. 3, (New York: Harcourt Brace Jovanovich, 1930), 404–5. For details on the rise of the mass media, see Edwin Emery, *The Press and America* (Englewood Cliffs, NJ: Prentice Hall, 1972); Theodore Peterson, *Magazines in the Twentieth Century* (Urbana: University of Illinois Press, 1964); and Stephen Fox, *The Mirror Makers* (New York: Morrow, 1984).

[31] For details, see Scott M. Cutlip, "The Nation's First Public Relations Agency," in *The Unseen Power,* 10–26. See also "The Nation's First Public Relations Firm," *Journalism Quarterly* 43 (Summer 1966). (It was, in fact, a publicity agency, not a public relations firm.)

[32] Cutlip, *The Unseen Power,* 11.

[33] Ray Stannard Baker, "Railroads on Trial," *McClure's Magazine* 26 (March 1906): 535–44. The story is also told in Weinberg and Weinberg's *The Muckrakers.* Baker worked with Ida Tarbell and Lincoln Steffens at *McClure's,* doing what critics called "muckraking journalism," to expose corruption in the railroads and financial institutions of the day.

[34] Cutlip, *The Unseen Power,* 16.

[35] "Department Press Agents," Hearing before Committee on Rules, House of Representatives, May 21, 1912, 62d Congress, 2d session (Washington, DC: Government Printing Office, 1912), 16. Also see William Kittle, "The Making of Public Opinion," *Arena* 41 (1909): 443–44.

[36] Ibid., 92–103.

[37] Ibid., 32–33.

[38] Gordon A. Moon II, "George F. Parker: A 'Near Miss' as First White House Press Chief," *Journalism Quarterly* 41 (Spring 1964): 183–90.

[39] Cutlip, *The Unseen Power,* 52–53.

[40] Quoted in Sherman Morse, "An Awakening on Wall Street," *American Magazine* 62 (September 1906): 460.

[41] Ivy L. Lee Papers, Princeton University Library. Lee's 1907 correspondence includes a letter from the president of Pennsylvania Railroad to a colleague in Southern Pacific, saying that the time had come to take measures to "place our case before the public."

[42] Ivy L. Lee, *Publicity: Some of the Things It Is and Is Not* (New York: Industries Publishing Company, 1925), 39.

[43] Ibid., 48.

[44] For testimony on this case, see *Investigation of Nazi and Other Propaganda: Public Hearings before a Subcommittee of the Committee on Un-American Activities, Hearing Number 73-NY-7* (Washington, DC: Government Printing Office, 1934); and *Trials of War Criminals before the Nuremberg Military Tribunal,* Volumes 7 and 8, Case Six, *U.S. v. Krauch,* "The I. G. Farben Case" (Washington, DC: Government Printing Office, 1963).

[45] Ray Eldon Hiebert, *Courtier to the Crowd: The Story of Ivy L. Lee and the Development of Public Relations* (Ames: Iowa State University Press, 1966), 310–311.

[46] See Noel L. Griese, "James D. Ellsworth, 1863–1940," *Public Relations Review* 4 (Summer 1978): 22–31.

[47] George Juergens, *News from the White House: The Presidential-Press Relationship in the Progressive Era* (Chicago: University of Chicago Press, 1981), 70.

[48] For more on the development of public relations in higher education, see Scott M. Cutlip, "Advertising Higher Education: The Early Years of College Public Relations," *College and University Journal* 9 (November 1970), part I, and 10 (January 1971), part II.

[49] For a full account of public relations' role in fund-raising, see Scott M. Cutlip, *Fund Raising in the United States: Its Role in America's Philanthropy* (New Brunswick, NJ: Rutgers University Press, 1965), and Kathleen S. Kelly, *Effective Fund-Raising Management* (Mahwah, NJ: Lawrence Erlbaum Associates, 1997), Part II, "Historical Context of Fund Raising."

50 James O. Mock and Cedric Larson, *Words That Won the War* (Princeton, NJ: Princeton University Press, 1939), 4.

51 *New York Times,* February 1, 1920, p. 9.

52 Harold D. Lasswell, *Propaganda Techniques in the World War* (New York: Alfred A. Knopf, 1927), 220.

53 John F. Budd, "Carl Byoir's Contributions to PR Are Worth Noting Despite Its US Demise," *PRWeek,* December 10, 2001, p. 10.

54 See Cutlip, *The Unseen Power,* 531–588, for detailed descriptions of the growth and tumultuous times of Carl Byoir & Associates.

55 Edward L. Bernays, *Biography of an Idea: Memoirs of Public Relations Counsel Edward L. Bernays* (New York: Simon & Schuster, 1965), 288.

56 Pamel J. Creedon, "Public Relations History Misses 'Her Story,'" *Journalism Educator* 44, no. 3 (Autumn 1989): 26–30.

57 Doris Fleischman Bernays, *A Wife Is Many Women* (New York: Crown, 1955), 171. As quoted by Creedon in "Public Relations History," p. 28.

58 Susan Henry, "Dissonant Notes of a Retiring Feminist: Doris E. Fleischman's Later Years," *Journal of Public Relations Research* 10, no. 1 (1998): 1. (In 1955, she identified herself as "Doris Fleischman Bernays" on the title page of her book, *A Wife Is Many Women*—as Henry's description of Fleischman's later life so vividly portrays.)

59 Hill's papers related to the Tobacco Industry Research Committee are available online from the Wisconsin Historical Society at www.ttlaonline.com/HKWIS/hksplash.htm.

60 Hill Papers (December 3, 1958, memo), as quoted in Cutlip, *The Unseen Power,* 518.

61 Cutlip, *The Unseen Power,* 487–88.

62 Ibid., 501.

63 George Griswold Jr., "How AT&T Public Relations Policies Developed," *Public Relations Quarterly* 12 (Fall 1967): 13. (A special issue devoted to AT&T's public relations.)

64 Noel L. Griese, *Arthur W. Page: Publisher, Public Relations Pioneer, Patriot* (Tucker, GA: Anvil Publishers, 2001), 229–230. This is *the* definitive biography of Page.

65 Cutlip, *The Unseen Power,* 527.

66 For a balanced view of Howe's contributions to FDR's career and his public relations ideas, see Alfred B. Rollins Jr., *Roosevelt and Howe* (New York: Alfred A. Knopf, 1962).

67 Marilyn Kern-Foxworth, "Minority Entrepreneurs Challenge the Barriers," *Public Relations Journal* 45, no. 8 (August 1989): 19.

68 Cutlip, *The Unseen Power,* 598.

69 For a quick study of the OWI, see Robert L. Bishop and LaMar S. Mackay, "Mysterious Silence, Lyrical Scream: Government Information in World War II," *Journalism Monographs* 19 (May 1971), based on their Ph.D. dissertations written at the University of Wisconsin.

70 Gordon W. Keisser, *The Marine Corps and Defense Unifications 1944–47* (Washington: National Defense University Press, 1982).

71 "Business Is Still in Trouble," *Fortune* 39 (May 1949) reflects business' postwar public relations problems. For a biting critique of some business efforts to deal with critics, see William H. Whyte, *Is Anybody Listening?* (New York: Simon & Schuster, 1952).

72 Personal letter to author (Broom), February 1, 2003. For more information about Traverse-Healy and the collection of his writings, go to www.pr-50years.co.uk/index.html.

73 Personal communication to the author, February 15, 2008.

74 Allen H. Center, Patrick Jackson, Stacey Smith, and Frank R. Stansberry, *Public Relations Practices: Managerial Case Studies and Problems,* 7th ed. (Upper Saddle River, NJ: Pearson Prentice Hall, 2008).

75 Rachel Carson, *Silent Spring* (Boston: Houghton Mifflin, 1962). A 25th anniversary edition of this landmark book was published in 1987.

76 Ralph Nader, *Unsafe at Any Speed: The Designed-In Dangers of the American Automobile* (New York: Grossman, 1965).

77 Saul D. Alinsky, *Rules for Radicals: A Pragmatic Primer for Realistic Radicals* (New York: Random House, 1971), 3.

78 Ibid., 177.

79 Jarol B. Manheim, *The Death of a Thousand Cuts: Corporate Campaigns and the Attack on the Corporation* (Mahwah, NJ: Lawrence Erlbaum Associates, 2001), 45–49.

80 Ibid., viii.

Additional Sources

Cutlip, Scott M. *Public Relations History: From the 17th to the 20th Century.* Hillsdale, NJ: Lawrence Erlbaum Associates, 1995.

Cutlip, Scott M. *The Unseen Power: Public Relations—A History.* Hillsdale, NJ: Lawrence Erlbaum Associates, 1994.

Hallahan, Kirk. "Ivy Lee and the Rockefellers' Response to the 1913–1914 Colorado Coal Strike," *Journal of Public Relations Research* 14, no. 4 (2002): 265–315.

Harrison, Shirley, and Kevin Moloney, "Comparing Two Public Relations Pioneers: American Ivy Lee and British John Elliot." *Public Relations Review*

30, no. 2 (2004), 207–215. Authors draw parallels between the careers of Ivy Lee and the first practitioner in Great Britain to have "public relations" in his job title.

Henry, Susan. "Dissonant Notes of a Retiring Feminist: Doris E. Fleischman's Later Years." *Journal of Public Relations Research* 10, no. 1 (1998): 1–33. Also by Henry, see "Anonymous in Her Own Name: Public Relations Pioneer Doris E. Fleischman." *Journalism History* 23, no. 2 (Summer 1997): 51–62.

Hon, Linda Childers. "To Redeem the Soul of America: Public Relations and the Civil Rights Movement." *Journal of Public Relations Research* 9, no. 3 (1997): 163–212.

Kern-Foxworth, Marilyn. "African-American Achievements in Public Relations." *Public Relations Journal* 47, no. 2 (February 1991): 18–19.

Lee, Mordecai, "When Congress Tried to Cut Pentagon Public Relations: A Lesson from History," *Public Relations Review* 26, no. 2 (Summer 2002), 131–154.

Olasky, Marvin N. *Corporate Public Relations: A New Historical Perspective.* Hillsdale, NJ: Lawrence Erlbaum Associates, 1987; and "The Development of Corporate Public Relations, 1850–1930." *Journalism Monograph* 102 (April 1987), by the same author. Olasky recasts the historical role of public relations as an attempt by corporations to limit competition.

Pearson, Ron. "Perspectives on Public Relations History." *Public Relations Review* 16, no. 3 (Fall 1990): 27–38.

Pratt, Cornelius B. "The 40-Year Tobacco Wars: Giving Public Relations a Black Eye?" *Public Relations Quarterly* 42, no. 4 (Winter 1997–98): 5–10.

"Public Relations in American History" (special issue). *Public Relations Review* 4 (Fall 1978). Lectures by historians Allan Nevins, Ray Allen Billington, Frank E. Vandiver, George F. G. Stanley, Eric F. Goldman, and Joe B. Frantz.

Raucher, Alan R. "Public Relations in Business: A Business of Public Relations." *Public Relations Review* 16, no. 3 (Fall 1990): 19–26.

Part 2

Foundations

Professionalism and Ethics

STUDY GUIDE After studying Chapter 5, you should be able to:

▶ Identify the five characteristics of professions.

▶ Describe the major professional organizations serving the field.

▶ Describe the program of study in public relations recommended by the Commission on Public Relations Education.

▶ Identify the major motivations behind concern for professional ethics in public relations practice.

▶ List and briefly discuss the positives of socially responsible public relations, as well as the major negatives attributed to public relations when it is not practiced in the public interest.

▶ Outline and apply some of the major articles from the Public Relations Society of America Code of Ethics.

▶ Outline the major arguments for and against licensing and accreditation of practitioners.

A s discussed in Chapter 1, many people confuse public relations with other departments, such as marketing, or with its parts, such as publicity. Furthermore, many people hold mistaken assumptions about public relations, believing it serves only organizational interests without regard for the public interest. For these reasons, improving the professionalism of public relations practice remains a key concern among most practitioners. They cannot do their jobs without the trust of the public and their organization's dominant coalition; they cannot earn their trust until they live up to professional standards.

Criteria of a Profession

As in other "professional" occupations, many in public relations work to earn status as members of a true profession. Attempts to achieve professional status might be considered selfish by some, but the results of increased professionalism benefit society as a whole. Professionalization institutionalizes the best practices and establishes standards of quality that serve the public interest. Professionalization has, by and large, brought us better health care; safer highways and bridges; better houses; faster cars and airplanes; safer air travel; and

Decision-making when faced with an ethical dilemma is easy: Do the right thing. Always.
—Alexander M. Cutler,[1]
Chairman and CEO, Eaton Corporation

If I have done my job well for the right purpose, my life has substance and meaning. If I have done my job poorly or for the wrong purpose, I have squandered my life, however much I have prospered.
—John Kultgen[2]

This chapter was revised in collaboration with Professor **Bey-Ling Sha,** Ph.D., APR, School of Journalism & Media Studies, San Diego State University. Previously, Dr. Sha taught at the University of Maryland–College Park and at the American University of Paris. She also served as a public affairs specialist with the U.S. Census Bureau, Washington, D.C., and as a consultant in public relations research and strategy for numerous public and private organizations.

higher standards in business, banking, and accounting. Add to this list more competent public relations counsel.

Assessing the progress of contemporary practice toward achieving professional status requires criteria. Indicators of professional status include:

1. Specialized educational preparation to acquire unique knowledge and skills
2. A body of theory-based knowledge, developed through research, that provides us with principles of appropriate public relations practice
3. Codes of ethics and standards of performance established and enforced by a self-governing association of colleagues
4. Autonomy in practice and acceptance of personal responsibility by practitioners
5. Recognition by the community of a unique and essential service

Before discussing each of these indicators of professional status, we examine some organizations that support professionalism in public relations.

Professional Organizations

The growth of professional associations reflects the serious efforts being made by many practitioners to surround the function with status and to advance its competence. Although these associations represent only a small portion of all those working in the public relations field, they exert considerable influence through their publications, conferences, seminars, awards programs, and advocacy for the practice. These organizations are international, national, regional, and specialized by area of practice—such as practitioners in health care, agriculture, or financial relations.

International Professional Organizations

The growth of public relations on a global scale makes it possible to have international professional societies devoted to public relations education, research, and professional standards. Groups of scholars such as the International Communication Association also have divisions devoted to public relations research and teaching among their ranks. Practitioners have organized several international societies, including the following.

IABC

International Association of Business Communicators (IABC) Progress toward increased professionalism and higher standards in public relations advanced with the emergence of the IABC as a strong organization. Founded in 1970 when the Association of Industrial Editors and the International Council of Industrial Editors merged, IABC grew from 3,500 members to more than 14,000 members today in over 70 countries (www.iabc.com). The IABC headquarters is in San Francisco. To advance the competence and ethics of this field, IABC created a professional development guide for practitioners to help them identify the skills and knowledge necessary for attaining career goals and an ethics review committee to enforce a code of ethics. The code of ethics (see Exhibit 5.1) emphasizes that the principles of professional communication—legal, ethical, and in good taste—apply worldwide.

International Public Relations Association (IPRA) When IPRA was formed in London in 1955, it had only 15 members in five countries. Membership in 2007

EXHIBIT 5.1

IABC Code of Ethics

Preface

Because hundreds of thousands of business communicators worldwide engage in activities that affect the lives of millions of people, and because this power carries with it significant social responsibilities, the International Association of Business Communicators developed the Code of Ethics for Professional Communicators. The Code is based on three different yet interrelated principles of professional communication that apply throughout the world.

These principles assume that just societies are governed by a profound respect for human rights and the rule of law; that ethics, the criteria for determining what is right and wrong, can be agreed upon by members of an organization; and, that understanding matters of taste requires sensitivity to cultural norms.

These principles are essential:

- Professional communication is legal.
- Professional communication is ethical.
- Professional communication is in good taste.

Recognizing these principles, members of IABC will

- engage in communication that is not only legal but also ethical and sensitive to cultural values and beliefs;
- engage in truthful, accurate and fair communication that facilitates respect and mutual understanding; and,
- adhere to the following articles of the IABC Code of Ethics for Professional Communicators.

Because conditions in the world are constantly changing, members of IABC will work to improve their individual competence and to increase the body of knowledge in the field with research and education.

Articles

1. Professional communicators uphold the credibility and dignity of their profession by practicing honest, candid and timely communication and by fostering the free flow of essential information in accord with the public interest.

2. Professional communicators disseminate accurate information and promptly correct any erroneous communication for which they may be responsible.

3. Professional communicators understand and support the principles of free speech, freedom of assembly, and access to an open marketplace of ideas; and, act accordingly.

4. Professional communicators are sensitive to cultural values and beliefs and engage in fair and balanced communication activities that foster and encourage mutual understanding.

5. Professional communicators refrain from taking part in any undertaking which the communicator considers to be unethical.

6. Professional communicators obey laws and public policies governing their professional activities and are sensitive to the spirit of all laws and regulations and, should any law or public policy be violated, for whatever reason, act promptly to correct the situation.

7. Professional communicators give credit for unique expressions borrowed from others and identify the sources and purposes of all information disseminated to the public.

8. Professional communicators protect confidential information and, at the same time, comply with all legal requirements for the disclosure of information affecting the welfare of others.

9. Professional communicators do not use confidential information gained as a result of professional activities for personal benefit and do not represent conflicting or competing interests without written consent of those involved.

10. Professional communicators do not accept undisclosed gifts or payments for professional services from anyone other than a client or employer.

11. Professional communicators do not guarantee results that are beyond the power of the practitioner to deliver.

12. Professional communicators are honest not only with others but also, and most importantly, with themselves as individuals; for a professional communicator seeks the truth and speaks that truth first to the self.

Courtesy International Association of Business Communicators. From www.iabc.com (October 2004).

French Stamp

totaled nearly 1,100 individuals in 100 countries (www.ipra.org). With administrative offices in the United Kingdom, IPRA is formally recognized by the United Nations, as well as by the Economic and Social Council (ECOSOC) and UNESCO. In 1965 it adopted an International Code of Ethics, called the "Code of Athens," which is based on the UN Declaration of Human Rights. To commemorate IPRA's 25th anniversary in 1980, the French Post Office Authority issued the first and only stamp dedicated to public relations. IPRA promotes professional recognition, high standards, and ethics among practitioners working in international aspects of public relations. In addition, it supports professional development and recognition in parts of the world where public relations is just developing and helps establish new national associations.

One of the newest international organizations in the field is the Global Alliance for Public Relations and Communication Management (http://www.globalpr.org). See Exhibit 5.2 for details on its founding.

EXHIBIT 5.2

The Global Alliance Supports "One Profession . . . One Voice"

Juan-Carlos Molleda, Ph.D.
Associate Professor
College of Journalism and
Communications
University of Florida

The Global Alliance for Public Relations and Communication Management (GA) provides leadership in unifying the world-wide trade community under a common vision: one profession, one voice. After three years of planning, the formal commitment to establish the GA was reached by 23 professional organizations at a meeting that followed the 2000 World Public Relations Congress cosponsored by PRSA and IPRA in Chicago.

The GA is a clearinghouse of national and international professional organizations that encourages debate regarding common issues facing the industry. Likewise, the GA works to set standards for the practice of public relations and provide venues and channels for increasing interactions among global practitioners. Because no individual membership is allowed, the national association is the GA's primary focus. The core offering of the GA allows member associations to share re-

sources and achieve greater unity through building constructive relationships.

In 2002, the GA became a registered nonprofit in London, initiated a formal election process for its leadership (a chairperson holds the position for two consecutive years), and structured seven committees: setting standards (i.e., ethics, accreditation, curriculum, industry tools, corporate social responsibility), sharing information and resources, advocacy, outreach, finance, marketing, and technology.

Relevant outcomes of these efforts include a Global Protocol of Ethics introduced in Rome in 2003; a study on regulations in Italy, South Africa, and the United Kingdom; a Position Statement on CSR in 2004, and a series of PR Landscapes profiling the industry, business, and political landscapes in countries around the world. In addition, the Global Alliance Scholarship offers education opportunities in association with the University of Lugano, Switzerland, and its Executive Master of Science in Communications Management to member-organization applicants, seminars/workshops on best practices in association management, and a report on core competencies in public relations and communications.

The GA convenes twice annually, once with the Executive Board and the other as a General Council meeting in which all association representatives are encouraged to participate. Meetings are held as a component of conferences and the World PR Festival organized by national association members.

Professor Molleda is public relations graduate coordinator at the University of Florida and coordinator of the PR Landscape project of the Global Alliance for Public Relations and Communication Management.

National Professional Organizations

Public Relations Society of America (PRSA)   The largest public relations professional organization in the world is headquartered in New York City. With the Public Relations Student Society of America (PRSSA) as its affiliated student organization, the PRSA has nearly 32,000 professional and student members. PRSA is organized into 109 chapters nationwide and 19 professional interest sections, and the organization traces its origins to three older associations established to bring together practitioners of this growing vocation (see Chapter 4, pages 110–111). Formed in 1947, PRSA fosters the exchange of ideas through its publications and meetings, promotes a sense of professionalism, provides opportunities for continuing education, and encourages ethical behavior and high standards of practice (www.prsa.org).

Canadian Public Relations Society (CPRS)   Founded in 1948, the same year as PRSA, CPRS has 2,000 national members in 16 local Societies (www.cprs.ca). One-third of the members are accredited. CPRS publishes a bi-monthly newsletter, *Communiqué*, and holds an annual conference. Headquartered in Toronto, Ontario, CPRS closely parallels PRSA in philosophy and programming. The local Societies also recruit and mentor junior and student members.

Chartered Institute of Public Relations (United Kingdom) (CIPR)   Also founded in 1948, London-based CIPR has regional and specialist groups (by type of practice) with 9,000 members (www.ipr.org.uk). It is the largest public relations professional association in Europe. Fifty-five percent of the membership work in-house, while the other 45 percent work in public relations consultancies. Long a leader in establishing and enforcing codes of professional and ethical conduct, and in encouraging academic preparation and professional development within the profession, CIPR publishes *Profile* six times a year (www.profile-extra.co.uk). It is a member of the Confederation Europeene des Relations Publiques and charter member of the Global Alliance for Public Relations and Communications Management.

Outside the United States, there are more than 100 national and regional associations of public relations practitioners in more than 70 countries. One of the oldest of these national associations, the Public Relations Institute of Australia, also was formed in 1947 (see Exhibit 5.3). As public relations gains recognition around the world, the number of professional associations in this field will continue to grow (see Exhibit 5.4).

Specialized, Regional, and Local Associations

The growing memberships of several specialized national organizations attest to the field's growing sense of common interests, developing esprit de corps, and professionalism. Almost every type of industry has an organization for its communicators, and many are organized by geographic location or demographic commonalities. For some examples, see Exhibit 5.5 (see page 126).

In addition, a number of "exclusive" professional groups have developed over the years, with varying degrees of impact in shaping the practice. These include the Wise Men, begun in 1938 by John W. Hill, Pendleton Dudley, and T. J. Ross; Public Relations Seminar, started in 1951 as an outgrowth of the National Conference of Business Public Relations Executives; and Pride and Alarm, founded in 1957 in New York. Exclusivity for the in-group is their hallmark, and these groups generally hold their meetings in private and off the record. Some are small, informal, and area-specific,

EXHIBIT 5.3

Public Relations Institute of Australia

Tracy Jones FPRIA
President, Public Relations
Institute of Australia, and
Managing Director, Creative
Territory Pty. Ltd., Darwin

The Public Relations Institute of Australia (PRIA) is the peak body for public relations and communication professionals in Australia. PRIA represents and provides professional support and recognition to over 2,500 individual practitioners, and more than 150 consultancies, across the states and territories.

Since 1947, it's been our role to promote and enhance the profession and its status to the broader community throughout Australia and to enforce the principles of ethical standards and represent public relations practitioners in the best interests of the profession.

Our members are drawn from in-house and agency practice across all sectors of the industry, from corporate to government to community. Individuals are required to meet strict criteria for full professional membership.

These include a PRIA accredited tertiary qualification and a minimum of three years' full-time practice, or a minimum of five years' full-time experience. All membership applications are peer reviewed by senior practitioners in each state and territory.

All members are required to make a personal, written commitment to a stringent Code of Ethics, governed by a senior group of practitioners known as the College of Fellows. Consultancy members also are governed by the Code of Ethics.

To be eligible for Registered Consultancy status, the PR agency principal must be a full professional member of the PRIA. Consultancy members are also bound by an additional Code of Practice covering client relations, fees and income, and general practice.

PRIA provides members with professional accreditation and recognition through our annual awards program. PRIA also provides members with privileged access to a range of resources, tools and professional support to help them develop the current role or the next.

Volunteer committees comprising members from each state and territory organise and run hundreds of networking, information, and training events and programs each year, to help improve members' professional skills, networks, and opportunities.

like the Houston group—Corporate Relations Roundtable. Others are large, formalized, and national or international.

The newest by-invitation-only group is the Arthur W. Page Society, formed in 1983 when deregulation splintered AT&T's public relations unit. The group's literature offers the vision statement (www.awpagesociety.com):

> The Arthur W. Page Society is committed to the belief that public relations as a function of executive management is central to the success of the corporation. The membership of the Society will embrace those individuals who epitomize the highest standards of public relations practice, as exemplified by the Page Principles. [See Exhibit 5.6, page 127]

Elite groups such as the Page Society attempt to provide leadership, continuity, and continued growth for the public relations function. They often encourage the role of the public relations practitioner as the ethical conscience of an organization, help mentor young public relations managers, and advance the role of public relations in management.

EXHIBIT 5.4

Public Relations in Sweden

Larsåke Larsson
Professor
Örebro University
Sweden

Public relations in Sweden started much later than in the United States, England, and Germany. Swedish public relations began during World War II, when the country was isolated because it was neutral, like Switzerland. The State Information Bureau was established during the war to spread information about national security matters and to promote thrifty manufacturing and housekeeping.

After the war, some government agencies and corporations, such as Swedish Rail, Swedish Post, and the National Board of Health, engaged public relations specialists. Public relations competence spread in the business sector in the 1950s under the title "press officer." The first counseling firms also came into being during this decade, but the public relations industry grew slowly in the following decades. Beginning in the late the 1970s, however, the function in all types of organizations began to grow, with particularly rapid growth in the 1990s. Counseling firms experienced a surge in growth as the twentieth century ended.

The Swedish public relations industry embraces about 10,000 professionals in a country with 9 million inhabitants. Almost half—4,500—belong to the Swedish Public Relations Association (Sveriges Informationsförening). When established in 1956, the group concentrated on listing members

from the private sector. In 1992, it merged with an association of public relations and information professionals in the public sector to form the current association.

Most professionals work in-house for companies, organizations, and state and local governmental authorities. The others are engaged as consultants at public relations firms. At least 1,000 consultants work in approximately 100 public relations firms, most of them in small firms, employing some few or a handful of people, while about one fourth of the consultants work for the three largest public relations firms. Several large firms are affiliates of international firms based in other countries.

Public relations in Sweden differs from the practice in many other countries in that approximately 40 percent work within the public/official sector. Secondly, most public relations professionals work in-house. A third feature specific to Nordic/Scandinavian public relations strategy is that programs often address the "general public" due to cultural tradition and laws that require the dissemination of public information.

Twelve state universities offer public relations education under a three-year general media and communication program. Students study public relations (often called "planned and strategic communication") for one to four semesters. A few private schools also offer public relations and advertising education.

Scholarly research in public relations is a specialty under the larger field of media and communication research. About twelve researchers study public relations, with most using qualitative methodology and employing a societal-critical perspective. These researchers are mostly active in the European Public Relations Education and Research Association (EUPRERA) (http://www.euprera.org).

Student Organizations

Development of the Public Relations Student Society of America under the auspices of PRSA has strengthened education and recruitment into the field in the United States. PRSSA's first chapter was chartered in 1968; today, PRSSA has 291 chapters at colleges and universities throughout the United States and one chapter in Argentina. The organization's purpose is "to cultivate a favorable and mutually advantageous relationship between students and professional public relations practitioners" (www.prssa.org). Since the mid-1970s, the organization has been completely governed by student leaders elected to the PRSSA National Committee by PRSSA delegates to the organization's annual national convention. Thus, PRSSA presents opportunities for training not only in public relations, but also in leadership.

EXHIBIT 5.5

Public Relations Professional Associations

International

Confédération Européenne des Relations Publiques, established in 1959 (www.cerp.org)

Federation of African Public Relations Associations, 1975 (www.fapra.org)

Global Alliance for Public Relations and Communication Management, 2000 (www.globalpr.org)

International Communications Consultancy Organisation, 1988 (www.iccopr.com)

Universal Accreditation Board, 1998 (www.praccreditation.org)

Nation-Based

Canadian Public Relations Society, established in 1948 (www.cprs.ca)

Chartered Institute of Public Relations (United Kingdom), 1948 (www.cipr.co.uk)

Deutschen Public Relations Gesellschaft (Germany), 1958 (www.dprg.de)

Federal Council of Professionals of Public Relations (Brazil), 1969 (www.conferp.org.br)

Information Presse & Communication (France), 1956 (www.infopressecom.org)

Public Relations Society of India, 1958 (www.prsi.co.in)

Public Relations Institute of Australia, 1947 (www.pria.com.au)

U.S.-Based, Specialization-Based

Agricultural Relations Council, established in 1953 (www.agrelationscouncil.org)

Association of Fundraising Professionals, 1960 (www.afpnet.org)

Council for Advancement and Support of Education, 1975 (www.case.org)

Hispanic Public Relations Association, 1984 (www.hpra-usa.org)

Issue Management Council, 1988 (www.issuemanagement.org)

National Black Public Relations Society, 1987 (www.nbprs.org)

National Investor Relations Institute, 1969 (www.niri.org)

National School Public Relations Association, 1935 (www.nspra.org)

Religion Communicators Council, 1929 (www.religioncommunicators.org)

In Transition

Women Executives in Public Relations (WEPR) and Advertising Women of New York (AWNY), in the process of merging, as of spring 2008.

IABC also sponsors student chapters (www.iabc.com/student); although IABC's student organization is smaller than that of PRSSA, it has the benefit of being international. Students worldwide are forming similar affiliates of their country's professional societies. In Russia, for example, more than 400 public relations majors at 67 universities met in Moscow in December 2003 to form the Russian Public Relations Student Association (RASSO), the student division of the Russian Public Relations Association (RASO).[3]

Professional Education

The establishment of pre-professional organizations for students is only one aspect of an aspiring professional's education in public relations. As a leading public relations practitioner told students at Ball State University, "Public relations will never reach the status of a profession as long as people can get into the field and prosper without having completed a fairly rigorous course of study in the field."[4] Established professions require extended periods of training to learn the knowledge and skills needed to practice, plus the completion of qualifying or board exams; generally

EXHIBIT 5.6

Arthur W. Page Principles

Arthur W. Page practiced seven principles of public relations management as a means of implementing his philosophy.

Tell the truth. Let the public know what's happening and provide an accurate picture of the company's character, ideals and practices.

Prove it with action. Public perception of an organization is determined 90 percent by what it does and 10 percent by what it says.

Listen to the customer. To serve the company well, understand what the public wants and needs. Keep top decision makers and other employees informed about public reaction to company products, policies and practices.

Manage for tomorrow. Anticipate public reaction and eliminate practices that create difficulties. Generate goodwill.

Conduct public relations as if the whole company depends on it. Corporate relations is a management function. No corporate strategy should be implemented without considering its impact on the public. The public relations professional is a policymaker capable of handling a wide range of corporate communications activities.

Realize a company's true character is expressed by its people. The strongest opinions—good or bad—about a company are shaped by the words and deeds of its employees. As a result, every employee—active or retired—is involved with public relations. It is the responsibility of corporate communications to support each employee's capability and desire to be an honest, knowledgeable ambassador to customers, friends, shareowners and public officials.

Remain calm, patient and good-humored. Lay the groundwork for public relations miracles with consistent and reasoned attention to information and contacts. This may be difficult with today's contentious 24-hour news cycles and endless number of watchdog organizations. But when a crisis arises, remember, cool heads communicate best.

_____

Courtesy Arthur W. Page Society. From http://www.awpagesociety.com/site/about/page_principles (April 2008).

the more rigorous the training and the more complex the knowledge, the higher the professional status.

Because preparation is standardized and demanding, those entering professions go through similar initiations to the values and expectations of practice. Their common socialization experience not only standardizes the practice, but also encourages commitment to lifelong careers and strong bonds with colleagues. Because of the commitment, time, and effort invested in acquiring the knowledge and skill base, professionals value achievement in the intellectual aspects of their fields.[5]

Degree Programs

Degree programs in public relations have seen tremendous growth over the last half century, and the numbers of students majoring in public relations continues to grow each year.[6] The first university-level public relations course was offered in 1923 and taught by Edward L. Bernays, who had just written *Crystallizing Public Opinion*, a foundational book for the field. Bernays taught the one-semester-credit course for two years in the journalism department of New York University's School of Commerce, Accounts, and Finance. In the United States, instruction in public relations quickly grew. By 1946, 30 colleges offered 47 courses.[7] In 1956 the PRSA made the first comprehensive survey of public relations education and found that the number of colleges offering courses had tripled in a decade.[8] Another survey financed by PRSA in 1970 identified 303 institutions offering one or more courses and increasing scholarly research activity.[9] The 1981 Commission on Public Relations Education estimated that 10,000 students were taking public relations courses at some 300 institutions.[10] Now, there are respected public relations programs at most major universities in countries around the globe.

The most recent Commission on Public Relations Education recommended that undergraduate public relations programs contain the following core content areas of study:

1. *Theory, Origin, Principles, and Professional Practice of Public Relations*—nature and role of public relations, history and development of the field, theories and principles underlying the practice, and societal forces affecting the profession and its practice.

2. *Public Relations Ethics and Law*—codes of ethics and standards of practice in public relations and in other professions; ethical issues and trends toward greater organizational transparency; and legal and regulatory compliance issues such as privacy, defamation, copyright, workplace diversity, product liability, and financial disclosure.

3. *Public Relations Research, Measurement, and Performance Evaluation*—quantitative and qualitative research designs, processes, tools, and techniques such as public opinion polls, surveys, experiments; fact-finding and applied research; observation and performance measurement; social, communication, and employee audits; issue tracking; focus groups and interviews; use of external research services and consultants; media clipping and analysis; and historical research.

4. *Public Relations Planning and Management*—techniques and models related to setting long- and short-term goals and objectives; designing strategies and tactics; segmenting publics and designing effective messages; analyzing problems and opportunities; communicating with top management; developing budgets; contingency planning for crises and disasters; managing issues, developing timetables and calendars; and assigning authority and responsibility.

5. *Public Relations Writing and Production*—communication theory; concepts and models for mass, interpersonal, employee, and internal communication; new and emerging communication technologies; organizational communication and dynamics; communication with diverse audiences and across cultures; persuasion and propaganda; controlled versus uncontrolled communication; and feedback systems.[11]

The Commission on Public Relations Education advised that these key courses be supported by a public relations internship and coursework focusing on tactical implementation, such as a writing or campaigns class. Finally, they also recommended directed electives in an area of "supporting coursework" in another discipline. The Commission also recommended business management and marketing, sociology, public administration, political science, and international business courses.[12]

Continuing Education

Professions require continuing education to keep practitioners current in theory and skills. The Public Relations Society of America (PRSA) and the International Association of Business Communicators (IABC) now require or encourage members to earn continuing education units (CEUs) through professional development seminars and workshops.

Requiring practitioners to maintain current expertise and skills, and to perform public service, moves the field even closer to the more established professions. Continuing education also demonstrates commitment to the lifetime of learning needed to provide clients with current and competent service, part of any profession's implicit contract with society.

Research and the Body of Knowledge

Professional higher education introduces aspiring practitioners to the body of theory, research, and skills on which the profession is based. Continuing education then keeps practitioners up to date on research developments that expand the body of knowledge. Not everyone, however, accepts the concept of a body of knowledge and the value of basic research. Few practitioners subscribe to or read the field's research journals, as many believe that experience is enough to guide their activity.

A sure sign of advancement toward professional status, however, is the increasing demand for research and critical examination of the conventional wisdom guiding the practice. Public relations problems in business and industry, for example, are every bit as tough and complicated as the problems faced by engineering, finance, production, or distribution. Practitioners must approach them as methodically and as thoroughly prepared as engineers, economists, and other managers approach their own. Such a scientific approach requires understanding based on a body of knowledge developed through extensive research. Hence, the oft said, "Nothing is more practical than a good theory."

Support for Research

Because professions draw on a specialized body of knowledge developed through research, practitioners are obligated to support the advancement of professional knowledge. Several organizations support research in public relations, including the Institute for Public Relations (IPR), the International Association of Business Communicators (IABC), the Public Relations Society of America (PRSA), and the Plank Center for Leadership in Public Relations.

In 1956, the PRSA chartered the Foundation for Public Relations Research and Education to advance professionalism in the field by funding research, disseminating scholarly writings, and promoting professional education. In 1989, this foundation separated from PRSA and changed its name to the Institute for Public Relations (IPR). Today an independent nonprofit based at the University of Florida, the IPR's mission is to support "the science beneath the art of public relations" (http://www.instituteforpr.org). To that end, the IPR funds public relations research projects and publishes their results online, makes academic research accessible to practitioners, recognizes outstanding scholarship, and awards undergraduate and graduate scholarships. The IPR also supports the Commission on Public Relations Measurement and Evaluation, founded in 1998, and the International Public Relations Commission, founded in 2005. In another key effort to support public relations research, the IPR sponsors, with the University of Miami and other organizations, the annual International Public Relations Research Conference, which draws top scholars from around the world to present cutting-edge research that pushes the boundaries of our body of knowledge.

In 1984, the Research Foundation of the International Association of Business Communicators (IABC) awarded the largest-to-date single grant for public relations research. Estimated to total more than $400,000, its "Excellence in Public

Relations and Communication Management" project explored the function's contributions to the bottom line and identified factors contributing to organizational success. Professor James Grunig, now retired from the University of Maryland, led a team of researchers from the United States and the United Kingdom that produced comprehensive reviews of theory and research and also collected data from more than 200 organizations in the United States, Canada, and the United Kingdom. This decade-long research project produced several principles of excellence in public relations, which many scholars and practitioners consider to benchmark the body of knowledge in our field.[13] Another important research project funded by the IABC Research Foundation in the 1980s was the "Velvet Ghetto" study, which benchmarked how women in public relations at that time often failed to advance to managerial roles (see Chapter 2, page 44).[14]

In 1990, the Public Relations Society of America reorganized its efforts to support research, creating the PRSA Foundation as a philanthropic arm "committed to the development of programs to advance public relations research, education and scholarships, while encouraging contributions from those who stand to benefit from its advancement." Each year, the PRSA Foundation offers the Jackson Jackson and Wagner Behavioral Science Prize, which recognizes a researcher "whose scholarly work enhances the understanding of the concepts and theories that contribute to the effectiveness of public relations practice" (http://www.prsafoundation.org). In addition, the foundation offers grants to support research from public relations academics, graduate students, and practitioners.

A relative newcomer in the effort to support research, the Plank Center for Leadership in public relations was established in 2005 at the University of Alabama. With generous funding from public relations pioneer Betsy Plank, often called the "First Lady of Public Relations" in the United States (see Chapter 4, pages 108–109), the Center supports various awards and scholarships, educational programs, and grants in leadership studies related to public relations (http://www.plankcenter.ua.edu).

The Body of Knowledge

The body of knowledge serving the field, as documented in scholarly and trade publications, often reflects a gap between the immediate information needs of practitioners and the theory-building research conducted by scholars. For example, the content of PRSA's *Public Relations Tactics* and IABC's *Communication World* primarily reflect practitioners' interest in day-to-day problems and techniques related to designing and implementing programs and what one practitioner called "news you can use." The independent *Public Relations Quarterly* features commentaries and scholarly analyses, book reviews, and regular columnists of interest to practitioners. PRSA's slick *Public Relations Strategist* quarterly addresses issues and trends of interest to public relations professionals and—according to the magazine's promotional literature—their peers, meaning "the chief executive officer, marketing managers, and financial and human resources executives." *PRWeek* updates practitioners with industry news and features, primarily focusing on marketing support efforts of public relations firms and corporate departments.

On the other hand, the scholarly journals—*Public Relations Review* and *Journal of Public Relations Research*—report research on the social context of public relations, factors of effectiveness, and theory development related to the practice. The scholarly literature also mirrors classic concerns of other emerging professions: preoccupation and introspection during the search for collective identity, justification, and recognition.[15]

In 2007, in an effort to bridge the gap between public relations practitioners and scholars, PRSA relaunched *Public Relations Journal* as an online publication in which researchers must spell out the implications of their work for public relations practice (http://www.prsa.org/prjournal). Potential articles are reviewed by scholars for their research rigor, as well as by practitioners for their practical relevance in the day-to-day work of public relations professionals. But despite all these trade and scholarly publication outlets, a majority of public relations analyses and research reports do not get published and widely disseminated. Most of the research conducted by and for public relations departments and firms is considered proprietary and is therefore not shared beyond the sponsoring organization.

Ethical Foundations of Professionalism

One key characteristic of professional education in any field is an emphasis on professional ethics. Yet, even as the majority of professionals in a field do their work ethically, there are always those few who harm the profession's reputation through their lack of ethics. News reports tell of insurance fraud, unnecessary medical tests, or risky but unnecessary surgery. Lawyers are known for filing absurd claims to harass, intimidate, or frustrate the judicial process. Dentists, pharmacists, accountants, and other professional occupations also have their share of scandal. In public relations, practitioners have been convicted of defrauding their clients, among other crimes.[16]

Ideally, professional societies or associations engage in self-policing to deter malfeasance, to enforce the collective morality, and to ensure that professionals will engage in what one writer calls "right conduct."[17] Surely, the primary goal is to protect the clients of professional services. At the same time, however, self-policing in the professions protects the professional franchise and maintains public trust and support for professional privilege.

Professional Ethics

Ethical conduct suggests that actions are consistent with moral norms in a society. In professions, the application of moral values in practice is referred to as "applied ethics."[18] Established professions translate widely shared ideas of right conduct into codes of ethics. These statements of applied ethics guide professional practice and provide the basis for enforcement and sanctions. For instance, an attorney convicted of perjury or witness tampering can be disbarred and no longer be allowed to practice law.

Why this concern for professional ethics and enforcement of codes of conduct? The answers are both simple and complex. The simple answer is to protect those who entrust their well-being to the professional. The more complex answer also includes concerns about protecting the profession itself: professional privilege, status, and collegiality.

The Imperative of Trust

Clients' relationships with professionals differ from their relationships with other providers of skills and services. For example, if you go to a hospital emergency room, you will most likely have some degree of confidence that the physicians and nurses are qualified and capable and, furthermore, that it is their ethical duty to perform with your best interests in mind. It is unlikely that you will delay their performance while you check their transcripts to make sure they took the appropriate courses and passed all their exams. Contrast your relationship with these doctors and nurses with the one you establish with a mechanic when your car needs repair service.

The difference centers on the nature of *fiduciary relationships*. When you seek the services of a professional, you put yourself—not just your things—at risk. Your well-being is subject to the judgment and actions of the professional. Professional privilege maintains confidentiality when you must reveal aspects of your person and behavior that normally remain private. In other words, you trust the professional with information and access that often are withheld from even your closest friends and family. Often, you actually entrust yourself and your possessions to the professional. That is, you enter a fiduciary relationship, meaning the professional holds you, and possibly your possessions, in trust and is obliged to act in your best interest. This obligation differentiates the professional from other occupations.[19]

Professional Privilege

Professionals traditionally hold privileged positions in society because of the value and trust inherent in fiduciary relationships. Additionally, professionals do work that is seen as especially valuable, in part because of the preparation and practice needed to develop the required knowledge and skills. Not only must professionals invest a great deal of time and effort to acquire their knowledge and skills, but they must also commit themselves to uphold the profession by honoring its obligations and values. For example, the Hippocratic oath, written in 400 B.C., obligates physicians to work for the benefit, not harm, of patients.

When professionals violate fiduciary relationships or otherwise exploit clients, or when they perform substandard practice, they threaten not only their client's welfare but also that of their entire profession. Professional privilege rests on the foundation of public trust and confidence in both the professional's expertise and right conduct.

To protect both clients and their own privileged positions in society, professions establish codes of ethics and standards of practice. These codes often have the weight of law and the power of state sanctions. The argument for codes and rigorous enforcement rests on the belief that professional work involves special and valuable knowledge and skill essential to the public good and is so complex that only those deemed qualified may engage in practice.[20]

Social Responsibility

Professions must also fulfill expectations and moral obligations at the level of society. Commitment to serve society applies to both individual practitioners and the profession collectively. It means that right conduct takes into account the welfare of the larger society as the professional helps clients solve problems. It also means that associations of professionals exercise collective power as moral agents for the betterment of society. One example of a "guerrilla marketing stunt" that failed to consider its potential impact on society occurred in January 2007, when a promotional campaign for a television show planted "briefcases with blinking lights in locations around 10 cities nationwide." In Boston, panicked citizens reported the devices to authorities, who shut down highways and bridges thinking terrorists were involved.[21]

Ultimately, public relations is judged by its impact on society. Public relations' value to society is enhanced when (1) it promotes the free, ethical competition of ideas, information, and education in the marketplace of public opinion; (2) it reveals the sources and goals of participants in the debate; and (3) it enforces high standards of conduct. Value to society is diminished when (1) it suppresses or otherwise limits competition of ideas; (2) it hides or ascribes to others the true sources of public relations efforts; and (3) it leaves unchallenged incompetent or unethical practice.

Positives The major positives of socially responsible public relations include the following.

1. Public relations improves professional practice by codifying and enforcing ethical conduct and standards of performance.
2. Public relations improves the conduct of organizations by stressing the need for public approval.
3. Public relations serves the public interest by making all points of view articulate in the public forum.
4. Public relations serves our segmented, scattered society by using communication and mediation to replace misinformation with information, discord with rapport.
5. Public relations fulfills its social responsibility to promote human welfare by helping social systems adapt to changing needs and environments.

Much good can be credited to ethical public relations practice, and opportunities for serving the public interest abound. Public relations' benefits are apparent in the billions of dollars raised to construct buildings, endow professorships, and provide scholarships in universities; in campaigns to eradicate disease and substance abuse, reduce poverty, improve nutrition, and house the homeless; in the lessening of ethnic, racial, and religious discrimination and conflict; in responsive economic enterprises providing profit for investors, jobs for employees, and goods and services for consumers; and in greater understanding of global problems and relations. The potential good inherent in ethical, effective public relations is limitless. So is the potential for dysfunction.

Negatives Three major negatives can be attributed to the practice.

1. Public relations gains advantages for and promotes special interests, sometimes at the cost of the public well-being.
2. Publicity clutters already choked channels of communication with the debris of pseudo-events and phony phrases that confuse or influence rather than clarify.
3. Public relations sometimes corrodes our channels of communication with cynicism and credibility gaps.

Too often the thrust of public relations is to obfuscate and obscure rather than to clarify complex public issues. Robert Heilbroner recognized public relations as a social force and charged it with a major part "in the general debasement of communications from which we suffer." He said,

> No one can quarrel with the essential function that public relations fills as a purveyor of genuine ideas and information. No one denies that many public relations men, working for corporations as well as for colleges or causes, honestly communicate things which are worth communication. Nor can anyone absolve public relations for loading the communications channels with noise. We read the news and suspect that behind it lies

the "news release." We encounter the reputation and ascribe it to publicity. Worst of all, we no longer credit good behavior with good motives, but cheapen it to the level of "good public relations."[22]

This social aspect of right conduct reminds us that both individual practitioners and the profession as a whole are entrusted with the welfare of larger society as a condition on how they serve clients. This aspect of ethics is referred to as the profession's "social responsibility." When choosing such work and life, one also takes on the social responsibility of the profession, as well as its knowledge, skills, trust, and privileges.

In summary, to qualify as a profession, practitioners—both individually and collectively—must operate as moral agents in society. Ethical professional practice requires placing public service and social responsibility over personal gains, as well as the ability to engage in a rational analysis of ethical dilemmas. To facilitate and encourage ethical conduct, professional associations establish codes of ethics and standards of practice to which they hold their members accountable. Thus, before we can discuss accountability in public relations, we first must understand codes of ethics.

Codes of Ethics

A basic requirement for professions is adherence to a set of professional norms, usually referred to as codes of ethics. Many practitioners are making an earnest effort to act morally and to advise their organization or clients as an ethical conscience of the company. Unfortunately, others see codes of ethics as obstacles to be avoided, window dressing, or nice-sounding puffery.[23] Even more unfortunately, sometimes codes of ethics are indeed just that. For example, one practitioner pointed out that "Enron's code of conduct was as well-written as any I've seen in the industry. . . . And yet, as we all know, it was window dressing."[24]

Codes of ethics may be established by specific employers or by professional associations. Thus, attempts to advance the ethics in public relations are reflected in the number of codes of professional standards for the practice. In the United States, the principal code is that of the Public Relations Society of America. PRSA's first Code of Professional Standards was adopted in 1954, and the newest iteration of the code appeared in 2000 (see Exhibit 5.7).

PRSA members agree to conduct their professional lives in accordance with the code of ethics. Compliance is enforced in confidential proceedings, following complaints of code violations by a PRSA member, by a nonmember, or through media exposure. An eleven-member national Board of Ethics and Professional Standards investigates complaints and makes recommendations on whether or not to bar individuals from membership or to expel members found in violation of the code.

Enforcement by PRSA's Board of Ethics and Professional Standards has been uneven over the years. Few cases get referred to the ethics panel. Most cases that are referred are dismissed due to lack of evidence, settled to the satisfaction of all parties, or dropped because the charged member died or simply resigned. One of the quirks in the code is that it applies only to members.

Adoption of a code of ethics does not automatically bring morality to a calling. Generally, having a code reflects a sincere desire to raise standards of ethical practice and to provide criteria to guide and judge individual behavior. But a code without commitment, training, and enforcement means little in practice. Thus, many public relations firms hold regular training sessions on ethical issues, such as conflicts of interest among commitments to various clients, transparency about whom firms are representing, buying advertising in a news medium that runs a positive

EXHIBIT 5.7

PRSA Member Code of Ethics

Professional Values

Advocacy. We serve the public interest by acting as responsible advocates for those we represent. We provide a voice in the marketplace of ideas, facts, and viewpoints to aid informed public debate.

Honesty. We adhere to the highest standards of accuracy and truth in advancing the interests of those we represent and in communicating with the public.

Expertise. We acquire and responsibly use specialized knowledge and experience. We advance the profession through continued professional development, research, and education. We build mutual understanding, credibility, and relationships among a wide array of institutions and audiences.

Independence. We provide objective counsel to those we represent. We are accountable for our actions.

Loyalty. We are faithful to those we represent, while honoring our obligation to serve the public interest.

Fairness. We deal fairly with clients, employers, competitors, peers, vendors, the media, and the general public. We respect all opinions and support the right of free expression.

Core Principles

Free Flow of Information

- Preserve the integrity of the process of communication.
- Be honest and accurate in all communications.
- Act promptly to correct erroneous communications for which the practitioner is responsible
- Preserve the free flow of unprejudiced information when giving or receiving gifts by ensuring that gifts are nominal, legal, and infrequent.

Competition

- Follow ethical hiring practices designed to respect the free and open competition without deliberately undermining a competitor.
- Preserve intellectual property rights in the marketplace.

Disclosure of Information

- Be honest and accurate in all communications.
- Act promptly to correct erroneous communications for which the practitioner is responsible.
- Investigate the truthfulness and accuracy of information released on behalf of those represented.

- Reveal the sponsors for causes and interests represented.
- Disclose financial interests (such as stock ownership) in a client's organization.
- Avoid deceptive practices.

Safeguard Confidences

- Safeguard the confidences and privacy rights of present, former, and prospective clients and employees.
- Protect privileged, confidential, or insider information gained from a client or organization.
- Immediately advise an appropriate authority if a member discovers that confidential information is being divulged by an employee of a client company or organization.

Conflicts of Interest

- Act in the best interests of the client or employer, even subordinating the member's personal interests.
- Avoid actions and circumstances that may appear to compromise good business judgment or create a conflict between personal and professional interests.
- Disclose promptly any existing or potential conflict of interest to affected clients or organizations.
- Encourage clients and customers to determine if a conflict exists after notifying all affected parties.

Enhancing the Profession

- Acknowledge that there is an obligation to protect and enhance the profession.
- Keep informed and educated about practices in the profession to ensure ethical conduct.
- Actively pursue personal professional development.
- Decline representation of clients or organizations that urge or require actions contrary to this Code.
- Accurately define what public relations activities can accomplish.
- Counsel subordinates in proper decision making.
- Require that subordinates adhere to the ethical requirements of the Code.
- Report ethical violations, whether committed by PRSA members or not, to the appropriate authority.

Courtesy Public Relations Society of America. From http://www.prsa.org/aboutUs/ethics/preamble_en.html (April 2008).

article about a client, and disclosure that one is speaking on behalf of a paying client when one uses blogs or creates anonymous Internet postings to promote a product or idea. Some firms—like CarryOn Communication based in Los Angeles—make a particular point of ensuring that employees understand the firm will support them in making ethical choices. As the company's managing director explained, "[Employees] know that they're not going to lose their jobs because the client asked them to do [something unethical that] they didn't want to . . . . [They] don't have to be bullied by the client."[25]

Further demonstrating their commitment to ethical practice, some public relations firms—Epley Associates, Inc.; Ketchum Public Relations; and Manning, Selvage & Lee—require new employees to sign an agreement that obligates them to practice according to the PRSA code, even if they are not themselves members of PRSA. Such agreements are similar to the PRSA Member Code of Ethics Pledge, which all members must sign:

> I pledge:
>
> To conduct myself professionally, with truth, accuracy, fairness and responsibility to the public; to improve my individual competence and advance the knowledge and proficiency of the profession through continuing research and education; and to adhere to the articles of the Member Code of Ethics for the practice of public relations as adopted by the governing Assembly of the Public Relations Society of America.
>
>   I understand and accept that there is a consequence for misconduct, up to and including membership revocation.[26]

A Canadian counselor pointed out that "Unfortunately, these codes have little real value unless they are accepted in turn by the employers of practitioners and applied to the conduct of the business itself."[27] Longtime leader and crusader for higher ethics in public relations Frank Wylie admonished, "We shouldn't allow ourselves to accept the lowest common denominator of behavior—the negative and retrogressive 'it won't really hurt anyone' philosophy. We must aspire to a better level of ethics, and we must persevere to achieve that goal."[28]

Another common pitfall is the idea, "If it isn't illegal, then it must be all right." This mistaken logic abrogates the moral duty of public relations practitioners to attorneys.[29] Public relations practice is fraught with ethical dilemmas, and practitioners must be prepared to evaluate them using the professional codes of ethics. (See Exhibit 5.8 for examples.)

In public relations scholarship, the debate about codes of ethics is ongoing. Some scholars see codes as unenforceable and voluntary, whereas others see them as necessary baselines for the practice. Public relations ethicists argue that the PRSA code is unenforceable, full of contradictions, and neither professional nor useful to practitioners.[30] Even though codes of ethics are held up as evidence of professional status, enforcement poses little threat or is easily subverted when the subject of enforcement simply drops his or her membership.

Some argue that codes of ethics only "preach to the choir" and do not help where they are actually needed: with ethics training and moral reasoning or moral development.[31] Others argue that codes institutionalize consistent guidelines for public relations practice around the world.[32] Whether a code is used or not often matters less than *who is responsible for making ethical decisions*. One ethicist concluded: "The bottom-line of ethical decision making in our field will continue to rest in the laps of individual practitioners."[33] Even though the culture of the organization in which a practitioner works often exerts subtle, but powerful, influence over

EXHIBIT 5.8

Public Relations Ethics: Situations for Discussion

Refer to the IABC Code of Ethics in Exhibit 5.1 and the PRSA Code of Ethics in Exhibit 5.7 to resolve the following situations.

Situation 1: Your firm is one of several under consideration by a prospective client planning to introduce a new service. The company anticipates severe opposition from certain groups and politicians. You are given confidential information as to the service and the company's plans for you to use while developing your firm's proposal. The company awards the contract to a competing firm. Can you disclose the information to the company's opposition?

Situation 2: Your firm publishes a newsletter directed to brokerage houses. A corporate executive—one of your clients—asks you to help make the company better known among stockbrokers. You publish a highly optimistic forecast of the company's business prospects, leaving out some information about problems. You also fail to indicate your firm's relationship with the company. Were you under any obligation to disclose this relationship? Should you print a correction that includes all the information you have about the company?

Situation 3: Your employer directs you to set up a supposedly independent citizens' organization to demonstrate support for a new real estate development that requires planning commission approval. The new organization will be financed secretly by your company and a group of contractors who will participate in building the homes. Is there anything wrong with establishing this organization?

Situation 4: Your employer asks you to give a series of talks in communities served by your company. You are to discuss the new plant being built and its operations. You visit the plant before giving the speech prepared by your immediate supervisor. During the tour you learn that several claims in the speech are not true. Can you give the speech as originally written?

Based on an article written by the late Donald B. McCammond, APR, while he served as chairman of PRSA's Board of Ethics and Professional Standards. "Ethics: The Right Choice," *Public Relations Journal* 43, no. 2 (February 1987): 8–10. Used with permission of *Public Relations Journal*.

---

individual behavior (see Chapter 9), professionals are "held responsible for improving the institutions administering those services."[34]

In other words, public relations professionals must behave ethically as individuals, as well as encourage their organizations to support ethical behavior. It is imperative that ethical behavior be authentic, institutionalized, and reinforced through codes of ethics, training, and sanctions within organizations. Lockheed Martin's director of communications, Gail Rymer, explained that "PR needs to be leaders in [ethics] because we are the people out front dealing with the media, with consumers, with the public. If we do business ethically, everything else will follow."[35]

Accountability: Licensing and Accreditation

Accountability in a profession means that practitioners must face up to the consequences of their actions. As noted earlier, codes of ethics put forth by public relations associations are not always useful for holding unethical practitioners accountable, because these codes only apply to association members, rather than to all practitioners, and because associations often do not have power to enforce or penalize transgressions against their own codes.

Another possible means of holding practitioners accountable for their actions is occupational licensure—the permission granted by the state or government to engage in a specific occupation. Brazil has used this method since 1967 to regulate the public relations industry in that country.[36] Practitioners who behave unethically or otherwise inappropriately in the execution of their professional duties can be removed from the profession by having their license revoked, much like doctors or lawyers guilty of malpractice can have their licenses taken away.

Pioneer counselor Edward L. Bernays was among the first to advocate licensing of public relations practitioners. In 1953 he argued, "In the entire history of professions, licensing standards and criteria and finally codes of ethics in public conduct have been necessary . . . to exclude those who are not properly qualified."[37] The indefatigable Bernays was still thumping the same drum more than 30 years later:

> We must get the two words, public relations, defined by law with licensing and registration of practitioners, as is the case with lawyers, medical doctors and other professionals. Today the term 'public relations' is in the public domain and anyone—many without training, education, or ethical behavior—is welcome to use it to describe what he or she professes to do.[38]

Yet practitioners in the United States remain divided on the feasibility and desirability of licensing.

Legal Considerations

The issue of licensing, whereby the government regulates who can practice public relations and who cannot, generates many questions and concerns for practitioners around the world. In the Unites States, licensing raises three basic constitutional issues: (1) the right of freedom of expression, (2) the right of the states to regulate occupations, and (3) the right of individuals to pursue occupations without unjustified state interference. Licensure must be justified on the grounds that it is crucial to the well-being and preservation of society.

In the United States, legal objections are raised in the debate over licensing. One is the problem of demonstrating a compelling state interest; another is safeguarding the practitioner's freedom of expression as guaranteed by the First Amendment to the U.S. Constitution. The right of the states to regulate occupations is based on the Tenth Amendment, which reserves for states the powers not specifically delegated to federal government. Therefore, the two broad reasons generally given for public relations licensure—protection of society and professionalization of practitioners—must be considered carefully in the light of "compelling state interest."

The argument for a compelling need to regulate public relations is weak in the eyes of the courts. Although public relations—like any occupation—has the potential for abuse, its actions may be no more dangerous to society as a whole than would be those exercised directly by the organization for whom the practitioner might act. And although public relations practice may be controversial in some instances, the courts have argued in cases such as *Adams v. Tanner*, 244 U.S. 590 (1917), and *Baker v. Daly*, 15 F. Supp.2d 881, that controversy is not sufficient cause to regulate. In fact, U.S. courts tend to rule in favor of public relations and media efforts to foster "vigorous public debate" and to protect the "watchdog of government." The argument that licensing would protect society is directly refuted in law. The U.S. courts have consistently found that even abusive communication merits protection under the First Amendment. Other nations, such as Australia, Germany, the Netherlands, and England, also tend to encourage free and open debate in the media as a means of societal expression.

The second argument for licensure—that it would professionalize the practice—also gets short shrift in the law. It may be a powerful professional argument, but it has no legal basis. In no case have the courts suggested that because licensing would be beneficial, it would be justifiable. Licensing cannot be imposed simply for the benefit of those in an occupational group, either to raise standards or to fence out competition.

Advocates counter that licensing would be voluntary, thereby avoiding conflicts with the constitutionally protected rights. Likewise, organizations cannot be forced to hire only licensed practitioners. Instead, state licensing would limit only the use of the title "*licensed* public relations practitioner" label, not restrict the right of free expression. Advocates also point out that employers and clients would soon learn the value of hiring licensed professionals. On the whole, it appears that licensure will not soon provide a means of elevating and standardizing the preparation, ethics, and competence of practitioners.

Accreditation

In the absence of state licensing, accreditation is one means of encouraging professionalism and accountability in public relations. Although accreditation programs from various professional organizations have existed for decades, only in 1998 did several groups join together to form the Universal Accreditation Board (www .praccreditation.org). The accreditation examination in public relations involves a portfolio presentation and panel interview with three accredited practitioners, as well as a rigorous, four-hour, computer-based test. Successful candidates earn the right to put the professional designation of "APR" or "Accredited in Public Relations" after their name on all professional documents. To retain their accredited status, professionals also must earn 10 points every three years through education, professional development, and public service activities.

A 2005 salary survey indicated that "accredited public relations professionals earn 20 percent more than those who are not [accredited]—that is, on average, $102,031 versus $85,272." [39] Financial considerations aside, accreditation may offer other benefits, such as setting a standard for ethical practice and helping practitioners connect public relations efforts with organizational goals. Accreditation is also a way to reconnect with fundamental public relations skills and principles, to indicate that one is serious about the profession, and to advance in the field, because some firms will not promote employees beyond a certain level unless they are accredited.[40] Yet, the fact remains that many employers do not care whether the practitioners they hire are accredited, just as many do not care whether potential employees have any public relations education.

Advocates of accreditation have proposed consolidation of the many accreditation programs under a single certification program. The Universal Accreditation Board was a large step toward that goal. A single, well-publicized, and strongly enforced accreditation program backed by strong ethics codes is a significant advance toward professional status. Current practice, however, continues to be guided by weak voluntary codes and splintered efforts by different associations and societies. For example, the IABC continues its own accreditation program that leads to the "ABC" or "Accredited Business Communicator" designation. Absence of a single, credible accreditation or certification agency weakens claims of professionalism and high ethical standards, which in turn affects the ability of public relations to gain community recognition of its role in organizations and society.

Winning Acceptance and Stature

Today, public relations still falls short of public acceptance as a true profession. The field has a recommended, standardized educational curriculum, but even those who do not study public relations can enter the profession. Journals and books report a research-based body of knowledge, but many practitioners remain ignorant of basic

EXHIBIT 5.9

Public Relations in China: Rapid Growth and Great Potential

Ming Anxiang
Professor, Institute of Journalism & Communication
Chinese Academy of Social Sciences
Executive Vice-Chairman, China Public Relations Association
(CPRA)

With China's 2001 entrance into the World Trade Organization (WTO) and hosting of the 2008 Summer Olympics, organizations ranging from major corporations to different government agencies recognize the importance of professional public relations practice.

From Intrinsic Ancient Practice to Imported Modern Concept

Many Chinese scholars consider public relations to be a common phenomenon of human behavior that has been practiced in China since ancient times. For example, during China's Spring and Autumn Period (770–476 B.C.), as well as the Warring States Period (475–221 B.C.), Chinese politicians used sophisticated skills and techniques of persuasion and mediation to lobby among the states. On the other hand, Chinese scholars of public relations agree that, as a modern concept and practice in China, public relations was imported mainly from the United States in the form of public relations departments within international hotels such as the Hilton and the Sheraton in Guangzhou and Beijing after China opened to the outside world in the early 1980s.

In 1984, I led a group to study concepts of Western public relations and investigate the practice in foreign and local corporations on China's mainland; the results of this study were published on December 26, 1984, in one of the most important Chinese national newspapers, *Economic Daily*. In 1986, other researchers and I published the first Chinese text on public relations, using the U.S. "bible of public relations"—*Effective Public Relations*—as our number-one reference book. Since then, hundreds of books about public relations have been published in China, including printings of two editions of *Effective Public Relations* in Chinese.

Established in 1987 as the Public Relations Society of China (PRSC), the China Public Relations Association (CPRA) today has about 1,000 members. Founded in 1991, the China International Public Relations Association (CIPRA) now has more than 1,000 members. There are also hundreds of professional public relations associations across all levels of government, more than 10,000 public relations firms, and more than 100,000 public relations practitioners. Around 10,000 Chinese universities or colleges offer public relations courses.

From Confused Concept to Professional Practice

Until the mid-1990s, many corporate managers, public relations practitioners, and even some teachers—not to mention ordinary people—confused public relations with advertising and marketing, or defined it using the negative aspects of Chinese traditional "guanxi"—the use of personal connections to achieve an end. Today, however, there is greater recognition that media coverage, effective events execution, strategic planning, corporate positioning, issues management and crisis communication are important elements of professional public relations practice.

Beijing's bid to host the 2008 Olympic Games was the first time that Chinese central and municipal governments—in collaboration with Chinese and international public relations organizations and consultants—consciously and successfully employed modern public relations. Other successes followed, such as Shanghai's hosting of Asia Pacific Economic Cooperation (APEC) in 2002 and its successful 2003 bid to host Expo 2010.

After more than two decades of rapid economic growth, China has enormous media resources in place for modern public relations practice, including more than 2,000 newspapers (almost half of them dailies), 400 million TV sets, 500 million radio receivers, and 1.2 billion TV viewers and radio listeners. There are 162 million Internet users, 371 million fixed telephones, and 531 million mobile phones.

According to a recent survey by CIPRA, the average operating income in 2006 of the top 20 international and local PR firms on China's mainland was RMB ¥ 80.7 million, a 27 percent increase over last year. The estimated operating income of China's public relations service industry as a whole (excluding Taiwan as well as the Special Administrative Regions [SARs] of Hong Kong and Macao) was RMB ¥ 8 billion (more than USD$1 billion) in 2006, a 33 percent increase over the previous year. The future of public relations in China looks very bright.

principles grounded in theory. There are professional associations with codes of ethics, but the latter apply only to association members. There is no uniform process for holding practitioners accountable for their work, although accreditation is an important step in that direction. And although public relations provides an important and necessary service, giving voice to a variety of organizations in the marketplace of ideas, many people still view public relations as "spin-doctoring" or "media manipulation," in short, as a practice dedicated to special interests at the expense of the public interest.

Thus, the field continues to attract some practitioners who are more interested in manipulating opinions than in building true relationships with stakeholders. There is ample evidence that the function is not fully and widely understood, and confusion exists even among its practitioners and students.[41] In sum, the field still attracts many who cannot qualify *morally*, through a commitment to ethical practice, or *functionally*, through knowledge and expertise gained in specialized education. Fortunately, the ranks of those who meet these requirements are growing rapidly.

Professionalism and ethics go hand in hand. One without the other falls short of the ideal: Ethics without competence is meaningless; competence without ethics is directionless—and even dangerous. European scholar Hans-Martin Sass makes the point clearly:

> Ethics and expertise belong together; only together do they constitute true professionalism and provide a morally acceptable foundation for professional fiduciary services. The client . . . expects experienced expertise in making good technical and good moral judgments.[42]

Whether public relations qualifies as a profession ultimately will depend on the extent to which its practitioners use their unique positions as *rigorously professional* and *ethical counselors* to create genuine dialogue between organizations' managers and their publics.

Toward a Promising Future

More than a century ago a handful of pioneers staked claim to what is now called public relations. Moves to professionalize the practice and to accept the nobility of serving the public interest continue to strengthen educational programs, build the body of knowledge, and raise the standards of ethics and acceptable behavior. Consequently, public relations continues to progress professionally and to provide opportunities to achieve professional status to those with the necessary ethics, commitment, knowledge, and skills, all over the world (see Exhibit 5.9). Practitioners committed to high standards of ethics and professionalism will distinguish public relations practice from other skilled occupations and make it a calling serving the public interest.

Notes

[1] Alexander M. Cutler, "Doing Business Right," in *Building Trust—Leading CEOs Speak Out: How They Create It, Strengthen It, Sustain It* (New York: The Arthur W. Page Society, 2004), 70.

[2] John Kultgen, *Ethics and Professionalism* (Philadelphia: University of Pennsylvania Press, 1988), 371.

[3] "Russian PR Students Establish Association," *PR Tactics* (March 2004): 30.

[4] David Ferguson, "A Practitioner Looks at Public Relations Education," 1987 Vern C. Schranz Distinguished Lecture in Public Relations (Ball State University, Muncie, IN).

[5] Eliot Freidson, "Nourishing Professionalism," in *Ethics, Trust, and the Professions*, ed. Edmund D. Pellegrino, Robert M. Veatch, and John P. Langan, 193–220 (Washington, DC: Georgetown University Press, 1991).

[6] Keith F. Johnson and Billy I. Ross, "Advertising and Public Relations Education: A Five-Year Review." *Journalism & Mass Communication Educator*, Vol. 55, Issue 1 (Spring 2000): 66–72.

[7] Hale Nelson, "Training for Public Relations," *Public Relations Journal* 12, no. 9 (September 1956).

[8] Ray Eldon Hiebert, *Trends in Public Relations Education, 1964–1970* (New York: Foundation for Public Relations Research and Education, 1970). Also see "PR in Classroom," *Public Relations Journal* 26 (September 1970).

[9] Kenneth O. Smith, "Report of the 1981 Commission on Public Relations Education," *Public Relations Review* 8 (Summer 1982): 66–68.

[10] William P. Ehling and Betsy Plank, *Design for Undergraduate Public Relations Education* (Chicago: Commission on Undergraduate Public Relations Education, 1987).

[11] Judy VanSlyke Turk, ed. *The Professional Bond: Public Relations Education for the 21st Century*. (Report of the Commission on Public Relations Education, November 2006): 45–46.

[12] Ibid., 43–44.

[13] The IABC Excellence study research team included Professor David M. Dozier, San Diego State University; Professor William P. Ehling, Syracuse University; Professor James E. Grunig, Professor Larissa A. Grunig, University of Maryland; and public relations consultants Fred C. Repper (now deceased), and Jon White, Bedford, UK. Books reporting the project results include James E. Grunig, ed., *Excellence in Public Relations and Communication Management: Contributions to Effective Organizations* (Hillsdale, NJ: Lawrence Erlbaum Associates, 1992); David M. Dozier, *Manager's Guide to Excellence in Public Relations and Communication Management* (Mahwah, NJ: Lawrence Erlbaum Associates, 1995); and Larissa A. Grunig, James E. Grunig, and David M. Dozier, *Excellent Public Relations and Effective Organizations: A Study of Communication Management in Three Countries* (Mahwah, NJ: Lawrence Erlbaum Associates, 2002).

[14] Elizabeth L. Toth and Carolyn G. Cline (Eds.), *Beyond the Velvet Ghetto* (San Francisco: IABC Research Foundation, 1989).

[15] Glen M. Broom, Mark S. Cox, Elizabeth A. Krueger, and Carol M. Liebler, "The Gap between Professional and Research Agendas in Public Relations Journals," *Public Relations Research Annual* 1 (1989): 141–54.

[16] Randi Schmelzer, "Dowie Gets Prison Time," *PR Week* (February 5, 2007), 1.

[17] R. M. Veatch, "The Danger of Virtue," *Journal of Medicine and Philosophy* 13 (1988): 445–46.

[18] Baruch Brody, *Ethics and Its Applications* (New York: Harcourt Brace Jovanovich, 1983).

[19] Robert Sokolowski, "The Fiduciary Relationship and the Nature of Professions," in *Ethics, Trust, and the Professions: Philosophical and Cultural Aspects*, ed. Edmund D. Pellegrino, Robert M. Veatch, and John P. Langan, 23–43 (Washington, DC: Georgetown University Press, 1991).

[20] For more detailed discussion of the bases for professional privilege, see Freidson, "Nourishing Professionalism."

[21] Erica Iacono, "Turner Enlists PR Aid as Publicity Stunt Goes Awry," *PR Week* (February 5, 2007), 1.

[22] Robert Heilbroner, "Public Relations: The Invisible Sell," in Reo M. Christenson and Robert O. McWilliams, *Voice of the People*, 2d ed., 485 (New York: McGraw-Hill, 1967).

[23] Shannon A. Bowen and Robert L. Heath, "Issues Management, Systems, and Rhetoric: Exploring the Distinction Between Ethical and Legal Guidelines at Enron," *Journal of Public Affairs*, Vol. 5, Issue 2 (May 2005): 84–98.

[24] "Reconnecting Main Street to Wall Street: How Business Regains Credibility," *Journal: Page One Teleconferences 2001–2002* (August 13, 2002), 39, Arthur W. Page Society.

[25] Ted McKenna, "For Firm and Staff Alike, Ethics are Good Business," *PR Week* (May 21, 2007), 7.

[26] Public Relations Society of America, *The Blue Book* (New York: PRSA, 2004), B19. Also available at www.prsa.org/aboutUs/ethics/preamble_en.html.

[27] Leonard Knott, *Plain Talk about Public Relations* (Toronto: McClelland and Stewart, 1961), 3. Written by one who pioneered and shaped the practice in Canada.

[28] Frank Wylie, "Professional Ethics and Other Misconceptions." Address before the Publicity Club of Chicago, April 20, 1977.

[29] Bowen and Heath, "Issues Management, Systems, and Rhetoric."

[30] Michael Parkinson, "The PRSA Code of Professional Standards and Member Code of Ethics: Why They Are Neither Professional nor Ethical," *Public Relations Quarterly* 46, no. 3 (2001): 27–31; and Donald K. Wright, "Enforcement Dilemma: Voluntary Nature of Public Relations Codes," *Public Relations Review* 19, no. 1 (1993): 13–20.

[31] Larissa A. Grunig, "Toward the Philosophy of Public Relations," in *Rhetorical and Critical Approaches to Public Relations*, ed. Elizabeth. L. Toth and Robert L. Heath (Hillsdale, NJ: Lawrence Erlbaum Associates, 1992), 65–91.

[32] Kathy R. Fitzpatrick, "The Role of Public Relations in the Institutionalization of Ethics," *Public Relations Review* 22, no. 3 (1996): 249–58; and Dean Kruckeberg, "Universal

Ethics Code: Both Possible and Feasible," *Public Relations Review* 19, no. 1 (1993): 21–31.

[33] Donald K. Wright, "Ethics Research in Public Relations: An Overview," *Public Relations Review* 15, no. 2 (Summer 1989): 4.

[34] John Kultgen, *Ethics and Professionalism* (Philadelphia: University of Pennsylvania Press, 1988), 248.

[35] Alison Stateman, "The 2006 State of the Profession Opinion Survey: Exploring Perceptions, Issues, Trends, and Challenges," *PR Tactics* (March 2007), 24.

[36] Juan-Carlos Molleda and Andreia Athaydes, "Public Relations Licensing in Brazil: Evolution and the Views of Professionals," *Public Relations Review*, Vol. 29, Issue 3 (September 2003): 271–279.

[37] Edward L. Bernays, "Should Public Relations Counsel Be Licensed?" *Printers Ink* (December 25, 1953).

[38] Edward L. Bernays, "The Case for Licensing PR Practitioners," *Public Relations Quarterly* 28 (Spring 1983): 32.

[39] "Professional Accreditation: Does It Push the Needle?" *PRNews* (September 25, 2006), 1.

[40] Randi Schmelzer, "Accreditation Receives High Marks from Most Firms," *PR Week* (May 28, 2007), 7.

[41] Christopher Spicer, "Images of PR in the Print Media," *Journal of Public Relations Research* 5, no. 1 (1993): 47–61.

[42] Hans-Martin Sass, "Professional Organizations and Professional Ethics: A European View," in *Ethics, Trust, and the Professions*, ed. Edmund D. Pellegrino, Robert M. Veatch, and John P. Langan, 270–71 (Washington, DC: Georgetown University Press, 1991).

Additional Sources

Bivins, Thomas. *Mixed Media: Moral Distinctions in Advertising, Public Relations, and Journalism.* Mahwah, NJ: Lawrence Erlbaum, 2004. Examines the difference between morals and ethics.

Building Trust—Leading CEOs Speak Out: How They Create It, Strengthen It, Sustain It. New York: The Arthur W. Page Society, 2004.

Craig, David A., "The Case: Wal-Mart Public Relations in the Blogosphere," *Journal of Mass Media Ethics*, Vol. 22, Issue 2/3 (2007): 215–218. Examines case of bloggers hired by a public relations firm to disseminate positive information about Wal-Mart.

Curtin, Patricia A., and Lois A. Boynton. "Ethics in Public Relations: Theory and Practice." In *Handbook of Public Relations*, edited by Robert L. Heath, 411–22. Thousand Oaks, CA: Sage, 2001.

Fitzpatrick, Kathy R., and Carolyn Bronstein. *Ethics in Public Relations: Responsible Advocacy.* Thousand Oaks, CA: Sage, 2006.

Gale, Kendra, and Kristie Bunton, "Assessing the Impact of Ethics Instruction on Advertising and Public Relations Graduates," *Journalism & Mass Communication Educator*, Vol. 60, Issue 3 (Autumn 2005): 272–285.

Gower, Karla K. *Legal and Ethical Restraints on Public Relations.* Prospect Heights, IL: Waveland Press, 2003. A practical guide to common situations.

Huang, Yi-Hui. "Should a Public Relations Code of Ethics Be Enforced?" *Journal of Business Ethics* 31, no. 3 (2001): 259–70.

Larsson, Larsåke, "Public Trust in the PR Industry and Its Actors," *Journal of Communication Management*, Vol. 11, Issue 3 (2007): 222–234. Reports annual surveys of public opinion in Sweden with regards to the trustworthiness of public relations practitioners.

Stoker, Kevin, "Loyalty in Public Relations: When Does It Cross the Line Between Virtue and Vice?" *Journal of Mass Media Ethics*, Vol. 20, Issue 4 (2005): 269–287. Examines the concept of loyalty, one of the professional values in the PRSA Code of Ethics.

Wright, Donald K., ed. "Special Issue: Ethics in Public Relations." *Public Relations Review* 15, no. 2 (Summer 1989).

Legal Considerations

6

STUDY GUIDE   After studying Chapter 6, you should be able to:

▶ Summarize the basic structure of law in the United States and its relevance to the practice of public relations.

▶ Outline the major principles of the First Amendment pertaining to freedom of speech and press.

▶ Describe permissible federal regulation of First Amendment–protected expression in election communication, lobbying, communication

between labor and management, and financial public relations/investor relations.

▶ Outline constitutional protection and permissible federal regulation of copyright and trademark law.

▶ Define and explain the major provisions of libel law and privacy law relevant to public relations work.

Public relations practitioners do not operate in a societal vacuum. Accordingly, they need to know how to evaluate situations involving legal issues if they want to succeed in their jobs. This may come as a surprise to those who subscribe to the common misconceptions that law is incomprehensible to those who are not lawyers and that law is only narrowly applicable or relevant to public relations.

Clearly, this chapter alone cannot provide everything a practitioner needs to know. Instead, it presents a summary of major legal issues affecting public relations work. It is important to remember, however, that public relations practitioners *do not practice law*, but knowledge of the law will help them avoid legal pitfalls and work with their organizations' legal staff in situations that require collaboration.

It is the purpose of the First Amendment to preserve an uninhibited marketplace of ideas in which truth will ultimately prevail.
—*Supreme Court Justice Byron White*

What Is Law?

Fundamentally, **law** is that system of rules that governs society.

In the U.S. government structure, both the **executive and legislative branches make law,** whereas the **judicial branch interprets law** to ensure that it complies with existing statutes and ultimately the U.S. Constitution. The U.S. legal structure includes (1) federal laws—made by the president and the Congress, along with *regulations* produced by federal government agencies—as well as (2) state laws enacted by governors, legislatures, and administrative

This chapter was written in collaboration with **Martin Kruming**, J.D., San Diego, California. Kruming is a private practice lawyer, editor of *San Diego Lawyer* (San Diego County Bar Association journal), and journalism lecturer in the School of Journalism and Media Studies, San Diego State University. (The chapter includes work done for the ninth edition by Associate Professor Barbara K. Petersen, Ph.D., University of South Florida, Tampa.)

EXHIBIT 6.1

Law Sources Hierarchy

Constitutional law represents the basic legal charters of the federal and state governments, spelling out basic legal principles, rights, and authorities. The federal Constitution is the final arbiter of constitutional law, because no law in conflict with the U.S. Constitution can be enforced by the government.

Statutory law is that body of statutes and ordinances written and passed by legislative bodies at the federal, state, and local levels.

Administrative law includes rules and decisions of the numerous governmental agencies established by statute to write and enforce administrative rules in regulated areas and activities, such as communication (Federal Communications Commission), advertising and trade (Federal Trade Commission), public trading of stocks (Securities and Exchange Commission), and communication between labor and management (National Labor Relations Board).

Executive actions are made by the top elected government official at the federal level (president), state level (governor), city level (mayor), and so forth.

Common law in the United States derives from the accumulation of court rulings over time and is based on English common law. There is no federal common law, however, because each state has its own judicial traditions that are subject to changing conditions and values.

Law of equity is a part of common law, but there are no jury decisions, only rulings by judges.

agencies in each of the 50 states. The U.S. Constitution, the fundamental source of all law in the United States, provides a minimum set of rights to which any state constitution may add for its residents.

To illustrate the relationship between federal and state law, Exhibit 6.1 presents the sources of law in the United States organized in the hierarchy of their authority over one another. Knowing where a particular law originates as well as what other type of law can supersede it will help practitioners better evaluate the impact of any single part of the law on public relations work.

Federal and state courts are separated into criminal courts—to review laws against actions that harm "the state" (society in general), such as murder and theft—and civil courts, to resolve disputes between private individuals, such as defamation and privacy invasion. Most legal decisions affecting public relations work occur in civil court.

Public Relations and the First Amendment

Congress shall make no law respecting an establishment of religion, or prohibiting the free exercise thereof; or abridging the freedom of speech; or of the press; or the right of the people peaceably to assemble, and to petition the Government for a redress of grievances.

The power of the First Amendment to the U.S. Constitution is uniquely American. Adopted in 1791, it was not until early in the twentieth century that U.S. Supreme Court decisions began to reveal its power. [1]

There is no such category as "public relations speech" in the lexicon of the courts or First Amendment scholars. But that does not mean that the U.S. Supreme

Court has no knowledge of the field. In fact, Petersen and Lang's content analysis of U.S. Supreme Court decisions from 1766 through 1999 concluded that "over the years, the justices have had a much better understanding of the public relations practice than has the typical citizen"; that there is a strong association of public relations with the highly protected speech used in lobbying the government for redress of grievances; and that the justices know the similarities as well as differences between public relations and marketing.[2] Petersen and Lang found

> The strong First Amendment connection with public relations tactics such as publicity campaigns. . . . Even when the justices pointed out publicity practices they deemed unethical, they still emphasized the fact that constitutionally, such practices are protected alongside other contentious exchanges in the marketplace of ideas.[3]

Public relations practitioners who know when to invoke their clients' rights under the First Amendment to the U.S. Constitution, and when to caution clients that certain speech activities can be limited by the government, will not only better serve their clients but also provide higher quality public relations counsel.

As an example, under the Beef Promotion and Research Act, cattle producers were required to help fund generic beef ads even though some of them might have disagreed with the ads. The Livestock Marketing Association sued the Department of Agriculture claiming an infringement on their right of free speech. However, the U.S. Supreme Court ruled in 2005 that the advertising was government speech and therefore the government could not be sued.[4]

Public Relations Access to Mass Media

Public relations practitioners have a symbiotic relationship with journalists.[5] To achieve "free publicity" for their work, practitioners need access to the news media to disseminate the ideas, information, or causes of organizations and clients they represent. Journalists rely on information in press releases for articles about newsworthy events in their communities. However, First Amendment protection of press rights means that journalists can choose whether or not they will use a particular press release, or interview a particular person, or print letters to the editor. Even commercial speech gets this type of First Amendment protection, meaning mass media companies have the choice to publish or not publish a particular category of advertisements.

A new legal twist on the journalist/public relations practitioner relationship came about in the early 1990s because of a U.S. Supreme Court decision about the way journalists treat their sources of information. Drawing on a previously obscure part of the law, journalists must keep the promises they make to their sources; in this case, it was a public relations political consultant. If the source suffers harm because the promise was not kept, judges will apply principles of fundamental fairness to hold the journalists accountable.

This was obviously not good news for journalists, but it presents a potential boon to public relations practitioners and others who are misquoted or misunderstood by the media and suffer some personal harm to their reputations. Communications between attorneys and clients, doctors and patients, and priests and parishioners—among others—are privileged, meaning that the confidentiality of their conversations is protected. However, there is no such legal privilege for communications between public relations practitioners and their clients.

Print Media

Public relations practitioners need to know that First Amendment protection of press freedom means that no citizen has a guaranteed right to require the print media to publish specific information. In 1974, the U.S. Supreme Court declared unconstitutional a Florida statute requiring a newspaper to give a candidate for public office free space to reply to criticism. The Court said the state government should not be allowed to compel a newspaper to print something that its editors would not have chosen, because this would interfere with the editorial control that First Amendment press freedom protects. [6]

Broadcast Media

In an apparent contradiction of First Amendment principles, U.S. broadcast media have been subject to government regulation since their inception, providing several opportunities for public relations practitioners to gain access to this medium.

It is important to note that "broadcasting" means only *over-the-air signals* that are capable of being received by a television or radio with the use of a simple antenna and are thus accessible to people who do not have cable or satellite service. Federal government regulation of the technological aspects of broadcasting began early in the twentieth century under the jurisdiction of the Secretary of Commerce and Labor,[7] with the original justification for government oversight borrowed from the Interstate Commerce Commission—public interest, convenience, and necessity.[8] That standard continues today under the control of the Federal Communications Commission (FCC).

The FCC was created by the **Communications Act of 1934**, which gave the agency the power to make and enforce programming policies for broadcasting and issue, renew, or deny licenses to individual station operators. An early challenge to the FCC's power to regulate program content, on the grounds that this violated the First Amendment, was rejected by the U.S. Supreme Court, which ruled, ". . . the right of free speech does not include . . . the right to use the facilities of radio without a license."[9]

The basic justification for regulating broadcast content that the Supreme Court has accepted over the years is based on the 1934 congressional assertion that the U.S. airwaves are owned by the public and are a scarce resource that needs to be protected. Accordingly, those who receive licenses to use this limited resource must be trustees for all those who do not get to operate a broadcast station.

Cable Systems

Cable technology was developed in the late 1940s and applied to broadcasting by Community Antenna Television Systems (CATVs), whose primary purpose was to improve a community's reception of available but hard to receive over-the-air broadcast signals. The CATVs were not licensed by the FCC, but instead were awarded state and local government franchises to serve a particular geographic location. There was no specific cable legislation at that time, and the FCC had statutory authority only to regulate broadcasting. The U.S. Supreme Court ruled that cable regulation was necessary to ensure "fair, efficient, and equitable" broadcasting service, and that the FCC had the authority to do so because the Communications Act of 1934 required the commission to take action "reasonably ancillary" (connected) to its responsibility to regulate broadcasting.[10] Ultimately, the courts made it clear that cable operators have more First Amendment rights than do broadcasters, though cable still falls far short of the constitutional freedom of expression rights granted the print media.[11]

In 1984, Congress enacted the Cable Communication Policy Act giving the FCC jurisdictional authority over cable, deregulating rates and program choices, and providing benefits for cities and counties regarding franchise fees. This act also required cable applicants to set aside channels on its systems for public, educational, and governmental access. These public access channels also provide valuable tools for public relations practitioners who need to reach particular publics directly through a mass medium, such as giving citizens opportunities to observe city council meetings and other local government activities.

The Internet

The 1997 Supreme Court decision *Reno v. American Civil Liberties Union* made it clear that speech on the Internet was fully protected by the First Amendment.[12] The decision overturned the Communications Decency Act (CDA) of 1996, in which Congress tried to regulate indecency on the Internet by forbidding the operation of certain Web sites. The Court found that the law to contain unconstitutional content regulation was both vague and overbroad. The justices ultimately decided that the Internet was more like the traditional public forum, concluding, "As the most participatory form of mass speech yet developed, the Internet deserves the highest protection from government intrusion."[13] This gives public relations practitioners "free rein" to use the Internet to send unmediated communication to various constituencies.

The Children's Internet Protection Act (CIPA) of 2000 requires public schools and libraries that receive some federal money for Internet use to install "technology prevention measures," meaning filters, on computers used by those 17 or younger to block material that is obscene, or is child pornography, or is "harmful to minors." The Supreme Court upheld this legislation regulating Internet speech as constitutional. Libraries that do not comply risk losing their share of federal funding for computers in libraries.

Access to Government Information and Meetings

Access to government-controlled information is important to every citizen because the legal presumption in a democracy is that such accounts belong to the people, not the government. Thus, to encourage open government and an informed electorate, the federal government and all 50 states have statutes governing open records and meetings.

The structure of laws at the state level is similar to that of the federal statutes, but the extent of access varies considerably from state to state. Accordingly, this section will discuss only the U.S. federal laws, and public relations practitioners must study on their own the access laws of the particular state or nation in which they do business. A compilation of access laws for all 50 states is available online through the Marion Brechner Citizen Access Project (http//www.citizenaccess.org).

It might surprise some that the heaviest users of open access laws are not journalists. Various estimates over the years of *who* requests government records the most agree that it is business, with approximately one-half of all requests each year. Journalist requests make up only about one-quarter of the requests, with the remaining one-quarter made by the general citizenry. Indeed, the U.S. Supreme Court has ruled in several decisions that the media's right of access to government sources of information is only as extensive as that of the public.[14] Most important is the fact that the U.S. Supreme Court has ruled there is no First Amendment or other federal constitutional right of media access to government-controlled information.[15]

Public relations practitioners in government organizations must be fully informed about both federal and state open access legislation because they are responsible for responding appropriately to requests for access to information and meetings relevant to their particular agencies. Practitioners must also make sure that the officials with whom they work are aware of their obligations under both federal and state laws.

The federal **Freedom of Information Act (FOIA) of 1966** was a bipartisan effort in the U.S. Congress to promote full disclosure from the executive branch of government. It applies to "any executive department, military department, government corporation, government controlled corporation or other establishment in the executive branch of the federal government. . . , or any independent regulatory agency." The act applies only to records, meaning *tangible* items of information such as documents, but not to *intangible* information, meaning agency employees are not required to answer any questions. The **1996 Electronic Freedom of Information Act** added access to digital information (e.g., computer databases) held by those federal government agencies subject to the FOIA.

The federal FOIA specifies nine categories of exemptions from disclosure, giving government employees discretion to decide if they should provide access to items in these categories. The nine categories of exemptions are national security, agency rules and procedures, statutory exemptions, confidential business information, agency memoranda, personnel or medical, law enforcement investigations, banking reports, and information about oil and gas wells.[16]

Corporate Political Expression

First Amendment protection is considered to be an individual right in our democracy. However, a more complex question of great importance to public relations practitioners is whether the organizations they represent also have constitutional rights for "political speech." Historically, U.S. Supreme Court decisions have afforded corporations *some* of the same legal rights as individuals, but courts have also upheld many restrictions on corporate legal rights. The same is true in First Amendment jurisprudence. Corporations regularly engage in First Amendment protected "commercial speech" (i.e., advertising), but as noted previously, such speech is protected at a lower level than is "political speech."

In the precedent-setting decision defining corporate political speech rights, *First National Bank of Boston v. Bellotti*, the Supreme Court ruled that the First Amendment protects "political speech" regardless of who (individual or corporation) is speaking.[17] The case in question involved a Massachusetts statute prohibiting corporations from trying to influence a ballot item that did not relate directly to their businesses. First National Bank and four other companies wanted to buy advertising to oppose a referendum on establishing a state personal income tax.

In striking down the statute, the U.S. Supreme Court said that the inherent worth of speech that informs the public "does not depend upon the identity of its source, whether corporation, association, union, or individual."[18] The justices dismissed the argument that corporations were too powerful to be allowed participation in the marketplace of ideas. However, the Court did not say that corporate political speech rights were equal to individual rights. Rather, the Court said the proper question is not whether corporations have First Amendment rights but whether the state statute abridges free expression. The Court struck down the statute because it prohibited political expression that "was at the heart of the First

Amendment's protection." An advertisement expressing a view on a tax referendum, said the justices, "is the type of speech indispensable to decision making in a democracy, and this is no less true because the speech comes from a corporation rather than an individual."[19]

Two other important Supreme Court decisions regarding corporate speech rights dealt with energy utility companies that were subject to state regulations, and the matters in dispute were traditional public relations activities. For example, in 1980, the Court struck down a New York Public Service Commission ruling that barred regulated utilities from including messages about public issues in a customer's monthly bill mailing. Consolidated Edison Company had included in its bills a pamphlet advocating nuclear power as the best alternative for large-scale energy generation, but opponents of nuclear power did not want a government-regulated utility to participate in this political debate. The Court ruled that Consolidated Edison could publish its perspective on the issue precisely because its customers should have access to a variety of viewpoints on this controversial topic.[20]

Three years later in California, a special-interest group called The Utility Reform Network (TURN), which opposed large-scale energy generation, wanted to include its opinions and fund-raising appeals in monthly billing notices sent out by Pacific Gas & Electric Company to its customers. The High Court ruled that the company did not need to disseminate speech with which it did not agree. In other words, as it does for individuals, the First Amendment also protects the right of corporations *not* to speak.[21]

Even though the Supreme Court has recognized some speech rights for corporations, many instances remain in which such rights are restricted by government regulations that have been justified by the long-standing fear of the potential corrupting influence of business. Such regulations mean the government has demonstrated a *compelling interest* to regulate corporate political speech. Four major areas of federal legislation limiting corporate speech that are relevant to public relations include political elections, lobbying, labor organization communication with management, and securities trading.

The **Bipartisan Campaign Reform Act of 2002 (BCRA)**—commonly referred to as "McCain-Feingold"—regulates political election contributions. As Exhibit 6.2 shows, the three main provisions of the BCRA are "soft money" prohibitions (money donated to political parties for "party building" purposes), increases in contribution limits, and limits on "electioneering communications" (commercials that support or oppose a candidate without explicitly urging that candidate's election or defeat).

Lobbying

Because of the fear that lobbyists for groups could corrupt the lawmaking process, Congress passed several laws regulating lobbyists' attempts to influence legislation and regulations directly. Because lobbying has been one of the fastest growing specialties in public relations practice, these regulations are important to practitioners.

Lobbyists for organizations were first required to disclose their activities under Title III, the **Federal Regulation of Lobbying Act of 1946**.[22] Lobbyists were required to register with Congress, file quarterly financial statements detailing their lobbying expenses and sources of income, and report any articles or editorials the lobbyist had caused to be published to influence legislation. In 1953 and 1954 decisions, the U.S. Supreme Court narrowed the law so that it applied only to people and organizations whose main purpose was to influence legislation through "direct

EXHIBIT 6.2

Campaign Finance Reform

Bipartisan Campaign Reform Act (BCRA) of 2002 [in effect since November 6, 2002]

- **Soft Money Prohibition ["soft money" donated to political parties for "party building" purposes]**

Corporations and labor unions may not *contribute* or make *expenditures* on behalf of the national political party committees or Leadership PACs (set up by federal candidates and officeholders as nonprofit organizations raising funds for the campaigns of those particular federal candidates or officeholders).

Only individuals and federal PACs, subject to federal limits, may *contribute* to the national parties and Leadership PACs, though state parties may continue to give $25,000 under federal hard dollar limits to the national parties.

Corporations and labor unions may still *contribute* to state and local organizations as permitted under state law, although these organizations are limited in how they can use money raised outside the federal limits.

Members of Congress may no longer solicit funds for *soft money* accounts, including for their own Leadership PACs and for state and local parties.

Members of Congress may raise no more than $20,000 per individual donor for *voter registration and get-out-the-vote (GOTV) efforts* by 501(c) (general nonprofit) and Section 527 (nonprofit political) organizations, but they may continue to solicit funds for a nonprofit organization's *non*-political activities.

- **Post-BCRA Contribution Limits**

An individual may *contribute* no more than $2,000 per election (the primary and general count separately) to any one federal candidate (twice the previous limit).

The contribution limit to a federal candidate may be increased to $3,000 per election if the candidate's opponent spends a specified amount of his or her personal funds on the race.

An individual may *contribute* no more than $5,000 per calendar year to any one federal PAC (no change).

An individual may *contribute* no more than $25,000 per calendar year to a national political party committee.

An individual may *contribute* no more than $10,000/ calendar year to the federal account of a state political party.

During the two-year election cycle, an individual may *contribute* no more than $95,000, *of which*

No more than $37,500 may be contributed to federal candidates, and

No more than $57,500 may be contributed to national political parties and federal PACs, *of which* no more than $37,500 may be contributed to federal PACs, state/local party committees.

Contribution limits to candidates and national party committees are indexed for inflation while contribution limits to PACs are not.

- **Limits on "Electioneering Communications" ("issue ads") [commercials that support or oppose a candidate without explicitly urging that candidate's election or defeat]**

Radio or television advertising that refers to a *federal candidate* and is made within 60 days of a general election and within 30 days of a primary is an "electioneering communication."

Corporations, trade associations, and labor unions may only run "electioneering communications" through their PACs, using hard money contributions.

Any entity making "electioneering communications" must file a *disclosure report* with the FEC listing those who *gave* more than $1,000 for the communication and those who *received* more than $200 relative to the advertisement.

communication with members of Congress on pending or proposed federal legislation."[23] Concerns continued, however, that the lobbying legislation was inadequate to control all instances of potential corruption.

To more effectively regulate lobbying and protect public confidence in government, Congress enacted the **Lobbying Disclosure Act of 1995,** with updated definitions, disclosure requirements, and restrictions.[24]

A *lobbyist* is someone employed or retained by a client who makes more than one contact on behalf of that client and spends at least 20 percent of her/his time during a six-month period providing that service to the client.

A *lobbying firm* is an entity that has at least one person who was hired to represent someone other than her/his employer. The term also applies to self-employed individuals who represent other people or entities.

A *lobbying contact* is defined as a communication, either oral or written, on behalf of a client to a covered executive or legislative branch official regarding legislation, rules, regulations, grants, loans, permits, programs, or the nomination of anyone subject to Senate confirmation.[25]

Lobbying includes direct pressure on members of Congress through an "artificially stimulated letter writing campaign."[26] But lobbying does not include general public relations campaigns designed to sway public opinion and to activate constituents, thereby increasing pressure on legislators and government agencies. So-called "grassroots lobbying" is part of an organization's First Amendment right to express itself on public issues.[27] It is distinguished from the type of lobbying that requires registration by the fact that it is not "direct" contact with government officials. Nor does lobbying include testimony before a committee of Congress (because such testimony is invited by the legislators), or magazines and newspapers that in the ordinary course of business publish news items and editorials urging the passage or defeat of legislation.[28]

Lobbyists and lobbying firms must register with the Secretary of the Senate and the Clerk of the House and must report names, addresses, places of business, and phone numbers of their own business, their clients, and anyone else who contributes more than $10,000 in a six-month period to lobbying activities conducted by the registrant. In addition, all registrants must file reports twice a year, providing "good faith estimates" of the amounts paid by clients or spent on lobbying.[29] Lobbying laws also apply to nonprofit charitable, educational, and other tax-exempt organizations. Nonprofit organizations that engage in lobbying are prohibited from receiving federal grants, awards, contracts, and loans.

The law allows nonprofit charitable, educational, and other tax-exempt organizations to simply file a copy of their IRS Form 990, which reports lobbying expenditures, rather than requiring them to file a separate report. Nonprofit organizations that engage in lobbying are prohibited from receiving federal grants, awards, contracts, and loans.[30] The act exempts public officials, the working press, and those who provide testimony before congressional committees. It also excludes those whose total work for a client consists of less than 20 percent of the activities qualifying as lobbying.

All public relations practitioners working for "foreign principals" must register under the **Foreign Agents Registration Act of 1938** (FARA), whether or not they lobby U.S. government officials.[31] The law requires all persons who work as agents of foreign governments, companies, or political parties to register within 10 days with the U.S. Attorney General. Congress passed FARA because members believed "the spotlight of pitiless publicity will serve as a deterrent to the spread of pernicious propaganda. We feel that our people are entitled to know the sources of any such efforts, and the person or persons or agencies carrying on such work in the United States."[32]

The Lobbying Disclosure Act of 1995 also applies to the Foreign Agents Registration Act. The law defines a "foreign agent" as anyone in the United States who works as a "public relations counsel, publicity agent, information service employee, or political consultant," acting "at the order, request, or under the direction or control" of a "foreign principal," which could be a government, political party, business, or other organization.[33] Information materials produced by foreign agents are defined as any communication designed to influence the American public about political interests or policies of a foreign government; to influence U.S. foreign policy; to promote racial, religious, or social tensions; or to advocate the forceful overthrow of other Western Hemisphere countries.[34] Foreign agents must label lobbying materials as "political propaganda" being distributed by a registered foreign agent. They also must provide copies to the U.S. Attorney General.

Labor Relations

Public relations specialists whose work involves communication between unions and management must comply with the provisions of the **National Labor Relations Act of 1935** (Wagner Act) and the **Labor Management Relations Act of 1947** (Taft-Hartley Act). The 1935 statute created the independent, federal National Labor Relations Board (NLRB) to administer laws governing relations between unions and employers in the private sector. These prohibit both unions and management from engaging in unfair labor practices, primarily by forbidding coercive expression during political elections and also by forbidding management from interfering with labor's right to organize and to bargain collectively once a union is established.

Representative Elections

In 1941, the U.S. Supreme Court ruled that an employer could not be barred "from expressing its view on labor policies." The employer, the Court said, is free "to take any side it may choose" on a controversial labor issue as long as the employer does not restrain or coerce his employees.[35] This ruling has major implications for public relations work in internal communication.

Management does not engage in an unfair labor practice if it communicates to employees through speeches, talks, and letters to tell workers about the strike history of the union, the likely dues and assessments, and the merits of working for a company without a union. But management cannot threaten to fire or punish employees because of union activities, make promises of special benefits to influence votes, spy on union meetings, or call employees separately to discuss the union. Management also cannot urge employees individually to vote against the union.

Collective Bargaining

The Labor Management Relations Act of 1947 also requires companies and unions to enter negotiations with open minds and with a willingness to reach an agreement. Practitioners sometimes deal with management that is unwilling to meet or is unreasonably firm in its offers, or with unions that engage in unfair labor practices or make equally unreasonable demands. The NLRB regularly publishes fact sheets, press releases, and case summaries of the Board's actions on its Web site "News Room" (http://www.nlrb.gov).

Regulation of Publicly Owned Companies

Public relations specialists whose work involves communication by publicly owned companies must comply with the **Securities Act of 1933** and the **Securities Exchange Act of 1934,** which were enacted in response to the great stock market crash of 1929.

The 1933 act restricts corporate communication before and during the period that new securities offerings are being registered.[36] The Securities and Exchange Commission Act of 1934, which regulates trading of securities after their initial distribution, requires periodic reporting about a company.[37] The 1934 statute also created the independent, federal **Securities and Exchange Commission (SEC)** to enforce the newly passed securities laws, to promote stability in the markets, and most important of all, to protect investors. The **Investment Company Act of 1940** and the **Investment Advisers Act of 1940** regulate investment companies and advisers.[38] In addition, practitioners in this field are subject to the disclosure rules of the stock exchange that lists their company's stock.

Financial public relations, sometimes called "investor relations," requires public practitioners to also have in-depth knowledge of corporate finance, accounting, and law.[39] Under the SEC's "integrated disclosure system," corporations in which members of the public own shares must continuously provide information that affects the understanding of stockholders and investors about the financial position and prospectus of a company. Accordingly, practitioners must issue press releases, draft speeches, and write quarterly and annual reports to achieve the "adequate and accurate information" required under federal law. Public relations practitioners keep current with changes in securities regulations by regularly visiting the SEC's Web site (http://www.sec.gov).

Disclosure requirements take two forms—that mandated by statute, and that required to avoid fraud. Both the Securities Act of 1933 and the Securities and Exchange Act of 1934 mandate disclosure by "senior officials" of a corporation, defined as "any director, executive officer, investor relations or public relations officer, or other person with similar functions."[40]

The 1933 Securities Act requires filings with the Securities and Exchange Commission when securities are offered to the public. The law requires that companies provide "material information" about new security offerings so that investors can make purchasing decisions based on facts. Information is considered "material" if the information is likely to have a significant effect on securities prices or if it is likely to be considered important by a reasonable investor when making decisions to buy, hold, or sell shares. The Securities Act also requires a company to register its stock with the Securities and Exchange Commission and to provide detailed information about its financial history and prospects. Furthermore, it prohibits a company from offering to sell or to buy a security before the security is registered with the SEC.

The Private Securities Litigation Reform Act of 1995 made several reforms to the Securities Act of 1933 and the Securities Exchange Act of 1934, primarily in restricting such abusive litigation practices as routine filing of class action lawsuits against public companies following sharp drops in stock prices and abuse of the discovery process by plaintiffs' attorneys to extort settlements from publicly traded companies that might be willing to settle simply to avoid costly litigation.[41] Additionally, the act created a new "Safe Harbor for Forward-Looking Statements" to encourage dissemination of information without fear of litigation. Companies may be protected from liability for predictions about earnings and performance as long as such forecasts are tempered by "meaningful" cautionary statements telling investors why the projections might fail to come true.[42]

The Securities Exchange Act of 1934 mandates disclosure to ensure that investors have accurate information during the trading of securities. Section 13 of the act requires companies registered with the SEC to file quarterly, annual, and other reports with the SEC.

In addition to writing annual reports, public relations professionals are likely to have an important role in issuing proxy materials and organizing the company's annual meetings. Proxies are the statements companies must provide to tell share-holders when and where the annual meeting will be held and what business will be conducted. Stockholders who cannot attend the meeting can vote their shares by proxy—giving specific directions in writing about how their votes are to be cast. The financial relations practitioner may have a hand in writing management policy pro-posals, publishing them in the proxy statements, and organizing and conducting the annual meeting at which proposals will be voted upon. During proxy fights, in which a group of shareholders tries to sway votes to oppose management, the public rela-tions practitioner may help choose issues, plan appeals to stockholders, and buy ed-itorial advertising to promote management's positions.

Practitioners also participate in the "continuous disclosure" required by the se-curities laws and the rules of the stock exchanges. Companies must provide "current reports" within 15 days of any material change in the company such as shifts in the control of the company, acquisition or disposition of assets, bankruptcy or receiver-ship, changes in the company's certifying accountants and financial statements, and resignations of directors.

Simply issuing a press release may not be sufficient to fulfill the disclosure re-quirements. The American Stock Exchange disclosure policies, for example, require a company, "at a minimum," to release announcements of material information si-multaneously to the national business and financial news wire services, the national news wire services, the *New York Times*, the *Wall Street Journal, Moody's In-vestors Service,* and *Standard & Poor's Corporation*. Appropriate disclosure procedure depends on the size of a company and the dispersion of its stockholders, but the basic principle remains the same—public statements must be truthful.

Securities regulations also prohibit fraud in securities trading.[43] In order for there to be fraud in the buying and selling of securities, it is usually necessary to show that insiders are using nonpublic information to help them trade securities profitably or that insiders are "tipping" friends and clients with information that gives them an unfair advantage over the average investor. "Insiders" barred from tipping or trading on information not available to the public include corporate ex-ecutives, public relations personnel, outside accountants, lawyers, outside public re-lations counsel, and other professionals with access to corporate plans.

A combination of new federal legislation (**Sarbanes–Oxley Act of 2002**) and Securities and Exchange Commission and New York Stock Exchange rules imple-mented since November 2003 update SEC regulations and further ensure compliance. The new rules increase transparency and timeliness, hold top management account-able for financial reports, and make sure insiders cannot exercise unfair advantage in either their compensation or stock trading. Some of the most visible changes are:

1. Prohibit independent auditing firms from also engaging in business consulting assignments for the client. For example, at Enron, then-Arthur Andersen collected $27 million per year in consulting fees and $25 million per year in auditing fees. In effect, the same consulting company that helped set up business operations and investments would later examine these as "outside auditors." The conflict of interest was obvious, as was the case in dozens of other corporation–auditor relationships.[44]

2. Establish a Public Company Accounting Oversight Board to ensure uniform legal behavior by companies' outside auditors.

3. Require the quarterly and annual financial reports be signed by a company's chief executive officer and chief financial officer, who are then personally accountable for any mistakes in the reports.

4. Prohibit company loans to directors and officers.

5. Mandate statutory maximum sentences for eleven types of financial crimes. For example, conviction on a charge of mail fraud or shredding/changing records in order to obstruct a federal investigation each can mean 20 years in prison and a fine of $250,000.[45]

Copyright and Trademark Law

Legal protection for "intellectual property," so called because it refers to rights in intangible products of the mind or intellect, is found in the U.S. Constitution.[46] The two parts of this body of law most relevant for public relations work are copyright law and trademark law, both of which apply to creative works regardless of the medium in which they are expressed (print, broadcast, Internet).

Copyright

Copyright protection has the multiple goals of providing economic incentive for creative people to produce original work and for publishers to distribute those works, and also to preserve the public interest by guaranteeing that the right to use the works without restrictions will eventually be passed to all people.

The statutory definition of copyright is that it subsists in "original works of authorship fixed in any tangible medium of expression . . . from which they can be perceived, reproduced, or otherwise communicated."[47] Public ownership of creative material exists—that is, it is in the "public domain"—when a copyright has expired, when an author has never claimed copyright, and when the materials involved were produced by government employees on government-paid time.[48]

The eight categories of works that can be copyrighted are literary works (includes databases, computer programs); musical works; dramatic works, pantomimes and choreographic works; pictorial, graphic, and sculptural works; motion pictures and other audiovisual works; sound recordings; and architectural works created after 1990.

Copyright law requires public relations practitioners to check the copyright date of each work to determine which copyright act applies and then to calculate from that date when the work will pass into the "public domain," when it can be used without restriction (see Table 6.1).

A copyright exists automatically the moment a work is created and copyright notice is placed on the work. The copyright notice must have three elements: (1) the word "Copyright," or the abbreviation "Copr.," or the copyright symbol ©; (2) the year of first publication; and (3) the name of the copyright owner. An example of a correct copyright notice is "© 2009 by Jane Q. Citizen." However, formal registration is necessary for a copyright owner to bring suit for infringement, but that formal registration can be made after the infringement has occurred.[49]

Generally, copyright belongs to the "author" of the work. However, when an author publishes a book, at least some of the rights of ownership transfer to the publisher, who purchases the rights to reproduce and distribute the book. Depending on the terms of a publisher's contract, an author might be able to negotiate to retain some copyright rights, for example, adaptation rights.

Who owns the copyright when an individual completes a "work for hire" is a complex issue. The Copyright Act includes two different definitions of this term.[50] In the first, the phrase refers to works made by an employee as part of his/her employment, in which case copyright ownership belongs to the employer. The second definition refers to "a work specially ordered or commissioned," such as that produced

TABLE 6.1
Term of Copyright
Ownership

	Personal Authors	Corporate Authors, Works for Hire, and Anonymous Authors
1909 Copyright Act (original protection given 1909–1976)	75 years from date of copyright	75 years from date of copyright
1976 Copyright Act (original protection given 1977–present)	Lifetime + 70 years	95 years after first publication *or* 120 years from creation, whichever occurs first
Visual art created after 1990	Lifetime of artist only	*Not applicable*

by freelance writers, and who owns the copyright depends on whether the person creating the work is considered an "employee" of the organization that commissioned the work or an "independent contractor."

In a 1989 decision, the U.S. Supreme Court set the guidelines for something to be considered a freelancer's work product, rather than the intellectual property of the employer.[51] Essentially, if an independent contractor wants to keep control of the copyright for something produced as a "work for hire," the person must have a written agreement signed by all parties specifying this ownership.

The "Fair Use" Doctrine allows limited portions of an original work to be used or copied before falling into the public domain. (See Table 6.2 for guidelines.) The following factors determine whether someone may freely use the copyrighted material:

> The purpose and character of the use, including whether such use is of a commercial nature or is for nonprofit educational purposes; the nature of the copyrighted work; the amount and substantiality of the portion used in relation to the copyrighted work as a whole; and the effect of the use upon the potential market for or value of the copyrighted work.[52]

TABLE 6.2
Copyright Permission
Guidelines

Seek Copyright Permission If You:	Generally You Do Not Have to If You:
Reproduce an article from a magazine or newspaper and distribute it at a trade show or use as a promotional handout.	Reproduce excerpt from that article and send it to a few coworkers or friends, or an outside vendor.
E-mail the article to a large number of clients, potential clients, colleagues, etc.	E-mail excerpt from the article to a few clients, potential clients, colleagues, etc.
Put the entire article up on your Web site or Intranet.	Post excerpt from the article and link to the original source of the article.
Publish the entire article in an internal newsletter or blog.	Publish excerpt from the article in an internal newsletter or blog.

SOURCE: Adapted from "Copyright Compliance: What Every Media Relations Professional Needs to Know." Livingston, NJ: BurrellesLuce (February 14, 2008). Downloaded February 26, 2008, from www.burrellesluce.com/copyright1.

Infringement of copyright involves a violation of one or more of copyright "rights" of an owner. Legally, the copyright owner must show proof of three elements—originality of the work, probable access by the infringer, and substantial similarity of the unauthorized work to the original.[53] In a case involving file-sharing, the U.S. Supreme Court held that developers of this type of software may be liable for copyright infringement for the actions of their end users.[54]

Trademarks

The Lanham Act of 1946 and its amendments protect **trademarks**—words, names, and symbols used by companies to identify and distinguish their goods or services from those of another. A trademark can be a product brand name such as Kleenex. A **trade name,** on the other hand, identifies the commercial name of the producer. Thus, Kimberly-Clark Corporation, a trade name, manufactures Kleenex™ tissues, a trademark. A **service mark** differs from a trademark only in that it identifies a source of services, rather than a source of goods. For example, *ServiceMaster* is a registered name for a company that provides cleaning services.

Trademark rights are created through adoption and use of the mark on goods in trade. Trademark rights are protected under common law, but registration of a trademark with the U.S. Patent and Trademark Office creates presumptions of ownership that are important should infringement be claimed. Application for trademark registration can be filed before or after the mark is used in commerce, but usually after a commercial research firm has confirmed that no other party has registered the name, phrase, or logo intended as a trademark.

The formal trademark application process includes filing a written application form with a drawing of the trademark, paying the filing fee, and providing three examples of how the trademark is being used. The ® symbol or the phrase "Registered in U.S. Patent and Trademark Office" indicates a completed trademark registration. Often, the "TM" subscript is used when the registration is pending for a mark identifying a product, whereas "SM" is used to identify a service mark. The completed trademark registration lasts for 10 years, with 10-year renewals granted for as long as the mark is used in commerce.

Trademark enforcement is limited to situations that have a likelihood of confusion or deception or a probability that the public will be misled because of the use of confusingly similar marks. Also subject to enforcement are situations where the use of a trademark would tarnish or dilute its value. For example, the Coca-Cola Company formally objected to associations of its soft drinks with the abbreviation "coke" meaning cocaine.[55]

Owners of trademarks frequently run advertisements in such specialty publications as *Editor and Publisher* reminding journalists and public relations practitioners to use trademarks as adjectives, not as nouns or verbs, and to use capital letters when referring to their products. For example, people may use a Xerox photocopier, but they cannot "Xerox" a document. Penalties for infringement are specified in the federal trademark law. In a successful infringement suit, the trademark owner is allowed to recover *treble damages*. This means the persons who infringed the trademark must pay the owner three times the infringer's profits from using the mark or three times any damages sustained by the legal owner, *whichever is greater,* plus reasonable attorney's fees to cover the costs of the trademark action. Furthermore, whatever materials have been created using the infringed trademark "shall be delivered up and destroyed."[56]

Tort Law: Libel and Privacy Invasion

In civil law, a tort is anything considered legally wrong that one party does to harm another, such as defaming someone's reputation or invading someone's privacy. If a legal remedy is sought for that wrong, the party committing the offense becomes the "defendant," who is sued for monetary damages by the person who was harmed, or the "plaintiff."

Practitioners responsible for writing news releases, speeches, corporate reports, newsletters, brochures, and other communications need to be constantly aware that pictures and statements could defame someone or invade someone's privacy. Because tort law varies among the states, it is imperative for practitioners to know and understand the applicability of state law regarding libel or privacy lawsuits in their states. To begin that process, practitioners can make use of a free legal information service on the Internet at http://www.findlaw.com.

Libel

Libel is a legal action designed to compensate someone whose reputation or standing in the community has been wrongfully damaged, essentially the definition of **defamation.** Technically, libel is written defamation, whereas slander is spoken defamation, but that distinction became blurred after the advent of broadcasting. Accordingly, this section will use the term **libel** generically to discuss both types of legal actions.

Any individual, business, nonprofit organization (e.g., church), or unincorporated association (e.g., labor union) has the right to sue for libel. Government institutions cannot bring suit for criticism of their official conduct because it is a fundamental First Amendment right of citizens to criticize government action, but public officials may sue as individuals when they think their reputations have been subjected to defamatory statements that cause injury or actual damage.

Because defamation is a matter of personal reputation, individuals cannot sue on behalf of relatives or friends, and large groups of people cannot sue for damage to the group as a whole.[57]

Attorney Johnny Cochran, who led the "Dream Team" legal defense of O. J. Simpson, had sued a former client for defamation after he had picketed his offices and carried signs containing obscenities and insults. Cochran obtained a permanent injunction but upon Cochran's death, the U.S. Supreme Court ruled "the injunction amounts to an overly broad prior restraint upon speech, lacking plausible justification." The Court ruled in 2005 to vacate the injunction.[58]

Suing may not be the wisest course, however. Corporations and executives considering suits against critics whom they believe have defamed them must consider the public relations ramifications of their suits in the court of public opinion as well as their chances of winning in a court of law. Moreover, public practitioners must remind thin-skinned executives that the First Amendment protects caustic and even false comments that can arise from public discussion of controversial issues.

In all libel actions, the **plaintiff** (i.e., the person or institution whose reputation has been wrongfully harmed) has the **burden of proof** (responsibility) that libel exists. This means plaintiffs must demonstrate in court proceedings that they have evidence for all the elements of the libel suit according to a particular state's laws, or the courts will not allow the lawsuit to go forward. Though specific requirements for bringing a libel suit may differ among the states, there are key elements that are the same nationwide.

- **Defamation** is at the core of a libel lawsuit. It is defined as an intentional false communication . . . that injures another's reputation or good name.[59]

- **Publication** of defamatory communication means there must be a witness to the matter. For a nonmedia defendant (i.e., a public relations practitioner), only one person is necessary other than the plaintiff and defendant to see or hear the defamatory communication. For mass media defendants (i.e., newspaper, TV station), the publication burden is presumed to be met. Publication can occur in public relations brochures, newsletters, fiction, yard signs, interoffice memos, conversations, interviews, business letters, e-mail, and Web sites. Any individual who repeats the libelous statement can also be sued.

- **Identification** of the plaintiff in the defamatory communication is required in a libel lawsuit. Plaintiffs must prove that the defamatory language is "of or concerning" them, and that at least one reader/viewer/listener could identify them. Many libel cases involve naming the wrong person because of careless reporting or writing by the defendant. People can also be identified without actually being named (e.g., providing a job description).

- **Retraction** requested by the plaintiff is required in most states before any legal action can commence. Generally, the plaintiff must serve written notice to the defendant that communication contains the specific statements alleged to be defamatory. There is no obligation for the defendant to publish a retraction, but many state laws will reduce certain damage awards if retraction occurs.

- **Fault** is the most complex and most misunderstood element of a plaintiff's burden of proof in libel law. "Fault" is defined as "negligence; an error or defect of judgment or of conduct; any deviation from prudence, duty, or rectitude; any shortcoming, or neglect of care or performance resulting from inattention, incapacity, or perversity. . . ."[60] For purposes of the present discussion, fault can be considered to be some sort of "mistake." The degree of fault (how serious was the mistake) that must be proved depends on who is suing whom, as well as what is the content of the alleged defamation.

Before 1964, all that was required in state libel laws was whether the plaintiff could provide evidence of defamation, identification, and publication. There was no real defense available to persons being sued, and there were no different standards of proof based on who was the plaintiff or the defendant or what was the contentious issue. However, a 1964 landmark U.S. Supreme Court decision, *New York Times v. Sullivan*,[61] was the first of several High Court decisions that added First Amendment standards to libel law nationwide, so that **when the plaintiff is a public official,** criticism of official government action is not stifled.[62] The resulting categorization applies to both libel and privacy actions nationwide.

- *Public Official.* As defined by the Supreme Court these are government employees who have, or appear to the public to have, substantial responsibility for or decision-making control in governmental affairs.[63] Not all public employees are public officials, but only those who hold positions that invite greater public scrutiny (e.g., city tax assessor, county medical examiner, public university president).

- *Public Figure.* As defined by the Supreme Court in *Gertz v. Welch*,[64] these are people who invite attention and comment and thus voluntarily expose themselves to an increased risk of public scrutiny and possibly, to defamatory falsehoods.

- *Private Figures.* Also defined by the Supreme Court in *Gertz v. Welch*, private persons are more vulnerable to injury and can thus suffer more irreparable damage to their reputations. The *standard of proof required* for the lawsuit to go forward is set, because the Supreme Court ruled that public officials and public figures should have a higher standard than private persons.

- *Actual Malice.* In the *New York Times* decision, the Court ruled that the constitutional guarantees require a federal rule that prohibits a *public official* from recovering damages for a defamatory falsehood relating to his official conduct unless he proves that the statement was made with "actual malice." That means the false statement is made with knowledge that it was false or with reckless disregard to its truthfulness. In subsequent decisions, the Court ruled that this should also be the standard of proof for public figures.

- *Negligence.* In most states, the standard of proof for private figures is the failure to act as a reasonable person would in similar circumstances. Examples include the failure to verify statements, or to misinterpret court records.

In all libel actions, the **defendant** has a number of legal defenses available to counter a libel lawsuit.

- *Summary Judgment.* If a defendant believes that a plaintiff does not have sufficient evidence to meet a libel action's burden of proof, she or he can ask the judge before trial to issue a "summary judgment" in favor of the defendant.

- *Statute of Limitations.* There is a limited time in which a plaintiff can bring a lawsuit for libel, as established by each state's libel statute—ranging from one to three years.

- *Truth.* It is really quite difficult to have sufficient evidence for a defendant to prove in court that statements published about the plaintiff are *literally* true. Perhaps the defendant's witnesses refuse to testify, or perhaps either the witnesses or the defendant do not seem credible to the jury.

- *Privilege.* In tort law, privilege is defined as "the ability to act contrary to another individual's legal right without that individual having legal redress for the consequences of that act."[65] By definition, therefore, actions that are classified as privileged cannot be libelous. Two types of privilege are classified in libel law.

- *Opinion Defenses.* The definition of libel includes the requirement that there be a false statement of *fact,* with fact defined as something that is provably true or false. Pure opinion by definition is an expression of belief or judgment, not an assertion of fact. Traditionally, courts protected opinion from successful libel lawsuits because the punishment of opinion involves the punishment of ideas, and this is at the heart of First Amendment protection for speech and press freedom.

The standard of fault necessary for the plaintiff to prove to receive compensatory damages varies from state to state, with the average libel award close to $1 million. However, about 75 percent of jury awards nationwide end up being reduced or thrown out when the trial court's decision is appealed. Accordingly, public relations practitioners should pay close attention to appeals of court decisions in libel actions in their states to best understand how to model their own activities.

Privacy

Legal scholars divide the law of privacy into four different torts, each of which is "an interference with the right of the plaintiff . . . 'to be let alone.'"[66]

1. **Intrusion** upon the plaintiff's seclusion or solitude, or into her/his private affairs.
2. **Public disclosure** of embarrassing private facts about the plaintiff.

3. Publicity that places the plaintiff in a **false light** in the public eye.
4. **Appropriation** of the plaintiff's name or likeness for the advantage of the defendant.

In privacy legal actions, the defendant has a number of legal defenses available to counter an invasion of privacy lawsuit. These legal tactics are primarily used by media defendants, though they are also relevant for situations in which public relations practitioners are the defendants.

The U.S. Supreme Court has acknowledged that the publication of some private information is protected by the First Amendment. The Court has allowed publication of most truthful information that was lawfully obtained from official government records or court proceedings.[67] Common law provides broad protection for publication of newsworthy information, and that *newsworthiness outweighs privacy interests in stories of public interest involving public officials or public figures participating in public proceedings*. The newsworthiness defense also overrides the privacy interests of private individuals—the key is not the status of a person as a public or private figure, but rather, the status of an event as being newsworthy.

Public relations practitioners typically get **formal consent** for anything that is not obviously newsworthy, and especially for disclosing very private facts. The necessary components of such formal consent are that it be written, that it states the names of all parties to the agreement, that it states the scope and duration of the terms of the agreement, and that it provides for consideration or payment.[68] Practitioners must make sure the appropriate person signs the consent form, keeping in mind that minors and mentally disabled persons cannot give legal consent.

Other Legal Issues

Litigation Public Relations

The increased recognition of the impact of public opinion on organizations involved in legal controversies spawned the development of a specialty practice area in public relations called "litigation public relations." Those practicing litigation public relations help organizations address important interests that extend beyond legal concerns. For example, a company might be concerned about the effect of litigation on its shareholders and the price of its stock, on its employees and the company's effort to recruit, on its customers and the sale of its products, and on its relationships with industry partners such as distributors and suppliers and others. In short, because the damage caused outside the courtroom can be greater than that incurred in resolving the legal issues, it is in a company's best interest to seek both legal and public relations counsel.

Whether practitioners are knowledgeable or not, legal considerations often define, limit, and regulate modern public relations practice. Public relations practitioners themselves are not immune from lawsuits, and so the increasing need for malpractice insurance is understandable. Many consider it a cost of doing business in today's litigious society, similar to the malpractice insurance carried by lawyers, doctors, accountants and other professionals.

Contract Law

Legal issues also guide the business practices of public relations professionals. Contract law in particular calls for frequent specialized legal counsel. For example, when an advertising agency successfully sued when more than half the employees left with most of the agency's business in 1954, employment contracts began to routinely contain "noncompete" clauses. The principle established was that employees cannot use their employer's time and facilities to develop their own separate business. For example, Manning, Selvage & Lee sued three former executives in the Atlanta office—Glen Jackson, Boling Spalding, and Joseph Ledlie—who quit to start their own firm, Jackson Spalding Ledlie. The two firms settled out of court.[69]

In the majority of cases, however, the courts have not upheld noncompete clauses in employment contracts, favoring employees over their former employers seeking damages. Most contractual noncompete agreements apparently fail to meet one or more of three tests. First, they must be reasonable, being no broader than necessary to protect the legitimate business interests of the employer without placing undue restriction on an employee's ability to earn a living. Second, they must be supported by some monetary consideration, such as the offer of employment, raise, promotion, or continuing employment. Third, they must protect only the employer's legitimate business interests, such as unique products and services, trade secrets, and goodwill. Attempts to eliminate competition or other purposes not related to the three tests usually mean that courts will not uphold noncompete clauses.[70]

Postscript

It is important to remember that *public relations practitioners do not practice law*. However, sound knowledge of the law will help practitioners work in partnership with legal personnel so that lawyers do not try to do public relations work without the practitioner's involvement.

Notes

[1] See, e.g., the opposing positions taken by Justice Oliver Wendell Holmes regarding the kind of speech that would constitute a "clear and present danger" to the nation and therefore would not be protected by the First Amendment, as presented in two U.S. Supreme Court decisions regarding alleged violations by dissidents of the Espionage Act of 1917 and its 1918 Amendment. *Schenck v. U.S.*, 249 U.S. 47 (1919), and *Abrams v. U.S.*, 250 U.S. 616 (1919).

[2] Barbara K. Petersen and Allison R. Lang. "A 200-Year Analysis of U.S. Supreme Court Interpretations of Public Relations." A paper presented to the Law Division of the Association for Education in Journalism and Mass Communications (AEJMC) Southeast Colloquium, Chapel Hill, NC, March 16–18, 2000: 49, 50, 60.

[3] Ibid., 49.

[4] *Mike Johanns, Secretary of Agriculture, et al. v. Livestock Marketing Association; Nebraska Marketing Association, et al.*, 544 U.S. 550 (2005).

[5] In a recent study of how journalists view their relationships with public relations practitioners, the respondents estimated that 44 percent of the content of the U.S. news media is subsidized by practitioners. Lynne M. Sallot and Elizabeth A. Johnson, "War and Peace Between Journalists and Public Relations Practitioners: Working Together to Set, Frame and Build the Public Agenda 1991–2003." A paper presented to the Public Relations Division of the Association for Education in Journalism and Mass Communications (AEJMC), Annual Convention, Toronto, Canada, August 4–7, 2004.

[6] *Miami Herald Publishing Co. v. Tornillo,* 418 U.S. 241 (1974): 256.

[7] Wireless Ship Act of 1910, Radio Act of 1912, and Federal Radio Act of 1927.

[8] *Black's Law,* s.v. "public interest" and s.v. "public convenience and necessity." *Public interest* is "something in which the public, the community at large, has some pecuniary interests, or some interest by their legal rights or liabilities are affected." *Public convenience and necessity* is the common criterion used in public utility matters when a board or agency is faced with a petition for action at the request of the utility.

[9] *NBC v. FCC,* 319 U.S. 190, (1943).

[10] *U.S. v. Southwestern Cable Co.,* 392 U.S. 157 (1968).

[11] See, e.g., *Wilkinson v. Jones,* 800 F.2d 989, *aff'd without opinion,* 480 U.S. 926 (1987), in which the federal courts

declared the Utah Cable TV Programming Decency Act an overbroad restriction of cable system operators' First Amendment rights to choose programming. Likewise, provisions in the Cable TV Consumer Protection & Competition Act of 1992 to ban "indecency" on cable were found to violate the First Amendment (*Denver Area Educational Telecommunications Consortium, Inc. v. FCC*, 518 U.S. 727, 1996). Indecency is not the same as obscenity, which was declared outside the protection of the First Amendment in *Miller v. California*, 413 U.S. 15 (1973). Instead, the FCC defined indecency as something that depicts or describes sexual or excretory activities or organs in a patently offensive manner and that is offensive to the contemporary community standards for the broadcasting medium. The U.S. Supreme Court supported the FCC's ban on indecency on broadcasting in *FCC v. Pacifica Foundation*, 438 U.S. 726 (1978) because the agency believed broadcasting is a uniquely pervasive presence in the lives of all Americans, even in the privacy of the home, and because "broadcasting is uniquely accessible to children, even those too young to read." In *Wilkinson*, the Court ruled the opposite was true for cable.

[12] 521 U.S. 844 (1997).

[13] Ibid., 863.

[14] *Saxbe v. Washington Post Co.,* 417 U.S. 843 (1974); *Houchins v. KQED*, 438 U.S. 1 (1978); *Pell v. Procunier*, 417 U.S. 817 (1984).

[15] *Branzburg v. Hayes,* 408 U.S. 665 (1972).

[16] The U.S. Supreme Court reviewed FOIA's exemptions and found them constitutional since federal agencies are *not required* to withhold documents, though they *may* do so under their own discretion. *Chrysler Corp. v. Brown*, 441 U.S. 281 (1979)

[17] *First National Bank of Boston v. Bellotti,* 435 U.S. 765 (1978).

[18] Ibid., 777.

[19] Ibid., 776–777.

[20] *Consolidated Edison Co. of New York v. Public Service Commission of New York*, 447 U.S. 530, 535 (1980).

[21] *Pacific Gas & Electric Co. v. Public Utilities Commission of California*, 475 U.S. 1 (1986).

[22] 2 U.S.C. sec. 261 et seq. (1988).

[23] *U.S. v. Harris,* 347 U.S. 612, 620 (1954).

[24] The Senate passed S1060, 98-0, July 25, 1995. The House passed HR2564, 421-0, then cleared S1060, Nov. 29, 1995. President Clinton signed S1060 into law (PL 104-65), Dec. 19, 1995.

[25] "Lawmakers Enact Lobbying Reforms," Congressional Quarterly 1995 Almanac: 104th Congress (Washington, DC: Congressional Quarterly, 1996), sec. 1, 40.

[26] *U.S. v. Harris,* 347 U.S. 612, 620 (1954).

[27] *U.S. v. Rumely*, 345 U.S. 41, 47 (1953). However, if a powerful corporation uses a public relations campaign to do damage to another, it may run afoul of antitrust laws. In *Eastern Railroad Presidents Conference v. Noerr* (365 U.S. 127, 1961), the U.S. Supreme Court ruled that antitrust laws, which prohibit anticompetitive restraints of trade, do not bar corporations from joining with public relations counsel in a "no-holds-barred" public relations campaign to affect legislation. The Court said railroads could try through public opinion to kill legislation favored by truckers. However, the Court said there may be situations where a publicity campaign, "ostensibly directed toward influencing governmental action, is a mere sham to cover . . . an attempt to interfere directly with the business relationships of a competitor" (365 U.S. 127, 144, (1961).

[28] 2 U.S.C. sec. 267 (1988).

[29] "Lawmakers Enact Lobbying Reforms," *Congressional Quarterly 1995 Almanac: 104 Congress* (Washington, DC: Congressional Quarterly, 1996), sec. 1, 40.

[30] For example, the law precludes the most powerful lobbying organization in Washington, D.C.—the American Association of Retired Persons (AARP)—from receiving such government largess because it lobbies the federal government on Social Security, Medicare, taxes, and other issues important to its members.

[31] 22 U.S.C. sec 611 et seq. (1988). See original Act at 52 U.S. Statutes at Large, pp. 631–33, or PL 583, 8 June 1938.

[32] Congressman Emanuel Celler summarized legislators' motivations for passing FARA in 83 Cong. Rec. 7, 8022 (1938).

[33] 22 U.S.C. sec. 611 (c)(1)(iii) (1988).

[34] 22 U.S.C. secs. 611, 614 (1988).

[35] *National Labor Relations Board v. Virginia Electric & Power Co.,* 314 U.S. 469, 477 (1941).

[36] 15 U.S.C. sec. 77a et seq. (1988).

[37] 15 U.S.C. sec. 78a et seq. (1988).

[38] 15 U.S.C. sec. 80a-1 et seq. (1988) and 15 U.S.C. sec. 80b-1 et seq. (1988).

[39] See Barbara K. Petersen and Hugh J. Martin, "CEO Perceptions of Investor Relations as a Public Relations Function: An Exploratory Study." *Journal of Public Relations Research 8*(3) 1996, 173–209. CEO respondents in the study reported here did not perceive public relations knowledge as relevant for conducting effective investor relations programs, but instead, preferred to have them supervised and conducted by financial affairs executives and departments.

[40] 17 CFR 243.101(f).

[41] Private Securities Litigation Reform Act of 1995, Pub. L. No. 104-67, 109 Stat. 737 (1995).

[42] See Mary S. Diemer, "Reforms Change Landscape of Securities Litigation," *Litigation News* 21, no. 3 (March 1996): 1, 4.

[43] *Black's,* s.v. "fraud." Anything calculated to deceive, whether by a single act or combination, or by suppression of truth, or suggestion of what is false, whether it be by direct falsehood or innuendo, by speech or silence, word of mouth, or look or gesture. . . ." Bad faith" and "fraud" are synonymous, and also synonyms of dishonesty, infidelity, faithlessness, perfidy, unfairness, etc.

[44] Steve Liesman, Jonathan Weil, and Michael Schroeder, "Accounting Woes Spark Calls for Change—Suddenly, Everyone Has a Fix for a Tarnished Industry," *Wall Street Journal Europe,* February 7, 2002, 3.

[45] "Maximum Penalties for Crimes Under the Sarbanes-Oxley Act of 2002," *Journal Record* (Oklahoma City, Okla.), July 31, 2002, 1.

[46] U.S. Constitution, Article I, Section 8.

[47] 17 U.S.C., Sec. 102.

[48] 17 U.S.C., Sec. 101, 105.

[49] *Salinger v. Random House, Inc.,* 811 F.2d 90 (2d Cir. 1987), *cert. denied,* 484 U.S. 890 (1987). The author J. D. Salinger did not register his copyright of unpublished letters until after he became aware that they were scheduled to be published in a forthcoming book.

[50] *Supra note* 123.

[51] *Community for Creative Non-Violence v. Reid,* 476 U.S. 693 (1989).

[52] Copyright Act of 1976, 17 U.S.C., Sec. 107.

[53] 17 U.S.C., Sec. 506(a). Plagiarism and photocopying are two ways to show substantial similarity.

[54] *MGM Studios, Inc. v. Grokster, Ltd.,* 545 U.S. 913 (2005).

[55] In *Coca-Cola Co. v. Gemini Rising, Inc.,* 346 F. Supp. 1183 (E.D.N.Y. 1972), a federal court stopped a company from selling posters that were printed in the colors and type of script used by Coca Cola to identify its drinks, but that instead urged people to "enjoy cocaine."

[56] 15 U.S.C.S. Sec. 1117 (2004).

[57] According to the *Restatement (Second) of Torts,* 560, "liability exists when the group is so small that the matter can reasonably be understood to refer to an individual or the circumstances reasonably lead to the conclusion that there is a particular reference to one person."

[58] *Tory v. Cochran,* 544 U.S. 734 (2005).

[59] *Black's,* s.v. "defamation."

[60] *Black's,* s.v. "fault."

[61] *New York Times v. Sullivan,* 376 U.S. 255 (1964).

[62] In *New York Times* (Ibid at 270), the Court said that the United States has "a profound national commitment to the principle that debate on public issues should be uninhibited, robust, and wide-open, and that it may well include vehement, caustic, and sometimes unpleasantly sharp attacks on government and public officials."

[63] 383 U.S. 75 (1966).

[64] 418 U.S. 323 (1974).

[65] *Black's,* s.v. "privilege."

[66] William L. Prosser, *48 Calif. L. Rev.* 383 (1960)

[67] *Cox Broadcasting Corp. v. Cohn,* 420 U.S. 469 (1975).

[68] Traditionally, participants in public relations photographs or films are given a token "consideration" such as a one-dollar bill.

[69] "MS&L, JSL of Atlanta Settle Lawsuit," *Jack O'Dwyer's Newsletter* 30, no. 13 (March 26, 1997): 7.

[70] "Are Non-Compete Clauses Enforceable?" *Public Relations Tactics* 4, no. 12 (December 1997): 10.

Additional Sources

Black's Law Dictionary (8th ed). Garner, Byran A., ed. St. Paul, MN: West, 2004.

Fitzpatrick, Kathy R. "Public Relations and the Law: A Survey of Practitioners." *Public Relations Review,* 22, no. 1 (Spring 1996): 1–8.

Fitzpatrick, Kathy R., and Maureen Shubow Rubin. "Public Relations vs. Legal Strategies in Organizational Crisis Decisions." *Public Relations Review,* 21, no. 1 (Spring 1995): 21–33.

Gower, Karla K. *Legal and Ethical Restraints on Public Relations.* Prospect Heights, IL: Waveland Press, 2003.

Middleton, Kent R., and William E. Lee. *The Law of Public Communication,* 7th ed. Boston: Allyn & Bacon, 2008.

Roschwalb, Susanne A., and Richard A Stach. *Litigation Public Relations: Courting Public Opinion.* Littleton, CO: Fred B. Rothman, 1995. Judges, lawyers, and public relations specialists present cases to illustrate such public relations involvement as strategy, publicity, and media relations during legal processes.

Wren, Christopher G., and Jill Robinson Wren. *The Legal Research Manual: A Game Plan for Legal Research and Analysis.* Madison, WI: Legal Education, 1999. A user-friendly instruction guide to help the beginner conduct legal research.

Zelezny, John D. *Communications Law: Liberties, Restraints, and Modern Media,* 5th ed. Belmont, CA: Wadsworth, 2006.

Theoretical Underpinnings: Adjustment and Adaptation

7

STUDY GUIDE   After studying Chapter 7, you should be able to:

▶ Define a system and explain how systems theory is useful for explaining how concepts of adjustment and adaptation apply to public relations.

▶ Explain the differences between open and closed systems, using notions of reactive and proactive public relations.

▶ Define systems theory concepts—homeostasis, static and dynamic states, morphogenesis, negative and positive feedback, and cybernetics.

▶ Diagram, label, and explain the open systems model of public relations.

This chapter presents a theoretical model for public relations. Such a framework is necessary for understanding, organizing, and integrating the many activities and purposes of public relations. In addition, the professionalization of the field requires a body of knowledge grounded in theory.

As defined in Chapter 1, public relations deals with the *relationships* that organizations build and maintain with publics. These relationships are subjected to political, social, economic, and technological change pressures in an ever-changing environment. Careful assessment and tracking of these forces is essential if organizations are to steer a safe, steady course through uncharted territory in the increasingly global community. Why are Costco and Nordstrom strong retail organizations, and why are Montgomery Ward department stores and Woolworth's 400 five-and-dime stores gone from the scene? To paraphrase Darwin, it is not the powerful organizations that will survive, it is those able to adjust and adapt to a changing world.

The Ecological Approach

This was the first public relations book to suggest using a social systems perspective when in 1952 it introduced the concept of *ecology* to public relations. Borrowed from the life sciences, the term introduced students and practitioners to public relations as dealing with the *interdependence* of organizations and others in their environments. Viewed in this perspective, public relations' essential role is to help organizations adjust and adapt to changes in their environments.

Organizations depend on their environments for many things: charters to operate, personnel, funds to operate and grow, freedom to pursue missions, and too many others to list. To prosper and endure, all organizations must (1) accept the public responsibility imposed by an increasingly interdependent society; (2) communicate, despite multiplying barriers, with publics that are often distant and diverse; and (3) achieve integration into the communities that they

Our organizations are living systems, existing in a turbulent environment that constantly tests their abilities to survive . . . the forces of fierce global competition, dizzying technological advances, vacillating economies, and highly sophisticated and demanding customers.
—Carol Kinsey Goman[1]

The key ideas of system theory are amazingly coherent and consistent, and they have had a major impact on many fields, including communication.
—Stephen Littlejohn and Karen A. Foss[2]

were created to serve. The first point represents the source of public relations think-ing in management. The second point explains the growth of public relations as a specialized staff function. The third point states the goal of both management and the specialized practice.

In short, *the job of public relations is to help organizations adjust and adapt to their environments*. Public relations counselors monitor public opinion, social change, political movements, cultural shifts, technological developments, and even the natural environment. They then interpret these environmental factors and work with management to develop strategic plans of organizational change and responsiveness.

Years ago, author and futurist Alvin Toffler foresaw a more dynamic environ-ment emerging from what he called the "technology-driven Information Age." He said the changes would include "new family styles; changed ways of working, loving, and living; a new economy; new political conflicts; and beyond all this an altered consciousness as well."[3] The revolution in information and communication is not so much about technology as it is the social consequences of the new communication systems, according to communication scholar Frederick Williams: "Never before in history have so many people had so much information at their fingertips."[4]

Public relations specialists must anticipate and monitor such changes in an or-ganization's environment and help interpret them to management. The successful public relations counselor constantly surveys the environment, always trying to ex-tend vision further beyond the horizon and trying to increase both the size and the resolution of the picture of present and future realities. In essence, such attempts to see clearly and to anticipate are designed to give the organization time to plan, an opportunity to be *proactive* rather than simply *reactive* to environmental changes.

Specific changes and forces at play must be identified, studied, and understood for particular situations and organizational settings. At the same time, however, overriding basic changes drive other change pressures and produce consequences for all organizations, such as the tragic events of September 11, 2001, and the contin-uing efforts to rid the world of terrorism.

Tracking the Trends

This discussion of major trends and changes is far from complete, but it indicates how major forces affect organizations. It simply is not possible to build an omnibus list that would cover all situations. Instead, the role of public relations is to track and analyze the specific trends and forces at play in particular situations that affect their organizations.

For example, how will the growing animal rights movement affect an organiza-tion's ability to accomplish its mission? The *Los Angeles Times Magazine* reported that the Norfolk, Virginia–based animal rights group People for the Ethical Treatment of Animals (PETA) "has grown from humble origins to an 800-pound gorilla . . .the largest organization of its kind. . . ."[5] PETA's Web site claims 1.8 million "members and supporters" worldwide. Cosmetics manufacturers, medical research laboratories, meat packers, and even federal government agencies have had to factor the views of this new activist force into their decision making.

The animal rights movement forced Avon, Estée Lauder, Benetton, and Tonka Toy Company, among others, to stop testing products on rabbits, guinea pigs, and other animals. It forced the National Institutes of Health to close a research clinic that used animals in research and the Pentagon to halt wound tests on animals. Slaughterhouses in Texas and California were ordered shut after PETA pressure. PETA is also winning the battle for public opinion, as an overwhelming majority support animal rights and think it should be illegal to kill animals for fur or use animals in cosmetics research.

Education reform provides another example of change pressure: As more and more Americans enter the job market with deficient basic writing, math, and problem-solving skills, American industry slips further behind in the competitive global marketplace. At the same time, parents must cope with ever-increasing costs for postsecondary education. Then-RJR Nabisco Corporation (now split into separate tobacco and food companies—Altria Group, Philip Morris International, and Kraft Foods) matched employees' annual contributions to a tax-deferred educational savings plan. RJR Nabisco contributed up to $4,000 toward the costs of college, everything from a two-year college to an Ivy League university. Many other companies have "adopted" schools to help promote improvement in the educational system. Others have started their own basic education programs in an attempt to equip employees with basic job skills. For example, Shell Oil Company began the Shell Youth Training Academy to help prepare inner-city youth for college and jobs (see Chapter 15 and Figure 15.2).

Concern about global warming has reenergized the environmental movement. One survey found that 85 percent of U.S. consumers are willing to change brands or consumption habits in order to better serve society and the environment.[6] The "Tappening" campaign is an example of trying to pressure a corporation to change a product—bottled water. Organizers of the "Message in a Bottle" campaign asked consumers to insert environmental messages in one million water bottles to be delivered to the CEO of Coca-Cola Company, the owner of the Dasani bottled water brand.[7] Organizations and products that damage the environment face increased criticism, scrutiny, and threat of regulation.

Few organizations escape the change pressures brought on by the education crisis, the changing family, new technology, the "eco-movement," globalization, or other major issues and trends. (See Exhibit 7.1.)

EXHIBIT 7.1

Tracking Trends and Issues

Kerry Tucker, Chairman,
Nuffer, Smith, Tucker, Inc.,
San Diego, CA.

Picture yourself as the captain of the starship *Enterprise*.

You want to be sure that you have a radar system that can accurately anticipate fast-moving meteors and the location of nearby planets to avoid impending disasters.

While moving through space at warp speeds, you don't want to wait until these obstacles are in sight to adjust your course and keep the ship out of danger.

The same is true about an organization—your organization—facing a meteor shower of issues in today's rapidly changing environment.

As issues affecting your organization arise, it is best to have a radar system in place that will help management anticipate trends and issues likely to affect your organization and its publics, rather than waiting until it's too late to do anything except react defensively.

If you are in public relations, you must start being more systematic in the tracking and management of issues. If you don't, someone else in your organization will. It's a prerequisite for organizational survival.

Even the starship *Enterprise* would find it difficult to navigate through the turbulent issues environment most organizations face today.

Used with permission.

A Systems Perspective

This discussion of changes and their impact on organizations suggests a systems perspective for public relations. The systems perspective applies because mutually dependent relationships are established and maintained between organizations and their publics.

The concepts of adjustment and adaptation, as well as our definition of public relations, employ concepts and propositions from systems theory. For example, a university is part of a system composed of alumni, donors, neighbors, employers, high school counselors and teachers, and other universities in the area, to name but a few of the many publics. Even the simplest definition of a system—a set of interdependent parts—illustrates this perspective. However, an extended definition serves as the basis for applying systems theory to public relations: **A system is a set of interacting units that endures through time within an established boundary by responding and adjusting to change pressures from the environment to achieve and maintain goal states.**

In the case of public relations, the set of interacting units includes the organization and the stakeholders with which it has or will have relations. They are somehow mutually affected or involved. Unlike physical and biological systems, however, social systems are not especially dependent on the physical closeness of component parts. Rather, organization–public interactions define systems. In other words, an organization–publics system consists of an organization and the people involved with and affected by the organization, and vice versa. Whereas the organizational component in the system is relatively easy to define, publics are abstractions defined by the public relations manager applying the systems approach. In fact, different publics, and therefore a different system boundary, must be defined for each situation or problem.

This principle of systems theory can be illustrated by comparing a university's publics when the goal is recruiting students as opposed to when the goal is raising money for a new digital media center for the mass communication school. The student recruitment campaign might include college-bound high school students, their parents, high school counselors, students currently enrolled at the university, and alumni. Because the university tends to attract students from a particular region or segments of the population, program planners would have to identify the geographic and sociographic territory to be covered in the recruitment effort. In effect, each of these decisions defines the components and boundary of the system for the student recruitment program.

The capital campaign for the new digital media center at the same university, on the other hand, calls for a different definition of the organization–publics system. Program planners would determine what groups or entities are most interested in such a facility or most likely to benefit from its presence on campus. Surely the local media community would include potential donors. In cities far from the campus, corporate foundations that have historically funded innovative communication education programs would be included as prospective contributors. More specifically, digital media hardware and software companies that produce related products would be identified as a third public for this campaign. Not all alumni are likely contributors, but those who have succeeded in professions calling for digital media skills could be selected from the alumni list to make up a fourth public.

In both situations, definitions of the publics include those with whom the organization must establish and maintain enduring and mutually beneficial relationships. Most relationships, however, extend well beyond the period of such specific campaigns. Therefore, even though relationships must be defined specifically for each situation and program goal, they also must be viewed in the larger context of the university's overall public relations program.

Public relations efforts, then, are part of an organization's *purposive* and, therefore, *managed* behavior to achieve goals. For example, a fire that destroys a museum certainly has an impact on the museum's relationships with donors and others. Such an unplanned event, however, clearly is not part of the public relations program. On the other hand, the fund-raising campaign, groundbreaking ceremony, and grand opening gala are public relations responses to the situation created by the fire. These events are intended to establish or maintain relationships necessary for rebuilding the museum.

In some cases, goals can be achieved by simply maintaining existing relationships in the face of changing conditions. More likely, however, organizations must continually adjust their relationships with publics in response to an ever-changing social milieu. Because organization–publics systems exist in changing environments, they must be capable of adapting their goals and relationships to accommodate change pressures from their complex and dynamic settings. A classic case of adjustment and adaptation is the redirection of March of Dimes fund raising and research to birth defects after the polio vaccine eliminated the disease for which the organization–publics system was originally created.

Environmental Change Pressures

Systems theorists typically define the environment as anything that generates change pressures—information, energy, and matter inputs—on a system. Environmental inputs to organization–publics systems take many forms. For example, news coverage of the American Red Cross Katrina relief efforts headlined alleged abuses and missteps—missing rented cars, generators, computers, and donated supplies; and the use of convicted felons as volunteers in the disaster area. The charges certainly affected the charity's relationships with donors and local Red Cross chapters who had raised more than $2 billion to fund relief activities. And the impact was not limited to the American Red Cross, as all charities braced for a donor backlash, greater public scrutiny, and even government investigations of the high salaries and generous benefits packages of nonprofit organizations' executives.

Soon after the August 2005 Katrina disaster, the American Red Cross made headlines in the nation's news media: "Counterparts Excoriate Red Cross Katrina Effort" (the *Washington Post*), "Red Cross Shifting Internal Charges over Katrina Aid" (the *New York Times*), and "American Red Cross Troubles" (PBS *News Hour*). The perception of abuses by the charity continued well after Katrina when the ousted CEO, Marsha Evans, was awarded a severance package worth $780,000 by the organization's governing board. According to records released by the Senate Finance Committee, the Red Cross also had paid out about $2.8 million in severance, bonuses, and delayed compensation to five other Red Cross executives in the prior seven years.[8] Soon after, Iowa Senator Charles E. Grassley, chairman of the Senate Finance Committee, was on record threatening to rewrite or revoke the organization's charter if it did not thoroughly change its operations.[9]

In fact, the governance of the American Red Cross did get changed. On May 11, 2007, President George W. Bush signed into law H.R. 1681, the American National Red Cross Governance Modernization Act. This set of reforms resulted from a comprehensive assessment of Red Cross governance launched on February 24, 2006, by its board of governors. The Red Cross dealt with the threat to its survival as all functional systems do—by changing its structure and processes of governance and operations. In April 2008, the governing board appointed former AT&T executive Gail J. McGovern president and CEO of the storied but troubled charity.

Changes in educational levels and values of those entering the local workforce affect relationships between a local manufacturing company and labor unions, community groups, local government, and other employers in the area. Shifts in university students' majors—from history and classics to business and communication, for example—put stress on the rather rigidly structured faculty and resources at a university. Changes in the university in turn affect relationships with its various publics: prospective students, current students, faculty, alumni, trustees, donors, legislators, and prospective employers of graduating students. Relationships with other institutions of higher education will change as the universities compete for history majors and refer business students to each other's campuses.

Even "an insignificant leak" of radioactive water in a power utility's nuclear-generating reactor puts stress on a utility's relationships with regulators, antinuclear citizen groups, and the financial community. Media coverage of protest groups picketing tuna-canning companies because their fishing practices killed dolphins had almost immediate effects. Sales slumped, government scrutiny increased, children and parents alike erroneously accused the companies of killing "Flipper" for profit, and activists attached protest stickers to the product on grocery store shelves. Socially conscious investors sold tuna stock as prices plummeted.

These examples illustrate that change pressures on organization–publics systems come from many types of environmental sources. In turn, organization–publics relationships change in response to these environmental pressures. If they do not change, old relationships become dysfunctional because the organization acts and reacts in ways inappropriate to the new circumstances. If they are unmanaged and nonpurposive in their responses to environmental changes, systems tend to degenerate to maximum disorder, what systems theorists call "entropy." In social systems, this means that coordinated behavior to attain mutually beneficial goals is no longer possible. Simply put, systems break up. Public relations is charged with keeping organizational relationships in tune with the mutual interests and goals of organizations and their publics.

Subsystems and Suprasystems

To this point, a system has been defined as including the organization and its publics. Similarly, the organization is itself composed of a set of interacting units. From this perspective, the organization can also be viewed as a system. Because organizations exist in dynamic social settings, they must modify internal processes and restructure themselves in response to changing environments. In the absence of such adjustment and adaptation, organizations—just like any other social systems—become out of step with the world around them. As counselors to line management, the public relations staff is charged with keeping the organization sensitive to environmental changes, anticipating as well as reacting to change pressures.

Likewise, the organization–publics system can be part of a larger set of interacting units, thus viewed as a component of a higher-order social system. For example, the local American Red Cross–publics system is but one component of a community's charitable social services system. It is also only one subsystem in the national system of affiliates, which in turn is but one component of the nation's charitable social services system. Eventually, of course, one could project this series of ever-larger systems to the highest level on earth, the world. Many public relations specialists work at the level of the private enterprise system, health-care system, educational system, or international development system, to name but a few examples of regional, national, and international systems.

The systems perspective, then, suggests that the level and definition of the system must be appropriate to the concern or the problem situation. A component—a subsystem—in one system may be itself analyzed as a system in another context. Likewise, a system defined as such for one purpose may be but a component or subsystem in a higher-order suprasystem when the reason for the analysis changes.

For example, when reorganizing the local Red Cross' internal structure and programming, the organization is viewed as the system and the publics are viewed as parts of the environment. When the American Red Cross crisis made headlines, however, each of the 700 local Red Cross chapters and their publics became local systems subject to forces at play in the larger environmental context. Likewise, the national American Red Cross, made up of national headquarters in Washington, D.C., and all 700 local chapters, can be viewed as but one component in the national or international charity system. And the charities taken as a group are but one component in the larger set of tax-exempt, nonprofit organizations some have referred to as the "third sector" of the economy.

Systems theorist James G. Miller uses the concept of higher-order systems to define a system's environment:

> The immediate environment is the suprasystem minus the system itself. The entire environment includes this plus the suprasystem and systems at all higher levels which contain it. In order to survive, the system must interact with and adjust to its environment, the other parts of the suprasystem. These processes alter both the system and its environment. It is not surprising that characteristically living systems adapt to their environment and, in return, mold it. The result is that, after some period of interaction, each in some sense becomes a mirror of the other.[10]

Organizations as Systems

Miller says "living systems" engage in exchanges with their environments, producing changes in both the systems and their environments. Such imagery of exchange processes, structural change, and adaptation captures the essence of the public relations function in organizations. Specifically, public relations is part of what organization theorists call the *adaptive* subsystem, as distinct from the *production*, *supportive-disposal*, *maintenance*, and *managerial subsystems*.[11] The latter—the managerial subsystem—is defined as "direction, adjudication, and control" of the other subsystems.

Adaptive subsystems vary in their sensitivity to their environments, just as do the public relations functions within organizations. Some organizations actively monitor their social environments and make adjustments based on what is learned. An example is a church that begins offering single-parent counseling and social events in response to the growing number of households headed by divorced and single parents. On the other hand, given public concerns about health-care costs and excessive corporate profits, how sensitive was the pharmaceutical company that charged 100 times more for a drug when it was used to treat human cancer than when the same drug was sold as an antiparasitic agent for farm animals? Or how sensitive was Wal-Mart—the world's largest retailer—when it tried to recover medical expense benefits from a brain-injured former employee disabled in a highway collision with a tractor-trailer truck? Wal-Mart's lawsuit demanded all the remaining funds from a settlement with the trucker. The funds were in a trust to provide now-required 24-hour long-term care in a nursing home. (After much critical media attention, the company dropped the lawsuit and apologized to the family for "any additional stress" caused by the lawsuit. Too late, damage done.)

The amount of resources, time, and effort an organization devotes to monitoring its environment is determined by

1. The degree of conflict or competition with the external environment, typically related to the extent of involvement with and dependence on government
2. The degree of dependence on internal support and unity
3. The degree to which internal operations and the external environment are believed to be rationalized, that is, characterized by predictable uniformities and therefore subject to planned influence, and affecting all of these
4. The size and structure of the organization, its heterogeneity of membership and diversity of goals, its centralization of authority[12]

Organizational adjustment and adaptation to new conditions depend in part on how open organizations are to their environments. Differences in how sensitive organizations are to their environments provide a useful basis for further systems analysis of the public relations function.

Open and Closed Systems

All systems—mechanical, organic, and social—can be classified in terms of the nature and amount of interchange with their environments. The continuum ranges from closed systems on one extreme to open systems on the other. *Closed systems* have impermeable boundaries, so they cannot exchange matter, energy, or information with their environments. *Open systems,* on the other hand, exchange inputs and outputs through boundaries that are permeable. Of course, social systems cannot be completely closed or totally open, so they are either *relatively open* or *relatively closed.* The distinction is important.

The extent to which systems are closed indicates their insensitivity to their environments. Closed systems do not take in new matter, energy, or information. In short, closed systems do not adapt to external change and eventually disintegrate. On the other hand, open systems are responsive to environmental changes. Survival and growth of open systems depend on interchange with their environment. The most successful organizations are "especially adroit at continually responding to change of any sort in their environments."[13]

Open systems adjust and adapt to counteract or accommodate environmental variations. Inputs from the environment can be reactions to a system's own outputs or the result of changes independent of system outputs. In either case, inputs have an impact on system goal states, those conditions the system holds as "ideal" or "desired." Inputs can cause deviations from these system goal states. When that happens, feedback within a system causes adjustments in both system *structure* (what the system is) and *processes* (what the system does).

Adjustments are intended to reduce, maintain, or increase the deviations from goal states. The output of adjustments can be directed internally, externally, or both. Internal outputs change or maintain goal states. External outputs change or maintain environmental conditions. Which type of output should public relations stress? That depends, because "there is no property of an organization that is good in any absolute sense; all are relative to some given environment, or to some given set of

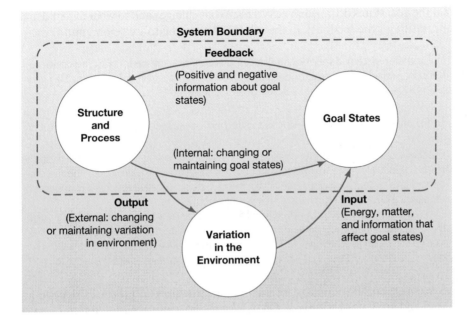

FIGURE 7.1

Open Systems Model

threats and disturbances, or to some given set of problems."[14] Will an open system adjust effectively? Not necessarily, for "there is maladjustment as well as adjustment; the function concept only poses the question of adequacy but does not settle it beforehand."[15] Figure 7.1 depicts the cyclical nature of an open system's interchange with its environment, assessment and reassessment, and adjustment and adaptation essential to the system maintenance and change.

The ultimate goal of systems, of course, is survival. But because they exist in changing environments, open systems must continually adjust to maintain states of equilibrium or balance. The conditions necessary for survival are represented as the "goal states" in the model. Paradoxically, open systems must continually change to remain the same, an enduring set of interacting units. To differentiate the *dynamic* states of relatively open systems from the *static states* of relatively closed systems, systems theorists refer to the changeable goal states as "homeostasis." This term is used "to avoid the static connotations of equilibrium and to bring out the dynamic, processual, potential-maintaining properties of basically unstable . . . systems."[16] The person credited with coining the term "homeostasis" said it "does not imply something set and immobile, as stagnation," but rather "a condition which may vary."[17]

Homeostasis, then, refers to goal states in Figure 7.1 that, although relatively stable, are subject to change as a result of system inputs. For example, your academic department attempts to maintain a certain student population, but that goal may change if the state reduces the university's budget. The student census goal could be increased if new resources are added, such as a newly endowed lectureship made possible by wealthy alumni. Yet another term is needed, however, to describe other changes characteristic of open systems that adjust and adapt to environmental inputs.

Whereas homeostasis represents the maintenance of dynamic system goal states, *morphogenesis* refers to changes in the structure and process element in the open systems model in Figure 7.1. For example, press and public criticism of how the state fair is being managed prompts the board of directors to appoint a new administrator and to reorganize the business office. In addition, the board revises procedures for awarding contracts. Notice that the structure and processes may change even if the goal states do not, and vice versa. What changes and to what extent depends on the nature of the feedback in the system. According to Littlejohn and Foss,

> In a complex system, a series of feedback loops connects the parts. . . . In a positive relationship, variables increase or decrease together. In a negative relationship, they vary inversely, so that as one increases, the other decreases.[18]

In an earlier edition of his book, Littlejohn explained feedback more fully:

> Feedback can be classified as positive or negative, depending on the way the system responds to it. *Negative feedback* is an error message indicating deviation, and the system adjusts by reducing or counteracting the deviation. Negative feedback is important for balance because it maintains a steady state.
>   A system can also respond by amplifying or maintaining deviation, in which case the feedback is *positive*. This kind of interaction is important to morphogenesis, or system growth such as learning . . . [T]he response to negative feedback is "cut back, slow down, discontinue." Response to positive feedback is "increase, maintain, keep going."[19]

Systems, then, adjust and adapt their goals, structures, or processes, depending on the kind and amount of feedback. Open systems not only generate different types of feedback as a result of system inputs, but they also exhibit more flexibility in adjusting to inputs. Choices among alternative adaptive strategies are made on the basis of which ones are most effective in helping the system maintain or achieve system goals in the context of environmental change pressures. As one systems theorist put it, "All systems are adaptive, and the real question is what they are adaptive to and to what extent."[20]

Cybernetics in Open Systems

Study of this input–output self-regulation process in systems is referred to as **cybernetics**. Buckley's general cybernetic model (Figure 7.2) portrays what tends to occur or would occur ("were it not for complicating factors") in goal-seeking systems. The model contains five elements: (1) goals established in a control center; (2) outputs related to the goals, which have an impact on the state of the system and its environment; (3) feedback to the control center on the effects of the output; (4) a comparison of the new system state with the goal state; and (5) control center determination of the need for corrective output.[21]

Cybernetic control systems used for navigation on space shuttles, airplanes, and ships are good examples. Early in the twentieth century, sailors called the first such

FIGURE 7.2

Cybernetics in Open Systems

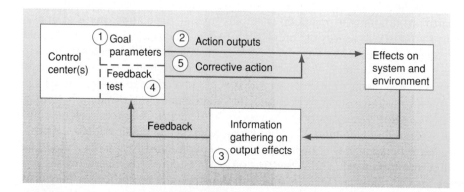

navigational system "iron mike." This relatively simple cybernetic system contained a course-setting device, a course indicator to signal discrepancies from the set course, and a mechanism for activating the rudder to make course corrections. Compare that with the sophisticated cybernetic control system on the most advanced and largest sailing ship, the 617-foot *Wind Surf:*

> A hard gust of wind generates pressure on the sails. The extent of that increase in pressure is measured, and the computer instructs the sheets, which are attached to the clews of the sails, to slacken off—spilling the incremental wind and thereby easing the tension. Simultaneously, the computer instructs the windward seawater ballast to ingest more water, while the leeward ballast chamber rushes to empty its supply of water. It is most terribly important to do all of this before the ship lists over more than two degrees, that being, [on *Wind Surf*] the limit of official toleration. If the ship were to heel more than two degrees, passengers might notice that they were under sail, and that isn't really the idea, on the world's largest sailboat. So that everything described above happens within approximately three seconds.[22]

Even a thermostat-furnace system can be described as a cybernetic system. Just as does *Wind Surf*, this system responds (corrective actions) to deviations from the goal state (the temperature set in the thermostat). Its responses, however, include either production or cessation of heat or cold: turning the furnace on or off, or turning the air conditioner on or off. Similarly, relatively simple organisms have limited options for dealing with variations in their environments. For example, the cuttlefish (Figure 7.3)—a squid-like marine mollusk—first takes on the appearance of whatever surface it is on. If the threat—whatever it is—persists, the cuttlefish indiscriminately squirts an inky fluid, apparently to conceal itself or to confuse whatever it senses is a threat in its surroundings. Change the threat—real or perceived—and the response is always the same.

Organizations, much like the *Wind Surf*, have so many more sophisticated options available for dealing with environmental change that they make turning on the heat and squirting ink seem primitive. Or do they? Some public relations programs are routine to the point that, regardless of the problem and without regard to environmental conditions, the response is to issue a press release and other communications "telling our story." In other words, the response is both predetermined and applied

FIGURE 7.3
Cuttlefish

indiscriminately from situation to situation, and it involves no real consideration of what the threat is—real or not. Maybe the cuttlefish's strategy for squirting ink at threats to conceal itself and confuse them is not unique to that species!

Simple mechanical cybernetic systems and living organisms typically do not change structurally except when pushed to the limit of system tolerance. For example, even though the cuttlefish makes cosmetic changes to blend in with its environment, structural change is not an option when it confronts threats in its surroundings. Social systems and complex cybernetic systems such as those used in "smart buildings," on the other hand, have the capacity to use cybernetic self-regulation to make relatively major structural changes. Such changes help the system to adapt to new environmental conditions or to modify outputs to change or neutralize the sources of change pressure. This interchange between systems and their environments is characteristic of open systems and makes *morphogenesis*—purposive changes in structure and process—possible. In short, open systems have the capacity to adjust and adapt to constantly changing environments.

Another quality of open systems becomes apparent when social systems are compared with mechanical systems and many living organisms. Simple, relatively closed systems react to outside events only if the input—change pressure—is sufficient to penetrate the system boundary. Complex, relatively open systems monitor, and in some cases actively probe, their environments to detect and predict changing conditions. In other words, sophisticated open systems *anticipate* changes in their environments and initiate corrective actions designed to counteract or neutralize the changes before they become major problems.

Public relations exhibits a similar range of closed versus open approaches. When public relations practitioners get together, they often use the terms *reactive* and *proactive* to describe programs. Reactive programs employ relatively closed systems approaches to program planning and management. Like the cuttlefish squirting ink, a reactive public relations program activates only when disturbed (see Figure 7.4). For example, *Forbes* magazine suggested that Weyerhaeuser's management philosophy "minimizes outside pressures for performance on management."

FIGURE 7.4

Reactive Public Relations

Courtesy Doug Marlette.

The magazine went on to say, "The company is structured in ways that once made sense but no longer do." According to *Forbes*, the longtime chairman's (the founder's great-grandson) "reaction to criticism was to shrug it off," hiring from the outside "was nearly taboo," and "change moves at a glacial pace in this company." Completing the picture of a relatively closed systems approach, the magazine reported that company representatives "declined to talk with *Forbes* for this story, citing among other things a negative story that ran 13 years ago. Like an elephant, Weyerhaeuser never forgets. Like an elephant, it is also hard to turn around."[23]

Similarly, apparently Amarillo city officials and the Texas beef industry were operating in the reactive mode of relatively closed systems when they dealt with Oprah Winfrey, the nation's top-rated talk show host. Oprah taped her show in Amarillo while defending herself in court against charges that she had defamed beef during a program about "mad cow disease." Texas cattlemen and the Texas Beef Group sued. Chamber of Commerce leaders decided not to welcome Oprah and forbade Chamber employees to attend tapings of the program. Oprah won in the court of law and in the court of public opinion, increasing her position as one of the most popular talk show hosts on television. City officials missed an opportunity to put the city in a good light when they refused to cooperate with Oprah's staff and did not provide information about Amarillo and its attractions. Typical of such closed systems' responses, the mayor was quoted afterward as saying, "I didn't realize the depth and breadth of Oprah's popularity."[24]

Exhibiting the telltale signs of a closed system, the beef industry responded with similar denial and "ink squirting" when confronted with the clear evidence that mad cow disease had been found in a cow slaughtered in the United States. Industry groups resisted calls for increased inspection and screening of cattle being slaughtered for human consumption and for an end to adding parts of slaughtered animals to cattle feed. The beef industry and its friends in government agencies have continued to resist increased inspections and tighter controls over the beef that enters the food system, even as other cases of mad cow disease were discovered. The routine, defensive tactics and resistance to structural change represent a system slow to adjust to environmental change. In other words, collectively, the beef industry appears to operate as a relatively closed system.

Proactive programs, in contrast, use their early-warning "radar" to gather information, to make adjustments, and to generate internal and external output to prevent or avoid problems. In contrast to the beef industry, pistachio growers in California responded as an open, self-correcting system when increased levels of mold were found in their product. The California Pistachio Commission—representing growers—asked the Agriculture Department to lower allowable levels of mold and to increase inspections, demonstrating an ability to take in new information and a willingness to change structure and process.

Sadly, even what appears to be a relatively open system in one aspect of its life may be vulnerable to environmental change in other areas. For example, the California Pistachio Commission was eliminated in 2007 by a vote led by the state's largest grower because the commission's $6 million advertising budget—to which all growers were obliged to contribute—promoted pistachios as a commodity. The large growers wanted instead to promote their own branded pistachios. According to the large grower's representative on the CPC marketing committee:

> We've been working with the CPC to try and change their perspective on things [with limited success]. . . . We know our [own] programs are effective in generating consumer interest and demand that goes well beyond the generic programs.[25]

Digital Research Technologies' announcement that it would no longer merely issue a steady stream of press releases is another example of an organization changing from a closed systems approach to public relations to a more open systems model. Instead of indiscriminately squirting ink like a cuttlefish, the computer software company adopted a proactive open systems approach. To that end Digital Research not only retained a public relations firm but also added the firm's head to its board of directors. The first step in the new approach was a series of strategic planning sessions—a proactive response.

Similarly, even a power utility, long thought of as the corporate equivalent of an elephant, can behave as a proactive open system. For example, while other utilities were fighting acid rain regulations and legislation, Minneapolis-based Northern States Power Company had already factored pollution control and reduction into operations. "Their policy is to exceed every environmental requirement that's placed on them," according to a Minnesota pollution-control agency program chief. Northern States, for example, to comply with new emission regulations, started buying low-sulfur Western coal years before it needed to. By doing so it locked in prices and transportation costs well into the twenty-first century. Meanwhile, other Midwest utilities continued to burn the cheaper, high-sulfur Midwestern and Eastern coals. As a result, these coal-burning utilities paid premium prices for the cleaner-burning Western coal. Northern States also installed scrubbers to clean sulfur from smoke and gases emerging from its furnaces and continued to improve their efficiency. Utilities that waited paid more than five times as much for scrubbers. The company's president and chief executive took the long view: "You have to be environmentally responsible to have a hope for success or longevity."[26] He could have added "environmentally *responsive*."

Open Systems Model of Public Relations

Output of a steady stream of press releases and other traditional reactive public relations responses clearly is suggestive of closed systems thinking. This all-too-common approach to public relations is apparently based on several assumptions: (1) that the purpose of public relations is limited to effecting changes in the environment, (2) that persuasive communication can make those changes happen, (3) that message placements in the media are all powerful, and more mistakenly, (4) that organizations do not need to change themselves in order to solve public relations problems. Such thinking reminds one of the cuttlefish and furnace thermostat systems. On the other hand, an open systems approach casts public relations in the role of bringing about mutual changes in both environments and organizations as a result of environmental inputs.

Bell and Bell referred to the reactive approach to public relations as *functionary* and the open systems appraoch as *functional*. In their view, the functionary role is similar to a closed systems approach:

> Public relations functionaries attempt to preserve and promote a favorable image of the organization in the community on the hypothesis that if the organization is "liked" the public will continue to absorb the organization's outputs. Such functionaries are only concerned with supplying information about the organization to the environment and not with supplying information to the organization about the environment. Because functionaries do not supply feedback information, they do not function in decision-making or even in advisory roles in relation to environmental concerns. Therefore, *they have little to say about **what** is said; they are mainly concerned with **how** things are said.*[27]

In this approach to public relations, the emphasis is on maintaining the status quo within the organization while effecting change in the organization's publics. The goal of building and maintaining relations between the organization and its publics is to bring the publics into line with the organization's plans.

In contrast, a functional view of public relations calls for an open systems approach, changing both the organization and the environment. Relations between the organization and its publics are maintained or changed on the basis of reciprocal output–feedback adjustment. In the functional approach:

> [Public relations] has the potential to act in an advisory capacity and to have impact on decision-making. This potential in turn leads to some control over its own domain in

EXHIBIT 7.2

Adjustment and Adaptation—"Ma Bell" Style

Before government and media turned their attention toward Microsoft's alleged domination of the software industry, maybe no organizational change received as much attention as did the court-ordered divestiture of the Bell System. On January 1, 1984, the then-107-year-old American Telephone and Telegraph split into eight separate companies: AT&T and seven regional companies. The old AT&T had been the world's largest company, secure in its position as a virtual monopoly and employer of almost a million "telephone people." It began with the famous words of Alexander Graham Bell, "Mr. Watson, come here. I want to see you." Its continuing transformation stands as an extreme example of system adjustment and adaptation to a changed environment.

Even during the long court fight against divestiture, AT&T was planning a new structure to respond to the new legal, social, economic, and technological environments. AT&T's chairman had decided that the fight would have gone on for years with little hope of avoiding the inevitable breakup. When it happened, advertisements announced, "We've been working to make the biggest change in our lives a small change in yours."

The response should have been anticipated: Theodore N. Vail, twice chairman of AT&T—1878 to 1887 and 1907 to 1920—pioneered in making the corporation responsive to its social setting. He did not fight public regulation and hired James D. Ellsworth to begin a public relations program that responded to public interests. Arthur W. Page succeeded Ellsworth. Page's philosophy of public relations and corporate social responsibility endures (see Exhibit 5.4).

By the early 1990s, AT&T and the seven regional companies had broadened their missions and product lines well beyond what was once thought of as "the telephone company." They manufactured computers and other communication equipment, expanded their publishing businesses, diversified their communication services, and became leaders in the generation and transmission of information. Cable television companies, other manufacturers, publishers, and other telephone

companies faced not one, but eight competitors. By the late 1990s, mergers had reduced the number of regional "integrated telcos" to five, and AT&T had once again divested, spinning off its Bell Laboratories to form a new company—Lucent Technologies—and spinning off former cash register manufacturer NCR as a computer company. AT&T also began building high-speed fiber-optic voice and data transmission networks, and even reentered the local telephone service business in 1999 by linking its operations with Time Warner's millions of cable television lines. In 2005, SBC purchased AT&T for $16 billion and took on AT&T's more widely recognized name. The merged company added SBC's Internet services to AT&T's business and long-distance services. As one observer said, "SBC is now a part of AT&T." Who bought whom?

In short, AT&T transformed itself into a powerful player in a new digital, wireless, and multimedia environment. It is no longer "The Telephone Company" or "Ma Bell." The old AT&T adjusted and adapted to business changes regulatory changes, and Technology changes.

It was not an easy transition, however. Longtime AT&T consultant Chester Burger recalls that in the early 1980s there were 1,700 full-time public relations specialists on AT&T's payroll with a total budget of about $170 million. Much of the public relations effort was to defend the company's historic monopoly in providing telephone service and the equipment that could be connected to the system. Burger concludes, however, that (1) public relations strategy can't overcome broad social factors, (2) it is easy to convince yourself that corporate self-interest coincides with the public interest, and (3) technology is changing the world.

Simply put, AT&T either had to change or it would have followed other corporate dinosaurs into extinction.

Source: Adapted in part from Chester Burger, APR, Fellow PRSA, "Last Word: When Public Relations Fails," *The Public Relations Strategist* 3, no. 3 (Fall 1997): 56.

times of crisis and, as a sensing device, public relations can be effective in preventing many potential crisis situations. Management properly remains the "large wheel" but the small wheel that is public relations may occasionally be capable of influencing the larger one. If observations of external and internal environments indicate that a policy or practice is detrimental to the best interests of the organization (and, increasingly, society) management can be encouraged to adjust.[28]

The functionary approach casts public relations practitioners in the technician role discussed in Chapter 2. In this limited role, they monitor the environment (if at all) to make communication output more effective, not to make changes within the organization. In organizations in which public relations operates in the functional mode, on the other hand, practitioners become part of top management, "the dominant coalition."

> Practitioners with the knowledge, training, and experience to practice a two-way model of public relations are more likely to be included in the organization's dominant coalition. They also are more likely to have power in that coalition rather than to serve it in an advisory role. When public relations managers have power in the dominant coalition, they can influence organizational ideology and the choice of publics in the environment for which strategic public relations programs are planned. At that point, public relations practitioners can fulfill a communication counseling and management role—and truly practice the profession defined for them in public relations textbooks but seldom fulfilled in the real world.[29]

In effect, public relations practiced in the closed systems (functionary) model attempts to maintain the status quo within organizations while directing change efforts at the environment. When public relations is part of organizations' strategic attempts to adjust and adapt to their dynamic environments, the practice reflects the open systems (functional) model.

The open systems approach radically changes how public relations is widely practiced. Whereas the more common functionary version attempts to exercise control over environmental forces, the open systems model views adjustment and adaptation as the more realistic and appropriate responses. Most definitions of organizational environment suggest that it includes factors outside organizational boundaries and often outside organizations' control. An organization's particular environment includes those "constituencies that can positively or negatively influence the organization's effectiveness. It is unique to each organization and it changes with conditions."[30]

The open systems model uses "two-way symmetric" approaches, meaning that communication is two way and that information exchange causes changes on both sides of organization–public relationships. The difference between one-way and two-way communication led the Grunigs to propose yet another way to describe closed and open systems public relations: craft public relations versus professional public relations.

> Practitioners of craft public relations seem to believe that their job consists solely of the application of communication techniques and as an end in itself. To them, the purpose of public relations simply is to get publicity or information into the media or other channels of communication. Practitioners of professional public relations, in contrast, rely on a body of knowledge as well as technique and see public relations as having a strategic purpose for an organization: to manage conflict and build relationships with strategic publics that limit the autonomy of the organization.[31]

Both approaches emphasize the primary role of communication in social systems. As Buckley put it, "the interrelations characterizing higher levels (of systems) come to depend more and more on the transmission of **information**—a principle fundamental to modern complex system analysis."[32]

Applying the open systems approach to public relations first and foremost calls for purposeful sensing of the environment to anticipate and detect changes that affect organizational relationships with publics. Following an open systems approach, public relations must be selectively sensitive to specifically defined publics that are mutually affected or involved by organizational policies, procedures, and actions. The open systems model of public relations calls for research skills to monitor publics and other environmental forces, as well as forces within organizations.

Open systems public relations also has the capacity to initiate corrective actions within organizations and direct programs to affect knowledge, predisposition, and behavior of both internal and external publics. The outcomes sought are maintenance or achievement of goals that reflect the mutual interests of organizations and their publics. Those found in conflict with mutual interests are changed or eliminated, *before* they become issues or problems. Proactive corrective action may be the major and most useful aspect of the open systems model of public relations. Steps taken in advance reduce both the amount of effort required and the trauma associated with crisis-oriented reactive public relations.

Thus, organizations employing open systems public relations maintain their relationships by adjusting and adapting themselves and their publics to ever-changing social, political, and economic environments. Figure 7.5 shows the open systems model applied to public relations.

As early as 1923, in one of the earliest public relations books, *Crystallizing Public Opinion*, Edward L. Bernays wrote about the role of the "public relations counsel" in a democratic society. Expressing a model of public relations similar to our open systems approach, he said that the public relations counsel recognizes changes in the organization's social setting and advises clients or employers how the organization should change itself and respond so as to establish a "common meeting ground." Not many years later, Harwood Childs said that the function of public relations is to "reconcile or adjust in the public interest" those aspects of organizations that have social significance. This concept of public relations, based on the open systems theoretical

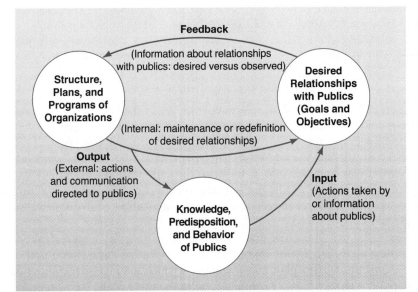

FIGURE 7.5

Open Systems Model of Public Relations

EXHIBIT 7.3

Good Theory Drives Best Practice

James Everett, Ph.D.,
Interim Provost
University of Alaska Southeast
Juneau, Alaska

The importance of a good theory is that it guides our thinking, informs our practice, and sets imperatives for refining our understanding. The adjustment and adaptation model of public relations is in many ways a centrifugal force in public relations because it fulfills these obligations to thinking and practice, but equally, points toward how to do both better.

While some see theory as a barrier to effective action, in fact it is a necessary, if usually tacit, precursor to such action. In this context, the adjustment and adaptation model refines our understanding of the significance and functional role of public relations in organizations by moving the boundaries of practice beyond prescriptive, journalistic output toward a new horizon of responsibilities linked to management decision making. In this role, the boundary-spanning nature of public relations creates a core operational activity that serves as a "mind in the middle" to provide critical monitoring and knowledge management functions through which the organization interprets its environment and creates sustainable relationships with stakeholders.

The adjustment and adaptation model, first built in this text two decades ago, anticipated the contemporary turn in sociology and the management disciplines to organizational ecology for describing the relationship of organizations to their social environments. Today, the insight offered by those early statements of public relations as an applied discipline set within organizational ecology remains one of the essential challenges for building our discipline in the twenty-first century.

In applied social sciences like public relations, good theory also helps provide an understanding of the teaching and learning requirements that eventually become what philosopher T. S. Kuhn called the discipline's "textbook tradition." Here the adjustment and adaptation model clearly differentiates the education and training of students and practitioners from the discipline's journalistic past. The model establishes the tenet that the quality of communication between an organization and stakeholder publics is a necessary but insufficient requirement of good practice.

Perhaps more fundamentally, the model stipulates that good practice must include the capacity to monitor and interpret the organization's social environment. Under these terms, contemporary public relations education should emphasize construction of a professional "portfolio" that, in addition to writing skills, includes skills related to measurement, analysis, and predicative modelling. The implications of the adjustment and adaptation model are that such skills are critical to practitioners who are called on to describe, explain, and influence the nature of such realities as public opinion in the organization's social environment and cultural elements within the organization that are inertial barriers to adaptation.

Additionally, practitioners who must defend program strategy and related budgets do so by the capacity to measure the effects of public relations programs on target publics. Such skill sets require commitments to lifelong learning by practitioners whose work is inextricably linked to the challenging problems of social influence, organizational legitimacy, and collective behavior. Those problems ensure not only the viability of our discipline in the twenty-first century, but also the value of its central theoretical model.

model, serves as the basis for the many activities under the banner of public relations and spells out its essential role in organizations and society (see Exhibit 7.3).

In the final analysis, public relations practitioners are applied social and behavioral scientists working as part of a strategic plan. According to employee communication expert Paul Sanchez at Watson Wyatt Communication Consulting Practice, a public relations plan "also tilts the balance toward proactive communication, thus avoiding wasted time on purely reactive communication that does not support strategic goals."[33]

Working on behalf of their organizations and in the public interest, public relations professionals are *agents* and *managers of change*, both inside and outside their organizations. They plan and facilitate organizational and social adjustment and adaptation using primarily communication, the topic of the next chapter.

Notes

1 Carol Kinsey Goman, "Energizing a Restructured Work Force," *Communication World* 14, no. 3 (February 1997): 55–57.

2 Stephen W. Littlejohn and Karen A. Foss, *Theories of Human Communication*, 9th ed. (Belmont, CA: Thompson Wadsworth, 2008), 40.

3 Alvin Toffler, *The Third Wave* (New York: Bantam Books, 1980), paperback, 9. See also Toffler's *Future Shock*.

4 Frederick Williams, *The New Communications*, 3d ed. (Belmont, CA: Wadsworth, 1992), 340.

5 Howard Rosenberg, "Fighting Tooth and Claw: Ingrid Newkirk's Combative Style and Headline-Grabbing Stunts Have Shaken Up the Animal-Rights Movement," *Los Angeles Times Magazine*, March 22, 1992, p. 18.

6 Irene Chang, "Edelman Ups Social Impact in Latest Unit," *PRWeek*, 26 November 2007, 6.

7 Aarti Shah, "Eco-Group to Take on Bottled Water Makers," Ibid.

8 Jacqueline L. Salmon, "Red Cross Gave Ousted Executive $780,000 Deal," *The Washington Post*, March 4, 2006, A9. (Downloaded April 3, 2008, at http://www.washingtonpost.com.)

9 Stephanie Strom, "Red Cross Sifting Internal Charges over Katrina Aid," *The New York Times*, March 24, 2006. (Downloaded April 3, 2008, at http://www.nytimes.com/2006/03/24/national/nationalspecial/24cross.html.)

10 James G. Miller, *Living Systems* (New York: McGraw-Hill, 1978), 29–30. This 1,100-page book is the most complete reference on systems theory. More readable and probably cited more is Ludwig von Bertalanffy, *General Systems Theory: Foundations, Development, Applications*, rev. ed. (New York: George Braziller, 1968).

11 For more complete explications of these subsystems, see landmark books by Chris Argyris, *Integrating the Individual and the Organization* (New York: John Wiley and Sons, 1964), and Daniel Katz and Robert L. Kahn, *The Social Psychology of Organizations* (New York: John Wiley and Sons, 1966), 39–47.

12 Harold L. Wilensky, *Organizational Intelligence: Knowledge and Policy in Government and Industry* (New York: Basic Books, 1967), 10.

13 Thomas J. Peters and Robert H. Waterman Jr., *In Search of Excellence* (New York: Harper and Row, 1982), 12.

14 R. Ashby, "Principles of the Self-Organizing System," in *Principles of Self-Organization*, ed. H. Von Foerster and G. W. Zopf (New York: Pergamon Press, 1962), 266.

15 Siegfried F. Nadel, *Foundations of Social Anthropology* (London: Cohen and West, 1951), 375.

16 Walter Buckley, *Sociology and Modern Systems Theory* (Englewood Cliffs, NJ: Prentice Hall, 1967), 14.

17 Walter B. Cannon, *The Wisdom of the Body* (New York: W. W. Norton, 1939), 24.

18 Littlejohn and Foss, *Theories of Human Communication*, 40.

19 Stephen W. Littlejohn, *Theories of Human Communication*, 7th ed. (Belmont, CA: Wadsworth/Thompson Learning, 2002), 45.

20 Lotfi A. Zadeh, as quoted by George J. Klir, *Facets of Systems Science* (New York: Plenum Press, 1991), 143.

21 Buckley, *Sociology and Modern Systems Theory*, 172–76. Cybernetic theory of self-regulating systems was first detailed in Norbert Wiener's *Cybernetics* (Cambridge, MA: MIT Press, 1948) and revised in a 1961 second edition (New York: John Wiley and Sons).

22 William F. Buckley Jr., "Haut Boat," *Forbes FYI* (March 16, 1992), 88 and 90. The ship was renamed *Wind Surf* in 2000 (from *Club Med 1*).

23 John H. Taylor, "Rip Van Weyerhaeuser," *Forbes* 148, no. 10 (October 28, 1992): 38–40. The story reported changes in top management, structure, and incentive programs to make the company more responsive and profitable.

24 Billy Layne Smith, "When Oprah's Cattle Battle Came to Amarillo," *Public Relations Tactics* 5, no. 4 (April 1998): 1, 9, and 27.

25 Hilary Potkewitz, "Shelling Out: Billionaire Grower Goes to War with Pistachio Commission," *Los Angeles Business Journal* (November 14, 2005), 14 April 2008, http://www.thefreelibrary.com/Shelling+out:+billionaire+grower+goes+to+war+with+pistachio+commission-a0139523890.

26 Steve Weiner, "Profit without Pollution," *Forbes* 139, no. 11 (May 18, 1987): 46.

27 Sue H. Bell and Eugene C. Bell, "Public Relations: Functional or Functionary?" *Public Relations Review* 2, no. 2 (Summer 1976): 51–52.

28 Ibid., 53.

29 James E. Grunig and Larissa Schneider Grunig, "Toward a Theory of the Public Relations Behavior of Organizations: Review of a Program of Research," *Public Relations Research Annual* 1 (1989): 60.

30 Stephen P. Robbins, *Organization Theory: Structure, Design, and Applications*, 3rd ed. (Englewood Cliffs, NJ: Prentice Hall, 1990), 207.

31 James E. Grunig and Larissa A. Grunig, chapter 11, "Models of Public Relations and Communication," in *Excellence in Public Relations and Communication Management*, ed. James E. Grunig (Hillsdale, NJ: Lawrence Erlbaum Associates, 1992), 312.

32 Buckley, *Sociology and Modern Systems Theory*, 47.

33 Paul Sanchez, "Agents for Change," *Communication World* 14, no. 3 (February 1997): 53.

Additional Sources

Adams, Tyrone L., and Norman E. Clark. *The Internet: Effective Online Communication.* New York: Thomson Wadsworth, 2001. Discusses how communication theory and principles apply to the Internet.

Cadwallader, Mervyn L. "The Cybernetic Analysis of Change in Complex Social Organizations." In *Communication and Culture: Readings in the Codes of Human Interaction*, edited by Alfred G. Smith, 396–401. New York: Holt, Rinehart and Winston, 1966.

Cancel, Amanda E., Glen T. Cameron, Lynne M. Sallot, and Michael A. Mitrook. "It Depends: A Contingency Theory of Accommodation in Public Relations." *Journal of Public Relations Research* 9, no. 1 (1997): 31–63. Presents a theory of sources of variance in the degree of accommodation in public relations practice, in contrast to Grunig's normative two-way symmetrical model.

Churchman, C. West. *The Systems Approach.* New York: Dell, 1979. Applies systems approach to management and decision making.

Dozier, David M., with Larissa A. Grunig and James E. Grunig. *Manager's Guide to Excellence in Public Relations and Communication Management.* Mahwah, NJ: Lawrence Erlbaum Associates, 1995. Deals with power and change in organizations, building linkages to and working with top management, and qualities of public relations excellence.

Grunig, Larissa A., James E. Grunig, and David M. Dozier. *Excellent Public Relations and Effective Organizations: A Study of Communication Management in Three Countries* (Mahwah, NJ: Lawrence Erlbaum Associates, 2002). Provides evidence supporting systems approach to public relations "excellence."

Hage, Jerald. *Theories of Organizations: Form, Process, and Transformation.* New York: John Wiley and Sons (Wiley-Interscience), 1980. Remains a classic work on organizations as adaptive systems.

Heath, Robert L., and Douglas D. Abel. "Proactive Response to Citizen Risk Concerns: Increasing Citizens' Knowledge of Emergency Response Practices." *Journal of Public Relations Research* 8, no. 3 (1996): 151–71.

Kotter, John P. *Leading Change.* Boston: Harvard Business School Press, 1996. Outlines eight-step process for organizational change, as well as the obstacles communicators and managers must overcome in change efforts.

Kuhn, Alfred J. *Organizational Cybernetics and Business Policy: System Design for Performance Control.* University Park: Pennsylvania State University Press, 1986. Presents a seven-phase model for applying systems theory to the design and management of complex business organizations. Uses General Motors as a case study.

Monge, Peter R. "Systems Theory and Research in the Study of Organizational Communication: The Correspondence Problem." *Human Communication Research* 8 (Spring 1982): 245–61.

Rapoport, Anatol. *General Systems Theory: Essential Concepts and Applications.* Tunbridge Wells, UK: Abacus, 1985.

Communication and Public Opinion

8

STUDY GUIDE   After studying Chapter 8, you should be able to:

► Identify the first task of public relations communications in the crowded message environment.

► Define communication as a two-way process of exchanging signals to inform, persuade, and instruct within intrapersonal, interpersonal, and social contexts.

► Diagram the communication model, and label and briefly discuss its elements.

► List and briefly discuss the four major categories of public relations communication effects.

► Identify and discuss the five dimensions of public opinion.

► Outline the three dimensions that differentiate *latent* publics from *active* publics.

► Define *attitude* and *opinion*, and distinguish between them.

► Diagram and explain the model of individual orientation and the model of coorientation.

► Define the four states of coorientational consensus.

The force of public opinion has steadily gained strength around the world as mass communication has become a global phenomenon. Governments and institutions formerly somewhat isolated from the glare of media attention and public scrutiny now see their actions or inaction reported via international news media. For example, international pressure against China increased after media reports and bloggers confirmed the crackdown on protestors in Tibet calling for an end to Chinese rule. The pressure mounted with news of sympathetic protestors in Istanbul, London, Paris, San Francisco, and other cities disrupting Olympic torch relays leading up to the 2008 Summer Olympics.

Other issues, however, fail to catch the attention of busy, distracted, and media-saturated publics. For example, the war in western Sudan, Darfur, failed to capture much attention, even while the country's militia employed a "scorched earth policy," committed genocidal atrocities (more than 200,000 people killed), and engaged in other crimes against humanity. More than 2.5 million Sudanese have been displaced, many crossing the border to Chad for protection.[3]

Almost instantaneous global media coverage is possible today, making mass communication a rapidly changing and far-reaching phenomenon. Satellite signals and the Internet distribute images of suicide bombings, starving children, and terrorist beheadings, causing a convergence of attention on events around the world—a lone student blocking a column of military tanks in Beijing's Tiananmen Square and the destruction of Saddam Hussein statues after the fall of Baghdad. Media have expanded the "world outside" and increased the number of "pictures in our heads," to borrow from Walter Lippmann.[4] The

No human capability has been more fundamental to the development of civilization than the ability to collect, share, and apply knowledge. Civilization has been possible only through the process of human communication.
—Frederick Williams[1]

Publicity is a great purifier because it sets in action the forces of public opinion, and in this country public opinion controls the courses of the nation.
—Charles Evans Hughes,[2] 11th Chief Justice, U.S. Supreme Court (1930–1941)

media themselves have multiplied to the point that competition for audience attention has never been greater. The nature of "news" itself is changing, as competitive media outlets—traditional and new—pursue even more unique, distant, novel, interesting, entertaining, and sensational information to attract audiences worldwide.

The Battle for Attention

In the United States alone, book publishers issue more than 60,000 new titles each year. During the same year, typical U.S. adults and teens watch television for 63 days and spend 41 days listening to radio, and about a week each on the Internet, newspapers, and recorded music.[5] There are at least 19,500 magazines in the United States, 13,977 radio stations, more than 8,000 daily and weekly newspapers, 1,759 television stations, ubiquitous signage and billboards, Internet pop-ups, and new media technologies too numerous to count.[6] Each competes for audience attention. Estimating how many messages each of us is exposed to each day by all these media has become a complex game of probabilities. No doubt each of us is exposed to hundreds, even thousands, of messages each day.

You chose to read this section of *Effective Public Relations,* but more likely during the rest of the day you are exposed to many more messages, most of which you do not seek out. You probably screen out many because you have little or no interest in the content. You skip some because you do not have time to pay attention. You miss others simply because you are preoccupied with something else and "tune out." In short, getting your attention is the goal of a fierce competition. The contenders include advertisers, news media, entertainment media, political parties and politicians, and all manner of other special interest groups.

To defend against the onslaught of attention seekers, people become choosy, even resistant. As a result of this onslaught of messages and information overload, few messages get their attention. Even fewer have an impact. No wonder some communication scholars refer to "the obstinate audience."[7]

Public relations communications compete in this crowded message environment. The first task is to get the *attention* of target publics. The second is to stimulate *interest* in message content. The third is to build a *desire* and *intention* to act on the message. And the fourth is to direct the *action* of those who behave consistent with the message. Unfortunately, the communication process is not as simple as many apparently believe.

Dissemination versus Communication

The myth of communication suggests that sending a message is the same as communicating a message. In essence, *dissemination* is confused with *communication*. This confusion is apparent in public relations when practitioners offer media placements (clippings, "mentions," cable placements, broadcast logs, etc.) as evidence that communication has occurred. These practitioners probably subscribe to the communication model introduced by information scientists Shannon and Weaver, based on their work for Bell Telephone Laboratories in the late 1940s.[8]

Shannon and Weaver's model consists of an information source, message or signal, channel, and receiver or destination. Not surprisingly, because of their telephone perspective, the communication process produces relatively few and simple problems. *Technical* problems arise when the signal or channel limits or distorts the message being transmitted from the source to the sender. *Semantic* or *fidelity* problems occur when the receiver's perception of the message and meaning are not the same as those intended by the sender. *Influence* problems indicate that the sender's message did not produce the desired result on the part of the receiver. As Weaver wrote,

> The questions to be studied in a communication system have to do with the amount of information, the capacity of the communication channel, the coding process that may be used to change a message into a signal and the effects of noise.[9]

But as public relations practitioners know, however, communication with target publics is much more complicated than this set of questions suggests. As the late Wilbur Schramm pointed out, communication is complicated by *people*:

> Communication (*human* communication, at least) is *something people do*. It has no life of its own. There is no magic about it except what people in the communication relationship put into it. There is no meaning in a message except what the people put into it. When one studies communication, therefore, one studies people—relating to each other and to their groups, organizations, and societies, influencing each other, being influenced, informing and being informed, teaching and being taught, entertaining and being entertained—by means of certain signs which exist separately from either of them. To understand the human communication process one must understand how people relate to each other.[10]

This is no simple task. In fact, Schramm's concept of communication requires a two-way-process model in which sender and receiver operate within the contexts of their respective frames of reference, their relationship, and the social situation.

As Figure 8.1 illustrates, **communication is a reciprocal process of exchanging signals to inform, persuade, or instruct, based on shared meanings and conditioned by the communicators' relationship and the social context.**

The process of *informing* involves four steps: (1) attracting attention to the communication, (2) achieving acceptance of the message, (3) having it interpreted as intended, and (4) getting the message stored for later use. The process of *persuasion* goes beyond active learning to a fifth step—accepting change: yielding to the wishes or point of view of the sender. The more demanding process of

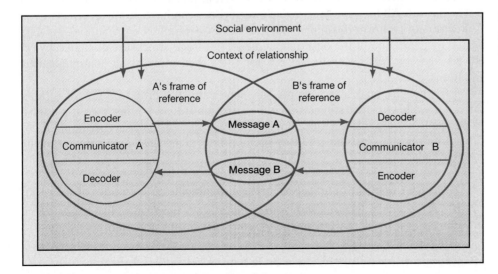

FIGURE 8.1

Communication Process Model

instruction adds a sixth step: stimulating active learning and practice. Clearly, barriers to achieving the outcomes of informing, instruction, and persuasion increase with the addition of the fifth and sixth steps in the processes.[11]

Elements of the Communication Model

Early communication researchers studied the individual elements in the communication process model to determine the effect of each on the process. Most studies dealt with persuasion as the desired outcome, but more recent studies have expanded the range of effects studied.

The Sender

Characteristics of message sources affect receivers' initial acceptance of the message but have little effect on long-term message impact. Hovland and his colleagues called this long-term source impact the "sleeper effect."[12] For example, according to the theory of source credibility and attractiveness, safe-sex messages promoting prevention of HIV infection among college students are more readily accepted as believable when presented by highly credible sources, such as a recognized medical authority, than when presented by peers.

More recent research suggests both short-term and long-term source impact. Source credibility amplifies the value of information, according to one scholar. The theory suggests that the perceived status, reliability, and expertness of the source add weight to messages. Multiplying the three source characteristics by each other yields the weight factor of the source in the communication process.[13]

Researchers have concluded that although source characteristics affect the communication process, their impact varies from situation to situation, from topic to topic, and from time to time. At a minimum, however, source characteristics affect receivers' initial receptivity to messages.

The Message

Message characteristics surely have an impact in the communication process, but many communication scholars say, "Meaning is in people, not words." This observation leads naturally to the conclusion that different people receiving the same message may interpret it differently, attribute different meanings to it, and react to it in different ways. All the same, message characteristics can have powerful effects, even if they do not conform to simple and direct cause-and-effect explanations. As suggested by the notion of the obstinate audience, message effects are mediated by receivers, thereby frustrating the search for rules that apply in all communication situations.

Early persuasion research on message characteristics produced few such rules, but did provide guidance still used in public relations today. For instance, if you wish to persuade, should the message contain only one side of the issue, or should it address both sides of an argument? Research findings generally support the following recommendations:

1. If receivers oppose your position, present arguments on both sides of the issue.
2. If receivers already agree with your position, your message will have greater impact—probably reinforcement—if you present only arguments consistent with the receivers' views.
3. If receivers are well educated, include both sides of the argument.

4. If you use messages containing both sides of the argument, do not leave out relevant arguments on the opposing side, or receivers who notice the omission will grow suspicious of your presentation.[14]

5. If receivers are likely to be exposed later to persuasive messages countering your position, use two-sided messages to "inoculate" the audience to build resistance to the later messages.[15]

Research on message effects suggests that gaining compliance is a complicated process, however. If the message source has little power or control to exercise over the receiver, then persuasion becomes the primary strategy. If, on the other hand, the sender has power or control, then instruction or direction becomes the relevant strategy. Research on the impact of message characteristics also supports the general conclusion from the previous section: Message impact is mediated or conditioned by receivers. For example, the classic study of order of presentation—"primacy" versus "recency"—demonstrated that the first part of the message has the greatest effect on receivers with low initial interest. The last part of the message has the greatest effect on those with high initial interest.[16]

Another line of message research initiated by Hovland and his associates at Yale University dealt with the use of fear to achieve compliance. After conducting an experiment using messages about dental hygiene, Janis and Feshback concluded that low-fear messages produce more compliance than do high-fear messages. High-fear messages apparently produce defensive reactions in the receiver that led to distortion, denial, or rejection of the message.[17] Some recent research on fear appeals, however, suggests a much more complicated relationship in which several factors influence the relationship between fear messages and subsequent compliance.

For example, high-fear messages about the dangers of smoking and of venereal disease, when combined with believable recommendations, produce high scores on intended compliance. Three factors affect the impact of fear messages: (1) the seriousness or harmfulness of the subject, (2) the likelihood or probability of the feared event, and (3) the efficacy of the recommended course of action. Apparently receivers evaluate fear-producing messages on these three characteristics before making a decision to adopt recommended courses of action. Researchers refer to this decision process as "protection motivation."[18]

In the final analysis, however, many characteristics of the source, receiver, and communication situation mediate the impact of messages on receivers. One writer concluded,

> When main-effect findings demonstrated relationships between the selected variable and some measure of attitude/behavior change, additional variables such as source characteristics, power, and receiver variables were investigated.[19]

The Medium or Channel

New technologies for delivering messages challenge conventional wisdom. For example, in many organizations, e-mail has changed communication within organizations and even across national boundaries. Meetings take place in a variety of virtual or digital formats, changing the nature of the interaction but providing benefits in cost and convenience.

Communication scholars and practitioners historically have considered face-to-face interpersonal communication the most direct, powerful, and preferred method for exchanging information. In contrast with mass communication, interpersonal communication involves as few as two communicators (typically in close proximity), uses many senses, and provides immediate feedback. This description of the interpersonal communication situation, however, does not take into account the possibility that mass media messages may be directed to only a few in a very specific public. Likewise, physical proximity can be less important than the nature of the relationship between communicators, what one scholar calls the "intimacy-transcends-distance phenomenon." What began as impersonal communication when people initially exchanged messages can become interpersonal communication as the communicators develop a relationship.[20]

Extending time and distance, however, often requires using message delivery systems other than in-person presentations. In much of contemporary society, face-to-face contacts give way to mediated transmissions. Spoken words give way to written communication. Individually addressed letters give way to targeted publications. Printed publications give way to broadcast words and pictures. Broadcast messages give way to networks of computers carrying digital signals translated into all manner of information. Choosing the right *medium* (singular) or *media* (plural) requires an understanding of media and media effects.

The Receivers

Communication models—and public relations programs—often mistakenly consider the audience passive recipients at the end of a message transmission process. This tradition continues even though research evidence and constant references to "two-way" suggest a different model and role for the audience.

In early mass communication studies, however, mass society audiences were viewed as vulnerable to messages and media manipulated by those in control. Critics saw people as alienated and isolated from the kind of strong social and psychological forces found in traditional societies, as a consequence of industrialization, urbanization, and modernization. However, the evidence gathered on audience effects suggests a more active receiver. The Yale persuasion experiments demonstrated that receivers are not uniformly influenced by messages designed to change attitudes. For example, receivers who value group membership are relatively unaffected by messages espousing positions counter to those of the group. Those who are persistently aggressive toward others tend to be resistant to persuasive messages. On the other hand, receivers with low self-esteem and feelings of social inadequacy are influenced more by persuasive messages than are people with high self-esteem and feelings of indifference toward others.[21] These differences in impact place a great responsibility on the communicator to target messages to specific and well-defined publics.

In short, the notion of a monolithic and passive mass audience does not describe reality. A more accurate description suggests selected active receivers processing messages designed for the few, not the masses:

> Since audiences are known to be evasive at best and recalcitrant at worst, efforts are directed at targeting messages for different audience segments and promoting audience involvement wherever possible.[22]

Context of the Relationship

Communication occurs within the context of the communicators' relationship. The range of such relationships includes close and intimate relationships as well as formal, competitive, and conflictual interpersonal relationships in a variety of settings.

The point, of course, is that the relationship itself affects much about the communication process.

All relational communication reflects four basic dimensions: (1) emotional arousal, composure, and formality; (2) intimacy and similarity; (3) immediacy or liking; and (4) dominance–submission.[23] For example, a supervisor announces changes in work schedules for student assistants without consulting with the students (the first dimension just listed) by posting the new schedule on the office bulletin board (the second dimension). The notice also expresses the supervisor's hope that the new schedule does not inconvenience any of the assistants (the third dimension) but indicates that the supervisor has the power to establish work schedules (the fourth dimension).

Not surprisingly, nonverbal behaviors play important roles in relational communication. *Proximity* communicates intimacy, attraction, trust, caring, dominance, persuasiveness, and aggressiveness. *Smiling* communicates emotional arousal, composure, formality, intimacy, and liking. *Touching* suggests intimacy. *Eye contact* intensifies the other nonverbal behaviors.[24] Obviously, these interpretations of nonverbal behaviors do not take into account cultural differences. For example, in Navajo and some Asian cultures, eye contact can be interpreted as a sign of disrespect or challenge. In some cultures, touching in public is taboo.

Whether verbal or nonverbal, communication in relationships helps the parties make predictions about others in the relationship. Communication reduces uncertainty about the probable outcomes of future exchanges and provides a basis for the continuing relationship. Understanding the communication process, however, requires not only an understanding of the relationship between the communicators but also the larger social context within which communication occurs.

The Social Environment

Communication affects and is affected by the social setting. Thus, communication occurs as a structured process within evolving systems of related components and activities. Social systems include families, groups, organizations, and all kinds of collectivities that are at the same time both producers and products of communication.

For example, when people think they can achieve something through joint action that they cannot accomplish individually, they form groups. Communication in groups depends on the nature of the group (primary versus secondary, formal versus informal, task-oriented versus experiential), characteristics of group members, group size, group structure, group cohesiveness, and group purpose.[25]

Successful group decision making requires accomplishing four tasks: (1) developing an adequate and accurate assessment of the problem, (2) developing a shared and complete understanding of the goal and the criteria for success, (3) agreeing on the positive outcomes of decisions, and (4) agreeing on the negative outcomes of decisions. Decision-making effectiveness, therefore, depends on the extent to which members' communication helps achieve these group functions.[26]

Organizations impose additional layers of complexity and constraints on communication. Forces at play in the larger society affect how all communicators—individuals, groups, and organizations—approach their publics, shape the content of their messages, define communication goals, and condition audience responses. Recall our ongoing connection to systems theory: All elements of a system are interdependent and mutually influenced by forces in their environment. In short, communication—when it occurs—results from a complex reciprocal process in which communicators try to inform, persuade, or negotiate within the contexts of their relationships and the larger social setting.

Communication Effects

Communication effects have long been the object of concern and study. The range of effects runs the gamut from early concerns about "all-powerful" media to "no effects." Hypothesized unlimited effects of movies on helpless children motivated the Payne Fund studies of the 1920s. Maybe critics simply feared too much. After ambitious public persuasion and political campaigns in the 1940s and 1950s produced disappointing results, many concluded that mass communication has almost no impact. Maybe the campaign planners simply asked too much of mass communication. More recent evidence supports theories in which mass communication effects occur under specified conditions. Apparently, the answer depends on what question you ask.

Creating Perceptions of the World Around Us

Early theorists cast mass communication's role as telling about events, things, people, and places that could not be directly experienced by most. Walter Lippmann said it best when he wrote about "the world outside and the pictures in our heads." He described a "triangular relationship" between the scene of action (interpreted to include people, places, actions, and the entire range of possible phenomena), perceptions of that scene, and responses based on the perceptions. The last side of the triangle is complete when the responses have an impact on the original scene of action. Mass media fit in the model between the scene of action and audience perceptions (see Figure 8.2).[27]

Lippmann pointed out that most of us cannot or do not have direct access to much of the world; it is "out of reach, out of sight, out of mind." The mass media help us create a "trustworthy picture" of the world that is beyond our reach and direct experience. His notions of media impact on public perceptions not only set the stage for studying mass communication effects but also arguably established the conceptual basis for much of what later became public relations.

Communication scholar George Gerbner followed up on Lippman's work. His studies of television viewing led to what he called "cultivation theory"—the homogenizing effect of creating a shared culture.[28] For example, those who watch a great deal of television have a different picture of the world—social reality—than do

FIGURE 8.2

Mass Media in Public Opinion Formation

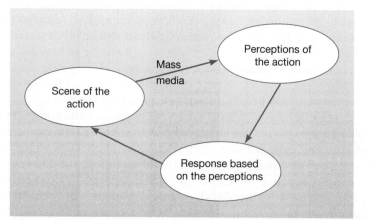

those who do not watch much television. Heavy viewers see the world as portrayed on television, not as it really is. The most dramatic example of the effect is referred to as the "mean world syndrome," meaning that heavy television viewers see the world as more dangerous and less trustworthy, and view it more pessimistically than do light viewers. Maybe the most dramatic of the cultivation theory studies was the finding that senior citizens who watch a great deal of television see the world outside their homes as too dangerous to venture into, even though reality has little relationship to the levels of muggings, purse snatchings, robberies, murders, etc., portrayed on television. In sum, the findings show that the effect of television viewing is less one of individual impact as it is of a collective impact on culture and people's views of the world around them.[29]

Setting the Agenda

The "agenda-setting" theory of mass communication effects also builds on Lippmann's notion of media impact by distinguishing between *what we think about* and *what we think*. The difference is that the former includes what we know about (cognition), whereas the latter refers to our opinions and feelings (predisposition). Early agenda-setting theory suggested that mass media can have a substantial and important impact on the cognitive level without affecting predisposition.[30] But it should be clear that even if media are limited to this one effect, setting the agenda is not a trivial consequence.

For example, early explorations of agenda setting by the press during presidential elections found that relative media emphasis on issues has a cumulative effect on the electorate. The same issues, with the same relative emphasis as that given by the media, make up the voters' agenda. In other words, the issues considered least to most important by voters reflect patterns of media coverage rather than a particular political agenda. Furthermore, the relative number of people concerned about issues parallels the relative media emphasis of those issues. Media and public agendas were most similar during the early stages of the campaign and for those issues least likely to be within people's direct experience.[31]

Imagine the potential consequences of media agenda setting. First of all, media coverage can elevate the public standing of issues, people, organizations, institutions, and so forth. Second, changes in the amount of media attention can lead to changes in public priorities. Third, the more concerned people are about something, the more they tend to learn about it, the stronger their opinions are of it, and the more they tend to take action on it. (Notice, however, that the agenda-setting theory does not predict what information they will seek, which way their opinions will change, or what types of actions they will take.) Fourth, media coverage can affect the agenda priorities of some specific and important publics, such as legislators, regulators, and other policy makers.

In summary, mass communication can affect public opinion by raising the salience of issues and positions taken by people and groups in the news.[32] Furthermore, like Lippmann's theory of media effects, the agenda-setting theory contributes to the conceptual foundation for public relations mass communication.

For public relations practitioners, getting an issue onto the media agenda can be a good thing (i.e., when you want to raise awareness of an issue) or a bad thing (e.g., when something embarrassing, dangerous, or illegal happens at your organization). Being aware of the power of media agenda setting is a key to the strategic management of public relations communication. Public relations can contribute tremendously to the effectiveness of the organization when it carefully and strategically considers its own issues in regard to the media agenda. Often, public relations saves an organization money and resources by resolving a problem before it gets onto the media agenda. In other instances, getting an issue onto the media agenda is a crucial part of press agentry and a valuable method of creating symmetrical dialogue on an issue.

Two concepts in agenda-setting theory and research are especially useful in public relations:

1. *Issue salience* determines the *prominence* and *penetration* the issue has with the audience, or how well it resonates with each public. People care the most about issues that are close to their own interests. Researchers found that frequency of discussion was the single largest predictor of issue salience. Interpersonal communication enhanced the agenda-setting effect of the media or interfered with the agenda-setting effect when the interpersonal discussion conflicted with media content.[33]

2. *Cognitive priming* describes the personal experience or *connection* someone has with an issue. Researchers thought that a person with little or no personal experience on an issue must rely on the media for information. Scholars initially expected to find that the media had weak or no agenda-setting effect on issues with which people had personal experience. To the contrary, they found support for the cognitive priming hypothesis, which states that previous or personal exposure to an issue stimulates interest in that issue's media coverage, thus enhancing the agenda-setting effects.[34]

Researchers McCombs and Shaw have reformulated and expanded agenda-setting theory, however: "Media not only tell us what to think about, but how to think about it, and, consequently, what to think."[35] Indeed, this new theory of mediated, powerful effects provides a promising theoretical framework for application in the practice of public relations. In what is referred to as "second-level agenda-building and agenda-setting effects," researchers Kiousis and Mitrook concluded:

> In addition to object salience, the contemporary explication of second-level agenda setting has linked the concept with framing by suggesting that news media attention can influence how people think about a topic by selecting and placing emphasis on certain attributes and ignoring others. . . . If media, for example, emphasize the integrity of a political candidate in news stories, public descriptions of that candidate should also stress his or her integrity.[36]

The implications for public relations communication is made explicit by McCombs and Reynolds's summary statement about the expanded concept of agenda setting:

> How the media frame an issue or political candidate—which attributes are selected either as the central organizing idea or as the aspects of the topic presented to the audience—is a powerful agenda-setting role.[37]

McCombs elaborated how the process works:

> The agenda-setting influence of the press results in large measure from the repetition of the major issues in the news day after day. The public learns about the issues on the press agenda with little effort on their part, and considering the incidental nature of this learning, issues move rather quickly from the press agenda to the public agenda.[38]

Diffusing Information and Innovation

Beyond setting the issue agenda, research findings in a variety of settings show that mass communication facilitates social interaction and change. Sources may come from different social, economic, and educational backgrounds but are accessible through the media. The media, then, provide information from sources that would otherwise not be available through interpersonal networks in which "like talks to like." Once people get information from the media, however, they enter conversations armed with useful new information. What we learn from the mass media often determines what we talk about with others, providing the common ground needed to begin conversation: "Did you see in this morning's paper that . . . ?" or "Can you believe Jay Leno has already announced his retirement?" In effect, mass media provide information to those who seek it and supply information needed for subsequent interpersonal communication, thereby diffusing information to others.[39]

Diffusion of information and innovation theory explains this process. Characteristics of innovation—or new ideas—as well as characteristics of the adopters influence the adoption process. Ideas or innovations are more readily adopted if they are (1) more advantageous than the current situation, (2) compatible with previous experience and other aspects of the situation, (3) simple, (4) easily tried, and (5) observable with readily apparent outcomes. "Innovators" are the first to adopt new ideas, followed by "early adopters," "early majority," "late majority," and "laggards." Characteristics of the individuals in each of the categories vary with the nature of change being adopted and the context.[40]

Early diffusion of innovation studies identified *opinion leaders* as key components if gaining acceptance of new ideas and practices. In effect, these people tend to get their information from media sources and then become themselves the source to others in their network.[41] Researchers identified leaders who had influence on a specific issue, while others wielded influence over a range of issues. The two-step flow model has given way to the multi-step flow model, in which there may be many different steps and actors in decisions to adopt an innovation or idea.[42] Whatever the number of steps or links in the network, it is safe to conclude that people are important in the process of diffusion of innovation:

> Interpersonal influence is very important in this process. People raise awareness of the innovation as they talk with one another about it. They share opinions, discuss their experience with the innovation, sometimes advocate its use, and sometimes resist it.[43]

Diffusion and adoption processes illustrate the impact that mass communication has on interpersonal communication and networks. More important, they show how mass and interpersonal communication interact in social systems and in social change.

Defining Social Support

"Spiral of silence" theory suggests a phenomenon commonly referred to as "the silent majority." Individuals who think their opinion conflicts with the opinions of most other people tend to remain silent on an issue. Carried to an extreme, even if a majority actually agree but do not individually recognize social support, their silence and inactivity can lead to the erroneous conclusion that not many people support a particular view. On the other hand, individuals who think that many others share their view or that the number of people who agree is growing rapidly are more likely to express their views. Under these conditions, a vocal minority that sees itself on the winning side can appear to represent a widely shared perspective. In either case, as Lippmann pointed out more than 50 years before the spiral of silence theory, people "respond as powerfully to fictions as they do to realities, and . . . in many cases they help to create the very fictions to which they respond."[44]

In essence, public opinion arises as individuals collectively discern support for their views through personal interaction and by attending to the mass media. Individuals observe and assess their social environments, estimating the distributions of opinions, evaluating the strength and chances of success for each, and determining the social sanctions and costs associated with each. The spiral begins when individuals choose to remain silent or decide to express their views. It continues as others observe the presence or absence of support for their own views. It gains apparent legitimacy when increasing numbers of individuals translate their observations into either public silence or expression. It is reinforced when the media cover the views being displayed most forcefully and most frequently and do not make an effort to determine the actual distribution of views.

Media coverage can reflect, enforce, or challenge the spiral of silence effect on public opinion. But understanding the dynamics of individuals' collective observations of their social environments and public opinion translates rather directly into public relations practice. Examples include public information campaigns designed to break the spirals of silence associated with domestic violence, sexual harassment, and stalking, to list only a few. In each instance, and for many other public issues, mass communication plays a key role in redefining socially accepted expression and behavior.

As illustrated in Figure 8.3, mass media messages can provide individuals pictures of their social environment, of whether there is social approval or disapproval of their views or actions. This "sociocultural model" of communication effects suggests that "messages presented via the mass media may provide the appearance of consensus regarding orientation and action with respect to a given object or goal of persuasion."[45]

To sum up, the late communication scholar Everett Rogers concluded: ". . . [T]he media can have strong effects, especially when the media messages stimulate interpersonal communication about a topic through intermedia processes."[46]

Publics and Their Opinions

Nineteenth-century writer and first editor of *Atlantic Monthly* James Russell Lowell said, "The pressure of public opinion is like the atmosphere. You can't see it, but all the same it is sixteen pounds to the square inch." Lowell's words have even more relevance now. Public opinion has never been more powerful, more fragmented, more volatile, and more exploited and manipulated. For example, researchers studying U.S.

FIGURE 8.3

Sociocultural Model of Persuasion

Source: Melvin L. De Fleur and Sandra J. Ball-Rokeach, *Theories of Mass Communication,* 4th ed. (New York: Longman, 1982), p. 225.

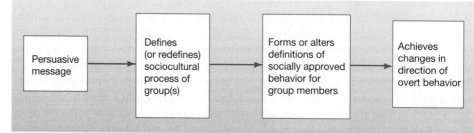

presidential campaign coverage found ample evidence of "a powerful relationship between news media coverage and public opinion in presidential elections."[47]

Public opinion polls have long guided politics, government programs, entertainment programming, and even corporate decision making. In short, much as Lowell suggested, public opinion is an always present, dynamic force. It is part of public relations' mission to help organizations recognize, understand, and deal with this powerful influence in their environments.

This is not an easy task, however. As the former vice president of AT&T said:

> Public opinion is not necessarily logical; it is amorphous, ambivalent, contradictory, volatile. Consequently, those of us who would hope to influence public opinion can only expect that our efforts, over time, may nudge the consensus toward some reasonable perception of the issues.[48]

Organizations of all types must deal with *real* and *perceived* public opinion as they establish and maintain relationships with their many internal and external publics. But organizations are the actors; public opinion is simply the "energizer" of their actions.

> (Public opinion) is . . . an expression of social energy that integrates individual actors into social groupings in ways that affect the polity. This understanding takes the concept of public opinion out of metaphysics and . . . avoids reducing it to a set of discrete individualized observations that cannot account for its composite sociopolitical significance.[49]

Definition of Public Opinion

The common notion of public opinion holds that it is simply the aggregation of individual views on some issue. This "individual agreement" approach to defining public opinion, however, misses the point that it is *public.* Individual cognition may or may not represent the *consensus,* or "thinking together," that more fully represents the kinds of opinions that form and are formed by public discussion among those sharing a "sense of commonness."

Thus, public opinion represents more than the collected views held by a particular category of individuals at one point in time. Public opinion is not adequately defined as simply a *state* of individual cognition. Instead, it reflects a dynamic *process* in which ideas are "expressed, adjusted, and compromised en route to collective determination of a course of action."[50] Public opinion is found among publics, or groups of communicating people who have some common interest. They collectively hold a view of an issue, why it is a cause for concern, and what can or should be done in the situation. The process is, unquestionably, ongoing.

In practice, however, both researchers and public relations practitioners take "snapshots" of public opinion, essentially freezing the process at one point in time so as to describe it and compare it with opinion at other times. Their surveys too often measure only direction and intensity, ignoring three other important dimensions:

1. **Direction** of opinion indicates the evaluative quality of a predisposition, telling us the "positive-negative-neutral," "for-against-undecided," or "pro-con-it-depends" evaluation of publics. In its simplest form, direction is a yes–no answer to a survey question. Media frequently report public opinion survey results as simply the percentages for or against some issue, proposition, or candidate. For example, stories reporting poll results, popularity, margin, and other indicators of the direction of public opinion about the candidates dominated coverage of

the 1996 U.S. presidential campaign, comprising 38 percent of all stories.[51] (Character stories were second at 18 percent.) Direction clearly represents the most basic and most frequently used measure of public opinion.

2. **Intensity** measures show how strongly people feel about their opinions, whatever the direction. For example, pollsters ask registered voters to indicate "on a scale of 1 to 10" how strongly they felt about a wide range of issues related to the election. Likewise, surveys often ask respondents to indicate whether they "strongly disagree/disagree/neutral/agree/strongly agree" with a statement. This question format is a common means of measuring both direction and intensity of feelings. Intensity measures provide an initial estimate of the relative strength of predisposition. Intensity and direction are often reported to indicate not only how people feel about issues, but also how deeply they hold the feelings. For instance, the issue of abortion commonly polarizes publics based on the intensity of their beliefs.

3. **Stability** refers to how long respondents have held or will hold the same direction and intensity of feelings. Measures of stability require observations taken at two or more points in time. Think of this dimension as something like the charts that track stock prices or temperature patterns over time. In effect, the stability measure provides evidence of how reactive public opinion is to events or other information.

4. **Informational support** refers to how much knowledge people hold about the object of opinion. For example, voters who have little information about candidates tend to focus on who they see as being involved or associated with a candidate and how they think the candidate would affect them personally. Better-informed voters, in contrast, "are more likely to ignore consideration of the specific groups involved in favor of a more general interpretation of the issue."[52]

Other researchers studying a mayoral election found that those more informed about issues hold stronger opinions about the issues, but the direction of the opinions is not easily predicted. Furthermore, those with more knowledge and strong opinions are more likely to vote and to contact local officials.[53]

Absence of "information mass" behind an opinion on relatively nonpartisan issues may indicate that the direction and intensity are susceptible to change. For example, if Monsanto finds that public opinion against field testing of genetically engineered plants is not well informed, the company could mount a public information campaign designed to educate community members about the risks and benefits involved, taking care to frame the messages in the context of who is affected and involved (including the consensus views of community leaders), as well as how the field tests will affect those in the community— potential risks (if any) and benefits.

5. **Social support** measures provide evidence of the extent to which people think their opinions are shared by others in their social milieu. The persuasion model in Figure 8.3 indicates the power of perceptions of social approval or disapproval. Pollsters probing this dimension of public opinion ask respondents to report their impressions of what significant others think about an issue or to estimate the distribution of public opinion on the issue under study. In effect, measures of social support show how people define the nature of the consensus on issues.

The social context of opinion may be simply the tendency to think that other people are more influenced by media or events than ourselves.

Researchers have found "third-person effects"—people tend to underestimate media impact on themselves and overestimate impact on others. Such effects could have consequences in how public policy is determined (protecting those perceived to be vulnerable others), or how political campaigns are conducted (influencing easily persuaded voters). Researcher Richard Perloff discussed the implications of the third-person effect:

> Social life is strengthened when individuals recognize that their perceptions of other people are not always accurate and that their fellow citizens are more capable of separating out the political wheat from the chaff than they typically assume. In a fragmented era, it is particularly important to reduce people's inclination to psychologically separate themselves from others and to encourage individuals to view others and the self through the same sets of lenses.[54]

Think of both informational and social support as giving predisposition weight and inertia. If, for example, people with a strong opinion on an issue hold a lot of information—pro and con—about that issue and see their particular position as being widely shared, then the direction and expression of the opinion are not likely to change. Just as the direction of a bowling ball is little affected by the air movement created by an air conditioner, opinions with much informational and social support have great mass and are not susceptible to easy or quick change. On the other hand, even strongly held opinions can change if they are not backed by information and perceived social support. They can change direction as frequently and rapidly as a ping-pong ball in a hurricane!

Describing and understanding public opinion requires greater measurement sensitivity and depth than the simple yes–no questions often used in telephone polling. Public opinion reflects a dynamic process of interpersonal and media communication on issues among groups of people who have the capacity to act in similar ways. "Thinking together" often leads to "acting together," the real reason for understanding public opinion.

Publics

First of all, *practitioners of public relations must discard notions about "the general public."* Sociographic and demographic variables, such as age, education, and income, naturally segment society into very large groups. Add to that the many different ethnic, racial, religious, geographic, political, occupational, social, and special-interest groupings and the result is that the concept of a general or mass public holds little, if any, value in public relations. Rather, effective programs communicate and build relationships with *specifically defined "target publics"* or *"strategic publics."* Without such specific definitions and detailed information about intended audiences of messages, how do program planners measure public opinion, establish program objectives, develop meaningful message and action strategies, select media to deliver messages selectively and effectively, and determine whether the program worked?

Philosopher and educator John Dewey defined a public as an active social unit consisting of all those affected who recognize a common problem for which they can seek common solutions. He wrote that publics were formed when "recognition of evil consequence brought about a common interest." Without communication, however, it "will remain shadowy and formless, seeking spasmodically for itself, but seizing and holding its shadow rather than its substance."[55]

Grunig expands Dewey's concept by outlining three factors that move *latent publics* to become communicating *active publics* through Grunig's situational theory of publics:

1. *Problem recognition* represents the extent to which people are aware that something is missing or amiss in a situation, thereby knowing that they need information.
2. *Constraint recognition* represents the extent to which people see themselves limited by external factors, versus seeing that they can do something about the situation. If people think they can make a difference or have an effect on the problem situation, they will seek information to make plans for action.
3. *Level of involvement* represents the extent to which people see themselves being involved and affected by a situation. In other words, the more they see themselves connected to a situation, the more likely they will communicate about it.[56]

These three variables are measured against how active or passive the communication behavior of a public is. Active communication behavior is called *information seeking* because people in that group are likely to seek information on the issue. Passive communication behavior is called *information processing* because a passive audience may or may not attend to a message.

After testing his "situational theory of publics" on a variety of environmental issues, Grunig concludes that environmental publics defined according to their communication behavioral similarities are not the same as those identified by demographic attributes or attitudes.[57] He consistently finds four types of publics:

1. *All-issue publics* are active on all issues.
2. *Apathetic publics* are inattentive and inactive on all issues.
3. *Single-issue publics* are active on one or a limited number of related issues. (Such publics include "pro-life," environmental, and animal rights groups.)
4. *Hot-issue publics* are active after media expose almost everyone, and the issue becomes the topic of widespread social conversation. (Mattel's recall of lead-painted toys created publics after attracting extensive media attention.)[58]

As suggested by Grunig's situational theory of publics, messages must be individually tailored to fit the information needs of different publics, based on how active or passive their communication behavior is and what are issues of importance to them. Useful definitions of publics go beyond demographics or "psychographics" to include relevant indicators of common recognition of mutual interests and situational variables that tie certain individuals, but not others, to specific situations or issues. In other words, publics result from specific issues or situations, not shared cross-situational traits. Dewey said,

> [When] a church, a trade union, a business corporation, or an educational institution conducts itself so as to affect large numbers outside of itself, those who are affected form a public which endeavors to act through suitable structures, and thus to organize itself for oversight and regulation.[59]

Specific issues and situations determine each public's composition, size, and range of responses. For example, an organization's philanthropic donation to support construction of a controversial abstract sculpture in a park can activate many individuals to respond in a variety of ways. Some, if not most, of those who see themselves affected by the organization's charity probably have no direct contact with the organization making the donation and do not live near the park. On the other hand, if the same organization proposes a complex restructuring of its long-term debt, then probably only a few top executives who fear being presented early retirements, financial analysts, and institutional investors may respond to the proposed changes.

From the perspective of the publics that come into existence in the two situations, a wider range of publics and a greater number of people are moved to react in a variety of ways by the charitable contribution than by the restructuring proposal. It is conceivable, however, that the long-term "evil consequences" of financial restructuring will have a much greater impact on the community than will the existence of a piece of public art. For specific issues, specific publics arise that have differing information needs, values, and priorities than other publics of the same organization. For this reason, public relations practitioners target specific messages to strategic publics; they know that the public receiving the information will care about the issue and attend to the message.

Individual Orientations and Coorientation

The different publics and reactions stimulated by the two situations in the previous scenarios suggest both individual and shared orientations. Individual orientations, however, do not become public opinion until they are shared—or perceived to be shared—by others. The realization, rightly or wrongly, that an individual's views of a situation are similar to those held by others evokes a sense of identification among individuals and the perception of a common interest. In other words, individual *orientations* include perceptions of issues or objects in one's environment, as well as perceptions of significant others' views of those same issues or objects. When two or more individuals' orientations include the same issues or objects and each other, they are in a state of *coorientation*.

Orientation

Individuals hold opinions of varying degrees of relevance and intensity. Individuals assign value to objects in their environment on the basis of both their previous history with the objects and their assessment of the objects in the current context (see Figure 8.4). The former value is *salience,* or the feelings about an object derived from an individual's experiences and reinforcements from previous situations. Salience refers to what the individual brings to a situation as a result of history. The second source of value is *pertinence,* which refers to the relative value of an object found by making object-by-object comparisons on the basis of some attribute or attributes. Pertinence value can vary depending on which attribute is used to make the comparison or what other objects are used in the comparison.[60] In other words, salience indicates how individuals feel about an object, independent of the situation, whereas pertinence depends on how the individual defines the situation. To describe and understand an individual's opinion about some object, then, you have to measure both salience and pertinence. The distinction helps clarify the relationship between attitudes and opinions.

An *attitude* is the cross-situational predisposition or preference with respect to an object or issue. Attitudes predispose individuals to respond in certain ways from

FIGURE 8.4

Model of Individual
Orientation

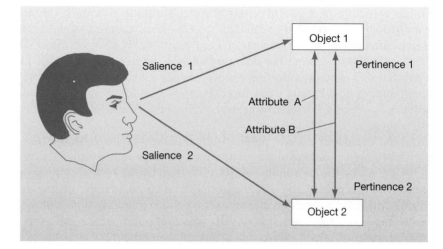

one situation to another, based on a lifetime of accumulating and evaluating information and experiences. Crespi substitutes "attitudinal system" when referring to what others call "attitude." He defines attitude systems as comprising four components:

1. Evaluative frames of reference (values and interests)
2. Cognition (knowledge and beliefs)
3. Affection (feelings) (Because many use the term *attitude* as referring only or primarily to the affective mode, whereas others use *attitude* more generally, an added benefit of adopting this nomenclature is that it avoids confusing the affective response mode with the entire system.)
4. Conation (behavioral intentions)[61]

On the other hand, an *opinion* is the judgment expressed about an object in a particular situation or given a specific set of circumstances. Opinions tend to reflect an individual's related attitudes but also take into account aspects of the current situation.

Scholars have generally distinguished between attitudes and opinions in two ways:

> First, opinions are generally considered to be verbal, or otherwise overt responses to a specific stimulus (an issue), while attitudes are more basic global tendencies to respond favorably or unfavorably to a general class of stimuli. While opinions are largely situational, attitudes are more enduring with a person across situations. Second, opinions are considered to be more cognitive and somewhat less affective in their makeup. . . . An attitude is an immediate, intuitive orientation while an opinion is a thought-out, reasoned choice between alternatives for action in a social matrix.[62]

The notion that opinions are expressed makes them important to the formation and study of public opinion. On the other hand, unexpressed intrapersonal predisposition does not affect public opinion formation. Not until attitudes are expressed through opinions in discussion or other public communication do they have an impact on the processes of forming and changing public opinion. That opinions are public expressions establishes public opinion as a social phenomenon.

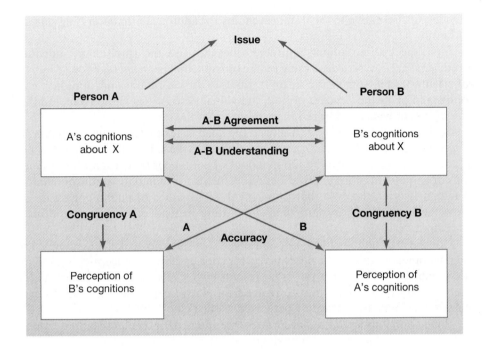

FIGURE 8.5

Model of Coorientation

Source: Adapted from Jack M. McLeon and Steven H. Chaffee, "Interpersonal Approaches to Communication Research," in *Interpersonal Perception and Communication,* ed. Steven H. Chaffee and Jack M. McLeod, special edition of *American Behavioral Scientist,* 16, no. 4 (March–April 1973), pp. 483–88.

Coorientation

The social or interpersonal concept of public opinion requires two or more individuals oriented to and communicating about an object of mutual interest. In other words, they are "cooriented" to something in common and to each other.

The coorientational model in Figure 8.5 illustrates the *intrapersonal* and *interpersonal* elements of communication relationships.[63] First, the intrapersonal construct of *congruency* describes the extent to which your own views match your estimate of another's views on the same issue. Some refer to this variable as "perceived agreement." On the basis of this estimate, you formulate strategies for dealing with the other person or for spontaneously responding in interactions.

The extent to which you accurately estimate another's views determines the appropriateness of your actions. Each of us recalls instances in which we misjudged another person's position on some issue of mutual interest and responded to them inappropriately until we learned what the person really thought about the issue. *Accuracy,* then, represents the extent to which your estimate matches the other person's actual views. Because it requires a comparison of observations taken from two different people, accuracy represents an interpersonal construct.

The other interpersonal constructs include *agreement* and *understanding.* Agreement represents the extent to which two or more persons share *similar evaluations* of an issue of mutual interest. Understanding measures the *similarities in the definitions* held by two or more persons. In terms used in the individual orientation paradigm, agreement compares saliences, whereas understanding compares pertinences.

Coorientational Consensus

By including many individuals simultaneously oriented to issues of mutual concern and interest, the interpersonal coorientational model is extended to large social groupings. A coorientational concept of public opinion in communities and society provides an alternative to the usual psychological approaches to describing states of consensus.

First, the coorientational approach does not use the traditional "individual agreement" approach to describing public opinion, that is, an aggregation of individual orientations to some issue or topic. Instead, the coorientational approach casts public opinion as the product of both individual perceptions on an issue and their perceptions of what significant others think about the same issue.

Social scientists long ago recognized the need to take into account *perceptions of agreement* in addition to *actual agreement*. Scheff, for one, argued that perceptions of agreement can be independent of actual agreement and that perceptions of agreement more likely affect public behavior than does actual agreement. In fact, it is often the case that those involved in issues of public debate do not know the state of actual agreement, operating instead on their perceptions of agreement.[64]

Conceiving public opinion—or consensus—in this way makes it a complex social phenomenon that can be described using coorientational concepts. For example, the state of *monolithic consensus* represents high levels of actual agreement accurately recognized as such by those involved. *Dissensus* exists when high levels of actual disagreement are accurately perceived as such (see Table 8.1).

Public opinion based on inaccurate perceptions of agreement is more troublesome in relationships. Unlike actual agreement or disagreement, however, inaccurate perceptions are at least subject to change as a result of effective communication. For example, after extended interaction, two or more persons may simply agree to disagree. At least they each know where the other stands on the issue. The same cannot be said about situations based on inaccurate perceptions of each other's views.

False consensus exists when there is actual disagreement but the majority of those involved think they agree. *Pluralistic ignorance* represents the state of public opinion in which a majority perceive little agreement, but in fact there is widespread agreement. When those involved do not accurately recognize the state of actual agreement, they act on the basis of their inaccurate perceptions. In the cases of false consensus and pluralistic ignorance, their responses and public expressions (that is, public opinion) are not consistent with the actual distribution of individual orientations on issues of common interest. Accurate perceptions of others' views, however, are surely the most likely outcome of public communication and the greatest motivation for maintaining communication in society and in relationships.

TABLE 8.1

Types of Coorientational Consensus

	Perceives That Majority Also Agrees on Issue	Perceives That Majority Does Not Agree on Issue
Majority actually agrees on issue	Monolithic Consensus	Pluralistic Ignorance
Majority does not agree on issue	False Consensus	Dissensus

Source: Adapted from Thomas J. Scheff, "Toward a Sociological Model of Consensus," *American Sociological Review* 32, no. 1 (February 1967), p. 39.

What may appear as logical in the context of this discussion, however, apparently is not widely recognized by those who commission or practice public relations. Instead of trying to increase the accuracy of cross perceptions in social relationships, most communication efforts attempt to influence levels of agreement or to "engineer consent." But actual agreement can exist independent of perceptions of agreement, leading to Scheff's more useful definition of coorientational public opinion:

> Complete consensus on an issue exists in a group [read "public"] when there is an infinite series of reciprocating understandings between the members of the group [read "public"] concerning the issue. I know that you know that I know, and so on.[65] (Words in brackets added.)

In the context of public relations, the coorientational approach to consensus and relationships is also useful for describing the nature of organization–public relationships.

Coorientational Relationships

The coorientational approach helps identify three public relations problems that call for rather straightforward communication strategies:

1. An organization and a public hold different definitions of an issue. They simply are not talking about the same thing when they engage in communication about "the issue." They are talking about different issues.
2. The organization's perceptions of a public's views of an issue (evaluations and/or definitions) do not match the public's actual views. Organizational management makes decisions about a public based on inaccurate estimates of the public's views. Not surprisingly, the relationship suffers when members of that public are subjected to the organization's actions and communications.
3. Members of a public hold inaccurate perceptions of an organization's positions on an issue of mutual concern. Public responses to the organization's management, its products, its actions and procedures, and so forth are based on inaccurate estimates of management policy and values.

Note that in all cases, the nature of the organization–public relationship is threatened by differing definitions and inaccurate perceptions, not by disagreement over the issue itself. None of the situations calls for communication designed to change the level of agreement–disagreement on the issue. Communication that helps create shared definitions and increase accuracy improves the relationship and makes each side's dealings with the other more appropriate (see Figure 8.6).

For example, even though the Army Corps of Engineers communicated the advantages of a proposed flood-control project to the various publics who would be affected, they apparently did not do the same for the project's disadvantages. Convinced that the various publics supported the project, the Corps scheduled what was to be the final public hearing for project approval. Project planners were surprised by the suspicions, concerns, objections, and uncertainties expressed at the hearing. The project was delayed for the additional meetings and negotiations needed to improve accuracy in both the Corps's and publics' perceptions of the project and one another's views.[66] Had the Corps initially used the coorientational approach to assess public opinion of the project, they might have identified their relationship problems and taken steps to avoid the costly delays.

FIGURE 8.6

Coorientational Model of
Organization–Public
Relationships

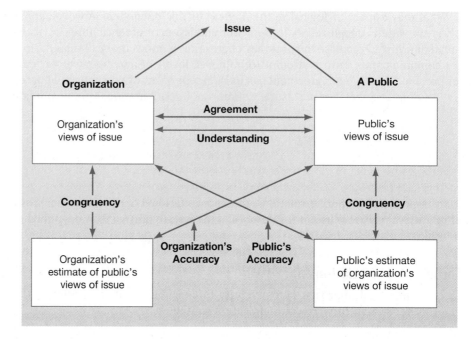

As this example illustrates, the coorientational approach serves three major purposes in public relations planning. First, coorientational measures provide the information needed to identify and describe problems in organization–public relationships. Rather than defining problems in ways that limit strategies to those designed to increase agreement by changing public perceptions, this approach calls for an assessment of all parties' views in order to understand relationships.

Second, coorientational measures provide useful guidance for planning appropriate messages and responses to correct organization–public relationship problems. Coorientational assessments of relationships can lead to atypical, yet efficient, solutions. For example, imagine that the analysis shows that management has an inaccurate perception of a public's views on an issue and as a result is proposing what will be an inappropriate action or response. Simply reporting the public's actual views on the issue to management may be the only corrective action needed.

Third, repeated use of coorientational measures indicates how the relationship changes as a result of the communication and other corrective actions. In other words, agreement, understanding, congruency, and accuracy serve as outcome criteria for assessing the impact of public relations efforts on organization–public relationships.[67]

In conclusion, public relations establishes and maintains relationships between organizations and their publics by—but not limited to—facilitating two-way communication. The communication, however, may have less impact on the extent to which parties agree or disagree than on the accuracy of their cross-perceptions of each other's views. In the final analysis, Lippmann's "pictures in our heads" of the "world outside" include our estimates of what others think. These perceptions of social reality lead to the formation of active publics and condition actions toward others, both other individuals and other organizations. Researchers studying how people interact with their computer, television, and new media arrived at the same conclusion: "What *seems* to be true is often more influential than what really is true.

. . . *Perceptions* are far more influential than reality defined more objectively."[68] As Lippmann said, "That is why until we know what others think they know, we cannot truly understand their acts."[69]

Communication, then, not only moves information from one party in a relationship to another but also defines the relationships and social environment within which all people function: as students, citizens, employees, managers, and policy makers. Not surprisingly, the media of communication—the topic of the next two chapters—play essential roles in shaping both issues and their social contexts. Mass media make possible the thinking together that shapes and represents the states of consensus in complex organizations, in communities, and in the larger global society.

Notes

1 Frederick Williams, *The New Communications*, 3d ed. (Belmont, CA: Wadsworth, 1992), 9.

2 "Brainy Quote," BrainyMedia.com. 15 April 2008, http://www.brainyquote.com/quotes/quotes/c/charleseva118640.html. Hughes served as 36th governor of New York (1907–1910); Associate Justice, U.S. Supreme Court (1910–1916); and 44th Secretary of State (1921–1925).

3 Raphael G. Satter, "Activists Mark Darfur Anniversary," Associated Press Online (13 April 2008), 15 April 2008, http://ap.google.com/article/ALeqM5hiOLjJP2On81d9 P1e44FQb6Xv2JAD90158900.

4 Walter Lippmann, *Public Opinion* (New York: Harcourt, Brace and Company, 1922), 3 and 4.

5 "Media Usage and Consumer Spending: 2000–2009," *Statistical Abstract of the United States: 2007*. U.S. Census Bureau. 15 April 2008.

6 See Chapter 10 for more details about new and traditional media.

7 Paul F. Lazarsfeld, Bernard Berelson, and Hazel Gaudet, *The People's Choice: How the Voter Makes Up His Mind in a Presidential Campaign*, 3d ed. (New York: Columbia University Press, 1968), 151.

8 Warren Weaver, "The Mathematics of Communication," in *Communication and Culture: Reading in the Codes of Human Interaction*, ed. Alfred G. Smith (New York: Holt, Rinehart and Winston, 1966), 17. Reprinted from *Scientific American*, 181 (1949): 11–15. Original theory published in Claude E. Shannon and Warren Weaver, *The Mathematical Theory of Communication* (Urbana: University of Illinois Press, 1949).

9 Ibid., 17.

10 Wilbur Schramm, "The Nature of Communication Between Humans," in *The Process and Effects of Mass Communication*, rev. ed., ed. Wilbur Schramm and Donald F. Roberts (Urbana: University of Illinois Press, 1971), 17.

11 Ibid., 38–47.

12 Carl I. Hovland, Irving L. Janis, and Harold H. Kelley, *Communication and Persuasion* (New Haven: Yale University Press, 1953). The World War II "Yale studies" provided the foundation for persuasion theory still used for designing both persuasion effects research and public communication campaigns.

13 Norman H. Anderson, "Integration Theory and Attitude Change," *Psychological Review* 78, no. 3 (May 1971): 171–206.

14 Adapted from Carl I. Hovland, Arthur A. Lumsdaine, and Fred D. Sheffield, "The Effect of Presenting 'One Side' versus 'Both Sides' in Changing Opinions on a Controversial Subject," in *Experiments on Mass Communication*, 201–27 (Princeton: Princeton University Press, 1949). Also in Schramm and Roberts, *The Process and Effects of Mass Communication*, 467–84.

15 Arthur A. Lumsdaine and Irving L. Janis, "Resistance to 'Counterpropaganda' Produced by One-Sided and Two-Sided 'Propaganda' Presentations," *Public Opinion Quarterly* 17, no. 3 (1953): 311–18. See also William J. McGuire, "Persuasion, Resistance, and Attitude Change," in *Handbook of Communication*, ed. Ithiel de Sola Pool and others, 216–52 (Skokie, IL: Rand McNally, 1973).

16 Carl I. Hovland, ed., *The Order of Presentation in Persuasion* (New Haven: Yale University Press, 1957). Reports series of experiments from the Yale studies of message effects in persuasion. The order of presentation, however, turned out to be a relatively minor factor in the communication process, inspiring little research over the years.

17 Reported in Hovland, Janis, and Kelley, *Communication and Persuasion*.

18 Ronald W. Rogers, "A Protection Motivation Theory of Fear Appeals and Attitude Change," *Journal of Psychology* 91 (September 1975): 93–114. See also Rogers and C. R. Mewborn, "Fear Appeals and Attitude Change: Effects of a Threat's Noxiousness, Probability of Occurrence, and the Efficacy of Coping Responses," *Journal of Personality and Social Psychology* 34, no. 1 (July 1976): 54–61.

[19] Michael Burgoon, "Messages and Persuasive Effects," in *Message Effects in Communication Science: Sage Annual Reviews of Communication Research* 17, ed. James J. Bradac (Newbury Park, CA: Sage Publications, 1989), 157.

[20] See Gerald R. Miller, "Interpersonal Communication," chapter 5 in *Human Communication: Theory and Research*, ed. Gordon L. Dahnke and Glen W. Clatterbuck, 91–122 (Belmont, CA: Wadsworth, 1990), for a review of interpersonal communication.

[21] Summary of "Developing Frameworks for Studying Mass Communication," chapter 1 in Lowery and DeFleur, *Milestones in Mass Communication Research*, 1–29.

[22] Brenda Dervin, "Audience as Listener and Learner, Teacher and Confidante: The Sense-Making Approach," in *Public Communication Campaigns*, 2d ed., ed. Ronald E. Rice and Charles K. Atkin (Newbury Park, CA: Sage Publications, 1989), 69.

[23] See Chapter 7, "The Relationship," in Stephen W. Littlejohn and Karen A. Foss. *Theories of Human Communication*, 8th ed. (Belmont, CA: Thomson Wadsworth, 2005), 186–212, for detailed discussion of theory about communication relationships.

[24] Ibid.

[25] Marvin E. Shaw and Dennis S. Gouran, "Group Dynamics and Communication," in *Human Communication: Theory and Research*, ed. Gordon L. Dahnke and Glen W. Clatterbuck, 123–55 (Belmont, CA: Wadsworth, 1990).

[26] Randy Y. Hirokawa, "Group Communication and Decision Making Performance: A Continued Test of the Functional Perspective," *Human Communication Research* 14, no. 4 (Summer 1988): 487–515.

[27] Walter Lippmann, "The World Outside and the Pictures in Our Heads," chapter 1, *Public Opinion* (New York: Harcourt, Brace and Company, 1922). Reprinted in *The Process and Effects of Mass Communication*, rev. ed., edited by Schramm and Roberts, 265–86.

[28] George Gerbner, "Toward 'Cultural Indicators': The Analysis of Mass Mediated Message Systems," *AV Communication Review* 17, no. 2 (1970): 137–148.

[29] Nancy Signorielli, "Television's Mean and Dangerous World: A Continuation of the Cultural Indicators Perspective," in *Cultivation Analysis: New Dimensions in Media Effects Research*, ed. Nancy Signorielle and Michael Morgan (Newbury Park, CA: Sage, 1990): 85–106.

[30] Maxwell E. McCombs and Donald L. Shaw, "The Agenda-Setting Function of Mass Media," *Public Opinion Quarterly* 36, no. 2 (Summer 1972): 176–87. First of many reports of media agenda-setting effects on a variety of issues in a variety of settings.

[31] Maxwell McCombs, Edna Einsiedel, and David Weaver, *Contemporary Public Opinion: Issues and the News* (Hillsdale, NJ: Lawrence Erlbaum Associates, 1991), 12–17.

[32] Ibid., 17–21.

[33] Wayne Wanta and Y. C. Wu, "Interpersonal Communication and the Agenda-Setting Process," *Journalism Quarterly* 69, no. 4 (1992): 847–855.

[34] David Demers, "Issue Obtrusiveness and the Agenda-Setting Effects of National Network News," *Communication Research* 16, no. 6, (1989): 793–812.

[35] Maxwell E. McCombs and Donald L. Shaw, "The Evolution of Agenda-Setting Research: Twenty-Five Years in the Marketplace of Ideas," *Journal of Communication* 43, no. 2 (1993): 65.

[36] Spiro Kiousis and Michael Mitrook, "First- and Second-Level Agenda-Building and Agenda-Setting Effects: Exploring the Linkages Among Candidate News Releases, Media Coverage, and Public Opinion During the 2002 Florida Gubernatorial Election," *Journal of Public Relations Research* 18 (3): 269.

[37] Maxwell McCombs and Amy Reynolds, "News Influence on Our Pictures of the World," in *Media Effects: Advances in Theory and Research*, 2nd ed., ed. Jennings Bryant and Dolf Zillmann (Mahwah, NJ: Lawrence Erlbaum Associates, 2002), 12.

[38] Maxwell McCombs, "The Agenda-Setting Function of the Press," in *The Press*, eds. Geneva Overholser and Kathleen Hall Jamieson (Oxford, U.K.: Oxford University Press, 2005),159.

[39] Steven H. Chaffee, "The Interpersonal Context of Mass Communication," in *Current Perspectives in Mass Communication Research*, vol. 1, ed. F. Gerald Kline and Phillip J. Tichenor (Beverly Hills, CA: Sage Publications, 1972), 95–120.

[40] Everett M. Rogers, "Communication and Social Change," in *Human Communication*, ed. Dahnke and Clatterbuck, 259–71.

[41] Elihu Katz, "The Two-Step Flow of Communication," *Public Opinion Quarterly* 21 (1957): 61–78.

[42] Everett M. Rogers, *Diffusion of Innovation* (New York: Free Press, 1995), 290–304.

[43] Stephen W. Littlejohn and Karen A. Foss, *Theories of Human Communication*, 9th ed. (Belmont, CA: Thomson Wadsworth, 2008), 322.

[44] Elizabeth Noelle-Neumann, "The Spiral of Silence: A Theory of Public Opinion," *Journal of Communication* 24, (1974): 24–51. Later published in book form, *The Spiral of Silence: Public Opinion—Our Social Skin* (Chicago: University of Chicago Press, 1984).

[45] Lippmann, *Public Opinion*, 14.

[46] Everett M. Rogers, "Intermedia Processes and Powerful Media Effects," in *Media Effects,* ed. Bryant and Zillmann: 211.

47 Melvin L. DeFleur and Sandra J. Ball-Rokeach, *Theories of Mass Communication*, 4th ed. (New York: Longman, 1982), 226.

48 Edward M. Block, "How Public Opinion Is Formed," *Public Relations Review* 3, no. 3 (Fall 1977): 15.

49 Irving Crespi, *The Public Opinion Process: How the People Speak* (Mahwah, NJ: Lawrence Erlbaum Associates, 1997): 10.

50 Vincent Price and Donald F. Roberts, "Public Opinion Processes," in *Handbook of Communication Science*, ed. Berger and Chaffee, 784.

51 David Domke, David P. Fan, Michael Fibison, Dhavan V. Shah, Steven S. Smith, and Mark D. Watts, "News Media, Candidates and Issues, and Public Opinion in the 1996 Presidential Campaign," *Journalism & Mass Communication Quarterly* 74, no. 4 (Winter 1997): 733.

52 Dennis Chong, "Creating Common Frames of Reference on Political Issues," Chapter 8 in *Political Persuasion and Attitude Change*, ed. Diana C. Mutz, Paul M. Sniderman, and Richard A Brody (Ann Arbor: University of Michigan Press, 1996): 199.

53 Dan Drew and David Weaver, "Media Attention, Media Exposure, and Media Effects," *Journalism Quarterly* 67, no. 4 (Winter 1990): 740–48.

54 Richard M. Perloff, "The Third-Person Effect," in *Media Effects*. Ed. Bryant and Zillmann: 503. See also Vincent Price, Li-Ning Huang, and David Tewksbury, "Third-Person Effects of News Coverage: Orientations toward Media," *Journalism & Mass Communication Quarterly* 74, no. 3 (Autumn 1997): 525.

55 John Dewey, *The Public and Its Problems* (New York: Henry Holt and Company, 1927), 15–17.

56 James E. Grunig and Fred C. Repper, "Strategic Management, Publics, and Issues," in *Excellence in Public Relations and Communication Management*, ed. James E.

Grunig (Hillsdale, NJ: Lawrence Erlbaum Associates, 1992), 135–37.

57 See also James E. Grunig, "Communication Behaviors and Attitudes of Environmental Publics: Two Studies," *Journalism Monographs* 81 (March 1983): 40–41.

58 Grunig and Repper, "Strategic Management, Publics, and Issues," 139.

59 Dewey, *The Public and Its Problems*, 28–29.

60 Concepts and paradigm of individual orientation adapted from Richard F. Carter, "Communication and Affective Relations," *Journalism Quarterly* 42, no. 2 (Spring 1965): 203–12.

61 Crespi, *The Public Opinion Process*, 19.

62 Price and Roberts, "Public Opinion Processes," 787.

63 Model and coorientational concepts from Jack M. McLeod and Steven H. Chaffee, "Interpersonal Approaches to Communication Research," in *Interpersonal Perception and Communication*, edited by Steven H. Chaffee and Jack M. McLeod, special edition of *American Behavioral Scientist* 16, no. 4 (March–April 1973): 483–88.

64 Thomas J. Scheff, "Toward a Sociological Model of Consensus," *American Sociological Review* 32, no. 1 (February 1967): 32–46.

65 Ibid., 37.

66 Keith R. Stamm and John E. Bowes, "Communicating During an Environmental Decision," *Journal of Environmental Education* 3, no. 3 (Spring 1972): 49–56.

67 Glen M. Broom, "Coorientational Measurement of Public Issues," *Public Relations Review* 3, no. 4 (Winter 1977): 110–19. See also Glen M. Broom and David M. Dozier, *Using Research in Public Relations* (Englewood Cliffs, NJ: Prentice Hall, 1990): 36–39.

68 Byron Reeves and Clifford Nass, *The Media Equation* (Cambridge, UK: Cambridge University Press, 1996): 253.

69 Lippmann, *Public Opinion*, 13.

Additional Sources

Bryant, Jennings, and Dolf Zillmann. *Media Effects: Advances in Theory and Research,* 2nd ed. Mahwah, NJ: Lawrence Erlbaum Associates, 2002. Twenty-two chapters summarizing the major theory and research on media effects.

Dominick, Joseph R. *Dynamics of Mass Communications: Media in the Digital Age with Media World 2.0 DVD-ROM.* New York: McGraw-Hill, 2008. Covers iPods, blogs, broadband TV channels, user-generated content such as YouTube, social networking sites, and Web 2.0.

Ewen, Stuart. *PR! A Social History of Spin.* New York: Basic Books, 1997. Almost 500 pages outlining a critical view of how public relations evolved from the work and thoughts of Edward Bernays and Walter Lippmann.

Glasser, Theodore L., and Charles T. Salmon, eds. *Public Opinion and the Communication of Consent.* New York: Guilford Press, 1995. Assembles 17 chapters written by 30 leading scholars on the nature, contexts, processes, and impact of public opinion.

Knapp, Mark L., and Anita L. Vangelisti. *Interpersonal Communication and Human Relationships.* Boston: Allyn & Bacon, 1992. Summary of literature and theory related to dialogue, interaction rituals, relationships, and other aspects of relational communication.

Littlejohn, Stephen W., and Karen A. Foss. *Theories of Human Communication,* 9th ed. Belmont, CA:

Thomson Wadsworth, 2008. Readable summaries of major theorical paradigms guiding theory and practice.

Perloff, Richard M. *The Dynamics of Persuasion*. Mahwah, NJ: Lawrence Erlbaum Associates, 2003. Comprehensive introduction to persuasive communication and attitude change.

Reese, Stephen D., Oscar H. Gandy, Jr., and A. E. Grant. *Framing Public Life: Perspectives on Media and Our Understanding of the Social World*. Mahwah, NJ: Lawrence Erlbaum Associates, 2001. A compendium of research on mass media framing.

Riffe, Daniel, ed. "Advances in Media Effects: Framesetting and Frame Changing." Special issue of *Journalism & Mass Communication Quarterly* 83, no. 4 (Winter 2006). Five insightful articles on media messages and effects.

Van Ginneken, Jaap. *Collective Behavior and Public Opinion*. Mahwah, NJ: Lawrence Erlbaum Associates, 2003. Outlines new thinking on the dynamics of public opinion.

Wanta, Wayne. *The Public and the National Agenda: How People Learn about Important Issues.* Mahwah, NJ: Lawrence Erlbaum Associates, 1997. Examines agenda-setting effects by examining demographic, psychological, and behavioral influences. Provides exhaustive list of agenda-setting references.

Internal Relations and Employee Communication

STUDY GUIDE After studying Chapter 9, you should be able to:

▶ Define internal and employee communication as a part of the public relations function, using the basic elements of the definition of public relations.

▶ Argue convincingly for the importance of the internal relations function.

▶ Discuss the impact of organizational culture on internal communication.

▶ Apply systems theory to internal relations.

▶ Discuss some of the regulatory and business contexts for internal relations.

▶ Explain the major purposes of employee communication.

▶ Describe nonmediated and mediated means of communicating with internal publics.

Public relations deals with the relationships among organizations and all types of publics on whom its success or failure depends. You probably think of public relations as communicating with external publics. However, the internal publics—employees—are any organization's most important publics.

This chapter discusses how public relations contributes to effective communication *within* an organization, also referred to as "internal relations." Communication inside an organization is arguably even more important than external communication, because the organization has to function effectively in attaining its goals in order to survive. In short, "timely, complete, and accurate corporate communication and face-to-face managerial communication can help to secure employee action in favor of company goals."[2]

Internal relations means building and maintaining relationships with all the publics inside an organization, including production line workers, managers and supervisors, administrative staff, and facilities and maintenance support, to name but a few. For example, a former CEO of General Motors (GM) identified internal communication as a "top three priority" because it is so vital to organizational success.[3] As one practitioner put it, "an organization's most important audience is, has been and always will be its employees."[4]

The first part of this chapter discusses how organizational culture and worldviews are important concepts for internal relations and the cultural contexts in which employee communication takes place. The second section addresses some of the problems and challenges faced in internal relations, including the regulatory and business contexts in which employee

As leaders, we must accept the challenge to create a work environment that sets the world-class standard where individual differences not only are recognized and valued, but indeed embraced because of the richness they bring to thinking, creating, problem solving, and understanding our customers and communities.
—*Marilyn Laurie,*[1] *Executive Vice President, Public Relations (Retired), AT&T*

This chapter was revised in collaboration with Professor **Bey-Ling Sha**, Ph.D., APR, School of Journalism and Media Studies, San Diego State University. Previously, Dr. Sha taught at the University of Maryland–College Park and at the American University of Paris. She also served as a public affairs specialist with the U.S. Census Bureau, Washington, D.C., and as a consultant in public relations research and strategy for numerous public and private organizations.

communication takes place. The chapter concludes with a review of some commonly employed means by which public relations practitioners conduct internal relations—in particular, the nonmediated and mediated contexts for employee communication.

Importance of Internal Relations

An organization's most important relationships are those with employees at all levels. The terms *internal publics* and *employee publics* refer to both managers and the people being supervised. These publics represent an organization's greatest resource—its people. According to Alvie Smith, former director of corporate communications at General Motors, two factors are changing internal communication with employees and enhancing management's respect for this part of the public relations function:

1. *The value of understanding, teamwork, and commitment by employees in achieving bottom-line results.* These positive aspects of worker behavior are strongly influenced by effective, way-of-life interactive communications throughout the organization.

2. *The need to build a strong manager communication network, one that makes every supervisor at every level accountable for communicating effectively with his or her employees.* This needs to be more than just job-related information and should include key business and public issues affecting the total organization.[5] [Emphasis added.]

Organizations miss out on a sizable share of their human resource potential because they do not put a high priority on effective, two-way communication—the foundation for management–employee relations and overall job performance. Smith calls the consequence "slothing on the job":

> The ugly truth is that employee disloyalty and lack of commitment to organizational goals may be costing American businesses more than $50 billion a year . . . the cost of absenteeism, labor grievances, production interruptions, poor quality, repair and warranty expenses. Perhaps most costly of all is inaction by employees who withhold their best efforts and ideas; who cruise along with just passable performance.[6]

The coordination and mediation necessary for dealing with employees today put the public relations staff, with its communication knowledge and skills, square in the middle of managing internal relationships. For example, former Delta Air Lines chairman and CEO Ronald W. Allen, who rose through the ranks by running departments such as human resources and training, saw his primary job as cultivating a motivated and loyal workforce.[7]

Day-to-day working relationships involve a great deal of contact, but effective employee communication develops in a climate of trust and honesty.[8] Ideally, working relationships are characterized by at least seven conditions:

1. Confidence and trust between employer and employees
2. Honest, candid information flowing freely up, down, and sideways in the organization
3. Satisfying status and participation for each person
4. Continuity of work without strife

5. Healthy or safe surroundings
6. Success for the enterprise
7. Optimism about the future

The chief executive must establish this culture and endorse it as formal policy. Even with such support from the top, however, many barriers stand in the way of free-flowing, two-way communication in organizations.

Opinion Research Corporation has tracked employee opinions of organizational internal communication since 1950. Large majorities consistently give their organizations favorable scores on credibility, but fewer than half say their organizations do a good job of "letting them know what is going on," or *downward communication* (management to employee). Less than half also give high marks to their organization's willingness to "listen to their views," or *upward communication* (employee to management). Face-to-face communication with an "open-door policy" is the primary medium for encouraging *upward, two-way communication* and for building good working relationships with employees.

Balancing the needs for employee satisfaction with the success of the enterprise is but one aspect of the continuous adjustment and reconciliation in employer–employee relationships—especially in multicultural settings. As a part of the larger public relations function, however, **the goal of internal relations is to establish and maintain mutually beneficial relationships between an organization and the employees on whom its success or failure depends.**

Cultural Contexts

Understanding the internal communication of any organization requires analysis of the culture of that organization. Some who study organizational culture define it as the shared meanings and assumptions of group members.[9] Others focus on culture as a common values system or the behavioral norms in the organization.[10] Organizational culture is an important consideration because it has a significant impact on the model of public relations an organization practices and on the internal communications that follow.

Organizational culture is defined as follows:

> Organizational culture is the sum total of shared values, symbols, meanings, beliefs, assumptions, and expectations that organize and integrate a group of people who work together.[11]

The culture of an organization is often what defines it as different from other organizations, and—if managed properly—can be a valuable asset in building cohesion and teamwork inside the organization, resulting in organizational effectiveness—reaching its goals. Organizational culture defines the values and norms used by decision makers in an organization. Worldviews and organizational culture define the range of responses preferred in any given issue situation. Although it is often unspoken, organizational culture is a powerful influence on individual behaviors within an organization.

Dimensions of Culture

Dimensions of culture are ways in which culture can be classified and explained. One of the most well-known studies of various cultural dimensions was conducted by Hofstede.[12] Although Hofstede's work focused on national cultures, the dimensions that he articulated can be applied to organizational cultures as well, because organizations often reflect the national cultures in which they operate.

The first dimension of culture articulated by Hofstede is the concept of *power-distance*, which is the extent to which people see inequities as natural and unchangeable. An organization with high power-distance is one in which managers and employees see themselves as inherently different from each other. Employees respect managers simply because of the position they hold within the organization, and promotion from the lower employee levels to the managerial levels would be unusual. In contrast, a low power-distance organization is one in which managers and employees see each other as equals, despite their different positions within the organization. In these organizations, there are no special bathrooms for high-level managers or different dining areas in the company cafeteria for workers of different positions.

For the public relations practitioner charged with communicating internally, the power-distance dimension suggests how organizational messages should be disseminated. In a high power-distance organization, communication might emphasize the power and authority of the top manager giving the information. For example, in South Korea, which has high power-distance in both its corporate and national cultures, there is high social distance between managers and employees, and managers can control the organization's communication system without "interference" from employees.[13]

In contrast, in a low power-distance organization, information might be better received if the manager emphasized similarities between him- or herself and the employees in terms of goals, values, or concerns. For example, many corporations in the United States, a traditionally low power-distance country, have instituted company blogs in which employees interact directly with CEOs, speaking to them as social equals, asking them hard questions, and expecting timely answers.[14]

Hofstede's second dimension of culture is *individualism*, or the extent to which people put their own individual needs ahead of the needs of the group. Organizations with strong individualistic cultures reward employees on the basis of their personal achievements, and there is competition among employees to gain that individual recognition. On the other hand, organizations weak in individualism are strong in collectivism, emphasizing the needs and accomplishments of teams of employees and focusing on the goals of the group instead of the goals of the individual.

For employee communication messages, the public relations practitioner in a highly individualistic culture might emphasize the actions that employees can take as individuals in order to accomplish something, say, a successful recycling program. In a more collectivist culture, public relations messages might instead focus on how recycling is a team responsibility that benefits everyone in the organization. As another example, in one study of an international public relations firm, employees from cultures high in individualism preferred less standardization of their work activities.[15] In other words, they wanted to do their jobs their own way.

Third, Hofstede identified *uncertainty avoidance* as a cultural dimension that explains the extent to which people prefer organizational communication and structures that reduce their social anxiety. In companies with high uncertainty avoidance, employees tend to prefer "clear requirements and instructions," to follow organizational rules, to take fewer risks, and to demonstrate more loyalty to the employer.[16] In a low uncertainty avoidance culture, people feel more tolerant of ambiguous situations, have lower resistance to change, and show greater interest in taking risks. Organizations with low uncertainty avoidance are more likely to engage in two-way public relations activities; in other words, they do not feel threatened by input from their environment.[17]

Finally, Hofstede's fourth dimension of culture, which he called *masculinity*, describes behaviors that are traditionally (or stereotypically) "masculine," such as aggressiveness and independence. An organization that is high in masculinity rewards competitiveness and initiative. On the other hand, an organization that is low in masculinity rewards nurturing and cooperation, i.e., traditionally or stereotypically "feminine" characteristics. For the public relations practitioner, employee communication must reflect organizational values to be effective, and this dimension of culture offers one way to characterize those values. Thus, in an organization with high masculinity, an employee communication program to encourage production might offer a competition between individuals or departments. In an organization with low masculinity, the same employee communication program might point out how increasing the production rate enhances or nurtures employees' sense of self-esteem.

Applying Systems Theory to Internal Relations

Chapter 7 outlined the ecological approach to public relations and how organizations can be relatively open or closed systems. This approach applies as well to internal communication as it does to external communication. To review, open systems are organizations that receive input from the environment and adjust themselves in response to that input. Closed systems are organizations that do not receive input from the environment; as a result, they are less likely to be able to adapt to environmental changes.

For internal communication, whether an organization is open or closed is related to its "worldview," or the basic value and belief system prevalent in an organization. Generally, the worldview of the organizational leadership, i.e., the dominant coalition (see Chapter 3), shapes the worldview of the organization as a whole through internal communication. Public relations researchers have identified two primary types of worldviews—symmetrical and asymmetrical.[18]

An *asymmetrical worldview* is one in which an organization's goal is to get what it wants without having to change the way it does business internally. This worldview focuses almost exclusively on the goals of the organization, and the culture is to resist change, much like the culture of a closed system. In an asymmetrical worldview, power in decision making tends to remain on the side of the organization and is not shared with publics.

A *symmetrical worldview* incorporates the ideas of negotiation, conflict resolution, and compromise in an organization's operating procedures. The organization is not only self-oriented, but also oriented on satisfying the interests of strategic publics. Therefore, desires and goals are set in a shared fashion by incorporating some of what the publics want. Change occurs on both sides of the relationship—a give-and-take on behalf of both organization and its publics. Change may not always be balanced in every instance, but both the organization and its publics are open to adopting or adapting to the views of the other through dialogue and negotiation. In other words, an organization with a symmetrical worldview tends to function as an open system.

Symmetrical and asymmetrical worldviews produce different organizational cultures—authoritarian and participative. These two organizational cultures have direct and indirect effects on the nature and flow of internal communication in the organization.

Authoritarian Organizational Culture   An authoritarian organizational culture arises from an asymmetrical worldview. In this type of culture, communication processes are *structured* and *formalized* within a decision-making hierarchy. Military organizations typically are examples of authoritarian organizational cultures.

In authoritarian organizational cultures, decisions are made at the top levels of the organization and implemented by those at lower levels. Decision making is *centralized* at the highest level of the organization, and input is typically not sought from middle- and lower-level employees. An authoritarian organizational culture usually stresses *individual accountability* for an area of limited scope, and organizational departments are independent, rather than interdependent. Authoritarian cultures are often based on the idea of a "mechanistic" or "mechanical" organizational structure, in which tasks are routinized and there is a *high division of labor*. For example, at Amazon.com, one employee is responsible for sealing and labeling boxes as they roll off the stocking line, while another employee stacks the boxes in the warehouse where they wait to be shipped. There is little role for dialogue or feedback in an authoritarian organizational culture, because the input of employees is not seen as vital in management.[19]

Communication in authoritarian cultures, therefore, takes on the form of disseminating the ideas and goals decided by upper management to various internal employee publics, such as midlevel and lower-level management, administrative and support staff, supervisors, skilled laborers, and unskilled laborers. This means that communication is generally one-sided—or asymmetrical—in that management directs employees, but little communication flows from employees back to management. Furthermore, what little communication does flow from employees to management is unlikely to result in the managers' changing their minds to accommodate employee concerns. Efficiency is valued over innovation in many authoritarian cultures due to the emphasis on uniform output of a product or standardized provision of a service.

Authoritarian cultures, like other closed systems, tend to resist change. Input from publics is viewed as a threat to authority rather than as an opportunity for change. These organizations also resist sharing power with "outsiders." Even internal publics face recalcitrant management in an authoritarian culture, leading to high employee turnover and lower levels of job satisfaction than reported in other types of organizational cultures.

Participative Organizational Culture   Participative organizational cultures are based on a symmetrical worldview that values *dialogue* and the exchange of input between the organization and its publics. *Teamwork* is valued, and emphasis is placed on the collective rather than the individual, meaning that the organization and employees share goals. A participative organizational culture values innovation and seeks input from employees and other stakeholder groups to ensure a thorough analysis of decisions and policy. Organizational departments are often integrated or multifunctional and emphasize open communication across different departments.[20]

A participative organizational culture values information and seeks input from internal publics; in other words, it functions as an open system with respect to employees, their opinions, and their concerns. Feedback and upward communication allow employees and those at lower levels of an organization to have a voice in management decision making. Feedback is encouraged and sought; furthermore, feedback is taken seriously and can lead to organizational change. In the language of systems theory (see Chapter 8), the organization engages in morphogenesis to maintain homeostasis. This type of culture is organic, as opposed to mechanistic, as parts of the team work together in an environment that encourages and rewards *innovation*.

In participative organizational cultures, decisions are made in a decentralized manner—across varying levels of the organization—and implemented by those who hold responsibility over a specific area. Innovative ideas can come from any level of the organization, from the manufacturing line to top management, or from the person who fills potholes in city streets to the head of the city street department. Feedback at all levels of the organization is sought and valued. One effect of a participative organizational culture is increased teamwork and higher value placed on employees at all levels.

At one company, the CEO established an employee advisory board to advise management on ways to be more environmentally friendly. Employees were eager to join the board, and many of its recommendations to help the company "go green" were implemented. According to the CEO, "employees will always be happier in an environment where they feel that they are being listened to and that their opinions count."[21]

In short, whether described using Hofstede's dimensions of culture or organizational worldviews, organizational culture has significant impact on internal relations and employee communication. Efforts to communicate with employees can only be successful when they account for and work with an organization's culture and worldviews. (See Exhibit 9.1 on page 220 for one approach to accounting for cultural factors in multinational organizations.)

Regulatory and Business Contexts

Internal relations involves more than communicating with employee publics in isolation; there are legal and business realities in which and about which employee communication takes place.

Safety and Compliance

Every organization must comply with the governing standards of the country in which it operates, even if the organization operates locations in many nations. The different standards for each country must be followed, or the organization can face severe penalties and fines from regulators. Internal relations specialists work hard at making sure the standards of each country are known and communicated internally in a global organization with locations around the world. Saying "that isn't the way things are done in our home country" holds no weight with foreign governments, and their regulations can vary tremendously from an organization's "standard operating procedure" at home. Every country has the equivalent of taxes, labor laws that govern workers, operational laws that govern workplace safety, and environmental laws concerning waste and transportation of materials. These laws are in addition to what the organization must also handle externally, such as import and export regulations, competition, and other civil and criminal laws.

Internal relations staff also educates employees about compliance with government regulations. Employees need to understand the rules under which they are required to operate in order to maximize their own safety. In the United States, one primary responsibility of the internal relations function is to communicate Occupational Safety and Health Administration (OSHA) worker safety standards required by the government. The U.S. Department of Labor requires organizations to hang posters in the workplace that list federal, state, and OSHA standards. These posters, which are usually displayed on bulletin boards or near time clocks or lockers, include topics such as minimum wage, safety standards, hand washing, and wearing protective equipment. OSHA governs everything from requiring hard hats in

EXHIBIT 9.1

Co-acculturation in Multinational Organizations

Suman Lee, Ph.D.,
Assistant Professor
Greenlee School of
Journalism and
Communication
Iowa State University

Doing business in the new global economy has created new kinds of organizations—multinational/multicultural organizations. It is now commonplace for multinational companies to include two or more cultures under a single corporate umbrella. In the multinational corporate setting, managers and workers are cultural strangers; each group with its own patterns of cognitive, affective, and behavioral structures and processes. Because of such cultural differences, multinational companies face unique challenges, and sometimes more serious manager–worker relationship problems, than do companies operating in their home settings.

For example, there can be problems in training new employees and in communication between managers and workers. Misconceptions led by cultural differences can interfere with the integration of new workers and cause higher turnover. In this regard, success or failure of a multinational company cannot be explained by economic factors alone. Effective communication and mutually beneficial relationships between cultural groups, especially manager–worker relationships, also serve as significant indicators of successful operation of multinational companies in the global economy.

Co-acculturation is a theoretical model for examining relationships between managers and workers in a multicultural, multinational organization. **Co-acculturation** can be defined as *simultaneous orientation toward each other and toward aspects of each other's culture.*

Co-acculturation combines and extends concepts derived from acculturation theory and the concept of coorientational consensus. Co-acculturation is not one individual's or one group's acculturation to a fixed and given host culture, such as when immigrants and international students "acculturate" to a host-country's culture. Rather, it represents *mutual and relational acculturation* between two or more cultural groups.

For example, Samsung Tijuana Park is a manufacturing plant in Mexico with expatriated Korean managers and resi-

dent Mexican workers. In this situation, both Koreans and Mexicans simultaneously acculturate to each other's cultures. Relationships in the co-acculturation paradigm require three measures: agreement, congruency, and accuracy.

Co-acculturation agreement is the comparison of one cultural group's view with the views held by the other group toward the same behavioral artifacts of culture. It represents the degree to which the cultural groups share the similar evaluations of the cultural artifacts. Therefore, co-acculturation agreement indicates the degree of cultural similarity between groups. **Co-acculturation congruency** is the comparison of one's own view on cultural aspects with his or her estimates of the other cultural group's view on the same dimensions. **Co-acculturation accuracy** is the degree to which members of different cultural groups estimate the other group's perceptions correctly. Improving co-acculturation agreement, congruency, and accuracy is a common goal for public relations programs.

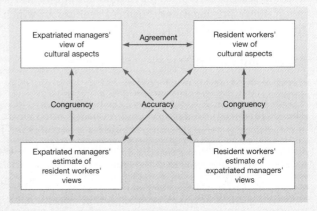

Co-acculturation theory has potential practical applications. Co-acculturation synthesizing acculturation theory and coorientational model has heuristic value not only in multinational organizations, but also in organizations undergoing merger or acquisition, as well as other organizations that employ from different cultural groups.

To some extent, public relations practitioners function as cultural messengers within and outside an organization. As globalization makes work settings much more culturally diverse, it will become the bigger challenge for public relations practitioners to facilitate communication within an organization. Co-acculturation provides a paradigm for understanding this challenge.

construction areas to the quality of air in office buildings. For example, OSHA regulates work conditions and safety of those handling the printing chemicals used to produce this book.

The Environmental Protection Agency (EPA) is another U.S. government agency that regulates disposal and transportation of goods, especially those deemed hazardous in nature, such as petroleum products, industrial chemicals such as DMSO or benzene, or pesticides. Many hazardous chemicals are used in manufacturing, so they must be produced at a chemical plant, are transported to the manufacturing site, and are eventually discarded after use. For example, textile dying and manufacturing plants often have large, concrete "settling ponds" in which used dyestuff is treated to decompose over time into biodegradable sediment. Or, Dow Chemical uses benzene, a highly poisonous solvent if airborne, and must maintain sensitive benzene monitors and alarms throughout its facility in case of accidental leaks. The EPA regulates sites such as these, and many others, for environmental safety compliance.

So, in many organizations, another important task of internal relations provides communication support to ensure that environmental regulations and worker safety standards are maintained. Responsible internal communication about these issues can be a matter of life and death and can help prevent the accidents and violations that damage organizational reputations.

Labor Relations

Another significant task of internal relations is interacting with hourly employees, some of whom belong to labor unions. The relationship with labor is a vital relationship on which the success or failure of the organization literally depends. This relationship cannot—and should not—be taken for granted. Maintenance of the relationship with labor constitutes a large part of an internal relations specialist's work, especially in organizations with a "unionized shop."

There is an inherent and undeniable tension between the roles of management and labor. This tension is the basis for many schools of thought in sociology and economics, in which labor and management are seen as adversaries locked in an eternal battle between the "haves" and the "have nots." Out of this socioeconomic theory arises the tension that exists in everyday relations with labor. There is a core value that labor enacts work and management controls work. Controlling resource allocations—money and number of jobs—is a main function of management, but workers would also like a voice in this process, and that is where internal relations comes into play.

Relationships with unionized workers and their unions must be attended to continually, and internal relations specialists facilitate and help maintain those relationships. Some assume that human resources (HR) is in charge of this organizational function, but the role of HR typically is limited to hiring, firing, training, and benefits. If a union is thinking of striking, it is the public relations function in management (usually the internal relations specialist) who first learns of the discontent. It is also the responsibility of internal relations to communicate about matters of dissention and try to find ways to resolve labor–management relationship problems. Although unions often draw much attention, the savvy internal relations manager accords just as much time and attention to communicating with nonunionized labor. (See Chapter 6 for legal considerations in labor–management communication.)

Organizational Change: Mergers, Acquisitions, and Layoffs

Internal communication specialists have important strategic responsibilities during organizational change. Communication during periods of change and uncertainty is

EXHIBIT 9.2

Communicating Organizational Change

David B. McKinney, APR, ABC
Public Affairs Manager
Shell Chemical Company,
Deer Park, Texas

Employees who learn from the local TV news that their company has just been acquired or the plant where they make widgets is shutting down have a right to be upset. After all, who has a greater personal and emotional stake in an organization than those who actually work there?

A line from a popular song proclaims: "The winds of change are always blowing." Today's business environment is characterized by frequent and unexpected change, with few certainties as to the future of the organization or individual jobs. At the same time, the abundance of and reliance on electronic communications, particularly e-mail and the intranet, is creating an information overload for all levels of employees.

Ironically, information breakdowns often occur when *effective* internal communication is the most critical: during workplace change or uncertainty such as layoffs, mergers, product recalls, and scandals. Addressing employee concerns, distraction and resistance requires attention to *content* (*what* is being communicated), and understanding the role of available *tools* or *mediums* (*how, where,* and *when* information is delivered). Additional challenges include how quickly management should respond; how much information should be given; and how employee support is gained and maintained. Objectives should be to keep up staff morale, boost staff's enthusiasm and interest in their jobs, and show what is being done to help those who lose their jobs.

Shell International Ltd. takes a three-phase approach to communicating change: Phase 1 has to do with "unfreezing" or acknowledging the passing of the old and celebration of the new. Phase 2 addresses "changing" or cognitive restructuring, which is timing critical (denial/resistance/exploration/commitment). Phase 3 is "refreezing" or commitment—reward, training, and validation. Understanding these phases can remove fear and uncertainty, limit rumors, and restore a sense of control.

Every step of the way, internal communication must support business objectives, generate internal community spirit to raise and maintain morale, and be honest and open. Employees should be given the information they want and need, as well as being told what management wants to say. **During workplace change or uncertainty, employees want to know what it means for them**: do they have a job, where will they work, why are the changes happening and how will it improve the business? The focus should be on face-to-face communication because it is, by far, the most effective. Other methods, such as e-mail, newsletters, and the intranet, can be used to raise awareness and share information, saving face-to-face discussion for debate, clarifying understanding, and private feedback—not for information dumping.

Internal communication is often overshadowed in the context of overall communication efforts. Attention typically is targeted toward external relations with media, investors, government agencies, the community, and other stakeholders. However, organizational change or uncertainty requires a communication plan that is sensitive to employees and acknowledges their potential impact as communication ambassadors for the organization as they interact with families, neighbors, and others in the community. Armed with factual information, informed employees are less likely to be discontent or engage in rumors and speculation—usually negative— caused by lack of, bad, or no "official" information.

As the song reminds us, the winds of change are always blowing. Effective, conscientious management ensures that when change occurs, the information winds blow to and from employees, facilitating two-way dialogue early, often, and in a credible, open manner.

Courtesy David B. McKinney and Shell International Ltd.

more than just "hand-holding," as it plays an important role in helping employees cope with uncertainty and adjust to change (see Exhibit 9.2).

In situations such as a merger or acquisition, internal publics of all levels immediately have a need for communication about the future of their position in the organization. These situations tend to produce anxiety, especially for those not involved in the discussions and decisions that led to organizational change. The role of internal relations should be to guide the merger or acquisition communication with internal publics in a forthright and expedient manner, dealing with questions and uncertainties in an honest manner. Often, if employees know that a decision is still under consideration, their anxiety will be less than if they know nothing at all. Again, "We are still working that out" is a better answer than "No comment."

Publics with a high level of involvement in the organization will have a greater need for information in times of uncertainty than in normal times, and internal relations should respond immediately and proactively. For example, a sharp drop in stock prices can cause both employees and investors to become concerned and to want accurate information rapidly. This information must be truthful.

In the Enron case, top executives were selling their own stock while assuring employees that the company was not losing value. This is an abhorrent example of allowing circumstances to dominate truth—rather than allowing truth to decide circumstances. It is the responsibility of the internal relations manager to be honest and forthcoming with information to internal publics, even when it means pushing recalcitrant top management to do the right thing.

During reorganization and layoffs, the responsible organization responds by helping employees to the greatest extent that it can. For instance, when a manufacturing site is to move, the company could pay to relocate employees to the new location or provide them with job search assistance and retraining. This is how Johnson & Johnson responded when the company sold a surgical scrubs facility that had employed many mentally challenged persons in garment folding and packing. The company worked with the buyer to make sure that this community outreach initiative was continued and then helped place some of the displaced workers in other Johnson & Johnson facilities.

Communicating Internally

Employee communication serves three main purposes. First, internal communication is meant to acculturate employees or to get them to understand and internalize the organization's culture and values. Second, internal communication serves as a way to inform employees of organizational developments, happenings, and news. Finally, internal communication is a way for the organization to listen to its employees, to hear employees' concerns and questions. All of these purposes can be served in any of a variety of ways, and new technology increasingly affects the manner in which employee communication occurs.

Acculturating Employees

Efforts to acculturate employees start from the moment a new person is hired. Usually, no distinction is made between information about organizational culture that is provided to internal and external publics. This congruence of internal and external messaging has two benefits; first, it ensures that employees get the same information about organizational culture as everyone else, and second, it helps to attract new employees who already believe in the organization's culture and values. Organizational culture is often articulated in vision statements, mission statements, policy documents, ethics statements, and training manuals.

Vision Statements   Vision statements provide an overview of organizational goals in the broadest sense. Although mission statements are better known, vision statements are the starting point for developing a more specific organizational mission. The terms *mission statement* and *vision statement* are closely related; however, there are basic differences between the two concepts.

The vision statement represents a future goal that outlines general priorities for where the organization is headed. An effective vision statement answers the basic questions: "Why does this organization exist?" and "What would we like to accomplish?" A shared vision is an integral part of the culture of an organization and is communicated through internal relations. If employees share a common vision and clearly defined goals, the organization can make more strategic and effective decisions than they can without a clear vision. *A vision statement spells out the future goal and strategy of an organization.*

Vision statements are important tools of internal relations, particularly for helping manage reactions to changes in the environment. A well-planned vision statement gives employees an idea of what the organization will strive for in the future, the values it holds, and the areas of the business that will be of most strategic importance—ranging from strategies as diverse as research and development of new products to maintaining market share or developing relationships with new distributors.

A vision statement is usually created at the highest level of the organization by the CEO or other members of the dominant coalition. One danger here is that creating a vision statement in the top level of the organization alone misses the opportunity to engage internal publics in the discussion of organizational mission. Employees often report that feelings of pride, ownership, and responsibility are fostered when many participants work together at creating a vision statement.[22] Participating in the process can create a "shared vision" of the organization's future throughout the organization (see Figure 9.1).

Mission Statements   The mission statement answers the question: "How are we different from our competitors?" For this reason, they are sometimes called "competitive advantage statements." They convey goals, organizational structure and strategy, legitimacy, values, participation and ownership among employees, leadership, responsibility to the community, ethical priorities, and commitment to publics and stakeholders. Although mission statements and vision statements are similar, mission statements are more specific and operational than are vision statements. *The mission*

FIGURE 9.1

Row Boats Cartoon

Courtesy Harold Smith, Asheville, NC.

statement helps employees set priorities and goals, so that all members of the or-ganization are committed to achieving the mission specified in the statement.

Mission statements encourage members in an organization to focus on its strengths by emphasizing areas and attributes in which it has success. The focus fostered by a compelling mission statement can provide a competitive advantage. It does so by allowing members of the organization to remain "on strategy," both in conducting their responsibilities and in allocating resources. Without a clearly defined mission statement, an organization might make decisions that are well intentioned, but that do not emphasize the unique competitive strengths of the organization. By building on what it does well, an organization reinvests resources in the areas where it is strongest and thus become less dependent on the areas in which it is weaker, giving it an overall competitive advantage.

An organization whose mission focuses on providing the highest quality product would have a different strategic mission than an organization focused on creating the most innovative products, or another that offers the most inexpensive merchandise. For example, Kia Motors' mission statement is "Provide high-quality, high-value vehicles at prices well below the competition . . ." (www.kia.com). Kia's internal communication emphasizes value and pricing. On the other hand, Porsche's philosophy as a company starts with the "Porsche Principle . . . What counts here are quality, environmental protection, safety. And, naturally, fascination." (http://www.porsche.com/usa). Whereas Kia emphasizes quality and economy, Porsche emphasizes uniqueness and cachet. Each mission statement spells out to employees what the organization values and rewards. (See Exhibit 12.1.)

There is little standardization of content and style among mission statements, but top-performing organizations almost always subscribe to exemplary statements of vision and mission.[23] In short, a clear vision for the future and a thoroughly articulated mission are vital to organizational success.

Policy Documents   Organizational policy and procedures are communicated through various channels to employees. Most organizations have an employee handbook telling how to implement policies and procedures in common situations. For example, many organizations have a policy regarding employee nondisclosure of confidential or privileged information. Manuals often specify the internal policies and the governmental laws that regulate the organization, such as antitrust laws and rules to prevent insider trading of stocks.

Policy manuals are generally exhaustive documents in book or electronic form that specify rights, responsibilities, and bureaucratic channels for procedures. A policy manual might include the procedure for reporting a sexual harassment situation or other problematic issue for employees, as well as routine procedures for requesting a promotion or personal use of office computers. A major drawback of this medium is that most policy manuals are little used because of their sheer length and complex content. For example, the Faculty Handbook for the University of Houston is an Adobe™ pdf document of more than 300 pages. Because of the presentation's detail and complexity, many employees refer to the policy manual only as a last resort. However, policy manuals can be effective tools of internal communication if they are well written, concise, interesting, and organized.

Ethics Statements   Another common policy document is a *code of ethics*. By definition, an ethics document provides a guide to organizational management's values, priorities, standards, and policy. The ethics statement spells out in clear terms the ethical parameters used by the organization in evaluating decision options. A well-written code of ethics provides more concrete guidance and priorities than does a vision or mission statement, but it is much briefer than a policy manual. Codes of ethics, also known as ethics statements, credos, principles, beliefs, values, or standards, are officially adopted and formalized statements that the organization adopts as its guide for ethical decision making. Johnson & Johnson's credo is an outstanding example of an ethics statement (http://www.jnj.com/our_company/our_credo/ index.htm).

Training Materials   Materials used in the orientation and training process help socialize new employees into the culture of the organization. The socialization process is a means of learning the values, standards, and norms of the organization, as well as what is expected in relation to job responsibilities. An employee is acculturated when he or she internalizes the values of the organization and begins to identify him- or herself as part of the organization. *Socializing and acculturating new employees are important aspects of internal relations.*

New employee *orientation* at every level of the organization, from labor to executive management, can cover topics in the policy manual, benefits, and related procedures.

Training provides internal relations staff an opportunity to help the human resources department to socialize and to acculturate employees at all levels of the organization. Employees need to be taught what is expected of them and the standards and methods to be used in that evaluation. Doing so builds more consistent organizational decision making, which can make maintaining relationships with publics easier. Providing rigorous training and setting clear expectations for employees also allows them to proceed in their responsibilities with the confidence that the organization will stand behind them when they act in accordance with its values.

Informing Employees Using Nonmediated Communication

The heart of communication inside an organization is in-person verbal communication. Employees prefer direct communication from their superiors over e-mail, peers, news media, or any other form.[24] Studies also show that the most memorable and effective type of message delivery for employees is traditional face-to-face communication. Verbal communication has a significant impact on organizational culture and deserves attention, even though it is often an informal medium.[25]

The "Grapevine"   The grapevine is neither a formal nor a controlled medium, but *word of mouth* is often the quickest means for communicating information. The grapevine is a potent line of communication, but is also dangerous because the information it carries is often unreliable or "enhanced." And e-mail makes the grapevine work with the speed of electrons!

Sometimes the grapevine is actually harmful, or threatens to be. Rumors of downsizing and layoffs, of a hostile takeover by a competitor, of friction among officials, of sexual harassment charges, or of bad blood between factions can cause dissension within the organization with the speed of a wildfire. Rumors can travel far beyond the organization, becoming more and more distorted as they spread.

Surveys conducted by consulting firm Towers Perrin found the grapevine second only to immediate supervisors as employees' most frequent source of organizational information. Nine out of ten surveyed, however, rated their immediate supervisor as the "preferred source" of information, often noting a preference for face-to-face communication, and ranked the grapevine as the least preferred source.

The public relations staff usually stays tuned in to the grapevine. When trouble brews, they squelch the gossip by releasing the full facts. Too often, however, the grapevine is the source of misinformation. *The lesson for the public relations practitioner is that the grapevine will fill the information gaps left by an inadequate internal communication program.* The informal, uncontrolled channels take over when the formal, controlled channels do not meet the need and demand for information.

Meetings, Teleconferences, and Videoconferences   Meetings bring people together, providing opportunities to both speak and listen, a method of two-way communication. Work group meetings, quality control circles, and participative management sessions are examples of small, task-oriented meetings. Face-to-face meetings are expensive in time away from routine tasks and sometimes include travel expenses. However, meetings are economical in the long run because of both the ideas they produce and their team-building effects. Employees prefer face-to-face communication on many topics—from organizational goals to financial and competitor information.[26]

Just as with other communication strategies, a meeting requires specific objectives, careful planning and staging, and skillful direction. Exchange of viewpoints can be open but controlled so that the meeting does not drag or get diverted from its purpose. Effectiveness depends on the conveyor's ability to lead and articulate. For some meetings, specially trained group-process facilitators serve this vital role, while participants delve into important content issues. One school of thought is that important meetings involving people of different levels trying to resolve conflicts, to address crises, or to make critical decisions should be guided by a process facilitator so that power, content, and process are not vested in one person—the boss.

For large gatherings, particularly those bringing together the entire employee force or important external publics, the public relations staff is called on to help plan the meeting. At Google, global communications director David Krane explained that public relations activities fall into five "buckets"; these include media relations, traditional corporate communications, issues management and public affairs, internal communication, and international communication. For internal communication, Google has held "Thank God It's Friday" (TGIF) meetings each week since its founding. When the organization had fewer than 100 employees, these meetings "always took place in an open space within the office and always near food." Today, with thousands of employees all over the world, Google holds TGIF meetings using videocasting. Furthermore, to accommodate those employees whose weekends have already started by the meeting time, the videocast is recorded, so that those not able to attend can replay the meeting later.[27]

As the Google example shows, many organizations use the latest technologies to bring ideas and people together. Some major global corporations have created state-of-the-art electronic meeting systems capable of connecting people around the world instantaneously to work together on a single problem. Another reason for using these meeting technologies is to reach people at many locations all at the same time with the same message. For example, key speakers unable to take time to travel to participate in person can address meetings via teleconferencing, videoconferencing, or podcasting. The savings in travel time and costs, meeting facilities, and boarding of participants can more than offset the costs of technology. However, traditional, face-to-face meetings are still highly valued and a preferred means of communication by employees, especially when their input on an issue is sought.

Informing Employees Using Mediated Communication

Mediated communication with today's employees ranges from the traditional newsletter to such newer forms as intranet and e-mail.

Employee Publications   Despite new communication technology, printed publications remain the primary media for internal communication in most organizations. Imagine the competition for attention these publications must overcome, given the amount of information that people are exposed to on a daily basis. The usual goals of such publications include

1. Keeping employees informed of the organization's strategy and goals
2. Providing employees the information they need to perform their assignments well
3. Encouraging employees to maintain and enhance the organization's standards for and commitment to quality improvement, increased efficiency, improved service, and greater social responsibility
4. Recognizing employees' achievements and successes
5. Creating an opportunity for two-way communication to generate employee feedback, questions, and concerns

Each publication, each issue, each printed word is part of a coordinated employee communication program designed to achieve these and other goals set in response to particular organizational settings and situations. Because of their impact, permanence, and reference value, printed words remain the workhorses of employee communication.

An organizational publication can take the form of a simple newsletter, a Web site, an intranet, a regularly distributed e-mail, a newspaper, a magazine, or a "magapaper" that combines the format of a newspaper with the style of a magazine. Many are high-quality, four-color publications (see Figure 9.2). Some companies now publish corporate history books, using them to tell stories about the company, its founders, and its employees.[28]

All organizational publications have these characteristics in common: They satisfy the organizational need to go on record with its positions and to communicate information essential for achieving organizational objectives; they permit the organization to deliver messages to specific target publics; and they let the organization communicate in its own words, in its own way, without interruption or alteration. In short, they give the organization a means of *controlled* communication.

The organizational publication is versatile. It can be edited to serve the narrow interests of its sponsor. It can be edited to shed light on issues important to employees and other publics. Most often it combines editorial content that both espouses the sponsor's point of view and addresses concerns of targeted publics. (Without the latter, of course, it would die for lack of readers outside the inner circle of top management.)

Organizational publications are directed to many publics, but the most common use is in employee communication. Practitioners responding to surveys usually rate employees as a primary audience for organizational publications. The major advantage of publications is their ability to deliver specific and detailed information to narrowly defined target publics who have an interest in the issues being discussed. As a result, many organizations have several employee publications, each designed to meet the information needs of different employee publics. For example, because about half of Callaway Vineyards' employees speak Spanish, it prints its employee publication in both English and Spanish. Ciba Geigy Canada Ltd. publishes its employee publications in both English and French. The front cover and pages to the center staple are in one language; flip the publication, and the back cover becomes the front cover for the half published in the other language.

FIGURE 9.2

DyStar Employee Publications

Courtesy DyStar, Frankfurt, Germany.

Many organizations construct their publications as *two-way* communication—inviting questions, seeking input and comments, and conducting surveys, then reporting the results. This requires the full cooperation of top management because of the time required to respond to questions and the expense of conducting surveys. Two-way communication also demands a climate of trust. Employees are often reluctant to submit questions or write for publication, so that sometimes comments are solicited anonymously. Nonetheless, internal publications provide an excellent mechanism for feedback and responsive communication. Comment cards provide a greater sense of anonymity to employees than do Web sites or intranet systems with feedback forms, because those people who want to comment anonymously sometimes fear that electronic communication will be traced back to them.

Printed newsletters remain the "workhorse" of employee communication, even in the computer and intranet age. They are the most common form of periodical publication. Because of readily available and inexpensive desktop publishing technology, newsletters are relatively easy, fast, and inexpensive to produce. As a result, most organizations rely on newsletters to communicate news in a timely and targeted fashion.

Printed publications are also important because not all employees have computer access. For example, at Walgreens—a drugstore company—only 10 percent of employees have daily access to a computer. The company's corporate magazine, *Walgreen World*, targets the organization's front-line employees who have daily contact with Walgreens shoppers. Numbering about 150,000, these employees represent a diverse group, from teenagers working the cash registers to near-retirees filling prescriptions in the pharmacy. Reader surveys from the company indicate that 64 percent of the magazine's target audience reads the employee publication during lunch or breaks—quite an achievement considering that these employees have access to all the popular magazines being sold in the store![29]

Inserts and Enclosures   Anyone who has received bills from utilities or oil companies knows about inserts and enclosures. A common form of insert is the "payroll stuffer" that goes into paycheck envelopes or gets direct deposit receipts. The insert is a valuable medium for appealing to natural constituencies for support and for important notices and news. Examples include calls for employees or stockholders to write to legislators in support of an organization's stand on a public policy issue, to recruit contributions to charitable organizations, or to notify of changes in benefits or procedures.

One obvious advantage of the insert is that the message goes to a strategically targeted public that is predisposed to be interested in the message. Readership and receptivity can be high. Another advantage is economy. A small, lightweight printed insert need not add to postage.

Published Speeches, Position Papers, and Backgrounders   Expressing an organization's position by electronically posting CEO speeches and position statements on an organizational Web site is a common method of communicating with both external and internal publics. Making such documents available on the Web site or intranet gives employees easy access to quotes and position statements and helps them follow developments and to more effectively represent the organization's positions in their communities. Reprinting CEO speeches or news articles in their entirety provides access to employees to the ideas of the CEO that they will probably not have on a personal basis.

Position papers and backgrounders also help employees understand new assignments quickly and might prevent them from exploring previously tried approaches to problems on the issue if they are familiar with the history of the situation. The downside of this information is that generally only publics with a need for information will seek it out. Information seekers benefit from such information, but internal relations must also encourage other employees to visit the publications archive.

Another method of extending the reach of limited-circulation materials is reprinting publications. With permission from the original publications, favorable publicity, analyses of important issues, and other relevant media coverage of interest to an organization's stakeholder publics can be reprinted and distributed. This adds control to what would otherwise be uncontrolled media coverage. Reprints can be added to the organizational archive for employees to continue referring to as necessary.

Bulletin Boards   The use of bulletin boards is widespread and here to stay. If there were no other reason, laws requiring the posting of an ever-increasing number of notices (OSHA and Homeland Security notices, for example) would preserve this medium. Bulletin boards represent both physical spaces that display traditional notices as well as electronic notices. Bulletin boards offer a good public place to corroborate information with brief messages. They provide quick access for making announcements and countering rumors from both internal and external sources.

In order to be effective, bulletin boards need to have regular attention and to be updated often. Seeing the same notice again and again becomes an annoyance and soon leads to inattention. The same category applies to notices, posters, and placards on walls or columns in work areas. The themes of such postings are usually safety, health, housekeeping, productivity, and security. Keep in mind that many of these items are required by regulations, and the specific mandated wording leaves little room for creativity. Employees get used to these items as part of the environment and often pay little attention to them. Therefore, other forms of internal communication are often needed to supplement bulletin boards and notices in a creative manner to remind employees of the message or to heighten awareness.

Intranets   Intranet postings are for internal use, because only employees can access the Internet-like system. The intranet can contain an e-mail system, electronic employee publications, policy manuals, electronic bulletin boards, and many sources of shared information such as project data. Having information available as an electronic document, such as a procedures manual, allows employees to search the document using key terms.

Using an intranet makes employees more productive because information can be located quickly and shared easily. Approximately three-fourths of American businesses use an intranet system because:

1. It disseminates information widely and rapidly.
2. An intranet empowers employees by providing them with ready access to the information they need.
3. It overcomes geography, so that people in distant locations can work together on projects. Communication is likely to be more frequent and more two-way in a work group that uses an intranet.[30]

Senior vice president of IBM Jon Iwata said that during a restructuring, "We figured out that what employees want is one intranet where everything is logically integrated. They don't want to hop around 8,000 sites; they want to stay in one place and have everything come to them. That requires all kinds of collaboration inside the company." He estimated that its intranet saved the organization a $2 billion cost of operation savings in a few years of use.[31] Similarly, in 2007, Motorola finished a two-year process of consolidating more than 25 separate company intranets and 5,000 employee blogs into a single site. The result? The intranet site failure rate dropped from 53 percent to only 3 percent, productivity increased, and employee collaboration flourished.[32]

Despite their advantages, intranets can create concern in internal relations. The advent of "spyware," or software that monitors everything a PC does, raises the issue of privacy. Many versions of snooping software can be installed on a machine without the knowledge of the user, and some can even be placed and activated on the computer surreptitiously via e-mail.[33] Employees might feel less empowered, and mistrusted, if their every move on the computer is monitored, although this approach can prevent policy infractions such as employee use of scandalous Web sites. However the ethical and legal issues of computer surveillance are handled, internal publics should be involved in and aware of the decision.

A second problem for an intranet system is that hackers could sabotage, disrupt, or steal information by electronically breaking into the site. Web sites can be hijacked internally by employee hackers or accessed externally to redirect those trying to enter a legitimate site. For these reasons, security of intranet and Internet sites are major concerns. Potential threats should be communicated about immediately.

Hotlines   Hotlines or toll-free phone numbers are also used in internal relations for disseminating basic information. For example, Johnson & Johnson employees use a toll-free hotline to dial for emergency or weather information, such as closing due to ice or heavy snow. This information is also sent to radio stations, but the hotline provides employees a convenient and expedient source of organizational information.

E-Mail   Perhaps the most ubiquitous form of employee communication today is the e-mail. E-mails and e-newsletters "push" information to the attention of employees, thus making them preferable for internal communication compared to electronic channels like intranets and Web sites, where employees must take the initiative to "pull" the information they seek.[34]

New Media   As new technology changes communication, public relations practitioners have adjusted their strategies for reaching internal publics. For example, Southwest Airlines uses CEO podcasts to connect the chief executive with rank-and-file employees.[35] UPS celebrated its 100th birthday not only by inviting 100 employees from all over the country to the company's Seattle headquarters, but also by giving the invitees the chance to share their experience with colleagues, friends, and family using blogs and video from the party.[36] Some public relations firms even use Facebook to strengthen employee relationships, with colleagues also becoming one another's "friends."[37]

Listening to Employees

When organizational culture is participative, employees are given opportunities to communicate their questions and concerns to the management. As noted earlier, this feedback can be sought in meetings or by using employee publications and e-mails. However, one challenge to getting feedback from employees is that people often do not want to ask questions for fear of being labeled a "troublemaker." To overcome this challenge, some organizations provide hotlines and toll-free phone numbers, as noted earlier, which allow employees to call with concerns or even as an anonymous whistle-blower source to report fraud. Anonymous e-mail systems are also used as "tip-off" hotlines in which employees can report wrongdoing for further investigation without the stigma of being named the "whistle-blower."

For example, in the United States, section 301(4)(B) of the Sarbanes Oxley Act requires publicly held (i.e., stock issuing) organizations to have an anonymous system that allows for reporting "questionable" accounting and management practices. As a result, companies that act as third-party call centers have become popular because they guarantee source anonymity and have a consistent method of interviewing callers and documenting claims for further investigation. For a good example, visit www.tnwinc.com, a company that says it provides whistle-blower service to 50 percent of the largest American businesses.

Hotlines should not be limited to whistle-blower alerts, however. They can also be helpful for identifying trends within the organization that are problematic and need resolution before they rise to the level of an issue or crisis. The concerns reported on a hotline can range from work schedule conflicts with picking up children before the daycare center closes, to exposing someone padding an expense account report, to accusations of sexual harassment.

Another way for organizations to listen to their employees is to provide the services of an *ombudsman* or *ombuds officer*. This person is charged with giving employees the opportunity to share their concerns and resolve them through informal mediation. For example, an ombuds officer can help prevent an employee sexual harassment lawsuit by helping to negotiate a satisfactory resolution for both the accuser and the alleged harasser. Information provided to the ombuds officer usually is considered confidential, as well as a good way to monitor emerging trends and potential problems the organization may be facing.

More information on ways in which organizations can listen to their employees, as well as to other organizational stakeholders, is provided in Chapter 11, with discussions of various informal and formal methods of collecting data, or conducting research. An understanding of research is important for public relations practitioners, including those responsible for internal communication.[38] Increasing numbers of organizations are conducting surveys to measure a variety of concerns, from employees' levels of engagement with the organization to whether a supervisor covered job basics during orientation.[39]

This chapter did not cover all the internal media available to practitioners. The intent here was to introduce the major media and employee communication channels used in internal relations. Controlled media are the primary means for communicating with internal publics. The composition and concentration of internal publics makes them relatively easy to reach with controlled media such as employee publications and the intranet, as well as with nonmediated efforts. Because external publics are often large and dispersed, sometimes making controlled media impractical, uncontrolled media and other communication targeted at external publics are topics in the next chapter.

Notes

[1] Marilyn Laurie, "Managing a Diverse Workforce in a Changing Corporate Environment," in *The Handbook of Strategic Public Relations and Integrated Communications*, ed. Clarke L. Caywood (New York: McGraw-Hill, 1997), 232.

[2] Julie O'Neil and Sean Williams, *Measuring the Impact of Employee Communication on Employee Comprehension and Action: A Case Study of a Major International Firm*. Paper presented to the International Public Relations Research Conference, Miami, Florida, March 2008.

[3] Jonah Bloom, "Internal Communications Is Key Ingredient to Growing Starbucks Worldwide," *PR Week* (September 16, 2002): 8.

[4] Jay Rayburn, "A Matter of Trust (and More): Bringing Employees Back into the Company Fold," *PR Tactics* (March 2007), 21.

[5] Alvie L. Smith in letter to authors, March 28, 1993.

[6] Alvie L. Smith, "Getting Managers Off Their Butts and into the Communication Game," *Communication World* 9, no. 1 (January 1992): 35.

[7] Linda Grant, "The Ascent of Delta," *Los Angeles Times Magazine* (June 16, 1991): 17–19, 32–33.

[8] Paul Holmes. "Employers Must Be Up Front with Employees, Who Are Well Equipped to Cut through the Spin," *PR Week* (January 19, 2004): 9.

[9] Eric M. Eisenberg and Patricia Riley, "Organizational Culture," in *The New Handbook of Organizational Communication,* ed. Fred M. Jablin and Linda L. Putnam (Thousand Oaks, CA: Sage, 2001), 291–322.

[10] Geert Hofstede, *Culture's Consequences: International Differences in Work-Related Values* (Newbury Park, CA: Sage, 1980).

[11] Larissa A. Grunig, James E. Grunig, and David M. Dozier, *Excellent Public Relations and Effective Organizations: A Study of Communication Management in Three Countries* (Mahwah, NJ: Lawrence Erlbaum Associates, 2002), 482.

[12] Hofstede, 1980.

[13] Chung, Eunkyung, and Seongjung Jeong, "The Relationship Between Crisis Management System and Cross-Cultural Analysis in South Korea and U.S. Multinational Corporations." Paper presented to the International Public Relations Research Conference (March 2008), Miami, FL.

[14] Allen, Justin, "Kraft Opens Virtual Door to C-Suite." 27 March 2008. http://ragan.com; Steve Crescenzo, "Bob Evans' CEO Blog Is a Crucial Internal Communication Tool." 17 April 2008. http://ragan.com.

[15] Newburry, William, and Nevena Yakova, "Standardization Preferences: A Function of National Culture, Work Interdependence and Local Embeddedness," *Journal of International Business Studies*, Vol. 37, Issue 1 (January 2006), 44.

[16] Hofstede, 1980, 176–177.

[17] Shoemake, Barbara Rene, *Cultural Determinants of Public Relations Practice: A Study of Foreign and U.S.-Owned Companies in the United States.* Doctoral dissertation, University of Alabama, 1995.

[18] James E. Grunig and Jon White, "The Effect of Worldviews on Public Relations Theory and Practice," in *Excellence in Public Relations and Communication Management*, ed. James E. Grunig (Hillsdale, NJ: Lawrence Erlbaum Associates, 1992), 31–64.

[19] Krishnamurthy Sriramesh, James E. Grunig, and Jody Buffington, "Corporate Culture and Public Relations," in *Excellence in Public Relations and Communication Management*, ed. James E. Grunig (Hillsdale, NJ: Lawrence Erlbaum Associates, 1992), 577–595; Stephen P. Robbins, *Organization Theory: Structure, Design, and Applications*, 3rd ed. (Englewood Cliffs, NJ: Prentice Hall, 1990).

[20] David M. Dozier, with Larissa A. Grunig, and James E. Grunig. *Manager's Guide to Excellence in Public Relations and Communication Management* (Mahwah, NJ: Lawrence Erlbaum Associates, 1995), 15.

[21] Sarah McAdams, "Going Green Boosts Employee Morale," 4 December 2007, http:/ragan.com.

[22] Robert L. Heath, *Management of Corporate Communication: From Interpersonal Contacts to External Affairs* (Hillsdale, NJ: Lawrence Erlbaum Associates, 1994).

[23] Patrick E. Murphy, *Eighty Exemplary Ethics Statements* (Notre Dame, IN: University of Notre Dame Press, 1998).

[24] O'Neil, 23.

[25] Angela D. Sinickas, "Intranets, Anyone?" *Communication World* (January–February, 2004): 30–34.

[26] Ibid., 31.

[27] Keith O'Brien, "From Startup to Tech Titan," *PR Week* (March 26, 2007), 17–18.

[28] Ray Gaulke, "Company Histories Engage, Inform Key Stakeholders," *PR Week* (June 6, 2005), 8.

[29] Sarah McAdams, "*Walgreen World*: An Internal Magazine More Popular Than *People*," 29 January 2008, http://ragan.com.

[30] "Intranets Revolutionize How Companies Operate and Communicate," *Ragan's Intranet Report* 10, no. 10 (1996): 1–8, 1.

[31] "Interview with Jon Iwata: Employee Comms Vital to How IBM's Work Gets Done," *PR Week* (May 17, 2004), 7.

[32] Bill Sweetland, "Motorola Consolidates Dozens of Intranets into One." 4 March 2008, http://ragan.com.

[33] John Schwartz, "Snoop Software Is Generating Privacy Concerns," *New York Times* (October 10, 2003), C1.

[34] Angela D. Sinickas, "The Role of Intranets and Other E-Channels in Employee Communication Preferences," *Journal of Website Promotion* 1, Issue 1 (April 2005), 31–51.

[35] Steve Crescenzo, "Southwest Podcast Connects Employees with CEO." 18 December 2007. http://ragan.com.

[36] Steve Crescenzo, "UPS Celebrates Centennial with Social Media," 19 December 2007. http://ragan.com.

[37] Alexandra Bruell, "Facebook Helps Firms Strengthen Staff Bonds," *PR Week* (November 26, 2007), 1.

[38] Rayburn, 21.

[39] Erin White, "How Surveying Workers Can Pay Off," *The Wall Street Journal* (June 18, 2007), B3.

Additional Sources

Davis, Alison (Ed.). *21 Strategies for Improving Employee Communication: Smart Tips for Communicators.* Glen Rock, NJ: Davis, 2005. Includes tips for measuring communication and communicating change using e-mail.

Grunig, Larissa A., James E. Grunig, and David M. Dozier. *Excellent Public Relations and Effective Organizations: A Study of Communication Management in Three Countries.* Mahwah, NJ: Lawrence Erlbaum Associates, 2002. Chapter 11 reports findings on organizational culture, gender and diversity, knowledge, CEO value, and organizational structure.

Hickson, Mark III, and Don W. Stacks. *Organizational Communication in the Personal Context.* Needham Heights, MA: Allyn & Bacon, 1998. Outlines role of communication in organization, tracing the function from the employee's perspective "from interview to retirement."

Holz, Shel. *Corporate Conversations: A Guide to Crafting Effective and Appropriate Internal Communications.* New York: American Management Association, 2004. Explains types of employee communications and covers both traditional and new communication tools.

Schneid, Thomas D. *Corporate Safety Compliance: OSHA, Ethics, and the Law.* Boca Raton, FL: Taylor & Francis, 2008. Explains OSHA inspection procedures, ways to manage compliance, and legal penalties and defenses.

External Media and Media Relations

STUDY GUIDE After studying Chapter 10, you should be able to:

▶ Discuss the major controlled and uncontrolled media used for communicating with external publics.

▶ Outline how technology-based new media affect external communication practices.

▶ Define the relationship between practitioners and journalists as being mutually dependent and mutually beneficial, but as sometimes adversarial.

▶ Outline basic guidelines for building good media relations and working with the press.

Practitioners of public relations use printed words, spoken words, images, and combinations of all these communication forms. They use both controlled media and uncontrolled media to communicate with their organizations' many publics. *Controlled* media include those in which practitioners have the say over what is said, how it is said, when it is said, and—to some extent—to whom it is said. *Uncontrolled* media are those over which practitioners have no direct role in decisions about media content. Instead, media gatekeepers decide if something is reported, what is reported, how it is reported, when it is reported, and to whom it is reported.

Technology has changed our notions about media, especially the concept of mass media. Three key changes with implications for public relations are that (1) audiences have become fragmented, choosing ever smaller niche media for their own unique needs, as opposed to being part of an undifferentiated mass; (2) audiences are more active, choosing two-way media that permit interactivity, as opposed to one-way media that permitted only passive reception of information; and (3) a "journalist" today is anybody with a camera cell phone and Internet access, as opposed to a trained professional who reports the news.

What follows is a snapshot of the major media used in public relations. The first part of this chapter examines the traditional media used primarily for—but not limited to—reaching large and dispersed publics. The second part of the chapter summarizes some of the new media developments that are challenging traditional public relations practice. The chapter concludes with a discussion of media relations, one of public relations' primary assignments.

Every newspaper when it reaches the reader is the result of a whole series of selections as to what items shall be printed, in what position they shall be printed, how much space each shall occupy, what emphasis each shall have. There are no objective standards here. There are conventions.[1]
—Walter Lippmann, 1922

The Internet gives you the power to end-run reporters, editors, and even complete news organizations when you really need to communicate directly with important audiences.[2]
—Shirley Fulton and Al Guyant, 2002

This chapter was revised in collaboration with Professor **Bey-Ling Sha**, Ph.D., APR, School of Journalism and Media Studies, San Diego State University.

Traditional Media, New Uses

Traditional mass media have long provided economical, effective methods of communicating with large and widely dispersed publics. Consequently, work in public relations requires understanding of and skills in using newspapers, magazines, trade publications, AM and FM radio, television, cable, books, and so on. To handle this part of the job, practitioners must understand the role of information, the various media and their production requirements, and the values of the gatekeepers who control access.

Practitioners also need to understand that media are constrained by their mechanical requirements, their values, their rules, and—for many—the necessity of "delivering" an audience to advertisers. Today's communicators are confronted with a paradox: Multiplying channels of communication permit a sharper focus of messages, but greatly escalate competition for audience attention. Furthermore, audiences today are more fragmented than in generations past, and they are also more active in the selection of which media messages get their attention.

Mass media reach into nearly every home and workplace, showering citizens with far more messages than they can absorb. General and specialized media appear to represent an easily used means of disseminating ideas and information to publics, but this can be deceptive. Just because these media distribute messages and have audiences does not mean that the messages are received, accepted, or acted upon.

Additionally, the traditional mass media have a relatively fixed capacity; newspapers and magazines have a limited number of columns for editorial matter, and there are only 24 hours in a broadcast day. Hence, any one of these media cannot possibly convey all the news and information available. Receivers also have limited time and attention to give to the millions of messages. In a media world crammed with messages, only a tiny fraction gets past the door and into the home. Even fewer get attention. Fewer yet have impact.

Nonetheless, institutionalized power is largely exercised through control of the means and content of mass communication. Mass media constitute the key components in a nation's public-information system, a system in which public relations practitioners play an increasingly important role as sources of an increasing proportion of the content. Many sources compete for access to media, however, so practitioners must continually adjust their communication strategy to rapidly changing media and audiences.

Despite the advent of new media technologies, the idea that "traditional media are dead" is a myth. In fact, a media usage survey by Ketchum PR shows that 73.6 percent of consumers tune in to their local television news, 71.4 percent watch major network news, and 68.9 percent read the local newspaper.[3] Thus, this chapter discusses traditional media at length, because they remain the bread and butter of much public relations practice.

Newspapers

Newspapers remain the workhorse of the public information system. When people think of publicity, they almost instinctively think of the newspaper. And for good reason, because newspaper coverage remains the foundation of most information programs.

Daily, weekend, Sunday, weekly, semiweekly, ethnic, labor, religious, scholastic, and foreign-language newspapers are most frequently read by the most literate people, whether online or in hard copy. For the most influential citizens, those "opinion leaders" discussed in Chapter 8, reading the newspaper is as much a daily habit as eating and sleeping. In fact, one study found that "readers of newspaper Web sites are 52 percent more likely to share their opinions than those who do not visit newspaper sites."[4] As a result, the influence of the world's great newspapers is also great. Journalism scholar and educator John C. Merrill refers to these as the "internationally elite newspapers":

> Such papers—mainly dailies—are read by the world's intellectuals, political and opinion leaders, and cosmopolitan, concerned citizens of various countries. They are directed at a fairly homogeneous audience globally and have a greater interest in international relations and the arts and humanities than the general run of mass-appeal papers. They are well-informed, articulate papers that thoughtful people the world over take seriously.[5]

U.S. papers on Merrill's list of elite dailies include the *New York Times, Los Angeles Times, Washington Post*, and *Christian Science Monitor*. His European list includes *Le Monde* in France, *Neue Zürcher Zeitung* in Switzerland, *El País* in Spain, *Daily Telegraph* in England, and *Svenska Dagbladet* in Sweden. Asia's elite dailies include Japan's *Asahi Shimbun* and *Mainichi Shimbun*, and India's *Times of India* and *Statesman*. According to Merrill, "The elite papers recognize that they will not reach many people, but they seek to have an impact that no other medium does on the serious, intellectual, opinion-leading segment of the world community."[6] On the other hand, *USA Today* and the *Wall Street Journal* reach both large U.S. and international audiences, with 2.3 and 2.1 million subscribers, respectively.[7]

Newspapers are a moving force in society. As the late Supreme Court Justice Felix Frankfurter once said: "To an extent far beyond the public's own realization, public opinion is shaped by the kind, the volume, and the quality of the news columns." Nor should editorial endorsement be totally discounted. For example, when last-minute challenges threatened to bring to a halt the "Block E" downtown revitalization project in Minneapolis, public relations firm Carmichael Lynch Spong helped place an opinion piece written with the city mayor in the *Star Tribune*, the major daily in Minnesota. Within days, the paper's editorial staff wrote a similarly supportive editorial. The project proceeded without serious opposition and delay.

Newspaper scholars have suggested that the power of the press comes from its dissemination of information and its impact on public interest in important issues (see Chapter 8 for discussion of the agenda-setting function). For example, newspaper readers' opinions about candidates for public office are affected by whether the local newspaper covered those candidates positively or negatively.[8] Although no longer the primary news medium for the majority of Americans, newspapers remain a powerful force in shaping the public agenda and influencing the outcome of debate.

Since the early part of the twentieth century until World War II, when newspapers were the prime source of news and entertainment, the number of daily newspapers has declined. The number began to stabilize in the 1950s and remained about the same through the mid-1970s. For example, there were 1,772 daily papers in 1950, with only 16 fewer, 1,756, in 1975. Today, however, the number has dropped to only 1,437 dailies because of mergers and discontinued editions.[9]

Newspaper circulation in the United States peaked in 1993 at almost 63 million. Circulation dropped below 52 million in 2006, but is slightly more than 53 million on Sundays.[10] The number of daily newspaper readers per copy remains relatively stable at 2.3, but has increased during the past decade to almost 2.6 for Sunday newspapers.[11] There are 101 daily newspapers in Canada, with a total circulation of

4.8 million. In both countries, the major change was from evening editions to morning editions. Whereas in 1980, only about one out of five daily newspapers had morning editions, now more than half are morning papers—58 percent in the United States and 55 percent in Canada.[12]

Although the number of dailies continues to decline and circulation dropped almost 2 percent in 2006, worldwide newspaper circulation continues to grow. Circulation topped 510 million subscribers in 2006 for 11,142 newspapers worldwide, an increase of 2 percent over 2005. South America led the world with an increase of 4.6 percent in subscriptions for daily newspapers.[13]

Figures compiled by the Newspaper Association of America show that each day approximately 51 percent of all adults read a daily newspaper and 58 percent read a newspaper each Sunday. However, only 37 percent of 18- to 24-year-olds read a newspaper daily, compared to more than 68 percent of those 65 and older. On the other hand, more than 56 percent of all readers have college degrees.[14] Newspapers tend to attract disproportionately white readers, however, as only 32 percent of Hispanic adults and 48 percent of African Americans read a daily newspaper.[15]

A study of newspaper readers in Brazil identified five types: *Instrumental readers* use newspapers to get information they think will be useful for daily living. Reading is purely an information-seeking activity to understand what is happening and why it is happening. *Opinion makers* use newspapers to get advice and guidance for forming and validating opinion. Newspapers help them make up their minds on issues and provide insight on what others are thinking. *Pleasure readers* use newspaper reading as an enjoyable habit. They see newspapers as a source of enjoyment and reading as an end in itself, not as a means for accomplishing some other purpose. *Ego boosters* use newspapers as a source of information for impressing others. They read to enhance their self-image and status with others. *Scanners* use newspapers for many and varied reasons, but there is no single motivation or pattern strong enough to suggest they belong in one of the other four types.[16]

The number and circulation of weekly and other newspapers published less than four times each week has rebounded in recent years. There are 6,659 "weeklies" with a circulation of almost 50 million.[17] Most weeklies emphasize *local* news about government, nonprofit organizations, schools, sports, business developments, and personal news. Likewise, births, weddings, anniversaries, and obituaries are big news. As many will tell you, they read the obituaries first. Public relations practitioners, walled in by skyscrapers and stuck in traffic jams or crowded mass transit, should not forget the people in rural, small-town, and suburban settings or the newspapers that help shape their opinions. In fact, many executives (with public relations assistance) write "specials to . . ." for the opinion–editorial pages of these papers to express views on issues relevant to local operations and the organization's interests beyond the local setting.

The Sunday paper generally gets a more intensive and leisurely reading. It tends to emphasize feature material—stories without a time element—with stories often more like those in a magazine than in a daily paper. In addition, practitioners should not overlook the national Sunday supplement magazines and local weekend magazines published by large-city newspapers. For example, 400 Sunday newspapers distribute *Parade Magazine,* with a circulation of 32 million and almost 71 million readers. The second-largest Sunday supplement is Gannett Co., Inc.'s *USA Weekend,* which is distributed by 600 newspapers each weekend. It has a circulation of more than 23 million and 49 million readers.[18]

Newspaper space allocated to news has decreased in recent years, at least relative to the increased glut of information pouring into newsrooms. Typically newspapers devote about 50 percent of their space to editorial matter, some as little as 25 percent. The rest is advertising (averaging 46 percent) and unpaid public service (4 percent). Local news makes up the largest proportion of editorial content—about 75 percent of all news published.

The **strengths** of newspapers are many. No other medium offers comparable audience size and breadth day in and day out, or the range and depth of content. Most newspapers are produced in local communities and are indigenous to those communities. They have a firsthand intimacy with their local publics. The local YMCA can reach its community publics through its local newspaper. The state health department can reach its publics through the state's daily and weekly newspapers. A commercial concern with regional distribution can reach its publics using a regional selection of newspapers. Similarly, a national organization can reach many national audiences with newspapers. In short, the local connections give newspapers a perceived credibility that is hard to match.

Technology has changed not only the content of newspapers, but also their organizational structures and how they process news and information (see Exhibit 10.1). About 37 percent of U.S. residents with Web access now read online newspapers. The nearly 54 million online readers are younger than readers of the newsprint editions, and also are more likely to shop and do their banking online.[19] Online editions and other innovative newspaper products have expanded the newspaper "footprint"—

> the combined reach of the full portfolio of a newspaper's products. In many cases, the newspaper brand reaches far beyond just the readers of the core product, the traditional newspaper. By combining the local paper with Web sites and other products, the newspaper brand connects with its audience in more ways, expanding the footprint.[20]

Wire Services and News Syndicates

News wire services economically and effectively distribute human-interest stories and spot news to state, regional, national, or international media. Publicity with a local angle can be directed to individual media where the information is relevant. For timely stories not limited to a locale, placing them on the wires increases the likelihood of immediate and widespread coverage. Being carried by a wire service also increases the acceptability of the practitioner's copy. A well-written wire story can reach newspaper readers, radio listeners, and TV viewers across the nation or around the world. Transmitting millions of words and pictures daily, wire services are influential beyond calculation. Access to these networks is through the nearest bureau or "stringer" correspondent.

Each of the two major wire services in the United States operates international, national, regional, state, and local bureaus. In addition to their newspaper subscribers, both serve online and broadcast customers with news copy and audio feeds. Both sell their news reporting services and products to media worldwide.

The Associated Press, founded in 1846 and headquartered in New York City, has 4,100 employees working in 243 bureaus in 97 countries. "AP"—as it is better known—sends news in six languages to almost 17,000 media subscribers in 121 countries. As the AP Web site boasts, "On any given day, more than half the world's population sees news from AP." It is a not-for-profit cooperative owned by 1,500 member newspapers. Subscribers in the United States include almost 1,700 newspapers, 5,000 radio and television stations, and 850 AP Radio Network affiliates. In addition, AP markets its news services and content to nonmedia clients. Beginning

EXHIBIT 10.1

Newspapers Try to Find Their Way in Changing Times

Bill Furlow, Partner*
Furlow Communications
Natchez, Mississippi

This is a trying era for newspapers as competition from new media erodes their readership and consolidation of ownership threatens their independence. Newsroom staffs are shrinking, and the willingness to invest in the most expensive types of reporting appears to be in retreat.

Nevertheless, newspapers remain a bread-and-butter information source for millions of people and are still the best way to communicate many stories.

The line between newspapers and other media has grown quite thin, as nearly every paper has an online edition that is not bound by print production schedules. Stories written for the paper become "repurposed" and are disseminated in other media.

The joint ownership of broadcast stations and papers in the same city has led to Web sites that combine the resources of sister media. And larger papers routinely send "news alerts" to their e-mail subscribers anytime the interest rates fall, the president makes a Cabinet appointment, or the latest teen movie star gets busted for drug possession.

Because reporters troll Google and Yahoo news sources as much as anyone, viral marketing that begins on the Internet can cross over into mainstream print media. Bad news will do the same (a reason not to ignore rumors and negative chat online). When planning a public relations campaign or warding off a crisis, it's important to have a comprehensive strategy that addresses new and traditional media.

For the organization trying to tell a controversial or complex story, newspapers have one big advantage over blogs and social media—editors. The fact that professional journalists act as filters between the sources of news and the readers adds balance and credibility to a report, at least in theory. Links to favorable newspaper stories can be included in e-mails and Web sites to good effect.

Unlike many of their urban counterparts, community papers and small-city dailies continue to occupy unique niches that make them essential to a well-informed public and profitable for their owners. These small papers should not be overlooked because they speak to an audience of friends, neighbors, employees, customers, competitors, regulators, and even shareholders that clients care about deeply.

As the next generation of reporters begins to replace the baby-boomers who retire from journalism or take buy-out packages offered by their corporate owners, it will be critical to develop tactics to deal with the greening of the American newspaper.

Public relations practitioners often face the challenge of dealing with newspaper reporters who are young, inexperienced, and may not have had the best ethics training in college. It's frustrating when key reporters lack even basic background on a story and their editors seem equally devoid of institutional memory. It's infuriating when they become seduced by one side in a controversy before completing their basic reporting. And it's mind-blowing when they print accusations without seeking response.

These situations require a carrot-and-stick approach. The carrot is the pledge to cooperate with a reporter fully, to run down the answers to every question, to respond honestly and not to stonewall. The stick is the insistence that the reporter get the facts right, provide an opportunity to answer every negative statement made by others, and to keep an open mind until all reporting is done.

Among the reasons newspapers remain important to us is that we can work with them. Their reporters don't hide behind clever YouTube or blog names. We can call them on the phone. Their e-mail addresses are generally in the paper or online. And not only do their stories inform their own readers, but their Web editions provide information for bloggers as well. That's why we must hold them to the highest standards and not accept sloppy, lazy, or unfair reporting without speaking out—loudly and firmly.

Although the influence of newspapers has undoubtedly been diluted, the newspaper remains the greatest random access information device ever created. While their owners, editors, and business leaders try to redefine their role in the evolving information industry, those who practice public relations also must stay attuned to their changing needs and work with them for our mutual benefit.

---

*Furlow is a former *Los Angeles Times* reporter and editor. Furlow Communications (http://www.furlowcommunications.com/) specializes in crisis and strategic communications.

in early 1993, AP began transmitting publicity photos for a fee, putting it in direct competition with the publicity wire services. (See www.ap.org.)

United Press International (UPI) is headquartered in Washington, D.C., and has been owned since 2000 by global multimedia company News World Communications. It was formed in 1958 by the merger of United Press (founded in 1907 by newspaper magnate E. W. Scripps) and William Randolph Hearst's International News Service. UPI operates under the principles that it provides an independent coverage of world news, and that any newspaper or news organization may purchase the news product. In addition to English, it provides Middle East news coverage in Arabic and Latin America coverage in Spanish. UPI maintains offices in Beirut, Hong Kong, London, Santiago, Seoul, and Tokyo. (See www.upi.com.)

The world's largest international news agency is London-based Reuters, with more than 2,400 editorial staff, journalists, photographers, and videographers working in 196 bureaus in 131 countries. Best known for its news products, about 90 percent of Reuters' revenue comes from its financial services business, with more than 370,000 financial professionals as subscribers (see http://www.about.reuters.com). Founded in 1851 as an independent company, it was acquired in April 2008 by Stamford, Connecticut–based Thomson Corporation, an international information services company.[21]

Internationally, Agence France-Presse (France), New China News Agency (People's Republic of China), and Kyodo (Japan) are a few of the major news services providing news and features for not only newspapers, but also radio, television, magazines, and private subscribers. These are large organizations with reporters, editors, and other staff in most major capitals and market centers.

Newspapers also subscribe to news services from the *New York Times*, *Washington Post*, *Los Angeles Times*, The McClatchy Company (formerly Knight-Ridder), and newspaper syndicates such as King Features Syndicate, National Newspaper Syndicate, News America Syndicate, United Features Syndicate, and Newspaper Enterprises Syndicate.

Much like the news wire services, commercial public relations wires provide news from organizations and public relations firms. Practitioners use these distribution services to speed time-critical press releases simultaneously into newsrooms worldwide.

PR Newswire (PRN) introduced electronic distribution of news releases in New York City in 1954. PRN now has 26 offices in the United States and 14 other countries (see http://www.prnewswire.com). Other public relations wires copied the concept, starting competing national systems in the United States, Canada, and England, followed by worldwide news-release distribution systems. For example, Business Wire began operations in 1961 and grew rapidly, totaling 26 U.S. offices and adding offices in Belgium, London, and Frankfurt at the beginning of the twenty-first century. In 2006, Business Wire became a wholly owned subsidiary of Warren Buffett's Berkshire Hathaway (see http://www.businesswire.com).

Although they differ greatly in size, all these services operate in essentially the same way: charging clients to electronically transmit print, photographs, audio, and video new releases, as well as regulatory postings, to the media and other organizations. Clients pay fees based on the extent and type of distribution ordered, but media receive these news services at no charge. In addition, public relations wire services also sell monitoring and measurement services, providing clients metrics indicating the extent of message dissemination, media placement, and potential audience size.

Because they offer fast, simultaneous transmission to the media, practitioners use these wires to send news ranging from major corporate developments and earnings

PR Newswire
United Business Media

reports, sporting events, and obituaries to invitations to press conferences. They are especially useful in times of emergency. For example, a baby food manufacturer had to urgently distribute a product recall to many media outlets quickly and simultaneously when glass shards were found in one shipment of food products.

Another large portion of print and electronic media content is supplied by the feature, photo, and specialized news syndicates. As in the case of the wire services, placement of a feature or a picture with a syndicate ensures wide, economical distribution and increases the acceptability of material. Most syndicates also distribute columns and comics. For example, United Feature Syndicate distributes columns and commentaries, editorial cartoons, and comic strips. Offerings include Scott Adams's popular "Dilbert," the late Charles Schulz's "Peanuts," and Greg Evans's "Luann." Syndicates charge fees based on each client's circulation or audience size.

As in the case of paid publicity wires, there are also feature services that supply newspapers and periodicals with material without charge. Sponsoring clients pay the bill. Typical is North American Precis Syndicate, Inc. (NAPS), with offices in New York, Washington, Atlanta, Chicago, San Francisco, and Los Angeles. In its "Featurettes" service, NAPS distributes consumer news and information for 750 public relations firms, corporations, associations, and government public affairs offices to more than 7,000 to dailies, weeklies, monthlies, shoppers, and dotcoms. NAPS' "Consumer Science News & Notes" radio and television service distributes paper scripts, MP3 and PDS files of scripts, CDs, and DVDs of consumer topics posted on the company's Web site. (See http://www.napsnet.com.)

Magazines

More than 19,500 magazines and specialized publications published in the United States offer effective specialized channels of communication to narrowly defined audiences.[22] Variations in content and audience appeal are almost limitless and ever changing, attracting 322 million subscriptions.[23] In 2006 alone, hopeful publishers launched 324 new magazines, but typically only one in 10 is successful in the long run.[24] Some do not make it to the first issue. Others fail after the first year or two, disappointing enthusiastic publishers who had visions of attracting both subscribers and advertisers.

One author claims that the first magazine was "America's only national medium," referring to the *Saturday Evening Post,* first published in 1821. Long before, Benjamin Franklin published *General Magazine* in February 1741. Technically, Andrew Bradford's *American Magazine* was the first American magazine, because it appeared in print three days before Franklin's magazine. Historians generally agree, however, that Franklin originated the concept of a magazine.[25]

Magazines provide an array and variety of communication media to reach audiences who share common interests, including through the Web sites now produced by 60 percent of consumer magazines.[26] Circulation giants such as *AARP The Magazine, Reader's Digest, TV Guide, Better Homes and Gardens, National Geographic, Good Housekeeping, Family Circle, Ladies Home Journal, Woman's Day, Time,* and *People* reach large national audiences. More narrowly targeted magazines include *Cooking Light, More, Rolling Stone, Wired, Wine Spectator,* and *Architectural Digest.* Trade and business magazine include *Hoard's Dairyman, Women's Wear Daily, The Economist, BusinessWeek, Fortune,* and *Forbes.* The sports-recreation-hobby magazines category includes *Golf Digest, Field & Stream, Motor Trend, Popular Science, Snowboarder,* and *Outdoor Life.* Clearly, magazines enable communicators to target specific messages to specific audiences.

The changing magazine market—from general to specialized publications—reflects the nation's changing interests and lifestyles. There is a magazine or periodical catering to almost every interest, vocation, and hobby. Advances in offset printing and computerized production have stimulated circulation and advertising revenues by giving advertisers options for buying targeted portions of the total circulation. Regional advertising in such national magazines as *Time* and *Newsweek,* for example, allows advertisers to advertise to a market within a market, even local markets.

Thousands of business and professional publications serve the specialized needs of professional groups, trade associations, and business and industry. These publications generally use prepared news releases if the content serves their readers' economic or professional needs. Each of these publications caters to a carefully defined audience, usually representing the membership lists of the organization publishing the magazine. Examples include PRSA's *The Strategist,* IABC's *Communication World,* and the American Medical Association's *American Medical News*. In addition to collecting subscription fees built into membership fees, many of these publications carry advertising for products and services specific to readers' occupations or professional practices.

Magazines offer several advantages: Opinion leaders read magazines. For example, one study showed that fashion opinion leaders were more likely to read fashion magazines than were non–opinion leaders on fashion-related topics.[27] Also, young and diverse populations read magazines. For example, 83 percent of African American adults read magazines, as do 75 percent of Hispanics/Latinos. Nearly eight out of ten teenagers (78 percent) read magazines.[28]

Magazines provide more durable information than newspapers. Magazine readers have the opportunity to read, reread, discuss, and debate the information gleaned from this source. Readers with special interests turn to magazines for in-depth treatment of topics, such as when older citizens report that magazines are second only to health care specialists as a source for health information. Magazines shape opinions, create preferences for fashions and products, influence house designs and decoration, help set standards for professions and businesses, and enlist political support. And even though most magazines are now available online, about three-quarter of readers—across generational lines—indicated that they still enjoy reading actual, hard copy magazines.[29]

Practitioners study magazines' topics, styles, policies, trends, formats, and so forth, and then apply this knowledge by slanting news and features to specific magazines. They generally do not submit unsolicited material, however. Rather, they work on a tip or query basis when they have something that would have reader appeal. They submit story outlines or feature suggestions. If one is accepted, a practitioner works with the magazine's staff or freelance writers to develop the story. The practitioner's job is to sell ideas to editors and then to cooperate with writers and photographers, who build the ideas into articles.

Magazine publicity placement is almost essential for organizations seeking to influence national or specialized audiences. Yet many practitioners fail in their efforts to get such publicity because they do not understand the lead time of national magazines and the stiff competition for space. The competition comes from the magazine's own editors and staff writers, frequent contributors, and freelance writers who write regularly for national magazines.

Practitioners sometimes overlook working with freelancers. Freelance writers who regularly sell to national magazines are interested in a story about an institution, a person, or an event that possesses at least one of these three qualities: (1) national importance or significance; (2) elements of struggle, conflict, contest, or drama; or (3) anecdotal enrichment and entertainment value. In other words, give the story to a freelance writer. The experienced freelancer known to the magazine gets a check from the magazine and the practitioner gets a publicity placement in a magazine.

Radio

Radio offers a wide range of publicity possibilities. It is a mobile medium suited to a mobile people. (Newspaper people like to point out that their medium is also "mobile," and batteries are not required.) It reaches the bedroom and breakfast table in the morning; rides to and from work in the car; goes along to the beach, to the woods, and on fishing trips; and lulls us to sleep at night—a flexibility no other medium can match.

Radio listening in the United States remains relatively constant at almost three hours a day, or about 19 hours each week. At any given time, almost half are listening in vehicles (47 percent), with the next largest segment listening at home (35 percent). During the course of a typical week, about 81 percent will listen to radio in their vehicles. Every day, more than 72 percent of those 12 years old and older listen to radio, and almost 93 percent listen during each week—reaching a weekly audience of 233 million listeners 12 years and older. Many begin and end their days listening to radio, with the "News/Talk/Information" (all news, all sports, news and talk, and all talk) format the most popular choice of more than 17 percent of all listeners.[30]

Also, in 2008, about 33 million Americans aged 12 and older listened to the radio via the Internet, up from 29 million online radio listeners the previous year. Of those online radio listeners, 63 percent had a profile on a social networking site such as MySpace, Facebook, or Linked-In.[31] This information illustrates how old media, with new uses and users, continue to be relevant to public relations practice.

The Federal Communications Commission (FCC) lists 13,977 licensed radio stations in the United States, of which 2,892 are public "educational" FM stations. There are 4,776 AM stations and 6,309 FM stations.[32] In the early 1970s, AM stations attracted three-fourths of the audience. By the early 1990s, more than three-fourths of the total radio listening audience tuned to FM stations. The AM dial is so crowded that nearly half the AM stations ("daytimers") have to shut down 15 minutes after sunset to avoid interfering with others' signals. FM also gained listeners because of its high-quality, static-free stereo sound, which coincided with the development of noise-free recordings. Subscription satellite radio is the fastest-growing option, because it is usually free of advertisements and offers an array of format choices.

Public relations practitioners use radio news releases and audio feeds sent to stations through networks such as CNNRadio (http://www.cnn.com), North American Network (Bethesda, MD, http://www.radiospace.com/about.htm), and News Broadcast Network (New York City, http://www.newsbroadcastnetwork.com). Distribution is over the Internet or telephone lines to stations targeted by region and format. CNNRadio, for example, distributes to 2,000 affiliated stations worldwide 24 hours a day with four minutes of news on the hour, two-minute updates 30 minutes later, and one-minute news cutaways. To increase local station airings, some audio news services also provide interviews or sound bites that stations then localize.

Even though it is a "mass" medium, radio possesses the qualities of a direct, personal touch, because it uses the spoken word, for the most part, to convey its message. Broadcast pioneer Arthur Godfrey understood this intimate quality when he decided that other radio speakers were reading to, not talking with their audiences. He decided that he would always have a mental image of talking to only one person on the other side of the microphone.

Indeed, radio is a person-to-person medium that flourishes on conversation. Call-in talk shows now help set the public agenda and provide a forum for public debate on many local and national issues. The potential impact is great. For example, listeners of radio talk shows tend over time to reflect the political orientations of show hosts. For years, conservative commentator Rush Limbaugh had a national radio audience of dedicated listeners, and in the 2000 presidential election, listening to that program was "strongly associated with preference for Bush," the Republican candidate.[33]

Almost every major city has its own radio all-talk shows that capitalize on local conflict, sensational topics, and legitimate public debate of important issues. Increased emphasis on the discussion format opens up many possibilities for practitioners. Popular talk shows and telephone interviews focusing on controversial issues have an almost insatiable appetite for guests with a message—however controversial it may be.

Public service time seldom is prime listening time, but it is not without value. Since the Federal Communications Commission relaxed its public service requirements for broadcasters, many stations have reduced the number of public service and other nonrevenue programs they broadcast. Yet most stations provide some free time to nonprofit agencies as part of the station's community relations program. In non–prime time the competition for airtime is less intense than during the more desirable—and salable—drive time and other high-listenership hours. That is not to say, however, that an effective program cannot attract and hold listeners even in prime time.

An effective way is to provide radio (and television) *public service announcements* (PSAs)—10 seconds, 30 seconds, or 60 seconds in length. A PSA is any announcement that promotes programs and services of government and voluntary agencies, for which no payment is made to the station. Stations set their own standards, but most use well-prepared PSAs. And they can be effective. For example, the Ad Council produces and distributes PSAs promoting use of seat belts, booster seats, and baby seats, no doubt saving many lives. Local, regional, and state groups promote recycling, storm water pollution prevention, and litter reduction. (For one example, see "Don't Mess with Texas," http://www.dontmesswithtexas.org).

Television

The communication phenomenon of the twentieth century was television. No other medium matches television's ability to provide a window on the world. What other medium could transmit live coverage from the international space station as an astronaut and cosmonaut make repairs outside the craft? How could any other medium convey the sights, sounds, and feelings of war as the embedded journalists did during the Iraq war? And most vivid of all, what other medium could convey the horror of the airliners crashing into the World Trade Center towers in New York City?

A medium that uses the printed word, spoken word, pictures in motion, color, music, animation, and sound effects—all blended into one message—possesses immeasurable potency. As discussed in Chapter 8, television's ability to shape our views of the world is explicated by cultivation theory. Television offers a vast range of possibilities for telling a story, from a terse, 60-second video on a TV newscast, to a half-hour or one-hour documentary film, to 24-hour coverage of a crisis such as the World Trade Center terrorist attacks, to a miniseries extended over several evenings or weeks. Satellites transmit news from any place on the globe, making the powerful, pervasive impact of television a worldwide phenomenon. Television took the lead from newspapers in 1963 as the primary source of news in the United States.

In the United States, 1,759 TV stations broadcast almost around the clock to nearly every household.[34] An average of more than 104 cable channels per household give viewers more options than they can carefully consider.[35] The average time a television is on in a household surpasses the length of a typical workday—8 hours and 14 minutes.[36] Children spend an average of almost three and a half hours each day watching television.[37] They grow up using the remote control to explore a seemingly endless array of program services such as Disney, Discovery, Black Entertainment Television (BET), TNT, HBO, CNN, and C-SPAN, to name but a few.

This is our most intimate mass medium, yet it can attract half the population to watch Janet Jackson "perform" her infamous "wardrobe malfunction" during a Super Bowl halftime. Television rears our young, serves as the prime source of news and entertainment for most Americans, and provides a powerful soapbox from which citizens' protests can be communicated to the nation and the world. This medium has greatly altered national election campaigns and diminished the role of the political parties.

Researchers in Germany, for example, found that TV newscasts not only caused changes in awareness of problems, but also had consequences on voting intentions.[38] National and international wire services and global TV news networks have created a truly global forum. Events made large by TV shape public opinion worldwide.

Television greatly heightens citizen awareness of the conduct of public institutions. It also creates a sense of frustration for citizens, who witness much that they cannot control—be it the war in Iraq, collapse of the World Trade Center towers, Coast Guard cutters intercepting boats overloaded with Haitian refugees, bloated stomachs of starving children and refugees in Sudan, anti-abortion protesters blockading the entrance to a health-care clinic, the wretched life of homeless families, or developers scraping hillsides flat to build more look-alike houses. In fact, some research has documented "compassion fatigue," meaning that people who are exposed constantly to bad news on television just get tired of hearing about it and become less prone to doing something about it.[39]

Even with the popularity of the Internet, television remains an integral part of our lives; one study found that 46 percent of consumers who go online regularly visit the Web site of a television network.[40]

Heavy reliance on TV news as a primary source of news disturbs thoughtful observers who know that the limits of time and dominance of dramatic pictures inevitably oversimplify and distort the news. For example, evening network shows, watched by millions of people each night, must tell the story of the world in 4,000 words or less, the equivalent of four columns in a standard-sized newspaper. A "major" story gets 58 seconds. Before retiring from the *MacNeil-Lehrer News Hour* on PBS (now the *News Hour*), Robert MacNeil bluntly admitted,

> In most of the stories television cares to cover there is always the "right bit," the most violent, the most bloody, the most pathetic, the most tragic, the most wonderful, the most awful moment. Getting the effective "bit" is what television news is all about.[41]

The wide range of news stories and time pressures in television news, coupled with today's news values and technology, produces a compound of fiction and fact in terse fragments to viewers around the world. One problem in journalism today is that news media often are citing other news media as sources of information, rather than verifying the news independently. Local television stations also contract with news services and independent journalists in other cities worldwide for news feeds reported under the banner of the local station. Not only is the source of the news ambiguous, or even misleading, but also so may be the journalistic integrity of the "news." This is especially evident when the "news" is about the trials and tribulations of the remaining "survivors," or about the stars *de jour* in the latest "reality" series.

Practitioners "pitch" story ideas to TV producers. Producers then decide if an author's new book is reviewed, if the author is interviewed, or if a personality appears on network shows such as NBC's *Today* and CBS's *Late Show with David Letterman,* or on syndicated shows such as *Oprah, Live with Regis and Kelly,* and *Ellen DeGeneres* (or similar local programs). Perhaps the most common technique for placing a message on television, however, is providing video for news or documentary programs in the form of a video news release (VNR).

TV Guide blew the whistle on VNRs used in newscasts without viewers being informed that the video was provided by an outside source. The magazine referred to the video press releases as "fake news," suggesting that VNRs blur the line between news and commercials.[42] Others have expressed concern that VNRs can be aired without first having passed journalistic standards for verifying accuracy, can be shown without identifying the source, can be used to manipulate media content in favor of the VNR source, and can violate generally accepted ethical principles in public relations and journalism.[43] In fact, however, local television news directors are pressed to fill ever-larger "news holes" with smaller staffs and budgets. Consequently, local news operations are increasingly dependent on public relations sources, although they are loathe to admit that reality.

Bob Kimmel of News Broadcast Network (New York City VNR producer) lists techniques to increase the chances that stations will use a VNR:

1. Don't mix natural sound with voice-over narration.
2. Don't overuse stills as a substitute for action video.
3. Don't place titles of "supers" on the video news segment itself. Provide the information separately so stations can insert titles in their regular fonts and styles.
4. Don't use fancy special effects and repetitive dissolves not ordinarily used in news packages.
5. Don't commercialize the VNR with blatant product or service presentations.
6. Don't put your own reporter on the screen.
7. Don't produce a VNR unless you have a news story or a timely feature of general interest.[44]

"At one time, VNRs were assailed by TV journalists because they too closely resembled advertisements. VNRs are under attack today, video experts say, because they deliver what they promise: news!"[45]

More frequently, satellite transmission makes it possible to instantaneously distribute public relations messages. The satellite media tour (SMT) has replaced the time-consuming and expensive city hopping that was formerly part of political campaigns, crisis communication programs (see Tylenol Exhibit 1.3), movie openings, product launches, and breaking news.

Turn on any morning news show and you see anchors interviewing doctors, writers, entertainers, CEOs and other experts. Most of the time the interviews are via satellite from locations other than the anchors' TV stations. . . . In the course of two or three hours, a typical SMT can cover 12 to 20 stations.[46]

SMTs work best when local stations cannot produce the same story themselves, when the story fits morning programming before being bumped by breaking news, and when the story calls for top management appearances on the global television medium.

Cable and Satellite Television

Television comes into our homes not only through the publicly accessible networks, but also via cable and satellite, with increasing competition among these delivery systems. The growth of cable and satellite television with its 500-channel-capacity and high-definition capabilities has profoundly altered the nation's communication and viewing patterns. Cable was born in 1948, when the first community-antenna television (CATV) system was built in a small Pennsylvania community that suffered from poor television reception. Advertising-supported cable channels collectively now have more than have a greater share of the television audience than do the broadcast networks—52 percent to 48 percent.[47] It was Cable News Network's (CNN) live coverage of the 1986 Challenger disaster; the round-the-clock coverage of the 1991 Gulf War and 2003 Iraq War; and 24-hour coverage of the September 11, 2001, World Trade Center and Pentagon attacks, however, that made cable news a major player in the global information system. CNN coverage was so complete that several network affiliates and many independent stations carried CNN reports and still contract for news packages.

As new technology expands the channel-carrying capacity and converts systems to on-demand programming, cable and satellite TV may become only part of the packages of services carried. Cable companies offer interactive services such as shopping, banking, information databases, local and long-distance telephone services, and emergency alert connections to police and fire departments. Digital and video recorders, currently in 17 percent of households, and other personal video recorders give viewers flexibility as to when they watch programs, called "time-shifted viewing."[48]

Fiber-optic and asymmetric digital subscriber line (DSL) networks link viewers 24 hours a day directly to central computers to retrieve and send information. Just as futurists had predicted, the line between television, telephone, other media, and home computers has blurred as both information and entertainment services are delivered to homes over wire and wireless systems. The next section examines some of these new media and the challenges they present for public relations practice.

New Media, New Challenges

The Internet represents the most ubiquitous leading edge of the communication revolution in that nearly all new media are Internet-based. For public relations practitioners, the new media environment offers at least three challenges: (1) staying abreast of technological developments in new media; (2) conducting media relations with untraditional "journalists"; and (3) representing organizations in the new media environment.

Dealing with New Technology

Although many recognize that new media technology changes how public relations is practiced, the rapidity of change illustrates how practitioners are scrambling to adjust. Consequently, the Institute for Public Relations and WORLDCOM Public Relations Group commissioned a study of the Internet's impact on public relations. Although the findings may not impress college students, they document a major change in the practice in the twenty-first century. The conclusions include the following:

- Almost all public relations professionals (98 percent) agree that advances in technology such as e-mail and the Internet have changed how they do their jobs.

- Almost all (91 percent) also say that they now stay in touch with more people in their business and professional environments than they did before e-mail.

- Most (90 percent) agree that the ability to send instantaneous written communication and to access real-time information via the Internet has accelerated decision making in news journalism.

- Public relations professionals typically spend between 15 and 19 hours online each week, and go online 5.8 days during an average week. One in three (33 percent) say they are online every day.

- Sixty-nine percent chose an Internet-connected computer when asked what medium they would choose if they were stranded alone somewhere for an extended period of time and could have access to only one medium.[49]

Handling Bloggers and Citizen Journalists

This study also indicated that "one of the greatest advantages of the Internet as a public relations medium is the reality it has . . . to provide direct and immediate access to specific target audiences, thus bypassing journalists and traditional news media."[50] On the other hand, this also means that practitioners must work with non-traditional media gatekeepers and influencers—such as bloggers—who have the ability to shape an organization's digital environment.

For example, when the Democrats met in Denver and the Republicans in Minneapolis–Saint Paul for their national conventions in 2008, bloggers worked as "credentialed media" alongside reporters from the traditional news organizations. But of course, bloggers did not have to attend the conventions in order to become publishers of news and opinion about the issues, speakers, and candidates. For those in virtual communities of like-thinking participants, blogs have become the sources of choice in the interconnected and digitalized cyberspace.

According to technorati.com, a site that tracks online traffic and provides news of interest to technophiles, there were more than 112.8 million blogs in April 2008, and more than 175,000 new blogs were being added each day to what the company calls the World Live Web, that part of the World Wide Web that is constantly changing due to "citizen media" (http://technorati.com). Public relations practitioners are increasingly monitoring the "blogosphere," but their relationship with bloggers remains tenuous because "bloggers want 100 percent access, and PR people want control. The level of transparency that bloggers think they should [get] is higher [than the level media expect]."[51] Nevertheless, blogs remain a useful tool for practitioners trying to reach Web-savvy publics, both by attracting blog coverage and by creating their own blogs as part of a communication strategy.

Finally, public relations practitioners must acknowledge that new technology today means that anyone with a camera phone can "report" the news. Often called citizen journalists, these individuals are invited even by mainstream media outlets such as CNN to share the news in their communities by sending in video clips to major news outlets for possible dissemination to a wide audience. For example, when a gunman killed 32 students and faculty members at Virginia Tech on April 16, 2007, much of the world's first view of the tragedy came from video taken by students on the scene, crouching in the bushes as police officers ran toward the sound of gunfire.

This kind of citizen journalism via cell phones and the Internet has the potential not only to inform our communities, but also to promote democracy around the world by empowering individuals to share their voices. For example, after a terrorist attack in Madrid, angry text messages about the conservative government's poor response to the crisis resulted in the Socialist party winning the next election.[52] Similarly, when exit polls in the 2002 presidential election in South Korea showed that the candidate most popular with young voters, Roh Moo Hyun, was losing . . .

> His supporters hit the chat rooms to drum up support. Within minutes more than 800,000 e-mails were sent to mobiles to urge supporters to go out and vote. . . . By 2 p.m., Roh took the lead and went on to win the election. A man with little support from either the mainstream media or the nation's conglomerates sashayed into office on an Internet on-ramp.[53]

Doing the Job in a Virtual World

Obviously, new media are not used merely to disseminate information one-way, from the organization to the public. Rather, new media allow for participation of the public in what one author called "unmediated conversations" in which "the empowerment of the Internet has magnified the intensity of opinions and made everyone an expert capable of transmitting his or her feelings at will through such content-sharing channels as YouTube, Twitter, Jaiku and Facebook, among many others."[54] For public relations practitioners, this means building relationships with organizational publics not only in the real world, but also in the virtual world (see Exhibit 10.2).

EXHIBIT 10.2

Leveraging New Media to Share Your Message

Rachel Kay, Principal
Rachel Kay Public Relations*
San Diego, California

The Web is often the fastest way to reach the most people, but it can sometimes be difficult to move beyond traditional print and broadcast media, and to understand the potential the Internet holds. New buzzwords like "viral," "blog," and "social networking" indicate how the pace and practice of public relations has changed. It is imperative to understand the challenges and risks in the era of Internet communication.

The term "blogging" was coined to describe a handful of cyber personalities sharing their views on a topic of interest. Initially lacking the credibility of traditional journalists, their online diaries were simply a platform for their own musings. Along came a slew of powerful characters, including Michael Arrington, founder of tech blog TechCrunch, who could propel a struggling start-up to stardom as quickly he could bury one. And, others like public relations gurus Richard Laermer and Kevin Dugan, whose Bad Pitch Blog broadcasts the names of publicists accused of poor pitch tactics. However, pop culture blogger Perez Hilton could be called the most influential blogger of our time, whose no-holds barred celebrity commentary captivated millions. Commanding millions of site views every day, PerezHilton.com is the source for Hollywood fans eager for the scoop, playing an integral role in elevating the craft of blogging to the credible and powerful forum it is today. The tabloid blogger also broadcasts a radio entertainment "news mini-show," Radio Perez, during morning and evening drive times in Los Angeles, New York, Chicago, and other large U.S. cities.

How does a public relations practitioner leverage that influence? Just like any journalist, bloggers seek truthful information, and they want it first. Above all else the information must be appropriate to the blogger's subject. Read the blog and understand his or her opinions, goals and audience. Unlike the fact-based nature of newspapers and broadcast news, blogs are often more opinion-based, so it is important to make sure you see eye-to-eye. Some bloggers will publish your letter with contact information if they aren't happy with the contents, so tread carefully. In addition, the real-time nature of blogging means public relations professionals must monitor online news constantly so they can react quickly. Finally, unlike most reporters, bloggers do not list their phone numbers, so the cleverly crafted pitch is essential to communicate the importance of your story idea. Rarely do you have a follow-up second chance.

Social networking also has boomed in recent years, due to the popularity of sites like MySpace and Facebook where people can connect through personalized pages. Hundreds of these sites exist, such as Deviant Art, which attracts aspiring artists, and Dogster, which brings our furry friends together. Publicists are eager to enter these tight-knit communities as a way to reach a targeted group of consumers. While social networks frown on blatant promotion, befriending owners of groups can help get a foot in the door. For example, Parfums Givenchy held a viral marketing campaign powered by Brickfish, in which logo design campaign participants had the chance to win a trip to meet actress and model Liv Tyler. The promotions team reached out to the leaders of Liv Tyler fan groups, assemblies of beauty mavens, and "fashionistas" on social networking sites. Those few people eagerly shared the information of interest with thousands. In addition, many organizations create branded MySpace and Facebook pages as a way to interact with their publics and to deliver consistent messages.

Relevancy and—most importantly—authenticity are key. Get the right content in front of the right audience and you'll succeed; spam them with disingenuous messages or irrelevant rubbish and you will almost certainly fall flat. Social network users are not media professionals. Rather, users are seeking a sense of community with likeminded "friends," and can easily create camaraderie in support or against an organization or service.

The word "viral" elicits visions of engaging millions of consumers with a touch of a button. A video might get millions of views on YouTube, but the challenge is igniting a viral campaign. Today, engineers are harnessing the power of virality and discovering ways to quantify it. Brickfish powers campaigns that collect user-generated content (UGC) from consumers and give them the tools to share it with peers through e-mail, instant messaging, and by posting it on social networking sites. The consumer-to-consumer approach gives more credibility to the brand message. A "Viral Map" also shows where each viral piece of content traveled and how many times people viewed it, measures most in public relations and advertising have not yet mastered.

A viral campaign puts communication in the hands of Internet users, significantly reducing the source organization's control over the message. The public relations professional must make the original message a clear representation of the brand or organization so that it translates authentically as it passes from user-to-user in a completely unique fashion. In addition, viral campaigns must be incredibly engaging in order to stand out among the thousands of spam and chain emails. Careerbuilder.com's "Monk-e-mail" campaign is an example of the reach that viral campaign can hold. Users use the goofy tool to send silly messages to friends, igniting the Web with the company's name to keep it top-of-mind to job seekers. Because the campaign was unique in its approach, millions engaged in the campaign, propagating the brand across the Internet. Out-of-the box thinking is imperative to propel virality, and practitioners must be more creative than ever before.

What are the implications of these evolving new media tools for public relations practitioners? The translation of information is much more volatile, so practitioners have more responsibility for messages and the organization's reputation. The Internet can be much less forgiving than traditional forms of press, so it is imperative to research and understand your target public, and to be receptive to all forms of feedback. Information, either positive or negative, can be updated almost instantaneously so have a process in place to ensure accurate communication in order to leverage that speed. The Internet tools also provide ways to quickly combat negative situations, be it quickly easing the fears of a product recall or communicating a recovery strategy in times of financial angst.

The Internet continues to develop as a medium for reaching consumers, and it is critical for publicists to keep up with the changing technology to stay competitive. While it is impossible to predict the future, it is safe to assume that today's "new media" will soon be "old" as tools and techniques evolve.

---

*Rachel Kay Public Relations is an independent public relations consultancy, servicing numerous products and services, including Brickfish.

For example, Diegoland contracted with Southern California–based CIM Incorporated to bridge the virtual and real worlds by helping companies and organizations in San Diego to build a presence in Second Life, a virtual world (http://secondlife.com). The organizations in Diegoland attract avatar visitors from all over the world, which promotes their own business as well as San Diego as a destination. The crossover between the real and virtual worlds is growing so rapidly that even presidential candidates have headquarters in Second Life, and many of the world's leading corporations (including many major media outlets) have established a presence in the medium.

As an example of publicity via new technologies, the March of Dimes turned to YouTube and various social networking sites to promote its contest for "a user-generated video PSA with a grand prize of $5,000 and placement on TV stations across the country." The idea was that users who had experienced the challenge of having a premature baby would be best at explaining to others the importance of preventing premature births.[55] The effort was at once both educational (about the subject) and relational (for the March of Dimes with key stakeholders).

Another concern for public relations practitioners today is ensuring that the organizations they represent can be found by those interested in them. Thus, SEO (search engine optimization) has become another tool in the practitioner's toolkit. Basically, SEO involves figuring out how to get an organization's name to come up at the top of the list generated by a user's online search on a specific topic. One study showed that search engines drive Internet traffic for 84 percent of users.[56] Google—one of the most popular search engines in the United States—produces search results using proprietary software called PageRank, which ranks sites based on links, clicks, matching texts, and other complicated features.[57] But one thing that search engines do not do is ensure the veracity of the information contained in the sites they sort.

Of course, information—truthful or not—spreads rapidly online, and savvy practitioners know that they need to be vigilant in scanning the digital media environment, "where rogue opinions can flourish and multiply."[58] This means that public relations practitioners must constantly monitor organizational reputations online; as one writer put it, "It used to be enough to read the morning papers on the way to work. That's no longer a sufficient defense."[59]

Trying to document developments in new media technology produces information with the shelf life of lettuce. By the time this chapter is published, no doubt some of the examples may be passé. However, the overriding conclusion is obvious: Rapidly evolving technology will change how media are used to communicate *with* stakeholder publics. The key for public relations is that the new technology promotes *interactive communication,* the essence of building and maintaining relationships.

Working with the Media

Knowing about the media—knowing how to work with each medium, produce content for each, meet the deadlines of each, adhere to specific style requirements, and address each medium's audience—is a major part of many practitioners' jobs. Practitioners must build and maintain relationships of mutual respect and trust with media gatekeepers. These relationships, although mutually beneficial, remain adversarial at their core, because journalists and practitioners are not in the same business and often do not have the same communication goals.

The Person in the Middle

To be effective in the go-between and mediating roles, practitioners must have the confidence of both their organization's management and the media. This is not an easy job. CEOs and other line managers are naturally suspicious of the media, just as journalists are by nature questioning and somewhat untrusting of those they put in the spotlight. Practitioners and others in organizations complain: "Why does the press always sensationalize things?" "Journalists never get things right." "I didn't say that!" "They take things out of context or twist things to fit their story." For example, the Queen of England's late father, King George VI, collected newspaper clippings in a scrapbook titled "Things my daughters never did."[60] And that was before the days of *Star* and *National Enquirer*!

Journalists counter: "That organization never tells the truth!" "We don't get to talk with the person who has the real story and real news." "What we get is PR fluff." "You get the feeling they're trying to hide something." "Spacegrabbers!"

This is not breaking news. The conflict between journalists and public relations practitioners has a long history of contradiction:

> Journalists wanted information to be easily available, yet resented the men and women who made it available. By the mid twentieth century, journalists were dependent upon PR practitioners for a large percentage of the stories appearing in newspapers. But admitting their dependence would shatter cherished ideals. Journalists were proud of their ability to uncover stories, verify details, and expose sham. Thus, they were unlikely to admit their dependence, lack of skepticism, failure to verify, and failure to expose every sham.[61]

The adversarial—sometimes even hostile—feelings that exist between practitioners and journalists often spill over into public debate. Herbert Schmertz, Mobil Corporation vice president of public affairs in the 1980s, criticized journalists and media performance by providing what he called "constructive, responsible criticism."[62] Mobil periodically used its advocacy advertising to criticize the media (see Figure 10.1), to which Schmertz credits substantial progress in improving print coverage of his corporation and business in general. He saved his harshest criticism for television news and:

> The questionable values that afflict TV journalism—the slavery to ratings . . . the pandering to the lowest common denominator...the emotional presentation to entice a larger audience . . . the subversion of news values to entertainment values . . . the ruthless compression of facts to fit preordained timetables.[63]

Schmertz was not alone in his criticism. General Motors counterattacked when an NBC News reporter staged accidents and fires involving GM's full-sized pickups manufactured from 1973 through 1987. The report aired on "Dateline NBC" under the title "Waiting to Explode." Exhibit 10.3 summarizes this case in which NBC admitted fault and apologized to viewers and to GM.

Others share the acrimony. When Meg Greenfield was *Washington Post* editorial page editor, she issued a memo barring practitioners entry to editorial offices: "We don't want any of that damned crowd around here." Subsequently, *Post* executive editor Ben Bradlee extended the ban, forbidding reporters to talk to public relations sources, a directive quickly ignored because reporters depend on public relations sources for news leads.[64] In fact, 90 percent of journalists admit to getting story ideas from news releases, and 89 percent say they rely on public relations

Mobil Corporation's Advertisement on "The Myth of Open Airwaves."

4. The myth of the open airwaves

There is a simple, yet overwhelming, difference between the print media and television journalism. Newspapers and magazines offer regular access to their pages to those who wish to rebut what has been printed. The major television networks do not.

Access to television is supposed to be governed largely by the Federal Communications Commission's Fairness Doctrine. That doctrine owes its existence to the theory that the airwaves are a scarce resource and must therefore be allocated among potential users. The doctrine requires owners of broadcast licenses "...to encourage and implement the broadcast of all sides of controversial public issues..." and to play "...a conscious and positive role in bringing about the balanced presentation of the opposing viewpoints." In theory, the Fairness Doctrine doesn't preclude anything. In reality, the networks have turned it into a doctrine of unfairness.

Under a mandate to present all sides of a public issue, the networks confine debate through controls imposed by their own news departments. Through their news staffs, the networks exercise total control over the agenda of issues, and who may speak to the public. Unfortunately, the result of this network control, with no system or forum for rebuttal, has resulted in a narrow and selective discussion of major public issues—and the systematic exclusion or distortion of many viewpoints.

Mobil has often been denied the opportunity to rebut inaccurate television news broadcasts. Frequently, the broadcasts appeared at times when critical energy legislation was under debate in Congress—legislation regarding oil company divestiture, natural gas deregulation, oil decontrol, and the "windfall profit" tax. At such times, the networks' systematic exclusion of ideas and information impaired the public's ability to rationally decide fundamental policy issues.

Other companies have experienced similar frustrations in their attempts to gain adequate airtime to rebut erroneous television newscasts. Kaiser Aluminum & Chemical Corporation had to threaten a slander suit and had to ask the FCC to order ABC to give it time to respond to charges made on a 1980 *20/20* segment, before ABC finally gave the company the opportunity for an unedited reply. It took more than a year, however, before the rebuttal was aired on prime-time TV.

In response to a 1979 CBS *60 Minutes* broadcast, Illinois Power Company produced its own tape to point out the network's distortions. Called "60 Minutes/Our Reply," the power company's rebuttal exposed the bias of the broadcast by including CBS film footage not included in the original segment. The program has been widely shown to various groups across the country, but it has not been aired on television.

The networks not only block rebuttals, they refuse to air advertisements on "controversial" issues, and have rejected Mobil advocacy commercials since 1974—despite evidence that public support for issue advertising is strong. (Network policies would preclude the very message you are currently reading.) A 1980 survey by the Opinion Research Corporation found that 85 percent of the American public think corporations should be allowed to present their views on controversial matters in television commercials. And most independent stations and network affiliates have opened their doors to advocacy advertising, without creating the chaos the networks profess to fear.

As the Supreme Court affirmed in its 1978 *Bellotti* decision: "The press does not have a monopoly on either the First Amendment or the ability to enlighten."

Mobil

© 1983 Mobil Corporation

Courtesy Mobil Corporation.

EXHIBIT 10.3

General Motors versus NBC News

Alvie L. Smith, APR
Director of Corporate
Communications (retired)
General Motors Corporation

The Situation

In November 1992, a 16-minute segment entitled "Waiting to Explode" on the television news magazine *Dateline NBC* focused on what it called the unsafe design of GM full-sized pickups built from 1973 through 1987. The show included a one-minute segment of "unscientific" demonstration crashes conducted by the Institute for Safety Analysis (ISA) in which one truck catches fire after being struck in the side by a car.

Seventeen million viewers saw apparent visual support for interviews with safety experts who claimed that the trucks were vulnerable to fires and explosions because of fuel tank design and placement.

The television segment also included interviews with the parents of a 17-year-old who was killed when his pickup was broadsided by a car driven by a drunken driver. GM officially complained to NBC that the show was "grossly unfair, misleading, and irresponsible."

In February 1993, the jury found GM "negligent" and awarded the parents $105.2 million. GM appealed, claiming that the 70-miles-per-hour impact into the cab, not the fire, killed the truck driver.

Although NBC and ISA claimed that the test vehicles had been destroyed after the demonstration crashes, GM investigators found them and got court approval to study the vehicles to recreate the demonstrations and results.

GM's Response

In a February 8, 1993, press conference in Detroit, GM's chief counsel presented a well-researched refutation of the *Dateline NBC* segment. GM locations throughout the world and North American dealers received the press conference via satellite. Hundreds of videotapes of the press conference

were distributed. While displaying the crash truck fuel tank and slow-motion sequences of the crash, GM's counsel pointed out major deceptions in the report and test crash:

1. NBC did not tell viewers that incendiary rocket devices were taped under the trucks and timed to go off on impact to ignite any spilled gasoline.
2. The fuel tank had been "topped off" before the test and fitted with a nonstandard cap that allowed gasoline to escape as the incendiary device was fired.
3. There was no puncture of the gas tank, as had been claimed in the NBC report.
4. Impact speed in the demonstration were significantly higher than those NBC reported: one at 39 miles per hour, not 30, and the other at least 47, not 40.

GM filed a lawsuit against NBC and ISA for defaming its reputation. This was the first such action in GM's history.

NBC's Response

NBC carried highlights of GM's charges in its February 8 newscast, but NBC News President Michael Gartner defended the segment. On February 10, however, *Dateline NBC* coanchors Jane Pauley and Stone Phillips read a lengthy retraction negotiated by NBC and GM that day. NBC did not contest any of GM's accusations. "NBC deeply regrets using the one-minute crash segment," Phillips said. "We apologize to our viewers and to GM."

Results

GM accepted NBC's apology and dropped the lawsuit, with the provision that NBC pay GM's research expenses, about $2 million. Quick acceptance of NBC's apology and dropping legal action took the matter out of the media spotlight. In March 1993, Gartner resigned from *NBC News* and three other executives were fired. A group of independent lawyers hired by NBC had scathing criticism for the show's producers. NBC announced it would reorganize its procedures to ensure future accuracy and fairness. *Detroit Free Press* columnist Steven Brill wrote: "NBC's candid apology was a pivotal event in the annals of journalism—a refreshing reversal of the usual arrogance and stonewalling and hiding behind a justifiably permissive law."

contacts for information.[65] Researchers in the United Kingdom recently learned that about three of every five stories in British newspapers, and radio and television news reports came from reprinted or rewritten press releases. They said their findings "illustrate that journalists' reliance on these news sources is extensive and raises significant questions concerning claims to journalistic independence in UK news media and journalists' role as a fourth estate."[66]

Thus, practitioners and journalists operate in a mutually dependent and mutually beneficial relationship, sometimes as adversaries and sometimes as colleagues cooperating in each of their own self-interests. Not as frequently, but occasionally, the news media are manipulated by practitioners, who may have more resources, as well as controlling access to news sources. With at least equal frequency, news media frustrate practitioners in their attempts to get information to publics.

In short, there is a dynamic tension in the relationship between practitioners and journalists that is "firmly embedded in journalistic culture."[67] Often, however, neither employers nor journalists understand the practitioner's liaison role in establishing and maintaining media relations.

Guidelines for Good Media Relations

The underlying conflicts of interest and of mission necessarily make the practitioner–journalist relationship adversarial. The practitioner advancing a particular cause or organization stands in stark contrast to the journalist's drive to dig up news through good reporting and journalistic initiative. Given the experience of at least a century, the adversarial relationship appears to serve the public interest and the needs of the public information system.

The sound approach for organizations and practitioners is to view media relations as an investment. Accuracy and fairness in press coverage does not result from reporters' work alone. Ultimately, the relationship between practitioners and journalists has an impact on the quality of news coverage about organizations.[68] Those relationships can best be achieved when practitioners follow a few basic rules:

1. *Shoot squarely.*   It is not just politically correct to counsel "honesty is the best policy" in dealing with the press; it is good business and good common sense. Jerry Dalton Jr., past PRSA national president, says the practitioner's most important asset in dealing with the media is credibility: "It must be earned, usually over a period of time. It means simply that a reporter can trust [the practitioner] totally, and vice versa. It means never lying. If you can't, for some legitimate reason, speak the truth, then say nothing."[69]

   Journalists point out that good and bad news tend to even out over time, so if practitioners are honest with bad news, then they are more likely to be trusted with good news. Another fundamental principle is that a practitioner cannot favor one news outlet at the expense of others; in fact, this is explicitly prohibited by the PRSA Code of Ethics' core principle of "fair competition" (see Chapter 5). The safest rule is that spot news should go out to all relevant media as fast as possible, letting the media determine the cycle in which it breaks. Less time-sensitive feature material should be alternated evenly among the competitors. As a corollary, practitioners must protect journalistic initiative. For example, if a reporter gets a tip and asks for information, the story belongs to that journalist. The same information should not be given to other outlets unless they come after it. This is a policy with which no reporter can justly quarrel, because each of them would demand the same protection for their scoops.

2. *Give service.*   The quickest, surest way to gain the cooperation of journalists is to provide them with newsworthy, interesting, and timely stories and pictures that they want, when they want them, and in a form they can readily use. Author Carole Howard suggests, "Be a reporter's reporter. When asked for information, do not hesitate to ask enough questions so you have a full understanding of the story the reporter is working on."[70]

Journalists work with fixed and sometimes tight deadlines. Practitioners who hope to place stories in the news media must know and adhere to media lead times. Again, Howard advises:

> Learn the regular and late-breaking deadlines of all the media that normally cover your organization. A reporter's life is controlled by very short deadlines, especially in the broadcast and Internet media, and you must meet the reporter's deadline or your information is useless.[71]

Journalists also count on and cooperate with the practitioner who willingly responds to a midnight call for a photo and biographical sketch of an executive who just died. News, a highly perishable commodity, occurs around the clock, as do news deadlines in the global media environment. Therefore, some practitioners are on call around the clock. Howard suggests keeping key materials at home, for as Dalton points out, "News doesn't wait—for anyone or anything."

3. *Do not beg or whine.*   Nothing irritates journalists and their editors and news directors more than the practitioner who begs to have stories used or complains about story treatment. Journalists have finely developed senses of journalistic objectivity and news value. If information is not sufficiently newsworthy on its own merits to attract their interest, no amount of begging and whining can change the quality of that information. Some practitioners (or their interns!) call journalists to ask, "Did you receive my release?" One online editor succinctly states how most journalists react to such follow-calls: "Assume that whatever it was you sent, we got it. If you don't hear back from us, we're not interested."[72]

Nothing, however, is more offensive to a journalist than a practitioner who tries to pressure the editorial staff to use a story, change a story treatment, or kill a story by holding hostage the organization's advertising business. That kind of pressure does not work when up against journalistic integrity and will surely lead to resentment or to an immediate public response.

Threats to "pull our advertising" can lead to banner headlines or lead stories on the evening news, pitting the media against a corporate bully. The rule of thumb is that advertising belongs in the advertising department, and news—good and bad—is for journalists to report in news columns and newscasts. Journalists refer to the "fire wall" between the two. Even though Reuters does not accept advertising, the international wire service's "Trust Principles" statement summarizes this journalistic value in no uncertain terms: "The integrity, independence and freedom from bias of Reuters shall at all times be fully preserved."

4. *Do not ask for "kills."*   Practitioners have no right to ask the press to suppress or kill a story. It seldom works, is unprofessional, and brings only ill will. To journalists, this is a crude insult and an abuse of the First Amendment. It is asking journalists to betray their public trust. The best way to keep unfavorable stories out of the press is to prevent situations that produce such stories.

At the same time, there are occasions when it is perfectly legitimate to request a delay in publication or to explain to the press any part of the story that might be damaging to the public interest. For example, hospital public relations staff cannot release the names and condition of accident or crime victims before the next of kin have been notified or without permission of the patient or family. Likewise the Departments of Defense and Homeland Security do not release, or may legitimately request media to delay releasing, information potentially compromising to military operations or threatening to public safety. Then again, in the latter cases, some will remind us of what California U.S. Senator Hiram Johnson said in 1917: "The first casualty when war comes is truth."[73] That is why public relations specialists in those organizations establish and maintain relationships of trust with their media counterparts. (See Chapter 16 on government public affairs.)

However, if the press reports an inaccurate or misleading story, ask for a correction. Many news media, in the interest of their own public relations, have adopted policies of publishing or broadcasting corrections, albeit often in an inconspicuous manner. At the same time, practitioners also should ask that the erroneous information be corrected in the computer database—what used to be called the "morgue" or library—so the information does not get repeated in subsequent stories.

Some organizations provide updated background information about the organization, its finances, its products or services, or executives to media so it will be in the file when stories break. For example, the Pharmaceutical Manufacturers' Association sends a file of information to news outlets with this note: "If your files on the prescription drug industry don't include the information in this folder, your files may be incomplete." Many organizations send annual fact books to the media, although increasing numbers of organizations simply include a media section on their Web site, as this is easier to keep updated than hard copies of anything. (See http://www.census.gov and click on "newsroom" for one example.).

5. *Do not flood the media.*   Study and experience teach the boundaries of newsworthiness, and common sense dictates respect for them. If a financial editor receives information appropriate for the sports or real estate editor, the financial editor loses respect for the practitioner who engages in blanketing the media with releases. The best advice includes the following: (1) stick to what journalists will consider news, (2) keep media mailing lists current, and (3) send to only one—the most appropriate—journalist at each news medium.

To document how much his reporters and editors have to cull each day, Paul Steiger, then the *Wall Street Journal*'s New York managing editor, asked the 17 domestic bureau managers to save for one day all news materials they received. They collected press releases, public relations wire stories, faxes, and letters, but not news sent over the Internet. The stack of boxes and bins in Steiger's office was more than 2 feet high and 10 feet long.[74] A similar avalanche of public relations materials reaches newsrooms around the globe. Not all of it will get through the careful scrutiny of media gatekeepers, and they quickly learn which sources provide information with real news value.

Guidelines for Working with the Press

Former CBS news reporter and long-time counselor Chester Burger says the press "is often unfair, unreasonable, and simply wrong. But even if it isn't our friend, it is the best friend the nation has, and we should be thankful for it."[75] Based on notions of a free and independent press, as well as principles of sound public relations practice, seasoned practitioners offer the following guidelines for working with the press:

1. *Talk from the viewpoint of the public's interest, not the organization's.*   The soft-drink bottler who launches a campaign to collect and recycle bottles can frankly admit that it does not want to irritate the public by having its product litter the landscape.

2. *Make the news easy to read and use.*   Use a short, punchy headline to attract attention and give potential users an indication of the topic. Do not use jargon, unfamiliar acronyms, or technical terms. Personal pronouns, names, and quotations make your copy easier to read and more interesting. Put the name, address, and phone number of the news source and contact at the top of releases.

3. *If you do not want some statement quoted, do not make it.*   Spokespersons should avoid talking "off the record," because such statements may well wind up published without the source identified. Some news organizations forbid reporters to accept such information. Moreover, it is absolutely too late to qualify something as off the record after you make a statement to a reporter.

4. *State the most important fact at the beginning.*   A manager's logical presentation may first list the facts that led to a decision, but news reporters want the decision. The first-level response to a reporter's question is a short summary of your position or newsworthy announcement. The second-level response includes a concrete example or evidence to back up your first statement. If the reporter persists, return to the first-level summary statement.

5. *Do not argue with a reporter or lose your cool.*   Understand that journalists seek an interesting story and will go to great lengths to get the story. To paraphrase an old public relations maxim, do not argue with people who buy printers ink by the barrel or with people who own the transmitter or cable system; these people have the final say.

6. *If a question contains offensive language or simply words you do not like, do not repeat them even to deny them.*   Along the line of having final say, reporters also can select quotes, portions of quotes, or even single words for the final story. Reporters often use the gambit of putting words into subject's mouths, such as, "Do you mean . . . ?" or "Is what you are really saying . . . ?"

7. *If the reporter asks a direct question, give an equally direct answer.*   Feeling pressure to say something more than what is called for by a question is a common error. If the appropriate answer is "yes" or "no," give the correct response and say no more. Some reporters will remain silent after getting an answer in hopes that the subject will volunteer more information. Assume that the camera is on at all times; otherwise the unguarded comment will be the sound bite on the evening news! Media adviser Roger Ailes's rule of thumb is that the tougher the question, the shorter the answer should be.

8. *If spokespersons do not know the answer to a question, they should simply say, "I don't know, but I'll get the answer for you."*   This is a commitment to follow through by providing the information as quickly as possible. Better yet, prepare for the interview by anticipating what questions will be asked, by developing succinct answers, and by rehearsing with someone playing the role of the reporter.

9. *Tell the truth, even if it hurts.*   Do not think for a moment that bad news will go away or that the media will miss it. Treat it as you would any other

story: Prepare as if it were good news and take it to the media. Not only does that mean that you will keep some control over the story and how it is covered, but it also means that you are not on the defensive, making yourself vulnerable to charges of trying to hide the facts or of having been exposed by the media. This may be the most difficult position to sell to those in top management, who often see the practitioner's job as keeping bad news out of the media.

10. *Do not call a press conference unless you have what reporters consider news.*   When is a news conference justified? Seldom. In fact, call a news conference only when there is no other means to get an important breaking story to the media in a timely fashion. Examples include important controversial matters such as labor—management disputes and settlements, important political announcements, and major policy changes affecting large numbers of people. The determining factor is the need to give reporters an opportunity to ask questions and pursue the story rather than simply issuing a statement or making an announcement (see Figure 10.2). Complex matters that require backgrounding and detailed explanation, such as a technological breakthrough, may justify a press conference. Simple, straightforward, or noncontroversial announcements rarely justify the expense and effort of media coverage. And finally, if you do call a press conference, follow the suggestions outlined in steps 1 through 9.[76]

Working with International Media

When working with news media from other countries, public relations practitioners must follow not only the same basic principles discussed in this chapter, but also keep in mind linguistic, cultural, and political differences. William Hachten categorized media systems around the world into five types:[77]

1. *Authoritarian.*   The media are subordinate to the state, which controls the press and restricts what they can cover. An example of this would be the media system in Iraq under now-deposed dictator Saddam Hussein.

FIGURE 10.2

Pentagon Press Secretary Geoff Morrell Briefs Press, January 2008

Courtesy Department of Defense. Photo by R. D. Ward.

2. *Communist.*   The state controls the media and requires it to espouse and promote Marxist ideals and philosophy. Media in Cuba and China are examples of this type of system.

3. *Revolutionary.*   This media system often exists clandestinely in conjuction with authoritarian or communist media systems. Characterized by its effort to spread information suppressed by the state media, the revolutionary media system today is often Internet-based, such as Web sites in China or Singapore that get shut down for disseminating information not authorized by the government.

4. *Western.*   Despite its name, this media system can be found in any country where the news media are free to report on whatever they wish, as long as they balance that right with their social responsibility, for example, by not reporting inaccurate or misleading information.

5. *Developmental.*   Found in so-called "third-world countries," this media system is relatively free, as long as it supports national goals toward development. One example is the media system in India, where news channels are unrestricted, while social programming encourages such government initiatives as the elimination of the traditional caste system.

Although Hachten's classification might seem somewhat dated today, it remains useful in reminding public relations practitioners that they cannot conduct media relations abroad the way they do at home. Other tips include being careful of cultural differences and sensitive issues (for example, some Chinese media resist company news releases with boilerplate statements about corporate social responsibility); translating all documents into appropriate languages (for example, mainland China, Hong Kong, and Taiwan require three distinct types of Chinese characters); refraining from potentially insulting language (for example, saying your U.S.-made product is "the best," when the country you are targeting produces something similar); and including local information and sources whenever possible.[78]

These suggestions can help practitioners build and maintain good relations with journalists in the news media, at home and around the world. Because of the crucial gatekeeper role played by reporters and editors in print, broadcast, and online media, practitioners have little choice but to earn and keep the respect of journalists. At the same time, although the public has a right to public information, there are limits. Some information is confidential, and some information cannot be disclosed because of individual privacy or because of the proprietary nature of the information in a competitive business environment.

Also, sometimes, news may be *embargoed*, meaning that information is made available to credentialed journalists with the understanding that they will not share it with a wider audience until given permission to do so. An example of embargoed news occurred in February 2008, when an Australian magazine "broke the embargo"—without authorization—about Britain's Prince Harry serving with his British Army unit in Afghanistan. When the news broke, Prince Harry was recalled home amid concerns for his safety and that of his military unit. Whether the news media were right to honor the embargo, denying people the right to know the prince was serving in Afghanistan, was the subject of subsequent debate among journalists.[79]

For the public relations practitioner, knowing how to keep control of the agenda when dealing with the press is part of the media training required for all those acting as spokespersons and managers of media relations. In the final analysis, however, the practitioner–journalist relationship is an adversarial relationship. After being accused of doing something immoral by teaching people how to deal with the press, Roger Ailes told a journalism seminar:

> We always advise our clients to tell the truth. But the thing that disturbs me most is that you are here in journalism school learning how to ask the questions, yet you would deny a person the right to learn how to answer those questions.[80]

Part of the motivation for giving managers media training is that the top executives in many organizations are public figures without training or experience in dealing with this aspect of their public life. Some suggest that CEOs are obliged to deal with the media and to face the public when their organizations make important decisions or are involved in crises that have impact beyond the organization. This obligation applies equally to leaders in corporations, nonprofit agencies, health and health-care organizations, educational institutions, government, and all other organizations concerned about their relationships with publics.

Because a free press plays a central role in a free society, this is the era of the media-savvy top executive. Media training designed to help executives deal directly with the press is a responsibility of the public relations department and an essential investment in building and maintaining good media relations, whether with traditional or new media outlets.

Notes

[1] Walter Lippmann, *Public Opinion* (New York: Harcourt, Brace, 1922), 354.

[2] Shirley Fulton and Al Guyant, *Beat the Press* (Salt Lake City, UT: American Book Business Press, 2002), 215.

[3] Susan Brophy, "Myth One: Traditional Media Are Dead," *Media Myths & Realities: 2006 Media Usage Survey* (Ketchum and the University of Southern California).

[4] "Newspaper Site Readers Spread the Word: The Well-Informed Make Great Evangelists," *eMarketer* (December 13, 2007), http://www.emarketer.com.

[5] John C. Merrill, "Global Elite: A Newspaper Community of Reason," in "World Media," special issue of *Gannett Center Journal* 4, no. 4 (Fall 1990): 93.

[6] Ibid., 101.

[7] Andrew LaVallee, "Newspaper-Circulation Drop Sharpens," *The Wall Street Journal* (April 29, 2008), B1.

[8] Kim, Kihan, and Maxwell McCombs, "News Story Descriptions and the Public's Opinions of Political Candidates," *Journalism & Mass Communication Quarterly,* Vol. 84, Issue 2 (Summer 2007): 299–314.

[9] "The Source: Newspapers by the Numbers—2006" (Vienna, VA: Newspaper Association of America, 2008), http://www.naa.org/thesource/14.asp#number. (Updated tables originally published in "The Source.")

[10] Ibid.

[11] Ibid., 21. (Original version available online at http://www.naa.org/thesource.)

[12] Updated tables online at http://www.naa.org/thesource/14.asp#number and http://www.naa.org/thesource/16.asp#number.

[13] "The Facts about Newspapers in 2007 . . . Not the Myths," World Association of Newspapers (online), http://www.comminit.com/en/node/244060. Downloaded March 25, 2008.

[14] Updated table online at http://www.naa.org/thesource/7.asp.

[15] "The Source: Newspapers by the Numbers—2006," 14, 16.

[16] A. Carlos Ruotolo, "A Typology of Newspaper Readers," *Journalism Quarterly* 65, no. 1 (Spring 1988): 126–30.

[17] Updated table online at http://www.naa.org/thesource/16.asp.

[18] *Parade Magazine* online at http://www.parade.com/parade_facts.html and *USA Weekend* online at http://usaweekend.com/about/index.html. Downloaded March 28, 2008.

[19] "The Source: Newspapers by the Numbers—2006," 34, 36.

[20] Ibid., 27.

[21] Available online at http://www.thomson.com/content/pr/corp/acquisitions_divestitures/265015?view=Print. Downloaded March 29, 2008.

22 "The Magazine Handbook: A Comprehensive Guide—2007/08" (New York: Magazine Publishers of America, 2007), 5. (Online at http://www.magazine.org.)

23 Ibid., 12.

24 Ibid., 7.

25 Shirley Biagi, *Media/Impact: An Introduction to Mass Media*, 4th ed. (Belmont, CA: Wadsworth, 1999), 66–67.

26 "The Magazine Handbook," 6.

27 Eric Vernette, "Targeting Women's Clothing Fashion Opinion Leaders in Media Planning: An Application for Magazines," *Journal of Advertising Research*. Vol. 44, Iss. 1 (New York: March 2004): 90.

28 Ibid., 68.

29 Gregory Solman, " 'Old Media' Still Resonate, Survey Says," AdWeek.com, August 14, 2007, n.p.

30 "Radio Marketing Guide & Fact Book: 2007–2008" (New York: Radio Advertising Bureau, 2007), http://www.rab.com/public/MediaFacts/factbook.cfm?type=nm.

31 Infinite Dial 2008: Radio's Digital Platforms, Arbitron and Edison Media Research, Somerville, NJ.

32 Federal Communications Commission, "Broadcast Station Totals as of December 31, 2007," http://www.fcc.gov/mb/audio/totals/index.html.

33 David C. Barker and Adam B. Lawrence, "Media Favoritism and Presidential Nominations: Reviving the Direct Effects Model," *Political Communication,* Vol. 23, Iss. 1 (Washington: Jan-Mar 2006), 41.

34 Ibid.

35 "FastTrax," Cabletelevision Advertising Bureau, online at http://www.onetvworld.org/main/index.shtml.

36 "Media Trends Track," Television Bureau of Advertising, online at http://www.tvb.org/nav/build_frameset.aspx.

37 Ibid.

38 Hans-Bernd Brosius and Hans Mathias Kepplinger, "Beyond Agenda-Setting: The Influence of Partisanship and Television Reporting on the Electorate's Voting Intentions," *Journalism Quarterly* 69, no. 4 (Winter 1992): 893–901.

39 Katherine N. Kinnick, Dean M. Krugman, and Glen T. Cameron, "Compassion Fatigue: Communication and Burnout Toward Social Problems," *Journalism & Mass Communication Quarterly,* Vol. 73 Issue 3 (Autumn 1996): 687–707.

40 Solman, n.p.

41 Robert MacNeil, *The Right Place at the Right Time* (Boston: Little, Brown, 1982), 129.

42 David Lieberman, "Fake News," *TV Guide* 40, no. 8 (February 22, 1992), 10–14, 16, and 26.

43 K. Tim Wulfemeyer and Lowell Frazier, "The Ethics of Video News Releases: A Qualitative Analysis," *Journal of Mass Media Ethics* 7, no. 3 (1992): 151–68.

44 "Ten Tips on How to Get Your VNR Aired," *Communication World* 9, no. 9 (September 1992): 10.

45 Adam Shell, "VNRs: In the News," *Public Relations Journal* 48, no. 12 (December 1992): 21.

46 Monica Jennings, "Creating SMTs That Deliver," *Public Relations Tactics* (July 2003), 16.

47 "Research SnapShots," Cabletelevision Advertising Bureau, online at http://www.onetvworld.org/main/index.shtml.

48 Ibid.

49 Donald K. Wright (Principal Investigator), "The Magic Communication Machine: Examining the Internet's Impact on Public Relations, Journalism, and the Public" (Gainesville, FL: The Institute for Public Relations, 2001), 37–39. (Online at http://www.instituteforpr.com/internet_new_technology.phtm.)

50 Ibid., 36.

51 Tanya Lewis, "Rules of Engagement Change with Blogs," *PR Week,* September 10, 2007, 15.

52 John M. Eger, "Technologies of Freedom," *Government Technology,* July 2, 2007, n.p.

53 Benjamin Fulford, "Korea's Weird Wired World," *Forbes,* July 21, 2003, 92–93.

54 Mike Greece, "Tempering Public Opinion in the Internet Age: When Everyone Is an Expert," *The Public Relations Strategist* (Winter 2008): 19–20.

55 Randi Schmelzer, "March of Dimes Eyes YouTube in New Effort," *PR Week,* July 30, 2007, 2.

56 Solman, n.p.

57 Karl Greenberg, "When Google Works Too Well," *Marketing Daily,* April 30, 2007, n.p.

58 Greece, 21.

59 Ibid.

60 Donald Trelford, "50 Years of Covering the Queen," *IPI Global Journalist* 8, no. 3 (Third Quarter, 2002): 17–19. Magazine published by the International Press Institute, University of Missouri, Columbia.

61 Denise E. DeLorme and Fred Fedler, "Journalists' Hostility toward Public Relations: An Historical Analysis," *Public Relations Review* 29, no. 2 (June 2003), 113.

62 "Inquiry: Press Can't Have the Right to Lie," *USA Today,* November 4, 1983, 11A.

63 Herbert Schmertz, "The Press and Morality." Remarks to Guild Hall Discussion Series, East Hampton, NY, July 12, 1983.

64 "Flack Attack: The *Post* Spurns P.R. 'Wolves,'" *Time,* May 10, 1982, p. 101; and Carl Cannon, "The Great Flack Flap," *Washington Journalism Review* 4 (September 1982): 35.

[65] "Journalists Rely on PR Contacts, Corporate Web Sites for Reporting, Survey Says," *PR Tactics and The Strategist Online* (November 19, 2007), http://www.prsa.org.

[66] Justin Lewis, Andrew Williams, and Bob Franklin, "A Compromised Fourth Estate? *Journalism Studies* 9, no. 1 (February 2008), 1–20. 24 April 2008. http://search .ebscohost.com/login.aspx?direct=true&db=ufh&AN= 28829440&site=ehost-live (abstract). Also reported in "Harper's Index," *Harper's Magazine* (May 2008), 15.

[67] Michael Ryan and David L. Martinson, "Journalists and Public Relations Practitioners: Why the Antagonism?" *Journalism Quarterly* 65, no. 1 (Spring 1988): 139.

[68] Mark S. Cox, "Media Relations and the Content of Business News" (Master of Science in Mass Communication thesis, San Diego State University, May 1983).

[69] H. J. Dalton Jr., personal letter and enclosure—"50 Basic Thoughts on Good News Media Relations" (undated presentation to Veterans Administration public affairs training seminar).

[70] Carole M. Howard, "Working with Reporters: Mastering the Fundamentals to Build Long-Term Relationships," *Public Relations Quarterly* 49, no. 1 (Spring 2004): 37.

[71] Ibid., 36–37.

[72] "Have You Read My Release?" *PRWeek*, September 17, 2001, 21.

[73] Coy Callison, "Media Relations and the Internet: How *Fortune* Company Web Sites Assist Journalists in News Gathering," *Public Relations Review* 29, no. 1 (March 2003): 33.

[74] "News Is Stacked Up at Wall St. Journal," *Jack O'Dwyer's Newsletter*, August 26, 1992, p. 4.

[75] Chester Burger, "Phony Communication Is Worse Than None at All." Arthur W. Page Society Hall of Fame induction speech, Amelia Island, FL, September 23, 1992.

[76] Adapted from Roger Ailes (with Jon Kraushar), *You Are the Message: Secrets of the Master Communicators* (Homewood, IL: Dow Jones-Irwin, 1988); Chester Burger, "How to Meet the Press," *Harvard Business Review,* July–August 1975; Christel K. Beard and H. J. Dalton Jr., "The Power of Positive Press," *Sales and Marketing Management,* January 1991: 37–43; Dalton, "50 Basic Thoughts on Good News Media Relations"; and Howard, "Working with Reporters."

[77] William A. Hachten, *The World News Prism: Changing Media, Clashing Ideologies* (Ames, IA: Iowa State University Press), 1981.

[78] Tanya Lewis, "What's Mandarin for 'Press Release'?" *PRWeek,* February 12, 2007, 18.

[79] "Media's Embargo on 'Harry's War' Sparks Debate," *Reuters,* February 29, 2008. http://www.reuters.com/article/ asiaCrisis/idUSL29380997.

[80] Ailes, *You Are the Message,* 165.

Additional Sources

Carstarphen, Meta G., and Richard A. Wells. *Writing PR: A Multimedia Approach.* Boston: Pearson Education/Allyn & Bacon, 2004.

Connolly, Diane, with Debra L. Mason (ed.). *Reporting on Religion: A Primer on Journalism's Best Beat.* Westerville, Ohio: Religion Newswriters Association, 2006. Available online at http://www.rna.org. Provides useful guide for and best practices when writing about the world's religions.

Diggs-Brown, Barbara. *The PR Styleguide: Formats for Public Relations Practice.* Belmont, CA: Thomson Wadsworth, 2006.

Fulton, Shirley, and Al Guyant. *Beat the Press.* Salt Lake City, UT: American Book Business Press, 2002. Outlines strategy and tactics for dealing with the media.

Hachten, William A. *The Troubles of Journalism: A Critical Look at What's Right and Wrong with the Press,* 3rd ed. Mahwah, NJ: Lawrence Erlbaum, 2004.

Howard, Carole M., and Wilma K. Mathews. *On Deadline: Managing Media Relations,* 4th ed. Prospect Heights, IL: Waveland Press, 2006. Summarizes how to deal with reporters, prepare spokespersons, and other aspects of effective media relations.

Kelleher, Tom. *Public Relations Online: Lasting Concepts for Changing Media.* Thousand Oaks, CA: Sage, 2007. Applies basic public relations principles to the online environment.

Overholser, Geneva, and Kathleen Hall Jamieson, (eds.). *The Press.* Oxford, U.K.: Oxford University Press, 2005. Encyclopedic collection of essays about the role and function of the press in the United States and about the essential role of journalism in democracy.

"The State of the News Media 2008: An Annual Report on American Journalism." The Project for Excellence in Journalism, Washington, D.C. http://www.stateof thenewsmedia.org/2008.

Part 3

Management Process

Step One: Defining Public Relations Problems

STUDY GUIDE   After studying Chapter 11, you should be able to:

▶ Outline the four-step problem-solving process as it applies to public relations.

▶ Define research, identify its major purpose as reducing uncertainty in decision making, and discuss why it is essential in public relations program management.

▶ Diagram and explain the "benchmarks model" of using research to plan, manage, and evaluate public relations programs.

▶ Describe the attributes of useful problem statements.

▶ Differentiate between informal ("exploratory") and formal methods of research, giving examples of both.

Dr. Edward Robinson wrote the obituary for the "seat-of-the-pants" approach to doing public relations in 1969. He saw the public relations practitioner as "an applied social and behavioral scientist" using "research to help in the problem-solving process." He may have been a bit premature in his assessment, however, when he wrote those words in the first public relations research book. Intuitive, individualistic approaches to problem solving often still guide the practice in many settings, even though, as Robinson wrote, research is "the most powerful tool available to the applied practitioner."[3]

The open systems approach discussed in Chapter 7 combines research-based problem solving and proactive strategic planning. From its origins as the art of reacting to outside threats to organizations, public relations has evolved into an applied science anticipating threats and managing organization-public relationships. No longer do hunches, gut feelings, and personal experiences, alone or in combination, serve as an adequate basis for public relations programs. And rarely do top managers or clients—many holding MBAs—accept on faith alone a practitioner's recommendations or simple assertions that there is a problem or that a program was successful. The question will be, "Where's the evidence? Show me the data."

The old "flying by the seat of the pants" approach to solving public relations problems is over.
—Edward J. Robinson[1]

The savvy PR person will have at least a basic understanding of different types of research and the sorts of information the different forms of research can provide.
—Mark Weiner[2]

Management Process

In its most advanced form, public relations is a scientifically managed part of an organization's problem-solving and change processes. Practitioners of this type of public relations use theory and the best available evidence in a four-step problem-solving process:

1. *Defining the problem (or opportunity).*   This first step involves probing and monitoring knowledge, opinions, attitudes, and behaviors of those

concerned with and affected by the acts and policies of an organization. In essence, this is an organization's intelligence function. It provides the foundation for all the other steps in the problem-solving process by determining, "What's happening now?"

2. *Planning and programming.*   Information gathered in the first step is used to make decisions about program publics, objectives, action and communication strategies, tactics, and goals. This involves factoring the findings from the first step into the policies and programs of the organization. This second step in the process answers, "Based on what we have learned about the situation, what should we change, do, or say?"

3. *Taking action and communicating.*   The third step involves implementing the program of action and communication designed to achieve the specific objectives for each of the publics to accomplish the program goal. The questions in this step are, "Who should do and say it, and when, where, and how?"

4. *Evaluating the program.*   The final step in the process involves assessing the preparation, implementation, and results of the program. Adjustments are made while the program is being implemented, based on evaluation feedback on how it is or is not working. Programs are continued or stopped after learning, "How are we doing, or how did we do?"

Each step is as important as the others, but the process begins with gathering intelligence to diagnose the problem. Information and understanding developed in the first step motivate and guide subsequent steps in the process. In practice, of course, diagnosis, planning, implementation, and evaluation cannot be so neatly compartmentalized, because the process is continuous and cyclical and is applied in a dynamic setting. Figure 11.1 shows the continuous, overlapping, and cyclical nature of public relations problem solving.

How an oil company's public relations staff managed a problem situation some years ago illustrates the four-step process. The company decided to close one of its sales divisions as part of a reorganization to increase efficiency. This meant that 600 employees would have to move or find new jobs, the community where the division was located would suffer economic loss, customers of the sales division would be concerned about getting equally good service under the new setup, and investors would be curious about how the move would affect the stock price.

The first task was to marshal all the facts through research so that the move could be explained and justified in terms of those concerned. The next step was to plan the announcement. Timing was important. The news had to be broken swiftly, before rumors started, released simultaneously to all those affected, and communicated in such a way as to explain satisfactorily the necessity and wisdom of the change.

Materials included a procedure memorandum to guide the staff, a presentation script for meetings, letters to several different groups of employees, letters to all dealers, a news release, a statement on banking arrangements for community banks, a general office letter, and plans for meetings. The news was released in a coordinated program of meetings, letters, and media coverage.

Finally, evaluation focused on the adequacy of the department's original assessment of the problem situation; monitoring the program as it was being implemented, with an eye to improving procedures; and assessing the reactions of those affected by and concerned about the move. The lessons learned were put to good use a few years later when the company closed a plant in another location, demonstrating how systematic research and evaluation improves the practice over time.

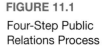

FIGURE 11.1

Four-Step Public Relations Process

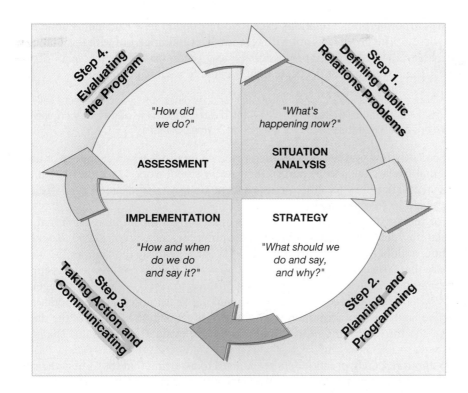

Obviously, this is an oversimplified presentation of what actually happened. The process includes many smaller steps within each of the four major steps represented in the model. These will be outlined in greater detail in this and the following three chapters. This chapter will describe the research and fact-finding methods necessary for beginning the strategic planning process.

Role of Research in Strategic Planning

Monitoring the social environment is not only the first step in the process; it is also the most difficult. The fable of the elephant and the six blind men of "Indostan" illustrates the challenge: Each blind man encounters only a single part of the beast and describes the elephant based on that limited information. For example, the one who grabs the trunk concludes, "The Elephant is very like a snake!" The one who feels the knee says, "'Tis clear enough the Elephant is very like a tree!" This process continues, with each experiencing only a portion of the elephant. In the end, each was partly right and mostly wrong about the nature of the beast but argued "loud and long" based on his respective encounter with the elephant.[4] Without researching a problem situation, practitioners run the risk of acting like the six blind men from Indostan.

Surveys of practitioners routinely show that research training tops the list of needed professional continuing education. Practitioners often say that they do not do more research because they lack funds and have too little time. A better explanation of why so little research is used in public relations, however, is a combination of (1) many practitioners do not know how to conduct and use research and (2) some employers and clients do not think that research is necessary, so they do not demand it.

As one corporate public relations executive responded in a Ketchum Public Relations survey, "The problem is not with research methodology, but with the inability—or perhaps laziness—of PR professionals who prefer to fly by the seats of their pants."[5] The Excellence Project researchers came to a similar conclusion:

> Public relations less often conducts research or uses other formal approaches to gathering information for strategic planning—an indication that many communication units are not qualified to make a full contribution to strategic planning.[6]

Until recently, few practitioners studied research methods while in college or anticipated that research would be part of their professional work. Once they began professional practice, they felt little pressure from employers and clients, who often did not demand or fund research.

For years, executives and practitioners alike bought the popular myth that public relations deals with intangibles that cannot be measured. David Rockland, Ketchum's global research director, says, "What I hear all the time is, 'You can't measure that. You can't test that. Let's just go with our gut.'"[7] With each passing day it becomes increasingly difficult to sell that position to results-oriented management (many with MBA degrees) accustomed to making decisions based on evidence and objective analysis. A practitioner in a nonprofit organization attributes "the decline of PR . . . to the lack of monitoring and substantive evaluation of results. That's why PR is seen by CEOs as 'fluff.'"[8]

Without research, practitioners are limited to asserting that they know the situation and can recommend a solution. With research and analysis, they can present and advocate proposals supported by evidence and theory. In this context, *research is the systematic gathering of information to describe and understand situations and to check out assumptions about publics and public relations consequences*. It is the scientific alternative to tenacity, authority, and intuition. Its main purpose is to reduce uncertainty in decision making. Even though it cannot answer all the questions or sway all decisions, methodical, systematic research is the foundation of effective public relations throughout the process. For example, research is used before, during, and after the program. The research benchmarks model illustrates the continuous nature of how research is used to plan, manage, and evaluate public relations programs:

Before the program begins, research is used to define the problem situation and formulate the program strategy—represented by the Time_1 stake in Figure 11.2.

FIGURE 11.2

Research Benchmarks Model

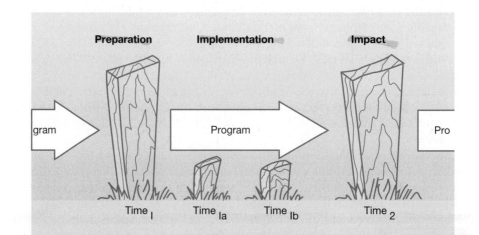

During the program, research is used to monitor the program in progress in order to reformulate (adjust) the strategy or fine-tune the tactics—represented by the Time 1_a and Time 1_b stakes. *After* the program, research is used to measure and document overall program impact and effectiveness—represented by the $Time_2$ stake in the model. Of course, $Time_2$ becomes the $Time_1$ benchmark for the next program cycle.

Research Attitude

Computers and management information specialists have greatly increased organizations' abilities to gather, process, transfer, and interpret information. The increase in MBA-prepared, information-conscious middle and upper managers intensifies the pressure on public relations for accountability. In short, a research orientation is necessary for those practicing public relations in the information age. An early researcher who helped build the automotive industry, C. F. Kettering, once described this attitude toward research in these words:

> Research is a high-hat word that scares a lot of people. It need not. It is rather simple. Essentially, it is nothing but a state of mind—a friendly, welcoming attitude toward change. Going out to look for change, instead of waiting for it to come. Research . . . is an effort to do things better and not be caught asleep at the switch. The research state of mind can apply to anything. Personal affairs or any kind of business, big or little. It is the problem-solving mind as contrasted with the let-well-enough-alone mind. It is the composer mind, instead of the fiddler mind; it is the "tomorrow" mind instead of the "yesterday" mind.[9]

Research is no longer a specialized activity delegated to "chi-square types" tucked away in the bowels of an organization. As Rossi and Freeman said: "It is also a political and management activity, an input into the complex mosaic from which emerge policy decisions and allocations for the planning, design, implementation, and continuation of programs to better the human condition."[10]

Modern managers are a fact-minded lot; they want figures. In many organizations, these executives tend to be isolated from problems by cadres of specialists and subordinates. When the public relations aspect of organizational problems must be brought home to them, the research-based approach is most effective. As other parts of organizations such as marketing, finance, and personnel have adapted a research-based approach, so must public relations. In fact, research findings suggest a strong linkage between doing research and earning one of the few seats at the management strategy table. Studies of practitioners show that participation in management increases if practitioners do research:

> In particular, their role is as environmental scanners, providing information needed about strategic publics affected by managerial decisions. They get this information through formal research and various informal methods of gaining information about organizational constituencies.[11]

Listening as Systematic Research

The International Listening Association defines "listening" as "the process of receiving, constructing meaning from, and responding to spoken and/or nonverbal messages." Effective public relations starts with listening, which requires openness and systematic effort. Too often, what purports to be communication is simply opposing ideas passing each other in different one-way channels, for example, in a management-versus-labor bargaining situation with each side merely wanting to score points, not listening to the other's views. As Wilbur Schramm explained, "Feedback is a powerful tool. When it does not exist or is delayed or feeble . . . then the situation engenders doubt and concern in the communicator, and frustration and sometimes hostility in the audience."[12] Also using his words, "Feedback tells the communicator how his message is being received."[13]

Listening is not an easy task. Channels from the worker out in the plant or from the alumnus in Seattle must be created and kept open. Failure to listen often leads to purposeless "communications" on issues that do not exist to publics that are not there. Unless you know the orientation, predisposition, and language of your audience—learned through empathetic listening—you are not likely to communicate effectively. Research is simply one method of structuring systematic listening into the communication process (see Exhibit 11.1).

An able listener of another time, Abraham Lincoln, knew the importance of listening. Twice a week, Lincoln set aside a time for conversations with ordinary folk: housewives, farmers, merchants, and pension seekers. He listened patiently to what they had to say, no matter how humble their circumstances or how trivial their business. A military aide once protested to the president that he was wasting valuable time on these unimportant people. Lincoln rebuked him, saying, "I tell you, Major . . . that I call these receptions my public opinion bath . . . the effect, as a whole is renovating and invigorating."[14] Today the White House has sophisticated and elaborate methods for monitoring constituent opinion: daily analyses of media (traditional and new) and mail content, sophisticated voice mail and e-mail tabulations, as well as regular public opinion polls (not to mention the apparently unlimited ability of the federal government to "listen" in on all telephone calls during President George W. Bush's administration).

Prudence dictates the systematic listening to an organization's publics through scientific research. Yet many organizations fail to utilize this public relations tool fully. In some, two-way communication is seen as organized back talk and a potential threat, rather than an essential tool of modern management. More likely, systematic listening to obtain reliable feedback is limited because it takes effort and skill. The amount of information input, however, determines the extent to which an organization operates as an open rather than as a closed system in dealing with problems.

Defining Public Relations Problems

In closed systems, of course, problems are allowed to define themselves, often as crises. The public relations effort then necessarily reverts to "firefighting" rather than "fire prevention." Examples include spending millions of dollars to counter proposals made by dissident stockholders; paying millions of dollars for advertising time and space to apologize for past actions and to announce corrective measures; and suffering costly construction delays because activist citizen groups resorted to legal action to stop proposed, yet unexplained, projects.

Such situations have long histories, and sometimes neither side recalls what caused the blowup. Heading off such blowups is part of the task. The earlier a complaint is caught, the easier it is to handle. Continuous fact-finding uncovers many problems while they are still small enough to permit corrective action and

EXHIBIT 11.1

Walter Barlow on Research as Listening

*Walter G. Barlow, President
Research Strategies Corporation*

At the end of a meeting with the CEO of a large corporation some years ago, he asked me, "Son, tell me, just what kind of 'racket' are you in?"

I replied, "Well, if you will let me ask a few questions, I think I can demonstrate what I do, but I warn you, the questions might cause you to throw me out of this office."

"Go ahead," he said.

"Well, how much of your business day would you say is spent in communication of some sort—having a conversation like this, attending meetings and conferences, reading reports, calling on the phone, and all the rest?"

He thought for a moment and replied, "You have pretty much described how I spend all of my time. I'm either communicating in some way, preparing for it, or seriously thinking about it."

That warmed me up a bit, because I felt safe to proceed. "Well, you have just told me that your time, valued at about $800,000 in salary last year, is spent in the *process* of communication. Now, tell me, in this communication, do you do all the talking?"

He smiled right away, "Of course not!"

"Would you say you spend, say, 40 percent of your communicating time in listening, or taking in information in some way?"

"That would probably be about right. I know I talk a lot, but I do listen too."

"Suppose I had asked the top fifty executives in your company the same question, do you think I would have gotten agreement on at least 40 percent?"

Again, he replied immediately, "I damned well hope you would."

"Now, we have established something else, and that is that you allocate around $320,000 of your base salary to the process of listening, and if I multiplied that 40 percent times the salaries of the fifty others, we would have a figure in the millions."

He was now totally absorbed in the interchange. "Yes, I see. I had never thought of it that way."

Here I had a chance to move in with the clincher: "Well, I happen to know that your advertising budget is in the neighborhood of $35 million, and if we added in all the other corporate 'talking,' we would certainly come up with a figure over $100 million." I had his total attention now.

"And just how much does your corporation spend in listening? Is it any wonder that from time to time you must feel that nobody really understands you?"

I did not get an answer to the question, because the point had been made: whatever listening was going on had to be a tiny fraction of the talking, a situation he would never have brooked in his personal corporate life.

"Well, corporations like yours can't listen like you're doing now. The only way we have found yet to do that is through scientifically planned research. It can reflect back to you how people are reacting to the corporate talking you do in so many ways."

"And that is the racket I am in: helping corporations close the loop and listen to their constituencies."

Courtesy Walter G. Barlow, President, Research Strategies Corporation, Princeton, NJ.

communication before becoming major public issues. The same attentive listening catches rumors before they become widespread and part of the public's perceptions of the organization.

Problem definition begins with someone making a value judgment that something is either wrong, soon could be wrong, or could be better. Implicit is the notion that organizational vision and mission statements, as well as goals, provide the criteria for making such judgments. Goal states serve as the basis for deciding if and when a real or potential problem exists. Once a judgment is made, however, the process becomes an objective, systematic research task designed to describe in detail the dimensions of the problem, the factors contributing to or alleviating the problem, and the stakeholders involved in or affected by the situation. In short, research is used to determine "What's happening now?"

Problem Statement

A useful problem statement summarizes what is known about the problem situation:

1. *It is written in the present tense, describing the current situation.* Avoid words such as "will," "could," and "should," because they address some desired future state, not "what's happening now."

2. *It describes the situation in specific and measurable terms,* detailing most of or all of the following:

   What is the source of concern?

   Where is this a problem?

   When is it a problem?

   Who is involved or affected?

   How are they involved or affected?

   Why is this a concern to the organization and its publics?

3. *A problem statement does not imply solutions or place blame.* If it does, program strategies are predetermined and limited, much like the cuttlefish's limited options for responding to its environment. The classic example of a problem statement that has an implied solution is the overused, "We have a communication problem." Communication is part of the solution, not the problem. What problem do you think communication will solve? Or, "Poor training of the field staff is the problem." It appears that someone has already determined that the training program needs to be improved. Maybe so, but what is the problem that makes someone jump to this solution and blame the training staff?

A problem could be that only 5 percent of new graduates join the alumni association during the first year following graduation, compared with 21 percent of all graduates, resulting in lost contact and reduced support for the university. Or in the case of a fund-raising effort for a new youth center, the problem could be that the building fund is $200,000 short of the amount needed to complete and equip the new gymnasium by the planned June 1 opening. If you had worked for one of the major oil companies several years ago, you might have been concerned about the "divestiture problem": A plurality (47 percent) of Americans agree with proposals to break up each of the major oil companies into four separate and competing operating companies, thus encouraging some in Congress to vote in favor of divestiture legislation.

Notice that each of these problem statements contains concrete measures of the problem situation based on objective research and documentation. Notice also that solutions are not implied, meaning that no particular strategy is suggested in any of the problem statements. In other words, communication may be part of the solution, but it is not stated as part of the problem. Finally, notice that the three examples describe the current situation—"What's happening now?"—not the future.

Situation Analysis

A problem statement represents a concise description of the situation, often written in a sentence or short paragraph. In contrast, a situation analysis is the unabridged collection of all that is known about the situation, its history, forces operating on it, and those involved or affected internally and externally. A situation analysis contains all the background information needed to expand upon and to illustrate in detail the meaning of a problem statement. In the process of analyzing the situation, one is able to clearly and specifically define and refine the problem statement. Typically, the definition process begins with a tentative problem statement, followed by investigation of the situation that then leads to refining the problem definition, and so on. The situation analysis results in what some practitioners call their "fact book"—the information assembled in three-ring binders or digital files.

Internal Factors   The section on *internal factors* deals with organizational policies, procedures, and actions related to the problem situation. Rather than direct all the attention to the publics and other external factors, a situation analysis begins with a thorough and searching review of perceptions and actions of key actors in the organization, structures and processes of organizational units relevant to the problem, and the history of the organization's involvement (see Exhibit 11.2).

The internal situation analysis also includes a "communication audit"—a systematic documentation of an organization's communication efforts for the purpose of understanding how it communicates with its publics. One practitioner describes the communication audit as follows:

> A complete analysis of an organization's communications—internal and/or external designed to "take a picture" of communication needs, policies, practices, and capabilities, and to uncover necessary data to allow top management to make informed, economical decisions about future objectives of the organization's communication.[15]

Consistent with the open systems model, practitioners do an audit to learn in detail how, what, and with whom they communicate. An audit provides decision makers a clear picture of what is currently done and a basis for deciding what changes need to be made.

EXHIBIT 11.2

Content of Situation Analysis: Part I—Internal Factors

1. Statements of the organization's mission, charter, bylaws, history, and structure

2. Lists, biographies, and photos of key officers, board members, managers, and so forth

3. Descriptions and histories of programs, products, services, and so forth

4. Statistics about resources, budget, staffing, sales, profits, stockholders, and so forth

5. Policy statements and procedures related to the problem situation

6. Position statements (quotations) by key executives regarding the problem situation

7. Description of how the organization currently handles the problem situation

8. Descriptions and lists of the organization's internal stakeholders

9. Lists of organizational media (two-way) for communicating with internal groups

Another essential part of the internal portion of a situation analysis is a constantly updated organizational almanac. This file not only serves as an essential organizational background reference when working on specific problems but also provides ideas and information for speeches, pamphlets, special reports, exhibits, and media requests. Most organizations do not have librarians or historians, so public relations departments often handle queries that cannot be answered by others. Journalists expect and need quick answers. Ready access to complete and accurate information on an organization, its history, performance, and managers can give the public relations department a start on crises or rumors in the making.

External Factors   After helping to develop an understanding of the organizational side of the problem situation, an analysis focuses on the *external factors*, both positive and negative. The starting point may be a systematic review of the history of the problem situation outside the organization. A situation analysis also calls for detailed study of who is currently involved or affected and how. Much of what is done under the banner of public relations research includes gathering information about stakeholders: what they know, how they feel, and what they do that is related to the problem (see Exhibit 11.3).

"Stakeholder analysis" is the process of identifying who is involved and who is affected in a situation. Stakeholders are the people—in the imagery of system theory—who are part of the same system as an organization. They are in interdependent relationships with an organization, meaning that what they know, feel, and do has an impact on the organization and vice versa. In the interest of building and maintaining mutually beneficial relationships, organizations undertake periodic stakeholder analyses to monitor how organizational policies, procedures, decisions, actions, and goals affect others. The different stakeholder groups can be ranked or

EXHIBIT 11.3

Content of Situation Analysis: Part II—External Factors

1. Clippings from newspaper, magazine, trade publication, newsletter, and online coverage of the organization and the problem situation

2. Reports, transcripts, and tapes of radio, television, and cable coverage

3. Content analyses of media coverage and Internet sources—Web sites, blogs, social media, etc.

4. Lists of media, journalists, columnists, talk-show hosts, freelance writers, online bloggers, Web sites, and producers who report news and features about the organization and issues related to the problem situation

5. Lists of and background information on individuals and groups who share the organization's concerns, interests, and positions on the problem situation (including their controlled internal and external media outlets)

6. Lists of and background information on individuals and groups who oppose the organization's concerns, interests,

and positions on the problem situation (including their controlled internal and external media outlets)

7. Results of surveys and public opinion polls related to the organization and the problem situation

8. Schedules of special events, observances, and other important dates related to the organization and the problem situation

9. Lists of government agencies, legislators, and other officials with regulatory and legislative power affecting the organization and the problem situation

10. Copies of relevant regulations, legislation, pending bills, referenda, government publications, and hearing reports

11. Copies of published research on topics related to the problem situation

12. Lists of important reference books, records, and directories, as well as their locations in the organization

rated according to the extent to which each is interdependent with an organization in a particular problem situation. Notice that not all those identified as stakeholders in a situation necessarily become target publics for the program designed to address a particular problem (the next chapter discusses defining publics).[16]

How could program planners set objectives for each of the publics if they do not know what people currently know about the issue at hand, what their related opinions are, and how they behave with respect to the issue? How could planners develop action and communication strategies without a detailed understanding of and empathy for the target publics? At least four additional questions must be answered through research:

1. How much do people use information in the problem situation? Communication is effective only if receivers see a need for information. The situation analysis research must determine to what extent different people actually feel a need for and use information related to a given problem situation.

2. What kinds of information do people use or seek? Whereas "why" questions make up 20 to 35 percent of the questions people typically ask in situations, these are the ones least likely to be answered successfully in communication programs. Programs that respond to audience needs rather than the interests of the source are based on knowledge of what information different people want.

3. How do people use information? Information is rarely an end in itself, because people use information in many different ways. Receivers see information as useful if they think that it relates to a specific action, topic, or plan they consider important. Rarely are they helped simply because they received general information.

4. What predicts information use? Demographics or other cross-situational characteristics often do not predict how people use information. Rather, where receivers are in the decision-making process with respect to a problem, and how they see themselves in the situation, determine whether or not they will use the information. In other words, planners must know how different individuals see themselves involved in or affected by the situation.[17]

The importance of situation-specific understanding of stakeholders is also evident in Van Leuven's "expectancy" theory of message and media selection:

(1) The user selects media and messages for his or her own rational-appearing and personally relevant purposes; (2) the user will attach his or her own personal meanings to a selected message; (3) the user's behavior reflects anticipated future communication satisfaction as well as a history of prior motivation, intentionality, and reinforcement.[18]

Researching the stakeholders before planning program strategies tests the accuracy of assumptions about who they are, what they know, how they feel about the situation, how they are involved or affected, what information they see as important, how they use it, and even how they get information. With that information in hand—and only then—can program planners write objectives for each public and develop strategies to achieve them.

Systematic definition and study of the stakeholders also is needed to determine an order of priority. Rarely do practitioners have the staff or money to mount programs directed to all stakeholders. Priorities must be assigned based on which of them are most central to the particular problem at hand and the program goal to be achieved, not based on past efforts or routine approaches unrelated to the current problem situation.

Increased understanding of the stakeholders helps determine their information needs and uses; thus, this understanding helps practitioners develop the appropriate message content. Researching their communication patterns and media preferences helps practitioners select the most effective and efficient media strategy for delivering those messages.

Only after the situation has been completely analyzed can practitioners set realistic program goals. Lacking complete and accurate information, practitioners can be guilty of overpromises and underdelivery. Without a complete understanding of the problem situation, practitioners run the risk of developing programs that do not address the major causes of the problem. No amount of public relations communication can change bad performance into good performance or socially irresponsible action into responsible behavior. Neither can it compensate for lack of integrity or persuade publics that an unfair or self-serving policy is fair and unselfish. Overenthusiastic selling of the public relations function often results from incomplete comprehension of the problem situation and leads to the appearance of program failure.

Researching the situation gives practitioners and their employers and clients the timely, complete, and accurate information they need to understand the problem, which serves as a basis for decision making. *Research is simply an attempt to reduce uncertainty,* or as one executive put it, "to help really see what's there to be seen."

SWOT Analysis   Detailed analyses of the internal and external factors in the problem situation provide practitioners with the information they need to assess organizational strengths (S) and weaknesses (W), and to identify the opportunities (O) and threats (T) in the external environment. In practice, practitioners refer to this approach to summarizing the situation analysis as "SWOT" or "TOWS" analysis. Several strategic implications logically flow from this analytic framework:

1. *SO* strategies build on organizational strengths to take advantage of opportunities in the external environment.

2. *ST* strategies also build on organizational strengths to counter threats in the external environment.

3. *WO* strategies attempt to minimize organizational weaknesses to take advantage of external opportunities.

4. *WT* strategies attempt to minimize both organizational weaknesses and environmental threats.[19]

Another analytic technique for summarizing the findings of a situation analysis is "force-field analysis," based on the theories of Kurt Lewin, which originated in the 1950s. Before researching the situation, practitioners and others on the management team brainstorm the negative forces contributing to or causing the problem, as well as the positive forces alleviating or solving the problem. The research on the internal and external forces helps determine the extent to which each contributes positively or negatively to the problem situation. Just as with SWOT analysis, the results of a force-field analysis lead to strategic decisions designed to minimize or neutralize the impact of negative forces and to maximize or enhance the contributions from positive forces.[20]

Research Process

The central roles of research in modern public relations, addressed further in Chapter 14, are introduced here. Sometimes practitioners do the research themselves. Other times practitioners hire research specialists or research firms to design the research, gather the information, or analyze the data. In either approach, practitioners must know the research process and concepts. Simply put, you cannot satisfactorily explain to someone else something you do not understand yourself. Ann H. Barkelew, former senior vice president and general manager of Fleishman-Hillard's Minneapolis office, says, "You cannot practice public relations today—successfully or effectively—without research."[21]

Scientists have developed a generally accepted approach to research. The process begins with a clear statement of the problem under investigation. Some choose to phrase the problem in the form of a question. Others pose hypothetical relationships between observable phenomena for testing and theory building. The next step is to develop the research design, the plan for making the observations related to the research problem. Is a survey needed? An experiment? Or will the observations be taken from published census reports? This is followed by the specific methods for gathering, analyzing, and interpreting data.[22]

Whereas two research projects are seldom the same in the specifics of how they are implemented, they share a common goal of increasing understanding of situations and society. The approach and methods chosen for a particular project will depend on the problem being addressed, the skills and preferences of the researcher, the available resources, and the constraints imposed by others or as a result of the situation. Informal and formal research methods differ primarily in their sample selection and sample size, as well as the generalizability of the findings they produce.

Informal or "Exploratory" Methods

Informal methods still dominate public relations research, even though highly developed social scientific methods are available. Informal methods can be useful, however, if practitioners recognize their weaknesses and purposes. The major problem—samples of unknown representativeness—results from how samples are selected. The issue is the extent to which the results from samples represent anybody other than the few from whom information was gathered. For example, the results may represent only the opinions of a vocal minority rather than the majority.

If viewed as methods for *detecting* and *exploring* problem situations and for pretesting research and program strategies, then informal methods serve valuable purposes. If the results are used as the basis for *describing* problem situations and stakeholders for program planning and evaluation, then these methods are misused. "Exploratory" best represents the probing nature of informal methods, as the findings may not be representative of the reality being studied.

The following sections describe some of the informal methods used in public relations.

Personal Contacts

In 1893 Lord Bryce said, "The best way in which the tendencies at work in any community can be best discovered and estimated is by moving freely about among all sorts and conditions of men." Politicians have been doing this for a long time. Skill in sizing up people's awareness, opinions, and attitudes has long been and always will be a prime qualification of public relations professionals.

For example, when management requested an employee communication campaign against drug abuse, a corporate practitioner, posing as a patient, checked into a drug treatment center and spent three days acquiring firsthand knowledge about drugs, their use, and their potential effects on employees. Others have worked in wheelchairs to gain perspective on what it is like to go for coffee breaks, use the bathroom, or complete other tasks in facilities not designed for easy access. Trade shows, community and professional meetings, or other occasions that attract stakeholders provide opportunities for practitioners to listen carefully and gain understanding.

A more structured use of personal contacts is exemplified by the annual shareholder meetings held each year by publicly owned corporations. For example, managers in one company visited shareholders in their homes after business hours. Each year management personnel in various locations personally talked with shareholders about the company's business. In another aggressive approach to getting feedback, a state highway department used a travel trailer as a mobile information center to collect citizens' views on proposed highway projects. The trailer provided an atmosphere for candid one-on-one discussions with highway personnel and gave people who are reluctant to speak in public meetings an opportunity to air their views.

Key Informants

Practitioners commonly talk with key informants, a variation on personal contacts. This approach involves selecting and interviewing knowledgeable leaders and experts. The interview typically takes the form of an open-ended discussion in which selected individuals are encouraged to talk about the problem or issue in their own terms. Because in-depth interviews with key informants take so long to complete and require such careful content analysis, the technique is limited to a relatively small number of respondents.

Many practitioners regularly consult influential people such as authors, editors, reporters, ministers, labor leaders, professors, civic leaders, bankers, and special-interest group leaders. Some have consulted bartenders and taxi drivers. The basis for selecting key informants is their perceived knowledge of an issue and their ability to represent others' views. The major limitation, of course, is that because they were selected purposely because they are seen to have special knowledge and leadership roles, by definition they do not reflect current views of followers. In-depth interviews with key informants often yield early warning signals on important issues, however.

Focus Groups and Community Forums

It is only a short step from personal contacts and key informants to asking groups for ideas and feedback. The range of groups runs from open town meetings, such as those used by the White House and candidates for U.S. president, to the highly structured and videotaped focus group, a technique commonly used in both public relations and consumer marketing research. For example, Twentieth Century Fox conducted focus groups to see how audiences felt about a little movie that a young director—George Lucas—wanted to call *Star Wars*.[23] An effective moderator who is an able interviewer and facilitator of group process is key to the success of these approaches.

Practitioners use focus groups and community forums to explore how people will react to proposals and to gather information useful for developing questionnaires to be used in more formal research methods. Unexpected insights are gained from the sometimes spirited dialogue among participants. Researchers call such information "serendipitous findings," but unanticipated reactions may be the best reason for using these informal research methods. It is better to learn such things before going to the field with a full-blown survey or program test.

Government agencies have long used this exploratory strategy to solicit information and participation. The USDA Forest Service, the Army Corps of Engineers, and the Environmental Protection Agency regularly conduct public meetings and hearings to get information and reactions to various project and program proposals. One of the lessons learned from their experiences is that community input must be sought early and often to keep agencies responsive to citizen interests. The findings from an experimental study of citizen input, however, found that sincere agency–citizen power sharing was more important than the timing of the input:

> The findings of this study provide strong empirical support for the conclusion that true power sharing in the public participation process causes increased levels of satisfaction with the decision-making process and with the final decision reached. At the same time, this study also provides strong empirical evidence that the timing of public participation (early vs. late) in the decision-making process exerts no measurable impact on the process and outcome satisfaction among publics.[24]

Focus groups represent a more structured approach. Typically, focus groups include 6 to 12 carefully selected representatives from a target public. They are asked to discuss a specific issue or program proposal in depth. Sessions are videotaped, and the recordings are carefully analyzed to catch the smallest detail in participants' comments. For example, one organization conducted focus group research to learn what middle school teachers want in curriculum materials provided by outside sources. One authority says the major strength of focus groups is the open, spontaneous, and detailed discussions they generate, even among people who did not know each other before the session began.[25] They can be planned, conducted, and analyzed in a matter of days, providing insights and understanding that can be factored into program planning.

Even when members of a group are carefully selected, as with information gained from personal contacts, the results cannot be used to make inferences to a larger population or public. Because the group is small, selection is usually not truly random, and the group-discussion context introduces an artificial setting, the results are not representative—in a scientific sense—of a public or the publics from which the participants were selected. As with other informal methods, focus groups are typically small groups of unknown representativeness.

Moderators also can have an effect on what and how the group discusses. In addition, those viewing and interpreting the session filter what is said through their own subjective perceptions. It is simply not appropriate to suggest that findings from this approach can be used in place of data gathered objectively from scientifically selected samples. The major uses are to identify and explore issues for further study in formal surveys and to pretest program strategies before full-blown field-testing.

Some marketers are using a new twist on the focus group—online community networks.[26] Instead of 6 to 12 people sitting in a room for a short time, organizations can create social networks of selected "representatives" to respond to questions, consider various proposals, try out new procedures, or even use products in development. The "group" can include hundreds, if not thousands, of participants. Organizations can keep different panels of participants for different kinds of issues. Questions about how representative these groups and the social-network experience are of the real world keep this approach in the informal exploratory category of information gathering.

Advisory Committees and Boards

A standing committee, panel, or board can sometimes be more useful than a single group session, particularly for long-running programs and issues. In some instances such a group can serve as a continuous feedback mechanism for detecting possible changes in public opinion on issues, even before they would show up in polls and surveys. There is a price, however, for using advisory committees and boards. Their advice must be given earnest consideration, or this method will backfire. Members quickly sense when they are being used for cosmetic purposes or being showcased to demonstrate concern for community input. Appoint such a committee or board only when the major motivation is to *sincerely* solicit input and guidance on a regular basis, and be prepared to act on the input.

Nonprofit organizations use this approach to tap the professional public relations community for both expertise and services. Almost every chapter of the United Way, Arthritis Foundation, Easter Seals, Salvation Army, and similar organizations has a public relations advisory committee. Committee service gives public relations practitioners a way to fulfill their public service obligation as professionals.

Other organizations, for-profit and nonprofit alike, use advisory committees and boards. For example, hospitals, chambers of commerce, and police departments typically use this method for gathering information. Although advisory committees and boards provide valuable information and guidance, they cannot substitute for formal approaches to determining the distribution of opinions and reactions among target publics. They also provide effective forums for increasing interaction, participation, and in-depth probing of issues. In other words, they too are exploratory techniques used to supplement more formal methods.

Ombudsman or Ombuds Officer

The ombuds officer in an organization is someone who listens to the concerns of internal organizational publics. This person may also review organizational policies and mediate disputes between the organization and its employees. The term *ombudsman* originated when the Swedish government established the first such position in 1713. Growing dissatisfaction with ever-longer lines of communication to increasingly isolated managers and bureaucrats has brought about widespread adoption of this informal information-gathering method in government agencies. In countless corporations the ombudsman concept has proved useful in providing feedback and ideas for solving problems while they are still manageable.

Two kinds of ombudsmen are used. One, true to the roots of the original, investigates and solves problems. The second, who at best parries problems, often is there to protect the bureaucracy and to create the illusion of a responsive organization. The former has independent authority to take action on complaints; the latter facilitates communication and seeks authority from others to implement remedies.[27]

The ombudsman's role and scope of its authority vary widely. Dow Chemical Company once established an "ombudswoman" to help promote the advancement of women in the company. At Bronx Community College the ombudsman, appointed by the president, acts as a conduit for student complaints but has no authority to make full-scale investigations. At the University of Nebraska–Lincoln, on the other hand, the ombudsman sees the job as "reporting to nobody and responsible to everyone." The U.S. Navy started its family ombudsman program in 1809 and sees the ombudsman's role as one of cutting governmental red tape and acting as liaison between interested parties and the Navy offices. The ombudsman "investigates organizational problems and makes recommendations for remedial action to improve the quality of administration and redress individual grievances." A large New York hospital employs, as do many hospitals, a "patient representative" to serve as an advocate of patients "to help them and their families find satisfactory solutions to problems."

In each of these settings, the ombudsman provides an effective means for facilitating greater management awareness of public reactions and views. If sincerely used and competently staffed, the ombudsman position can be an important means of obtaining organizational feedback, as well as for helping people get solutions for their problems and answers to their questions. But because this method relies on people who seek out the opportunity to make their feelings and complaints known—a self-selected sample—it also is an exploratory, informal approach to gathering information. Although information gathered by an ombudsman may not accurately describe the frequency or distribution of problems or concerns among the larger group, particularly among less assertive members, it can help detect that they exist for some.

Call-In Telephone Lines

Toll-free 800 numbers are commonly used to obtain instant feedback and to monitor the concerns and interests of various publics. Johnson & Johnson tracked telephone calls during the consumer panic associated with the seven deaths caused by cyanide-laced Extra-Strength Tylenol capsules. Similarly, Procter & Gamble (P&G) monitored more than 100,000 calls on its 800 number when a rumor was circulating that P&G promoted Satanism. The calls not only gave the companies opportunities to respond to concerned consumers but also provided constantly updated information on public concerns and reactions.

Companies also recognize the public relations value of giving consumers and customers access to the corporation and of answering questions directly. By doing so, consumer and customer hotlines provide companies feedback on their products, services, facilities, and employees. For example, General Electric's customer-service Answer Center gets more than 6,000 calls a day. Whirlpool Corporation, among the first to provide a customer call-in service in response to growing customer dissatisfaction, found that about 70 percent of its "Cool Line" service calls were from customers who wanted information on repairs.

Some organizations use this method to field questions from employees; some hospitals use it to provide information and take complaints from patients and their families; other health-care centers use toll-free numbers both to provide help and to determine the extent of health problems; and many government agencies use them to help citizens find their way through the bureaucratic maze.

To be effective, however, a call-in service must be used with sincerity. For example, the U.S. Bureau of Mines, acting in the wake of several major mine disasters, announced with great fanfare that it was installing hotline telephones at the entrance of every coal mine so that miners could alert the bureau if they found unsafe conditions. The bureau promised "instant action" on the reports. A few months later a reporter for the *Wall Street Journal* found that the bureau had not monitored the recorded calls for almost two months. The newspaper reported that bureau employees "had forgotten about the machine."

A pejorative description of radio talk shows, however, serves as a reminder of the danger in putting too much stock in analyses of telephone calls—"SLOP," which stands for a "self-selected listener opinion poll." Surely analyses of telephone calls can provide early evidence for detecting potential problems and public opinions. The caution, however, is that detecting problems and opinions cannot substitute for describing the frequency of problems or the distribution of opinions in an organizations' publics.

Mail and E-Mail Analyses

Another economical way of collecting information is periodic analysis of incoming mail—traditional and online. Stakeholders' correspondence reveals areas of favor and disfavor and information needs. Letter writers, however, tend to be critical rather than commendatory. Letters may serve as early warnings of ill will or problem relationships, but they do not reflect a cross section of public opinion or even the views of a particular public.

President John F. Kennedy borrowed a leaf from Franklin D. Roosevelt's book on keeping in touch with constituents. Kennedy directed that every 50th letter coming to the White House be brought to him. Periodic mail samples helped both these leaders bridge the moat surrounding the White House. Other chief executives in organizations of all kinds use daily or weekly reports on the mail to read the pulse of citizens' concerns and opinions. Many organizations file brief summaries of letters to track public concerns.

At its peak, Ford Motor Company's "We Listen Better" campaign brought in 18,000 letters a week from Ford owners. Letters were answered personally, not with form letters, which required a large investment in money and human resources. Comments, suggestions, and criticisms were carefully coded and keyed into a computer file. Printouts of the running tallies provided Ford executives useful information, even though the data came from a self-selected sample.

Similarly, the U.S. Census Bureau analyzed more than 12,000 e-mails from concerned residents about various issues related to the 2000 census. This analysis gave the agency a better idea of the census-related questions that people had, so that preparations could be made for the next census to address these concerns proactively.

The exploratory nature of mail analysis provides information useful for detecting concerns and problems before they become widespread. Those who feel so strongly about something that they take time to write letters or e-mails may not be representative of entire publics, but they may be the first of many to follow. In this role, those who write letters join those who call 800 numbers as early-warning signals of situations that need attention and may indicate a need for formal research.

Web 2.0 Online Sources

New communication technology creates opportunities for friend and foe to talk about each other, as well as about organizations, causes, and events. Prudent public relations practitioners now also monitor what is being said about their organizations online. Rumors on the Internet have the potential to influence labor negotiations, attract regulatory attention, drive stock prices up or down, and increase or decrease sales. Among those accessing messages on the Internet, an organization's reputation can be damaged, its brand franchise can suffer, and its hard-earned goodwill can be diminished.

Jackson and Stoakes referred to the Internet's "dark side, where the spread of false and misleading information can cause serious injury to an unprepared target." They recommend that public relations practitioners monitor the Internet to prevent a "cybercrisis" because "rumors that originate on the Internet often make their way into print and broadcast media before a company even knows they exist."[28] Some search engines that are particularly useful for scanning what is being said on the World Wide Web include www.google.com, www.yahoo.com, www.altavista.com, and www.askjeeves.com.

Chat rooms, online forums, discussion groups, and blog posts can be important sources of feedback. Many public relations practitioners now monitor the array of online social media in order to detect what is being said about the organization and important issues. Some professional research firms such as Nielsen BuzzMetrics and BuzzLogic have been established specifically to "harvest" online comments for clients and report what is said about brands, products, and organizations. "Buzz," as this online word-of-mouth (or "word-of-mouse") is called, represents the spontaneous comments of people interacting. Although target publics cannot be easily identified in Internet chat, online comment is a fast, free method of monitoring views and opinion.

Again, such searches are informal methods for *detecting* what is being said on the Internet; they cannot produce profiles of public opinion. And that may be the most important point: Monitoring online sources can help practitioners tap into the rapidly expanding channels of interactive communication and to intervene in the virtual conversation.

Field Reports

Many organizations have district agents, field representatives, or recruiters who live in and travel the territories served. These agents should be trained to listen and observe and be given an easy, regular means of reporting their observations. In this way they can serve as the eyes and ears of an organization.

Studies of organizational intelligence and communication demonstrate, however, that such representatives tend to "gild the lily" and to report what they think will set well with their bosses. This is particularly true if field staff know that their reports will pass through a gauntlet of superiors, the same people who hold power over their futures in the organization. For example, researchers studying "why employees are afraid to speak" in one organization concluded:

> Why? In a phrase, self-preservation. . . . [W]e found the innate protective instinct so powerful that it also inhibited speech that clearly would have been intended to help the organization. . . . A culture of collective myths proved chilling—for example, stories of individuals who had said something . . . were "suddenly gone from the company."[29]

In another example, attempting to assess the impact of a company's "progress week," management asked sales representatives to evaluate the program. Forty percent ventured no opinion. About half of those who did respond said the week's promotion had produced more favorable opinions of the company. A formal survey later found that only about one in 10 of the target population was inclined to be more favorable in their opinion of the company. After comparing the field reports with the survey results, it was clear that only 12 of the 42 grassroots observers accurately assessed the results of the promotion. The comparison serves as a reminder that all subjective reports such as field reports must be used with caution. Like the other informal methods, field reports serve best as an early warning to detect situations that may call for more thorough investigation.

Formal Methods

The purpose of both informal and formal methods is to gather accurate and useful information. Formal methods, however, are designed to gather data from scientifically representative samples using objective measures. Formal methods help answer questions about situations that simply cannot be answered adequately using informal approaches.

The danger is that practitioner–researchers can become more concerned about the methods used than the purpose of the study. As one writer put it, "In science as in love, concentration on technique is quite likely to lead to impotence." Those who get bogged down in research techniques at the expense of usefulness often spend time and resources to produce volumes of data that sit unused on shelves.

Formal methods are useful, however, only if the research question and objectives are clearly determined before selecting the research design. Other questions that need to be answered include:

1. What information is needed and why is it needed?
2. What publics should be targeted when gathering data?
3. When are the findings needed?
4. How will the findings be used?
5. How should the information be gathered? In other words, what is the most appropriate research method for gathering the information?
6. How will the findings be summarized and interpreted?
7. When and to whom will the findings be presented?
8. Who will be responsible for making sure that the findings are used? (See Figure 11.3.)

FIGURE 11.3

Flowchart for Designing a Research Project

Source: Glenn M. Broom and David M. Dozier, *Using Research in Public Relations: Applications to Program Management*. Englewood Cliffs, NJ: Prentice Hall, 1990, p. 97. Used with permission.

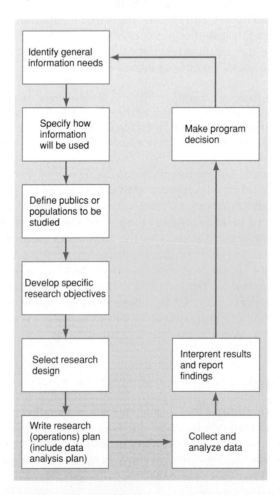

Done correctly, each formal approach can yield information that describes phenomena and situations within established ranges of accuracy and tolerance for error. These approaches also make it possible to use inferential statistics—the process of using data from representative samples to estimate characteristics of populations. In other words, systematic formal methods help practitioners to make accurate statements about publics based on evidence drawn from scientifically representative samples.

Successful public relations managers know about formal research methods and statistics. Public relations education at many universities now includes a research methods course as part of the curriculum. Continuing education programs for practitioners typically include offerings on how to use research in program planning, management, and evaluation. The following sections introduce some of commonly used methods and issues in conducting formal research.

Secondary Analysis and Online Databases

Doing research does not always call for gathering your own data. Secondary analysis reuses data gathered by someone else, often for other purposes.[30]

Numerous governmental and commercial organizations conduct national, regional, and local surveys. Some of these surveys track issues and trends. For example, the U.S. Census Bureau has a long history of developing standardized definitions, sampling techniques, sophisticated methods, and publications of findings. Within government, specialized departments have large research staffs tracking major developments and trends in agriculture, health, labor, business, the economy, and education, to name but a few of the areas under constant study.

Since the 1930s, major commercial polling firms such as those formed by A. C. Nielsen, George Gallup, Elmo Roper, and Louis Harris have made their names synonymous with measures of public opinion. Almost every major city has similar research firms tracking local public opinion trends and conducting marketing research. Major newspapers, television stations, and other news organizations regularly conduct their own surveys and report their results. The results of these surveys often can be segmented on the basis of geography, demographics, and other attributes relevant to public relations problem situations.

Also not to be overlooked are the survey research centers maintained by almost all major universities. Research conducted with public funds is often published and available for the asking. Most public agencies can provide listings of data sets and publications. For much less than the cost of conducting a survey, additional analyses of available data often can be done to help answer questions not asked in the original analysis.

Special-interest publications and scholarly journals regularly publish research data. A great deal of research is conducted to answer questions previously answered by competent researchers and reviewed by knowledgeable editorial boards. Online searches now make it easy and cost effective to search research literature for studies done on specific topics. It makes little sense to design and conduct research until after exploring the possibility that someone else has already done the work and published the results.

The most frequently used research approach to information gathering in public relations, however, is researching online databases. Some of the most-used databases include Lexis-Nexis (http://www.lexisnexis.com), Dun and Bradstreet (http://www.dnb.com), and Dow Jones News/Retrieval (http://www.dowjones.com). Practitioners use these services to access and search through news and technical publications, business information services, market research, financial reports, government records, and broadcast transcripts. Some online database companies customize services to meet the specific needs of subscribers. For example, to track the over-the-counter cold remedy field, the manager of information services at Ketchum Public Relations in New York subscribed to Dow Jones's customized service to get relevant information faxed to her office as soon as it went online. Lexis-Nexis will customize files for subscribers, making it easy for customers to access information without the usual cost of a conventional search of the entire database.

Content Analysis

Content analysis is the application of systematic procedures for objectively determining what is being reported in the media.[31] Press clippings and broadcast monitor reports, all available from commercial services, have long been used as the bases for content analyses. They indicate only what is being printed or broadcast, *not* what is read or heard. And they *do not* measure whether or not the audiences learned or believed message content. For example, a content analysis of newspaper clippings provides a useful measure of what messages are being placed in the media, but it does not indicate readership or impact.

Analyzing the editorials and letters to the editor may yield little more than the views of the editor and publisher. And the editorial page does not represent public opinion, as is made abundantly clear when candidates receiving newspaper endorsements do not win elections. As John Naisbitt demonstrated in his popular books on trends, however, content analysis can provide valuable insights into what is likely to be on the public agenda in the future. Recognizing the role of the media in reporting and influencing trends, in 1968 Naisbitt began publishing a quarterly newsletter, *Trend Report,* based on content analyses of 206 metropolitan newspapers. Many organizations worldwide now produce similar reports to give subscribers an early warning system for forecasting social and economic conditions, often long before they are apparent to most observers. The content analyses, however, cover newspapers, magazines, Web sites, blogs, books, television and cable news, newsletters, advertising, research journals, and many other sources depending on the trends or issues being tracked. Research firms providing content analysis reports in the United States and worldwide include Biz360, CARMA International, Cision (formerly Bacon's), CyberAlert, Cymfony, Echo Research, MediaTrack, Metrica, Millward Brown Prècis, Report International, VMS, and Vocus, as well as many other smaller and specialist companies.

Increasingly, public relations firms are helping their clients anticipate issues by either subscribing to issues-tracking services or by doing their own media content analyses. It is important to note, however, that these media content analyses employ a more systematic, formal method than the usual informal approaches used for monitoring the media. The key differences are the representativeness of the content selected for analysis and the objectivity used in measuring and coding the content.

Surveys

Surveys are systematic queries of subsets of the population under study. Surveys are administered in many ways, including by mail, in person, via telephone, and online. The adequacy of the administration method depends on the sampling procedures used, what questions are asked, and how the questions are asked.

Mailed Surveys   *Advantages* of mailed questionnaires—the most traditional method—include considerable savings of time and money, convenience for respondents because they determine when to answer the questions, greater assurance of anonymity, standardized wording, no interviewer bias, access to respondents not readily reached in person by interviewers, and opportunity for respondents to take time to gather information needed to complete the questionnaire. According to one professional, another advantage to using surveys for information gathering is that people view quantitative data as being accurate.[32]

The biggest *disadvantages* of mail surveys are that researchers have no control over who responds and that low response rates are typical. Whereas the original mailing list may have been a randomly selected and representative sample, unless all respond there is no assurance of an unbiased sample. Even a 90 percent response rate could be inadequate if those not responding represent a significant and uniform segment of the population being studied. Remember that elections are often won by fractions of a percent. There is no basis for the conventional wisdom that a 50 percent return is adequate. The unanswered question remains, which half of the sample did or did not respond?

Other disadvantages include lack of control over the conditions under which the questionnaire is completed, no assurance that the intended respondent completed the questionnaire, lack of flexibility in how questions are asked if the respondent does not understand what is being asked, and difficulties in getting and maintaining current mailing lists.

A variation of the mailed questionnaire takes the form of a page included in publications or distributed with other materials. Whereas the cost of a separate mailing is saved, all the advantages and disadvantages of the mailed questionnaire apply and in some cases are magnified.

In-Person Surveys   In-person, face-to-face administration of surveys gives researchers higher response rates compared to mail surveys, greater flexibility in dealing with the respondents, more control over conditions under which the questions are asked, increased control over the order and completeness of questioning, and opportunity to observe and record reactions not covered by the questionnaire. However, disadvantages include relatively greater research costs, the tendency of respondents to answer certain questions differently in the face of an interviewer, greater inconvenience imposed on respondents, less anonymity for respondents, increased difficulty in contacting those selected in the sample, and respondents' negative reactions resulting from misuse of survey approaches by salespersons and other solicitors posing as researchers. Furthermore, during both in-person and telephone survey administrations, the interviewers themselves can influence the information gathered, so interviewer training is an essential element of these approaches.

Telephone Surveys   Telephone interviews offer a faster and more cost-effective way to complete interview studies while providing somewhat greater anonymity to respondents. However, one major challenge for telephone-administered surveys is sample selection: More than 95 percent of households have telephones, but not all are listed in directories. Computer-assisted random digit dialing (RDD) has helped solve the sampling problem caused by incomplete directory listings. But even with the most sophisticated software, sampling phone numbers produces only about two working phone numbers for every three numbers dialed. The reasons for the relatively low—and dropping—rate of working phone numbers among those dialed are modems, faxes, and second and third lines. New area codes make frequent changes in the dialing software necessary, and special area codes for cell phones add to the challenge of finding respondents without inconveniencing them. So although the numbers selected for calls may be representative, answering machines and refusal rates have made it more difficult to obtain representative samples and have driven up telephone surveying costs.[33]

One common variation in the telephone survey is computer-assisted telephone interviews (CATI). In this method of survey administration, researchers enter respondents' answers directly into a computer system, which directs the flow of these complex surveys by skipping questions or asking supplemental ones depending on how respondents answer various "filter" questions. Another variation on the telephone survey is the IVR—interactive voice response—survey in which respondents call a number and complete the questionnaire at their convenience, responding verbally to questions asked by a computer, which in turn codes responses by recognizing key terms in participants' answers.

Self-Administered Surveys   Finally, the online administration of surveys is viewed by some researchers as the inevitable wave of the future. These methods may include graphics-based questionnaires that respondents access through a special URL and complete by clicking on various multiple-choice options, text-based questionnaires that are sent and completed via e-mail, or a combination in which an e-mailed note invites respondents to access a particular URL for participation in the survey. Advantages of the online administration of surveys include greater convenience for the respondent, as well as greater efficiency for the researcher, who can rely on computer systems to translate the data automatically into numeric form, rather than hand-coding each response.

Today, Web sites such as www.surveymonkey.com and www.zoomerang.com offer free downloadable sample survey questionnaires available for customizing. Some sites provide ready-made templates that can be easily customized and also offer automatic tabulation of the data collected. Mini-surveys and feedback forms for many purposes can be created and administered by practitioners with little formal research training.

However, one challenge for online survey administration remains—obtaining adequate sampling frames, or lists of e-mail addresses from which researchers can select their samples. Another challenge is low response rates, usually resulting from the junk mail filtering services provided on most e-mail accounts. The Council for Marketing and Opinion Research has even proposed a new method of calculating online response rates that would account for nonrespondents who never even see the initial request to participate in a survey.

Cross-Sectional versus Tread and Panel Surveys   Usually single surveys are conducted on *cross-section samples* of a population or public at a single point in time. If the study is designed to learn how people change over time or to track a process, however, a longitudinal study, either as a *panel study* or *trend study,* is the better approach. In panel studies the same respondents are interviewed several times during the study, are asked to complete a series of questionnaires on a fixed schedule, or are required to maintain a diary during the study period. For example, the "Baccalaureate and Beyond" study conducted by the National Center for Education Statistics surveyed the same group of bachelor's degree recipients over a period of 10 years. Two problems common to panel studies are that respondents drop out over the course of the project ("panel mortality") and that respondents become more attentive to the issues being examined because of the repeated contact with researchers ("sensitization"). A trend study uses different samples drawn from the same population to track change over time. Because different people are in the samples, however, not being able to attribute changes to particular types of people is the cost of solving panel mortality and sensitization problems. On the other hand, if the purpose is to track the distribution of public knowledge, opinion, or behavior over time, trend studies provide the most economical approach.

In summary, formal research methods follow the rules of science, use representative samples, and employ other systematic procedures for making the observations, taking the measurements, and analyzing the data. Like other skills based on specialized knowledge, doing formal research requires study and practice. Done correctly, however, formal research helps practitioners describe reality accurately. Research findings, combined with experience and judgment, provide the foundation for defining public relations problems and for designing programs to address those problems. In other words, research builds the information foundation necessary for effective public relations practice and management.

This chapter highlights only some of the approaches for gathering the informal and formal information needed to understand and define public relations problem situations. Whereas research is often viewed as a necessary step for evaluating program impact, it is equally necessary in the initial step of the problem-solving process—defining the problem situation. Not only does research provide the information necessary for understanding the problem, but also this "benchmark" description serves as the basis for monitoring the program in progress and for evaluating program effectiveness at the end of each program cycle. How can practitioners plan the program if they do not know what they are dealing with? How do they determine how the program is working if they do not know where they started? How do they know if the program failed or succeeded without having a baseline for comparison?

Research initiates, monitors, and concludes the problem-solving process. It is the essential ingredient that makes public relations a management function as well as a managed function.

Notes

[1] Edward J. Robinson, *Public Relations Research and Survey Research: Achieving Organizational Goals in a Communication Context* (New York: Appleton-Century-Crofts, 1969), ix. The first book devoted to using social science survey research methods in public relations.

[2] Mark Weiner, *Unleashing the Power of PR: A Contrarian's Guide to Marketing and Communication* (San Francisco, CA: Jossey-Bass, 2006): 50.

[3] Robinson, *Public Relations Research and Survey Research,* ix.

[4] From the fable "The Blind Men and the Elephant," by John Godfrey Saxe (1816–1887), quoted by Henry Mintzberg, "Strategy Formation: Schools of Thought," in *Perspectives on Strategic Management,* ed. James W. Fredrickson, 105–6 (New York: Harper Business Division of Harper & Row, 1990).

[5] Quoted in Walter K. Lindenmann, "Research, Evaluation, and Measurement: A National Perspective," *Public Relations Review* 16, no. 2 (Summer 1990): 14.

[6] Larissa A. Grunig, James E. Grunig, and David M. Dozier, *Excellent Public Relations and Effective Organizations: A Study of Communication Management in Three Countries* (Mahwah, NJ: Lawrence Erlbaum Associates, 2002), 58.

[7] Quoted in Sherri Deatherage Green. "Strategy by Numbers: Up-Front Research Doesn't Yet Have a Permanent Place in PR," *PRWeek* (August 4, 2003): 15.

[8] Lindenmann, ibid.

[9] C. F. Kettering, "More Music Please, Composers," *Saturday Evening Post* 211, no. 32 (1938).

[10] Peter H. Rossi and Howard E. Freeman, *Evaluation: A Systematic Approach,* 5th ed. (Newbury Park, CA: Sage Publications, 1993), 27.

[11] Grunig, Grunig, and Dozier, *Excellent Public Relations and Effective Organizations,* 191. See also David M. Dozier, "The Innovation of Research in Public Relations Practice: Review of a Program of Studies," *Public Relations Research Annual* 2 (1990): 3–28.

[12] Wilbur Schramm, *Men, Messages, and Media: A Look at Human Communication* (New York: Harper & Row, 1973), 51.

[13] Wilbur Schramm, "The Nature of Communication between Humans," in *The Process and Effects of Mass Communication*, rev. ed., ed. Wilbur Schramm and Donald F. Roberts, 26 (Urbana: University of Illinois Press, 1971).

[14] Carl Sandburg, *Abraham Lincoln: The War Years II* (New York: Harcourt, Brace and World, 1939): 236–37.

[15] Joseph A. Kopec, "The Communication Audit," *Public Relations Journal* 38, no. 5 (May 1982): 24.

[16] For more on the distinction between "stakeholders" and "publics," see James E. Grunig and Fred C. Repper, "Strategic Management, Publics, and Issues," in *Excellence in Public Relations and Communications Management*, 127–46 (Hillsdale, NJ: Lawrence Erlbaum Associates, 1992).

[17] Adapted from Brenda Dervin, "Audience as Listener and Learner, Teacher and Confidante: The Sense Making Approach," in *Public Communication Campaigns,* 2nd ed., ed. Ronald E. Rice and Charles K. Atkin, 67–86 (Newbury Park, CA: Sage Publications, 1989).

[18] Jim Van Leuven, "Expectancy Theory in Media and Message Selection," *Communication Research* 8, no. 4 (October 1981): 431.

[19] Heinz Weihrich, "The TOWS Matrix: A Tool for Situational Analysis," in *Strategic Planning: Models and Analytical Techniques,* ed. Robert G. Dyson, 17–36 (Chichester, UK: John Wiley and Sons, 1990).

[20] Kerry Tucker and Doris Derelian, *Public Relations Writing: A Planned Approach for Creating Results* (Englewood Cliffs, NJ: Prentice Hall, 1989), 41–46.

[21] Glen M. Broom and David M. Dozier, *Using Research in Public Relations: Applications to Program Management* (Englewood Cliffs, NJ: Prentice Hall, 1990), 20.

[22] For more detailed discussion of research methods, see Broom and Dozier, *Using Research in Public Relations*, or Don W. Stacks, *Primer of Public Relations Research* (New York: Guilford Press, 2002).

[23] "Flashbacks: Name That Gold Mine," *Forbes* (June 10, 2002): 60.

[24] Kristina Ray, David M. Dozier, Glen M. Broom, and C. Richard Hofstetter, "Public Participation: An Experimental Test of Stage of Involvement and Power Sharing on Satisfaction." Paper presented to the Association for Education in Journalism and Mass Communication, 2 August 2006, San Francisco, California, p. 18.

[25] Larissa A. Grunig, "Using Focus Group Research in Public Relations," *Public Relations Review* 16, no. 2 (Summer 1990): 36–37.

[26] Emily Steel, "The New Focus Groups: Online Networks," *Wall Street Journal,* 14 January 2008: B6.

[27] For an account of the origins and uses of the ombudsman concept, see Donald C. Rowat, ed., *The Ombudsman: Citizen's Defender,* 2nd ed. (London: George Allen and Unwin, 1968).

[28] Amy Jackson and Unity Stoakes, "Internet Vigilance: Monitoring Public Opinion Online," *Public Relations Tactics,* November 1997, p. 12.

[29] James R. Detert and Amy C. Edmondson, "Why Employees Are Afraid to Speak," *Harvard Business Review* (May 1, 2007). 6 May 2007, http://harvardbusinessonline .hbsp.harvard.edu/hbsp/hbr/articles/.

[30] David W. Stewart and Michael A. Kamins, *Secondary Research: Information Sources and Methods,* 2nd ed. (Newbury Park, CA: Sage Publications, 1993). Discusses how to locate information from various sources, including government agencies, online information search services, and CD-ROM delivery systems.

[31] For more detailed descriptions of content analysis procedures, see Robert P. Weber, *Basic Content Analysis* (Beverly Hills, CA: Sage Publications, 1985); and Guido H. Stempel III, "Content Analysis," in *Research Methods in Mass Communication,* ed. Guido H. Stempel III and Bruce H. Westley, 119–31 (Englewood Cliffs, NJ: Prentice Hall, 1981).

[32] Margaret Grisdela. "Create Surveys That Get the Press Calling," *Public Relations Tactics* (April 2003): 11.

[33] Terrence Coen, "Improve Phoneroom Efficiency," *The Frame,* November 1997, p. 1. (Quarterly newsletter published by Survey Sampling, Inc., Fairfield, CT.)

Additional Sources

Broom, Glen M., and David M. Dozier. *Using Research in Public Relations: Applications to Program Management*. Englewood Cliffs, NJ: Prentice Hall, 1990.

Fink, Arlene. *How to Analyze Survey Data* (The Survey Kit, Vol. 8) and *How to Report on Surveys* (The Survey Kit, Vol. 9). Thousand Oaks, CA: Sage Publications, 1995.

Greenbaum, Thomas L. *The Handbook for Focus Group Research,* 2nd ed. Thousand Oaks, CA: Sage Publications, 1997. Author summarizes 20 years of experience in focus group research.

Hyman, Herbert H. *Secondary Analysis of Sample Surveys: Principles, Procedures, and Potentialities*. New York: John Wiley and Sons, 1972. Considered the classic reference on doing secondary analyses.

Lavrakas, Paul J. *Telephone Survey Methods,* 2nd ed. Newbury Park, CA: Sage Publications, 1993. Outlines the use of new technology for conducting telephone research, sampling techniques, supervising interviewers, and securing cooperation of respondents.

Lavrakas, Paul J. *Encyclopedia of Survey Research Methods*. Thousand Oaks, CA: Sage Publications, 2008. Includes more than 600 sections covering all aspects of survey research methods, definitions, and biographies. Edited by former chief research for the Nielsen Company.

Miller, Delbert C., and Neil J. Salkind. *Handbook of Research Design and Social Measurement*, 6th ed. Thousand Oaks, CA: Sage Publications, 2002. Presents valuable guides on how to do research and provides selected scales and indices. This may be the most complete reference on social science research methods.

Stacks, Don W. *Primer of Public Relations Research*. New York: The Guilford Press, 2002. A welcome addition to the growing body of literature on research in the practice.

Weiner, Mark. *Unleashing the Power of PR: A Contrarian's Guide to Marketing and Communication*. San Francisco, CA: Jossey-Bass, 2006. Outlines a research-driven approach to managing and evaluating public relations programs.

relations components—become dynamic documents that reflect the open systems approach discussed in Chapter 7.

Reliance on research findings as the basis for strategic planning to achieve effective public relations varies widely. Walter Lindenmann, former senior vice president and director of research at Ketchum Public Relations in New York, surveyed practitioners to learn how many use research as the basis for program planning. Seventy-five percent of all those surveyed reported that they "occasionally" or "frequently" do research specifically for the purpose of planning. Counselors were most likely to use research, 89 percent, whereas practitioners in nonprofit settings were least likely, 68 percent.[8]

Another study concludes that practitioners' use of strategic thinking and program evaluation are correlated with the number of social science, statistics, and computer courses taken by practitioners. Seat-of-the-pants approaches are not correlated with taking social science, statistics, or computer software courses. Furthermore, the more practitioners engage in various types of research, the more likely they are to approach their work as managers and to be involved in management decision making.[9] As one practitioner put it, "If you don't have information to take to the table, then you don't get invited to the table [management meetings]."

Management Expectations

In many organizations, top management limits public relations participation in management decision making. "Many public relations people fantasize their roles in strategic planning, but few are really involved in any meaningful fashion," according to a principal of a major public relations firm.[10] Responding to management expectations requires practitioners to think outside the boundaries of public relations by analyzing and understanding the needs and concerns of operating units. In short, line managers expect public relations efforts to help achieve organizational goals, or in the words of some managers, "affect the bottom line."

Longtime AT&T public relations executive Ed Block outlined a CEO's expectations of the chief public relations officer:

> In this role, I need someone with an exquisite public relations "gut" combined with a comprehensive knowledge of the business and its external and internal environment. I want someone who is in touch with the "soul" of the business, someone who shares my vision and understands my sensibilities. I don't need a "handler" or a gatekeeper. I need someone whose counsel, over time, will influence my thinking in broad terms, not someone who hectors me on every piddling issue that crosses my desk. I also want someone whose counsel is sought out by others in top management because it is timely and thoughtful and helpful—not because it comes from someone who has special access to me.[11]

In the digital age of instant communication and online databases, the days of playing hunches and simply replaying the past as the primary bases for planning are history. Others in the organization may make strategic decisions based on financial, legal, or technical considerations and data. It is the responsibility of the public relations practitioner to anticipate the impact of those decisions on various stakeholder groups. In the words of another telephone company executive, "We lead an issues management group that functions as an early warning sentinel for the corporation." He credits the environmental scanning and "up-front counseling" for public relations' companywide acceptance in the strategic planning process. "Or to put it another way," he concludes, "we help plan the parade, not just carry the shovels afterward!"[12] AT&T's former CEO and chairman, Robert E. Allen, made the same point, "I need PR people at my side, not in my wake."[13]

Prudent long-range planning, anticipating conceivable developments, is more likely to result in the following:

1. An integrated program in which the total effort results in definite accomplishments toward specific goals
2. Increased management participation and support
3. A program emphasis that is positive rather than defensive
4. Careful deliberation on choice of themes, timing, and tactics

Even though the values of planning are evident and widely acknowledged, there is too little emphasis on this step in public relations. The following appear to be the main obstacles:

1. Failure of employers and clients to include the practitioner in deliberations that lead to policies and programs; a failure often born of lack of confidence in the public relations officer or counselor
2. Perception of public relations by some managers and practitioners as simply communication support—primarily at the tactical level—to achieve others' strategic goals
3. Absence of clearly agreed-upon objectives for target publics in the public relations program
4. Inadequate time because of the pressures of reacting to daily problems
5. Frustrations and delays that practitioners encounter in getting internal clearance and in coordinating with other departments

Despite the problems, in the final analysis management expects public relations to help manage threats from the environment, to enhance the organization's competitive edge (usually in the form of marketing support), and—most important—to protect an organization's most important assets, its good name and reputation. "Buildings depreciate, patents expire, but, properly managed, a company's name and reputation grow in value every year."[14]

Often the health of the bottom line depends on the health of an organization's reputation. An organization's market share, its ability to attract and retain valuable employees, its attractiveness to prospective donors and members, its autonomy and freedom to carry out its missions, and even its stock price are affected by its reputation among various stakeholders. Management expects the public relations unit to manage the organization's reputation and good standing with the same strategic thinking that goes into managing other assets.

Counselor Davis Young says there is no quick and easy way to build an organization's reputation:

If you want people to regard your organization highly, that must be a priority to which you allocate both time and money, one for which you plan and budget as you would for any aspect of your business. . . . It may take years to build a reputation but only a moment to destroy one. . . . A reputation is a priceless asset to be protected and managed at all times.[15]

Strategic Management

Strategic management represents the open systems approach to public relations rather than the closed systems, reactive approach. One counselor defines strategic management as "a process that enables any organization—company, association, nonprofit, or government agency—to identify its long-term opportunities and threats, mobilize its assets to address them, and carry out a successful implementation strategy."[16]

Strategic planning in public relations involves making decisions about program goals and objectives, identifying key publics, setting policies or rules to guide selection of strategy, and determining strategy. There must be a close linkage between the overall program goal, the objectives established for each of the publics, and the strategies selected. The key point is that strategy is selected to achieve a particular outcome (as stated in a goal or objective). On the other hand, if you don't care where you end up, any route will get you there.

Public relations practitioners work with other managers to develop strategic program plans. Although each program calls for specifically tailored and unique elements, the overall approach is similar from plan to plan. The planning and programming process typically includes the following steps:

1. *Defining roles and missions.*   Determining the nature and scope of the work to be performed

2. *Determining key results areas.*   Determining where to invest time, energy, and talent

3. *Identifying and specifying indicators of effectiveness.*   Determining measurable factors on which objectives may be set

4. *Selecting and setting objectives.*   Determining results to be achieved

5. *Preparing action plans.*   Determining how to achieve specific objectives

   a. *Programming.*   Establishing a sequence of actions to follow in reaching objectives

   b. *Scheduling.*   Establishing time requirements for objectives and action steps

   c. *Budgeting.*   Determining and assigning the resources required to reach objectives

   d. *Fixing accountability.*   Determining who will see to the accomplishment of objectives and action steps

   e. *Reviewing and reconciling.*   Testing and revising a tentative plan, as needed, prior to commitment to action

6. *Establishing controls.*   Ensuring the effective accomplishment of objectives

7. *Communicating.*   Determining the organizational communications necessary for achieving understanding and commitment in the previous six steps

8. *Implementing.*   Securing agreement among all key people regarding who and what needs to be committed to the effort, what approach will work best, who needs to be involved, and what action steps need to be taken immediately[17]

Mission Statements

The four-step public relations process outlined in Chapters 11 through 14 is based on the assumption that the organization has clearly defined its overall mission and goals and that public relations is part of the plan to achieve them.

Most organizations have documents that spell out their goals and objectives, both long-range and immediate. The purpose is to state succinctly why an organization exists, such as Merck Pharmaceuticals' "We are in the business of preserving and improving human life." Mission statements typically make public commitments of citizenship obligations and social responsibility. They often give the organization's attitude in dealing with its employees, members, clients, neighbors, and donors. They may state the organization's posture on government regulation or environmental issues, explain how it measures its own progress, and so on. In short, they are idealistic and inspirational statements designed to give those in the organization a sense of purpose and direction (see Exhibit 12.1).

EXHIBIT 12.1

Mission Statements

Weyerhaeuser Company (Tacoma, Washington)

Our Vision. The Best Forest Products Company in the World.

Our Strategies. We shall achieve our vision by: Making Total Quality the Weyerhaeuser way of doing business. Relentless pursuit of full customer satisfaction. Empowering Weyerhaeuser people. Leading the industry in forest management and manufacturing excellence. Producing superior returns for our shareholders.

Our Values. Customers: We listen to our customers and improve our products and services to meet their present and future needs. **People:** Our success depends upon high-performing people working together in a safe and healthy workplace where diversity, development and teamwork are valued and recognized. **Accountability:** We expect superior performance and are accountable for our actions and results. Our leaders set clear goals and expectations, are supportive, and provide and seek frequent feedback. **Citizenship:** We support the communities where we do business, hold ourselves to the highest standards of ethical conduct and environmental responsibility, and communicate openly with Weyerhaeuser people and the public. **Financial Responsibility:** We are prudent and effective in the use of the resources entrusted to us.

Johnson & Johnson

Our Credo. We believe our first responsibility is to the doctors, nurses and patients, to mothers and fathers and all others who use our products and services. In meeting their needs everything we do must be of high quality. We must constantly strive to reduce our costs in order to maintain reasonable prices. Customers' orders must be serviced promptly and accurately. Our suppliers and distributors must have an opportunity to make a fair profit.

We are responsible to our employees, the men and women who work with us throughout the world. Everyone must be considered as an individual. We must respect their dignity and recognize their merit. They must have a sense of security in their jobs. Compensation must be fair and adequate, and working conditions clean, orderly and safe. We must be mindful of ways to help our employees fulfill their family responsibilities. Employees must feel free to make suggestions and complaints. There must be equal opportunity for employment, development and advancement for those qualified. We must provide competent management, and their actions must be just and ethical.

We are responsible to the communities in which we live and work and to the world community as well. We must be good citizens—support good works and charities and bear our fair share of taxes. We must encourage civic improvements and better health and education. We must maintain in good order the property we are privileged to use, protecting the environment and natural resources.

Our final responsibility is to our stockholders. Business must make a sound profit. We must experiment with new ideas. Research must be carried on, innovative programs developed and mistakes paid for. New equipment must be purchased, new facilities provided and new products launched. Reserves must be created to provide for adverse times. When we operate according to these principles, the stockholders should realize a fair return.

Mission statements without management commitment and support, however, become simply cosmetic additions to brochures, reports, and speeches. The challenge is to instill a sense of mission, values, and behavior standards throughout an organization. Each organization has to define its own unique mission, matching its strategy and values, and creating its own culture.[18]

Whether these documents are kept private for competitive or security reasons or are open statements of mission, standards of conduct, or specific purposes, public relations staff are privy to them. In organizations where no such statements have been set down, there is an urgent need for the top public relations officer to propose one.

Mission statements of organizational goals, obligations, values, and social responsibility serve two important purposes in public relations: First, they commit the whole organization to accountability, and that means visibility or communication of some sort. Second, the attitudes expressed provide a framework in which public relations can devise its goals and objectives, build its budgets, direct its talents, devise its programs, and assess its impact.

The mission statement for the public relations function builds on the organization's mission statement. Typically the mission of public relations is to help the organization achieve its mission by doing the following:

1. Collecting and analyzing information on the changing knowledge, opinions, and behaviors of key publics and stakeholder groups

2. Serving as the central source of information about an organization and as the official channel of communication between an organization and its publics

3. Communicating significant information, opinions, and interpretations to keep an organization's publics and other stakeholders aware of organizational policies and actions

4. Coordinating activities that affect an organization's relationships with its publics and other stakeholder groups (Review Figure 3.3.)

To the extent that these activities and an organization's mission are connected to measurable goals and objectives, then public relations is part of management. To attain organizational maturity, the public relations function must be mainstreamed in every sense, not a sideshow, and have management agreement of a clear-cut charter, or mission.

Management by Objectives

As executives have become sophisticated in the ways of public relations, they have become more demanding. Most organizations operate on the basis of management by objectives (MBO) or, as others term it, management by objectives and results (MOR). Simply put, MBO systematically applies effective management techniques to running an organization. It specifies the outcomes (consequences, results, impact) to be achieved, thereby establishing the criteria for selecting strategies, monitoring performance and progress, and evaluating program effectiveness.

As now applied, MBO operates at two levels of outcomes: goals and objectives. Goals are summative statements that spell out the overall outcomes of a program. Such a program may involve many different parts of an organization as well as many different strategies. Goals state what the coordinated effort is intended to accomplish and by when it will be accomplished. Goals establish what will be accomplished if the objectives set for each of the publics are achieved.

Objectives represent the specific knowledge, opinion, and behavioral outcomes to be achieved for each well-defined target public, what some call "key results." The outcome criteria take the form of measurable program effects to be achieved by specified dates. In practice, objectives do the following:

1. Give focus and direction for developing program strategies and tactics
2. Provide guidance and motivation to those implementing the program
3. Spell out the criteria for monitoring progress and for assessing impact

An organization's overall goals provide the outcome criteria for unit and individual goals, including those for the public relations department. Just as an organization has a written MBO plan, so should public relations have a long-range MBO plan on paper. A separate document should give guidance within the department. Just as managers or general officers are periodically subject to performance review by a superior officer, so is the public relations manager. If line departments and other staff functions hold annual conferences to reenergize the staff, so should public relations. Most important, however, public relations must operate within and as part of an organization's overall MBO plan, must be held accountable in the same way as other functions, and must show how public relations contributes to the achievement of the organization's mission and goals.

Strategy and Tactics

The terms *strategy* and *tactics* are often confused. Borrowed from the military, *strategy* involves the crucial decisions of a war or campaign, such as whether to rely on missiles or aerial bombardment. Strategy represents the overall game plan. *Tactics* are decisions made during the course of battle. Tactics represent on-the-spot decisions necessitated because of developments as the strategic plan is implemented. In effect, tactics are the decisions or actions taken to make the strategy fit the reality and contingencies of the field of battle.

In public relations practice, however, *strategy* typically refers to the overall concept, approach, or general plan for the program designed to achieve a goal. *Tactics* refer to the operational level: the actual events, media, and methods used to implement the strategy. Long-time public relations leader and counselor John Beardsley summed up the difference this way: "Stragegy is the plan or plans that a business or other organization uses to get where it wants to go. Strategy is a ladder leading to a goal. Tactics are the steps on the ladder."[19] For example, the Wisconsin Milk Marketing Board's (WMMB) successful program to pass a referendum illustrates the difference between strategies and tactics.

WMMB wanted to win dairy producers' support for increasing, from 5 to 10 cents per hundredweight of milk produced, the amount directed to state and regional promotions of dairy products. Congress mandated that dairy farmers nationwide contribute 15 cents for each hundredweight of milk they sell to do research and to promote the sale of dairy products. Of the mandatory checkoff, 5 cents goes to the National Dairy Promotion and Research Board, and 5 cents goes to state or regional organizations. Dairy farmers then choose which organization gets the other 5 cents, often called the "middle nickel." WMMB wanted Wisconsin producers to direct the discretionary 5 cents to the state organization.

Program strategies included reinforcing the producers' belief in the need to build markets for Wisconsin dairy products; demonstrating WMMB's successes in marketing, research, and education; and enlisting influential third-party endorsements to reach targeted groups of producers. Tactics included check stuffers, newsletters, informational meetings, an 800–telephone number information service, the annual report, and exhibit booths at Farm Progress Days and the World Dairy Expo. The effect of these strategies and tactics was that 93 percent of the producers who cast ballots in the referendum voted in favor of directing the middle nickel to WMMB.

Reasons for Planning

Preparing a plan does not guarantee success, but it greatly enhances its chances. Strategic planning, however, is not universally accepted as part of public relations practice. The excuses practitioners give for not planning are similar to those offered by other managers:

1. *"We don't have time."* Practitioners who feel that they are already overloaded with work offer this excuse. Of course, they are missing the point that those with a plan typically make better use of their time, thus making time spent planning a wise investment.

2. *"Why plan when things are changing so fast?"* Plans get modified in light of changing circumstances; they are not cast in concrete. Having a plan, however, provides the baseline from which modifications can be made with full awareness that changes in strategy and direction are occurring. In fact, the more turbulent the environment, the greater the need to chart the changing course to the desired result, to have a plan. When is a plan more important, in calm seas or in rough, stormy seas?

3. *"We get paid for results, not for planning."* Many public relations practitioners tend to be oriented more to activities than to strategic planning. A dollar spent on research and planning is often viewed as a dollar not available for implementing program activities. This orientation generally leads to counting activities rather than results that count. In fact, clients and bosses pay practitioners for results that happen according to a plan to achieve goals—outcomes.

4. *"We're doing okay without a plan."* Short-term success can change to failure if conditions change. For example, it is easy to see how an injury to a football team's star quarterback can change an entire football season. Such was the case in a business setting when the founder and CEO of a new and successful computer company died in an automobile accident the very day the company's stock went public. The stock offer was withdrawn until new management was in place. A few weeks later the company stock was again offered but commanded a substantially lower price. Soon thereafter, Eagle Computer went out of business. Part of planning involves building in strategies for handling contingencies, such as industrial accidents and other operational crises; top management decisions that attract media and public scrutiny; changes in management and other key personnel; and charges by government agencies, consumer groups, unions, or whistle-blowers.[20]

Planning is for the purpose of making something happen or preventing it from happening, for the purpose of exploiting a situation or remedying one. Public relations practice is engaged more often in trying to create a viewpoint or a happening than trying to prevent one and trying to take advantage of an opportunity more often than trying to remedy an undesired situation. There remain, however, many situations and occasions when remedial public relations measures are required because preventive measures were not taken or were taken but failed.

Public relations calls for long-term planning and programming in many areas, such as public policy and social problems, but crises often give birth to public relations planning. Preventive public relations is tied most often to long-term planning. Remedial public relations actions tend to be of short duration and have minimal time for planning. The immediate need quite often is to pick up the pieces of a negative situation or to exploit a positive one. The latter works best if done within the framework of a long-term plan that includes strategies for such contingencies.

Writing the Program

Writing the program is a challenge. When the program meshes with organizational goals, the employer knows that the public relations practitioner understands what management is trying to do and is part of the management team. Counselor Jim Lukaszewski paraphrases the CEO's position: "Please spare me from another amateur corporate strategist—the person who doesn't have a clue about how the company operates, my goals, or our critical strategic needs; but who yaps at me every day and calls it strategy."[21]

The task of writing an overall program or a proposal would rarely fall on a new member of a staff. It is important, however, that all members understand how proposals and presentations evolve. By seeing how all the parts come together, all members are better able to perform their own segment or specialty when programs are implemented. Plans and programs are generally infused with enthusiasm. That helps get approval by employers and clients. But overenthusiasm carries with it the serious danger of overpromising: "This employee communication program has everything necessary to eliminate the turnover problem." Those are dangerous words. Suppose the program falls short, reducing employee turnover by "only" 50 percent? Ordinarily such a reduction might be considered an acceptable performance, but evaluated against the unrealistic earlier statement, it might be considered not up to the level promised.

Program Plan

A public relations plan starts with the organization's mission statement. It proceeds from the specific role assigned to it in the form of a public relations mission. It engages in whatever fact-finding is indicated, as discussed in Chapter 11. An orderly investigative process involves the following four aspects of a situation analysis:

1. *A searching look backward.*   There is no organization, no problem, no opportunity without a history. Learning that history is the first step. In a newly created entity, who founded it? For what purpose? Is it time for an anniversary event, an institutional museum, a biography of the founder? Can public relations help? Background information is also essential if public relations is brought into an entity to deal with a pressing problem. What is the background of the problem? What has happened that has caused public relations to be involved in a new or different way? Public relations problems, too, have a history.

2. *A wide look around.*   Where there has been no ongoing monitoring of public opinion toward the organization, that is the next step. How do employees feel about the conditions of their employment, their leadership? How do the neighbors feel about the presence and conduct of the organization? Is there a breakdown in understanding between the organization and any of its

constituent publics? Is there a resentment simmering somewhere? In a crunch, on whom could the organization depend? In that crunch, what groups would delight in the troubles or embarrassment of the organization?

3. *A deep look inside.*   Every organization has a character and a personality. Both tend to be reflections of those who control the organization by their ownership, management, votes, membership, or tenure or in some other way. Character can be discovered by examining the policies set down and by determining if day-to-day actions square with the words. Personality is evident in the style of administration: centralized authority or generous delegation, openness and candor or secretiveness and suspicion. It is portrayed by contemporary or traditional decor and equipment, open or closed doors on executive offices, symbols of stature, approachability of officials, and whether communication is formalized, as by memo, or casual, as by phone. The practitioner needs to know what makes the organization tick and whether it ticks with convictions, values, and standards that the practitioner can share and honestly promote.

4. *A long, long look ahead.*   Is the mission of the organization realistically attainable? Can public relations planning and programming fit in? Can they make a practical contribution? Will this organization be around in 10 years? Will it be larger and more solidly entrenched, or will it be engaged in a slow retreat toward oblivion? What are the pros and cons? What are the forces that will affect the organization's chances for success or failure? Are the game and the outcome worth getting involved?

Implementing these steps has been greatly enhanced by advances in technology and resources. Online databases, for example, as well as increasingly sophisticated issue-tracking techniques and services enable practitioners to meet executives' demands for data as a basis for planning. These data are used to build the foundation of the program: the problem statement and situation analysis (discussed in Chapter 11) and the program goal. The final plan (or proposal) typically includes the ten components outlined in Exhibit 12.2.

Action and Communication Strategy

Public relations has matured into the role of helping organizations decide not only *how to say it* and *what to say*, but *what to do*, according to Harold Burson. In its infancy and into the 1960s, public relations simply crafted and distributed the message handed down from management. Reflecting their view of public relations, management asked, "How do I say it?" In response to the social changes of the 1960s, organizations and their CEOs were increasingly held accountable on such issues as public and employee safety, equal opportunity, and the environment. In addition to how to say something, management asked public relations, "What shall I say?" Beginning in the 1980s, however, public relations entered a third stage; in addition to asking communication questions, management now asked, "What do I do?"[22]

Burson attributes this new role to unavoidable and increasingly detailed public scrutiny of what organizations do and say. This scrutiny has intensified in the wake of numerous corporate scandals, such as those of Enron, Tyco, and WorldCom; controversial responses by the Federal Emergency Management Agency (FEMA) and the American Red Cross after Hurricane Katrina; and "performance-enhancing" drugs in sports. Public response is also quick because of almost instantaneous worldwide communication. Modern communication technology closes the loop between

EXHIBIT 12.2

Public Relations Strategic Planning Outline

Four-Step Process	Strategic Planning Steps and Program Outline
A. Defining the Problem (Chapter 11)	**1.** The Problem, Concern, or Opportunity "What's happening now?" **2.** Situation Analysis (Internal and External) "What positive and negative forces are operating (SWOT analysis)?" "Who is involved and/or affected?" "How are they involved and/or affected?"
B. Planning and Programming (Chapter 12)	**3.** Program Goal "What is the desired situation?" "By when?" **4.** Strategy "What is the overall action and communication plan for achieving the program goal? "What is the budget available to implement the program? **5.** Target Publics and Objectives "Who—internal and external—must the program respond to, reach, and affect?" "What must be achieved with each public to accomplish the program goal?"
C. Taking Action and Communicating (Chapter 13)	**6.** Action Tactics "What changes must be made to achieve the outcomes stated in the objectives?" **7.** Communication Tactics "What message content must be communicated to achieve the outcomes stated in the objectives?" "What media best deliver that content to the target publics?" **8.** Program Implementation Plans "Who will be responsible for implementing each of the action and communication tactics?" "What is the sequence of events and the schedule?"
D. Evaluating the Program (Chapter 14)	**9.** Evaluation Plans "How will the outcomes specified in the program goal and objectives be measured?" **10.** Feedback and Program Adjustment "How will the results of the evaluations be reported to program managers and used to make program changes?"

message and behavior to the point that they are almost one and the same: What an organization does can be reported as quickly as what the organization says. As a result, all organizations need public relations more than ever to help determine what to do and what to say.[23] That constitutes action and communication strategy.

Role of Working Theory

The program strategy represents someone's working theory of what has to be done to achieve a desired outcome. In the words and form of a theoretical statement, "If we implement this action and communication plan, then we will achieve these outcomes with our publics, which should lead to accomplishing the program goal." Theory also determines the selection of tactics. Someone's working theory (strategy) guides how a special event is designed, how a newsletter or press release is worded, and how a community function is conducted. The theory that guides how each tactic is executed represents the practitioner's idea of what will cause a desired result. So when people say a program is "all theory," they are right! They are talking about the thinking behind strategy.

The role of theory is obvious, although not always made explicit, at every step of the planning process. Otherwise how would decisions be made? For example, theory clearly guides the process when writing program objectives and determining the strategies to achieve them.

For example, the goal of an employee communication program is to reduce the number of employees seriously injured or killed while driving to and from work and while driving on the job. The situation analysis background research shows that traffic accidents are the leading cause of workplace fatalities and cost U.S. employers almost $55 billion annually. The federal Department of Transportation estimates that 2,000 people die each year in work-related crashes, or 40 percent of all workplace deaths. Investigation shows that a surprisingly large percentage of employees do not wear seat belts while driving or when a passenger. Program planners decide to develop a program to increase seat belt use among employees. Clearly, their *working theory* is that getting employees to increase seat belt use will lead to a reduction in serious injuries and deaths.

The situation analysis research also shows, however, that delivery drivers are the ones most frequently injured or killed in accidents, and that the accidents occur during work hours. Program planners decide that to have the greatest impact on solving the problem and achieving the program goal, the program of action and communication should target delivery drivers and car parking-lot attendants—the major *program strategy*. Planners then outline what each of the two publics must learn from the program, what opinions each must hold after the program, and what each must do to reach the goal of increased seat belt use: another complex theoretical model of what the program must achieve. Their working theory follows the "learn-feel-do" causal sequence that guides most public communication programs:

Information Gain ⇒ Opinion Change ⇒ Behavioral Change

The working theory is made explicit when stated in the form of objectives for the two target publics. After the objectives are written, planners then turn to developing tactics to cause the sequence of outcomes specified by the objectives. If during implementation or after the program, the expected (theorized) outcomes are not being achieved, then program planners must decide whether their theory (read "strategy") was flawed or whether the program implementation was flawed.

Indeed, the wise practitioner keeps track of the conditions under which theorized cause-and-effect relationships appear to work and when those assumptions about the linkages between program activities and program effects do not occur. For example, did the third-party endorsements used in the Wisconsin Milk Marketing Board referendum campaign actually make a difference in the number of votes cast in favor of the middle-nickel checkoff? If so, maybe the strategy can be generalized to other programs. If not, are dairy producers unique and more resistant to such endorsements?

In summary, working theory drives every program decision, whether the assumptions about the causal relationships behind the decisions are made explicit or not. Practitioners are continually devising and testing their working theories. Those who can bridge the gap between theory and practice are the ones most likely to achieve management positions in the twenty-first century.[24]

Defining Target Publics

First in developing the strategy, practitioners must select and define the target publics publics from among all the stakeholders. The target publics, however, are abstractions imposed by program planners, as they typically do not exist as monolithic real groups. Planners must *reify* publics so as to develop the objectives, strategies, and tactics necessary for implementing a program. Reification means treating an abstraction as if it exists as a concrete or material entity. The "general public" is the grandest and least useful reification of all; there simply is no such thing. Given unlimited resources, practitioners could avoid the need to reify by targeting individuals, but that is seldom possible. Useful and practical definitions of publics, then, necessarily represent some degree of reification.

The usual demographic and cross-situational approaches to defining publics typically provide minimal useful guidance for developing program strategy. Simply listing general categories of potential stakeholder groups gives those planning and implementing a program little information about how people in each of the categories uniquely contribute to or are affected by the problem situation and organization.

Stakeholder categories such as employees, stockholders, alumni, consumers, community groups, government, and so forth, each may contain what public relations scholar James Grunig calls "nonpublics, latent publics, aware publics, and active publics."[25] *Nonpublics* are people who do not face a problem or situation in which they are mutually involved with or affected by either an organization or other people. Their level of involvement is so low that they have no impact on the organization, and the organization has no recognizable impact on them. *Latent publics* include people who are simply unaware of their connections to others and an organization with respect to some issue or other problem situation. *Aware publics* are those people who recognize that they are somehow affected by or involved in a problem situation shared by others but have not communicated about it with others. When they begin to communicate and organize to do something about the situation, they become *active publics*.

Useful definitions describe program publics on the basis of how people are involved in or affected by the problem situation or issue, who they are, where they live, what relevant organizations they belong to, what they do that is relevant to the situation, and so forth. The definitions derive from the particular situation for which a public relations intervention is being planned.

For example, suppose that a university has the goal of increasing the number of incoming freshmen for the next academic year. The target publics for the program might include staff members in the admissions and academic advising offices (internal publics), high school students and others who have written or called academic departments requesting information about particular majors, high school seniors with grade point averages of at least 3.0 in high schools within 100 miles of the university, parents of targeted student publics, and high school guidance counselors in those same schools. When a local newspaper accuses two starting football players at the same university of receiving bogus academic credit for summer work experience, however, the public relations office will define different target publics for the university's response. It is obvious that different people, with different kinds of connections to the university, are involved in and affected by the potential crisis in the university's football program.

Following are approaches used alone and in combination to define target publics from among the various stakeholder groups:

1. *Geographics*—natural or political boundaries—indicate where to find people but give little useful insight about important differences within the boundaries. This approach is useful for selecting media outlets and allocating program resources according to population density. ZIP codes, telephone area codes, city limits, county lines, voting districts, and so forth are examples of the geographic approach to defining publics.

2. *Demographics*—gender, income, age, marital status, education—are the most frequently used individual characteristics but provide little understanding of why or how people are involved or affected. Demographics and geographics help practitioners make the first cut, but without additional information about how people are involved or affected by an issue, problem, or situation, they usually give little guidance to developing strategy and tactics.

3. *Psychographics*—psychological and lifestyle characteristics (cross-situational) widely used under the name "VALS"—segment adults on the basis of "psychological maturity" and personality traits assumed to predict behavior. Knowing about lifestyle and values is useful, but typically only when combined with other attributes that tie the segments to something related to a particular situation.

4. *Covert power*—behind-the-scenes political or economic power—describes people at the top of a power pyramid who operate across situations. They exert power over others on a wide range of issues but often not in ways easily observed. Identifying these people requires a combination of careful observation over time, interviews with others in the problem situation, analyses of documents that record or track the exercise of covert power, or any combination of the three.

5. *Position* uses the positions held by individuals, not attributes of the individuals themselves, to identify target publics. People are identified as important in a particular situation because of the roles they play in positions of influence in those situations. The positions they hold make them important players in the efforts to achieve program goals and objectives.

6. *Reputation* identifies "knowledgeables" or "influentials" based on others' perceptions of these individuals. These publics are referred to as "opinion leaders" or "influencers," but they are defined as such by people in the situation of interest and are not to be confused by the cross-situational covert power group or defined as opinion leaders by the observer using some cross-situational definition.

7. *Membership* uses appearance on an organizational roster, list, or affiliation as the attribute relevant to a particular situation. For example, membership in a professional association or special-interest group signals a person's involvement in a situation, not the individual attributes of the member. Usually members receive controlled media from the organization with whom they are affiliated.

8. *Role in the decision process* calls for observing the decision-making process to learn who plays what roles in influencing decisions in a particular situation. This approach helps identify the most active among the active publics, those who really make decisions, take action, and communicate. Again, knowing their individual attributes can be less important than knowing how they behave in the process that leads to decisions related to the issue or problem of interest.

In short, defining publics by superficial characteristics alone is insufficient. *The key to defining publics strategically is to identify how people are involved and affected in the situation for which the program intervention is being developed.* That requires greater information-gathering efforts than simply putting labels on groups of people who appear to have something in common. Program planners can develop specific and responsive program objectives and strategies if they know what different people know about an issue or situation, how they feel about it, and what they do that is either contributing to it or reacting to it. This understanding of what they know, how they feel, and what they do, combined with who and where they are, provides the basis for writing useful program objectives for each target public.

Writing Program Objectives

Objectives spell out the key results that must be achieved with each public to reach the program goal. In practice, objectives

1. Give focus and direction to those developing program strategy and tactics.

2. Provide guidance and motivation to those charged with implementing the program.

3. Spell out the outcome criteria to be used for monitoring and evaluating the program.

All too often, however, public relations program "objectives" either describe the tactic, or means, rather than the consequences, or ends, to be achieved. For example, "To mail out 12 monthly issues of . . ." and "To inform people about . . ." both describe activities, not results. Objectives should outline the intended *impact* of the 12 issues and of the effort to inform.

Objectives also make concrete the working theory behind the program, usually in the "learn-feel-do" causal sequence. Program objectives for each public specify the desired outcomes and in what sequence, by what dates, and in what magnitude they are needed to achieve the overall program goal (see Exhibit 12.3). The more specific the objectives, then the more precise everything that follows. Following are examples of useful program objectives for the three levels of outcomes:

1. *Knowledge outcome:*   By July 1, to increase the number of local homeowners from 13 percent to 27 percent who know that wildland fires destroyed 2,500 homes during the past three fire seasons.

EXHIBIT 12.3

Sample Program Goal and Objectives

Program Goal

To reduce the number of delivery drivers seriously injured or killed while driving on the job from a five-year average of five per year to no more than two in the next fiscal year.

Objectives for Delivery Drivers

1. To increase, within 6 weeks after starting the program, the percentage of drivers from 8 percent to at least 90 percent who are aware that in a typical year four company delivery drivers are seriously injured and one is killed while driving on the job.

2. To increase, within 2 months after starting the program, the percentage of drivers from 5 percent to at least 80 percent who know that 55 percent of all fatalities and 65 percent of all injuries from vehicle crashes could be prevented if seat belts were used properly.

3. To increase, within 2 months after starting the program, drivers' awareness to at least 85 percent that 95 percent of all city employees, police, and emergency vehicle drivers use shoulder restraints and seat belts any time they drive on the same city streets.

4. To reduce, within 3 months after starting the program, the number of drivers from 67 percent to less than 25 percent who feel that using seat belts while driving adds to delivery time and extends the time needed to complete routes.

5. To decrease, by the end of the third month after the program begins, the number of drivers from 70 percent to less than 35 percent who "agree" or "strongly agree" with the statement that their own safe driving prevents serious driving accidents to the point that seat belts are not necessary.

6. To increase the percentage of drivers who use seat belts from the current 51 percent to at least 70 percent within 3 months after the program begins, to at least 80 percent within 5 months, and to at least 90 percent by the end of the first year.

7. After the 90 percent level of use is achieved, to maintain that level of seat belt use among all permanent and all temporary replacement drivers.

2. *Predisposition (opinion or attitude) outcome:* To increase neighboring property owners' confidence in our ability to conduct field tests safely from a mean confidence rating of 2.7 to 3.5 by January 15.

3. *Behavioral outcome:* To increase the percentage of employees who use seat belts when driving on the job from the current 51 percent to at least 70 percent within 30 days after the program begins.

These examples illustrate the elements and form of useful program objectives:

1. Begin with "to" followed by a verb describing the direction to the intended outcome. There are three possibilities: "to increase," "to decrease," and "to maintain."

2. Specify the outcome to be achieved. Again, there are three possible categories of what is to be maintained or changed: what people are aware of, know, or understand (knowledge outcomes); how people feel (predisposition outcomes); and what people do (behavioral outcomes). Each objective should spell out a single, specific outcome.

3. State the magnitude of change or level to be maintained in measurable terms. To provide useful and verifiable outcome criteria, objectives must be stated in quantifiable terms. Surely the levels must be realistic and consistent with the resources available to those implementing the program. Experience and judgment, plus evidence from the situation analysis research, provide the bases for setting the levels of outcomes to be achieved. Without benchmark data, judgment dominates when setting the outcome levels.

4. Set the target date for when the outcome is to be achieved. Dates stated in the objectives follow the working theory of the sequence of what has to happen. Typically, outcomes must be achieved in order, with one necessary before another. Each successive outcome is a logical consequence of the previous outcomes. Dates also provide guidance for those developing strategies and tactics, even down to deciding when to schedule communications and events.

Without objectives, programs drift according to the whims and desires of clients and employers, and the intuitions and preferences of practitioners. People in power choose program strategy and tactics because they like them, not because they are logically related to intended outcomes. Practitioners select strategy and tactics because of habit, because of comfort based on previous experience, or because something worked last time.

Objectives should be in writing, with copies available to each person working on the program. Objectives become the primary basis for developing and implementing program strategy and tactics. Objectives should be discussed frequently, because they provide the guidance for planning, managing, and evaluating program elements and the overall program. As the topic of staff discussions, objectives keep the program on track. As conditions change, program planners change the objectives to reflect the evolving program environment. After all, objectives provide the road map, derived from the working theory, to the desired goal.

Planning for Program Implementation

Plans, if they are to be carried out effectively, must be monitored at each step of the way. Preparation and follow-up support are necessary to ensure a return on the investment made in planning and programming. Anticipation and follow-through on plans are just as important in the practice of public relations as in sports.

Writing Planning Scenarios

Writing planning scenarios is the art of forecasting and describing the range of possible future states. Scenarios provide either longitudinal or cross-sectional summative statements about the future for the purpose of planning. Forecasters working in the Rand Corporation in the 1950s were the first to refer to "scenario writing" when describing their more qualitative approach to forecasting the future. The process differs from more traditional quantitative forecasting in that planners develop a number of plausible predictions of the future rather than relying on a single projection as the basis for charting strategy.[26]

The origins of scenario writing are more qualitative than quantitative. In fact, the pioneer of the technique said that the most important parts of the process are "simply to think about the problem" and to engage in "systematic conjecture."[27] The goal is to help clients anticipate more than one possible future state and plan for events that may have no history on which to build.

Futurists generally agree that the range of useful scenarios is two to four, but that the ideal number is three. And although the labels may vary, they represent high-, low-, and middle-ground future states, with the middle-ground scenario often viewed as the one most likely to occur. Some experienced planners, however, argue that to avoid the appearance of assigning probabilities, scenarios should be titled according to some major theme or major attribute. The danger of labeling one scenario as "most likely" or "probable" is that program planners tend to develop strategy for only that one possible future state, thereby defeating the purpose of having developed scenarios. After all, the purpose of writing scenarios is to construct descriptions of possible future states so that contingency planning can help prepare for the range of possibilities.

The greater the future uncertainty, the greater the need for planning scenarios. Predictions based on historical data, traditional forecasting models, and trend analyses may not meet the needs of public relations planners who must be prepared for the unexpected. This is not to say that one would be wise to abandon traditional quantitative methods, however.

Anticipating Disasters and Crises

A common type of planning scenario involves anticipating the worst things that could possibly happen to an organization; this is crisis planning. According to one practitioner, an effective corporate crisis communications plan is essential because "[I]t's only a matter of time before all companies experience an organizational or product crisis that could threaten their performance—or their very future."[28] Crisis communication scholar Kathleen Fearn-Banks summarized the need for planning: ". . . Successful crisis communication depends on crisis anticipation and thorough planning as well as open and honest policies with stakeholders and the news media."[29]

Whereas public relations practitioners typically cannot predict a specific disaster or crisis, they can anticipate that the unexpected will occur. It is the "unexpected" nature of events that creates a crisis situation: "An organizational crisis is a low-probability, high-impact event that threatens the viability of the organization and is characterized by ambiguity of cause, effect, and means of resolution, as well as by a belief that decisions must be made swiftly."[30]

First, though, practitioners must determine the types of crises, because the response depends in part on the type and probable duration of a particular crisis. One scholar of crisis management categorized eight types of crises caused by either management failures or environmental forces: natural, technological, confrontation, malevolence, skewed management values, deception, management misconduct, and business and economic.[31] Somewhat in jest, some use the "banana index" to describe crises: *green*—new and emerging issues and problem situations; *yellow*—current and ripe; and *brown*—old and moldy. A more serious attempt to define crises also uses time as the critical variable:

1. *Immediate crises*—the most dreaded type—happen so suddenly and unexpectedly that there is little or no time for research and planning. Examples include a plane crash, product tampering, death of a key officer, fire, earthquake, bomb scare, and workplace shooting by a disgruntled former employee. These call for working out in advance a consensus among top management for a general plan on how to react to such crises to avoid confusion, conflict, and delay.

2. *Emerging crises* allow more time for research and planning, but they may erupt suddenly after brewing for long periods. Examples include employee dissatisfaction and low morale, sexual harassment in the workplace, substance abuse on the job, and overcharges on government contracts. The challenge is to convince top management to take corrective action before the crisis reaches the critical stage.

3. *Sustained crises* are those that persist for months or even years despite the best efforts of management. Rumors or speculation get reported in the media

or circulated by word of mouth, outside the control of public relations. No amount of denial or countering seems to stop the rumor or purge the news database, meaning that reporters working on a new story will see the old story and may repeat the misinformation. Examples include persistent rumors of eminent downsizing, suggestions that Procter & Gamble's logo contains Satanic symbolism, and the charges of promiscuity that plagued President Bill Clinton throughout his two terms in office.[32] (This paragraph is an example of how such rumors get repeated to new audiences!)

Most organizations know how to deal with operational crises internally. It is the "unplanned visibility" following such crises, however, that can turn them into events that threaten reputation, credibility, and market position.[33] A quick public response is critical because, as a former vice president for CNN says, "If you don't respond quickly to what happens, you create a vacuum. And everyone else—the news media, your competitors—is going to step into that vacuum and tell your story the way they want to tell it, not the way you want it to be told."[34]

An example of how a slow response can harm the organization is the way the Catholic Church took a long time to address the issue of child sexual abuse by its priests. Because the organizational leadership was slow to acknowledge the problem and take timely steps to address it, the church lost the trust and financial support of many of its members.[35]

Common mistakes in handling crises include the following:

1. *Hesitation*—which leads to public perception of confusion, callousness, incompetence, or lack of preparation

2. *Obfuscation*—which leads to the perception of dishonesty and insensitivity

3. *Retaliation*—which increases tension and intensifies emotions rather than reducing them

4. *Prevarication or equivocation*—which creates the biggest problem, because nothing substitutes for truth

5. *Pontification*—which creates vulnerability by taking a high-handed approach without really dealing with the issue at hand

6. *Confrontation*—which provides others visibility by keeping the issue alive, giving them a platform, and giving them more to respond to

7. *Litigation*—which guarantees even greater visibility and may eliminate more reasonable solutions[36]

The key to anticipating and avoiding crises is assessing what can go wrong, what can affect people or the environment, and what will create visibility. Guidelines for preparing for public relations crises include the following:

1. Identify things that can go wrong and become highly visible; assess vulnerabilities throughout the organization.

2. Assign priorities based on which vulnerabilities are most urgent and most likely.

3. Draft questions, answers, and resolutions for each potential crisis scenario.

4. Focus on the two most important tasks—what to do and what to say—during the first critical hours following a crisis.

   a. Guidelines for "what to do" may include a telephone call tree showing the order in which key decision makers need to be informed.

    b. Guidelines for "what to say" may include "Q&As" that list questions likely to be asked by reporters and other publics, as well as the appropriate answers to these questions, and "standby statements" that are stock organizational positions regarding possible scenarios, with situation-specific information left blank to be filled in once the crisis occurs.

5. Develop a strategy to contain and counteract, not react and respond.[37]

The deadliest campus shooting in history at Virginia Polytechnic Institute and State University—Virginia Tech—highlighted the value of having a well-developed crisis plan. A student went on a shooting rampage, killing 32 students and faculty before killing himself. More than 500 journalists with 125 satellite trucks descended on the campus within hours. Larry Hincker, the university relations (read "public relations") leader charged with managing the crisis communication and media relations, said, "One of the first things you learn is you have to have a plan in place. It doesn't matter whether it's sophisticated or simple—you've got to have one. Frankly, the simpler the plan, the better."[38] Even with his plan at hand, Hincker also pointed out the need to react and adjust as the crisis unfolds:

> I violated crisis communications 101, which says appoint a single spokesperson and only that person interacts with the media. I had 500 journalists on this campus; that was not going to work. The second thing is that this crisis was so complex, so fast moving, that I was the one constant. I was the only person who was at all 10 of those press conferences, but I brought in the different experts.[39]

Successful handling of this and other crises requires an ability to anticipate possible emergencies and vulnerabilities, skills in planning strategy for responding to possible emergency scenarios, recognition of the early stages of crises, and the capacity to respond immediately as part of a systematic crisis management planning process (see Exhibit 12.4). Crisis management expert Lukaszewski adds, "The first challenge is always to make certain that the company, organization, or individual being advised behaves in a way that community, victim, and public expectations are met. If that happens, it's amazing how much of the rest takes care of itself."[40]

Establishing an Information Center

Many organizations have discovered the dangers of rumors and the need to provide authentic information. When a crisis arises, it suddenly becomes apparent that some seemingly unimportant facets of an operation have been overlooked and must be given hurried attention. Inevitably one such area of weakness is the availability of information. A knee-jerk response usually results in a jerry-built rumor center that operates through the crisis period, then fades away without serious thought until the next crisis comes.

Planning for an information center requires taking into account three major considerations. First, the center must be recognized for what it is: a place where information moves from the institution directly to an organization's publics. It is not a media operation. To saddle an organization's media relations office with an added responsibility of answering questions from other publics reduces the effectiveness of both functions. Media and public information centers must be closely coordinated, but where the organization can afford it, they must be separate entities, each directed toward its own specific function.

Second, the center should be in two parts. Rumor centers are almost exclusively telephone operations. Of course, there must be an answering service or information center. So one group deals directly with the publics, taking questions and providing

EXHIBIT 12.4

Checklist for Crisis Communication

Do the Following:

✓ Get out your prepared crisis plan, call together the crisis management steering committee, call in experts to help analyze and explain the crisis, and open the lines of communication.

✓ Notify top management and refer them to the crisis plan. Give them the task of making impact projections in preparation for inquiries from employees, government agencies, and the media.

✓ Channel all inquiries to the designated spokesperson, who was selected and trained in advance as part of the crisis planning preparation. Notify receptionists, operators, secretaries, and others to direct all inquiries to the designated spokesperson without giving their own versions or opinions.

✓ Set up a news center for media and begin providing information as quickly as it becomes available. Provide information background packets, telephones, computers and printers, fax machines, and a place for television interviews away from the crisis scene.

✓ Be open and tell the full story. If you do not, someone else will and you will lose control as journalists turn to other sources and outside experts to fill in gaps in the story.

✓ Demonstrate the organization's concern for what is happening and for the people who are involved and affected. At the same time, explain what the organization is doing or planning to do to solve the problem.

✓ Have someone on call 24 hours a day and stay with the story as long as the media are interested.

✓ Reconvene the crisis management team afterward to summarize what happened, to review and evaluate how the plan worked, and to recommend improvements in the crisis plan.

On the Other Hand:

✓ Do not speculate publicly about what you do not know to be fact. And do not respond to reporters' questions designed to solicit speculation.

✓ Do not minimize the problem or try to underplay a serious situation. The press will find out the truth soon enough.

✓ Do not let the story dribble out bit by bit. Each new disclosure becomes a potential headline or lead story.

✓ Do not release information about people if it will violate their privacy or if it blames them for anything.

✓ Do not say "no comment" or make off-the-record comments. If you cannot say something on the record, then explain why and tell reporters when they can expect the information. If information is simply not available, say so and assure reporters that you will get it to them as soon as you can.

✓ Do not play favorites among the media or the reporters. Respect reporters' work by not undercutting their scoops and enterprise.

✓ Do not try to capitalize on media attention and interest by trying to promote the organization, cause, products, or services. Do not do what will be perceived as a self-serving pitch while in the crisis spotlight.

Adapted from Claudia Reinhardt, "Workshop: How to Handle a Crisis," *Public Relations Journal* 43, no. 11 (November 1987): 43–44. Used with permission of *Public Relations Journal*.

answers. If that group does not have the information, they promise to have it within a certain period of time. The second group, however, is a coordinating agency—the point of contact between the information center and the institution's staff and agencies. The coordinating agency goes to the organization's staff for information and checks material with the highest level of the administration for accuracy, coordinates it with the media relations office, and relays it to the center for use. Hence, all information flows through the coordinating agency, where it can be accounted for and logged. In addition to raw information—the factual material used to answer direct and simple questions—the coordinating agency should have qualified people available to speak on policy or to conduct philosophical discussions of current issues. As the sole source of material for the information center, this agency controls the center and what is being said to the various publics. Although not an official spokesperson, it does provide for a "one-voice" response to the institution's problems in a crisis situation.

Third, and perhaps the most important, any such center must have credibility established long before any crisis; it must be the accepted source of accurate information. This cannot be accomplished during the period of crisis alone. The flow of credible information must be established during routine times. The function must become an accepted part of the institution on a full-time, continuing basis, identical in crisis or routine situations. It must also, over an extended period, encourage both internal and external publics to use it with faith and confidence. This amounts to more than establishing a reputation for truth; it involves education.

Internally, all parts of the organization must be made aware that such a system exists and must be encouraged to use it to make information for which they are responsible available. At the same time, employees at every level in the organization must be advised to direct all calls to the information center. Crisis management specialist Lukaszewski warns,

> The most damaging information or story points will come from individuals who work with us or who have worked for us; from documents or studies that should never have been written or done; from hand-written notes in the margins of otherwise innocuous documents; or from dumb, colorful statements or phrases a spokesperson just couldn't resist saying.[41]

Such an information or fact center, operating normally over a long period of time, sets the pattern within an organization for quickly and efficiently moving information. If the organization is tuned to such an operation in routine times, the transition is far less shattering in troubled times. When all the pieces of the crisis management plan work, some crises are avoided or preempted, and others are managed in ways that minimize damage. Pearson and Clair outline a broader definition of success, however:

> Effective crisis management involves minimizing potential risk before a triggering event. In response to a triggering event, effective crisis management involves improvising and interacting by key stakeholders so that individual and collective sense making, shared meaning, and roles are reconstructed. Following a triggering event, effective crisis management entails individual and organizational readjustment of basic assumptions, as well as behavioral and emotional responses aimed at recovery and readjustment.[42]

An all-too common aspect of crises is rumor. Authors Doorley and Garcia say that left unaddressed, rumors "can cause significant reputational harm—sometimes even more harm than the crisis."[43] They go on to explain that rumors exist in the absence of evidence when some people take them to be true:

> Rumors arise and are believed when official information is lacking or is considered unreliable. Rumors can be avoided if companies recognize the need to provide sufficient clarifying information as early as possible in the life of a disruptive event.[44]

Procter & Gamble's handling of a wild rumor illustrates the difficulties of dealing with a pernicious rumor. "Word was" that P&G was in "league with Satan" and giving part of the corporation's money to the "church of Satan." Supposed evidence for such claims was Procter & Gamble's logo, which had evolved over almost two centuries, showing the man in the moon and 13 stars, the latter of which represented

Old

Revised

Current

the original 13 colonies. To deal with this rumor, the company went to the media, the pulpit, and the courts to stop the wild charges emanating from religious fanatics. But in April 1985, Procter & Gamble gave up the fight and announced that it would remove the logo from its products. In 1991, Procter & Gamble modernized its logo for the first time since 1930 but did not use it on products or in advertising for several years thereafter. The company now uses the letters-only version, because the rumor persists even after many attempts to discredit it and to explain the real meaning of the original logo.

Budgeting

There is as much art and artistry in public relations budgeting as there is science. Available literature on the subject is sparse. Few practitioners study accounting and finance as part of their professional education. Canadian practitioners rated budgeting as their weakest skill, with 60 percent reporting that they had never received financial training.[45] Other surveys of practitioners reveal that they typically use their computers for word processing and desktop publishing but not to manage financial data. Yet many of them manage budgets of $1 million or more.

No doubt practitioners in other countries suffer from the same deficiency in their professional preparation. At professional seminars, the most frequently mentioned guideline seems to be, "Always ask for more than you need." Of course the deliberate, habitual padding of budget requests is not peculiar to public relations. It has become part of the system but cannot be recommended as responsible management.

In established departments, budgets generally relate to one of four control factors. One is the total income or funds available to the enterprise, the second is the "competitive necessity," the third is the overall task or goal set for the organization, and the fourth is the profit or surplus over expenses.

When *total income* or *funds available* is the basis, as in marketing or fundraising activities, public relations is generally allocated a percentage. The percentage relates to the organization's total operating budget, to gross sales, to funds raised, or to funds allocated from taxes. When *competitive necessity* is the criterion, the amount spent by a similar charity or a competing organization is matched or exceeded. This method is very risky. The *task* or *goal* basis usually provides for public relations to have a share of the funding set aside to achieve the desired end result. For example, to achieve a fund-raising goal, a museum might increase the percentage of the operating budget allocated to "development" activities. The final approach—*profit*, based on how much money is "left over"—usually sets a fluctuating figure that can go up or down, depending on "the point at which we break even," or in a nonprofit operation, "the point at which we cover all expenses." Not only is it difficult to plan and staff under this option, but it also reinforces the impression that public relations is something you do only if you have money to spend after covering the essentials.

Budgeting is rarely a one-person job. Each specialist is called on to estimate and itemize variable costs that will be incurred to implement the public relations plan during the next budget year. Variable costs are those associated with projects and activities, such as printing, rent for special events facilities, speakers' fees, photographers, advertising, travel, and entertainment. The department head, or someone designated, adds the estimated variable costs to the unit's fixed costs, including such expenses as salaries and benefits, overhead for office space, phone, service, equipment leases, supplies, subscriptions, and service contracts. The next executive up the line evaluates the budgets from the departments for which he or she is responsible, negotiates and adjusts the budget requests to fit the total available or needed, and

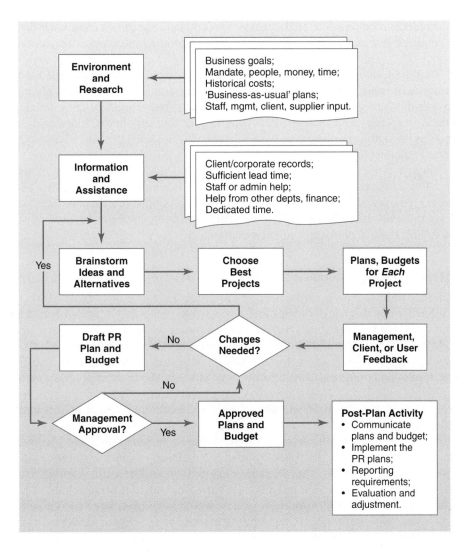

FIGURE 12.1

Public Relations
Budgeting and Planning
Flowchart

Source: Bob Delaney, APR,
SIRIS Counsulting, Missis-
sauga, Ontario, Canada.
Used with permission.

finally either approves or forwards the budgets to the next level for approval (see Figure 12.1).

Practitioners typically follow three guidelines:

1. *Know the cost of what you propose to buy.* If you plan to do a special mailing, find out the exact costs for photography and artwork, printing and folding, mailing lists, labeling and sorting, delivery, postage, and everything else needed to complete the job. Do not guess, because you will have to live within the budget that gets approved and deliver what was promised.

2. *Communicate the budget in terms of what it costs to achieve specific results.* The details of actual variable and fixed costs used to develop the budget may not be of interest to management or to a client. Managers who must approve the budget typically want to know how much it will cost to achieve goals and objectives. They look to you to manage the process in a cost-effective fashion.

3. *Use speadsheet software to manage the program.* Develop a master spreadsheet, as well as spreadsheets for individual projects. By tracking each

project and linking each to the master spreadsheet, you can estimate cash-flow requirements in advance and monitor expenditures against cost estimates.

Too often, budgets are put aside after they are approved and are not used as management tools. Used in conjunction with other elements of program planning, however, budgets provide guidance for scheduling staff resources, contracting for services, tracking project costs, and establishing accountability. Individual staff members, as well as the entire unit, should refer to the budget when assessing performance against expectations.

Budgets often play an important part in shaping and maintaining the relationship between the public relations staff and their clients and top management. In the final analysis, practitioners must have realistic budgets, must use them to direct staff efforts, must review them frequently with clients and top management, and must be able to link costs to performance and outcomes.

Pretesting Program Elements

Once the strategic plan is formulated, it should be tried on a pilot basis. Marketers have been doing this for decades. Only recently has pretesting a plan of action and communication become somewhat common in public relations.

Many qualitative and quantitative tools are available for pretesting efforts: interviews with opinion leaders, focus groups, controlled laboratory tests, and field tests in pilot communities. Careful pretests of strategy, tactics, and program materials provide estimates of how they will work, provide comparisons of alternatives to determine which works best, and detect possible backlash effects of unanticipated, unfavorable results.

Backlash effects can be avoided by conducting a response analysis. This means using a sample audience to observe immediate reaction to specific communication content. As an example, the Occupational Safety and Health Administration (OSHA) would have been spared much embarrassment had it pretested its 16-page booklet, "Safety with Beef Cattle." A pretest would have eliminated such nonsense warnings as, "Be careful not to step into the manure pits," "If your ladder is broken, do not climb it," and "Beams that are too low can hurt you."

Message pretesting also can help increase the understandability of the information for its intended audience. The symbolism chosen for a public relations document may represent perfect clarity to its creator but be both uninteresting and unintelligible to the reader. Or the symbol may be inappropriate, as when Caterpillar Tractor Company sent 10,000 calendars to its Saudi Arabia dealer, Zahid Tractor. When government inspectors opened the shipment they found that the calendar contained a picture of a village in Iceland showing a church with two crosses. Workers blotted out the crosses with heavy black markers because Christian symbols are forbidden in the devoutly Islamic nation. The blotches created 10,000 reminders of the need to pretest even the smallest detail in program communications and activities.

A few years ago an experimental program of health education was undertaken in an isolated Peruvian community high in the Andes. As part of the program, a film on the transmission of typhus by lice, featuring graphic close-up shots, was prepared and shown to the villagers. It became apparent that the message was not getting through. A survey of the people who had seen the film revealed that although they had many lice in their homes, they had never been bothered by the "giant" kind shown on the screen. To get results, appeals and symbols must be appropriate and understood.

A cautionary note on pretesting must be inserted. The stream of public opinion rushes along swiftly. An idea that worked well in a pretest might prove a fiasco upon widespread use because of a time lag. Seasons change and with them change people's concerns, recreational pursuits, and so forth. Overpowering and unexpected events can quickly alter the public opinion climate overnight; for example, the American Red Cross response to Hurricane Katrina dramatically changed the climate for fund-raising campaigns run by local Red Cross organizations. When using pretest results as a guide to communication programs, practitioners need to be as certain as possible that program conditions are similar to those that existed during the pretest and that pretest subjects are representative of the program target publics.

Selling the Plan

Research, analysis, precedents, and experience must be converted into program forms acceptable to those who are not public relations executives and to clients. Some are not sensitively attuned to public opinion. Some are cost oriented, or publicly gun shy, or both. Some do not commit comfortably to speculative expenditures with no guarantee of return. Some are nervous about issuing information to news media. Goals and objectives not tied directly to sales or profits are ephemeral to many. The more specific the institutional goals, the more specific and effective the public relations plan can be.

Selling the program proposal puts the practitioner's persuasive and technical communication skills to the test. It calls for effective writing, persuasive speaking, skillful use of presentation audiovisual materials, and careful reading of those around the conference table. But effective selling begins with an effective program proposal.

After a program has been approved at the policy level, it becomes necessary to familiarize colleagues with what is to follow. Otherwise, these important collaborators may wind up uninformed, like an outside counselor who is not allowed to participate in the planning. Then, they would not be able to do their part. They would not be in a position to solicit support from the people under their supervision.

Some generally accepted tenets related to introducing others to the public relations program merit noting. Explain the basic problems in terms of the harm that can be done if they are left unattended. Then, explain the immediate remedial measures in relation to long-term plans. Use similar case examples, precedents, and survey results to substantiate the plan. Eliminate personal opinion except as it applies to special knowledge of related cases. Relate the program to the climate in which the organization operates and that it hopes to enjoy in the future. Stress that the activities will have a desirable ultimate effect on public opinion. Keep explanations short and to the point. Be decisive and have conviction in the plan, qualities highly respected by administrators. And, as Lukaszewski advises, focus on the future: "The trusted strategic advisor can only be a force for tomorrow. The closer you are in tune with tomorrow, the more compatible you are likely to be with the leaders you are advising."[46]

It is important for future relationships that the programming agreed upon be a matter of record. Getting the plan on paper tends to make the planning and programming steps real and tangible for those charged with implementing the program. After all, "excellent strategists must have the executional capability to implement the strategy. . . . You can't divorce the two [strategy and implementation]."[47] Implementation is the topic of the next chapter.

Notes

[1] Jim Lukaszewski, "Let's Get Serious about Strategy," *strategy* I (Supplement to *pr reporter* newsletter), March 2, 1998, p. 1.

[2] Scott Adams. "Dilbert." Comic strip. *San Diego Union-Tribune,* 10 June 2007.

[3] David M. Dozier and Larissa A. Grunig, "The Organization of the Public Relations Function," in *Excellence in Public Relations and Communication Management,* ed. James E. Grunig, 412–13 (Hillsdale, NJ: Lawrence Erlbaum Associates, 1992).

[4] Jim Lukaszewski, *Why Should the Boss Listen to You? The Seven Disciplines of the Trusted Strategic Advisor* (San Francisco, CA: Jossey-Bass, 2008), 167.

[5] William J. Small, "Exxon Valdez: How to Spend Billions and Still Get a Black Eye," *Public Relations Review* 17, no. 1 (Spring 1991): 9–25.

[6] Stephen P. Robbins, *Organization Theory: Structure, Design, and Applications,* 3rd ed. (Englewood Cliffs, NJ: Prentice Hall, 1990), 121.

[7] Ibid., 121–23.

[8] Walter K. Lindenmann, "Research, Evaluation, and Measurement: A National Perspective," *Public Relations Review* 16, no. 2 (Summer 1990): 8.

[9] David M. Dozier, "The Innovation of Research in Public Relations Practice: Review of a Program of Studies," *Public Relations Annual* 2 (1990): 15–21.

[10] Robert W. Kinkead and Dena Winokur, "How Public Relations Professionals Help CEOs Make the Right Moves," *Public Relations Journal* 48, no. 10 (October 1992): 19.

[11] Ed Block, "Expectations of PR: A Colloquy," *Arthur W. Page Society Newsletter* 7, no. 2 (June 1991): 4.

[12] David M. Bicofsky of New York Telephone Company, quoted in Kinkead and Winokur, "How Public Relations Professionals Help CEOs," 23.

[13] Quoted in Dena Winokur and Robert W. Kinkead, "How Public Relations Fits into Corporate Strategy," *Public Relations Journal* 49, no. 5 (May 1993): 21.

[14] Kinkead and Winokur, "How Public Relations Professionals Help CEOs," 21.

[15] Davis Young, *Building Your Company's Good Name* (New York: American Management Association, 1996): 12.

[16] Paul S. Forbes, "Applying Strategic Management to Public Relations," *Public Relations Journal* 48, no. 3 (March 1992): 32.

[17] Adapted from George L. Morrisey, *Management by Objectives and Results for Business and Industry,* 2nd ed. (Reading, MA: Addison-Wesley, 1982), 107, 216–20.

[18] Andrew Campbell, "The Power of Mission: Aligning Strategy and Culture," *Planning Review* 20, no. 5 (September–October 1992): 10–12, 63.

[19] John Beardsley, "The Evolution of Strategy: Finding the True Nature of Strategic Thinking, *The Public Relations Strategist* (Fall 2007), 50.

[20] Adapted from Patrick J. Below, George L. Morrisey, and Betty L. Acomb, *The Executive Guide to Strategic Planning* (San Francisco: Jossey-Bass, 1987), 17–19; and Robert B. Irvine, "The Crisis Outlook for '92 and Beyond," *Public Relations Journal* 48, no. 10 (October 1992): 8, 34.

[21] Lukaszewski, "Let's Get Serious about Strategy," 2–3.

[22] Harold Burson, "Beyond 'PR': Redefining the Role of Public Relations," 29th Annual Distinguished Lecture of the Institute for Public Relations Research and Education, New York, October 2, 1990.

[23] Ibid.

[24] Winokur and Kinkead, "How Public Relations Fits into Corporate Strategy," 23.

[25] James E. Grunig and Fred C. Repper, "Strategic Management, Publics and Issues," in *Excellence in Public Relations and Communication Management,* ed. James Grunig (Hillsdale, NJ: Lawrence Erlbaum Associates, 1992), 127.

[26] Steven P. Schnaars, "How to Develop and Use Scenarios," in *Strategic Planning: Models and Analytical Techniques,* ed. Robert G. Dyson, 153–67 (Chichester, UK: John Wiley and Sons, 1990).

[27] Herman Kahn, *The Japanese Challenge* (New York: Thomas Y. Crowell, 1979), 5, as quoted in Schnaars, "How to Develop and Use Scenarios," 160.

[28] Andy Bowen, "Crisis Procedures That Stand the Test of Time," *PR Tactics* (August 2001): 16.

[29] Kathleen Fearn-Banks, *Crisis Communications: A Casebook Approach,* 2nd ed. (Mahwah, NJ: Lawrence Erlbaum Associates, 2002), 21.

[30] Christine M. Pearson and Judith A. Clair, "Reframing Crisis Management," *Academy of Management Review* 23, no. 2 (January 1998): 60.

[31] Otto Lerbinger, *The Crisis Manager: Facing Risk and Responsibility* (Hillsdale, NJ: Lawrence Erlbaum Associates, 1997), Part II.

[32] Adapted from Claudia Reinhardt, "Workshop: How to Handle a Crisis," *Public Relations Journal* 43, no. 11 (November 1987): 43–44.

[33] James E. Lukaszewski, "How to Handle a Public Relations Crisis," *World Executive's Digest* 12, no. 6 (June 1991): 68.

[34] David Bernkopf, quoted in Jeff Siegel, "Damage Control: How Prepared Are You for an Unforseen Disaster?" *Southwest Airlines Spirit* (October 2003): 52.

[35] James Burnett, "Crisis and the Cross," *PRWeek* (April 22, 2002): 17.

[36] Adapted from Lukaszewski, "How to Handle a Public Relations Crisis," 68–69.

[37] Ibid.

[38] Francis Ward-Johnson, "Preserving the Hokie Spirit at Virginia Tech," *The Public Relations Strategist* (Summer 2007): 8.

[39] Ibid., 10.

[40] James E. Lukaszewski, "Becoming a Crisis Guru," *The Public Relations Strategist* (Summer 2007): 45.

[41] James E. Lukaszewski, "A Primer on the News Magazine Shows," *Executive Action* (January/February/March 1997). Quote from The Lukaszewski Group Inc. newsletter. Used with permission.

[42] Pearson and Clair, "Reframing Crisis Management," p. 66.

[43] John Doorley and Helio Fred Garcia, "Rumor Has It: Understanding and Managing Rumors," *The Public Relations Strategist* (Summer 2007): 27. Article excerpted from Doorley and Garcia's book, *Reputation Management: The Key to Successful Public Relations and Corporate Communication* (New York: Taylor & Francis Group, 2007).

[44] Ibid., 29.

[45] Bob Delaney and Michael Lewis, "Planning and Budgeting for Public Relations Professionals." Paper presented to the 1990 Annual Conference of the Canadian Public Relations Society, June 1990.

[46] Lukaszewski, *Why Should the Boss Listen to You?* p. 12.

[47] Jack Bergen, Quoted in Alan Crawford, "Selling Strategic: Strategic PR Is All the Rage. What Is It and Why Is It Happening?" *PRWeek* (July 9, 2001): 19.

Additional Sources

Doorley, John, and Helio Fred Garcia, *Reputation Management: The Key to Successful Public Relations and Corporate Communication.* New York: Taylor & Francis Group, 2007. Provides practical guidance on dealing with threats to organizations' most important nonhuman asset—their reputations—written by two reputation-management experts.

Dozier, David M., with Larissa A. Grunig and James E. Grunig. *Manager's Guide to Excellence in Public Relations and Communication Management.* Mahwah, NJ: Lawrence Erlbaum Associates, 1995. Chapter 2 outlines "knowing how to manage strategically" as necessary to practicing public relations excellence.

Fearn-Banks, Kathleen. *Crisis Communications: A Casebook Approach*, 2nd ed. Mahwah, NJ: Lawrence Erlbaum Associates, 2002. Presents theory and practice of crisis communication, as well as case studies of how problems can turn into crises, then catastrophes, if not managed effectively.

Lerbinger, Otto. *The Crisis Manager: Facing Risk and Responsibility*. Mahwah, NJ: Lawrence Erlbaum Associates, 1997. Builds case for central role of communication in the management of crises.

Lukaszewski, James E. "Establishing Individual and Corporate Crisis Communication Standards: The Principles and Protocols." *Public Relations Quarterly* 42, no. 3 (Fall 1997): 7–14. Summarizes lessons learned by crisis communication management expert.

Pavlik, John. "Mapping the Consequences of Technology on Public Relations." Paper published by the Institute for Public Relations (September 2007). Available online at http://www.instituteforpr.org. Part I discusses technology's impact on how public relations practitioners do their work.

Rice, Ronald E., and Charles K. Atkin, eds. *Public Information Campaigns*, 3rd ed. Thousand Oaks, CA: Sage Publications, 2001. Useful reference for students and practitioners with interests in government, politics, and public health.

Schwarts, Peter. *The Art of the Long View*. New York: Currency Doubleday, 1996. Originally published in 1991, this remains the definitive guide for scenario building, and the author remains one of the leading strategists.

Smith, Ronald D. *Strategic Planning for Public Relations*, 2nd ed. Mahwah, NJ: Lawrence Erlbaum Associates, 2005. Detailed, step-by-step application of planning process to implementing public relations program.

Step Three: Taking Action and Communicating

The third step of program management advances the public relations process from strategy—the conceptual stage—to putting the program into operation—implementation. Once the problem has been defined and a solution worked out, the next steps are *action* and *communication*.

The Action Program

In the words of an old adage, "Actions speak louder than words." Yet many people in management, and unfortunately even some in public relations, believe the myth that communication alone can solve most public relations problems. Typically, however, public relations problems result from something done, not something said. The exception is when the "something said" becomes an event itself, such as when someone in authority or in a prominent position makes a sexist remark, racial slur, or other bigoted comment. For example, during a 2006 campaign rally, former U.S. senator and Virginia governor George Allen was shown in a cell-phone video using a word that is a racial slur in much of Africa to address an opposing candidate's supporter. He apologized, but it was too late. The Republican senatorial (and possible presidential) candidate became a victim of his own words, widely distributed worldwide by the 24/7 media. Even more problematic is when such a comment appears in official organizational communications.

Acting Responsively and Responsibly

It stands to reason that if something that was done caused the problem, then something must be done to solve the problem. In other words, corrective action is necessary to eliminate the original source of the problem. An example of the need for corrective action is a university that had difficulties attracting

Words are merely words, and they can be purely cosmetic if they aren't backed by convictions, actions, and policies.[1]
—*Harold Burson*

In all such settings and outcomes, there are winners and losers. More and more, it is the ability to control information and its flow that determines who is which.[2]
—*Jarol B. Manheim*

freshmen. Investigators discovered that the word was out, "Don't go to State, freshmen can't get classes." Sure enough, freshmen had the lowest priority for registering for classes. Even when admitted to the university, they ended up attending two-year community colleges in order to get required general education classes. Only after the university gave freshmen registration priority did the number of first-year students increase significantly.

Another example is the Bureau of Land Management's (BLM) "wild horse problem." The BLM, part of the Department of the Interior, runs the program mandated by the Wild Horse and Burro Act of 1971 ("The Wild Horse Annie Act") to manage the wild horse and wild burro populations on federal lands. With no real predators, the wild herds can double every four years. Without proper management, the herds in 10 western states increase to be far too large for the range and invade grazing lands leased to ranchers. Since 1971, the BLM has rounded up 220,000 horses and burros and made them available through the "Adopt-a-Horse" program (see Figure 13.1).[3] Because not all horses and burros are desirable to potential adopters, who pay an adoption fee averaging $125 per horse or burro, the BLM waived adoption fees for ranchers who took large numbers of the surplus animals.

Animal-protection protesters charged the BLM with condoning the slaughter of wild horses, "our national heritage," by giving them to ranchers. They alleged that the ranchers shipped the animals directly to slaughterhouses, making a handsome profit in the process. BLM officials disavowed any role in the commercial slaughter of wild horses and burros for pet food, but questioned the wisdom of spending millions of dollars each year to board surplus captured horses at a time when government programs for the poor were being cut. Still the angry protests continued. No amount of communication strategy appeared to ease the problem. When BLM officials recognized that their fee-waiver program was a major contributing factor, the program was canceled. Moreover, the agency changed policy with respect to ownership—ranchers would not take title of adopted horses and burros for one year. For that year, even though the rancher is responsible for care and feeding, the animals remain public property and cannot be sold. Again, actions spoke louder than words.

Source: U.S. Department of the Interior Bureau of Land Management.

FIGURE 13.1

Public Affairs Specialist at Adoption Event

Courtesy California State Office, Bureau of Land Management, The Department of the Interior.

its own recruiting and training program. Before developing any external recruitment communications, ABPS changed how it operated its recruiting program. First, ABPS expanded the search area from the metropolitan Atlanta area to all Georgia. Second, it staffed an office specifically to handle recruiting. Third, ABPS equipped the office with the computer equipment necessary for expediting applications. These internal changes and the accompanying communication campaign resulted in more than 1,800 applicants and a net gain of 80 new officers on the force in one year. Previous attempts at statewide recruiting without the other changes in structure and processing had not reversed the attrition problem.

Action strategy concentrates on adjustment and adaptation *within* the organization. An opportunity to implement such changes, however, requires that both top management and practitioners define public relations as something much more than publicity and persuasive communication. As Harold Burson pointed out, in its mature form, public relations helps relationships determine what is done as well as what and how something is said. The case of Sybron Chemicals Inc., now owned by Pittsburg-based LANXESS Corporation, provides yet another illustration.

Sixty neighbors of the Birmingham, New Jersey, manufacturer of water purification resins were evacuated following the accidental release of a noxious chemical. A month later, two plant workers were seriously burned during a process accident. These accidents and the resulting publicity only heightened public concerns about odors from the plant, plant safety, and the lack of information about plant operations. Neighbors and a U.S. senator called for new state and federal controls. Some in the community demanded that the plant be closed.[6]

With public relations counsel, Sybron devised a strategy to "take immediate, effective and credible action regarding each of the concerns identified by neighbors, local officials and state regulatory officials." The company also decided to break with past practice and begin regularly communicating both what was happening and the results of corrective actions. Action strategies included hiring an independent engineering firm to solve odor and chemical-handling safety problems and to upgrade plant facilities. Communication strategy included forming the Sybron Neighborhood Involvement Council to promote face-to-face communication; issuing a quarterly newspaper, *Sybron Community Update*; holding the first Sybron open house and plant tour; and installing a computerized 24-hour phone system (PINS Hotline) that calls neighbors' homes if there is a problem and allows neighbors to call any time of day for updated information.[7]

A follow-up survey of neighbors indicated that 90 percent felt more secure about Sybron as a neighbor and almost all believed that the company had improved communication with its neighbors. A report describes the award-winning program as "the story of how a new commitment to corrective action and communications resulted in a complete turn-around, in just seven months, with state regulators praising Sybron's actions as a model for the entire chemical industry."[8]

"Sybron is certainly a textbook example of how a company can turn neighborhood fear and anger into trust and credibility," according to Christine Foschetti, then account executive at Sybron's public relations firm, Holt and Ross, Inc. Sybron's management first had to mount an action strategy that included significant odor-reduction efforts and substantial environmental improvements. According to Foschetti, "Without these two very important elements, the company's public outreach program would have been doomed to fail."[9]

The Special Case of Special Events

Special events occupy a special place in public relations practice, because they mix elements of both action and communication. Although they appear to be "scenes of the action," to borrow from Lippmann's "triangular relationship" model in Chapter 8, they typically are designed to get a *message* in the media. In fact, special events have drawn fire from some of the most learned critics, including historian and former Librarian of Congress Daniel Boorstin. He argued that what he called "pseudo-events" blur, rather than clarify, public issues, writing that "our whole system of public relations produces always more 'packaged' news, more pseudo-events."[10]

Boorstin said that such events are "planned, planted, or incited" to be reported by the media, they may or may not reflect the underlying reality, and they are intended to be self-fulfilling prophecies. "The news they make happen, the events they create, are somehow not quite real."[11] True, but not necessarily a threat to modern civilization. Practitioners use special events and "media events" to attract the attention of target publics directly and through media coverage. For example, public relations specialist Debra Lynn Ross produced "The Battle of the Hospital Chefs" to attract the attention of those attending an annual hospital services annual conference and to secure media coverage about the improved quality of hospital food (see Exhibit 13.2).

EXHIBIT 13.2

Special Event: The Battle of the Hospital Chefs

Sometimes you just have to seize a good opportunity and run with it despite the fact that there may be time and financial limitations. "The Battle of the Hospital Chefs" was one of those. Designed as a national competition to raise awareness of a growing hospital food trend—gourmet, heart-healthy dishes that are part of normal hospital fare—the first of its kind special event was created as a cooking challenge similar to the Iron Chef. The "Battle" was created to help target audiences put aside outdated ideas about hospital food.

Each year, Consorta, a health-care group purchasing and resource management organization, holds an educational conference for its members. The conference also features an exhibition hall that links more than 350 exhibiting companies with conference attendees.

While over the past years, the number of conference registrants representing the food and nutrition area has grown markedly, exhibitors in the food and nutrition area of the exhibition hall were under-represented. With fewer than 120 days left until the conference began, exhibit sales were not at the expected goal. We needed to find a "different hook" to bring these companies to the exhibit floor and actively engage them in demonstration cooking in the Food & Nutrition Pavilion.

We found our inspiration in hospital food.

A successful event would increase supplier participation and therefore revenue. It would also expand visibility for member hospitals and their foodservice efforts by debunking the outdated notion that hospital food is bad.

With a nod to the Food Network, "The Battle of the Hospital Chefs" was born.

The Corporate Communications team created The Battle as a unique competition that pitted three chefs from Consorta member hospitals against one another as they created tasty, heart-healthy, low-cost gourmet meals. Finalists would have one hour to prepare a healthy menu, which was judged on many attributes, including the fact that it had to cost less than $4.95 a plate. The three finalists, along with their sous chefs, received all-expense-paid trips to Chicago to compete for the top prize.

Prior to the competition, Consorta staff worked with the finalists and their respective public relations departments to create videos highlighting their facility and showing colleagues cheering on their finalist. The videos would be shown the day of the event as each finalist was introduced.

Consorta brought together a judging panel consisting of three celebrity Chicago chefs, and Consorta's president and its chief operating officer.

A four-page brochure featuring the finalists' recipes was produced for the media kit and used as a handout at the event. In addition, we created an event Web site that contained information on hospital foodservice trends, finalists and their recipes, the judges, as well as a media link with downloadable documents and photos.

The Battle aired live and was carried on the in-house TV channel for those who preferred watching from the comfort of their hotel room. We designed the cooking stations to be similar to those seen on television cooking shows, with mirrors positioned above the work surfaces so the audience could see technique and how things were assembled. While the chefs were preparing their courses, each of the celebrity judges presented a healthy cooking tip. The emcee also engaged the audience in a true/false game about healthy eating and participants won healthy food-related prizes. The drama of the event picked up as the time remaining was called out. In the end, William Reed's Macadamia Crusted Tilapia with sweet soy reduction and mint sauce, spicy cucumber slaw, sesame soba noodle salad, and tofu-berry smoothie wowed the judges, winning him the Gold Chef Award.

As part of Consorta's social responsibility efforts, donations in the names of the winning chef and the three celebrity judges were made to charities and a charity for the homeless program received all the new cooking equipment used at the event.

The event also proved tremendously successful for Consorta, meeting our goals and objectives:

- Signed 18 new food and nutrition suppliers as exhibitors for the next conference, exceeding goal by 80% and resulting in $60,000 additional revenue

- Increased attendance at the Food & Nutrition Pavilion by 38%, exceeding target of 20%

- Secured more than 12 million possible media impressions, including:

  1. Live broadcast coverage on Fox TV, and a 3 1/2-minute segment on *ABC World News Tonight*.

  2. National print coverage in the *Wall Street Journal*, *AARP The Magazine*, and the *Associated Press*. We also provided information for *Parade Magazine's* "What America Eats" issue.

  3. Local broadcast and print coverage in the *Chicago Sun Times* and in the finalists' local media.

  4. Coverage in trade magazines, including *Acute Care News, Chef, Seafood Business, Healthcare Foodservice Management.*

  5. Visits to www.hospitalchefs.com, which had 1,782 visitors, 6,958 page views, and 641 visitors who downloaded heart-healthy foods recipes.

"The Battle" proved that the title "Hospital Chef" is not an oxymoron. The event is now an annual competition at the conference and attracts more chefs and attention each year.

———————————

—Debra Lynn Ross. Director, Corporate Communications Consorta, Inc., Schaumburg, Illinois.

Although Boorstin primarily blamed journalists, practitioners produce the majority of pseudoevents covered by the media. Few would deny that events promoting a cause in the public interest or calling attention to newsworthy events have a legitimate place in public relations and the public information system. It is the phony events to promote dubious causes and to "hype" self-serving interests that justify criticism. Precious news space and time given to a celebrity's latest stunt, production of the world's largest sub sandwich, or an orchestrated confrontation of the opponents in the next wrestling or boxing match photo opportunity preempts explaining the complexities of the plight of the homeless, the national debt, the need for health-care reform, or international trade relations. Produced with the public interest foremost, however, special events contribute to clarification of public issues, not to their displacement, distortion, or obfuscation.

Action strategy puts into practice what Chapter 7 refers to as the open systems model, or what James Grunig calls "two-way symmetrical" public relations.[12] The first assumption basic to this approach is that change is as likely within the organization as it is on the part of the organization's publics. Another assumption of this approach is that changes result in win–win outcomes, meaning that both sides in an organization–public relationship can benefit. A third assumption that drives action strategy is suggested by the quote, "Clean up your act, not just your image." If public relations is to have an impact in shaping the mutually beneficial relationships necessary for organizational survival and success, it must participate in developing the action strategy and in coordinating this strategy with the communication efforts that follow.

The Communication Program

Action strategy necessarily makes up the main thrust of a program but represents the part of the public relations iceberg that might not show above the surface. Communication, typically the more visible component, serves as the program catalyst to interpret and support the action strategy. Chapter 8 outlines relevant communication theory and concepts that serve as the foundation for this section. What follow are fundamentals and principles for applying the theory to the practice.

Framing the Message

The first principle of framing message content for the communication effort is to know the client's or employer's position and the problem situation intimately. The second principle is to know the needs, interests, and concerns of the target publics. In the words of one practitioner, "Get smart and put yourself in the other party's shoes."[13]

Attempting to establish any single set of surefire rules for framing message content would be disappointing, if not futile. Such rules might appear perfect in principle yet be rendered ineffectual by an unseen characteristic of the audience; for example, a religious belief that bans certain foods. The timing could be bad. A carefully timed announcement of a new stock offering by an oil company was smothered in the news by revelations that the organization had used corporate funds for political campaigns in the United States and for bribes abroad. The audience could harbor an unspoken prejudice, such as confronts a Democrat campaigning in a Republican precinct. The wording of the message could be such that it does not square with the images in the heads of the audience, or perhaps the audience is not in a listening mood. Regardless of the specific barrier, standardized programming can generate results that are frustrating or futile.

Effective communication must be designed for the situation, time, place, and audience. It means careful selection of media and technique. For example, the annual spring migration of college students to Florida's beaches poses health problems for that state, among them the spread of venereal diseases. One year the Florida Health Department gave Frisbees™ carrying messages on how to recognize and prevent venereal diseases to students as they swarmed the Florida beaches. This is targeted communication. So is the campaign against teenagers drinking and driving in Tucson, Arizona: "Driving Drunk Will Put Your Lights Out"—a message framed in the imagery and language of the target public.

Advances in technology and specialized media have created a wealth of possibilities for serving the needs of special audiences. Practitioners would be well advised to think in terms of smaller and more circumscribed patterns of communication as they seek to modify or mobilize opinions. No communication or action, simply because it worked once before in a given situation, can be carted about like a trunk full of old clothes and fitted to a new situation. With rare exceptions, the clothes will not fit the second wearer. If nothing else, they will be out of style.

All public relations problems, however, do have people as a common denominator and require communication to bring the people and their viewpoints closer together. This applies whether the programming calls for news releases, institutional advertising, meetings, or any other tool of contact. Continuity is required in communication. So is repetition of a consistent message in simple form, careful selection of time, place, and method, and a variety of media that converge on the audience from several avenues.

Public relations, with its powerful and varied means of selectively disseminating targeted information, suffers from an overcapacity. Simon and Garfunkel sang in "The Sounds of Silence" that our problem is people talking without speaking, people hearing without listening. Likewise, practitioners must define audiences with great precision and must use different strategies and techniques to accomplish different goals. For example, different concerns and different levels of intensity about an issue call for different message strategies.

The following time-tested techniques help reduce the discrepancy between the communicator's position and the audience's attitudes.

1. Use the media most closely identified with the audience's position.
2. Use a communications source that enjoys high credibility for the audience *on the topic of communication*.
3. Play down the differences between the positions of the communicator and those of the audience.
4. Seek identification in vocabulary and anecdote with the audience *in an area removed from the issue*.
5. Establish the communicator's position as being the majority opinion, defining the majority from the audience itself.
6. Bring the audience's group identifications into play when those identifications will help develop a positive response. The converse is also true.
7. Modify the message to fit the organization's need.[14]

Besides framing their message for the target public, public relations practitioners must also frame their messages for the media. According to some estimates, 9 out of 10 news releases get discarded.[15] Practitioners can increase their chances of getting the attention of journalists by carefully adhering to the *Associated Press Stylebook* and using multimedia tools in the presentation of their messages.[16] Most importantly, framing the message for the media and media gatekeepers requires attention to news value. Traditional criteria applied by gatekeepers, who see their role as acting on behalf of media audiences, include the following.

1. *Audience impact*—the number of people affected, the seriousness of the consequence, the directness of cause and effect, and the immediacy of the effect. This criterion applies not only to news but also to other information.
2. *Proximity*—the distance between the audience and the problem or issue of concern. This criterion simply suggests that local connections or news angles increase news value.
3. *Timeliness*—perishability. Like bread, news gets stale. This criterion also explains why journalists and media compete to be first with the news but why print media cannot compete with broadcast media on timeliness. As a result, print media may be more interested in why and how than in when, although daily newspapers remain concerned with the timeliness of information.
4. *Prominence*—recognizable and well known. Almost by definition, celebrity and celebrities are of interest to large numbers of people; they are newsworthy.

Prominence means that journalists and their audiences are interested in the private lives of public organizations and figures.

5. *Novelty or oddity*—the unusual, bizarre, deviant, and offbeat. Some even define news as deviation from the normal. Journalists and editors know that people are attracted by and interested in what is new, unique, and unexpected.

6. *Conflict, drama, or excitement*—strikes, fights, disputes, wars, crime, politics, and sports. All too often, conflict is the major ingredient in news, not only because of its appeal to journalists but also because of media pandering to public interest in the sensational and uncertain. Conflict situations often have issues that are not clearly defined, uncertainty about what is right or wrong, and oversimplified versions of winners and losers.[17]

Defining news may not be that simple, however. Some contend that news is anything that affects the lives and interests or stimulates the concern and curiosity of a significant number of people. In the final analysis, the distinction between hard news and soft news changes to accommodate audience interests in an ever-expanding range of topics, including science, culture, environment, social change, and education, to name but a few. Day-to-day news selection by gatekeepers, however, may result more from routine, deadline pressures, mechanical requirements, and their perceptions of what other journalists are saying and doing.[18]

Public relations practitioners must frame their messages to make them *newsworthy*, by whatever standard (hence the requirement to know the media and media gatekeepers). Messages also must be *understandable*—uncomplicated, free of jargon, and simple to grasp. They must be topical or local to take advantage of audience interest in information that is both timely and close to home. Most important, however, is that the message must be *immediately actionable*. In the same way that the action strategy must be mutually beneficial, so must messages. The content should be framed in such a way that the information answers questions, responds to audience interests and concerns, and empowers members of the audience to act on their interests and concerns (see Figure 13.2, Trades Hall, Melbourne, Australia). The actionable quality deserves special attention.[19]

FIGURE 13.2

Message Framing— "Make James Hardie Pay!"

Journalists systematically tend to shy away from including "mobilizing information" in their news stories. This is the information about identification, location, and instruction or direction that audience members would need to act on their predisposition. One could speculate that journalists might feel that providing such information would be a departure from their perceived role of objective news reporters. When they include mobilizing information in stories about charities, other community drives, and crises, journalists may see this either as a forgivable departure, given the positive context, or as acceptable professional behavior.[20]

Another useful approach to framing the message is to use the "30-3-30" formula devised by the late author-scholar Clay Schoenfeld.[21] The first number means that many in the audience will give you no more than 30 seconds to get your audience's attention, meaning that your key points must be strong, positive, and dominantly displayed. The second number indicates that some will give you up to three minutes, meaning that you can count on bold lines, subheads, illustrations, photo captions, and even highlighted summary statements to carry the message. Thirty-minute audience members will spend the time necessary to get message content, even though the details are reported in small type. Maybe a 3-30-3 formula should replace Schoenfeld's optimistic 30-3-30 formula when framing most public relations messages.

Finally, framing the message strategy requires attention to four fundamental facts.

1. The audience consists of people. These people live, work, worship, and play in the framework of social institutions in cities, in suburbs, in villages, or on farms. Consequently, each person is subject to many influences, of which the communicator's message is typically only one small source of influence.

2. People tend to read, watch, or listen to communications that present points of view with which they are sympathetic or in which they have a personal stake. For example, communication scholarship has shown that people who are Republican tend to pay more attention to television ads featuring Republican candidates, whereas Democrats tend to pay more attention to ads featuring Democratic candidates.

3. Media create their separate communities. For example, those who read *Soldier of Fortune* and *The National Enquirer* are not likely to read *Scientific American* and *Architectural Digest*. Similarly, online chat rooms are a high-tech example of communities created by specialized media.

4. Media have a wide variety of effects on individual and collective knowledge, predisposition, and behavior, not all of which are readily measurable. Careful framing must take into account both the intended and unintended effects of message content.

Priming for Effect

Recent research explores what influence audience receptivity to message frames. *Priming* theory suggests that previously learned information affects how receptive people are to new messages and how they interpret new information. According to Wang, "The priming effect states that by making some issues more salient than others, a prime influences the standards by which a particular issue is judged."[22] After his experiment testing the effects of priming and framing, he concluded:

> When people read primed messages that offered an important issue but did not carry a specific evaluative implication, they consider the primes. When people read a news

report that offered a direct link between an issue and a target corporation and carried a specific evaluative implication, they tended to adopt this frame of reference in their own thinking based on their previous positions held toward the issue.[23]

In a related study, Bae and Cameron also found a similar effect, what they called the "conditioning effect of prior reputation." Participants in their experiment were exposed to fictitious news stories about a company's reputation and later to another news story describing the company's charitable gift to a nonprofit health organization. Those who read that the company had good reputation concluded that the charitable gift was a mutually beneficial gesture. In contrast, those who read that the company had a bad reputation inferred that the company's charitable giving was simply another self-serving behavior. They concluded (1) that if a company has a bad reputation, even prosocial activity "triggers severe public suspicion toward the company's overall strategy" and (2) that practitioners "commit to enhancing intrinsic trustworthiness" of the company before attempting to influence publics with prosocial messages.[24] Indeed, consistent with the apparent relationship between priming and framing, information held prior to new communication affected subsequent judgments.

Semantics

Semantics is the science of what words mean. Language is constantly changing, with new words appearing (such as "googled") and words dropping from use (such as "groovy"). The meanings of words can change (such as "politically correct"). Others take on so many meanings that they become almost meaningless (such as "bottom line" and "strategic planning," according to some in public relations!).

This is not a book about linguistics, but practitioners acknowledge the importance of semantics in public relations. The subject really deserves and gets a great deal of attention from men and women in public relations because they live by words and make their living by them. For example, Edward Bernays referred to the "semantic tyranny" represented by the title of what is widely recognized as one of history's greatest special events, "Light's Golden Jubilee," the celebration of the 50th anniversary of Thomas Edison's invention of the incandescent lightbulb. There is no escape for communicators from what T. S. Eliot described as "the intolerable wrestle with words and meanings." Practitioners must seek mastery of word meanings and nuances.

When communicating with diverse audiences, the challenge is further complicated by the need to translate English-language words with accuracy, yet with a careful eye toward semantics in the end-language. For example, when the U.S. Census Bureau wanted to encourage Hispanics to complete and return their census forms, the English-language tagline was "This is your future. Don't leave it blank." In the initial Spanish-language translation, "blank" became "blanco," which some Hispanic community leaders felt implied that failure to complete the ethnicity question on the census form would lead to Hispanics being counted as non-Hispanic Whites. Thus, the Census Bureau decided to go with the tagline "Es nuestro futuro. Hagase contar" ("This is our future. Make it count.") for its Spanish-language campaign.

In this midst of the wrestle with words—in any language—is the public relations practitioner. Studying the words that leap out of people's mouths, stare up from newspapers, and smile out from a television tube, the practitioner is expected to react and then to be able to tell what those words mean—not what they say, but what they really mean. Then the public relations specialist is expected to combine words and actions that will correct misunderstandings, educate where there is a lack of knowledge, and, in general, clear up confusion.

Practitioners are constantly making decisions about word meanings, so the basic importance of semantics must not be overlooked. Deciding what the refusal of people to work should be called represents a decision in semantics. Is it a strike, a work stoppage, or an outrage against the people? Cutbacks are referred to as "downsizing" or "rightsizing." Procter & Gamble called its notification that the company was about to cut 13,000 jobs and close 30 factories "the global initiative announcement." Weapons of mass destruction are called "peacekeepers," military invasions are referred to as "police actions," and new taxes are camouflaged as "revenue enhancements." Clearly, there is no one-to-one ratio between a word and its meaning. The same signs and word symbols have different meanings for different people.

In addition, they have two different kinds of meaning: *denotative* and *connotative*. Denotative meaning is the common dictionary meaning, generally accepted by most people with the same language and culture. Connotative meaning is the emotional or evaluative meaning we read into words because of our experience and background. For example, all people will agree that "dog" *denotes* a four-legged, usually furry, canine animal. For most people, dog *connotes* a friendly, faithful pet and usually awakens nostalgic memories about a childhood pet. To others, however, the word connotes a dangerous animal or the cause of dander that causes a severe allergic reaction. Another example is the word "bullfight." North and South Americans fully agree on what the term denotes, but its connotative meaning differs sharply for many people north and south of the United States–Mexico border.

Words can excite and inflame. For example, there is evidence that a mistake in translating a message sent by the Japanese government near the end of World War II may have triggered the bombing of Hiroshima and thus ushered in atomic warfare. The word "mokusatsu," used by Japan in response to the U.S. surrender ultimatum, was translated as "ignore" instead of its correct meaning, "withhold comment until a decision has been made." And some years ago, semantic difficulties caused a crisis between the United States and Panama: Panamanians interpreted the English verb "negotiate" as a commitment to work on a new treaty, the meaning of the Spanish verb "negociar." The U.S. State Department intended it simply in its noncommittal sense of "to discuss."

Words often become code words to convey an unspoken but unmistakable meaning; for instance, "right to life," "law and order," "reverse discrimination," and "ethnic purity of neighborhoods." Even the meaning of commonplace words cannot be taken for granted. For example, a professor used the word "fallacy" on an exam, only to find that many students did not know what the word meant.

Public relations people must be able to select and transmit for various audiences words that will be received as kinfolk. Think of the harm that has been done, the confusion created, by legal language. The same is true for the language of doctors, educators, the military, and government. Each has a special jargon not readily understandable to others: legalese, educationese, militarese, and governmentese. And besides jargon there are slang, dialects, slogans, and exaggerations. Practitioners must work with their counterparts in the press, radio, and television and on the platform to help straighten things out for their publics.

Poet Anne Sexton cautioned, "Words, like eggs, must be handled with care; once broken, they are beyond repair." Practitioners must have a flair for picturesque, memorable terms, and a feeling for words.

Symbols

Communication involves more than semantics; in large measure it uses *symbols* and *stereotypes*. The symbol offers a dramatic and direct means of persuasive communication with large numbers of people over long lines of communication. Symbols have been used since the dawn of history to compress and convey complex messages to the multitudes. The Star of David and the Cross of Christ remind us of this. Most people need the shorthand of symbols to deal with whatever is abstract, diffuse, or difficult.

Years ago, Lippmann explained the need met by symbols and stereotypes as "introducing (1) *definiteness* and *distinction* and (2) *consistency* or *stability* [emphasis his] of meaning into what otherwise is vague and wavering. . . . We tend to perceive that which we have picked out in the form stereotyped for us by our culture."[25] Here is a current example of Lippmann's point: "Pro-life" is a powerful symbol because it condenses an enormous amount of meaning, information, and experience.

The value and use of a venerated symbol is seen in the British monarchy. The greatly diminished British Commonwealth of Nations today is a free association of independent nations loosely held together, not by legal ties but by the symbol of the Queen of England. She symbolizes the traditional loyalties, the common interests, the traditional institutional forms held more or less in common, and the family ties.

Symbols play an important role in the public relations and fund-raising programs of health and welfare agencies. Probably the best-known symbol of the kind is the Red Cross, from which that agency takes its name. The Red Cross originated in Switzerland and created its symbol by reversing the white cross and red background of the Swiss flag. The upright sword of the American Cancer Society, chosen in a nationwide poster contest, was created to portray its crusading spirit. Another crusade, that of the National Lung Association, is symbolized by the Cross of Lorraine, which dates back to the Crusades.

One of the most effective symbols ever created is that of Smokey Bear, used by the U.S. Forest Service, the Association of State Foresters, and the Advertising Council to promote forest-fire prevention. The idea originated in 1944 with a group of foresters and advertising specialists concerned about the need to protect our forests. After experimenting with drawings of deer, squirrels, and other small animals to carry fire-prevention messages, they had the idea of using a bear. A bear—with its humanlike posture, its way of handling itself, and its universal appeal to young and old—seemed ideal to build into a persuasive symbol (see Figure 13.3).

The Smokey Bear symbol changed over the years, as did the appeals used in the public service announcements. More than five decades of public awareness campaigns have produced almost universal awareness of Smokey Bear, with 98 percent aided recall in some parts of the country. Surveys typically show that about 95 percent of adults and 85 percent of children recognize Smokey's message, "Only *you* can prevent forest fires." But even though the symbol enjoys widespread recognition, many of the young urban children exposed to Smokey Bear in school programs do not know what to do to prevent forest fires. The bear, however, remains a credible symbol of forest-fire prevention.[26]

Increasingly, for-profit and nonprofit organizations emphasize symbols (designs and logos) to create a public image and instant recognition or to capitalize on widespread public awareness and acceptance. A current example of the latter is the symbol for recycling, which marketers and organizations use to demonstrate their concern for the environment. In fact, another new term—*green*—has entered the language to describe communication and an action strategy shaped to demonstrate sensitivity and commitment to protecting the environment.

Surely symbols should be distinct, different, and in character for the institutions using them. However, a changing public climate governed by new and different values can make symbols obsolete or offensive. For example, new public sensitivity for

Smokey Bear

FIGURE 13.3

Smokey Bear

Courtesy U.S. Forest Service, The Advertising Council, and the National Association of State Foresters.

the rights and feelings of minority groups has forced the University of Illinois, Syracuse University, St. John's University, and Stanford University to abandon American Indian symbols and names for their athletic teams. Clearly, the universities and the tribes hold different views of the use of Native American symbols.[27] Florida State University continues to use the Seminole warrior Osceola as its symbol and calls its marching band the "Marching Chiefs," whose signature piece is the "War Chant." The university and the Seminole Tribe of Florida continue to collaborate on the appropriate use of symbol, in the face of continuing pressure to drop long-standing Indian symbols and mascots.

Barriers and Stereotypes

Barriers to understanding and to the clarity of messages exist in the communicator and the audience alike. As Lippmann noted, each person lives in the protective shelter of a cocoon of his or her own spinning. This cocoon insulates the individual from the incessant communication babble that is steadily increasing in intensity. There are social barriers, age barriers, language or vocabulary barriers, and political and economic barriers. There is also the race barrier; the barriers and distortions that block communication are seen starkly in the gulf between racial and ethnic groups in the multicultural American society. There is peer pressure exerted within groups, where "reality" is shared and interpreted. There is also the often-overlooked barrier of the audience's ability or willingness to absorb messages. Finally, there is the constant roar of competition for people's attention in the noisy public arena. Barriers are not the only complications in communication, however.

People have impressions about everything that touches their consciousness. All people live in a world of their own symbols. Public figures, for example, during their lifetimes and afterward, are known partly through a personality created by images fixed in the public imagination. Astronauts, politicians, rock stars, and sports heroes are good examples. Their families and associates know them as people entirely different from their public personalities. People who live on one side of town tend to know people on the other side of town, as well as those in remote cities, in a half-fictional, half-imagined way. The only feeling that people can have about an event they do not experience or a person they do not know is by their own mental image of the event or person, developed from fragmentary, secondary sources.

In communication, nothing raises more problems than the reality that most mass media audiences have limited access to the facts. With limited access, and with some information tending to confuse as much as it clarifies, people rely heavily on *stereotypes*. Specific and significant impressions become generalities. As Lippmann pointed out, the "pictures in our head" derive mainly from what we see and hear in the mass media. Certainly our impressions of the war on terrorism in Iraq and Afghanistan, a nuclear plants in Iran and Syria, and riots in Tibet, as well as our stereotypes of the people in each situation, came from cable and network television, blogs and social media, newsmagazines, newspapers, and radio.

Incomplete and distorted stereotypes pose public relations problems. For example, a newly elected president of the California State Bar announced that she would make addressing negative and distorted public stereotypes of lawyers her highest priority. Unfortunately for lawyers everywhere, however, cartoonists took advantage of her announcement by exploiting stereotypes in a new rash of cartoons portraying lawyers as snakes, vultures, wolves, sharks, and so forth. The media help create new stereotypes by reducing complex people, groups, countries, and situations to their simplest and most general—sometimes distorted—attributes.

Lippmann emphasized the sacrosanct regard that people have for stereotypes as "the core of our personal tradition, the defense of our position in society."

> They may not be a complete picture of the world, but they are a picture of a possible world to which we are adapted. In that world people and things have their well-known places, and do certain expected things. We feel at home there. We fit in. We are members. We know the way around. . . . The stereotypes are, therefore, highly charged with the feelings that are attached to them. They are the fortress of our tradition, and behind its defenses we can continue to feel ourselves safe in the position we occupy.[28]

Stereotypes, then, serve as a defense mechanism against having to exert the effort required to learn about and understand the uniqueness and details of each person, group, and situation. They also form a moral code from which personal standards of behavior are derived. Practitioners must learn to recognize the influence and the presence of symbols and stereotypes in what appear to be the contradictions and contrariness of public opinion. Symbols are used to counter symbols, and stereotypes are used to counter stereotypes.

There is yet another side to stereotypes, however. In the context of a multicultural society, media are trying to be more sensitive and respectful of differences based on age, gender, sexual orientation, race, body shape, and ethnicity. Some criticize efforts to purge the language of stereotypes as yielding to the "politically correct language" movement. They say the movement is headed by the kind of "thought police" George Orwell warned us about. Others see eliminating words and phrases that are pejorative stereotypes as a way to promote acceptance of diversity and to make media content more inclusive and less offensive.[29] To avoid having the words themselves become a public relations problem, practitioners must be sensitive to word choice. As one writer put it, "[t]argeting a multicultural audience takes more than a dictionary—it takes tact, understanding, and relevance."[30]

Putting It All Together in a Campaign

The difficulty of public information campaigns can be clearly seen in the battle to save us from polluted air, polluted water, and chemically dangerous foods. America's pioneer ecologist, Aldo Leopold, in his early years said, "[I]f the public were told how much harm ensues from unwise land-use, it would mend its ways." In his twilight years, he knew that this conclusion was based on three mistaken assumptions: that the public is listening or can be made to listen; that the public responds, or can be made to respond, to fear of harm; and that ways can be mended without any important change in the public itself.[31]

In an often-quoted article, Hyman and Sheatsley codified the major reasons why many information campaigns fail. They include the following:

1. There exists a hard core of chronic "know-nothings." These people are difficult to reach, no matter what the level or nature of the information.

2. Interested people acquire the most information. Motivation is essential to learning or assimilating knowledge, yet there are large groups in the population who admit that they have little or no interest in public issues.

3. People seek information that is compatible with their prior attitudes and avoid exposure to that which is not compatible.

4. People interpret the same information differently. Selective perception and interpretation of content follows exposure: Persons perceive, absorb, and remember content differently.

5. Information does not necessarily change attitudes. Changes in views or behavior following exposure to a message may be differentially affected by the individual's initial predisposition.[32]

Another researcher, Harold Mendelsohn, countered with an analysis of why information campaigns can succeed:

What little empirical experience we have accumulated from the past suggests that public information campaigns have relatively high success potentials:

1. If they are planned around the assumption that most of the publics to which they will be addressed will be either only mildly interested or not at all interested in what is communicated.

2. If middle-range goals which can be reasonably achieved as a consequence of exposure are set as specific objectives. Frequently it is equally important either to set up or to utilize environmental support systems to help sheer information giving become effective in influencing behavior.

3. If, after middle-range objectives are set, careful consideration is given to delineating specific targets in terms of their demographic and psychological attributes, their life-style, value and belief systems, and mass media habits. Here, it is important not only to determine the scope of prior indifference, but to uncover its roots as well.[33]

That public information campaigns can succeed has been demonstrated by numerous campaigns against smoking in public places, the highly successful effort by Mothers Against Drunk Driving (MADD), the "Back to Sleep" campaign by the National Institute of Child Health and Human Development, and American Cancer Society efforts promoting cancer detection and prevention, to name but a few. The jury is still out on campaigns to prevent HIV infections, to reduce drug abuse, and to promote social tolerance. But, according to a Hopi maxim, however, "The one who tells the stories rules the world."[34]

Disseminating the Message

Gaining acceptance of an idea or an innovation is more than simply beaming it to an audience through a mass medium or internal publication. To illuminate, communication must be aimed with the precision of a laser beam, not cast in all directions in the manner of a lightbulb. Even after many years of research, there is still not definitive evidence of a single model of how ideas are disseminated among people. Elmo Roper, after nearly 30 years of opinion research, formulated a hypothesis that has some value as a guide. His concentric-circle theory says that ideas penetrate to the whole public very slowly through a process similar to osmosis. Histories of public campaigns substantiate this. They move out in concentric circles from great thinkers to great disciples to great disseminators to lesser disseminators to the politically active to the politically inert. This hypothesis assumes that American society can be stratified as indicated and emphasizes the importance of using opinion leaders in the public relations process.

The rate of flow in the transmission and acceptance of ideas, however, is governed by many factors other than the characteristics of the people involved. These include Lippmann's "barriers to communication" and George Gallup's "regulators of absorption rate" illustrated in Figure 13.4.

The communication step in the public relations process often requires influencing knowledge, opinions, and actions among sizable and distant groups. The accelerating rate at which innovations are being invented, developed, and spread makes it vital that communicators be able to transfer information to those who need it. Examples include gaining public acceptance of using sunscreen lotions to protect against skin cancer; overcoming fear of technology, such as programming a DVD player or paying bills online; and getting high-risk publics to get blood pressure checkups. And the rate of adopting new technology is accelerating: "(In 1997) 100 million people logged onto the Internet, up from 40 million the year before. That is faster than the phone, TV, and radio were adopted. When President Clinton took office [in 1992] there were only 50 Web sites. Now [in 1998] 65,000 are being added . . . every hour."[35] Never mind, by 2006 there were more than 70 million blogs worldwide and 175,000 blogs and 1.6 million new postings being added each day—almost 19 every second.[36] Of course, these data are also history by the time this book is published.

Diffusion refers to this process by which new ideas and practices are spread to members of a social system. The U.S. Department of Agriculture has been working at this task longer than most. It learned from experience that getting new ideas

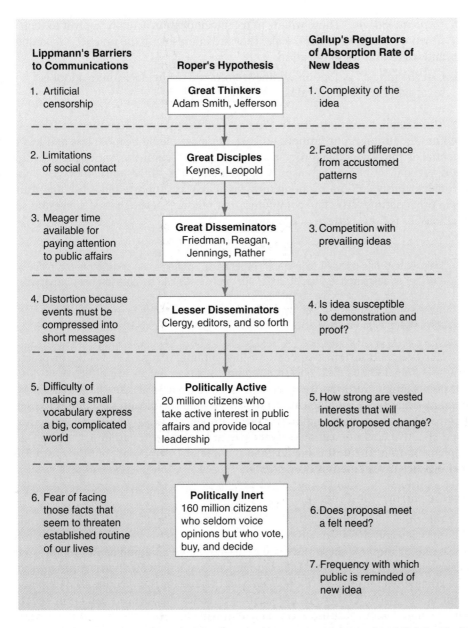

FIGURE 13.4

Communication Barriers and Dissemination

accepted involves more than simply discovering a new grain and publicizing it. It took 13 years to gain widespread adoption of hybrid seed corn on America's farms, for example. Out of their long experience and evaluation research, agricultural sociologists have concluded that acceptance goes through five stages:

1. *Knowledge.* People learn about an innovation and some gain understanding of what it is.

2. *Persuasion.* Potential adopters develop interest in the innovation. They seek more information and consider its general merits.

3. *Decision.* Potential adopters decide to adopt or reject the innovation after weighing its merits for their own situation.

4. *Implementation.* Those willing to try the innovation actually apply it to their situation, usually on a small scale. They are interested in the practice, techniques, and conditions for application.

5. *Confirmation.* Adoption is either reinforced or the decision to adopt is reversed based on the evaluation.[37]

Mass media have their greatest impact and usefulness in creating awareness in the knowledge stage. For farmers, at least, the mass media become less and less influential as the acceptance process advances toward confirmation of the adoption. Interpersonal influence increases with each step. This diffusion model, developed through extensive research among rural families, was supported in subsequent studies in other settings. The late communication scholar Steve Chaffee suggested several reasons for this pattern of diffusion:

> The media are comparatively rich in news content, whereas personal associates are likely to have had relevant "consumer" experience. Further, since consumption is partly a matter of defining one's social "self," other persons would be able to offer normative social guides to appropriate consumption patterns that the media cannot. Finally, some matters may not be dealt with by the media in sufficient depth or detail to satisfy personal information needs.[38]

Research conclusions demonstrate that communicating a new idea or practice can be a long, tedious task. Different communication tactics are effective at different points and in different ways. Influentials and opinion leaders have great power in many situations. Communicator must know what media and techniques to use at different stages and how to mobilize these influences effectively. In summary, however, effective communication is expensive in research, preparation, attention, and implementation. The cost is higher than is commonly supposed, but the cost of not making such investement is even greater.

Reconsidering the Process

The three elements common to all communication efforts are the source or sender, the message, and the destination or receiver. A communication breakdown can involve one or more of these three elements. Effective communication requires efficiency on the part of all three. The communicator must have *adequate information*. The communicator must have *credibility* in the eyes of the receiver. The communicator must be able to transmit information in codes the receiver can *comprehend*. The communicator must use a *channel* that will carry the message to the receiver. The message must be within the receiver's *capacity to comprehend* and be *relevant* to the receiver's interests or needs. Finally, the message must motivate the receiver's self-interest and cause a *response.*

Wise communicators see receivers not as passive subjects but as selective users of information for their own purposes. Too many public relations programs do not gauge the individual's role in the process. Public relations educator and scholar Doug Newsom says that practitioners should not use "the term 'audiences,' because it implies 'recipients' of messages instead of participants in communication."[39]

Words are symbols. There are words that serve as symbols for real objects—"table" and "chair"—thing words. There are words that are symbols of abstract ideas—such as "freedom" and "love"—nothing words. Children are taught, for example, that a furry little animal with long ears and a short, fuzzy tail is a "rabbit." Once the word and the little animal are associated, the word will always evoke the image of that creature. Word symbols for real objects are readily understood and agreed upon. This is not so with symbols for abstractions. Abstractions such as "pro-choice" or "pro-life" have no simple or universally accepted referents in the real world of objects. It is difficult for people to agree on an image of "free trade" when they cannot see, touch, hear, taste, or smell it. This difficulty goes right to the heart of the communication problem.

To communicate effectively, the sender's words and symbols must mean the same thing to the receiver that they do to the sender, a point made in Chapter 8. The word "communication" is derived from the Latin *communis*, meaning "common." So communication means establishing a sense of commonness. A sender can encode a message and a receiver decode it only in terms of their own experience and knowledge. But if there has been no common experience, then communication becomes virtually impossible. This explains a layperson's inability to understand an Einstein. It explains why—despite the tremendous flow of words to and from China—Americans and Chinese still have little understanding of each other.

Common knowledge and experience provide the connections. The greater the overlap in common interest and common experience, the easier it is to communicate. Many barriers impede achieving this overlap of commonness, but commonness in communication is essential to link people and purpose together in any cooperative system.

Public relations communication provides the climate for an action's acceptance and implementation, but it is only one element. For example, successful public campaigns against smoking, unsafe sex, drinking and driving, drug use, and careless use of fire in forests must be accompanied by action strategy that changes the problem situation and provides enforcement and social support.

Implementing the Strategy

The purpose of this chapter was to introduce some of the major considerations and principles of implementing public relations programs. However, entire books devoted to the topic cannot adequately cover the range of issues and practices related to putting the program in place. The chapter concludes with the venerable seven Cs of public relations communication:

1. *Credibility.* Communication starts with a climate of belief. This climate is built by performance on the part of the institution, reflecting an earnest desire to serve stakeholders and publics. Receivers must have confidence in the sender and high regard for the source's competence on the subject.

2. *Context.* A communications program must square with the realities of its environment. Mass media only supplement the words and deeds of daily living. The context must provide for participation and playback. It must confirm, not contradict, the message. Effective communication requires a supportive social environment, one largely set by the news media.

3. *Content.* The message must have meaning for receivers, and it must be compatible with their value system. It must have relevance to the receivers' situation. In general, people select those items of information that promise them the greatest rewards. The content determines the audience.

4. *Clarity.* The message must be put in simple terms. Words must mean the same to the receivers as to the sender. Complex issues must be compressed into themes, slogans, or stereotypes that have simplicity and clarity. The farther a

message has to travel, the simpler it must be. An organization must speak with one voice, not many voices.

5. *Continuity* and *consistency.* Communication is an unending process. It requires repetition to achieve penetration. Repetition—with variation—contributes to both learning and persuasion. The story must be consistent.

6. *Channels.* Established channels of communication should be used, channels that receivers use and respect. Creating new ones can be difficult, time consuming, and expensive. Different channels have different effects and serve effectively in different stages of the diffusion process. Selective channels are called for in reaching target publics. People associate different values with the many channels of communication.

7. *Capability of the audience.* Communication must take into account the capability of the audience. Communications are most effective when they require the least effort on the part of receivers. This involves factors of availability, habits, reading ability, and prior knowledge.

Communication and action are not the ends, but only the means to ends. The ends of public relations are the outcomes spelled out in program goals and objectives. Assessing the effectiveness of program strategy—the fourth step—is the topic of the next chapter.

Notes

[1] Harold Burson speech to Raymond Simon Institute for Public Relations, Utica College, Syracuse University, March 5, 1987.

[2] Jarol B. Manheim, *The Death of a Thousand Cuts* (Mahwah, NJ: Lawrence Erlbaum Associates, 2001), 308.

[3] "Wild Horse and Burro Management," Bureau of Land Management. 29 April 2007, http://www.blm.gov/wo/st/en/prog/wild_horse_and_burro.print.html.

[4] Don Etling, senior vice president, Fleishman-Hillard, quoted in Craig McGuire, "From the Top Down: A Sturdy Reputation Program Requires Buy-In from All Parts of a Corporation," *PRWeek* (January 19, 2004): 17.

[5] Norman R. Nager and T. Harrell Allen, *Public Relations Management by Objectives* (Lanham, MD: University Press of America, 1984), 241–42. (Originally published by Longman.)

[6] Caron Chess, Michal Tamuz, Alex Saville, and Michael Greenberg, "Reducing Uncertainty and Increasing Credibility: The Case of Sybron Chemicals Inc.," *Industrial Crisis Quarterly* 6, no. 1 (1992): 55–70.

[7] PINS Hotline is the registered trademark for the Prompt Inquiry and Notification System of the Environmental Affairs Institute, Inc., Edison, NJ.

[8] Public Relations Society of America, "1990 Silver Anvil Winners: Index and Summaries," New York, 1990, 1–2.

[9] Christine S. Foschetti, Edison, NJ, correspondence to the author, July 15, 1993.

[10] Daniel J. Boorstin, *The Image: A Guide to Pseudo-Events in America* (New York: Atheneum Publishers, 1961), 17. A 25th-anniversary edition of this classic was published in 1987 and published again as a "First Vintage Books Edition" in 1992.

[11] Ibid., 11.

[12] James E. Grunig, "Communication, Public Relations, and Effective Organizations: An Overview of the Book," in *Excellence in Public Relations and Communication Management*, ed. James E. Grunig (Hillsdale, NJ: Lawrence Erlbaum Associates, 1992), 18–19.

[13] A. C. Croft, "Delayed Action Allows Informed Response," *Public Relations Journal* 48, no. 5 (May 1992): 31.

[14] Eugene F. Lane, "Applied Behavioral Science," *Public Relations Journal* 23, no. 7 (July 1967): 6.

[15] Randy Hines and Joe Basso, "Do Editors a Favor: Use '*The Associated Press Stylebook*,'" *PR Tactics* (February 2003): 16.

[16] Ibid.; Sara Calabro, "Get the Smarts: Using Multimedia Releases," *PRWeek* (November 3, 2003): 26.

[17] Adapted from Brian S. Brooks, George Kennedy, Daryl R. Moen, and Don Ranly, *News Reporting and Writing*, 3rd ed. (New York: St. Martin's Press, 1988); and Brian S. Brooks, James L. Pinson, and Jean Gaddy Wilson, *Working with Words: A Handbook for Media Writers and Editors*, 6th ed. (Boston, MA: Bedford/St. Martin's, 2006), 310.

[18] Pamela J. Shoemaker, *Gatekeeping: Communication Concepts* 3 (Newbury Park, CA: Sage Publications, 1991), 50–52.

[19] For a detailed description of the James Hardie case, see Gwyneth Howell and Rohan Miller, "Spinning Out the Asbestos Agenda: How Big Business Uses Public Relations in Australia," *Public Relations Review* 32, no. 3 (September 2006): 261–266.

[20] James B. Lemert and Marguerite Gemson Ashman, "Extent of Mobilizing Information in Opinion and News Magazines," *Journalism Quarterly* 60, no. 4 (Winter 1983): 657–62.

[21] Clay Schoenfeld, "Thirty Seconds to Live," *Writer's Market*, February 1977, p. 29.

[22] Alex Wang, "Priming, Framing, and Position on Corporate Social Responsibility," *Journal of Public Relations Research* 19, no. 2 (2007): 124.

[23] Ibid., 143.

[24] Jiyang Bae and Glen T. Cameron, "Conditioning Effect of Prior Reputation on Perception of Corporate Giving," *Public Relations Review* 32, no. 2 (June 2006): 149.

[25] Walter Lippmann, *Public Opinion* (New York: Harcourt, Brace, 1922), 81.

[26] Smokey's history is summarized in *Public Communication Campaigns*, 2nd ed., edited by Ronald E. Rice and Charles K. Atkin (Newbury Park, CA: Sage Publications, 1989), 215–18.

[27] Jason Edward Black, "The 'Mascotting' of Native America: Construction, Commodity, and Assimilation," *American Indian Quarterly* 26:4 (2002): 605–622.

[28] Lippmann, *Public Opinion*, 95–96.

[29] Natasha Spring, "Freedom of Speech vs. Politically Correct Language," *Communication World* 9, no. 5 (April 1992): 34–38.

[30] Julia Hood, "Good Translations," *PRWeek* (August 18, 2003): 13.

[31] For the story of Leopold's career as an innovator and environmentalist, see Susan Flader, *Thinking Like a Mountain* (Columbia: University of Missouri Press, 1974).

[32] Herbert H. Hyman and Paul B. Sheatsley, "Some Reasons Why Information Campaigns Fail," *Public Opinion Quarterly* 11 (1947): 412–23.

[33] Harold Mendelsohn, "Why Information Campaigns Can Succeed," *Public Opinion Quarterly* 37 (Spring 1973): 50–61.

[34] Randolph Baker, "Calls for 'Reform' of Indian Gaming Present Strategic PR Challenge for Tribes with Casinos," *The Public Relations Strategist* 13, no. 3 ((Summer 2007): 61.

[35] William M. Daley, Secretary, U.S. Department of Commerce, Washington, DC, April 15, 1998, as quoted in *Collective Destiny* 2, no. 2 (April 1998): 1. *Collective Destiny* is a publication of the Japan–U.S. Telecommunications Research Institute, San Diego State University.

[36] John V. Pavlik, "Mapping the Consequences of Technology on Public Relations." Published by the Institute for Public Relations (September 2007), p. 6. Available online at http://www.instituteforpr.org.

[37] Everett M. Rogers, *Diffusion of Innovations*, 3rd ed. (New York: Free Press, 1983).

[38] Steven H. Chaffee, "The Interpersonal Context of Communication," in *Current Perspectives in Mass Communication Research*, ed. F. Gerald Kline and Phillip J. Tichenor (Beverly Hills, CA: Sage Publications, 1972), 103.

[39] Doug Newsom, Texas Christian University, as quoted in *pr reporter* 36, no. 17 (April 26, 1993): 4.

Additional Sources

Bivins, Thomas. *Public Relations Writing: The Essentials of Style and Format*, 5th ed. New York: McGraw-Hill, 2004. One of several good how-to books on preparing public relations and publicity materials—writing—based on a strategic plan.

Breakenridge, Deirdre. *PR 2.0: New Media, New Tools, New Audiences.* Upper Saddle River, NJ: Pearson Education/FT Press, 2008. Discusses social media tools available to public relations practitioners working primarily in the marketing context.

Carstarphen, Meta G., and Richard A. Wells. *Writing PR: A Multimedia Approach*. Boston: Pearson/Allyn & Bacon, 2004. Instructs on writing and designing messages for many media.

Guth, David, and Bonnie Poovey Short. *Strategic Writing: Multimedia Writing for Public Relations, Advertising and More*, 2nd ed. Boston, MA: Pearson/Allyn & Bacon, 2009. New edition updates user-friendly approach to writing across the disciplines.

Holtz, Shel. *Public Relations on the Net*, 2nd ed. New York: American Management Association, 2002. Looks at the impact of new technologies on communication with various stakeholders.

Newsom, Doug, and Jim Haynes. *Public Relations Writing: Form and Style*, 7th ed. Belmont, CA: Wadsworth, 2004. Instructs how to prepare and present information in the wide variety of public relations media.

Wilcox, Dennis L. *Public Relations Writing and Media Techniques*, 5th ed. Boston, MA: Pearson/Allyn & Bacon, 2005. Addresses a wide range of public relations writing assignments, including advertising, special events, conferences, meetings, and audiovisual presentations.

14

Step Four: Evaluating the Program

STUDY GUIDE   After studying Chapter 14, you should be able to:

▶ Define formative and summative evaluation research.

▶ Discuss how research is used to evaluate the preparation, implementation, and impact phases of public relations programs.

▶ Outline the recommended steps for conducting evaluation research.

▶ Outline the criteria used in evaluating the preparation, implementation, and impact phases of public relations programs.

▶ List and describe research methods commonly used for evaluating public relations programs.

N o topic dominates the practice as does program evaluation—the final step in the process. But not all practitioners "walk the talk," because systematic measurement and research lag behind practitioner interest in and rhetoric about program evaluation.

Increasingly, practitioners are being asked to document measurable results and returns from public relations programs compared with costs to demonstrate "return on investment" (ROI). Or, to paraphrase one practitioner, "The heat is on to meet the numbers." Public relations, like other staff and line functions, is being evaluated by how much it contributes to advancing the organization's mission and achieving organizational goals. Executives in all types of organizations, from the largest corporations to the smallest nonprofit groups, ask for evidence of program *impact*—particularly when old budgets are reviewed or new budgets are negotiated, when organizations are downsized to be more competitive, or when new management reviews and restructures operations and priorities.

The Push for Measurable Results

Top management's "results orientation" and "the heat to meet the numbers" account for much of the increased use of evaluation research to track program progress and to measure impact. Many executives look with suspicion at claims not supported with data. As Opinion Factor, Inc., CEO Richard Kuchinsky says, "One of the single most important steps in developing a communication

When you can measure what you are speaking about, and express it in numbers, you know something about it. But when you cannot measure it, when you cannot express it in numbers, your knowledge is of a meager and unsatisfactory kind.
—Lord Kelvin,[1]
British physicist

Evaluation is not simply a postmortem exercise but an ongoing process and a means for managing continual improvement in public relations.
—Mark Weiner,[2]
Public relations research executive

This chapter was written in collaboration with **Jim Macnamara**, Ph.D., FPRIA, Professor of Public Communication and Director of the Australian Centre for Public Communication, University of Technology, Sydney. Dr Macnamara has had a 30-year career in journalism, public relations, and research practice. Before taking his academic post in 2007, he was Group Research Director for Media Monitors and CARMA Asia Pacific and continues as a research consultant with the group.

program is to first conduct benchmark research and then track the program's effectiveness with follow-up studies."[3]

More sophisticated use of measurable outcome criteria in public relations objectives (see the "Management by Objectives" section of Chapter 12) also makes it possible to measure program impact. Few practitioners get by with the claim that program impact cannot be measured. The oft-used excuse that "it's intangible" is not supported when the financial and accounting sectors now measure "brand value," "goodwill," and "reputation" for the balance sheet. The trap of the "intangible" view is shown in the following exchange:

> We can't measure the results of public relations the way you measure other things.
>
> *Why not?*
>
> They're intangible. You can't actually see the results of public relations.
>
> *Why should I pay you for something that can't be detected—what you call "intangible results"?*
>
> Because public relations is different and can't be held to the same performance standards as other departments.
>
> *Well, OK. Here's your money.*
>
> Where? I don't see any money.
>
> *Of course not. It can't be detected—it's what you call "intangible."*

Knowledge outcomes, predisposition changes, and behavior can be measured. So what excuse justifies not knowing if the action and communication strategies are making progress toward achieving program objectives? What justifies not documenting how the program worked? What justifies not being able to say whether or not the problem has been solved?

Concurrent with increased interest in evaluation is rapid development of supportive literature. For example, Sage Publications has become the leading publisher of books and journals devoted to the general field of evaluation research. At least four books address using research in public relations programs.[4] *Public Relations Review* devoted entire issues to the topic.[5] Both the *Public Relations Review* and *Journal of Public Relations Research* periodically publish scholarly articles related to evaluation research. *Public Relations Tactics*, as well as *Communication World*, *PRWeek*, and *Public Relations Quarterly* regularly publish research and evaluation how-to features for practitioners. The International Public Relations Association published a Gold Paper on Evaluation.[6] The Institute for Public Relations in the United States regularly publishes articles and research papers on evaluation of public relations available free on its Web site (www.instituteforpr.org) and stages the annual Summit on Measurement. So lack of available published guidance is not a defense for not using research.

This body of literature serves as the basis for evaluation research courses now taught at many universities and included in a growing number of public relations curricula. As noted in Chapter 5, the Commission on Undergraduate Public Relations Education identified research for planning and evaluation as one of the five areas of study in the core curriculum.

Among senior practitioners, however, there are many who did not study research methods and even some who question whether research and evaluation are necessary. A 2001 Public Relations Society of America Internet survey of 4,200 members found "gut feel/intuition" was cited by 50 percent of practitioners as the second most frequently used method for planning and measuring results during the preceding two years, after press clippings, which were the leading method of measurement relied on by 82 percent of practitioners. Media content analysis was used by about one-third, with many citing advertising value equivalents ("AVEs") as a key metric. Surveys and focus groups were used by less than 25 percent of PRSA members, according to the survey.[7]

Some clients, some line managers, and even some public relations practitioners still do not budget for research or see research as an integral part of the process. One study of practitioners found that only 53 percent of respondents budgeted for public relations measurement programs, and 57 percent of those surveyed used only informal methods to measure the effectiveness of their work.[8] It seems that many practitioners are content with counting their media clips, according to many who work in public relations. If they feel it's working, they don't want to spend the money to find out otherwise. The trend is clear, however, as more are budgeting for research because top management is asking them to be more accountable.

An encouraging trend is that research is increasingly vital to firms seeking new business accounts. The ability to document baseline data and subsequent results gives firms a competitive edge. In short, good research is fundamental, not an extra. As practitioner Gary Barton, Monsanto Company (St. Louis), put it:

> In general, public relations people are being asked more and more by either their management or their clients to justify the expenditures for a project or the program. For example, after spending $200,000 or whatever for a program, they ask, "Did that change people's minds? Do they think differently now? Are they more aware of the company?" In other words, did it accomplish the objectives you said you were going to accomplish? That is the evaluative use of research at the end of the program. Without research, it is much harder to show results.[9]

An increasing number of public relations firms build evaluation research into the services they offer clients, either using their own staff, those of a research subsidiary, or those of a contractor. "Outsourcing" is a popular approach as most public relations firms do not staff a telephone survey center or keep data-entry specialists on payroll, choosing instead to contract with outside research firms to do most of their data gathering and compilation. Also, some research requires expertise that may not be present in a public relations department or consultancy firm.

Research firms such as CARMA International, Cision, Echo Research, Millward Brown Précis, and a growing number of others have staff trained in content analysis and familiar with quantitative and qualitative research methodology and statistics. Others such as Biz360, CyberAlert, Cymfony, and Vocus have expertise and sophisticated tools for searching and retrieving content from the Internet. Survey research firms in all major markets provide focus group and survey research capabilities to gather data to help evaluate programs. For example, Opinion Factor, Inc., in Murray, Utah, staffs "call centers" to conduct telephone surveys (see Figure 14.1).

In addition to acquiring expertise without having to employ full-time specialists internally, another benefit of using an independent research firm is the objectivity that a "third party" can bring to the research. Usually free from real or perceived vested interests (but not necessarily all), the findings of an independent researcher or research company can be viewed as more credible by management than are findings that practitioners present about their own work. Nevertheless, practitioners can use a range of do-it-yourself as well as outsourced research methods to gather information to help evaluate programs.

FIGURE 14.1
Telephone Survey Call
Center

Courtesy Opinion Factor, Inc.,
Murray, Utah.

Evaluation Research Process

As discussed in Chapter 11, research should be conducted for strategic planning, managing, and evaluating public relations programs. Research conducted before and during implementation to inform planning and program adjustment is called *formative* research. Research conducted postprogram to assess progress and to document program impact is called *summative* research. Others broadly refer to research conducted to evaluate public relations programs as "evaluation research" or simply as "measurement," which has become an industry buzzword.[10]

Evaluation researchers distinguish among the related terms *evaluation, measurement,* and *research:*

1. **Evaluation**—which literally means to determine the value of something—often refers to measurement conducted postprogram. But evaluation can and ideally should be conducted at multiple points throughout public relations programs. Evaluation can be carried out for a proposal, plan, or idea; or to identify current awareness levels *before* implementation of a program begins. Likewise, evaluation can be conducted *during* a program to assess progress and interim results. Thus, evaluation is not a single step *after* programs have been completed, but a process that can and should run throughout a program.

   Similarly, formative and summative research, while being separately identified because of their different objectives, are not discreet stand-alone activities; rather they are most effectively interconnected. Formative research obtains *benchmark* measures that are vital for evaluation as well as information to assist planning; summative research informs future strategic planning as well as evaluating current program activities. Much research is both formative and summative in that it helps guide planning and evaluation aspects of a program.

2. **Measurement**—while often used as a synonym for evaluation—refers specifically to the process of taking a measure of some defined criteria or phenomena. Measurement is part of both formative and summative research and is part of

evaluation. Without reliable measures, both planning and evaluation cannot be conducted with any precision.

3. **Research**—meaning conducting measurement in a systematic and controlled process that employs generally accepted standards of scientific inquiry—stands in sharp contrast to nonresearch approaches such as practitioner opinion ("gut feel"), casual observation, and anecdotal reports.

Rossi and Freeman used the terms "evaluation research" and "evaluation" interchangeably to represent "the systematic application of social research procedures for assessing the conceptualization, design, implementation, and utility of social intervention programs."[11] This definition emphasizes the focus of evaluation on the preparation, implementation, and impact of public relations programs. Furthermore, it explains the various stages by outlining the basic questions posed in evaluation:

Program conceptualization and design

What is the extent and distribution of the target problem and/or population?

Is the program designed in conformity with intended goals; is there a coherent rationale underlying it; and have chances of successful delivery been maximized?

What are projected or existing costs, and what is their relation to benefits and effectiveness?

Monitoring and accountability of program implementation

Is the program reaching the specified target population or target area?

Are the intervention efforts being conducted as specified in the program design?

Assessment of program utility: Impact and efficiency

Is the program effective in achieving its intended goals?

Can the results of the program be explained by some alternative process that does not include the program?

Is the program having some effects that were not intended?

What are the costs to deliver services and benefits to program participants?

Is the program an efficient use of resources, compared with alternative uses of the resources?[12]

Another important point to note is that evaluation research should be used to learn what happened and why, not to prove or justify something already done or decided. For example, one organization set up an evaluation project for the sole purpose of justifying the firing of its senior communication officer. In other cases, evaluation research is done by public relations and communication staff with a predetermined objective of supporting their decisions and programs. True evaluation research is done to gather information honestly and objectively to provide data for decision making with an open mind. "Symbolic" evaluation, on the other hand, is conducted to provide managers with supportive data from what can be called "pseudoresearch."[13]

Program managers use pseudoresearch for three reasons:

1. *Organizational politics:* Research is used solely to gain power, justify decisions already made, or serve as a scapegoat.
2. *Service promotion:* Pseudoresearch is undertaken, often in a slanted way, to promote products or services and impress clients or prospects.

3. *Personal satisfaction:* Pseudoresearch is done as an ego-bolstering activity to keep up with fads or to demonstrate acquired skills.[14]

In the long haul, these spurious efforts are self-defeating.

Overcoming Obstacles to Evaluation

Many practitioners profess good intentions to evaluate their programs, but fail in the face of what they see as insurmountable obstacles.

Industry research has identified the most commonly cited reasons for not conducting evaluation as cost (lack of budget) and lack of time. Although evaluation requires some degree of both, these are really just excuses, not reasons for carrying out evaluation. Walter Lindenmann says practitioners with limited budgets can and should "consider piggyback studies, secondary analysis, quick-tab polls, Internet surveys, or intercept interviews. Mail, fax, and e-mail studies are good for some purposes. Or, do your own field research."[15] First, outsourcing the work to outside vendors can reduce the time input of internal public relations staff to project briefing and supervision. Alternatively, if budget is not available for outsourcing and time is short, there are quick basic methods of evaluation research available that can provide the "best available evidence," as discussed in Chapter 11.

This is not to suggest that there are not obstacles or barriers to evaluation. Clearly there are—otherwise most or all practitioners would be carrying out evaluation, given the growing demand for accountability within management and competition for budget. The following barriers need to be overcome before practitioners can reach a position of being ready and able to implement program evaluation.

1. *Understanding communication, media effects theory, and audience effects.* There is not scope within this chapter to review the vast amount of research on communication, media effects, and audience effects. It has been shown that media and communication have impacts and effects in societies and in markets, such as the media's agenda-setting role discussed in Chapter 8. But it is important to note that early "injection" thinking based on transmission models of communication no longer hold currency for human communication. Messages are not simply transmitted from a sender via a medium to a receiver.[16] In reality, audiences ignore, reject, misinterpret, and reinterpret messages in various ways. A large body of research shows that *impact* cannot be assumed simply because information is disseminated to audiences. It is natural for professional communicators to be confident and enthusiastic about communication. But overcoming assumptions about audience impact and effects is fundamental to embracing and implementing program evaluation. Only then is evaluation seen as essential to identify what is working and what is not.

2. *Understanding the difference between processes (effort and outputs) and outcomes (impact and effects).* One of the major obstacles observed in reviewing public relations plans and program reports is that what are listed as "results" are often *outputs*—that is, what has been disseminated or implemented. Commonly, practitioners mistake the number of news releases distributed, the number of media clippings gained, the number of attendees at events, and so on as the end point of a program and markers of success. Even a cursory reflection reveals that these are not end points, but means to an end. This confusion is an obstacle to program evaluation in that it focuses evaluation on interim processes and fails to address the more important level of *outcomes*. This important distinction was brought home poignantly by former Microsoft senior executive Daniel Petre, when he was presented with a detailed report of a public relations firm's activities and output, and said: "I don't care how much work you have done and how much stuff you have put out. I want to know what impact you have had and what value you have contributed to our business."[17]

3. *Having "SMART" objectives.* Another major obstacle that prevents evaluation is program objectives that are broad and imprecise. Objectives need to be specific, measurable, achievable, realistic, and time-bound. Some replace "realistic" in the SMART acronym with "relevant," meaning objectives must be relevant to and aligned with the organization's overall goals and mission. A simple example such as "To increase awareness of ABC Corporation" is not SMART. Why? Because it does not identify what level of awareness exists now, among whom, by how much it is to be increased, or by when. A SMART version of this objective could be: "To increase awareness of ABC Corporation's emergence from bankruptcy from X percent to Y percent among financial analysts who track the industry group within the next 2 months." (Review Chapter 12's section on "Management by Objectives.")

4. *Being numeric as well as rhetorical.* It is a simple occupational characteristic that most public relations practitioners are educated and trained in arts and humanities. In broad terms, they deal in rhetoric—not in the colloquial sense of false words but in the Greek tradition of words used to inform and persuade. Few are numerically oriented. Conversely, studies show that management ranks are dominated by executives with numeric backgrounds, coming from fields such as accountancy and finance, sales and marketing, engineering, and so on. There is no easy way to address this, but practitioners need to learn basic skills in research to generate and present data to inform, support, test, and manage their programs.

To help overcome obstacles and secure management support for evaluation research, public relations managers must implement the following 10 steps:

1. *Establish agreement on the uses and purposes of the evaluation.* Without such agreement, research often produces volumes of unused and often useless data. Commit to paper the problem, concern, or question that motivates the research effort. Next, detail how research findings will be used. Such statements are doubly important when outside research specialists are hired to avoid buying "canned" or "off-the-shelf" services.

2. *Secure organizational commitment to evaluation* and make research basic to the program. Evaluation cannot be tacked on as an afterthought. Build research into the entire process, with sufficient resources to make it central to the problem definition, planning and programming, implementation, and evaluation steps.

3. *Develop consensus on using evaluation research within the department.* Even practitioners not eager to trade in their notions of public relations as intangible must be part of the effort. They have to accept the concept of evaluation research long enough to give the process time to work and must feel secure that research will not replace completely the lessons and insight gained from experience.

4. *Write program objectives in observable and measurable terms.* Without measurable outcomes specified in the program objectives, evaluation research

cannot be designed to evaluate program impact. If an objective cannot be evaluated, it is not useful. The evaluation imperative forces clarity and precision in the planning process, particularly when writing specific objectives for each of the target publics.

5. *Select the most appropriate criteria.* Objectives spell out intended outcomes. If increasing awareness of an organization's support of local charities is stated in an objective, for example, then column inches and favorable mentions in the media are inappropriate measures of the knowledge outcome sought. Identify what changes in knowledge, opinions, attitudes, and behaviors are specified in the objectives before gathering evidence. The same applies when the program seeks to maintain existing levels of desired states. (Review the "Writing Program Objectives" section of Chapter 12.)

6. *Determine the best way to gather evidence.* Surveys are not always the best way to find out about program impact. Sometimes organizational records contain the evidence needed. In other cases, a field experiment or case study may be the only way to test and evaluate a program. There is no single right way to gather data for evaluations. The method used depends on (1) the question and purposes motivating the evaluation; (2) the outcome criteria specified in the objectives; and (3) the cost of research resulting from the complexity of the program, setting, or both.

7. *Keep complete program records.* Program strategies and materials are real-world expressions of practitioners' working theories of cause and effect. Complete documentation helps identify what worked and what did not work. Records help reduce the impact of selection perception and personal bias when reconstructing the interventions and events that contributed to program success or failure.

8. *Use evaluation findings to manage the program.* Each cycle of the program process can be more effective than the preceding cycle if the results of evaluation are used to make adjustments. Problem statements and situation analyses should be more detailed and precise with the addition of new evidence from the evaluation. Revised goals and objectives should reflect what was learned. Action and communication strategies can be continued, fine-tuned, or discarded on the basis of knowledge of what did and did not work.

9. *Report evaluation results to management.* Develop a procedure for regularly reporting to line and staff managers. Documented results and adjustments based on evidence illustrate that public relations is being managed to contribute to achieving organizational goals. Evaluation also helps demonstrate how public relations contributes to the organization's "bottom line."

10. *Add to professional knowledge.* Scientific management of public relations leads to greater understanding of the process and its effects. Most program evaluation tend to be organization- and time-specific, but some findings are cross-situational. For example, findings about how many employees learned about a proposed reorganization from an article may be relevant only to that one article and organization. On the other hand, learning that employees want more information about organizational plans not only provides guidance for future issues of a particular newsletter but also may apply in other organizations. Sharing with colleagues the knowledge gained from relevant research distinguishes the professional practice from the aggregate of technical crafts practiced under the public relations rubric.

The evaluation process is not new; the need has long been recognized. To illustrate, here is what an early publicity specialist, Evart G. Routzahn, told the 1920 National Conference of Social Work:

> After the returns are all in—when the last meeting has been held, the final distribution or printed matter made, and all activities of the immediate effort have been recorded as history—is the time to put yourself and your methods through the third degree . . . with prayerful solicitude that you will be able to untangle the lessons to be applied to the next project.[18]

His counsel has only recently been fully accepted—if not always applied—in public relations, even though its merit has long been obvious.

Levels of Program Evaluation

Evaluation means different things to different practitioners. To some it is a letter from the boss or client complimenting the writing and photographs in a new brochure. To others, it is an award such as a Public Relations Society of America Silver Anvil trophy, an IABC Gold Quill Award, an International Public Relations Association (IPRA) Golden World Award, or similar recognitions from the Public Relations Institutes of the United Kingdom, Australia, Singapore, Malaysia, China, or wherever. To some it is clippings from newspapers around the world. To others the only meaningful evaluations are scientific measures of increased awareness, or changed opinions, attitudes, and behaviors. To those concerned about public policy or social problems, only evidence of economic, political, or social change satisfies their requirements for program evaluation. In fact, all these represent different levels of program evaluation.

Some researchers and public relations academics group these levels into stages of evaluation—*inputs, outputs,* and *outcomes.*[19] Tom Watson, who authored a book on evaluation of public relations with Paul Noble in the United Kingdom, refers to four stages—*inputs, outputs, impact,* and *effects*—in his "Unified Evaluation Model."[20] A high degree of consistency is evident in the various models of evaluation. In particular, all best-practice approaches recommend conducting evaluation in three stages: (1) preparation/inputs, (2) implementation/outputs, and (3) impact/outcomes/effects.

This approach does not make program evaluation more difficult or more time-consuming. To the contrary, it breaks evaluation into manageable stages. Also, very importantly, it breaks program evaluation into a strategically important sequence. If evaluation is skipped during the planning stage of a program or during the implementation stage, the chance of impact in line with desired objectives is much reduced. Early level 1 and level 2 evaluations often pick up problems that can be rectified, or identify opportunities that can be exploited.

Figure 14.2 shows the levels of program evaluation based on the **preparation, implementation**, and **impact** program phases.[21] The sequence represents typical, but not all, program elements or steps leading to problem resolution and social change.

Each phase in program evaluation contributes to increased understanding and adds information for assessing effectiveness. **Preparation evaluation** assesses the quality and adequacy of the information used to develop the program strategy and tactics. **Implementation evaluation** monitors the effort and progress as the program unfolds. **Impact evaluation** documents the consequences of the program

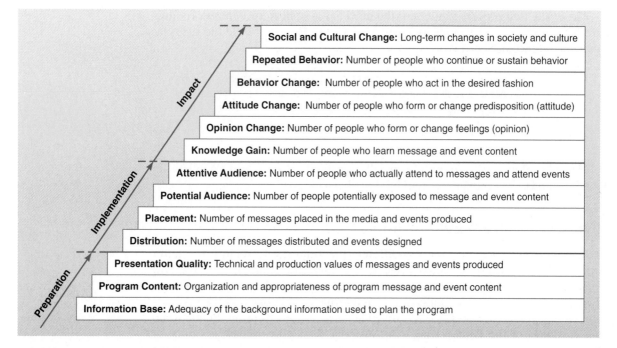

FIGURE 14.2

Phases and Levels for Evaluating Public Relations Programs

and provides feedback on the extent to which objectives and goals were achieved. No evaluation is complete without addressing criteria at each level.

A common error in program evaluation is substituting measures from one phase for those at another level. This is most clearly illustrated when practitioners use the number of news releases sent, brochures distributed, or meetings held (implementation efforts) to document alleged program effectiveness (impact). Or if asked to document program impact, they substitute publicity placements in the form of column inches or airtime, or Web site visits in terms of time spent and links chosen, for the changes in target publics' knowledge, predisposition, and behavior spelled out in program objectives. Evaluation researchers refer to this as the "substitution game." Somewhat analogously, magicians talk of "misdirecting" audience attention from what is really happening in order to create an illusion.

Preparation Criteria and Methods

Information Base.   During a program, practitioners periodically find that vital information was missing from the original situation analysis. Done systematically and recorded, this assessment represents an evaluation of the **adequacy of the background information** used for planning the program. Were key publics missed in the original determination of stakeholder groups? What assumptions about the publics proved to be in error? Did journalists request information that was not readily available in the background packet or fact book? What last-minute crises called for additional research and organization of information? Had all the key actors in the situation been identified? In effect, this part of the evaluation assesses the adequacy of the information gathering and intelligence steps in the preparation phase of the process.

Program Content.   The second step in evaluation addresses the **organization and appropriateness of program and message content**. Critical review of what is being said and what is being done occurs before implementation. Assessing the appropriateness of messages and program content with the advantage of hindsight gives guidance for future program efforts. For example, *pretesting* the content of brochures, Web sites, speeches, video scripts, and other materials can identify early on if it is appropriate to the target public. It goes without saying that this review should be done with the motivation of constructive criticism.

In politics campaign planners study their candidate's statements in blogs, speeches, and televised debates in light of media reactions and voter responses in follow-up polls. Did program message content match the problems, objectives, and media? Were communications accurate, timely, and appropriate for the intended publics? Were there adverse reactions to messages or actions? Did the events, corrective actions, and other activities support the program effort? Was enough done? Did the communication capitalize on and complement the action components of the program? Were staff and budget adequate for the task? This phase of the evaluation calls for a review of how well the program matches the demands of the situation.

Content analysis of materials produced, speeches and other presentations, as well as the "messages" communicated by activities and special events also provides information for determining the extent to which program content addresses the objectives spelled out for target publics and the overall program goal. Practitioners also use the results of content analyses of media coverage during the preparation stage. If certain media have been critical of an issue, these media may need to be targeted with a briefing or additional information. If some media on a target media list have never reported on a certain topic, alternative media with an interest in the subject may need to be targeted with the desired message content. (Content analysis will be explained in more detail under "Implementation Criteria and Methods.")

Presentation Quality.   Assessing the **technical and production values** of messages and other program elements constitutes the final step of preparation evaluation. Many professional societies' awards programs employ criteria from this step. The "best" annual report, the "most effective" overall program, and even the "outstanding" professional often are picked on the basis of style, format, and presentation of program materials. Best graphic design, best Web site, or best multimedia presentation are but three of dozens of award categories judged on the basis of production values and presentation merit. These often are the attributes that writing courses and professional workshops emphasize. This step in program evaluation considers the *quality* of professional performance in light of conventional wisdom and consensus among practitioners as to what is good and bad technique. Presentation quality is not judged by subjective criteria alone, however.

Readability tests are sometimes used to objectively assess message preparation. These tests, however, take into account only the approximate ease with which printed material can be read and comprehended; they do not consider the content, format, organization, and other elements of writing style. These factors, coupled with an understanding of what writers bring to their writing and readers bring to their reading, all shape the reception and impact of printed words. If used with this perspective in mind, readability tests are useful guides for making copy more readable and for increasing comprehension.

For example, the *Gunning Formula* is one commonly used method for measuring readability. Robert Gunning's Fog Index measures reading difficulty based on average sentence length and the percentage of words with three or more syllables.[22] The index is based on the number of whole sentences in at least two samples of text containing 100 words. Divide the number of words in the sentences by the number of whole sentences. Next, count the number of words with three or more syllables (but not counting capitalized words; those ending in "es" or "ed"; and those that combine simple words, such as *heretofore*). Enter the counts into the following formula.

$$\text{Fog Index} = 0.04 \times (\text{average number of words per sentence} + \text{number of long words per 100 words})$$

The Fog Index indicates the number of years of education needed to find copy easy to read (see Table 14.1).

Irving Fang's Easy Listening Formula (ELF) provides a comparable measure for estimating the "listenability" of broadcast copy, speeches, and other scripts. In fact, ELF scores correlate highly with print readability scores. Simply calculate the average number of syllables (above one per word) in sentences. The ELF score represents the approximate grade level required to follow and easily understand what is being said. Fang found that good television news copy averages below 12 on the ELF.[23]

Readability and listenability scores provide only rough indicators of how comprehensible messages are to target publics. Jargon, technical terms, and even dialect may make written material difficult to understand even when the Gunning or Fang indices indicate otherwise. These measures can help writers gauge the extent to which their copy matches audience needs for easy-to-read-and-understand messages. The measures simply give quantitative and objective indicators useful for monitoring one aspect of writing style.

Clearly, evaluation of the preparation phase of the program includes a mix of subjective and objective assessments of (1) the adequacy of the background research, (2) the organization and content of program materials, and (3) the packaging and presentation of program materials. The next phase of evaluation assesses the implementation of program activities and the dissemination of communication messages and materials to target publics.

Table 14.1

Interpretation of Gunning Fog Index

Fog Index	Grade Level	
17	College graduate	
16	College senior	
15	College junior	
14	College sophomore	
13	College freshman	
		"Danger line"
12	High school senior	
11	High school junior	
10	High school sophomore	
9	High school freshman	
8	Eighth grader	"Easy-reading range"
7	Seventh grader	
6	Sixth grader	

Source: Adapted from Robert Gunning, *The Technique of Clear Writing*, rev. ed. (New York: McGraw-Hill, 1968), 40.

Implementation Criteria and Methods

Public relations evaluations are most often done on the implementation phase. This level of evaluation typically involves counting the publications printed; news releases distributed; stories placed in the media; and readers, viewers, or listeners (potential and actual). The ease with which practitioners can amass large numbers of column inches or centimeters of press coverage, broadcast minutes, readers, viewers, attendees, and gross impressions probably accounts for widespread use—and misuse—of evaluations at this level.

Whereas records of program implementation are essential for program evaluation, measures at this level cannot be substituted for program impact. Evaluation researchers warn of substituting "countable activities" or recorded effort for achievement of program objectives. This amounts to using the amount of effort and resources expended (means) in place of measures of intended outcomes (ends). Without complete documentation and evaluation of the implementation phase of the program, however, practitioners cannot track what went right or wrong, and why.

Criteria and some methods for evaluating the communication portions of program implementation follow. Analogous evaluations must be done on the action components to complete the assessment of implementation.

Distribution.   This phase begins with keeping records of the **number of messages distributed**. This step is a straightforward documentation of how many letters, news releases, feature stories, publications, public service announcements, and other communications were produced and distributed. It also includes how many speeches, broadcast appearances, audiovisual presentations, and exhibits were used in the program. In other words, this step calls for documenting all the materials and activities produced and distributed. During the program, such records provide evidence that the program is being implemented as planned. Unsatisfactory results identified in subsequent steps may be traced back to the amount of the program directed to specific publics or to the program placement, the next criterion.

Placement.   Regardless of how much is produced and distributed, the **number of messages placed in the media** determines whether or not target publics have an opportunity for exposure. Clippings and broadcast logs have long been used to measure how many and what portions of news releases and public service announcements were used by media. Similarly, the number of organizations using a speakers' bureau, audiovisual presentations, and exhibits indicates effectiveness in getting messages placed in the intended channels of communication.

Evaluations at this level sometimes detect fatal flaws in program procedures. Lindenmann reports the case of a client who launched an expensive publicity campaign that produced little use of the materials sent to the media. A poll of the media found that the materials were not being used because the right people were not receiving them:

> The press contact list that the client had been using was sorely out of date. . . . Since the individuals to whom the materials were being sent were no longer at the media at which they were addressed, most of the materials were ending up in the garbage.[24]

Even the most effectively written materials have no chance of impact if they are not available to the intended publics.

Clipping and monitoring services such as Cision (a major European media monitoring and analysis firm that now owns Bacon's Information in the United

MEDIA MONITORS

States and Romeike in the United Kingdom); Burrelles*Luce* in the United States; Bowdens in Canada; Durrants, Precise Media Monitoring, and MediaTrack in the United Kingdom; and Media Monitors in Australia and Asia Pacific track national and international print and broadcast media placements for clients. Also, regional and local services in many areas provide documentation of media placements. Specialized monitoring firms track video news release (VNR) placements on television, and a number of firms now monitor the Internet to identify content placement and mentions in online media and Web sites. TNS Media Intelligence Cymfony, CyberAlert, and Vocus are examples of new technology monitoring companies that cover cyberspace.

With growing maturity and integration in the media intelligence and monitoring market, suppliers will increasingly offer complete services providing tracking of mainstream press, radio and television, online media editions, Web sites, blogs, and social media sites such as YouTube, MySpace, and Facebook. For instance, TNS Media Intelligence Cymfony's Orchestra platform/product allows users to view traditional and consumer-generated media in one Web-based application. Other providers are following suit.

Services vary in how they operate, but the general procedure calls for the client to provide key words and topics to watch for: organization's name, staff names, products or services, and even similar or competing organizations. Typically, the client also sends its monitoring service copies of news releases and broadcast scripts sent to the media.

Most local organizations maintain their own clipping files and placement records. Interns and entry-level practitioners often find "clipping the media" in their job descriptions. Rather than being a dreaded chore, however, it should be viewed as an opportunity to systematically study content and style preferences of the various media. Maintaining the clipping files also gives beginning practitioners opportunities to practice media surveillance and to learn about issues relevant to their organizations.

Clippings and similar media placement records have been overemphasized in public relations and too often they are misrepresented as measures of program impact. However, used properly, they are important elements of program implementation evaluation.

Increasingly clipping news stories is not seen as enough because it provides raw quantitative data on media coverage only. However, a large pile of clippings does not necessarily mean that the coverage was favorable, or that the organization's messages were effectively communicated. Some form of analysis is usually required to identify whether media coverage supported organizational objectives.

One measure all too often used to evaluate publicity media placement is "advertising value equivalents" (AVEs), also called "equivalent advertising value" or simply "advertising equivalency." This approach calculates how much money an organization would have had to pay to secure the same amount of space or time in the media as paid advertising. There is no theoretical or empirical basis for making the leap from editorial to paid advertising. In fact, the calculation of alleged advertising equivalents is seriously flawed and misleading on several grounds. So-called advertising equivalency measures are not justified for the following reasons:

1. Editorial publicity can be in nontarget or low priority media, whereas advertising is only placed in key media that reach target publics.

2. Editorial publicity also can be neutral or negative. Clearly, it is spurious to compare neutral and negative publicity with the best creative advertising.

Yet many AVE calculations do just this. Few proponents of AVEs employ methods that deduct neutral and negative articles and paragraphs, or sections within articles.

3. Editorial publicity often contains coverage of competitors, including favorable references to or comparisons with competitors. Advertising never favorably compares competitors and usually does not mention competitors.

4. Editorial publicity can be poorly positioned, which affects its impact. Advertising is almost always positioned prominently, often with guaranteed placement based on extra fees or through volume booking rewards.

5. Editorial publicity can be poorly presented. It may have ambiguous or misleading headlines, the organization's name or important information buried in the story, and outright errors. Advertising content is prepared by creative professionals and designed for maximum impact.

6. AVE calculations are usually based on casual advertising rates. These are usually higher than the rates negotiated for advertising campaigns, which further inflates the value of publicity used to calculate AVE.

7. AVE calculations actually measure cost, not "value." Even if editorial were to meet all the key criteria of advertising, the AVE totals represent the cost of buying equivalent media space and time for advertising. Clearly, AVE calculations also involve no effort to measure the impact or effect of the content. Unlike the claim being made for publicity AVE, advertising "value" is not measured in terms of what it cost. If it were, that would be suggesting that advertising is valuable simply because it cost $X million. Rather, advertisers use measures of audience reach, share of voice, recall of messages, as well as outcomes such as buying intentions, inquiries, leads, and sales generated. Value is determined by what is achieved, not what it cost.

Some practitioners apply multipliers ranging from two to 13 times the advertising cost to calculate a so-called "PR value," according to Walter Lindenmann.[25] Hallahan and Cameron both have studied third-party endorsement and source credibility, the bases of claims that editorial publicity can be as or more valuable than advertising. They found little research comparing the credibility of news and advertising, and studies they did find showed no consistent advantage of news over advertising.[26] Likewise, Grunig concluded, "The weightings for 'third party' endorsement are totally made up. Research does not support the idea that there is such a thing as third-party endorsement [effect]."[27]

Research reported at the Summit on Measurement further confirmed the fallacy of claims made about "ad equivalency" or the greater value of publicity over advertising. Researchers Michaelson and Stacks presented findings of an experiment in which they exposed a sample of 351 adults who read a newspaper at least once a week to similar advertising and editorial media content and then assessed their recall of key messages, brand awareness, beliefs about the promoted product, and their purchase intentions. They found that, at best, publicity can equal the effects of good advertising, concluding that the "increased value of public relations activities resulting in editorial coverage remains an assumption."[28]

Because the big numbers can be so impressive, however, many practitioners use AVEs and publicity multipliers as measures of "return on investment" to build their case for public relations "effectiveness." John Bergen, former president of the Council of Public Relations Firms and now senior vice president of Siemens Corporation, concluded, "AVE is a totally inappropriate measure of what we do."[29]

A more useful and rigorous way to evaluate media publicity is content analysis, which typically looks at variables such as:

- *Audience reach* (as already discussed).
- *Placement*—Where in the media did the content appear? Note that a page 1 story or lead item on television news is likely to have greater impact than a single-column "filler" buried on page 40 of a newspaper.
- *Prominence*—Is the organization mentioned in the headline, in the first paragraph, prominently throughout, or does it receive only passing mention?
- *Share of voice*—Is the organization reported in the whole story, half of it, or just in one or two paragraphs? How much space or time did competitors have in the story?
- *Issues or topics* reported—Is the story about an important issue of strategic importance, or a general reference?
- *Messages*—What messages were communicated in the story, both favorable and unfavorable?
- *Visuals* such as photos, video footage, or logos—Are any shown and, if so, how and in what context? A photo of a snarling CEO next to a headline saying the company is open to consultation communicates a clear message.

In addition to the above variables that are largely *quantitative*, media content analysis can include *qualitative* evaluation. This can use a coding system to evaluate the tone of articles and undertake further in-depth analysis of the messages communicated. Qualitative content analysis draws on research techniques from text analysis, discourse analysis, and semiotics (see Figure 14.3).

FIGURE 14.3

Publicity Content
Analysis Chart

Source: Courtesy Media
Monitors–CARMA Asia Pacific,
New South Wales, Australia.

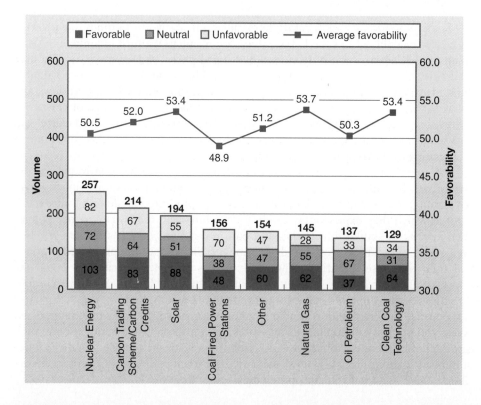

Potential Audience.   The next step in implementation evaluation is determining how many in the target publics received the messages the program is attempting to communicate; that is, **the number of people potentially exposed to program messages**. Care must be taken, however, to separate the *delivered audiences* from the *effective audience*. The delivered audience includes all potential readers, viewers, listeners, or those attending events. The effective audience represents only those who are in the target publics. Audience size is seldom the major consideration; rather, the makeup of the audience is more important to program evaluation. For example, placement or coverage in a prestigious publication may look impressive, but probably contributes little to program success if the target public is middle-income earners. Practitioners could capitalize on such placement by reprinting the article (with permission) and distributing it themselves to key publics. However, the expense of such a strategy usually makes placement in appropriate media initially a more cost-effective practice. The effective audience is called "audience reach" in advertising and this metric is relevant to public relations programs. Identifying target audience reach is a first basic step of media audience analysis.

Circulation figures and audience data are readily available for most publications and broadcast media. Most newspapers and major magazines belong to the Audit Bureau of Circulations (ABC), which publishes guaranteed circulation figures for member publications. Circulation departments of local newspapers and magazines regularly report the number of paid subscriptions, as well as audience size and characteristics. A. C. Nielsen and Arbitron report audience estimates for television stations in more than 200 market areas in the United States, as well as online audiences for these broadcast stations. Along with other companies, they also compile circulation and audience data in other countries. Some media individually report their claimed circulation or audience data in their own promotional materials, but audited data typically are more reliable.

Audience reach can be further analyzed by accessing demographic and even psychographic data. A number of media research companies collect and provide demographic breakdowns such as the number of 18–24-year-old males within a medium's total circulation or audience. This is important, for instance, if the client organization is targeting young males. Others segment audiences by socioeconomic strata or by attitudinal factors. For example, technology companies look for data on how many in media audiences are "early adopters" of technology rather than followers.

Companies such as Traffic Audit Bureau for Media Measurement (TAB) and Simmons Market Research Bureau report audience reach and frequency figures for outdoor advertising. These are based on local transportation authorities' "ridership" figures and can be used to estimate audience size for transit public service advertising placed inside buses, subways, and trains. Attendance figures for events, meetings, and exhibits also provide data to measure potential exposure to program messages.

However, while these data may indicate the number of people who have been exposed to messages, it is naïve to think that these figures alone indicate program effectiveness. Not unexpectedly, the next question should be, "Of those potentially exposed, how many actually paid attention to the message?"

Attentive Audience.   The **number of people who attend to messages and attend events**, that is, pay attention to them, constitutes the next criterion in program implementation evaluation. It is important to recognize that some people drive or ride past outdoor signage and do not see it, skip through newspapers without reading many of the articles, and have the television on but do not pay attention to all that is shown and reported. *Readership, listenership,* and *viewership* studies measure audience attention to media and messages. Readership studies, usually based on surveys or interviews, identify how many read publications, and what they read, how much they read, as well as who reads and who does not. Studies of broadcast audiences produce similar data on viewers and listeners. Numerous audience measurement firms now employ a range of metrics to indicate the number of people who attend to messages on the Internet in online media, blogs, and social media sites.

A well-known print advertising readership evaluation technique is Daniel Starch's recognition method used by Starch INRA Hooper, Inc. Results divide readers into three levels of readership. *Noted readers* simply recall having seen the advertisement. *Associated readers* also remember the name of the advertiser. *Read most* readers say that they read at least 50 percent of the copy and recall enough of the content to support their claim. This method is called "aided recall" because respondents are shown the advertising or other published material and then asked if they recall having read the material. A number of market research firms provide magazine and readership data. The National Newspaper Publishers Association and the Magazine Publishers of America also commission numerous readership studies to track audience characteristics and reading habits.

Audience research firms use four primary methods to measure radio and television audiences:

1. *Diary.* The diary method requires some member (or members) of the household to keep a written record or log of listening or viewing. This method has a built-in bias, because those who agree to participate may differ significantly from nonrespondents.

2. *Meter.* The meter method electronically records individual set tuning by frequency or channel and time of day. The information is sent over telephone lines to a central computer. This is the method used by both A. C. Nielsen and Arbitron in major cities for the "overnight" ratings reported for major television programs. A major problem with this method is that the meter cannot always reliably detect who (if anyone), or how many people, are watching or listening.

3. *People meter.* Audience measurement companies use sophisticated meters in an attempt to solve the missing-information problem of audimeters and television meters. Each person in a metered home has his or her button to push when watching television. The meter records who in the household is watching what program and feeds the information over telephone lines to the base computer. The people meter also is used in marketing research to report purchasing behavior and then to correlate purchases with television viewing. Not surprisingly, people tire of having to "punch in" and "punch out" and of entering all the other information requested, such as entering for small children too young to manage the technology that goes with living in a metered home. Another problem is that not all television sets in a home are metered, so the people meter yields incomplete reports of household viewing.

4. *Telephone interview.* The telephone interview method involves calls either during or following a given program to determine audience size and composition. The most common approach is the telephone coincidental survey, meaning that calls are made while the program is running. Answering machines, cell phones, caller-ID technology, and abusive and high-pressure telemarketers causing nonresponses are making it increasingly difficult to obtain representative samples using this technique.[30]

Readership studies of employee publications are also commonplace. For instance, Weyerhaeuser Corporate Communications tracks readership of the company-produced *Today* to learn how many employees read each of the stories, their interest in stories, the magazine's readability and appearance, and the perceived balance in how issues are reported. Sometimes readership studies produce surprising results. When Jim McBride surveyed San Diego Kaiser Permanente hospital and clinic employees, he found that fewer than half read anything in the employee newsletter. Readership was high among those who received the publication, but about half of all employees did not receive the newsletter. His findings prompted changes in the method of distribution, not changes in the content, which received high marks from readers. This case also illustrates the necessity of evaluating every step in the program implementation process.

If the preceding section addresses only measures of the **implementation** or outputs phase, what are appropriate measures of program **impact**? Program impact is the next phase of program evaluation.

Impact Criteria and Methods

Impact measures document the extent to which the outcomes spelled out in objectives for each target public and the overall program goal were achieved. In Chapter 11 the term "benchmark" was used to describe how *formative* research findings define the problem situation and establish the starting point for the program. *Intermediate* impact assessments monitor progress toward objectives and goals while the program is being implemented, and media analysis is an example of an intermediate or interim impact assessment. *Summative* impact assessments provide evidence of success or failure in reaching the planned ending point.

The benchmark model in Figure 14.4 illustrates the program evaluation cycle, showing how summative impact evaluations ($Time_2$) serve as formative evaluations ($Time_1$) for the next program cycle. The sections that follow describe only general guidelines and methods for impact assessment, because intended outcomes are unique to each program. Specific criteria for evaluating program effects should be clearly stated in the objectives that guided program preparation and implementation. For impact evaluation, these same criteria identify both the nature and the magnitude of changes in (or maintenance of) knowledge, predisposition, and behaviors of internal and external publics. These criteria were chosen because they were viewed as essential steps to achieving the overall program goal (working theory).

FIGURE 14.4

Benchmarks Evaluation Model

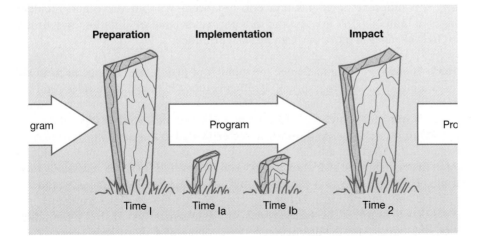

Preparation   Implementation   Impact

gram   Program   Pro

Time I   Time Ia   Time Ib   Time 2

Knowledge Gain. The first impact assessment measures **the number of people who learn message content**. This is clearly the logical follow-on from how many attended to the message. Most programs seek to communicate information to increase knowledge, awareness, and understanding among internal and external target publics. Increasing knowledge is often critical to increasing their interest or motivation, a sequence leading to taking action. What people know about your organization—regardless of where they got the information—affects how they feel and act and, therefore, the organization's relationships with them. What they do not know may be even more critical: As long as explorers believed that the world was flat, they dared not sail too far toward the horizon. Similarly, what people know or do not know about issues and events may influence opinions and behaviors relevant to organization-public relationships.

The key to evaluation of what people learned from a program (or concurrent sources) is to measure the same knowledge, awareness, and understanding variables that were measured before the program began. To determine change, comparisons must be made between at least two comparable measures: by repeating the measures among the same of similar people or by making comparable measures in a control group of similar people not exposed to the program. This same principle applies to all assessments of program impact.

For example, a gas and electricity utility evaluates an energy conservation information program designed in part to increase knowledge of how much energy is saved with proper insulation. The research design calls for comparing survey results from a sample of homeowners who received the information (treatment group) with results from a similar survey of homeowners who did not receive the information (control group). In another case, an employee communication specialist in a manufacturing organization evaluates a program to increase production employees' awareness of safety procedures by comparing precampaign and postcampaign survey results. Similar research designs are used to assess changes in opinions and attitudes.

Opinion Change. The gas and electric utility may also want to know **the number of people who change or form opinions** about the value of home energy conservation efforts. The manufacturer conducting the safety information program could be interested in increasing employee interest in on-the-job safety. Surveys used to measure changes in knowledge, awareness, and understanding also can be used to determine if a program had an impact on audience predisposition. Different questions would be required, however, because increased knowledge and opinion change are different outcomes and one can occur without the other. Similarly, changes in opinions that are specific to a particular issue or situation may or may not reflect changes in more basic underlying attitudes.

Attitude Change. Trying to change the **number of people who change or form attitudes** is a higher-order program impact than is opinion change. Attitudes represent broad, cross-situational predisposition. They are less subject to short-term change. They result from a lifetime of reinforcement and experience, so they typically require time and effort to change. And what you see expressed in a situation may or may not represent the underlying attitude. For example, just because a homeowner holds the opinion that adding attic insulation will save on energy bills does not necessarily mean that the person qualifies as a conservationist *attitudinally*. Determining whether or not people hold an attitude about energy conservation requires measuring their predisposition across many energy use issues and situations. (Review the "Orientation" section of Chapter 8 for the distinction between opinions and attitudes.)

Behavior Change.   The **number of people who act in the desired fashion**—behavioral change—likewise may or may not follow a sequence of knowledge and predisposition changes. Chain-link fences, for example, negate the need for information and persuasive communications designed to keep all but the most determined people from entering restricted areas. Seldom do public relations programs have such powers, so typically people must be informed and persuaded before behavioral changes occur. Assessments of program impact on behavior include self-reports of behavior through *surveys*, *direct observation* of people's actions, and *indirect observation* through the examination of official records or other "tracks" left by those engaging or not engaging in the behavior.

Surveys sometimes yield unreliable measures of behavior, especially if respondents are asked to report sensitive or socially acceptable actions. Not surprising, few employees willingly report that they ignored management policy. Folks tend to claim more viewing of public television programs than detected by other audience measures. Imagine how many students would admit to not doing assigned readings on the professor's class survey, or how many taxpayers would mark, "Yes, I cheated on last year's income taxes" on an IRS questionnaire! With validation questions built into the survey, however, many types of behavior can be measured using self-reports in surveys.

Examples of direct observation are turnstiles at events, head counts at meetings, tallies of telephone or mail responses, and participant observation. The local Red Cross or blood bank does not need to develop an elaborate measurement technique to determine how many people respond to a call for donations of a rare blood type. Nor does an organization hire a research consultant to learn if protestors stopped picketing the main lobby. Some public relations research executives have even considered using direct observation in the form of *ethnography*—observing people in their natural habitats, such as in their home or at the store—but this method can be expensive and sometimes difficult for clients to understand.[31]

Indirect methods for observing behavior include a social service agency's records of client appointments, a museum's maintenance records showing where worn floor tiles are most frequently replaced, and library checkout records. By studying these by-products of behavior, assessments are made about how many people used agency services, which areas or exhibits in the museum are most popular, and how many students checked out assigned public relations reference books. This type of observation technique is called "unobtrusive measures."[32] This approach to assessing impact does not depend on the cooperation of those being observed, and the measurement technique does not contaminate the behavior observed.

The National Park Service's "Keep Yosemite Bears Wild" campaign caused behavior change—as measured by indirect methods. The program educated campers about how their own behavior—feeding wild bears—was encouraging bears to become more aggressive in damaging people's cars and other property in their search for human food. The campaign strategy was "to shift responsibility for the situation to people by persuading visitors to act properly, rather than blaming the bears." As a result of the six-month campaign, incidents of property damage at Yosemite National Park fell from around 1,600 incidents in the previous year to 760. Property damage dropped to one third of previous levels. The property damage records served as an indirect indicator of changed human behavior (as well as changed bear behavior!).[33]

In summary, measures of behavior call for a combination of research skills and ingenuity to get valid evidence for the evaluation and to avoid influencing the behavior of those being observed.

Repeated Behavior.   Public relations programs are usually designed to increase **the number of people who continue or sustain the desired behavior**. Counts of the number of people who give up smoking on the day of the Great American Smokeout are not sufficient measures of program success for those wanting to decrease the number of people engaging in this health-threatening habit. As any reformed smoker will attest, success in quitting cannot be determined by checking only once shortly after a quit smoking campaign.

Likewise, the Australian government's National Skin Cancer Awareness Campaign is designed to get teenagers and young adults (other campaigns target other publics) to adopt five "normal and socially acceptable" sun protection behaviors:

1. Put on a broad-brimmed hat that shades your face, neck, and ears.
2. Wear sun-protective clothing that covers as much of your body as possible.
3. Seek shade.
4. Wear wrap-around sunglasses.
5. Apply SPF30+ broad spectrum water-resistant sunscreen liberally to clean dry skin, at least twenty minutes before being exposed to the sun, and reapply at least every two hours when outdoors.

Evaluation must include follow-up measures sometimes continuing for months or even years. United Nations family-planning programs are more interested in repeated use of contraceptive methods, not just short-term trials motivated by an educational movie and samples. The same applies to those interested in assessing the impact of safe-sex education programs among at-risk high school and college populations. Evaluating program success in changing long-term behavior calls for an extended period of observation and measurement to document program impact.

Goal Achieved.   At some point in this series of impact levels, the **program goal is achieved or the problem solved**. Election and referendum results, legislative victories or defeats, and fund balances provide summative indications of the success or failure of political, lobbying, and fund-raising programs, respectively. The program goal spells out the appropriate summative evaluation criteria. It should also be clear that evaluation must extend to this level, because it is possible that some or many of the intermediate impact outcomes may occur without the program goal being achieved. In other words, while each level may or may not be *necessary* in the process, no single level or even combination is a *sufficient* measure of goal achievement.

For example, the goal of an energy conservation program was to reduce total energy consumption. Increased knowledge of cost-saving practices, increased interest in energy conservation, and even changes in energy-use habits do not indicate success or failure in achieving the overall program goal. The utility reported program success this way:

> The average cost of all conservation advertising to provide you with information on how to save energy is about 11 cents per month per customer. An analysis conducted on the actual savings realized by customers through conservation indicates that the savings averaged $10 for each $1 spent on conservation advertising.

The utility's suggestion that the conversation advertising caused the savings illustrates a major problem in program evaluation—the tentative nature of cause-and-effect claims. To list but a few alternative explanations for reduced consumption, the drop in energy consumption occurred during a period of escalating energy costs, energy conservation was a topic of many news stories and features in the national and local media, and manufacturers were introducing more energy-efficient appliances. In the uncontrolled environment of most public relations programs, evaluation research only helps answer questions about impact. Definitive answers are elusive, but objectively and systematically gathered evidence certainly beats assertions and strengthens the case for or against claims of program success or failure. (See Figure 14.5 for a similar model of the hierarchy of program evaluation.)

Social and Cultural Change.   The ultimate summative evaluation of programs and the practice of public relations is their contribution to **positive social and cultural change**. To complete the range of impact assessments, we conclude with this step. Evaluation at this level is confounded by the passage of time and the existence of other causal factors and is usually left to scholars in sociology and anthropology. Early programs promoted settlement in the West. Health and nutrition education programs have both reduced infant mortality and extended life. Programs that resolved conflicts and built new relationships maintained the dynamic public consensus necessary for meeting human needs. Those in the calling derive their professional motivation and fulfill their social responsibility by being concerned about the impact of their work on society and culture. Both individual practitioners and the practice of public relations will be judged accordingly by future generations.

FIGURE 14.5

Pyramid Model of
PR Research

Copyright © Jim R. Mac–namara 1991 & 2001. Used with permission, Jim R. Mac–namara, CARMA International, Chippendale, NSW Australia.

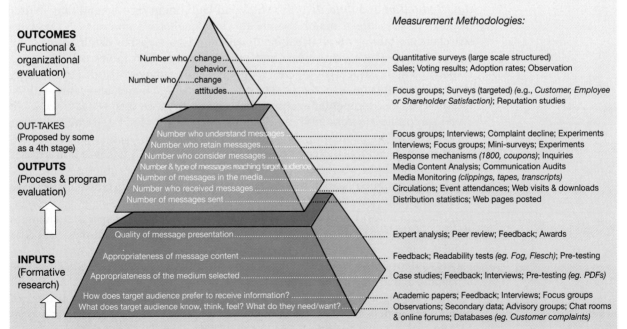

Macnamara's Pyramid Model of program evaluation also depicts a hierarchy of program evaluation similar to the levels described here.[34] Like the evaluation levels model in Figure 14.2, the Pyramid Model reads from the bottom up, the base representing the start point of the strategic planning and preparation process, culminating in achievement of the program goal. The pyramid metaphor is useful in conveying that, at the base when communication planning begins, practitioners have a large amount of information to assemble and a wide range of communication and action options. Selections and choices are made to direct certain messages at certain target audiences through certain media and, ultimately, achieve specific objectives and goals—the peak of the program or project.

Some have criticized both the evaluation levels and Pyramid models for not incorporating feedback loops. However, it is implicit in these models that findings from each stage of research are looped back into planning. The literature accompanying both models suggests that practitioners should not proceed to the next step unless formal and informal feedback gathered from the previous step has been incorporated into ongoing planning and management of the program. For instance, if early feedback or formal measurement (such as pretesting) finds that a selected medium is inappropriate, no practitioner would reasonably proceed to distribute information using that medium—at least one would hope not.

Another important feature of the Pyramid Model is the lists of the most common research methods for carrying out evaluation that are relevant to each stage of the process. Many of these have been mentioned and discussed throughout this and previous chapters.

Interpreting and Using Results of Evaluation

Two key steps in interpreting and making sense of data gained from research are *data reduction* and *data display*. Miles and Huberman recommend that "better displays of data are a major avenue to valid qualitative analysis."[35] These researchers are talking about breaking down data from statistics databases or large spreadsheets—which can be vast and overwhelming—into tables or charts that display the main categories, themes, groupings, and leading statistics. For instance, the data gained from a survey of staff and students at a major university with 40 questions on environmental health and safety ran to more than 60,000 rows in an Excel spreadsheet across multiple columns. The answers to closed-end questions were "reduced" by tabulating the most frequent responses from each, and the answers to open-end questions grouped into categories. Once this was done, tables and charts could be produced to display distilled data in meaningful summaries.

In this simplified format, researchers and practitioners can start to make sense of data and interpret what they mean to the organization management. Interpretation (hermeneutics) is a challenging field, and researchers learn special techniques to minimize the risks of overlooking and oversimplifying important data. But data reduction is essential whenever large amounts of data are collected, and data display is vital for both helping researchers and practitioners interpret the data, as well as helping management understand it.

Interpreting and applying the results of evaluation makes clear that the end point of research is not data. The ultimate aim is to learn what has worked and what has not, and if not, why, as well as what should be done. Data collected using valid and reliable methods provide a foundation of evidence upon which managers can make objective decisions and manage public relations scientifically.

Katie Paine made this point in *The Measurement Standard* when she wrote:

It's **what you *do* with the data that is the hard part**; that's what turns *numbers* into *measurement*. Measurement means providing highly accurate and reliable data, including human verification of results and extensive data checking to make sure that the results are what you think they are. **Finally, and perhaps most importantly, measurement means studying the data to figure out what it means and what it doesn't mean, and what the client should or shouldn't do as a result** [emphasis added].[36]

Even armed with evidence, practitioners need to exercise care when interpreting and using evaluation results. Three major interpretations are possible when the expected impact is not detected in the evaluations:

1. Even though preparation and implementation were adequate, **the theory behind the program strategy was faulty**. This type of failure is typified by the common notion that "telling our side" will win arguments. Remember the warning earlier in this chapter that we cannot assume communication will work. Often it does not for a range of reasons, some of which may be beyond the control of the communicator.

2. If the theory guiding the program was useful, then the absence of impact may be attributed to **program failure: errors made when preparing and/or implementing the program**.

3. It is also possible that the program succeeded in all respects but that the **evaluation methods did not detect the program impact**. Observations were made on the wrong people, the observations were not valid or used unreliable measures, or the effect was so elusive that it could not be detected using conventional measurement techniques.

In the final analysis, program evaluation requires knowledge of scientific research techniques, abilities to interpret data, and a willingness to learn from and apply findings.

Having undertaken evaluation, it is important that findings are not ignored in a bottom drawer or on a hard disk somewhere in the organization. "Selling" the results of evaluation can sometimes be just as or more difficult than selling evaluation research in the first place. But top management support and acceptance by practitioners are primary among the many structural, process, and organizational factors influencing the utilization of evaluation research in public relations. Following are some recommendations for increasing the probability that research will be accepted by senior management and become central to managing public relations.

1. Show how research findings relate to potential users' current concerns, policies, procedures, and practices before discussing long-term applications.

2. Maintain frequent and direct participation and communication with potential users and other stakeholders throughout the research.

3. Limit reports of research findings to either those with immediate application or those with implications for long-term changes. Save the other type of findings for another report and setting.

4. Report only implications that are logically derived from and supported by the data.

5. Use researchers with established credibility and integrity and avoid using people who might be seen by others as having a vested interest in the results.

6. Use research designs and methods that conform to rigorous scientific standards and technical soundness.

7. Emphasize corroborating information over information that contradicts users' expectations and frames of reference, minimize negative surprises, and avoid early closure on politically sensitive recommendations.

8. Enlist sponsorship of key managers in encouraging serious consideration and use of what was learned from the research.

9. Take the time and effort necessary to persuade potential users to consider and understand the findings and to help them apply what was learned from the research.

10. Conduct the research and use the findings in an ethical and socially responsible manner; respect basic human and civil rights.[37]

This chapter concludes with a reminder of an important point made at the beginning: that evaluation applies to the planning (inputs) phase, implementation (outputs) phase, as well as the impact (outcomes) phase of public programs. Effective program planning and effective program evaluation are inseparable and interrelated, as this quote attests:

> The sins of the program are often visited on the evaluation. When programs are well conceptualized and developed, with clearly defined goals and consistent methods of work, the lot of evaluation is relatively easy. But when the programs are disorganized, beset with disruptions, ineffectively designed, or poorly managed, the evaluation falls heir to the problems of the setting.[38]

Research should be seen as central to the management of public relations, not simply as the means by which practitioners are held accountable and the worth of their programs is assessed. As the benchmark model suggests, today's evaluation of program impact is tomorrow's baseline for the next program cycle. The late public relations executive Kalman B. Druck remarked: "I have found that research is too frequently used as an odometer rather than as a speedometer. Research is often used to tell us where we have been, not where we are going."[39]

Conducted well, evaluation research can tell practitioners both where they have been and where they are going, as well as give insights on how best to get there. And the research pays off in getting public relations to the management table. The evidence shows that use of evaluation research is associated with participation at senior management level. As Dozier reported:

> Practitioner participation in management decision making increases when the practitioner plays the manager role and conducts scientific, mixed, and information program research. . . . Participation in management decision making is increased when the practitioner does research, independent of manager role playing.[40]

But of course, that is not the real goal of evaluation research. Rather, the goal is to improve program effectiveness, which requires counseling skill beyond interpreting the data. As management expert Jim Lukaszewski summed up the goal:

> Showing the manager or boss how to put your advice into practice is essential. Most bosses learn how to work with advisors through trial and error. The best advisors always help their clients understand how to use the advice they receive from many different quarters.[41]

Notes

[1] Lord Kelvin, more correctly, First Baron Kelvin, was the British physicist, mathematician, and inventor William Thompson (1824–1907).

[2] Mark Weiner, *Unleashing the Power of PR: A Contrarian's Guide to Marketing and Communication* (San Francisco: Jossey-Bass, 2006): xvii.

[3] Personal communication with authors, January 10, 2008.

[4] E. W. Brody and Gerald C. Stone, *Public Relations Research* (New York: Praeger Publishers, 1989); Glen M. Broom and David M. Dozier, *Using Research in Public Relations: Applications to Program Management* (Englewood Cliffs, NJ: Prentice Hall, 1990); Don W. Stacks, *Primer of Public Relations Research* (New York: Guilford Press, 2002); and Tom Watson and Paul Noble, *Evaluating Public Relations: A Best Practice Guide to Planning, Research and Evaluation* (London: Kogan Page, 2005).

[5] *Public Relations Review* 16, no. 2 (Summer 1990), devoted entirely to "Using Research to Plan and Evaluate Public Relations."

[6] International Public Relations Association, "Public Relations Evaluation: Professional Accountability," Gold Paper Number 11 (London, 1994).

[7] Public Relations Society of America, "Media Relations Reality Check," online at http://www.prsa.com.

[8] Quoted by Deborah Hauss in "Setting Benchmarks Leads to Effective Programs," *Public Relations Journal* 49, no. 2 (February 1993): 16.

[9] Quoted in Broom and Dozier, *Using Research in Public Relations*, 11.

[10] John Guiniven, "Ask the Professor: Embracing Measurement," *PR Tactics* (August 2004): 6; Jeff Miller, "Media Measurement: It's More Than Looking at ROI," *O'Dwyer's PR Services Report* 18, no. 3 (March 2004): 13; "More Clients, Agencies Find the Value in Measurement," *PRWeek* (May 31, 2004): 7.

[11] Peter H. Rossi and Howard E. Freeman, *Evaluation: A Systematic Approach*, 5th ed. (Newbury Park, CA: Sage Publications, 1993), 5.

[12] Ibid., 34–41. The questions appeared in earlier editions.

[13] Broom and Dozier, *Using Research in Public Relations*, 299.

[14] Stewart A. Smith, "Research and Pseudo-Research in Marketing," *Harvard Business Review* 52, no. 2 (March–April 1974): 73–76.

[15] Walter K. Lindenmann, "Research Doesn't Have to Put you in the Poorhouse." Online at http://www.instituteforpr.com/measurement_and_evaluation.phtml?article_id=2001_poorhouse.

[16] Claude Shannon and Warren Weaver, *A Mathematical Model of Communication* (Urbana, IL: University of Illinois Press, 1949).

[17] Personal communication with the authors, date not known, 1991.

[18] Routzahn (1869–1939) was a social worker and foundation executive, associate director of the Russell Sage Foundation, 1912–1934. He also was the founding chairman of the Social Work Publicity Council, one of the first professional public relations groups. The quotation is from the 1920 National Conference of Social Work proceedings.

[19] Jim Macnamara's Pyramid Model of PR Research uses the terms *inputs, outputs,* and *outcomes.* Walter Lindenman discusses three levels—*outputs, outtakes, and outcomes*—in his "Guidelines for Measuring the Effectiveness of PR Programs and Activities" (Gainsville, FL: Institute for Public Relations, 2003). Available at http://www.instituteforpr.org/research_single/measuring_activities.

[20] Tom Watson presents his "Unified Model" in *Evaluating Public Relations*.

[21] The Planning, Implementation, and Impact Model of evaluation levels developed by Glen Broom first appeared in the sixth edition of *Effective Public Relations* (1985).

[22] Robert Gunning, *The Technique of Clear Writing*, rev. ed. (New York: McGraw-Hill, 1968), 38–40.

[23] Irving E. Fang, "The 'Easy Listening Formula,'" *Journal of Broadcasting* 11, no. 1 (Winter 1966–67): 63–68.

[24] Walter K. Lindenmann, "Dealing with the Major Obstacles to Implementing Public Relations Research," *Public Relations Quarterly* 28, no. 3 (Fall 1983): 12–16.

[25] Walter K. Lindenmann, "Guidelines and Standards for Measuring and Evaluating PR Effectiveness" (Gainesville, FL: Institute for Public Relations, 2003). Available online at http://www.instituteforpr.org/index.php/IPR/IPR_info/measuring_activities.

[26] Findings from studies by Glen T. Cameron, "Does Publicity Outperform Advertising? An Experimental Test of the Third-Party Endorsement," *Journal of Public Relations Research* 6, no. 3 (1994): 185–206; Kirk Hallahan, "Product Publicity: An Orphan of Marketing Research," in Esther Thorsen and Jeri Moore, eds., *Integrated Communication: The Search for Synergy in Communication Voices* (Mahwah, NJ: Lawrence Erlbaum Associates, 1996), 305–30; and Kirk Hallahan, "No Virginia, It's Not True What They Say About Publicity's Third-Party Endorsement Effect," *Public Relations Review* 25, no. 4 (1999): 331–50.

[27] Jim Grunig, International Public Relations Association e-group posting, August 4, 2000.

[28] David Michaelson and Don Stacks, "Exploring the Existence of the Multiplier: Initial Findings" paper presented to the Summit on Measurement, Institute for Public Relations, Portsmouth, NH (September 28, 2006) and online at

http://www.instituteforpr.org/index.php/IPR/research_single/exploring_the_comparative_communications/.

[29] "Is Ad Value Equivalency a Credible Measurement of PR's Effectiveness?" *PRWeek* (October 8, 2001): 10.

[30] Will Lester, "Hang-Ups Bedevil the Telephone Pollsters," *San Diego Union-Tribune* (November 30, 2002): A11.

[31] Sherri Deatherage Green, "A Question of Cost: Ethnography Raises the Research Bar (side box)," *PRWeek* (April 7, 2003): 17.

[32] Eugene J. Webb, Donald T. Campbell, Richard D. Schwartz, and Lee Sechrest, *Unobtrusive Measures: Nonreactive Research in the Social Sciences* (Chicago: Rand McNally, 1966).

[33] Aimee Grove, "Yosemite Puts Lid on Bear Market," *PRWeek* (June 12, 2000): 28.

[34] Jim Macnamara, *Jim Macnamara's Public Relations Handbook,* 5th ed. (Sydney: Archipelago Press, 2005), 243–312. Also published in Jim Macnamara, "Research and Evaluation," Chapter 5 in Candy Tymson and Peter Lazar, *The New Australian and New Zealand Public Relations Manual* (Sydney: Tymson Communications, 2005), 100–134; and in Jim Macnamara, "Research in Public Relations: A Review of the Use of Evaluation and Formative Research," *Asia Pacific Public Relations Journal* 1, no. 2 (1999): 107–33. First published in Jim Macnamara, "Evaluation: The Achilles Heel of the Public Relations Profession," *International Public Relations Review* 15, no. 4, (1992): 19.

[35] Mathew B. Miles and A. Michael Huberman, *Qualitative Data Analysis* (Newbury Park, CA: Sage Publications, 1994), 11.

[36] Katie Paine, "Companies That Do Fake Social Media Measurement," *The Measurement Standard* 6, no. 2 (June 2007), online at http://www.themeasurementstandard.com/issues/6-1-07/mm6-1-07.asp#menace.

[37] Broom and Dozier, *Using Research in Public Relations*, 302–13.

[38] Carol H. Weiss, "Between the Cup and the Lip," *Evaluation* 1, no. 1 (1973): 54.

[39] *Arthur W. Page Society Newsletter* 4, no. 1 (April 1988): 4.

[40] David Dozier, "The Innovation of Research in Public Relations Practice: Review of a Program of Studies." *Public Relations Research Annual* 2 (Lawrence Erlbaum Associates, 1990): 24.

[41] James E. Lukaszewski, *Why Whould the Boss Listen to You?* (San Francisco, CA: Jossey-Bass, 2008): xliii.

Additional Sources

Broom, Glen M., and David M. Dozier. *Using Research in Public Relations: Applications to Program Management.* Englewood Cliffs, NJ: Prentice Hall, 1990. Still the most comprehensive introduction to using research in public relations, he said immodestly.

Caroll, Tina, and Don W. Stacks. *Bibliography of Public Relations Measurement.* Gainesville, FL: Institute for Public Relations, 2004. Extensive list of measurement-related sources for public relations practitioners and educators of all levels.

Hon, Linda C. "Demonstrating Effectiveness in Public Relations: Goals, Objectives and Evaluation," *Journal of Public Relations Research*, 10 (1998): 103–135.

Lindenmann, Walter K. *Public Relations Research for Planning and Evaluation.* Gainesville, FL: Institute for Public Relations, 2003.

Miller, Delbert C., and Neil J. Salkind. *Handbook of Research Design and Social Measurement*, 6th ed. Thousand Oaks, CA: Sage Publications, 2002. An encyclopedic presentation of research methods, measurement scales, and references.

Olson, Beth. "Media Effects Research for Public Relations Practitioners." In *Handbook of Public Relations*, edited by Robert L. Heath, 269–278. Thousand Oaks, CA: Sage, 2001.

Rossi, Peter H., and Howard E. Freeman. *Evaluation: A Systematic Approach*, 5th ed. Newbury Park, CA: Sage Publications, 1993. Essential reading for those engaged in program evaluation.

Stacks, Don W. *Primer of Public Relations Research.* New York: Guilford Press, 2002. Comprehensive guide for using various research methods to manage public relations programs.

Weimer, Mark. *Unleashing the Power of PR: A Contrarian's Guide to Marketing and Communication.* San Francisco, CA: Jossey-Bass, 2006. Research-based practical guidebook for creating and implementing public relations programs.

Wimmer, Roger D., and Joseph R. Dominick. *Mass Media Research: An Introduction*, 8th ed. Belmont, CA: Wadsworth/Thompson Learning, 2006. Useful research methods reference for understanding and interpreting media research.

Part 4

The Practice

Business and Industry Public Relations

15

STUDY GUIDE   After studying Chapter 15, you should be able to:

▶ Describe the role of public relations in supporting profit-driven corporations.

▶ Discuss current business issues, such as corporate governance, executive compensation, and corporate social responsibility.

▶ Explain how the public relations function contributes to corporate well-being in the post-9/11 era of heightened security and increased threats from terrorism.

▶ Describe the crucial role of public relations in communicating with the financial community.

▶ Outline the role of philanthropy as a key element in corporate citizenship.

▶ Explain the increasing importance and constantly changing effect that new media can have on corporate reputation.

The first decade of the new millennium was a roller-coaster ride for corporate America. The twenty-first century arrived amid great optimism for growth, sustained profitability, and expansion into many new markets around the world. These new markets were essentially created by the the rise of what has now come to be known as the BRIC countries (Brazil, Russia, India, and China), some of them rich in raw materials but with relatively under-developed economies.

These great expectations quickly soured for most American corporations. One factor was the September 11, 2001, attacks on the World Trade Center and the Pentagon. The subsequent hyperfocus on homeland security and terrorism had multiple effects on the business sector.

First, the U.S. economy was already showing signs of weakness, and the infamous "9/11" helped shove the economy into a full-fledged recession. This, in turn, led to the loss of thousands of U.S. jobs as companies downsized to adjust for reduced profits.

A second economic reality was the exporting of thousands of American jobs to Third World countries, where increasing amounts of manufacturing are done for U.S. companies. Wal-Mart Corp., for example, buys 1 percent of China's gross domestic product annually.[1] More than 70 percent of Wal-Mart Stores' products come from China.[2]

A third factor causing economic uncertainty in American markets is the war on terrorism. In the space of three years, American troops were sent to

All business in a democratic country begins with public permission and exists by public approval.
—Arthur W. Page

This chapter was revised in collaboration with **MaryLee Sachs**, chairman, Hill Knowlton USA, and director, Worldwide Marketing Communications Practice, Hill Knowlton, Inc., New York. Before assuming her U.S. leadership role, she worked 17 years for H&K and Fleishman-Hillard in London. She began her public relations career in Southern California.

Afghanistan and Iraq to topple authoritarian governments. Particularly in Iraq, a quick military victory was followed by sustained insurgency that continued to claim American and Iraqi lives, among others. American companies, anxious to participate in the rebuilding of Afghanistan and Iraq, were soon faced with the realities of kidnapped and executed employees, often with grisly details posted on the World Wide Web. This, coupled with terrorist bombings in other nations, is not the stability large corporations seek when looking for new or expanded markets. The resulting conservatism may eventually be measured in billions of dollars of lost opportunities and flat earnings for many large companies.

Finally, the early years of the new millennium were marked with unprecedented corporate misconduct, victimized employees, indicted executives, and massive class-action suits by shareholders against senior management of various corporations. Eventually, news headlines featured jail time for numerous former executives who were part of overreported profits, understated expenses, and illusory offshore ventures that had the substance of a gallon of fog.

And what of the public relations roles in corporations affected by this collection of disappointing economic news, increased danger in world markets, and unbridled greed in executive suites? Have public relations officers been kept in the dark or have they abetted some of the schemes by dutifully writing their news releases and responding to media queries with barely plausible information? As this is written, only two public relations executives have fallen to bogus financial dealings: Doug Dowie, while GM of Fleishman-Hillard's Los Angeles office, was indicted and later found guilty of overbilling the city and other clients by more than $300,000. A federal jury convicted Dowie and John Stodder, the former manager of Fleishman-Hillard's public affairs department in Los Angeles, on charges of conspiracy and fraud, overbilling the city's Department of Water and Power from 2000 through 2004. Prosecutors reported the two also had inflated bills for the Port of Los Angeles, the Worldwide Church of God, and the architect Frank Gehry.[3]

Corporate public relations has only become more complex over the past several decades. And more than ever before, the issue of transparency by public relations executives has become crucial with the rise and spread of the digital tools made available by Web 2.0 and the increasing popularity and globality of social media. Although this has resulted in increased pressures, it has also created marvelous opportunities for the profession to demonstrate its abilities to help companies behave responsibly and solve complex problems, as long as public relations executives maintain high ethical values themselves.

The Profit Motive

Corporate America deals with a somewhat schizoid public view of what businesses do. On one point, there should be no mystery—corporations exist to make a profit and create value for their shareholders. Although not a mystery, this truism inevitably raises many questions:

- How did XYZ Company achieve a 55 percent increase in profits over the previous year?
- What portion of those increased earnings went to the shareholders vs. the management team, and how much of the new profitability will be used to improve the company's social responsibility obligations?

- Why did XYZ's chief executive receive $15 million in compensation in a year in which the company's earnings dropped by one-third?

- How many jobs were eliminated and/or exported to developing countries, and how much did this contribute to increased profits last year?

- Will increased earnings withstand public scrutiny in the aftermath of corporate misdeeds by Enron, Tyco International, ImClone, and others?

Beneficiaries of the focus on profits, its stockholders, are the "owners" of the company and can be identified in three distinct categories:

Individuals, sometimes referred to as "mom-and-pop investors," are those who may buy a few shares each month and might own several hundred shares of stock.

Institutional investors own 70 to 80 percent of all the shares in corporations. These are mutual funds, insurance companies, pension plans, and universities. It is not unusual for a $20 billion corporation to have two-thirds of its shares held by just 80 to 100 institutional investors.

The third category is less publicized than the other two. However, it is crucial for employees of a corporation to find out how much of its stock is held by its own *senior management* and *board of directors*. A CEO who decides to sell stock options in his or her company because of a lack of confidence that the firm will be successful sends a negative message. And, in a painfully logical manner, why should blue-collar or white-collar employees invest in their company's stock if the top 20 executives do not?

Ownership of stock is one of the cornerstones of American finance. Whether an investor owns shares directly, through a mutual fund or a 401(k) plan, or as part of a company pension plan, stock ownership makes a person part of yet another fundamental economic fact: Corporations create wealth. Properly managed and overseen by an alert board of directors, corporations make profits, thus increasing market value. Stock dividends paid quarterly provide additional rewards for investors, many of whom reinvest those dividends and turn them into additional shares of ownership.

There's nothing wrong with the profit motive. Nor is there anything fundamentally flawed with free enterprise. However, corporations are under greater scrutiny than at any time since the robber baron and arrogant monopoly eras of the late 1800s. Whether public relations practitioners consider this a "problem" or an "opportunity" will determine whether public trust can be maintained (or restored).

Public Relations in Corporate Organizations

Much has been written about the ideal organizational scheme to make optimum use of the public relations function. Most senior practitioners prefer reporting directly to the chief executive officer. This makes for the most informed and best-supported public relations officer because of the removal of "filters" in the form of organizational layers.

As much as it makes sense to report to the CEO, the reality is that all corporate functions have an argument for the same reporting relationship—human resources, legal, research and development, quality assurance, and others. Even an extraordinarily competent CEO will normally manage perhaps a dozen direct reports, and the heads of the profit sectors, the chief operating officer, and the chief financial officer are certain to be part of that direct staff.

In practice, the senior public relations officer is normally a vice president or a senior vice president reporting to one of the CEO's direct staff members. Titles can be misleading, though. One company might pay more attention to influence than to trappings such as job titles. Another might be hierarchy intensive, where several hundred executives will have titles of vice president or higher.

In practice, companies organize in a way that best suits their culture, tradition, market orientation, public profile, and other needs. A very large consumer products company with high name recognition would organize one way, whereas an equally large industrial company with only 200 to 300 key customers would have different needs and organize accordingly.

Experienced public relations professionals cite several factors that are more crucial than the reporting relationship:

- Through networking and organizational savvy, public relations practitioners realize that most decisions made in an organization come about through a consensus process. In decisions with some element of controversy, it's a certainty that marketing, manufacturing, the profit centers, legal, investor relations, and other functions will have legitimate stakes in the outcome. Public relations officers who have nurtured relationships with the heads of these departments will find they have more support when key decisions are finalized.

- Some senior public relations professionals allow pride to take precedence over ways to gain maximum influence, even if their arguments are carried forward by a boss who is "in the management tent." Though difficult for many to accept, it's a fact that if the practitioner isn't in the inner circle of 8 to 10 executives, he or she will want to report to the strongest available alternative.

- In every organization there are influential people, often with modest job titles, whose advice is highly valued by the CEO. Sometimes called "change agents," these people are extremely tuned in to the CEO's agenda and have an intuitive sense of what will (or won't) pass muster at that level. Once a public relations practitioner identifies these important colleagues, he or she must develop working relationships based on trust, sound processes, and insights about the way CEOs think and operate. Increasingly, social networking analysis tools can be used to track online internal conversations, thus helping to identify the real influencers in an organization.

For many reasons, public relations officers are loath to report to human resources (HR) or the legal department. HR is seldom a viable alternative, because its focus is primarily *internal*. The HR officer is being pressed by senior management to reduce the cost of employee health care or find ways to control absenteeism and turnover. Public relations frequently provides assistance in these areas but also has a much broader portfolio and is decidedly more *external* in focus.

Public relations practitioners will develop working relationships with the legal department, because litigation has become "America's second national pastime," trailing only baseball. Large companies are sued hundreds, perhaps thousands, of times each year in cases involving product liability, sexual harassment, wrongful termination, racial discrimination, breach of contract, and other issues. The plaintiffs' attorneys usually take the offense and make public allegations about company behavior or practices.

Companies with "green light" lawyers will work closely with public relations to determine what the two functions can do within the legal system to defend the company's good name. "Red light" lawyers, concerned mostly about risk, prefer a "no comment" position on virtually all media queries, mostly because they cannot predict what twists and turns a lawsuit may take.

Much has also been written about reporting to the marketing function. Critics of such arrangements say (sometimes with justification) that marketing executives are so narrowly focused on product sales, market share, pricing, and sales promotion that they seldom pay proper attention to the nonmarketing roles that are central to an organization's reputation and the public relations discipline that protects reputation. As in most such disputes, there are practitioners who have had ideal working relationships with marketing vice presidents *and* the freedom to serve their many other clients internally. No doubt, there are others who have seemed to fail in issues management or crisis communication roles because their boss would not allocate resources to anything not directly related to sales and marketing.

Corporate Social Responsibility

Corporations have always had obligations to the society in which they operate. Although true, the historical overview found elsewhere in this text has shown that many companies had to be forced to meet their obligations.

Historians may debate when social responsibility appeared on corporate radar screens. One view is that the obligations facing firms today probably got their start in the 1960s, as outlined in the "Period of Protests and Empowerment (1965–1985)" in Chapter 4.

In addition to the environmental, consumer, and civil rights movements in the 1960s and 1970s, the United States saw its first indicators that civil litigation was going to create hundreds of public issues. Individual and class-action suits were highly publicized, emotional claims were made, and corporations were usually the targets because they had both large assets and a tendency to become stationary targets for the litigators. This litigation frenzy has bankrupted many companies, especially those caught in asbestos-related cases, and caused other companies to shift business and research strategies because of a hostile public climate.

A major challenge for corporations is to understand widely varying definitions of social responsibility. There are fundamental tenets of a corporation's obligations to the society it serves, but where do the expectations end?

Answers may come in the form of federal legislation, judicial rulings, or simply the press of the workforce and/or public opinion. At present, there is probably consensus that a publicly traded corporation's social obligations include the following:

1. Provide a stable source of employment, with a visible commitment to diversity in hiring, promoting, and compensating workers at all levels.
2. Operate profitably and provide a reasonable return on investment to shareholders.
3. Establish and meet strategic objectives that provide for long-term growth and competitiveness.
4. Voluntarily comply with—or exceed—government regulations regarding health, safety, and the environment.
5. Set aside a reasonable amount of yearly revenue for philanthropic purposes.
6. Maintain comparable operating standards in every country where the company does business.
7. Participate actively in public policy processes affecting the company, its industry, and other stakeholders who are part of the "public interest."

The challenge is in defining what serves the public interest and meets shareholder demands or government requirements. This is where the board of directors should provide important assistance. Many corporations now have board committees focused on "corporate governance," "public interest," and "stakeholder relations." In most cases, these committees are composed of nonemployee directors (i.e., they are able to give senior management an outside-in view of public expectations and then ensure programs address those needs).

These decisions are often more complex than meets the eye. For example, a company may comply with current air quality standards at all its manufacturing plants. For an additional investment of $100 million, the company could go 10 percent beyond government regulations. Although this may be greeted with enthusiasm by advocacy groups and even neighbors in plant communities, it also means $100 million that cannot be used for other purposes—or go back to the stockholders in a dividend.

Or, a company may be operating an older plant that is marginally profitable. The most obvious economic decision is to close the plant and lay off the employees. But the company may have operated in the particular community for 60 years and have many second- and third-generation employees. In some cases, "the company is the town," and vice versa. Once again, social obligations may collide with economic realities and commitments to stockholders.

Many companies have had written operating philosophies for decades. These may be called something like "core values" or, as has been well documented, Johnson & Johnson's "Credo." After the corporate misconduct binge of 2001–2003, many firms developed new codes of conduct or guidelines for optimum business behavior.

The vital question, however, is how companies respond when violations of these codes occur. Often called an "acid test," the real gut wrenching occurs when a company discovers behavior that is in direct conflict with its code of conduct. What does the organization do? Does the company immediately cease the noncompliant behavior, fire the employee(s) involved in illegal and/or questionable activities ("zero-tolerance policy"), and take tangible steps to demonstrate the seriousness of the code? Or, for those willing to face considerable public criticism and cynicism—do nothing?

The public relations practitioner is, in many cases, the best interpreter of public concerns and reactions. These analyses may come in the form of survey data, newspaper editorial analyses, assessments of news coverage and online conversations or blogs, reaction from Capitol Hill, and, quite often, the internal buzz from employees discussing a new concern or opportunity.

Dozens of corporations have launched meaningful programs that partially contributed to their social obligations. Here are just a few.

The Chicago Bulls, a professional basketball franchise, demonstrates its commitment to metropolitan Chicago and surrounding areas. The effort serves both the Bulls and their primary publics—current and prospective ticket holders and community organizations that benefit from exposure to successful professional athletes. In the process, the Bulls and the National Basketball Association gain from positive impacts on community members.

The Bulls' multifaceted community effort includes the following programs:

- A "Read to Achieve" program is active in all NBA cities, but Chicago takes the program further. Each October, Bulls players start their new season with an event for young students at Chicago's Berto Center. Each month thereafter, the Bulls send players to libraries, schools, and youth centers to promote literacy as a key to success in the adult world (see Figure 15.1 and http://www.nba.com/bulls/community/schools.html).

FIGURE 15.1

**Chicago Bulls at Boys &
Girls Club**

Courtesy Chicago Bulls. Used
with permission.

- Special "Reading Time-Outs" are scheduled during the December holidays, on Martin Luther King Jr.'s birthday in January, and during February's Black History Month.

- The organization builds a new Reading and Learning Center each year at a school, library, youth center, or group home. For example, in April 2008, the Bulls opened a new Reading and Learning Center at Cook Elementary School on the city's south side. The center is designed to increase students' literacy skills by giving them access to books, computers, reference materials, and learning aids. Along with Bulls memorabilia, the renovated facility has new furniture (http://www.nba.com/bulls/community/cook_080415.html).

- In conjunction with the Chicago Public Schools, the Bulls host an annual spring Spelling Bee involving more than 30 schools. Winning foursomes are recognized at a Bulls halftime ceremony.

- Each year, the Bulls organization contributes more than 5,000 new books to local libraries, schools, youth centers, and clubs.

- For more than 15 years, the Bulls have sponsored "FestaBulls," dinner auctions that provide fan–player interaction and autograph sessions and raise nearly $150,000 per year for charity.

- Bob Love, a former Bull and three-time NBA All-Star, has served as the franchise's director of community affairs since 1991. He travels the country making some 300 presentations per year to encourage people to overcome their challenges. Love shares his personal experience of a haunting problem with stuttering that lasted from childhood until well into his professional career.

- The franchise's charitable arm, "CharitaBulls," contributed $4.5 million to build a Boys & Girls Club and Family Life Center in the western part of Chicago and named it for the late James Jordan, father of Michael Jordan, the most popular Bulls player in history. Current players contribute their time to the program.

IKEA Corporation, a Sweden-based furniture company, has attracted attention for its ability to deal early and decisively with social responsibility issues.

IKEA's first significant encounter with critics came over the issue of child labor in countries where suppliers were employing young children—in one case, Pakistani children, who were chained to their weaving looms. IKEA sent its carpeting business manager to Pakistan to investigate the charges. On arrival, the business manager terminated the supplier's contract and soon thereafter added a paragraph to all the company's supplier contracts prohibiting child labor from involvement with any IKEA product. For good measure, IKEA hired a consulting firm to monitor supplier compliance with the new policy.

IKEA then visited UNICEF, the International Labor Organization and individual unions to seek deeper solutions to the child labor issue. In the next several months, IKEA contributed more than $500,000 to support programs addressing child labor abuses.

The company also surprised industry observers by contributing $2.5 million to a coalition of advocacy groups to fund a global forestry mapping project and agreed with another group to sell no products made of old-growth teak, a Southeast Asian hardwood.

Newsweek had this to say about IKEA's efforts to address public scrutiny:

> In the end, IKEA's Teflon shield is less a product of luck and Swedishness than of hard work. It was forged in rapid response to crises, hardened by strategic retreat when necessary and covered by a policy of discreet silence—even when IKEA was trying to do the right thing. . . . IKEA has drafted a code of conduct for all 2,000 suppliers governing everything from overtime to recycling techniques. In-house inspectors around the globe will use a 59-item checklist to evaluate suppliers every two years.[4]

McDonald's Corporation defines social responsibility as "striving to do what is right, being a good neighbor in the community and integrating social and environmental priorities into restaurants and relationships with suppliers and business partners." Social responsibility is a key part of the company's heritage and business strategy.

From creating an independent advisory council on animal welfare, to working with suppliers to phase out the use of growth-promoting antibiotics in its dedicated poultry supply, measure environmental performance, and set goals for improvement, McDonald's also aims to be a pioneer in building social responsibility.

And McDonald's also takes responsibility for environmental impacts. Since 1990, the company has worked with suppliers to reduce the amount of material used in its packaging and increase the amount of recycled material in use. Many McDonald's restaurants around the world recycle used cooking oil and wastes such as corrugated paper packaging.

Community involvement is also a cornerstone of the McDonald's business approach, with a philanthropic focus on programs that benefit children. That was the impetus behind the creation of World Children's Day—a fund-raising event that takes place each November in McDonald's restaurants in more than 100 countries. Since its inception in 2002, World Children's Day has raised more than $27 million for Ronald McDonald House Charities and other nonprofit children's organizations.

Together with individual donors and other corporations, McDonald's, its owner/operators, and its suppliers are key supporters of Ronald McDonald House Charities and its three core programs.

The Ronald McDonald House program provides a home away from home for the families of seriously ill children being treated at nearby hospitals. Started in 1974 in Philadelphia, the program has grown to nearly 250 Ronald McDonald Houses in 24 countries and has helped more than 10 million families around the world.

Nearly 70 Ronald McDonald Family Rooms have been created in hospitals in nine countries to provide a place of respite within the walls of the hospital where the families of critically ill children can rest and relax.

The Ronald McDonald Care Mobile program delivers cost-effective medical, dental, and health-education services to children who are uninsured and/or unable to access quality health care. The program began in 2000 with the first site in Worcester, Massachusetts. By the end of 2007, the company had more than 32 Ronald McDonald Care Mobile programs in operation in Argentina, El Salvador, Poland, New Zealand, and the United States.[5]

Shell Oil is a major corporation owned primarily by British and Dutch interests, but it does business all over the world. Shell has a high profile in many U.S. communities and where Shell Oil Company (United States) does business, and it seeks to advance major and sustained social responsibility programs.

One of the most visible and successful programs has been the Shell Youth Training Academy (SYTA) that has operated primarily in Chicago, Houston, Los Angeles, and Oakland, California, since 1993. This program works with inner-city youth to prepare them for college and/or the workplace. In the first decade of the program, more than 2,500 high school students graduated from the SYTA program, and more than 90 percent of them were fully employed, in college, or both.

The Oakland phase of SYTA was founded in 1998 in conjunction with the Oakland Unified School District. In 2002, Shell Oil Company was named the Oakland Corporate Citizen of the Year, with U.S. Sen. Barbara Boxer (D-Calif.) presenting the award. Since its inception in 1992, the Oakland program has awarded nearly $1 million in scholarships to graduates of the SYTA program. (The Los Angeles 2004 graduates are shown in Figure 15.2.)

Habitat for Humanity is an excellent example of a nonprofit organization that benefits from the social responsibility efforts of many large and small corporations,

FIGURE 15.2

Shell Youth Training Academy Graduates

Courtesy Shell Oil Company. Used with permission.

as well as community-minded volunteers. The program was founded in 1976 by Millard and Linda Fuller. The couple, who had been very successful in the private sector, had "a vision of a world without homelessness and shacks."

The concept was—and is—to build houses with families in need, sell the houses to the families at cost and without interest, then cycle the mortgage payments back into the program to build more houses. As this is written, more than 225,000 homes have been built by families in partnership with one of Habitat's 2,100 active affiliates in more than 90 countries and all 50 of the United States, the District of Columbia, Guam, and Puerto Rico. Corporations such as Whirlpool Corp., Bank of America, Best Western, Marriott, Delta Airlines, Nissan, General Electric, Cisco Systems Foundation and many other companies and foundations have participated with employee voluntarism, donated equipment and building supplies, and other tactics. Former President Jimmy Carter has also been a very visible supporter of the effort.

Habitat for Humanity is now probably best known for its hurricane-response program in the wake of Hurricanes Katrina and Rita. The program was implemented to help low-income hurricane-affected families in Louisiana, Mississippi, Texas, and Alabama build permanent housing.

The Ashoka-Nike partnership promotes sports for social change. After years of implementing traditional community programs, Nike, Inc. launched a new level of community involvement with Ashoka, the world's largest community of social entrepreneurs. Its aim was to build a social marketplace where innovations are shared, new funds are mobilized, and human and social capital is exchanged in support of a global movement based on the power of sport to unleash human potential. Their goal was to inspire social change through the development of a vibrant, youth-led global "Let Me Play" society by 2011.

Together, Nike and Ashoka's Changemakers.net launched the collaborative "Sport for a Better World" competition to identify innovative and transformative ideas from around the world, and to accelerate their development, innovation, and potential for global impact (see Figure 15.3). Judged by leaders in the world of sport, including Olympians, leaders from international sports bodies, and Nike president

FIGURE 15.3

Sport for a Better World

Courtesy Ashoka's Changemaker
(http://www.change
makers.net/en-us/competition/
sports)

and CEO Mark Parker, winners of the competition were given small grants and received attention to help them build awareness and attract other funding. The first competition received entries from 69 countries on five continents.[6]

The foregoing are just a few of the thousands of initiatives undertaken each year by the corporate world. Some others include a $2 million grant by Hewlett-Packard (Canada) to create an endowed research chair in corporate social responsibility at York University's Schulich School of Business; a $500,000 contribution by ChevronTexaco to Harvard University for creation of a program to enhance corporate responsibility by addressing crucial global social, economic, and environmental issues; and creation of a Strategic Social Responsibility Section within the Public Relations Society of America.

Most recently there has been a much more pronounced push toward environmentalism and sustainability, driven in part by pressure being applied to the United States from other countries—witness discussions at the World Economic Development Forum in Davos, Switzerland, as well as campaigns that have originated in this country, such as those led by Al Gore and Leonardo DiCaprio.

Although corporations such as Procter & Gamble have long had policies related to sustainability, many newer companies have developed programs that support sustainable business development and infrastructure. Moreover, environmental concerns have spawned a new breed of companies and organizations such as Shai Agassi's "Project Better Place," an infrastructure solution for electric vehicles. Partnered with the Renault-Nissan Alliance, the partners announced in January 2008 that they will build the first pilot electric battery rechargeable grid system in Israel. The press conference was attended by Renault-Nissan CEO Carlos Ghosn, Israel President Shimon Perez, and Project Better Place CEO Shai Agassi (see Figure 15.4).[7]

These and countless other examples have some common denominators. The most obvious one is that no matter how much a corporation does in the public interest or how much money they spend on social and community causes, they will remain visible targets of advocacy groups on some basis. McDonald's, for example, has traditionally been regarded as one of the most responsible corporations in America. At the same time, it has been targeted by some groups for allegedly contributing to obesity among its customers. We live in contentious times, and for every good work,

FIGURE 15.4

"Project Better Place" in Israel

Courtesy Project Better Place, Palo Alto, California.

there is at least one offsetting critic group. Ultimately public opinion has to decide which arguments are most substantive. And, if it isn't already obvious, a corporation's good works have to be visible and sustained to be of any value. Public relations practitioners have the opportunity of finding ways to maximize good works and address critics.

Corporate Philanthropy

Companies have always wrestled with complex questions about their charitable giving programs: How much should we give? To whom? How closely should our grants be tied to our business purpose? Do we reduce charitable giving in an economic slowdown, even though recipient needs clearly increase? Do we give cash? Equipment? Loaned executive time? All of the above?

It may or may not be coincidental that America's most recent recession seemed to accelerate immediately after the events of September 11, 2001. There were already signs of an economic slowdown, but after the World Trade Center and Pentagon attacks, the slowdown became a crawl. When that happened, many companies deferred investments, cut outside expenses, and laid off employees not deemed essential. Though many management consultants advocate increasing, not decreasing, public relations efforts during slow economic times, the reverse continues to be the rule, not the exception. Most CEOs are willing to risk a loss of momentum and even a short-term loss of visibility and trust, simply based on short-term cost cutting.

Nevertheless, the corporate need for "enlightened self-interest" has not waned, particularly given incidents such as global catastrophes like the South Asian tsunami and Gulf Coast hurricanes. In response, giving by the almost 2,600 grant-making U.S. corporate foundations grew almost 7 percent in 2007 to a record $4.4 billion. This followed a 6 percent increase in 2006 and a 16.5 percent jump in funding in 2005. More than half of the corporate foundations responding to the Foundation Center's annual survey said they expected to increase their giving in 2008.[8]

In the 2000s, philanthropy has undergone fundamental changes. One is a much-tighter focus on strategic impact. For example:

> Companies have shifted their involvement from merely handing out annual checks to becoming directly involved in programs, and the results are encouraging. The best managed companies are focusing their community involvement in areas that draw upon skills and resources they use every day in their businesses. The days in which companies arbitrarily reacted to the solicitations—or, worse, supported organizations because the CEO or his spouse liked them—have passed.[9]

Following are examples of worthwhile—and strategic—philanthropic programs by large corporations.

1. Citigroup enhances financial literacy around the world. In tandem with nonprofit organizations, employee volunteers work with students on technology-driven simulated cases.[10]

2. American Express raised nearly $2 million for restoration of the Statue of Liberty by donating a portion of its charge card transactions. Over the three-month period of the program, American Express card use increased by 28 percent.[11]

3. When Joan Kroc, widow of Ray Kroc, founder of McDonald's, died in 2003, she left $200 million to National Public Radio. This bequest was the largest in NPR

history and actually amounted to twice the size of NPR's yearly operating budget at the time.[12]

4. The Timberland Company has a Path of Service program that commits up to 40 paid hours of an employee's annual time for community volunteerism. Twelve years after its launch, "The fully integrated program has now grown to give more than 200,000 hours of service through more than 200 social service agencies in . . . 73 American cities spanning 30 states, as well as 18 foreign countries."[13]

5. General Mills donated $2.5 million in cash and thousands of employee hours to an effort to convert the crime, drug, and gang-choked Minneapolis suburb of Hawthorne—just five miles from General Mills' headquarters—into a safe and livable community. The drop in crime rates and the demolition of crack houses to make way for a new elementary school are just a few indicators of success.[14]

Corporate Financial Relations

Chapters 1 and 6 discussed some of the responsibilities of financial public relations. Depending on whether this function reports to the chief financial officer or the vice president of public relations, several factors make this job one of the most demanding—and perhaps the least forgiving—jobs in an organization. Reasons include the following:

- Financial public relations serves many clients, including stockholders, financial analysts, pension fund managers, financial and business editors and reporters, the internal organization (CEO, CFO, controller, treasurer, investor relations director, general counsel, heads of business units, and others), the board of directors, and, in some cases, the Securities and Exchange Commission and the various stock exchanges (NASDQ, New York Stock Exchange, Tokyo Exchange, etc.). These audiences have widely varied expectations and always tight deadlines.

- Financial public relations is quite literally a zero-defect operation. Typographical errors in earnings statements, news releases regarding mergers or acquisitions, annual, or quarterly reports—all carefully proofread by many internal and external reviewers—are unacceptable.

- The financial community speaks its own dialect, and a public relations practitioner who is not conversant with the language of a balance sheet or SEC filing will be at a distinct disadvantage.

- A new practice is emerging—that of analyst relations—which increasingly is becoming a focal point for communications and influence. Usually part of investor relations or the larger corporate public relations function, analyst relations communicate with research analysts who track a particular stock or group of stocks for independent research and consulting firms.

- In a so-called bear market, with depressed stock prices reflecting a soft economy, financial public relations and investor relations professionals must deal with an increasingly anxious (even hostile) group of shareholders, sometimes called "the dissatisfied investor class."[15] The challenge is to persuade investors to ride out an economic slump *with* the company.

- Some of financial public relations' clientele may not check the company's stock price more than once a week. Others will check every hour, especially when the company has just announced news of some substance. Any time the stock price takes an unexpected dip of perhaps 3 to 10 percent, key clients will want to know why. It may result from an industry analyst writing a negative review of the company's earnings outlook. It could also be attributed to a large sell-off of stock (often called "profit taking") fueled by a recent rise in the company's stock price. Sometimes, however, the drop in the stock price can be attributed to something said (and perhaps misinterpreted) in response to a news media query. In this case, it doesn't really matter whether the "fault" lies with the public relations practitioner or the reporter.

- Financial public relations professionals have access to highly confidential and time-sensitive information that requires extraordinary discretion, lest the practitioner be guilty of insider trading or releasing information prematurely.

- The financial public relations manager is frequently chosen to answer media queries about the company CEO's compensation and perks. This may be the origin of the term "being between a rock and a hard place." Questions about "golden parachutes" (lucrative severance packages for departing CEOs) are especially difficult to explain to shareholders. So are questions asked in the context of "executive greed." The best of all worlds is to have the most profitable company and the best-paid CEO in an industry because his or her compensation is based on results. The flip side is having declining earnings when the CEO is collecting significantly increased base pay, bonuses, and stock options. All of this suggests that financial public relations managers need to be very "nimble."

- Another complex challenge is communicating about mergers, acquisitions, and divestitures. Loaded with SEC confidentiality implications and the need for formal shareholder approval, these situations require exquisite planning between two corporations, with numerous eventual publics to satisfy. The transactions often reflect good news for one party and not-so-good news for the other. Or, the "deal" may be good for both companies, though thousands of employees will lose their jobs when negotiations are consummated. In fact, when two companies of comparable size go through a merger, it is assumed that in two to three years, only 50 to 60 percent of the workforce will remain. And, there is growing evidence that mergers and/or acquisitions may not deliver the profits promised. In one study of 168 mergers between 1981 and 2001, takeovers by big firms were said to have "destroyed" $226 billion in shareholder value, whereas takeovers by small firms generated $8 billion in "shareholder wealth."[16]

Much of this section may read like a future obituary for a hard-working financial public relations professional. The good news is a definite flip side for those who succeed and master the world of financial communications. Those who prosper have a leg up on the competition for the next big communications job in the company. They have tackled some of the toughest tasks the company could dish out, and their victories are obvious. Some of the survivors will want to broaden their portfolio and parlay their communications successes into a job in one of the line business units. They may also find themselves in high demand by executive recruiters who never have enough outstanding financial public relations practitioners to present to their clients.

Business Misconduct

It's unlikely the American corporate sector has ever had a rockier ride than what began in 2001 with an economic recession and great unrest due to terrorism threats worldwide. At the same time, a large number of corporations and their leaders committed felonies and lost substantial levels of public trust (see Figure 15.5). Dire public

FIGURE 15.5

Corporate Greed

Courtesy Rex Babin, Sacramento Bee. Used with permission.

relations implications ensued, along with severe questions about whether each company's practitioners were even factors in damage control.

The cases appear to have many similarities. Each began with a revelation of inaccurate SEC filings, earnings statements, or listings of debt. Then various government agencies announced an investigation to determine if laws were broken. When the government was confident its case was solid, various high-profile defendants were arrested, usually at about 6 A.M. at their residences, and led away in handcuffs—with the news media informed well in advance.

The arrest scenario has occurred so often that it is known as the "Perp Walk." Next, the company's board files lawsuits against the management, their outside auditors, and anyone else responsible for the economic collapse. Eventually prosecutors and defense attorneys jawbone until there is agreement on a list of charges or a plea bargain that spares some defendants a trial. If the case goes to trial, the star witnesses are usually other company employees (or ex-employees), who themselves face criminal charges. In return for a guilty plea and agreement to testify against the "bigger fish," these lesser defendants cut years off their future imprisonment.

Following are short summaries of some recent cases (in alphabetical order).

Adelphia Communications Corp. John Rigas founded Adelphia in 1952 with $300 in capital. Adelphia eventually grew to be the sixth-largest cable television company in the United States and owner of a wide range of properties, including the National Hockey League Buffalo Sabres.

The company went public in 1986 and filed for bankruptcy in June 2002. In between, the Rigases went on personal spending binges with tens of millions of dollars in Adelphia funds. When John Rigas, sons Timothy and Michael, and two former Adelphia executives were arrested on July 24, 2002, and charged with 24 crimes, the company's stock had plunged from $28.80 to 15 cents per share in just seven months, costing investors about $60 billion.[17]

The Rigases' alleged misdeeds began about 1999 and included obtaining loans totaling $3.1 billion using Adelphia as the guarantor; artificially enhancing the company's balance sheet by adding 140,000 nonexistent cable subscribers; using $241 million in company funds to pay off personal loans; issuing inaccurate press releases and earnings reports;[18] buying more than 100 luxury residences in New York, Colorado, and Mexico; taking about $1 million per month in secret cash payments from the company in order to fund John Rigas's lavish lifestyle; and filing inaccurate financial reports in order to persuade investors that Adelphia was a better investment than was the case.[19]

During the defendants' trials in U.S. District Court in New York City, government prosecutors repeatedly returned to a common theme: The defendants had used Adelphia as their "personal piggy bank." John Rigas, who was 80 years old at the time, was sentenced to 15 years in prison. Son Timothy, then 49, was sentenced to 20 years in prison.

Enron. This company had a wild ride from a small natural gas pipeline company, rapid growth through acquisitions, development of a highly aggressive corporate culture, star status on Wall Street, revelations that its accounting and other business practices were flawed, Congressional investigations, criminal indictments, employee savings plans vaporized, a decline in its stock price from $84 per share to $0.26 per share in less than a year, bankruptcy, and eventual disappearance as one of America's publicly traded companies.

In its heyday, Enron was a $200-billion-a-year company, with 20,000 employees and assets of more than $60 billion.[20] It had innovative business projects all over the world. Unfortunately, some of them were shams, and once media, Congress, and the SEC began investigating Enron, the downfall was neither pretty nor slow.

When Enron stock began its decline, Enron management froze the employee savings plan to keep its rank-and-file workers from selling their stock at a time when senior management was dumping their shares and salvaging several hundred million dollars (see Figure 15.6). Portland General Corp., a subsidiary of Enron, purchased life insurance policies for all its employees, but the beneficiary of each policy

FIGURE 15.6

Enron Ethics

Courtesy Copley News Service, and Scott Stantis, 2004. Used with permission.

was the *company*, not the employees' survivors. Proceeds from these deals, known indelicately as "dead peasant" or "dead janitor" policies, provided about $80 million to a fund that provided bonuses and other benefits for its senior management team and directors.[21]

From a public relations standpoint, the Enron debacle was a classic example of all the wrong things to do. Key executives declined to testify in highly visible and televised Congressional hearings. Others offered implausible mea culpas to a cynical public. Jeffrey Skilling actually testified that as CEO he was unaware of many questionable practices that led to the investigations—at the same time that other ex-Enron officials were testifying that Skilling knew precise details of the transactions.[22]

In mid-2004, Enron won approval from a federal judge to emerge from bankruptcy, sell assets to pay creditors about 20 cents for every dollar they were owed (shareholders got nothing), and begin doing business under the name of **Prisma Energy International**—ironically returning to its roots as an energy and pipeline firm.[23] Former chairman and CEO Ken Lay died in July 2005 awaiting sentencing, after being found guilty of conspiracy and fraud. His successor, Skilling, was sentenced to more than 24 years in prison after helping guide the largest corporate fraud in history.

Arthur Andersen. If there is a corporate version of the death sentence, it aptly describes the fate of Arthur Andersen—once a respected Big Five accounting firm—now known as Accenture.

Enron relied heavily on Andersen for accounting and nonaccounting services. Ultimately, it was Andersen's involvement in helping craft some of the most troublesome business ventures and off-the-books financial dealings that eventually torpedoed Enron, too. The conflict of interest in establishing a business venture and then auditing its results apparently never occurred to Andersen.

When Enron came under intense public and government scrutiny, the Andersen team did a terribly ill-advised thing—they shredded thousands of documents investigators wanted to review. This ultimately led the senior Houston officer of Andersen, David B. Duncan, to refuse to testify before a House subcommittee without a grant of immunity. For this, Duncan was fired. Later, Duncan pleaded guilty to obstruction of justice and cooperated with prosecutors.

This pursuit was successful, as Andersen was convicted of obstruction of justice, fined $500,000, and put on probation for the part the company played in the Enron collapse.[24] Under U.S. law, this meant the firm could no longer audit publicly traded companies without special permission from the SEC. By that time, though, nearly 700 of Andersen's 2,300 audit customers had fired the firm.[25] Andersen's U.S. employment plunged from about 28,000 to fewer than 200, and about 100 of its 111 U.S. offices closed. On May 31, 2005, the U.S. Supreme Court unanimously overturned Arthur Andersen's conviction because "the jury instructions were flawed," but the damage had been done.[26]

Tyco. Dennis Kozlowski joined Tyco in 1975, becoming CEO in 1992 and credited with Tyco's massive expansion in the late 1990s. Tyco consistently beat Wall Street's expectations and, through a series of strategic mergers and acquisitions, ushered in an entirely new generation of mega-conglomerates. But in 2005, Kozlowski was convicted for misappropriation of Tyco's corporate funds, among other charges. He and ex-CFO Mark Swartz were found guilty of stealing hundreds of millions of dollars from the manufacturing conglomerate, taking bonuses worth more than $120 million without the approval of Tyco's directors, abusing an employee loan program, and misrepresenting the company's financial condition to investors to boost the stock price while selling $575 million in stock.[27] Both men were sentenced to 8 1/3 to 25 years and ordered to pay back $239 million in total fines and restitution.[28]

ImClone Systems Inc. Sam Waksal, founder and former CEO of ImClone, currently resides at the Schuylkill Federal Correctional Institution at Minersville, Pennsylvania, after being sentenced to seven years in prison for conspiracy, securities fraud, and bank fraud.

Waksal's problems started when the U.S. Food and Drug Administration on December 26, 2001, declined to give a speedy review of test data on a new ImClone cancer drug, Erbitux. The company was counting on the quick approval and a profit windfall in 2002 and beyond.

Waksal knew the bad news would send ImClone's stock price tumbling the next day. In order to help his father and daughter and, allegedly, his friend Martha Stewart avoid financial losses, he arranged for them to learn about the prospects of the stock tanking. Several people close to Waksal sold about $10 million worth of their ImClone stock and avoided big losses when the FDA announcement came. The company's stock dropped 16 percent that day. Between December 2001 and June 2002, ImClone stock value declined by about 90 percent.[29]

Martha Stewart. The most well-known person to be charged was Ms. Stewart, CEO and primary shareholder of Martha Stewart Living Omnimedia Inc. The federal government charged that she committed securities fraud and lied to investigators about circumstances of her sale of ImClone stock worth $229,000 (see previous paragraph) based on insider information from Waksal. In February 2004, U.S. District Court Judge Miriam Goldman Cedarbaum dismissed the securities fraud charge, ruling that "No reasonable juror can find beyond a reasonable doubt that the defendant lied for the purpose of influencing the market for the securities of her company."[30]

Stewart and her former stockbroker still faced charges of lying to investigators. On March 5, 2004, the jury found Stewart guilty of conspiracy, obstruction of justice, and lying to federal investigators. She was sentenced to five months in federal prison and fined $30,000 on July 16, 2004, but the sentence was deferred pending outcome of Stewart's appeal of her conviction. Judge Cedarbaum acknowledged receiving some 1,500 letters from Stewart supporters. One letter said, "It is apparent that you have helped many people outside of your own family and that you have a supportive family and hundreds of admirers." Addressing Stewart, Judge Cedarbaum said, "I believe that you have suffered, and will continue to suffer, enough."[31] She eventually served the five-month sentence, however.

WorldCom Inc. This is another case of a fabulously successful small-town entrepreneur who ran afoul of the law and saw an empire disintegrate.

WorldCom founder Bernie Ebbers established the company in Mississippi. After paying $37 billion for MCI, WorldCom became the second-largest long-distance carrier in the United States with total 2001 revenues of $21.3 billion. Then disaster struck in June 2002, when it was learned that WorldCom had treated $3.8 billion in *expenses* as *assets* for accounting purposes. Then it was learned that Ebbers had borrowed $408 million from the company to pay off personal debts, and he was forced to resign as CEO. WorldCom was left with a raft of regulatory and Congressional inquiries and the tricky job of explaining how such a large company could make a $9 billion "accounting mistake."[32]

In July 2001, the company filed a $104 billion bankruptcy, and by the end of 2002, its stock price had fallen from a high of $64.50 to less than a dollar. When Ebbers appeared before Congress, he made a single statement about his innocence and then cited the Fifth Amendment in refusing to answer any questions.

Former CFO Scott Sullivan was the sixth WorldCom executive to plead guilty to criminal charges, and he agreed to testify against Ebbers, his longtime boss. By this time, additional discoveries had pushed the amount of WorldCom's "accounting" misdeeds to $11 billion.[33] Ebbers was sentenced in July 2005 to 25 years in prison.

In short, the early years of the new millennium were not good times for corporate America or corporate public relations.

Remedies for Corporate Misbehavior

A combination of new federal legislation (the Sarbanes–Oxley Act of 2002) and Securities and Exchange Commission and New York Stock Exchange rules implemented since November 2003 has already provided some incentives and deterrents to ensure legal compliance by publicly held corporations. Some of the most visible changes are the following:

- "Separating the Siamese Twins" is a step to prohibit independent auditing firms from also engaging in business consulting assignments for the client. At Enron, Arthur Andersen collected $25 million per year in auditing fees, but $27 million per year in consulting fees—in effect, setting up the business operations, investments, and processes it would later examine as outside auditors. The conflict of interest was obvious, as was the case in dozens of other corporation–auditor relationships.[34]
- Creation of a Public Company Accounting Oversight Board is designed to ensure uniform legal behavior by companies' outside auditors.
- Quarterly and annual financial reports must be signed by a company's chief executive officer and chief financial officer, who are then personally accountable for any mistakes in the reports.
- Company loans to directors and officers are prohibited.
- Eleven types of financial crimes now carry statutory maximum sentences. For example, conviction on a charge of mail fraud or shredding/changing records in order to obstruct a federal investigation each can mean 20 years in prison and a fine of $250,000.[35]

Other remedies have not yet been implemented, though their logic is abundantly clear. For example,

- Make the financial penalties fit the crime. As the *Wall Street Journal* reported:

  SEC fines don't pose much of a deterrent now, either. Consider the SEC's $7 million fine against Arthur Andersen last year [2001] over its botched audits of Waste Management Inc. In the settled complaint—in which Andersen neither admitted nor denied wrongdoing—the SEC accused the firm of committing financial fraud by certifying financial statements that it knew were false and misleading. The commission's public-relations arm touted the fine as the largest against an accounting firm in U.S. history. But that $7 million was less than 10% of the $79 million that Waste Management paid Andersen in 2000 for audit and other services.[36]

- Several opinion leaders have advocated requiring any corporate executive or director who prospers financially from illegal behavior to *forfeit the entire amount of his or her gain*—perhaps with a penalty tacked on.
- Some Congressional hearings have discussed ways to reward "whistle-blowers" who take courageous stands and play a key role in ending criminal behavior.

One incentive would be to pay a percentage of ill-gotten gain to the whistle-blower. A reporter described the reasons for the new, stricter rules like this:

> The accounting scandals . . . undermined the most valuable commodity in the U.S. stock market: trust. For many investors, the accounting fraud at companies such as Enron, WorldCom and Tyco broke their belief in a system in which corporate leaders are supposed to honestly boost shareholder value, auditors are supposed to ensure the accuracy of financial reports, and boards of directors are supposed to make sure everyone is doing their jobs.[37]

Communications Misconduct

It has always been important for corporations to communicate responsibly and as transparently as possible with the media. But with the increasing prevalence and penetration of the Internet, corporations have been faced with new challenges and opportunities that have ramifications for all of their stakeholders, from employees to shareholders to employees, from customers to regulators.

Some organizations have exploited this new channel in ways that damaged their reputations. Following are two examples:

1. A Wal-Mart blog praising Wal-Mart, called "Wal-Marting Across America" and ostensibly created by a man and a woman traveling the country in an RV and staying in Wal-Mart parking lots, turned out to be underwritten by Working Families for Wal-Mart, a company-sponsored group organized by the Edelman public relations firm. Richard Edelman, president and CEO of the firm, apologized on his own blog: "I want to acknowledge our error in failing to be transparent about the identity of the two bloggers from the outset. This is 100% our responsibility and our error, not the client's."[38]

2. When Whole Foods CEO John Mackey posted opinions on a Yahoo stock-market forum under the pseudonym "Rahodeb" (an anagram of his wife's name, Deborah), he demonstrated a clear lack of transparency while rubbishing Wild Oats and cheering Whole Foods. He wrote, "No company would want to buy Wild Oats Markets . . . ," all the while planning for Whole Foods to purchase the Wild Oats chain.[39]

Most organizations have policies in place about how employees can engage with new forms of social media from a professional perspective, and there are some standard rule-of-thumb principles that focuses largely on transparency and respect.

Restoring Public Trust

Restoring public confidence in the nation's investment system will take years. Public relations practitioners can either view the task as hopeless—or as a once-in-a-career opportunity to really turn things around. Corporations will need the best thinking of public relations and other resources, as will stock exchanges, regulatory agencies, and individual officers and directors. (See Exhibit 15.1 for one company's strong code of business conduct.)

Apparently it can be done. The trade publication *PRWeek* chose a unique effort as its 2004 Campaign of the Year. The principals were Weber Shandwick, one of

EXHIBIT 15.1

UPS Code of Business Conduct

Public relations practitioners are no strangers to corporate mission and value statements. They write the documents, oversee writing by an outside consultant, or sit on a company committee that hammers out a draft, which then goes through a lengthy clearance process leading up to, and including, the board of directors. Unfortunately, many (if not most) such documents are full of passive language, platitudes and buzzwords, and attempts to satisfy every imaginable stakeholder group the company deals with.

A refreshing change is the Code of Business Conduct at UPS, the "brown" delivery company. The entire document can be found on the company's informative Web site (www.ups.com), but a review of the key elements is useful to future practitioners who may someday be doing the writing, with clear messages for would-be violators:

1. A brief, one-paragraph statement introducing the code of conduct.
2. A description of the reason for a code of conduct, including ways it relates to other company policies.
3. A message from Michael L. Eskew, chairman and CEO of the company, including this warning, "Employees who get results at the cost of violations of laws or through unscrupulous dealings do more than violate our standards—they challenge our ability to grow our business and undermine our reputation."
4. A statement of corporate values and management philosophies.
5. A "Checklist for Leading with Integrity," which asks a dozen questions employees should consider as they create an ethical work environment.
6. A description of the way the UPS Business Conduct Program is administered.
7. Encouragement to raise questions and voice concerns about possible violations of company policies, including access to a UPS Help Line that is available around the clock, seven days a week.
8. A clear statement about retaliation, or the fear of retaliation, for those who raise questions or voice concerns.
9. Additional statements on workplace environment, equal employment opportunity, workplace health and safety, substance abuse, and workplace violence, among others.
10. Policies on conflicts of interest, giving and/or receiving gifts and nonincidental entertainment, customer relationships, doing business with governments, and dealing with confidential information.
11. Antitrust and insider trading policies.
12. Policies on intellectual property, proprietary company information, and protection of trademarks.
13. A description of company political activities, processes, and contributions.

the largest public relations consulting firms in the world, and Foley & Lardner, a national law firm. The campaign was entitled, "The Corporate Governance Price Tag—Sarbanes–Oxley at What Cost?" Its fundamental objective was to clarify the confusion that reigned when the new federal legislation was enacted. Most important, the campaign emphasized what companies *could* do under the new law—not just those things that were prohibited.[40]

Terrorism and Corporate Security

In the first decade of this century, concerns about terrorism and corporate security are tightly entwined. The aftermath of the 9/11 attacks, suicide bombers in multiple nations of the world, continuing resistance to regime change in Iraq, and vulnerability of many U.S. industrial and other public facilities should have brought corporate security to a high state of readiness. Because companies and governments, for good reason, do not publicize their security precautions and contingency plans, one can only speculate about the amount of preparation given to possible terrorist acts that could cripple sectors of the U.S. economy or cause trauma to the populace.

Public relations practitioners will recognize a number of significant challenges in the war on terrorism and concern about homeland security:

- There has never been a time when crisis planning is more necessary. Though corporations are quick to say they are ready for "any contingency," experience shows that CEOs and other senior officers consider the chances of such misfortune to be very remote.

- Employees must be made aware of the reasons for annoying but necessary increased security precautions at company buildings and manufacturing operations. They must also feel assured the company is atop the concerns, so that productivity is not hampered.

- The best time to develop contingency plans and practice them in realistic crisis drills is when the terrorism threat is at a low point. When the Homeland Security needle showing the risk of terrorist attack reaches the orange or red levels, it is virtually too late to begin developing a crisis plan and/or capability.

- One fear of the Department of Homeland Security and White House planners is that a preoccupation with terrorism might make firms so risk averse that they will forego expansion plans and/or cease entry into foreign markets. This would have negative effects on the U.S. economy in the long run, but what CEO would invest several hundred million dollars in an unsettled part of the world in today's conditions?

- Security and crisis planners must recognize that terrorism risks come in many forms other than Al-Qaeda. Antiglobalization organizations, though seldom responsible for deaths, are quite adept at destroying property and disrupting operations through massive demonstrations. Animal rights activists, for example, continue to protest against corporate uses of test animals such as rats and mice—even those tests required by government regulations. A favorite tactic is to break into a laboratory at night and turn all the test animals loose, thus destroying research work done up to that point.

Dr. Murray Weidenbaum of Washington University, St. Louis, Missouri—distinguished educator, author, and public servant—has written extensively about terrorism's threats to international business. Some of his observations highlight the challenges to public and private organizations—and their public relations teams:

> The 1993 bombing of the World Trade Center killed six and injured more than 1,000 people. The cost to the conspirators, however, has been estimated at less than $50,000 in bomb materials and other expenses. The cost to the terrorists of the far more deadly September 11, 2001, attacks is estimated at $500,000—compared to over $135 billion of property losses, cleanup costs, and government bailouts that resulted.[41]

Globalization

At the heart of many protests against multinational companies today is a growing sense among activists that the globalization movement is benefiting only the rich, with no noticeable gains for the poor in the developing world. Consider the following:

- According to 2007 data from *Fortune* magazine and the World Development Indicators database of the World Bank, of the 150 largest economies in the world, 100 are now global corporations and only 50 are countries.

- Based on *Fortune*'s 2007 world's top corporations and IMF GDP data by country, the combined sales of the world's top 200 corporations is still greater than a quarter of the world's economic activity.

- The top 200 corporations' combined sales are bigger than the combined economies of all countries minus the largest 14; that is they surpass the combined economies of 177 countries. According to Rhett Butler of Mongabay.com, "With corporations now making up roughly two-thirds of the world's 150 largest entities, the private sector is arguably as important as governments in directing policy on climate change."[42]

- And in 2007, for the first time, half of the world's population lives in cities, with five of the planet's top 10 most populous cities being located in the burgeoning BRIC countries of Brazil, Russia, India, and China, according to Goldman Sachs. Sao Paulo, where 10 percent of Brazil's population lives, and Mumbai, home to 1.6 percent of India's citizens, are the largest of those BRIC cities. And Goldman Sachs predicts the middle class in BRIC countries will exceed 500 million by 2010.[43]

One crucial challenge to America is that the country is not nearly as revered and respected as it was in previous decades. John Paluszek, former national president of the Public Relations Society of America and senior counsel at Ketchum Public Affairs in New York City, told the Southern Connecticut Chapter of PRSA:

> [C]liché though it may be—there is truth in the axiom that perception is a form of reality. And, folks, America has been *perceived* in many places around the world as dominating. Our powerful economy and our military strength, our postmodern secular culture and our global communications capabilities—all taken together have a displacement effect in world affairs that is unavoidable.[44]

Paluszek also cited Benjamin Barber's book, *Jihad vs. McWorld*, in describing the current global unrest as:

> [N]othing less than the clash between globalism and tribalism that is reshaping the world. He [Barber] characterizes these two forces as creating a destructive "pincer" movement on the nation-state (especially those Middle Eastern and African states artificially created by the fiat of Western diplomats some 80 years ago, in the aftermath of World War I).[45]

Globalization is a weighty topic of current debate. Although public relations people may not provide the economic and social solutions to the gulf between the haves and have-nots, they may be able to sensitize managements and host governments to the mutual benefits of multinational capital, technology and management skills providing jobs, a manufacturing-based economy, and export prospects for operations in less-developed countries.

The public relations profession can help drive the global agenda, according to John Bergen, senior vice president, corporate affairs and marketing, Siemens Corporation:

> The increase in global issues, particularly climate change, is also driving the need for international public relations. American business executives are increasingly participating in global forums like the World Economic Forum in Davos, Switzerland, and the Clinton Global Initiative in New York. The Internet has also brought a global immediacy of news, whether it's happening in board rooms in Munich, Mumbai, or Miami.[46]

Notes

[1] Rowan Callick *(China Correspondent)*, "US-China Yawning Cultural Gap a Threat to Global Trade," *The Australian* (All-Round Country Edition, Finance Section), May 28, 2007, 33.

[2] "Unions Chide Wal-Mart on Chinese Goods," *The Record* (Bergen County, NJ), October 16, 2007, B03.

[3] Bloomberg News, "Two Guilty of Overbilling," *New York Times* (Business Section), May 17, 2006. 10 April 2008, http://www.nytimes.com/2006/05/17/business/17omnicom.html.

[4] Karen Lowry Miller, "The Teflon Shield," *Newsweek* (International Edition), March 12, 2001, 26.

[5] Ronald McDonald House Charities, "Ronald McDonald Care Mobile Program." 2 May 2008, http://www.rmhc.org/programs/ronald-mcdonald-care-mobile-program.

[6] Changemakers.net. Sport for a Better World Competition. Available online at http://www.changemakers.net/en-us/competition/sports.

[7] Earth2tech.com. January 21, 2008, http://earth2tech.com/2008/01/21/project-better-place-and-renault-nissan-charge-ahead-in-israel.

[8] "Key Facts on Corporate Foundations," Foundation Center (April 2008). May 3, 2008, http://foundationcenter.org/gainknowledge/research/nationaltrends.html.

[9] Paul Ostergard and Benjamin R. Barber, "Should Corporations Be Praised for Their Philanthropic Efforts?" *Across the Board*, May/June 2001, 44.

[10] Ibid.

[11] Daniel Gross, "A Company Scrambles to Keep its 'Strategic Philanthropy' Going," *New York Times*, November 12, 2001, G-26.

[12] Jacques Steinberg and Elizabeth Olson, "Billions and Billions Served, Hundreds of Millions Donated," *New York Times*, November 7, 2003, E1.

[13] Marc R. Benioff, "The End of Philanthropy: A New Model for Globalization," *Nonprofit World*, September/October 2002, 31.

[14] Michelle Conlin and Jessi Hempel, with Joshua Tanzer and David Polek, "The Corporate Donors: Business Week's First Annual Ranking of America's Most Philanthropic Companies," *Business Week*, December 1, 2003, 92.

[15] "Investor Relations—Taking a Fair Share of the Responsibility," *Strategic Direction*, July/August 2002, 13.

[16] William A. Niskanen, "The Real Governance Challenges," *Chief Executive*," December 2003, 46.

[17] Peter J. Howe, "Adelphia Founder, 2 Sons Arrested on Fraud Charges; Rigases Accused of Stealing Hundreds of Millions from Cable TV Company," *Boston Globe*, July 25, 2002, C1.

[18] Bill McAllister and Jennifer Beauprez, "Adelphia Founder, Two Sons Arrested in $60 Billion Swindle," *Denver Post*, July 25, 2002, A1.

[19] David Ho, "Adelphia Fraud Trial Under Way," *Atlanta Journal-Constitution*, March 2, 2004, C1.

[20] Allan Sloan, "Lights Out for Enron," *Newsweek*, December 10, 2001, 50.

[21] L. M. Sixel, "'Dead Peasant' Policies Benefit Top Executives," *Houston Chronicle*, April 24, 2002, 1.

[22] Gail Russell Chaddock, "The 'Inquisitors' Who Will Frame Enron Story; Tone and Import of Hill Probe is the Dictate of a Powerful Few Congressmen," *Christian Science Monitor*, February 12, 2002, 1.

[23] Kristen Hayes (Associated Press), "Enron Start-Over OK'd," *Deseret Morning News* (Salt Lake City, Utah), July 16, 2004, D12.

[24] Lee Hockstader, "Andersen Hit with Maximum Penalty; Judge Fines Firm $500,000, Puts It on Probation," *Washington Post*, October 17, 2002, E1.

[25] Grant Ringshaw, "End of the Road for Andersen: The Giant Accountancy Firm Is Doomed, Says Grant Ringshaw," *Sunday Telegraph* (London), June 16, 2002, 2.

[26] "Andersen's Enron Verdict Quashed," BBC News Channel (May 31, 2005). May 3, 2008, http://news.bbc.co.uk/1/hi/business/4596949.stm.

[27] Krysten Crawford, "Ex-Tyco CEO Kozlowski Found Guilty," *CNNMoney.com*, June 21, 2005. May 3, 2008, http://money.cnn.com/2005/06/17/news/newsmakers/tyco_trialoutcome/index.htm.

[28] Grace Wong, "Kozlowski Gets Up to 25 Years," *CNNMoney.com*, September 19, 2005. May 2, 2008, http://money.cnn.com/2005/09/19/news/newsmakers/kozlowski_sentence/index.htm.

[29] Justin Gillis and Ben White, "ImClone Scandal Tarnishes Biotech," *Washington Post*, August 9, 2002, E1.

[30] Thomas S. Mulligan, "Judge Drops Most Serious Stewart Charge," *Los Angeles Times*, February 28, 2004, C1.

[31] Constance L. Hays, "5 Months in Jail, and Stewart Vows, 'I'll be Back,'" *New York Times*, July 17, 2004, A1.

[32] Pia Sakar, "Year in Review; People in Crisis; WorldCom Unravels; Ex-CEO Bernie Ebbers Flew High, Fell Hard and Took the Telecom Giant with Him," *San Francisco Chronicle*, December 27, 2002, B1.

[33] Jayne O'Donnell, "Workaholic Sullivan Turns on Former Boss; Ex-WorldCom CFO Seen as an Enigma," *USA Today*, March 3, 2004, B3.

[34] Steve Liesman, Jonathan Weil, and Michael Schroeder, "Accounting Woes Spark Calls for Change—Suddenly, Everyone Has a Fix for a Tarnished Industry," *Wall Street Journal Europe*, February 7, 2002, 3.

Government and Public Affairs

16

STUDY GUIDE   After studying Chapter 16, you should be able to:

▶ List and discuss the seven major goals of government public affairs programs.

▶ Outline the three major barriers to effective public relations in government.

▶ Identify the major aspects of government–media relations.

▶ Describe public relations' role in the military.

Government public relations specialists—typically called "public affairs officers" in the United States and "information officers" in most other countries—are the critical link between the people and the government. The diversity of technical skills, organizational goals, and public activities of the function of government public affairs is far greater than of specialized and/or traditional public relations practices. And the paramount difference is the public advocacy role played by government communicators to government decision makers. Today's public affairs practitioner must possess a solid mix of communicative arts skills linked to a comprehensive understanding of the organization's culture, policies, practices, and constituents. The public affairs officer is an integral member of the organization's executive management team. Though it may be considered mere "wordsmithing," public affairs practitioners' believe their expanded responsibilities, as well as performing under statutory restrictions, justifies a distinction in name.

Whereas one public affairs specialist in the Internal Revenue Service conducts an information campaign explaining new user-friendly forms, another conducts an enrollment drive for pregnant women to take WIC (Women, Infants, and Children) nutrition education classes. Yet another practitioner writes an op-ed article describing the U.S. Department of Agriculture's "enhanced surveillance plan" to reduce consumers' anxieties toward "mad cow" disease in the U.S. beef industry. Simultaneously another practitioner prepares "infomercials" seeking to gain public compliance for stricter inspection measures launched by the Transportation Security Administration (TSA) to thwart terrorism. No matter the level of government in which one is engaged, a public affairs officer is available to inform the public about an elected official's programs or bureaucracy's doings.

In a very real sense, the purpose of public affairs itself closely matches that of democracy. Abundant and accurate information is used by effective democratic

> *A popular government without popular information or a means of acquiring it is but a prologue to a farce or tragedy, or perhaps both.*
> —*James Madison*

This chapter was written in collaboration with **George D. Lennon**, director for Public Affairs, the National Science Foundation. Prior to taking his current position, he was the national director of the Office of Communication, U.S. Forest Service, Washington, D.C. He is a retired lieutenant colonel, U.S. Army, where he held infantry command assignments and senior staff positions, and culminated his 21-year career as a strategic plans officer in the Office of the Secretary of Defense (Public Affairs).

governments to maintain responsive relationships with constituents, based on mutual understanding and continuing two-way communication.

The Goals of Public Affairs in Government

Government touches every aspect of society, and virtually every facet of government relies on, or is closely tied to, public affairs. (See Figure 16.1 for examples of related program materials.) The overall goals for government public affairs, regardless of the level and, to some extent, type of government, have at least seven purposes in common:

1. Informing constituents about the activities of a government agency.
2. Ensuring active cooperation in government programs—voting, curbside recycling, as well as compliance with regulatory programs—mandatory seat belt use, antismoking ordinances.

FIGURE 16.1

Print Materials from Government

Courtesy National Science Foundation; Office of Science and Technology, The White House; U.S. Army; U.S. Department of Homeland Security; and National Aeronautics and Space Agency.

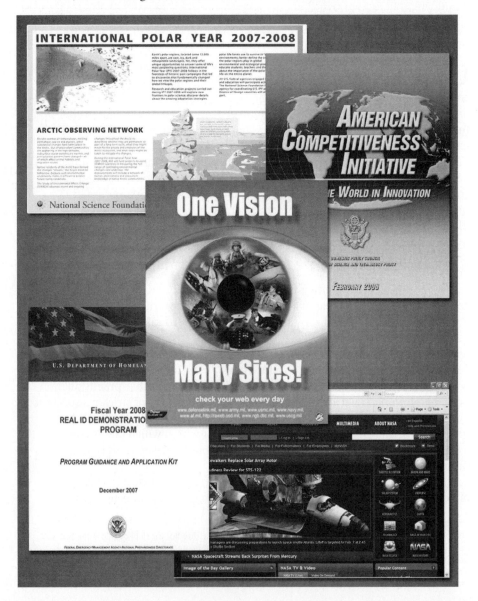

3. Fostering citizen support for established policies and programs—census participation, neighborhood crime watch programs, personal health awareness campaigns, support for disaster relief efforts.

4. Serving as the public's advocate to government administrators—conveying public opinion to decision makers, managing public issues within the organization, encouraging public accessibility to administration officials.

5. Managing information internally—preparing organization-focused newsletters, electronic bulletin boards, and the content of the organization's Internet site for employees.

6. Facilitating media relations—maintaining relationships with local press; serving as the organization's conduit for all media inquiries; educating the press on the organization, its practices, and its policies.

7. Building community and nation—using government-sponsored public-health campaigns and other public-security programs, and promoting a variety of social or development programs.

Informing Constituents

The primary job of government public affairs practitioners is to inform. A multitude of other roles and responsibilities—many of enormous importance and scope—are assigned to specific governmental practitioners, and ensuring the constant flow of information to persons outside and inside government is generally the top priority. And the information function can be global, as the need to inform could well extend beyond the nation's borders to allies or to warn enemies. Bear in mind, however, that political systems may enable or constrain this particular role, especially when communication efforts are directed outside a nation.

For the United States, every federal department and agency retains a public affairs function, ranging from a single individual to an organization as large, aggressive, and sophisticated as a top-tier public relations firm. Regardless of size, the focus is informing general and specific audiences about the organization's services. Usually, these activities are accomplished through external, internal, and general information services. These information transfers are predicated on informing and educating the public, not lobbying for a desired outcome. Likewise at levels below the federal government, the focus remains the same for all—to inform constituents about governmental activities and services. The exception to informing versus influencing a constituency occurs when information services are intended and disseminated to overseas audiences.

U.S. Department of State

The United States dramatically changed how it manages the flow and purpose of its overseas informational services on October 1, 1999. The U.S. government, consistent with the Foreign Affairs Reform and Restructuring Act of 1998, transferred the functions of the United States Information Agency (USIA) to the United States Department of State. (Until the transfer, the USIA had been an independent foreign affairs agency in the executive branch that reported directly to the U.S. president.) A multi-agency reorganization plan submitted to Congress on December 30, 1998, had presented a rationale for that transfer: "The infusion of USIA's strategic approach to diplomacy, open style, close ties with non-governmental organizations

(NGOs), technology for open communications, and skillful Internet use will make U.S. foreign policy more agile."[1]

An Overseas Presence Advisory Panel, established by the secretary of state, later weighed in, reporting in November 1999,

> The United States needs to revise and reform the methods by which it operates overseas to reflect and accommodate a more complex environment. In short, we need a new design that will address the demands of the 21st century as effectively as the old model addressed those of the past 50 years.[2]

The USIA had, since its creation in 1953, interpreted public opinion in more than 200 locations in more than 140 countries and provided analysis and commentary on overseas trends to the federal government. And that function justified the federal government's creation and management of media pools, the selective granting of media credentials, and the use of technology of image management to cultivate desired global images, to advance foreign policies, and to explain or defend international actions.[3]

USIA functions have been transferred largely to three bureaus and a bureau-equivalent office within the Department of State: the Bureau of Educational and Cultural Affairs (ECA), the Bureau of Public Affairs (PA), the Bureau of Intelligence and Research, and the Office of International Information Programs (IIP). All report to the secretary of state. A new position, undersecretary of state for Public Diplomacy and Public Affairs, has immediate responsibility for ECA, PA, and IIP. The IIP is the principal U.S. government organization for

> engaging, informing, and influencing key audiences around the world about U.S. policies, principles, and values—to provide a context for understanding U.S. policy, to help set the international agenda, to forge consensus on common approaches to global challenges, and to help shape the preferences of international actors.[4]

To achieve their purposes, ECA and IIP use personal contacts, speaker programs, the Internet, print media, radio, television, film, libraries, books, the arts, and exhibits to communicate the U.S. message abroad. To facilitate two-way communication, their programs include cultural and educational exchanges of scholars, journalists, students, and cultural groups around the world. In much of Europe and in the developing world, ministries, agencies, and institutes, similar in organization to that of the U.S. Department of State, are charged with image making, news gathering and dissemination, and information posturing to counter negative developments that have national or international implications—or both.

Globally, the former USIA was known as the United States Information Service (or USIS). In American embassies, the chief USIS officials were public affairs officers. They advised ambassadors and other diplomats on relevant public relations issues affecting U.S. interests and policy, and on embassy operations and relationships within host countries.

International Broadcasting

The international broadcasting functions of the former USIA are managed by an independent executive branch: the Broadcasting Board of Governors (BBG). BBG's nonmilitary international broadcasting reaches an estimated 100 million people each week in about 130 markets worldwide. BBG oversees the International Broadcasting Bureau, which in turn operates the following federal entities: the Voice of

FIGURE 16.2

Reporting Poppy
Cultivation in Afghanistan
Courtesy Voice of America.

America, Radio/TV Marti, and WorldNet Television. It also manages Radio Free Europe/Radio Liberty and Radio Free Asia, both of which operate as independent, nonprofit corporations, and program initiatives such as Radio Sawa, Radio Farda, and Afghanistan Radio Network (see Figure 16.2). Consistent with the act of 1998, the BBG and the secretary of state must respect the professional independence and integrity of the International Broadcasting Bureau and its services. The secretary sits on the board, providing information and guidance on foreign policy to the BBG and coordinating its efforts.

BBG launched Alhurra, a 24-hour Arabic-language satellite television news network in Springfield, Virginia, in February 2004. It also broadcasts from studios in the Middle East. The network broadcasts to at least 22 Middle Eastern countries in hopes of winning support for U.S. foreign policy in that region. Also at the same time BBG worked closely with the U.S. Department of Defense in Iraq to establish the Iraqi Media Network (IMN) as a symbol of a free press in that country. The purpose of IMN is to provide comprehensive, accurate, fair, and balanced news and to serve as an example to Iraqi journalists.

The USIA was perhaps best known for its radio broadcast network, the Voice of America, which began in World War II and was responsible for providing information to American troops and citizens in war areas. Its mandate was and remains to

1. Serve as an authoritative, accurate, objective, and comprehensive news source
2. Represent America by presenting a balanced and comprehensive projection of significant American thought and institutions
3. Present the policies of the United States clearly and effectively and present responsible discussions and opinions on those policies[5]

Jess T. Ford, director of International Affairs and Trade, in testimony before a House subcommittee, said that concerns have been raised, even among public affairs officers at the Department of State, about insufficient resources to conduct public diplomacy effectively.[6] Similarly at issue are treating public diplomacy in the Department of State differently from other functions;[7] reversing trends in audience decline, particularly in high-priority markets; using modern broadcast techniques to reach large audiences; allocating resources to focus on high-priority broadcast markets; and questioning the overall efficacy of U.S. international broadcasting efforts in helping the United States achieve its mission overseas.[8]

All in all, the public affairs practitioner, whether working overseas striving to responsibly expose American culture and values or as an agency representative focused on new policy direction, seeks to provide the targeted publics with the most up-to-date and accurate information available.

Ensuring Active Cooperation in Government Programs

How do citizens expand their knowledge about their civic obligations and duties? What actions should citizens take to fulfill them? Why is it important for citizens to comply with government regulations? And what changes in regulations are in the offing? These are some of the questions that frame governments' use of communication campaigns to remind Americans about the importance of, say, having infants immunized, funded health care benefits, personal security while traveling, or something as simple as changes in filing tax returns each year.

Without an informed and active citizenry, elected and appointed officials may lose touch with the true needs and interests of their constituents. Programs costing millions of dollars may be undertaken to address public needs that have been overestimated, while more pressing needs remain hidden. Special-interest politics may dominate decision making. Citizen discontent may linger just beneath the surface, then suddenly appear and be fueled by simplistic rhetoric in place of a deeper understanding of issues.

Even in emerging nations where governments tend not to be as directly responsive to citizen interests, public affairs is still used as a tactical information tool—albeit in much more constrained ways. The point is that the use of public affairs as a two-way symmetric activity—in which practitioners use public affairs to guide understanding of their publics—is a reflection of a nation's media freedom. The more independent the news media are of governmental control, the more freedom government public affairs specialists have to conduct public affairs responsively.

Paris-based Reporters Sans Frontières (Reporters Without Borders) produces an annual "Worldwide Press Freedom Index" that ranks countries based on their relative press freedom (online at www.rsf.org). Rankings reflect data collected from freedom of expression organisations worldwide, RFS's network of 130 correspondents, as well as journalists, researchers, jurists and human rights activists responding to 50 questions dealing with censorship and violence toward journalists. For the first time, Eritrea replaced North Korea as the country with the least free press. Iceland, Norway, and Estonia topped the list as countries with the greatest press freedom. The United States ranked only 48th among the 169 countries ranked. The freer a media system is, the more it engenders an environment in which public affairs practitioners may conduct their activities without undue government restrictions. Advances in the practice of public affairs have, therefore, tended to occur in countries in which media and communications are less under governmental interference and where civil order is not an issue.

The collapse of the Soviet Union led to the birth of 21 republics, a number of which, including Armenia, Azerbaijan, and Ingushetia, have had civil strife and in which "several barriers . . . stand in the way of public affairs maturation and growth."[9] In those new republics, "public affairs practitioners—often the 'new kids on the block' who are staff workers outside formal lines of authority—face uphill battles in gaining status within high-power-distance societies."[10]

The problems and pressures of society increasingly strain the machinery of government. Government is intended to provide services that would otherwise be impractical for individuals to provide, such as police and fire protection, wildlife preserves, civil and national defense, transportation systems, justice systems, social programs, and national museums. These programs, although administered by government officials, are responses to needs originating with ordinary citizens. As the needs of society have expanded in scope and complexity, government at all levels has also grown. Now some see government as no longer an extension of the people but rather as an adversary or "big brother." A labyrinth of bureaus, offices, departments, agencies, divisions, authorities, commissions, councils, boards, and committees has developed. Thousands of forms and reports are generated annually, most containing technical terms and jargon that inhibit many citizens' understanding and confidence in working effectively with government.

Much of the expansion of government in the United States may be attributed to two basic trends: First, increased population, social movements, business and economic activity, and technology have created new problems and issues that require regulatory attention and accompanying new procedures for the public. An example is the Transportation Security Administration's (TSA) public-education campaigns to inform travelers about security procedures at airports and train stations, and passport requirements.

Second, U.S. citizens have increasingly grown to expect more from all levels of government. What may start as an offhanded remark such as, "There ought to be a law against that!" often leads not just to new regulations but also to agencies set up to ensure that the new laws are obeyed. In the simpler times of our agrarian past, neighbors often worked together to build community projects, families were extended to include elderly grandparents, and food was grown locally. More than ever, government is viewed as the primary mechanism to address injustices and inequities in virtually all activities. Examples of governments' responsiveness to protect their citizens include the Fair Housing Act, which prohibits discrimination in the sale and rental of housing; labor laws that address discrimination in employment; and government-approved services such as Medicaid.

Fostering Citizen Participation and Support

Specific public affairs objectives vary from agency to agency, but the basic justification for government public affairs rests on two fundamental premises: (1) that a democratic government must report its activities to the citizens, and (2) that effective government administration requires active citizen participation and support. Even the staunchest critics of "government propaganda" concede that as government becomes more complex and ubiquitous, the challenge of maintaining citizen involvement and ensuring government responsiveness to societal needs becomes more difficult. Elected officials often claim credit for their election on their ability to keep a finger on the pulse of constituents. However, because of the sheer magnitude and complexity of the job, much of that responsibility falls to government public affairs specialists. In *Communicating for Results in Government*, James L. Garnett discussed the importance of straightforward communication with citizens:

> As with planning, budgeting, program evaluation, and other managerial tools, communication is important because it affects people's control over government. It influences employee morale and productivity and permeates all facets of government. Because government decisions and actions often affect more people and with greater consequences, communicating in government tends to be more important and often more difficult than communicating in business.[11]

Thus governments use communication to seek public understanding and their participation in assisting the less fortunate or disenfranchised as a measure toward building community. For example, the United States resettled thousands of Hmong refugees from camps in Southeast Asia and also declared them eligible for aid disbursed by the U.S. Department of Health and Human Services and by state governments. This effort required public affairs practitioners to operate simultaneously at cross-cultural, multiagency, and neighborhood levels as they sought to reduce residents' anxieties regarding the absorption of 60,000 Indochinese refugees into local communities.

The complexity of public affairs work is thus apparent in local government, which provides much community support for the new residents (see Figure 16.3). This level is closest to its constituents, both in the services it provides and in the accessibility of elected and appointed officials. Moreover, the growing influence of neighborhood-level activist groups places a unique burden on local governments:

> Although the neighborhood associations are infrequently direct initiators of new agenda items, they play an important secondary role in creating a policy-making environment that will be hospitable to some kinds of proposals and unkind to others. They incrementally alter agendas, force initiators to anticipate their preferences, and play a vital role in the planning process at both the neighborhood and citywide levels.[12]

Public Participation

Also frequently overlooked is government practitioners' responsibility in soliciting and motivating involvement of citizens in governmental decision-making processes. For example, in Australia, federal and state laws require citizen input in planning major infrastructure projects, making "community engagement" a fast-growing part of public relations practice Down Under. Finland, the Netherlands, and Spain have policies in place to promote representative input and to encourage community participation in government processes. In Asia, particularly when dealing with urban environments, governmental and agency reforms call for citizen participation.[13]

In the U.S. Federal Advisory Committee Act (FACA) of 1972, Congress formally recognized the benefits of seeking advice from, and assistance of, citizens. Although FACA is not a public participation statute, its perhaps unintended effect might very well achieve just that. FACA stimulates discussion of important public issues with private individuals, nongovernmental organizations, or the public at large. Thus, FACA allows for collaboration as a means of obtaining public involvement in a broad range of issues affecting federal policies and programs. Federal agencies establish or sponsor advisory groups (or committees) that (a) provide advice that is relevant, objective, and open to the public; (b) act promptly to complete their work; and (c) comply with reasonable cost controls and record-keeping requirements.

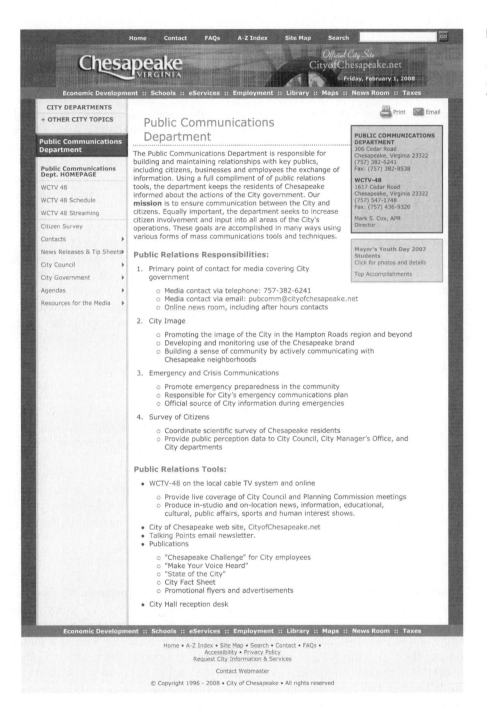

FIGURE 16.3

Public Relations in Chesapeake, Virginia

Courtesy City of Chesapeake, Virginia.

Often the major obstacle to such public involvement is internal, because elected officials and administrators may be reluctant to have their carefully formulated plans altered by the multitude of interests and viewpoints citizen involvement inevitably generates. In *Policy Studies Review*, Mary Kweit and Robert Kweit discussed the trade-offs inherent in encouraging citizen input:

> In the ideal bureaucracy there is no place for citizen participation. Citizens lack the technical expertise, are unfamiliar with bureaucratic routines, and are emotionally involved

in issues rather than being detached and rational. Citizens are outside the hierarchy and therefore hard to control. As a consequence, participation may increase the time needed to reach decisions as well as the level of conflict.[14]

Public Opinion Surveys

Scientific surveys, which provide snapshots of public opinions, are used increasingly in government. Politicians, especially those running for national office, have long relied on the Roper and Gallup polls, as well as privately commissioned surveys, for guidance in formulating campaign strategies. More recently citizen surveys have been used for identifying priorities for government. In addition, surveys are being used as the bottom line for government, whereby citizens' ratings of various services are the barometer of organizational success.

When used to set goals and priorities, citizen surveys prove to be an equalizer against well-funded special interests and lobbying groups. "The greatest strength of citizen surveys is that they have the potential to sample the viewpoints of all citizens—not simply those who choose to participate."[15] However, citizen surveys can be counterproductive when they are not properly administered, as when surveys ask citizens about subjects on which they have little or no knowledge, for example, how best to design a major highway or how to solve complex financial problems facing government. Not only could the results be meaningless, they may cause problems.

> A second serious problem with citizen surveys is that they can have some serious political repercussions. The public may express a negative view of whatever services are dutifully provided. Pressures may develop to enact whatever recommendations the public might suggest. And then, apart from the issues of effectiveness and political advisability, there is always the issue of cost. With budgets getting ever tighter, a citizen survey might easily seem like an unnecessary frill. The costs could be particularly onerous to small governments.[16]

Increasing involvement in programs and activities leads many government practitioners to use other tools and tactics often identical to those of private public relations firms and advertising agencies. Many of these efforts, when not properly explained, lead to criticism and additional scrutiny by both Congress and the press.

Serving as the Public's Advocate

Governments may be public institutions, but they are characteristically bureaucratic, sometimes riddled with process complexity, and often contradictory to the meaning of service. Except for campaigning, elected officials are routinely shrouded behind the machinery of their administration, rarely interacting with and understanding the day-to-day issues of their constituents. The public affairs officer bridges the desires of the official for accessibility with the people and in turn represents the people's values, opinions, and interest to that official. Public affairs officers provide the frontline "face" for an administration before the public through polling, interviewing, and maintaining constant contact in the community.

The practitioner straddles the need for communicating the organization's agenda and the need to communicate the public's desires, conflicting as they may be, back to the organization. For example, in the aftermath of the September 11, 2001, terrorist attacks in New York and Washington, United States–based airlines and the government took restrictive steps regarding passenger movement through airport terminals. Initially the public accepted the protracted screening process as necessary for better security, but in time sentiment soured to outright complaints of governmental bungling.

Public affairs officers in the Department of Transportation and TSA, the targets of this backlash, brought to their officials a well-researched argument to review the status quo despite accusations of being "soft on security." Management listened, and the screening processes were modified, which aided in repairing TSA's credibility.

Similarly, public affairs officers at the Consumer Product Safety Commission advocated consumer well-being by assisting in crafting and issuing a recall of 150 million toy bracelets and necklaces that have lead concentration by weight as high as 69 percent. (Paint with lead concentration of more than 0.06 percent by weight is prohibited from sale.) At the same time, they were communicating the overarching mission—the safety agenda—of the commission.

With the support of their officials, these government public affairs officers performed their traditional public information role, namely, disseminated objective information about their agency (public-information model), and, to a slightly lesser extent, used research to develop a basis for advising officials about the need to make changes internally (two-way symmetrical model). This mix of models suggests a mixed-motive approach in which organizations seek to balance their own interests with those of their stakeholders.[17]

For example, when the Forest Service surveyed its publics about their values with respect to public lands the results indicated two categories of mutual interest:

1. Socially responsible individual values—respondents have a strong orientation toward environmental protection.

2. Socially responsible management values—the public holds a moderately strong conservation and preservation ethic.[18]

Cast against the background of what the Forest Service knows about the values of its publics vis-à-vis use of public lands on a national scale, the agency's Lake Tahoe Basin Management Unit conducted several studies of Americans' outdoor use preferences in the Pacific Northwest. The findings indicated, for example, that residents in communities close to the Zephyr Cove Resort Campground on the eastern shore of South Lake Tahoe would like not just a closer recreational facility, but one that catered to their eclectic interests: hiking and biking trails and Internet and television use. A Forest Service–private interest partnership was established to raise funds to cover the renovation project, which demonstrated the reach and value of government public affairs. The agency also sought upgrades on water quality in the area, and, as a by-product of that effort, added water controls and containment ponds, which improved the overall visual experience for campground visitors.

The public affairs office at the Management Unit used public relations research techniques to determine the public's needs and then used the findings for planning the recreation facilities. Zephyr, then a run-down camping facility in a prized location, now has numerous upgrades that include improved water quality, Internet and television hook-ups, a laundry, and shower facilities.

Electronic Government and Citizen Participation

Governments in developed democracies, more so than those in developing countries, view information as a rights issue: that citizens are entitled to information on the workings of their government. In 2000, Sweden became the first country in the world to adopt a policy that promotes the civic and political uses of information and communication technology to enhance democracy.[19] That national policy will aid Sweden's focus toward becoming an electronic information-sharing society using the latest technology to communicate among citizens and between citizens and their government.

Even though the United States officially may not be an "information nation" in the same vein as Sweden, its federal government uses information and communication technologies to deliver a range of services and benefits to the American people and to encourage citizen participation in governance—electronic government ("e-gov" for short). (See Figure 16.4.)

Every federal agency and department today has established a direct electronic link to the public via an e-gov focus. The National Aeronautical and Space Administration (NASA) initiated a free and readily accessible download capability of images from space. This simple service has resulted in record electronic visits to NASA, permitting the space agency enviable opportunities to connect with the public on a one-to-one basis. The Forest Service's e-gov initiative includes delivering Web-based information to internal and external constituents on demand, improving public access to agency services, and responding quickly and accurately to information requests, including those made under the Freedom of Information Act and those for commonly requested products, records, data, and documents.

The National Science Foundation (NSF), the federal agency responsible for promulgating basic research in science and education, serves the public and its constituents almost exclusively via the Internet. From its Web site, www.nsf.gov, the agency provides announcements on all grants and proposals, educational and scientific findings, and supports a host of other informative sites. Capitalizing on the Internet, NSF has nearly quadrupled its service support to researchers and academe from ten years ago.

But there is an area in which e-gov may not be a reality for a while in the United States—in the exercise of a citizen's fundamental right to participate in the nation's democratic process. For example, electronic voting for six million military service personnel and other Americans living abroad remains far-fetched. Secure Electronic

FIGURE 16.4

U.S. Fish & Wildlife Screen

Courtesy U.S. Fish & Wildlife Service.

Registration and Voting Experiment, a voting initiative, has been criticized for design weaknesses and security flaws that make it an easy target for saboteurs, yet the current paper voting system does not serve the interests of U.S. voters abroad, if it prevents or discourages them from voting.[20]

Managing Information Internally

Communicating internally is yet another major function of government public affairs. Although such communication per se is common in organizations, it assumes a unique significance in government for two key reasons. First, because of the near-instantaneous public dissemination of an organization's statement, policy pronouncement, or action, it is critical that all echelons of the organization be aware of and conversant with the issues. Second, rumors or half-truths may be destructive or counterproductive to any organization, but it is absolutely disastrous to governmental organizations.

All federal agencies, even the Central Intelligence Agency, maintain a public reception area or information room staffed by information specialists at their office locations. These frontline employees meeting the public must be fully familiar with the organization's policies, proposed changes, and practices, and not merely focused on the local available services. Employees must be apprised of organizational developments not so much because they may have to field questions from the media—a responsibility primary for the public affairs practitioner—but because they work in the public domain and can better respond to public requests or concerns if they are current on the issues of the day. Their knowledge of issues fosters an immediate dissemination of key messages directly to a using or inquiring constituency.

The Department of Defense (DoD) has no equal when it comes to managing internal information, which only further strengthens its external image. Each base, post, ship, and camp has what is commonly referred to as a Command Information (CI) program. The CI staff gathers the most current local information of the day and provides it to military members and their families through newspapers, closed circuit/cable access television, Web sites, bulletin boards, and/or daily briefings. Nearly all military organizations have weekly newsletters, newcomer's magazines, and special announcement papers, and many are using an "in-house" electronic information service or intranet. Military members, their families, and on-base civilian employees are kept well informed on the local, national, and global issues of the day, prepared and provided by fellow service members. This top-driven, timely information reduces rumors and anxieties associated with not understanding the current situation. And it provides ready mouthpieces to the public explaining policies or action in "their own words."

Additionally, government agencies work in partnership with one another; therefore, keeping up to date on interagency activities has a symbiotic, interagency significance.

Forest Service employees, for example, collaborate extensively through the intranet with similar other agencies such as the U.S. Department of Agriculture and the U.S. Department of Interior—particularly the latter's Fish and Wildlife Service and its Bureau of Land Management. Forest Service employees, as well as those in Interior, must be well informed about predictions relevant to movements of wildfires, regional threats to specific endangered wildlife, or mitigating environmental damage due to human activities. Such knowledge enables all to play meaningful roles as partners in service to communities, to interest groups, and to the nation.

Facilitating Media Relations

Democratic traditions require that a nation's governmental agencies be accessible to the news media, hence media relations is a fundamental function of public affairs officers. The very nature of governmental programs makes their stakes so high that media interest is also high. Political theorist Jodi Dean succinctly captured the essence of that interest: "Democracy needs media."[21]

DoD's Directorate of Defense Information (DDI) and the National Media Desk of the Office of Communication in the Forest Service are good examples of executive officials recognizing the importance for immediate response to the media. The Forest Service's media desk was created specifically to meet media outlets' expectation for timely and accurate information about Forest Service policies, programs, and activities. The media desk directly supports the agency management objectives by facilitating opportunities for the press to participate in Forest Service programs that include reporting on wildfire suppression, timber extraction, and research venues through well-planned efforts and local coordination. It uses frequent media contact and early sharing of information to keep the attending press well informed about agency issues, resulting in more balanced and informed accounting by the journalists covering the agency.

DDI staff operate on a 24/7 basis and serve as the clearinghouse for all media directed queries to the Department of Defense. The communication lessons implemented following the Vietnam experience continue today as uniformed services support the media with open and unfettered access to their processes—transparency in government.

Building Community and Nation

Because the public affairs practice emphasizes relationship management,[22] much interest has been demonstrated in its role in community and national development and in regional interdependence.[23] Governments use national campaigns for development—in promoting health, fostering tribal or ethnic relations, creating an environment for international investment, providing opportunity for acquiring job skills, expanding international trade, and advancing international relations.

U.S. Programs

In the United States, the federal government launched one such campaign in response to the national prevalence of obesity: More than 64 percent of U.S. adults are medically overweight or obese, with nearly 31 percent—more than 61 million people—meeting criteria for obesity. Yet an estimated 44 million people lack health insurance, and an additional 36 million have no access to any form of health care because their communities have no physician offices or clinics. As a result, health communication on obesity becomes even more critical as perhaps the only channel to address an escalating public health issue.

To tackle what the U.S. Food and Drug Administration calls the "nation's obesity epidemic," the U.S. Department of Health and Human Services launched "Steps to a Healthier U.S.," a bold initiative to promote healthful lifestyles in communities. Several communities across the United States have information-and practice delivery partners: faith-based organizations; employee worksites; "patient navigators," who assist the uninsured and rural families to access health care; kids' networks; and other nonprofit organizations, all of which advocate and promote health and prevent disease.

In a similar vein, the U.S. National Cancer Institute launched a "5 A Day" national campaign in California as an interagency effort to increase consumption of fruits and vegetables to at least five servings daily. The campaign increased public awareness of the importance of eating five or more servings of fruits and vegetables and provided consumers specific information on how to include them in their eating patterns. The national multimedia effort included a 5 A Day logo, "5 A Day Month," subject matter experts available in the produce departments of grocery stores, television and radio spots, news releases, visits to churches and schools, dissemination projects, pitch letters, and fact sheets.

Other Nations

Globally, the United States along with many other nations responded quickly and without restrictions to aid victims in the aftermath of the catastrophic tsunami in the Indian Ocean on December 26, 2006. Notwithstanding previous political relationships with affected countries, nations poured in food supplies; medicines, medical equipment, and emergency response staffs; engineering equipment and operators; and general support in a global effort to restore the affected areas.

On a smaller, regional scale the United States and several other countries are engaged in nation-building efforts in countries such as Afghanistan, Iraq, Haiti, Sierra Leone, Bosnia, and Kosovo that have seen decades of political unrest and social instability. Public affairs plays an overarching role in those efforts, perhaps more extensively in Afghanistan and in Iraq than in other countries. Communication programs and counterpropaganda measures are being used to restore public safety and to reorganize security forces; to rebuild schools, colleges, and universities; to rebuild infrastructures; to organize grassroots democracy and representative government; to assist in skills building, particularly among Afghan women; and to imbue Iraqis, Afghans, ethnic Albanians, and Serbs with a new level of much-needed patriotism that transcends ethnic, tribal, and religious-sect boundaries. There has been progress, even as such nation-building efforts have been an incredibly difficult, if not a disheartening, undertaking because in those countries "nation-building has come to mostly mean the comprehensive occupation of collapsed or defeated states, the remaking of entire societies and sky-high, endless costs."[24]

On a continental scale, government public affairs is even more critical to the effectiveness of the European Union (EU), which admitted 10 additional member states on May 1, 2004. This union of 25 nations has vexing challenges that have major implications for government public affairs. Those challenges include the following.

1. Tensions that are building up around borders of new member states.

2. Concerns that the big three—Germany, Britain, and France—will dominate the Union, threatening the sovereignty, culture, and identity of poorer member states in Central and Eastern Europe.

3. Ideological debate over harmonization of EU tax policies that have already led to charges of "dumping" and to concerns about higher corporate-tax countries losing jobs and investment to the East, where the average corporate tax rate is significantly lower.

4. Divergence in economies that arises from differences in the robustness of member-states' economies. The 10 new members have per capita incomes about one-half those of the original 15 members.

5. Policy of a free movement of tourists and workers across national borders, as well as income gaps and disparate employment levels, which may result in a flight of skilled workers and a drain on social-security benefits.

A key message in the Union's information campaign is that the EU's membership provides a combined population of 450 million citizens—an enormous market for the movement of goods, services, and capital. As an aid toward promoting trust and understanding in the Union, and between it and the rest of the world, the Center for Transatlantic Relations at the Paul H. Nitze School of Advanced International Studies at Johns Hopkins University in the United States publishes a bimonthly publication, *Transatlantic: Europe, America & the World.*

In parts of the developing world that are ravaged by diseases, government-sponsored health campaigns use a variety of communication channels—public service announcements, radio soap operas, billboards, slogans, posters, singing groups, skits, murals, and social encounters—to inform citizens of the life-threatening consequences of HIV/AIDS or malaria and their implications for their national economies. Government-sponsored HIV-prevention programs in Uganda, one of a handful of success stories in sub-Saharan Africa, use an easily recognized national slogan as the centerpiece of a massive campaign to stem the spread of the disease.[25]

Malaysia uses communication campaigns in a variety of nation-building programs to foster interethnic relationships among its people of Malay, Chinese, and Indian ancestry.[26] And it uses nationally sponsored programs, development projects, and nationalist rhetoric, in light of the nation's history of ethnic conflicts, particularly those that came to a head between the Malays and Chinese in 1969.[27] Begun in the mid-1980s, the nation's Department of National Unity launched a Neighborliness Campaign to improve awareness on public safety and about social goals and to foster cooperation with other races at work, in communities, and in pursuit of national unity.

Similarly, one of the objectives of the Public Relations Organization of the Philippines—a professional organization of government information officers—is to assist the government to meet public needs, provide direction to the government's development-oriented information programs, and achieve national development.[28]

Barriers to Effective Government Public Affairs

Public affairs practitioners in government shape much of the meaningful dialogue necessary to make democracy work. Their work carries with it a civic obligation to serve as intermediaries between elected officials and staff and their citizen constituencies. Yet three major issues hamper the work of building and maintaining government and citizen relationships: questionable credibility, public apathy, and legislative hostility.

Questionable Credibility

The public's perceived believability and trustworthiness of public affairs practitioners in general, and governments in particular, have been an irksome issue for decades. Whenever communication practitioners are perceived to have questionable ethics, then it is logical to expect that the organizations they represent reflect practitioner values and ethics. Too often government public affairs is variously referred to as "just PR" or "propaganda machines" and its implementers as "spin doctors" or "flacks." These pejorative labels notwithstanding, the public affairs officer is often the first and probably only contact for a citizen seeking information about a program or relief from a problem or shoddy service.

Accentuating the perceived questionable credibility of public relations practitioners in general is the inevitable association of government information programs with the word "propaganda." Americans have long been deeply suspicious of anything with that label, particularly because this powerful technique has been used in other countries to gain and hold despotic control. Thus, public suspicion of information as "nothing but propaganda" is especially strong when the information comes from the government. This is reflected in a fear that government communication could become little more than tax-supported propaganda designed to persuade taxpayers to spend even more tax dollars. To shore up its credibility among citizens, the U.S. federal government recently took two key actions.

First, it approved the Electronic Freedom of Information Act Amendments of 1996 to harness technological innovations; to further open government to public advocacy groups, the news media, scientists, scholars, and others engaged in research; and to enhance public access to computerized government information.[29]

Second, it passed the Data Quality Act in 2001, which requires federal agencies to develop standards for using and disseminating substantively accurate, objective, and credible information and to develop supplementary guidelines for reviewing and disseminating scientific research information.

An example of government actions that could fuel the perception of questionable government communication was the assertion by the United States and some European governments that Iraq had weapons of mass destruction (WMD). Professor Edward Lordan argued that "the WMD claims have inevitably reduced the administration's credibility, nationally and internationally, at a time when trust is at a premium."[30] He further stated that the U.S. government's reinterpretation of its earlier statements on WMD exerted pressure on various administration units that resulted in new messages that had subtle shifts from earlier positions and were sometimes contradictory. Later developments added to public distrust: First, initial reports about the "heroic" death of U.S. Army Ranger and former National Football League (Phoenix Cardinals) star Pat Tillman in Afghanistan proved false. Second, in what the *San Francisco Chronicle* called the "big lie," the falsely reported circumstances of the capture of Army Quartermaster Private Jessica Lynch further undermined DoD credibility with the media and citizens worldwide. In fact, the failure to communicate accurately the circumstances of the Iraqi WMD program and other Iraqi war developments became defining examples of "spin" for the Bush administration.

The public shift from open support to public outcry was dramatically apparent in the aftermath of the release in July 2004 of United States and British government reports on their intelligence-gathering activities before the start of "Operation Iraqi Freedom." The perceived credibility of government information among citizens was that both governments may have fallen short of exercising their full responsibility to question the veracity of amassed intelligence. That failure may have further eroded citizens' doubts worldwide about the credibility of government-disseminated information. As a reflection of public perceptions of government communication, apathy looms large—the next topic.

Public Apathy

Unlike most business operations, government practitioners usually cannot target small segments of broad publics to achieve desired results and ignore the rest of the people. An automobile manufacturer, for example, may be satisfied with 10 or 20 percent of the car-buying adults in a country. Government seeks to serve *all* taxpayers, or at least as great a portion as possible. This is an extremely difficult task, complicated by the lack of interest among many citizens. One writer wrote that public apathy is a "groundswell" among Americans:

> The hard fact is that most Americans are contemptuous of politicians and cynical about the motives of government and business. The U.S. now ranks 23rd in voter participation among Western democracies, and the share of adults who vote in presidential elections has dropped 20 percent since 1960."[31]

An occasional wave of public apathy is an indisputable fact of public life. The percentage of eligible voters who participate in major national elections is invariably low, and the percentage of those voting in state and local elections is even lower. Only 49 percent of adults in the United States voted in the 1996 presidential election, and slightly more than 51 percent voted in the 2000 elections. The 2004 election saw a reversal due almost exclusively to the deep division between the two candidates causing both parties to aggressively get out the vote, resulting in the largest turnout since 1968—61 percent.

City councils, county boards of supervisors, citizen advisory boards, and commissions all struggle with apathy each time a public hearing is scheduled, frequently cutting meetings short when few, if any, citizens show up to voice an opinion. Local government agencies that appoint citizens to serve on advisory boards often have woefully few candidates from which to choose.

Contributing to public apathy are citizen frustration and a general sense of impotence toward government at all levels. Correct or not, the popular perception of government is one of gridlock, a maze of red tape, special interests, corruption, ineptitude, and partisan politics. A law degree is virtual prerequisite for elected officials at the federal and state levels. The system has grown too complicated for most citizens either to understand or to gain access to services easily. Simply adding a room or a back porch to a home often requires the help of an architect or development consultant to ensure that proper permits are acquired and that no environmental regulations are violated.

Paying taxes, especially to the federal government, creates citizen hostility that spills over into other areas of government not related to the collection of taxes. Despite the annual rhetoric calling for simplifying the filing of personal income tax forms, millions of Americans still must seek the assistance of accountants and tax-preparation experts. Beginning in late 1997, the public outcry reached a peak when the Internal Revenue Service became a target of public and legislative scrutiny because of charges of intimidation, invasion of privacy, and favoritism. In Senate hearings "hooded witnesses told horror stories about IRS abuse, and the agency was depicted as a heartless cell snatching money and property from regular working folks."[32]

Facing citizen hostility is not unusual for many government agencies, even when they are simply fulfilling their most basic responsibilities. For example, consider the challenges faced by wildlife park management officials in controlling the growing deer population. In the Gettysburg National Military Park (Pennsylvania), the deer population is about 12 times what the local forest can reasonably maintain, resulting in deer–human collisions and fatalities. Due to restrictive administrative rules, the National Park Service is limited in the steps it can take to reduce an obvious hazard, regardless of common sense demanding such action. There and elsewhere deer contribute to the spread of Lyme disease and cause damage to crops and grazing lands. Despite what many believe are humane actions to control the deer population, wildlife management opponents have been effective in promoting their cause in allowing deer to roam with few restrictions.

Legislative Hostility

The public affairs function has been established longer in government than in any other field of practice, yet it has never been totally effective or given the respect enjoyed by practitioners in the private sector. In government, as in other organizational settings, public affairs is a legitimate management function that helps make agencies, departments, and other public entities responsive to the citizens they serve. However, government practitioners often face more hostility and suspicion than do other practitioners. They have had a rocky status at the federal level, where Congress has been hostile to information activities in the federal executive branch.[33] This hostility stems from four fundamental and long-standing conflicts embedded in our democratic government:

1. The continuing struggle between the press, fighting for "the people's right to know," and the officials of government, who insist upon discretion in certain sensitive areas of the public business.

2. The unrelenting struggle for the balance of power between the legislative and executive branches of government. This contest is present whether it is between mayor and council, governor and legislature, or president and Congress.

3. The continuing struggle for power between the major political parties. The "out" party fears the power of an army of "propagandists" in keeping the "ins" in and the "outs" out.

4. The protests of industries, institutions, and other vested interests when threatened by proposed legislation or government regulation. They often disparage the use of public funds and government machinery to carry the day against them.

Government public affairs had been handicapped by opposition legislators who prevent maximum effectiveness and accurate accounting of the function's cost and ascertaining corporate value. Attacks on public affairs programs by legislators are less frequent than those by the press but perhaps more damaging.

Legislative opposition is often stimulated by other sources of hostility. The formidability of early federal public relations practices shocked the Congress and highly placed interest groups at the turn of the nineteenth century. Beginning in 1905 through 1909, the Forest Service—an obscure, newly established agency led by its first chief, Gifford Pinchot—aggressively and successfully curried the favor of key newspapers and special-interest groups to move his message of conservation and protection of the nation's public forests. Pinchot and his "press officers" took the conservation debate straight to the people and clearly reshaped the nation's attitude toward unchecked logging and use of public lands (see Figure 16.5). Finally, the Roosevelt–Pinchot campaign for land conservation sparked congressional reaction, thanks largely to the efforts of spokespersons of lumber interests, mine operators, and cattle grazers who had been exploiting the nation's public lands. Congressman Franklin Mondell of Wyoming, spokesman for sheep and cattle ranchers,

FIGURE 16.5

"Alaska" Editorial
Cartoon [Circa 1910]

Courtesy of U.S. Forest Service, Gifford Pinchot National
Forest, Vancouver, Washington.

Circa 1910 illustrating Gifford Pinchot's powerfull
use of the press to lobby for protection of Alaska's
forests.

won adoption of a 1908 amendment to the agricultural appropriation bill dealing
with the Forest Service, which read:

> That no part of this appropriation shall be paid or used for the purpose of paying for in
> whole or in part the preparation of any newspaper or magazine articles.[34]

Thus, the first effective use of public relations to promote acceptance of an administration's policies brought congressional restriction of the function in the executive branch. Congressional ire erupted next in 1910, when Joseph T. Robinson, a
representative from Arkansas, demanded an investigation of the Census Bureau for
employing a special agent at $8 per day in 1909. The agent was to explain to the

public the purpose of the 1910 census. Census Bureau Director E. Dana Durand insisted that it was essential, if the census was to be complete, that all citizens and aliens be reached—through newspapers, the foreign-language press, and agricultural weeklies—and be assured that their replies would not be used for taxation purposes. The committee, after hearing this, tacitly approved.

By 1912 the number of "publicity agents" employed by executive departments was growing, and some campaigns were not beyond reproach. In May 1912, Rep. John Nelson of Wisconsin gained passage of a House resolution to investigate meat inspection in the U.S. Department of Agriculture's Bureau of Animal Industry. Early in the hearings, Nelson was angered by a circular criticizing the resolution and defending the department; the pamphlet had been published before the hearings opened. He charged that the department was using publicity to discredit one of its accusers, and he introduced a House resolution to investigate "the expenditure of public moneys for press bureaus, postage, stationery, and employees by the Department of Agriculture and by other departments; and that said committee be directed to make recommendations to the House as to what steps are necessary to protect public funds from newspaper exploitations."[35] The resolution did not pass.

A year later the Civil Service Commission advertised for "a press agent to help boom the good roads movement" in the Office of Public Roads. The circular called for a "publicity expert" whose "affiliations with newspaper publishers and writers are extensive enough to secure publication of items prepared by him." The circular prompted Rep. Frederick H. Gillett to offer an amendment to an appropriations bill specifying that no money could be spent for publicity unless specifically authorized by Congress. It passed.

The 1913 Gillett Amendment remains embedded in law. It is only one of six restrictions on the function that has been written into U.S. codes and is a source of much confusion. As one government public affairs officer observed, "The amendment does not prohibit the use of publicity; it merely states that such funds be clearly identified."[36] He said that the 1913 amendment continues to intimidate those who work in government public affairs.

Legislative opposition to the function at all levels has led to legal restrictions, circumvention of budgetary procedures, and wasteful practices designed to conceal legitimate government functioning. Legislative hostility and self-serving posturing by elected and appointed officials also causes many competent professionals to shy away from government service.

Government–Media Relations

Since the very beginning of American government, the First Amendment to the Constitution has guaranteed freedom of the press. This freedom was vital to the founders of the new nation, so much so that Thomas Jefferson said, "Were it left to me to decide whether we should have a government without newspapers or newspapers without government, I should not hesitate a moment to prefer the latter."

Media Access to Government

Over the years, the constitutional freedoms guaranteed to the press have been expanded and clarified. Access to government information, in addition to the freedom to speak out or write freely about government, has been codified in freedom of information legislation and "sunshine laws." Except for well-defined areas, such as national security, litigation, certain personnel records, and so forth, virtually every piece of information maintained by the government is open to inspection by the press, as well as by the public. In most cases, a reporter can demand to see unfinished drafts of reports and handwritten notes if the reporter has specific knowledge of these and can request them with adequate specificity.

The right of access to government information and meetings is of paramount importance. Beyond just informing citizens about the official actions of government, the indispensable role of the press as the watchdog of government helps guarantee accountability, reduce corruption, and crystallize public issues and opinions. In addition, the watchdog press serves as the citizen's representative in the broad system of checks and balances. Consequently, government–press relationships often are adversarial. Government frequently argues that any large organization is more effective if it has a degree of privacy in formulating strategies. For example, in labor and contract negotiations or the purchase of land, privacy is needed to avoid giving the other side, often exempt from freedom of information laws, an unfair advantage. The press counters that the public's business should be conducted in the open to ensure that all activities are conducted ethically and in the public interest.

The idea of the news media having responsibilities beyond simply providing the facts and offering a few editorial columns is becoming more accepted. Sometimes labeled "public journalism" or "civic journalism," a more activist form of news coverage is being used by a growing number of media covering government agencies and programs.

Editors at the *Spokesman-Review* in Spokane, Washington, and at the *Virginian-Pilot* in Norfolk, Virginia, are examples of news media unabashedly seeking to affect the agenda of political and governmental discourse. The editors have convened public forums in their communities to discuss the same issues being discussed by legislative bodies, have sought out nonjournalists to write columns, and have generally attempted to increase the number of options and entities involved in government decision making.

The new role of these news organizations is not without criticism. Many government officials condemn the effort as ignorant of the basic principles of representative government. Many assert that American democracy is founded on the idea that most ordinary citizens—who do not have the time, expertise, or interest to fully research and understand complex and numerous issues facing governments—elect persons they trust to conduct the public's business. Reaching consensus, they argue, is a difficult, arduous process already criticized for its snail-like pace. Injecting additional entities with tremendous publicity powers but no legal accountability is counterproductive. Likewise, many journalists are fearful that by becoming newsmakers themselves, reporters and editors may lose the objectivity, independence, and courage to report on public issues.[37]

Government Dependence on Media

The relationship between journalists and government is simultaneously an unquestioned necessity and an obstacle to government communication with citizens. A shortage of media attention is rare, but it usually comes when government agencies want it least. On the other hand, when government agencies want media attention, journalists may decide that the information is not newsworthy or they are so busy working on other stories that they fail to notice a government news release.

The standards used by reporters and government communicators to define news are usually quite different. It is not surprising that much information considered by individual agencies to be of vital importance gets lost in the mountains of information generated by public affairs staffs. Besides, the news media do not have resources to cover all that is the public's stake in government, in part because there are not enough journalists on media payrolls to adequately track all the activities and developments in the many agencies at all levels of government.

Despite those difficulties, government still relies heavily on the news media to pass on important information, as exemplified in the U.S. military's decision to embed journalists in combat units during the Iraq war. (In the 1991 Gulf War, by contrast, journalists relied on reports from a few detached stringers or pool reporters.) Granted, such a decision had been criticized for its potential to compromise the objectivity of news reports filed by embedded journalists, to discourage journalists from expanding their reporting beyond that to which they have been officially embedded, and to create a climate conducive to "groupthink" that encourages journalists to march in lockstep in their reporting. But the U.S. Department of Defense, which organized the program, argued that giving journalists a front-row seat in a war zone would give them a bird's-eye view of war operations and lead to fuller and more comprehensive coverage (see Figure 16.6).

Historically, the concern was that journalists could undercut national security interest by giving "too much information to the enemy on the home front of public opinion," as Retired U.S. Army Colonel Robert Rigg, a paid consultant to the *Washington Post*, wrote in reference to the Vietnam War. [38] Journalists' experiences have been mixed, however. Christiane Amanpour, CNN news correspondent, thinks that embedding made the press uncritical of the administration: "I think the press was muzzled and I think the press self-muzzled. I'm sorry to say but certainly television, and perhaps to a certain extent my station, was intimidated by the administration and its foot soldiers at Fox News."[39] Susan Carruthers also cites a danger of such journalistic restraint:

> [S]elf-censorship is as real a threat to the free circulation of opinion and images in wartime as anything enacted by the state. Hence one increasingly visible anomaly, for "consumers" of news, is that our visual experience of war appears to be contracting

FIGURE 16.6

CNN War Coverage

even as the technological capacity to convey higher-definition images with greater immediacy expands.[40]

Some of the journalistic failings in the coverage of wars such as the Vietnam War and the Gulf War are apparent in more recent wars and conflicts. A content analysis of four U.S. newspapers—the *New York Times*, *Washington Post*, *Los Angeles Times*, and *Chicago Tribune*—shows the following major results:

1. Embedded journalists' newspaper stories about the military, its units, and personnel were more decontextualized and episodic than those of nonembedded journalists.
2. Embedded coverage of Operation Iraqi Freedom was more favorable in overall tone, both toward the military generally and toward its personnel, than that of nonembedded coverage.
3. The overall tone of embedded reports during Operation Iraqi Freedom was not more positive than that of other conflicts—Desert Storm and Enduring Freedom—that had limited use of embedded journalists.[41]

Thus, based on this study, embedding journalists in military combat influences both the nature and the tone of news coverage. More important, two implications must be noted. The first is that embedded journalists must conduct self-censorship, which could force them to abandon objective reporting and information disclosure. The second implication is that episodic framing of news, that is, absent contextual reporting, is not necessarily a plus in that it could pressure journalists to ignore the broader, fuller news events. Process or contextual reporting that delves into meaningful details of war would be more advantageous to both the government and citizens.

Media Reporting of Government

In days gone by, news of government was a relatively simple matter of personalities, oratorical political campaigns, trust busting, and the like. It was entirely different from reporting international trade and outsourcing, world affairs, nuclear energy and waste disposal, mental health, space travel, issues affecting equal opportunity, global warming and the environment, and terrorism. Interpreting the complexities of government requires trained specialists and often takes more time than news media deadlines permit. Hence, government public affairs specialists play an essential role in working with journalists to communicate with citizens.

The media have made much progress in their reporting of governments, but the need for governments to strengthen and supplement today's reporting by the media is greater than ever. Problems in media coverage of federal government are not always the fault of either the media or individual journalists. Rather, shortcomings in coverage are due to the magnitude of the task, as the size of the job is staggering. Washington dominates the nation's news system. News organizations, write Michael Grossman and Martha Kumar, "have become one of the principal forces on the national political scene, influencing the other major forces—the President, Congress, the bureaucracy, the parties, and the pressure groups—and in turn being influenced by them."[42]

Some in government do not think that the media measure up to their task. At no time in history did this point come through as clearly as during the news coverage of the Clinton administration. Allegations of past marijuana use, draft dodging, questionable real estate dealings, and other issues early in the Clinton presidency served as merely a warm-up for what was to follow, ultimately leading all the way to impeachment by the House of Representatives and trial in the Senate. The issues centered not on the job performance of the president but on his purported liaisons with a variety of women close to the White House and his comments regarding the accuracy of those allegations. All of this came at a time when the country was at peace, the economy was strong, and the president's approval ratings in the national polls remained near historic high levels.

Instead of reporting on the president's relationships with foreign heads of state, every major news organization repeatedly led with stories about Clinton's affairs with former government employees such as Paula Jones and Gennifer Flowers and White House intern Monica Lewinsky. Many questioned the role of the press in making activities that had once been considered too sensitive—and perhaps too insignificant—the dominant issue in the nation's headlines.

The increasing emphasis on sex and scandal in media reporting of government has been widely criticized.[43] Yet, such emphasis is unlikely to go away. For one thing, the proliferation of television news and information programming has spawned saturation coverage similar to the seemingly endless helicopter tracking of freeway chases with their inevitable endings. Cable news channels carry from beginning to end the press conferences of officials accompanied by their stern-looking spouses standing behind them as they admit to extramarital affairs or airport bathroom dalliances. Then, to fill time, the story nourishes itself on speculation, rumor, and the opinions of a staggering array of "reliable" sources and "experts," and the ubiquitous panels of "talking heads" and pundits. Government and Hollywood scandals appear to be the prime sources of much of the sensationalized, but often unimportant media coverage that fills the time and space that could have addressed more substantive news.

Military Public Affairs

Military public affairs is geared toward boosting public opinion about the armed forces, maintaining or improving personnel morale, procuring financial support for its programs, and nurturing public understanding and support. But the American public's view of, and relationship with, the military changed dramatically in the 1990s, threatening to weaken recruitment efforts and legislative support. Although the end of the Cold War offered renewed hope for a peaceful world, many internal issues facing the military made front-page news and lead stories for tabloid television programs. Some of the most noteworthy had little to do with national defense, security, nuclear weapons, or similar topics. Instead, the focus of many administrative and news media investigations was often on the sexual activities of members of the armed forces, from the lowest to the highest ranks.

Understandably, the military, like private-sector corporations, has had controversies and historical tensions with the media, "compelling the two actors to interact as antagonists."[44] How did the military respond to the vacuum in media coverage of its activities and programs and to the tension with the media? For one thing, it developed a Statement of Principle for telling its own story to the American public, for projecting its own brand of public affairs, and for guiding military–media relations: "The American public must be informed about the United States' military operations, and this information must be provided through both the news media and the government."[45] For another, the military exemplified that principle by expanding its embedding policy during "Operation Iraqi Freedom" (see Exhibit 16.1).

Captain David Westover, a U.S. Air Force public affairs officer, and Margot Lamme, a professor of public affairs at the University of Florida, found that that

EXHIBIT 16.1

Journalists Embedded on the *USS Constellation*

Lieutenant Commander
Wendy L. Snyder
Public Affairs Officer
Commander, Navy Region
Europe
Naples, Italy

In January 2003 approximately 35 journalists from around the world embedded aboard the U.S. Navy aircraft carrier *USS Constellation* (CV 64), one of three U.S. carriers deployed to the Persian Gulf for Operation Iraqi Freedom. I was the public affairs officer (PAO) for *USS Constellation*, and was responsible for the press embed while managing day-to-day public affairs for the ship and battle group.

Although general PAO functions working with the news media did not change, management of information did. The 24-hour deadlines and eagerness for information put a strain on my "day job" serving the admiral and the captain of the ship. Some reporters were demanding, others more accommodating. Live news coverage, new media deliverables, and the divergence of the operational tempo meant added work to get the message out.

Target audiences were vastly different. With journalists from around the globe, "home" meant the whole world. Language barriers often required more time to explain information after an interview or background on information for their news articles or broadcasts. Cultural differences meant more time was needed to explain the daily routine aboard ship. Smoking, for example, created quite a fuss initially when the journalists first arrived. Daily routine aboard ship for sailors who smoke means going to a designated area and only when they have time for a short break during their busy workday. Many journalists were not happy about this rule as they wanted to smoke whenever and wherever. When they were restricted from doing

their job because they were not willing to adhere to the ship's rules and regulations, however, for safety reasons, among others, they eventually came around.

Working on little to no sleep was difficult but the fact that we were all in the same boat allowed for a lighter side. The press corps, for example, showed me a news announcement they had received about "Operation Burning Candle." I had no information but spoke with the admiral anyway. He agreed to do a press conference. Without details, I was very nervous. (Never let an admiral go into a news conference on a subject that you know nothing about!) When everyone arrived, all cameras turned on me as the entire group (admiral included) cheered, "Happy Birthday, PAO! This is your Operation Burning Candle," and presented me with a cake.

Working closely with the news media under these circumstances gave me a new appreciation for their daily rigors. The same held true for reporters observing the PAO. Many said to me, "I had no idea . . ." and, "It amazes me how young the sailors are with such a great deal of responsibility!" (Note: The average age of a sailor working on the flight deck helping launch multimillion-dollar aircraft is about 20.)

Regardless of the challenges, it was an amazing experience and one that I think every military PAO should have at least once in a career to really appreciate how the two roles are vital in delivering the message. The news media need us and we need them.

Courtesy Glen M. Broom.

principle, when applied to embedded journalism, resulted in broad accomplishments for the military: unprecedented access, better understanding of military life, reporters also serving also as the link back home, greater trust that eased some tension, increased information exchange, and better military–media relationships.[46]

The military's programs and policies frequently are criticized in the news media. For example, gays in the military stirred considerable debate on the appropriateness of the "don't ask, don't tell" rule, an attempt to avoid discharging otherwise capable military personnel because of their sexual preferences. In a larger context, the military is often held to far higher standards of conduct and performance than the general population with very little tolerance for error or personal indiscretion. U.S. citizens expect the military to perform at its peak capabilities all of the time. Hence, an illicit affair by a senior military official becomes the main story of the day. Aware that it is always in the public's eye, the military pursues aggressive, community relations programs that permit it to tell its story from the "bottom up." One account the military seeks to tell is of its members' successes and opportunities and its overall value to society. As good neighbors to local jurisdictions, leaders of military bases serve in advisory roles to local governments and public enterprises. Through cooperative agreements resources such as recreational and sport facilities, use of classrooms and open space are shared or provided to local residents where permitted. Military rank and file members are encouraged to actively participate in their local communities as well. It is no coincidence there are higher percentages of Boy and Girl Scout troops, active participants in local civic organizations, and community-based after-school programs in communities that host military bases. Participation in parades, base and shipboard open houses, and military events such as flyovers or presenting the flag at public events permits the military to remind the citizenry that it is involved in their communities as a contributing element of security to the nation.

The task of ensuring these community relations programs as well as internal information and media relations remain effective falls to the military public affairs officer. The military has for at least two decades been carefully nurturing the professionalism of its public affairs staff and building better relations with its stakeholders. Many of the former journalists and the public affairs officers who fulfill the responsibilities of military public affairs were trained at the Defense Information School, Fort George G. Meade, in Maryland, or at universities offering undergraduate and graduate curricula in journalism and public relations.

For example, the Department of Defense entered into a contract with San Diego State University in 2005 to offer an accelerated master's degree program for active duty public affairs officers. The prime mover was the U.S. Navy, but students from the Air Force and Marines also are enrolled, with U.S. Army officers in line for future cohorts. A total of 37 officers completed master's degrees in the first three years of the program, with many also earning PRSA accreditation (APR) while in or shortly after the program. As Air Force Major Jonathan Riley said of the program from his new assignment in Air Force public affairs at the Pentagon: "I'm thinking at a level I wasn't thinking before I went into the program. I'm more strategic now and have more of a foundation in theory. This will help me in everything I do on the job, every day. It changes everything."[44]

Some recommend that both military public affairs and journalism use a vigorous educational program to understand the other side, endure frustrations and setbacks along the way, educate each other on the peculiarities of each other's culture, and build on similarities and mutual interests.[45] Holm argues that the military's public wounds have been self-inflicted and concludes that "it is essential that the military abandon its self-protective, reclusive nature when responding to the press.

In the absence of response, the American public will fill in the blanks, often not to the armed services' favor."[46]

Government as Business

Three developments have altered some of the basic philosophies of government and changed the way many government agencies integrate their activities into society:

1. An increasing awareness among government entities of the need to compete with other government agencies in the public and political arenas for scarce funding resources
2. A growing attitude among many observers that government should be run like a business, not a nonprofit charitable organization with unlimited resources
3. The increasing need of federal officials and the nation to seek the advice and assistance of U.S. citizens, which led in part to new regulations, issued July 19, 2001, that exempted some advisory groups from FACA regulations

Osborne and Gaebler point out that, unlike businesses, most public agencies do not get their funds directly from their clients or customers. Rather, funding decisions are made by city councils, legislatures, or elected boards. Agency heads therefore aim to please these bodies, not those they are designed to serve. Besides, their clients—unless they move to another city or state—have little choice in the services provided by government. Most businesses, on the other hand, must remain competitive and attempt to please their customers just to stay in business.[47]

In several other aspects, government operates in a competitive, businesslike environment, one in which public affairs plays a key role. Many government activities are being funded by corporate sponsorships, and public–private partnerships are favored by politicians and taxpayers alike. States and cities launch massive promotional campaigns to attract tourists and conventions that bring millions of dollars into communities. These dollars support local businesses, which in turn pay more taxes and keep the general tax rates down for residents. State and local governments also compete to attract new industry through advertising, participation in international trade shows, and tax incentives, thereby creating more jobs and opportunities for their residents and diversifying their tax base.

Public Affairs in Politics

For as long as there have been leaders in society, there has been a love–hate relationship between the governed and the governing. Politicians often spend much of their careers in service to fellow citizens only to be crudely thrown out of office when the political environment or the local newspaper editorial policies change. At the same time, another politician may lack high ethical standards, or may even be guilty of serious crimes, and yet be returned to office when reelection time comes. Such was the case with Marion Barry, then-mayor of Washington, D.C., who was videotaped by police using illegal narcotics, yet returned as mayor of the nation's capital.

The challenge to lead and to serve in the midst of constant conflict is a difficult one for any politician or organization. Cynicism about public affairs in government is greatest when associated with elected officials, or "politicians." Within an environment of skepticism, many view communication from elected officials as mere propaganda. Often many wonder whether the work of government is at its roots purely politics and running for reelection. For example, members of Congress use their franking privileges (free mailing) merely to communicate to their constituents back home.

Similarly, voters decided in California in 1988 that many elected officials were taking advantage of their agencies' publications to gain recognition and popularity. Proposition 73 was aimed at limiting campaign contributions, as well as prohibiting elected officials from using public funds to gain political advantage. Included in the new law was a provision that prohibited government agencies from mailing newsletters and other mass-produced publications if the publication included "the name, office, photograph, or other reference to an elected officer affiliated with the agency which produces or sends the mailing." The California Fair Political Practices Commission, the agency responsible for enforcement, later clarified the law to prohibit any publication that "features" an elected official. This includes—by the Commission's definition—material that "singles out the elected officer by the manner of display of his or her name or office in the layout of the document, such as by headlines, captions, type size, typeface, or type color."[48] Elected officials' photographs and signatures were also prohibited.

In fact, politics and government cannot be separated. Likewise, the role of public affairs in politics and government is inextricably interrelated. At no level of government is public affairs more important than in our cities, where government provides schools, fire and police protection, safe streets and public transportation, recreation facilities and programs, housing, and other vital services. Yet, even with cities in crisis, public affairs has been slow to develop and is often the target of tax protesters and politicians looking for easy targets to exploit.

As the practice in government matures and becomes increasingly professional, however, it is demonstrating its ability to make government more responsive to citizens' needs and concerns, gain acceptance of necessary programs, and make services widely available to those who need them. In short, the public affairs function in government is increasingly recognized as a truly essential element of effective government.

Notes

[1] "Reorganization Plan and Report," submitted to Congress on December 30, 1998. Available online at: http://www.state.gov/www/global/general_foreign_policy/rpt_981230_reorg1.html.

[2] U.S. Department of State, "America's Overseas Presence in the 21st Century: The Report of the Overseas Presence Advisory Panel," November 1999, 31.

[3] Michael Kunczik, *Images of Nations and International Public Relations* (Mahwah, NJ: Lawrence Erlbaum Associates, 1997): 230–233; Jarol B. Manheim, *Strategic Public Diplomacy and American Foreign Policy: The Evolution of Influence* (New York: Oxford University Press, 1994), 40–41.

[4] U.S. Department of State, "Public Diplomacy Worldwide," The Office of International Information Programs, Washington, D.C., n.d., 6.

[5] U.S. General Accounting Office, "U.S. International Broadcasting: New Strategic Approach Focuses on Reaching Large Audience But Lacks Measurable Program Goals," Report to the Committee on International Relations, House of Representatives (July 2003): 6.

[6] Jess T. Ford, "U.S. Public Diplomacy: State Department and the Broadcasting Board of Governors Expand Efforts in the Middle East But Face Significant Challenges," Testimony before the Subcommittee on National Security, Emerging Threats, and International Relations; Committee on Government Reform; House of Representatives, February 10, 2004.

[7] U.S. Advisory Commission on Public Diplomacy, "Consolidation of USIA into the State Department: An Assessment after One Year," October 2000.

[8] U.S. General Accounting Office, "New Strategic Approach Focuses on Reaching Large Audiences."

[9] Hugh M. Culbertson, "Around Europe: An Introduction," in Donn J. Tilson and Emmanuel C. Alozie, eds., *Toward the Common Good: Perspectives in International Public Relations* (Boston: Allyn & Bacon, 2004), 129.

[10] Ibid., 130.

[11] James L. Garnett, *Communicating for Results in Government* (San Francisco: Jossey-Bass, 1992), 14.

[12] Jeffrey M. Berry, Kent E. Portney, and Ken Thomson, *The Rebirth of Urban Democracy* (Washington, DC: Brookings Institution, 1993), 113.

[13] Kim A. Johnston, "A Typology of Community Engagement." Unpublished paper from Queensland University of Technology, Brisbane, Australia, 30 March 2007, p. 5.

[14] Mary Grisez Kweit and Robert W. Kweit, "The Politics of Policy Analysis: The Role of Citizen Participation in Analytic Decision Making," *Policy Studies Review* 3, no. 2 (February 1984): 32.

[15] Gregory Streib, "Dusting Off a Forgotten Management Tool: The Citizen Survey," *Public Management* 72, no. 7 (August 1990): 17.

[16] Ibid., p. 18.

[17] Priscilla Murphy, "The Limits of Symmetry: A Game Theory Approach to Symmetric and Asymmetric Public Relations," in *Public Relations Research Annual, Volume 3*, ed. James E. Grunig and Larissa A. Grunig, 115–131. (Hillsdale, NJ: Lawrence Erlbaum Associates, 1991).

[18] Deborah J. Shields, Ingred M. Martin, Wade E. Martin, and Michelle A. Haefele, "Survey Results of the American Public's Values, Objectives, Beliefs, and Attitudes Regarding Forests and Grasslands: A Technical Document Supporting the 2000 USDA Forest Service RPA Assessment," General Technical Report, RMRS-GTR-95 (Fort Collins, CO: USDA Forest Service, Rocky Mountain Research Station, September 2002): 22–24.

[19] Tobias Olsson, Håkan Sandström, and Peter Dahlgren, "An Information Society for Everyone?" *Gazette: The International Journal for Communication Studies* 65 (2003): 347–363.

[20] Shane Harris, "Voted Down: Why the Ultimate E-Government Effort Failed to Get Off the Ground," *Government Executive* (April 1, 2004): 34–38.

[21] Jodi Dean, "Making (It) Public," in *Public Affairs: Politics in the Age of Sex Scandals*, ed. Paul Apostolidis and Juliet A. Williams (Durham, NC: Duke University Press, 2004), 268.

[22] Robert L. Heath, ed., *Handbook of Public Relations* (Thousand Oaks, CA: Sage, 2001); John A. Ledingham and Stephen D. Bruning, eds., *Public Relations as Relationship Management: A Relational Approach to the Study and Practice of Public Relations* (Mahwah, NJ: Lawrence Erlbaum Associates, 2000).

[23] Maureen Taylor, "Toward a Public Relations Approach to Nation Building," *Journal of Public Relations Research* 12 (2000): 179–210; Maureen Taylor, "Media Relations in Bosnia: A Role for Public Relations in Building Civil Society," *Public Relations Review* (Spring 2000): 1–14; Hugh M. Culbertson and Ni Chen, eds., *International Public Relations: A Comparative Analysis* (Mahwah, NJ: Lawrence Erlbaum Associates, 1996).

[24] Morton Abramowitz and Heather Hurlburt, "The Shaky State of Nation-Building," *Washington Post*, July 11, 2004, B4.

[25] Helen Epstein, "The Fidelity Fix," *New York Times Magazine* (June 13, 2004): 54–59.

[26] Taylor, "Toward a Public Relations Approach."

[27] Ibid.

[28] Zenaida S. Panol, "Philippine Public Relations: An Industry and Practitioner Profile," *Public Relations Review* 26 (Summer 2000): 237–254.

[29] Martin E. Halstuk and Bill F. Chamberlin, "Open Government in the Digital Age: The Legislative History of How Congress Established a Right of Public Access to Electronic Information Held by Federal Agencies," *Journalism & Mass Communication Quarterly* 78 (Spring 2001): 45–64.

[30] Edward J. Lordan, "Mixed Messages: The Bush Administration Public Relations Campaign in the Iraqi War," *Public Relations Quarterly* 48 (Fall 2003): 11.

[31] Mark D. Uebling, "All-American Apathy," *American Demographics* 13, no. 11 (November 1991): 30.

[32] Keith Elliott Greenberg, "A Taxing Challenge: The IRS Works to Improve Its Image," *Public Relations Tactics* 5, no. 2 (February 1998): 27.

[33] Mordecai Lee, "The First Federal Public Information Service, 1920–1933: At the US Bureau of Efficiency!" *Public Relations Review* 29 (November 2003): 415–425.

[34] Congressional Record, 60th Congress, House Rules Committee, 1st sess., 1908, vol. 42, 4137. Historical data provided by Felice Michaels Levin.

[35] U.S. Congress, House Rules Committee, Hearing on H. Res 545, Department Press Agents, 62nd Cong. 2d sess., 1912, 3–4.

[36] David H. Brown, "Government Public Affairs—Its Own Worst Enemy," *Public Relations Quarterly* 26 (Spring 1981): 4.

[37] Christopher Conte, "Angels in the Newsroom," *Governing* 9, no. 11 (August 1996): 20.

[38] Colonel Robert B. Rigg, "How Not to Report a War," *Military Review* 49, no. 6 (June 1969): 15.

[39] Quoted in Ken Auletta, "Fortress Bush: How the White House Keeps the Press Under Control," *New Yorker*, January 19, 2004, 62.

[40] Susan L. Carruthers, *The Media at War: Communication and Conflict in the Twentieth Century"* (New York: St. Martin's Press, 2000), 275.

[41] Michael Pfau, Michel Haigh, Mitchell Gettle, Michael Donnelly, Gregory Scott, Dana Warr, and Elaine Wittenberg, "Embedding Journalists in Military Combat Units: Impact on Newspaper Story Frames and Tone," *Journalism & Mass Communication Quarterly* 81 (Spring 2004): 74–88.

[42] Michael Baruch Grossman and Martha Joynt Kumar, *Portraying the President* (Baltimore: Johns Hopkins University Press, 1981): 16.

[43] See, for example, Julie Yioutas and Ivana Segvic, "Revisiting the Clinton/Lewinsky Scandal: The Convergence of Agenda Setting and Framing," *Journalism & Mass Communication Quarterly* 80 (Autumn 2003): 571; Dean, "Making (It) Public."

[44] Erik Battenberg, "Surpassing Basic Training: San Diego State's Accelerated Master's in PR for Military Practitioners," *Public Relations Tactics* (October 2007): 43.

[45] Colonel Barry E. Willey, "The Military-Media Connection: For Better or Worse," *Military Review* 78, no. 6 (December 1998–February 1999): 16–20.

[46] Jason Holm, "Get Over It! Repairing the Military's Adversarial Relationship with the Press," *Military Review* 82, no. 1 (January–February 2002): 65.

[47] David Osborne and Ted Gaebler, *Reinventing Government: How the Entrepreneurial Spirit Is Transforming the Public Sector* (Reading, MA: Addison-Wesley, 1992), 166–167.

[48] Information supplied by the League of Cities in a March 1990 letter to California city managers. Also see California Government Code Sections 82041.5 and 89001.

Additional Sources

Althaus, Scott L. *Collective Preferences in Democratic Politics: Opinion Surveys and the Will of the People.* Cambridge, UK: Cambridge University Press, 2003. Focuses on the pitfalls of using polls to represent people's voices—or their collective preferences.

Artz, Lee, and Yahya R. Kamalipour, eds., *Bring 'Em On: Media and Politics in the U.S. War on Iraq.* Lanham, MD: Rowman & Littlefield, 2004. Presents an interplay among foreign policy, public relations, marketing, news media, and warfare within the context of the war in Iraq.

Berinsky, Adam J. *Silent Voices: Opinion Polls and Political Representation in America.* Princeton, NJ: Princeton University Press, 2004.

Creighton, James L. *The Public Participation Handbook: Making Better Decisions Through Citizen Involvement:* Hoboken, NJ: John Wiley & Sons, 2005

Henry, Nicholas. *Public Administration and Public Affairs.* 10th ed. Upper Saddle River, NJ: Prentice Hall, 2006.

Lerbinger, Otto. *Corporate Public Affairs: Interacting with Interest Groups, Media, and Government.* Hillside, NJ: Lawrence Erlbaum Associates (LEA Series), 2005.

McNabb, David E. *Research Methods in Public Administration and Nonprofit Management: Quantitative and Qualitative Approaches.* Armonk, NY: M. E. Sharpe, 2002.

Newland, Chester A. "Public Management and Reform in the United States." In *Public Sector Reform: An International Perspective,* edited by Brendan C. Nolan, 21–32. Houndmills, United Kingdom: Palgrave, 2001.

Smith, Jeffery A. *War and Press Freedom: The Problem of Prerogative Power.* New York: Oxford University Press, 1999. Discusses military–media relations from the French and American revolutions to the Cold War.

Sproule, J. Michael. *Propaganda and Democracy: The American Experience of Media and Mass Persuasion.* New York: Cambridge University Press, 2005.

Nonprofits, Trade Associations, and Nongovernmental Organizations

17

STUDY GUIDE   After studying Chapter 17, you should be able to:

▶ Describe the role of public relations in the nonprofit sector.

▶ Outline some of the major changes affecting nonprofit organizations, health care, and education.

▶ List and briefly discuss major changes in recent public relations practice in nonprofit organizations.

▶ Discuss the changing role of public relations in health-care organizations.

▶ Outline the major purposes of associations, professional societies, and labor unions.

▶ List the major public relations activities of associations and professional societies.

▶ Describe the major purposes of public relations in the labor movement.

Nonprofit organizations especially seem to allow for a broad array of activities and services that may not be provided otherwise.

More so in the United States than in any other country, voluntary nonprofit organizations provide many of the social, educational, cultural, and welfare services vital to society. In effect, the nonprofit sector fills the gaps in meeting the needs of society left unattended by the other two sectors— for-profit corporations and government agencies. Recognition of the role and importance of nonprofit organizations in society highlights the need for effective public relations in the "third sector."

The Third Sector

If you attend a state university, listen to public radio, visit museums, go to church, buy Girl Scout cookies, or give clothes and furniture to the Salvation Army, you have encountered a nonprofit organization.

Nonprofit organizations address a range of issues that affect people's lives, including health care, homelessness, environmental concerns, youth development, job training, arts and culture, education, and much more. They are organized to provide a variety of services and activities of public or private interest.

Nonprofit organizations did not always play such a large and significant role in U.S. society. There were only 12,500 charitable tax-exempt organizations not affiliated with churches in 1940, and only 32,000 in 1950.[2] Today there are nearly 1.5 million nonprofit organizations.[3]

This chapter was written in collaboration with **Jim McBride**, president of McBride Communications and lecturer in the School of Journalism and Media Studies at San Diego State University. He formerly served 22 years as director of Public Affairs and Communication for the Kaiser Permanente Medical Care Program, San Diego, California.

Defining Nonprofit Organizations

Nonprofit organizations exist as a special category of organizations in the tax code in recognition that society is "delegating public tasks to private groups."[4] Although there are various types of nonprofit organizations, and legal distinctions among them, they are all exempt from federal taxes. A definition of the nonprofit sector that can be applied in many countries includes five distinguishing features of such organizations:

1. *Organized.* In short, there is some institutionalized entity, meaning that the organization has a charter, regular meetings, officers, rules, or other indicators of relative permanence.

2. *Private.* Nonprofit organizations are institutionally separate from government, meaning that they are not agencies of or controlled by government, even if they receive government funding.

3. *Nonprofit distributing.* Nonprofit organizations do not attempt to generate profits for the owners or directors. This does not mean that nonprofit organizations cannot make a profit. Rather, it means that distributing the profits to those who manage or direct the enterprise is prohibited, hence the term *not-for-profit,* or *nonprofit.*

4. *Self-governing.* Nonprofit organizations govern themselves and their activities, meaning that they set their own procedures and are independent of external control. They have their own boards of directors and provide opportunities for citizen involvement without government control or direction.

5. *Voluntary.* At a minimum, there must be some voluntary participation in either the management of the organization or in the conduct of its program, meaning that there is some aspect of charitable contribution involved.

And although debate continues over whether or not the wide variety of charitable tax-exempt organizations truly represents a category that can be meaningfully defined, there is little question about the interdependence of government and the nonprofit sector.

For example, then-President George H. W. Bush asked Congress for $425 million to support his Points of Light Initiative to help fight drug abuse, illiteracy, homelessness, and other critical social problems. President Bush recognized that nonprofit organizations are essential to the quality of life and in some instances the very survival of many citizens: "I have always felt that private citizens, banding together to lift the lives of others, can give the extra special touch of compassion that government is simply incapable of providing."[5]

The Clinton administration continued to emphasize the essential role of nonprofit organizations in "building a bridge to the twenty-first century," and President George W. Bush identified the importance of the church community in addressing pressing community needs by encouraging "faith-based initiatives."

Volunteerism and Philanthropy

Philanthropy is the act of giving resources (money, volunteer time, etc.) to help individuals, causes, or organizations.[6] In many nonprofit organizations, volunteers mean the difference between providing services and closing down the organization. According to the Bureau of Labor Statistics, 61.2 million people volunteered at least once to do unpaid work through or for an organization between September 2005 and September 2006. The organizations for which these volunteers worked were most often religious (35 percent), followed by education or youth-related service (26 percent).[7]

Despite these impressive numbers, however, the number of volunteers and donated dollars are seldom enough to meet the increased demand for nonprofit organizations' services.

While the demand for government services continues to outpace revenues, state, county, and local budgets have been cut, causing even fewer staff and reduced resources for social services. This focuses attention on the importance of philanthropic support for nonprofit organizations—a key educational role for public relations to play.

Fortunately, charitable giving in America was $295 billion in 2006, a new record for generosity. This was a 4.2 percent increase over 2005 (see Figure 17.1 for contribution sources).[8]

According to Henry Goldstein, chair of Giving USA Foundation:

> People are motivated to give because they value the cause, whether it is religion, education, or international relief. Charitable giving above the 2 percent of gross domestic product is one demonstration of our nation's renewed commitment to the good works done by charities and congregations.[9]

The charitable giving was directed to several types of organizations, with religion and education being the largest beneficiaries. Figure 17.2 shows the types of organizations that received contributions.

Changing Climate

The nonprofit sector operates within a climate of change:

1. Government cutbacks continue to shift responsibility for public service and assistance to voluntary organizations.

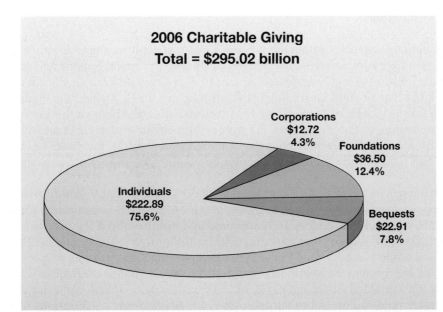

2006 Charitable Giving
Total = $295.02 billion

Corporations
$12.72
4.3%

Foundations
$36.50
12.4%

Individuals
$222.89
75.6%

Bequests
$22.91
7.8%

FIGURE 17.1

Charitable Giving by Source

Courtesy Giving USA 2007, Giving USA Foundation.

FIGURE 17.2

Charitable Giving by
Type of Recipient

Courtesy Giving USA 2007,
Giving USA Foundation.

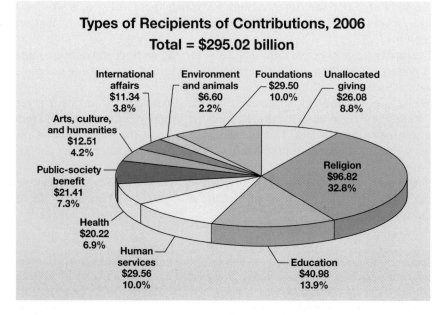

Types of Recipients of Contributions, 2006
Total = $295.02 billion

International affairs $11.34 3.8%

Environment and animals $6.60 2.2%

Foundations $29.50 10.0%

Unallocated giving $26.08 8.8%

Arts, culture, and humanities $12.51 4.2%

Public-society benefit $21.41 7.3%

Religion $96.82 32.8%

Health $20.22 6.9%

Human services $29.56 10.0%

Education $40.98 13.9%

2. Competition is intense among hospitals and charitable groups for financial donations and volunteer support.

3. Demand for social and support services exceeds available resources.

4. Diversity and cultural issues in the workplace and among target publics must be addressed.

5. There is growing public concern about the credibility and accountability of tax-exempt organizations and whether increased government regulation is needed.[10]

6. To address social problems, nonprofits are building collaborative relationships and developing strategic partnerships with corporate donors and media organizations.

Charitable agencies within the nonprofit sector are still reeling from exposés of six-figure executive salaries and charges of financial mismanagement and lavish spending. Even the highly respected American Red Cross suffered significant criticism and negative publicity for failing to distribute in a timely manner the funds donated for the victims of the September 11 terrorist attacks. Although this tarnished the reputation of the Red Cross, the agency brought in a new CEO and subsequently announced sweeping changes in how disaster victims can access needed help and financial resources (see Chapter 15 about subsequent Katrina response problems).[11]

Although there is some evidence that donors have a long memory when it comes to scandals and mistakes, the nonpartisan research organization Public Agenda reported that donors are passionate and positive about the charities and nonprofits they support, but concerned when these organizations market themselves like "big business." The Public Agenda report highlights the key role of honest, credible communications in instilling and maintaining public confidence.[12]

Reform-minded critics and public officials call for more effective policing of all charitable fund-raising and fuller disclosure of how nonprofit organizations spend

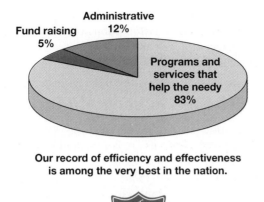

FIGURE 17.3

The Salvation Army
Contribution Solicitation
Brochure

their funds. Public relations is charged with both helping rebuild credibility and maintaining or trying to restore public confidence in the many charitable agencies and voluntary groups that serve the needs of so many. Figure 17.3 illustrates one organization's rebuttal.

As health-care costs and the cost of prescription medications continued to rise through the 1990s and 2000s, health insurance became less affordable and access to care diminished. The nation debated why health care costs so much; who will pay; who will be covered; what care will be available; and what are the roles of government, health insurance companies, health maintenance organizations (HMOs), private hospitals, doctors, nurses, and other caregivers.

Consumers, providers of health services and those who pay for health care—including the government—have demanded changes in the financing of health care. But some of these reform initiatives impacted quality of care and access to services, prompting the media to scrutinize the health industry. Early in 2007, for example, reporters from the *Washington Post* uncovered major problems with the outpatient care given to physically and emotionally wounded military veterans at Walter Reed Army Hospital. Veterans waited excessively long for medical appointments in buildings with mold, peeling paint, and mouse droppings.[13] The aftermath included resignations, firings, Congressional hearings, and a presidential apology.[14]

Questions about cost, access, and quality also dominated the public debate about education reform. Growing public concern prompted a major shift toward greater accountability in education. At the national level, for example, Congress passed the No Child Left Behind Act of 2001 to ensure quality education by, among other things, increasing accountability among schools and teachers, as well as requiring higher student scores—with financial consequences if performance standards are not met. Although many school superintendents across the country instituted standards of accountability, teachers unions and others lobbied for additional financing for schools as a better way to address educational problems.

Each year, numerous studies and countless initiatives examine every aspect of education. For example, "Quality Counts 2008: Tapping into Teaching," a report by *Education Week,* graded individual states on performance outcomes and policy efforts in areas such as chance for success index, college preparatory curriculum, and indicators for teacher quality. As the merits of the different reform proposals were debated, education administrators invited public relations specialists to work more closely with school districts, colleges and universities, and educational associations, as well as with parents and teachers.[15]

Role of Public Relations in Nonprofit Organizations

In short, following a historic pattern, public relations is often added, expanded, and elevated in stature when organizations are confronted by outside forces, threatened with funding cuts or outright elimination, or otherwise pressured to change or reform. The nonprofit sector faces all these crises in an environment of increasing competition for donations, diminishing government subsidies, and increasing demand for services.

In most nonprofit agencies public relations aims to

1. Define or "brand" the organization, gain acceptance of its mission, and protect its reputation.
2. Develop channels of communication with those an organization serves.
3. Create and maintain a favorable climate for fund raising.
4. Support the development and maintenance of public policy that is favorable to an organization's mission.
5. Inform and motivate key organizational constituents (such as employees, volunteers, and trustees) to dedicate themselves and work productively in support of an organization's mission, goals, and objectives.

Even though these objectives are common to most nonprofit organizations, the public relations tactics may differ greatly. For example, hospitals typically invest relatively more in public relations and associated programs such as marketing and development. In recent years, hospitals and health-care organizations have integrated public relations with marketing, as well as business development, government affairs, physician education, and even strategic planning.

To the extent that social and economic conditions require public support, public relations helps create the public policy environment, volunteer participation, and philanthropic support crucial to the survival of charitable organizations.

Health-care agencies, social service agencies, churches, educational institutions, and fine and performing arts groups all depend on public support (see Exhibit 17.1 for fund-raising principles).

The intense competition for limited resources in recent years has led to profound changes in how public relations is practiced in nonprofit organizations:

1. Integrating public relations with marketing and management by objectives have emerged as important parts of the communication strategy.
2. Nonprofit sector leaders (boards of directors or trustees and program managers) have raised the standards and stepped up pressure to engage professional public relations assistance—either hiring staff or outside consultants.
3. Recruiting volunteers and obtaining donations are standard expectations of the public relations role.
4. Paid advertising has emerged as a major controlled communications tactic for nonprofit organizations, particularly for the health-care industry.

EXHIBIT 17.1

Principles of Fund Raising

Preparation

1. The five essentials of a successful campaign are a strong case, effective leadership, conscientious workers, prospects willing and able to give, and sufficient funds to finance the campaign.
2. Committee work and publicity work should be coordinated and spelled out in detail in advance.
3. The cost of a campaign, within reasonable limits, should be estimated in advance.
4. All campaign activities should be given a time limit and specific deadlines.

Committee Work

1. The originating group, whether a committee or a board of directors, should be a representative body.
2. Strong leadership is a necessity.
3. The effectiveness of the group depends on the degree to which individuals accept responsibility.
4. Committees are better at critiquing than creating. Before asking for ideas or suggestions for a plan, give each member of the group a copy of the plan to critique.

Publicity

1. The first objective of publicity is to sell the idea; the second objective is to sell the means of its accomplishment.
2. Publicity materials should appeal both to the emotions and to the intellect.
3. Publicity must have continuity, with all the elements of a campaign tied together with a theme of common appeal

4. Publicity should proceed from the general to the specific. Interest in an idea proceeds from an appeal of general application.
5. Cheap publicity is expensive. Quality in publicity efforts pays dividends.
6. Publicity should be positive and not negative. Effective publicity always plays up elements of strength.

Campaign Operation

1. A campaign should solve immediate financial needs and lay a firm foundation for future campaigns.
2. Effective canvassing answers five questions: why, where, who, what, and how.
3. Campaigns should periodically reach milestones to arouse and maintain interest.
4. All canvassing, even for special gifts, should be conducted in an atmosphere of universality. Prospects typically ask, "What are others doing?"
5. Campaigns should be conducted under a steady and constant pressure and sense of urgency.
6. The time spent on a campaign varies directly with the size of the goal and inversely with the popularity of the appeal.
7. The direct appeal for help should be made when interest is at its peak.
8. There are four tests of the effectiveness of campaign operations: quality, quantity, cost, and time.
9. Campaign impact is determined by the degree to which the campaign objectives were achieved.

5. Strategic partnerships linking nonprofits with corporate donors and news media organizations have emerged to enhance the reputation of nonprofits and promote their services.
6. Technology—including Web sites, e-mail, social media, and portable communication devices—has extended the selectivity and reach of communication, but has raised questions about ethics, privacy, and legitimacy.

In addition to various relationship-building and communication functions, the public relations role includes support for the fund-raising effort.

Nonprofit organizations generate revenue from three major sources: *private charitable giving* (gifts from individuals, corporations, and foundations), *government support or payments* (grants and contracts or reimbursements for services), and *private fees and payments* (proceeds from the sale of services or products to the consumer). Nonprofit organizations in the United States generate 52 percent of their revenue from private fees and payments, 30 percent from government sources, and 19 percent from private charitable giving.[16]

These data make clear that nonprofits are dependent on multiple funding sources as well as strategic public relations planning to meet the social, cultural, educational, and health-care needs of society.

Foundations

Private and community grant-making foundations are part of the growing nonprofit sector. A foundation is a nongovernmental, nonprofit organization that uses its own funds to provide grants and financial assistance, primarily to other unrelated nonprofit agencies for educational, social, religious, cultural, or other charitable activities.[17]

There are two general types of foundations—private foundations and public foundations. Private foundations are funded by one source, whether an individual, a family, or a corporation. Public foundations, in contrast, receive funds from multiple sources, including private foundations, individuals, government agencies, and their own service fees. Unlike private foundations, public foundations must continue to seek money from many sources in order to keep their tax-exempt status.[18]

There are about 71,000 active private and public foundations in the United States, with assets totaling $550 billion. The largest foundation, by size of assets, is the Bill and Melinda Gates Foundation, which has more than $33 billion in assets. The Ford Foundation is the second largest with assets totaling $13.6 billion. Foundations have given grants, scholarships, and employee matching gifts totaling more than $38 billion.[19]

Social Service Agencies

Nonprofit social service agencies, sometimes called human service agencies, fill a vital role in the health, safety, and well-being of millions of Americans. These nonprofit agencies and programs fill needs that other organizations are unable to meet by providing services and resources that are not accessible or not readily available to those who need them. Social service programs typically are organized to provide parent and child programs, food and nutrition programs, shelter, services for the deaf and vision impaired, drug rehabilitation, services for the mentally ill or refugees, those suffering from depression, and much more. Programs such as Medicaid and Food Stamps are generally considered social welfare programs.

Although federal and state governments spend hundreds of billions on social welfare and social service programs annually, it is still not enough to meet the demand for services. In many communities, budget deficits are requiring cuts in government spending on social programs. The burden of funding community nonprofit agencies shifts to American philanthropy, as nonprofit agencies strive to do more with less (i.e., recruit more volunteers and seek additional donations to fund programs and services). Given this situation, enlightened nonprofit social service agencies realize that public relations expertise is required to achieve organizational goals such as maintaining existing funding and attracting new philanthropy, building a committed staff and mobilizing volunteers, educating legislators and key community leaders to gain their support, establishing strategic partnerships, and so on.

A decision that social service agencies face is whether to hire a public relations professional, contract with an outside firm for these services, or use internal staff and volunteers. Regardless of which choice is made, it is crucial for social service agencies to muster public support through a planned, strategic public relations program that will endure in good times or bad. Figure 17.4 shows a graphic illustration of the major responsibilities of the Salvation Army that have public relations implications.

Beyond the fund-raising challenge, communicating with potential beneficiaries of social services can be a challenge. Without professional public relations assistance, it may be difficult to reach the people who need services. Many do not know how to access available services or simply do not know that services are available. In addition, because agencies must respect the privacy of clients, publicity and media coverage may be limited. In ethnically diverse communities, communication must address cultural and language differences or low education levels. People with disabilities may present additional communication challenges.

The role of public relations in social service agencies is rich with possibilities and variety. It includes counseling executive directors and boards of directors about the role of communication, developing a planned program to address

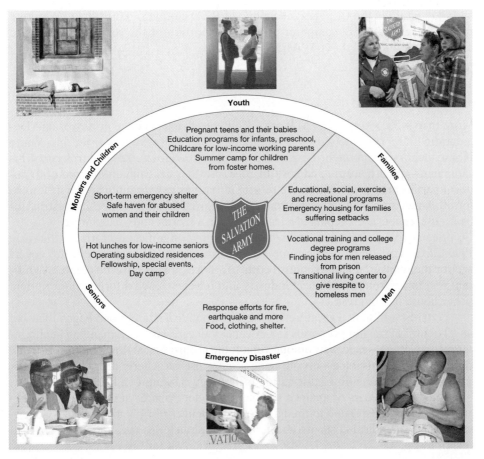

FIGURE 17.4

The Salvation Army
Doing the Most Good

Used with permission from The Salvation Army, San Diego. Photos by Suszi Woodroff Lacey and Tod Lilburn.

organizational issues and achieve goals, providing support for volunteer recruit-ment and fund-raising, and educating key publics about how agencies are building a healthier community.

To help accomplish their missions, nonprofits have increasingly developed strategic partnerships with news organizations, corporate donors, or others. Strategic partnerships often include a corporate donation used in part to fund a media cam-paign featuring a nonprofit agency. The donor gets positive publicity as a responsi-ble corporate neighbor; the news organization gets the funds and enhances its image as a community leader; and the nonprofit agency receives significant media cover-age to reach its target publics and tell its story.

The American Red Cross and FedEx Corporation have worked in partnership for many years—a partnership now commonly referred to as "cause marketing." FedEx uses its transportation expertise and provides shipping of disaster relief supplies to help the Red Cross respond to disasters around the world. In addition, FedEx donates $1 million in cash and in-kind services to the Red Cross annually.[20]

Cause marketing partners nonprofits with businesses to accomplish mutual goals such as funding for the nonprofit and an enhanced image for the business, which can lead to additional sales. Some cause marketing projects involve the design and sale of customized products.[21] For example, to raise money for The Global Fund, which fights HIV/AIDS in Africa, recording star Bono and Bobby Shriver, chairman of DATA (Debt, AIDS, Trade, Africa), teamed up with major businesses to produce "RED" branded products. A portion of the proceeds from the sale of RED products goes to The Global Fund. Apple Computer developed RED iPods and iPod Shuffles, the Gap designed a line of RED clothing, and Dell and Windows produced several RED computer products. A portion of the selling price goes to The Global Fund to fight HIV/AIDS.[22]

Health Care

More than a decade ago, Harris Wofford, a Pennsylvania college professor and De-mocratic state official, scored a stunning U.S. Senate victory over his White House–endorsed opponent by making health-care reform the centerpiece of his campaign—quality, access, and cost. In 2008, presidential candidates from both po-litical parties proposed health-care reform initiatives to guarantee health insurance for all Americans, make prescription drugs affordable, address obesity, restrict to-bacco use, encourage keeping electronic medical records, and much more.

Clearly, the health-care system in America needs significant reform. In the early 1990s, President Bill Clinton's complex proposal to expand access to health cover-age for the uninsured and to control costs for those already covered created signifi-cant resistance from the medical industry and never reached a formal floor vote in either house of Congress.

Congress and state legislatures changed the political strategy and began focusing on a handful of smaller proposals to reform health care, such as expanding health in-surance coverage—especially among vulnerable groups such as low-income Hispanic children and the disabled—encouraging greater use of generic drugs, adjusting tax credits, and exploring how information technology can improve health-care quality.

Still, despite years of analysis and health-policy debates at every level of gov-ernment, the issues related to the quality, access, and costs of health care remain un-resolved, and medical costs are accelerating at a much faster rate than the overall cost of living.

Health Care in Crisis

The crisis in health care has been with us for so long that some would say we always will be in a state of crisis. Sherry Glied, PhD, of Columbia University summarizes the crisis this way:

> In some senses we've always been in a health care crisis. . . . We have a real conflict between how much money we're willing to spend on health care and how much we want for that money, and that's a perpetual conflict.[23]

Quality and access to care are always important in health care, but costs have overwhelmed them as the dominant concern. Factors influencing the continuing rise in health-care costs include advancing medical technology, new treatments, skyrocketing medical malpractice rates, increasing government regulation, and surging costs of prescription drugs. Direct-to-consumer marketing of prescription drugs is creating demand where none previously existed.

An ongoing problem related to the costs of health care is the number of uninsured Americans, which increased in 2006 to 47 million—including almost 9 million children.[24] The number of uninsured has both financial and health implications. Without insurance, people may delay or not receive treatment, which can lead to more serious illness, which is usually more costly. When the uninsured cannot pay for the care received, hospitals seek government reimbursement, which may or may not be successful. Hospitals may absorb the cost of uncompensated care or may shift the costs to those with insurance. For example, in California, this cost-shifting results in a 10 percent increase in health premiums for those with health insurance.[25]

In addition to adequately funding health care, including care for the uninsured, health-care leaders and policy makers wrestle with additional complex issues like modernizing Medicare; attending to the special needs of the mentally ill and those with AIDS, Alzheimer's and Parkinson's; and preventing chronic conditions such as diabetes, obesity, and asthma.

Health-Care Public Relations and Marketing

Hospitals and health-care organizations must remain financially viable. If they do not make enough money to cover costs, they may face budget cuts, reduction in services, or layoffs, all of which could potentially affect the survival of hospitals and the health-care system.

To survive in this complex, competitive, and rapidly changing environment, health-care leaders have turned to public relations and marketing for help. Marketing identifies the wants and needs of a hospital's constituents and guides the organization toward effectively satisfying those wants and needs. This can be challenging for three reasons:

1. Generally, the payer for health services—an insurance company—has limited control over the purchase or cost of service.

2. It is usually the physician or other provider—rather than the patient—who chooses a hospital or orders services.

3. The services rendered can be painful and unpleasant, clearly making a distinction between wants and needs.

Like marketing, health-care public relations has evolved into a highly regarded management function that is expected to contribute to the "bottom line." Today's public relations professionals must understand the business and financing of health care, know about health-care issues, have an ability to think and plan strategically, possess research skills to monitor consumers' perceptions, and be able work as part of a team, especially with the marketing department. The increasing overlap among many health-care departments requires a working knowledge of other disciplines to facilitate decision making and more effective communication.

Public relations professionals are adapting to the digital age, in which traditional media are giving way to online media. Many hospitals create and maintain media centers on their Web sites to enable journalists and others to have access to a variety of health information as well as podcasts, videos, and photos. Internal communication quickly becomes external, and critics who blog can negatively affect an organization's brand or reputation. In this environment, public relations must counsel senior leaders, monitor multiple media, plan strategic communication, and help demonstrate value for their organizations.

Public relations and marketing, although distinct management functions, work closely together in today's health-care environment, utilizing their respective strengths to enhance the survival of health-care organizations.

Role of the News Media

In a 2005 Kaiser Family Foundation poll, Americans were asked to choose the most important health issue that the president of the United States and Congress should address. They named health-care costs (39 percent), access to care and insurance (23 percent), and senior citizens' issues (13 percent).[26]

Although the media cover health care as intensely as ever, it is the way they cover the news that is changing dramatically. The emergence of the Internet and availability of Web sites is causing a fundamental change in the nature of health-care media relations. Millions now use the Internet as a source of health information. Health-care organizations make their own news stories available to a worldwide audience by posting them on Web sites. Whether reporting on a breaking news story or just looking for story ideas, health reporters more frequently turn to company Web sites. Even news organizations have created their own Web sites, which is also changing the nature of health news reporting.

Even though technology offers many communication advantages to hospitals and health-care organizations, today's environment is still characterized by increased media scrutiny of health-care operations. According to Bruce Vladeck, then president of the United Hospital Fund:

> Of all the tasks of leadership in health-care organizations, maintaining communications between the organization and its communities is perhaps the most important.[27]

Although Web sites, paid advertising, community relations, interpersonal communication, publications, videos, CDs, and DVDs all play a role in reaching target publics, the mainstream mass media still play an important role in setting the health-care agenda, explaining health-care issues, and shaping the reputation of hospitals.

Just as in other industries, the keys to good media relations in hospital or health-care settings are honesty, rapid access to decision makers, and prompt response to inquiries. Most hospitals have an authorized spokesperson on call 24 hours a day to answer inquiries from the media. Journalists expect hospital administrators and senior leaders to be accessible—especially in crises. How the public relations staff responds to media needs in routine and crisis situations can have a lasting impact on the organization's reputation.

Media requests for hospitalized patient condition reports, however, have strained relationships between the media and public relations practitioners. The Health Insurance Portability and Accountability Act of 1996 (HIPPA), which went into effect in 2003, creates strict rules governing patient privacy rights. One of HIPPA's most notable restrictions is that the media must have a patient's first and last name before hospital officials can release patient condition reports. Without the patient's name, the hospital cannot even acknowledge that the patient is in the hospital.

HIPPA rules may prevent hospitals from responding to allegations made by disgruntled patients who take their complaint to the media or post them on the Internet (see Exhibit 17.2).

Whether adapting to legislation or responding to economic and social changes, public relations in the health industry has emerged in recent years as a vital member of the management team. Steven V. Seekins, former vice president of the American Medical Association and an accredited member of PRSA, identifies an increasingly important role for practitioners in health-care settings: "To make public relations indispensable to senior management, practitioners must stake out issues management as an area of expertise."[28] No doubt the complex and hotly contested public debate on how to make quality health care both affordable and available to all those in need will continue for years. All parties in the debate will call on public relations practitioners to help set the agenda and to contribute constructively to shaping public policy in health care.

Nongovernmental Organizations

In addition to delivering health care, providing grants and education, and other services, nonprofit and charitable organizations also advocate for public policy on behalf of the people they serve. The term *nongovernmental organization*, or

---

EXHIBIT 17.2

When Patients Go Public with Complaints

In a health-care environment characterized by diminishing public trust, increased litigation, a scrutinizing media, and a 24-hour news cycle, hospitals and health-care organizations find themselves the target of patient allegations about poor-quality care, denying access to care, failure to provide coverage of a procedure, and other issues.

Disgruntled patients may take their complaints to the media. If a patient's complaint sounds compelling, the media may decide to do a story. Unless the patient has a signed HIPPA consent form, the hospital cannot respond to the specific allegations, even if they are untrue. These patients also write letters to the editor, expressing their negative views of their experience at a health-care organization.

More and more, unhappy patients take matters into their own hands—with the help of technology. For example, they criticize the hospital or staff on blogs or post negative opinions on Web sites.

In these situations, how can an institution respond? That is a challenge facing public relations professionals today. Although HIPPA restricts the information hospitals can release about individuals, the hospital spokesperson should first express concern about the allegations and a strong commitment to look into them. The spokesperson can explain hospital policies and procedures or convey key general messages about quality of care or the expertise of the staff.

In addition, hospitals may choose to retain the services of companies that specialize in Internet-based monitoring of online media coverage as well as blogs and other discussion areas to find out what is being said about the organization. Knowing what is being said in these venues helps public relations professionals determine appropriate response options.

FIGURE 17.5

ConsumerFreedom.com Advocacy Advertisement

Courtesy The Center for Consumer Freedom, Washington, DC.

NGO, refers to a wide variety of institutions that may provide funding, technical advice, and advocacy for people in need. By focusing on a specific mission or cause and relying on the passionate support of committed volunteers, NGOs are able to address issues that others cannot or would not (see Figure 17.5).[29]

NGOs focus on a range of issues such as human rights, environmental protection, animal rights, disaster relief, racial equality, political freedom, and more. NGOs can range in size from large international groups to local "grass-roots" groups. They may be called membership or voluntary organizations, advocacy groups, development agencies, or mutual aid societies.[30]

A few examples of NGOs include:

1. Greenpeace and the Sierra Club, international organizations dedicated to protecting the environment

2. Alcoholics Anonymous, a voluntary worldwide fellowship of people who meet to attain and maintain sobriety

3. Red Cross, an international organization that mobilizes communities to help people prevent, prepare for, and respond to disasters

4. Salvation Army, a charitable and religious organization that cares for the poor and homeless

5. CORE, the Congress of Racial Equality, which promotes harmony among all people regardless of race, creed, sex, disability, sexual orientation, religion, or ethnic background

6. Human Rights Watch, an international organization dedicated to preventing discrimination, upholding political freedom, and publicizing human rights violations

7. Save the Children, an international relief and development organization, which works with families to create opportunities for children to live safe, healthy, and fulfilling lives

8. Girl Scouts of the USA, an organization dedicated to helping girls develop leadership, values, social conscience, and commitment about their self-worth

9. Catholic Church, the largest Christian church in the world that advocates for social justice around numerous issues including poverty, arms control, death penalty, refugees, and so on

10. American Civil Liberties Union, or ACLU, a nonprofit organization that works to ensure that rights and freedoms guaranteed in the U.S. Constitution are not denied to individuals

NGOs are not part of governments, but to achieve their missions, they may collaborate with governments or try to influence government policies to benefit to the poor and needy. For example, NGOs attempt to fill humanitarian needs in war zones like Iraq and Afghanistan because the U.S. military is not equipped to provide humanitarian or reconstruction aid.[31]

Not all governments are willing to cooperate with NGOs. Human Rights Watch is an independent NGO that monitors and reports on human rights violations, wherever they occur. It advocates for workers' rights to unionize, voting rights, the safety of prisoners, the right of free speech and a fair trial, against racism, and more. HRW became involved in Middle East politics when it charged Hezbollah with attacking civilians during its war with Israel. Rockets were fired into northern Israel resulting in civilian casualties. Lebanon quickly condemned Human Rights Watch, saying that its people were victims of Israel bombing of southern Lebanon.[32]

NGOs deliver humanitarian aid around the world, sometimes in dangerous places. In 2001 President Bush directed federal dollars to faith-based organizations to help them achieve their humanitarian missions. He doubled the percentage of U.S. foreign aid going to groups like Food for the Hungry, World Vision, and Catholic Relief Services to provide training in hygiene, childhood illness, AIDS relief in Africa, clean water in Third World countries, and so on. Many in Congress who advocate for separation of church and state challenged the president's initiative.[33]

Although NGOs conduct humanitarian missions, volunteers with NGOs still may face dangers. Workers for the Red Cross, United Nations, and other agencies have been attacked, captured, or killed. But while danger is a reality for agencies delivering these services, there are rewards as well. In 1999, the Nobel Peace Prize was presented to Doctors Without Borders, an NGO that delivers emergency medical assistance to people affected by war, epidemics, and disaster throughout the world.

Education

Education touches the lives of virtually every citizen. More than 75.7 million students ages 3 and older are enrolled in school.[34] In 2006 there were 6.8 million teachers in the United States, with 2.7 million teaching at the elementary and middle school level.[35] Federal, state, and local governments spent $497 billion dollars a year for elementary and high school education in 2004–2005.[36]

Access, Affordability, and Accountability

Since the 1980s, policy makers, business leaders, professionals, and parents have challenged the efficacy of public education. The public has debated education reform ever since. The emerging consensus seems to be that major structural change is needed to fix the system's most pressing challenges of access, affordability, and accountability.

Differences in access to college, for example, are significant. Just 60 percent of America's low-income children can expect to graduate from high school, and one in three can expect to enroll in college. To rectify this situation, many experts say that improvements must be made in academic preparation, including helping students to recognize the link between college graduation and their desired careers.[37]

Virtually everyone demands that schools be more accountable. Demands for accountability have moved far beyond student achievement scores to include calls for teacher competency tests and the institution of merit-based incentive pay. Taxpayers and legislators reject the notion that schools and universities will improve if given more funds. Educators and schools believe that demanding change without reallocating or adding additional resources will not work.

Funding is an ongoing challenge for schools, whether the K–12 level or college. In recent years, many states have not increased higher education budgets enough to cover increased costs and demands for classes, research, and off-campus services. When federal funds are available to help local schools, they generally come with requirements on how the funds can be spent.

On many college campuses, an increasing share of the cost is being covered by increases in student tuition and fees. Some schools have formed their own foundations and encourage public relations to become involved in fund raising, or "development," as it is often called.

Central to the difficult task facing public education is widespread concern that the money taxpayers spend on their schools and universities is not used effectively, and that educational outcomes are not satisfactory.

However, addressing these issues is not a simple task. Education reform involves many more dimensions, including parental involvement, the physical and emotional health of children, cultural diversity, class size, relevant programming, how technology is changing learning, transportation and access issues, overcoming financial barriers, and many more. Then there is the issue of public perceptions. While about half of those who graduate high school are prepared for college-level math and science, the reading and math scores in the early grades are at all-time highs for Hispanic and African American students.[38]

Public Relations for Public Schools

The major objectives of public relations for public schools include the following:

1. To increase awareness of educational issues, especially funding issues, to dispel misinformation and rumor (see Figure 17.6)
2. To cultivate relationships with key constituents to build public support and help ensure adequate funding, including donations where appropriate
3. To gain public acceptance of educational initiatives and support when making educational changes
4. To enhance the reputation of schools among key target audiences

FIGURE 17.6

Public School Literature

Courtesy Williamsburg–James City County Public Schools, Williamsburg, Virginia.

Public relations for education is expanding in scope, concept, and utilization. It has taken on increased importance as officials try to persuade taxpayers to raise school levies to cope with inflation or to pass bond issues for new buildings. In addition to helping schools address the financial issues, public relations directors help school officials deal with other crises. Some examples include responding to the pledge of allegiance debate and the broader separation of church and state issue, determining when freedom of expression becomes hate speech, responding to the changing educational needs of society, incorporating technology in the classroom, and clarifying the role of the school in social issues such as sex education and providing condoms on campus.

The relationships between educational institutions and the communities they serve are many, diverse, and complex. Key target audiences for education include parents and students, school staff and administration, business and community groups, and local news media.

1. *Parents play a key role in building support for adequate budgets.* Good relationships with parents start with frequent, frank communication between teachers and parents.

2. *School staff, from principal and teacher to custodian and school nurse, must become engaged in school public relations programs.* Many superintendents have organized advisory councils that include representatives from all categories of employees.

3. *Students may be the school system's most important public.* School executives should ensure that pupils are well informed about policies, that courses satisfy their needs and challenge their abilities, that individual attention is provided to those who need it, and that the overall atmosphere engenders pupil and parent pride in the school.

4. *Business community and school partnerships take many forms.* These can include adopt-a-school programs, resource sharing, consultation in management and technology, and advocacy with state and local governments to increase support for public schools.

5. *Community groups, such as neighbors, potential donors, and other concerned citizens.* These may be reached through Parent-Teacher Association (PTA) meetings, special events and forums, service clubs, church groups, Web sites, the media, and so on.

6. *Local news media, cable television, and Web sites are key to informing the public about local school challenges.* To obtain strategic news coverage, schools must be creative and persistent in sharing information about educational curriculum and policies.

7. *Board of education members who can act as intermediaries between school publics and the professional administrators.* It is essential that board members agree on an adequate statement of public relations policy.

Higher Education

Enrollment in colleges and universities continues to grow, with an estimated 17 million people enrolled in college in 2006.[39] The children of baby boomers are now graduating from high school and entering college, a trend that will continue for several years. In addition to increased numbers, the race and ethnic composition of college students is shifting with more African, Hispanic, and Asian Americans and foreign-born students enrolled in higher education.[40] The demand is increasing for more classes and newly added disciplines like information and technology science, as well as for more computers and Internet access. Although citizens do not want to spend more money on education, they also do not want to see classes cut. This creates challenges for higher education administrators as they hire faculty and staff, expand facilities, and add new technology.[41]

Higher education faces four continuing problems:

1. Financial support is insufficient and precarious.
2. Competition for qualified students is spirited and costly.

3. Government constraints and regulations make university administration difficult and costly.

4. Academic freedom and tenure are challenged by both internal and external stakeholders.

Higher education must "meet these issues head on," according to Gail Raiman, vice president for public affairs, National Association of Independent Colleges and Universities:

> Just as the media are being more aggressive in covering education, we must be more aggressive in educating the public and opinion leaders. We need to use clear language, not academic jargon. We have to go to these opinion leaders instead of waiting for them to come to us.[42]

Although change has always been slow in higher education, public relations offices are increasingly open to change. Researchers Christopher Simpson and Teresa Parrot concluded that a new and expanded communication office will beceome even more essential to colleges' and universities' long-term success. The new office, however, will:

> . . . centralize, or at least coordinate, all internal and external communications ranging from recruiting to fund raising to alumni participation and more traditional uses of media, publications and special events. And in each case, they must use state-of-the-art communications, and their achievements—or lack thereof—will be measured quantitatively.[43]

Today, colleges face public relations challenges unlike anything in the past. Public relations departments now align themselves closely with university advancement and alumni associations to strengthen fund-raising efforts and increase donations and financial gifts. In the past, improving access to a college education was a priority; today an equal emphasis is placed on helping students succeed and graduate. Graduation rate, for example, is one measure of accountability in higher education.

In addition, a great deal of time is spent on reputation management and enhancing the univertity's brand image, which includes building trust. Advances in communication technology now require universities to act quicker than ever before and during crises. For example, a shooting rampage at Virginia Tech University that left 33 people dead has raised expectations about how fast a university must notify students, parents, and the community as a whole about a campus crisis.

To achieve public relations goals in higher education, programs typically target the following key publics:

1. *Students.* Students are both a university's most important public and its most important public relations representatives.

2. *Faculty and staff.* Faculty and staff are important internal publics because of their critical roles in education and governance, and their role as representatives of the university to external constituencies.

3. *Alumni.* Alumni contributions are the single most important source of voluntary support in higher education.

4. *Community groups and business leaders.* Many colleges and universities are turning to the business sector to build new, mutually beneficial relationships.

5. *Government.* Public relations must build understanding and support in all levels of government, especially in education departments.

6. *Media.* Building positive media relations is an investment that pays off over the long term. But centralizing and coordinating the news flow from the campus can be difficult to achieve. A college or university "speaks" with many voices—the president and other administrators, the public information office, the student newspaper and radio station, the faculty, and the athletic director and coaches, to name but a few.

7. *Parents and others.* Parents are a ready-made nucleus of support. Other publics include prospective students and their parents, current and prospective donors, opinion leaders, philanthropic foundations, sister educational institutions worldwide, and professional organizations and scholarly societies.

College Presidents' Public Relations Role

Presidents must be effective communicators and mediators to balance the conflicting values and demands of key target publics. They must recognize that public relations is a required part of the job. Almost a third of university and college presidents say that they meet more frequently with their public relations officers than with any other member of the management team.[44] The president is the key to establishing the relationships and public support needed to fulfill higher education's mission in the new global society. As one former president said, "The president is the one best able to sell the entire institution."[45]

Churches and Other Nonprofit Organizations

Space does not allow detailed analysis of all nonprofit settings. Brief descriptions of some of the issues and pressures on churches, libraries, museums, and arts groups will illustrate how the practice of public relations is both as complex and as essential in these settings as in other nonprofit settings. Public relations plays a role in advocating for nonprofit organizations (see Figure 17.7).

Religion remains an important part of American life. According to the Pew Research Center for People and the Press, about 8 in 10 Americans have no doubt that God exists, and that prayer is important in their daily lives.[46]

Religion is a strong and growing force in the way Americans think about politics and government, but things are changing. The Pew survey reveals a growing gap in religious belief. For example, Republicans express greater religious commitment now than in the past 20 years, while Democrats express less. While 5 percent of Republicans say they are atheist, agnostic, or decline to state a religious preference, the number of Democrats in this category increased from 7 percent 20 years ago to 11 percent in 2007.[47]

Religion's increasing influence on political opinion and behavior rivals factors such as race, region, age, social class, and gender. Those who say religion plays a very important role in their lives are more conservative, but there is little indication of a coherent pattern of liberal belief associated with any major religion or religious group.[48]

The Pew study also reports a slow but steady decline in the number of Americans who support traditional or conservative values, while the public is increasingly accepting of homosexuality. For example, in 1987, 73 percent of white evangelic Protestants agreed that school boards had the right to fire homosexual teachers, compared to just 42 percent who felt that way in 2007.

"Meet J. Robert Anderson, Philanthropist"

FIGURE 17.7

"Meet J. Robert Anderson Philanthropist"

Courtesy The Advertising Council.

Meet J. Robert Anderson, philanthropist.

He's not a millionaire. In fact, he's not even rich. But he gives.

Most of the giving in this country doesn't come from the wealthy. Almost half of it comes from people who earn less than $20,000 a year. Everyday, ordinary people. Like the guy down the street. Or your next-door neighbor. Or 100 million others who, every year, give unselfishly just to help people.

And while those who give may sometimes go unnoticed, their contributions don't. Because in this country, when a lot of people give, it adds up to a lot.

It helps fund important research. It helps run community church programs. It helps support local charities.

It helps people out.

There are so many things in this country that could use your hand. Your time, your tal-ents, your money. What you give isn't so important. That you do give is. Because you don't have to

be rich to be a philanthropist. You just have to care.

A Public Service of This Publication & The Advertising Council

From the Advertising Council.

Organized religion is actively participating in social change efforts. For example, the nonprofit National Council of Churches has joined with 100 business leaders, religious groups, unions, insurers, consumer organizations, and provider groups to call on our nation's policy makers to dramatically overhaul the health-care system.[49]

Even in good times, however, the church is not immune from public relations crises. The child molestation scandal in the Catholic Church caused community outrage, as well as shock and sadness among churchgoers and the vast majority of priests and clergy. Some television evangelists and faith healers have been exposed as lavish spenders and frauds. The 2003 election of the Episcopal Church's first openly gay bishop, Gene Robinson, created a crisis within the church, with conservative and traditionalist bishops raising the possibility that the church would split over this issue.[50] Sure enough, the Diocese of San Joaquin voted December 8, 2007, to secede from the Episcopal Church and to join the Worldwide Anglican Communion. Similar controversy accompanied the 2006 election of Katherine Jefferts Schori as presiding bishop, because Jefferts Schori is a woman. Some dioceses—including the Diocese of San Joaquin—said they would reject her authority and asked to be assigned a different presiding bishop. Early in 2008, church leaders dismissed the conservative San Joaquin bishop in an attempt to regain control of that diocese.[51]

On top of such crises and activism, churches face increased competition for volunteer commitment and dollars. Slightly less than half the nation's population are regular churchgoers. Declining participation and the financial squeeze have underlined the importance of public relations to many church leaders. As a major force in society and social change, however, the church cannot avoid the spotlight. Virtually all the major denominations as well as many smaller churches and church-affiliated schools or hospitals have professional communicators on staff or public relations firms on retainer. With this professional help, churches are better able to respond to crises, convey strategic messages, enhance the image of churches, recruit new members, and strengthen the faith.

Although apparently much less controversial by their very nature and missions, libraries, museums, and arts groups also compete for public support in the form of volunteers, donations, and public funding. Many of these important institutions, which contribute so much to the quality of life, live in a financial straitjacket that does not permit adequate funding either for their programs or for professional public relations assistance.

Most public libraries in major cities have public relations departments, usually called public information departments. However, in smaller cities and suburbs, the public libraries may have very small staffs that do not include public relations expertise. At best, these libraries may take advantage of volunteer support and special events like National Library Week to achieve limited public relations objectives. To provide effective public relations support to its many small libraries, Wisconsin established the Coordinated Library Information Program, which provides the counsel of a public relations specialist to libraries in that state.

Similarly, arts groups face a constant battle to keep the financial wolf from the door. In recent years, both foundations and governments have cut support of cultural institutions and museums.

By necessity, nonprofit organizations recognize the importance of effective public relations and have come to rely on it to attract volunteers and to obtain funding from donors and other public and private sources. Without effective public relations, many nonprofits would have to close their doors, which in some cases would leave the most vulnerable members of society with nowhere to turn.

Associations and Societies

A trade association is an organization dedicated to promoting the interests and assisting the members of a particular industry. Associations exist to advance the interests of their members by offering educational and professional development, certification and standards, codes of ethics, information, research, a forum to discuss common issues, and community service or volunteer opportunities. Associations typically publish newsletters, magazines, and other publications. They often sponsor trade shows and hold conferences. People join associations because they want to work together on a common cause or interest such as to advance careers, help fight medical problems, pursue hobbies, and more.

There are several types of associations, including trade associations, professional societies, chambers of commerce, philanthropic or charitable organizations, and labor associations. To determine an exact number of associations it is helpful to distinguish the types. For example, according to the U.S. Bureau of Labor Statistics, there are 102,000 business, professional, and other membership organizations.[52] The online *Encyclopedia of Associations* profiles more than 135,000 associations worldwide, including more than 115,00 U.S. national, state, and local associations.[53]

Associations represent a significant economic impact, employing more than 1 million Americans in 2006 in a wide range of industries. Business and professional associations bring in about $33 billion in revenue annually.[54]

Types of Associations

Professional associations and *professional societies* typically represent individuals engaged in similar work based on common educational preparation or specialized knowledge. Examples include the American Nurses' Association, the American Bar Association, and the Public Relations Society of America. *Cause groups* and *special-interest groups* function as associations of individuals with a common interest or goal. Examples include the National Audubon Society and the American Automobile Association.

Membership in the more than 3,500 *trade associations* includes companies, firms, or other organizations engaged in similar activities. Business competitors associate in order to organize and implement mutual-assistance efforts and to expand or protect their industry. Examples include the Alliance of Automobile Manufacturers, with only nine members, and the National Automobile Dealers Association, with more than 19,700 new car and truck dealer members.

Producer associations and *commodity boards*, such as the National Dairy Promotion and Research Board and the National Livestock and Meat Board, represent the interests of their members and promote consumption of their commodities. For example, the Illinois Pork Producers Association represents the interests of the state's more than 4,000 pork producers and promotes consumer preference for pork.

Federations—also referred to as councils or institutes—typically include other associations. For example, the International Federation of Library Associations and Institutions has more than 1,700 member associations and individual institutions in 155 countries. The National Cotton Council of America represents associations of cotton producers, ginners, warehouse managers, merchants, and so on to unify their efforts to promote the cotton industry.

Federations of labor unions, such as the Teamsters and the American Federation of Labor and Congress of Industrial Organizations (AFL-CIO), represent many different occupational, trade, and craft unions. The AFL-CIO, for example, represents 56 national and international labor unions and more than 10 million members.[55]

Well-known national associations include the American Tobacco Institute, which represents a relatively small number of corporations but is a powerful association, and the YMCA of the USA with more than 20 million served and more than 560,000 volunteers.[56] One of the most influential associations in the United States, the AARP (formerly the American Associated of Retired Persons), flexed its muscle on behalf of just under 38 million members and championed the Medicare prescription drug bill.[57] The American Bar Association is an organization of more than 400,000 legal professionals that promotes improvements in the American system of justice.[58]

At the state level, the California Milk Advisory Board promotes consumption of dairy products on behalf of the state's dairy farmers and the California Milk

Processors Board promotes fluid milk consumption on behalf of the state's dairy processors. Another statewide dairy association, the Dairy Council of California (DCC), conducts nutrition education programs financed by both dairy farmers and dairy processors. In 2008, DCC had a budget of $6 million, 5 offices, 30 professionals working in nutrition education, and the services of the San Diego public relations firm of Nuffer, Smith, Tucker, Inc. Their educational programs are presented in elementary and secondary school classrooms, online and offline media, and through medical and nutrition communities.[59]

The resources dairy associations are able to direct to such activities illustrate the power of producer groups: Congress mandated that dairy farmers nationally contribute a 15-cent checkoff on every 100 pounds of milk produced to promote dairy products. Five cents of the checkoff goes to the National Dairy Promotion and Research Board, 5 cents goes to state or regional promotion organizations, and the remaining 5 cents (sometimes referred to as the "middle nickel") can go to either the national or state organization, depending on which one individual dairy farmers designate.[60] Likewise, pork producers pay 40 cents out of every $100 worth of pigs sold to fund pork promotion, education, and research.

The Problem of Serving Many Masters

In contrast to corporations and other organizations with clearly defined business interests, associations typically serve a variety of membership interests. Association staffs must attempt to meet membership demands and serve their interests externally but often must do so with little centralized power and authority. The challenge for public relations is to find the common ground and unifying positions that best represent member interests. Thus, associations are by nature limited to areas of action in which there is general agreement or a substantial majority in support of any initiatives taken on behalf of membership.

Associations log nearly 200 million volunteer hours with activities such as organizing blood drives for the American Red Cross, contributing to the United Way, delivering Meals On Wheels, staffing hotlines, and more. Associations also protect consumers by ensuring high professional standards, disseminating accurate information to those who need it most, or providing educational background on health care, tax reform, product safety, and other issues affecting Americans.

Growing Importance of Public Relations

Association public relations practitioners design and implement programs to address a variety of challenges:

1. To provide members with helpful information
2. To expand the association by recruiting new members
3. To harmonize member viewpoints by promoting positive positions
4. To promote the industry or profession
5. To influence government legislation and regulation
6. To improve products and services
7. To gain popular support and combat adverse publicity
8. To train recruits and provide continuing education for all members
9. To contribute to social progress by sponsoring public service programs

Labor Unions

Closely related to trade associations are labor unions. A labor union consists of a group of workers who organize to gain improvements in wages, benefits, and work conditions, such as flexibility for meeting job and family obligations and a voice in improving the quality of products and services produced by the companies for whom they work. Examples include the National Education Association, American Postal Workers Union, the International Association of Fire Fighters, the Screen Actors Guild, and the Communication Workers of America.

The American labor movement is credited with helping bring about many of the changes and legislation in civil rights, health, education, and employee rights that have occurred since the death of President Franklin Roosevelt. Labor's clout has diminished in recent years, however, because of changes in the workforce, a series of judicial rulings supportive of management, and declining public support of labor unions.

Organized labor unions, with a total membership of about 15.7 million in 2007, represent 12.1 percent of the American workforce. The union membership rate has steadily declined from a high of 20.1 percent in 1983, the first year for which comparable union data are available.[62]

Still, organized labor has shaped national public opinion and policy. Labor has a rich history of fighting against employer abuses since the early part of the twentieth century and today still stands up for civil and human rights, voting rights, access to health care, better working conditions, protection for immigrant workers, and more.

Organized labor's strong convictions have led to increased political influence. The "American Needs a Raise" campaign by the AFL-CIO has contributed to recent legislation raising the minimum wage. According to AFL-CIO President John Sweeney:

> Minimum-wage workers are doing some of the hardest, most-needed and most-dangerous work in America, with minimal or nonexistent benefits and unforgiving schedules that can mean job loss because of a sick child or transportation breakdown.[63]

But the development of a global economy and international trade agreements such as the North American Free Trade Agreement (NAFTA) has labor leaders concerned that jobs will be lost.

For example, a pilot program that allows a small number of Mexican trucks to travel freely on U.S. highways has prompted the Teamsters Union to launch a campaign to stop the Department of Transportation (DOT) from allowing this program. The union claims that Mexican trucks on U.S. highways represent a safety hazard and will eliminate U.S. jobs. The union efforts include a media outreach, rallies, posters, banners and bumper stickers, a leafleting campaign, and more.[64]

The Problem of Strikes

Through the years, workers have tried to improve living and working conditions. But when their demands were not met, they have sometimes refused to work—that is, go on strike. However, for a variety of political, economic, and social reasons, strikes are not as frequent as they were early in the twentieth century.

Following the bitter, four-month strike by 70,000 United Food and Commercial Workers in Southern California against three grocery firms, the spokesperson for one of the companies said, "I think the lesson coming out of Southern California is clear. No one wins in a strike."[65]

The biggest impediment to a prolonged strike is the growing recognition that strikes may damage both sides. For example, workers only make money when they work, a company that is struck is less able to produce products or serve clients, and customers go elsewhere. When the strike is settled, contractual gains may not offset financial losses, customers may not return, and jobs may be lost permanently.

Despite the risks, inconveniences and costs involved, the strike weapon is still considered essential to labor's success. Media coverage tends to feature picket lines, angry strikers, and vocal labor leaders. Management, on the other hand, is somewhat restricted by law as to what it can say and do. (Review the section in Chapter 6 on the National Labor Act of 1935 and the Taft-Hartley Act of 1947.)

On the surface, it would be easy to advise unions not to go on strike because of the impact on public opinion and on relations with management. But strategic public relations in the labor movement often calls for leveraging labor's position of power in ways that will not be universally popular but that will achieve labor's goals for members.

The Challenge for Labor

In recent years unions have been debating the best ways to reverse the trend of declining membership while finding ways to increase the power of workers. Stephen Lerner, assistant to the president of one of the nation's largest unions, Service Employees International Union (SEIU), suggests that unions need to reorganize for greater effectiveness: "Traditional organizing doesn't let you do enough fast enough, so that's why we don't do it any more. How do we get bigger, faster and grow? We should do all sorts of experiments."[66] Unions would organize faster and be more powerful, according to Lerner, if they merged and realigned to focus on perhaps 15 distinct industries, such as durable manufacturing, retail trade, or finance.

Some argue that if unions are to survive, they must become more productive partners with business. American Rights at Work, an educational and advocacy organization dedicated to improving the climate for America's workers, features four such companies that it says treat workers with respect. They are Harley Davidson, Inc., Cingular Wireless LLC (now AT&T), Ford Motor Co., and Kaiser Permanente, all of which bring the notion of labor management "partnerships" to the workplace.[67]

Recognizing that organized labor must change with the changing environment, David Pearce Snyder says:

> We in America are reinventing our corporations, reinventing government, reinventing labor relations, reinventing health care and public education. We are reinventing all of our great institutions, and when we are all done, we will have reinvented America. The other industrial nations are beginning to reinvent themselves as well. Eventually, the whole world will be reinvented.[68]

The Role of Public Relations

Organized labor's approach to public relations has changed since the early days of George Meany, the first president of the AFL/CIO, who for 25 years was labor's clearly identifiable and unquestioned spokesperson. Today, the skills of public relations specialists and others have been augmented and honed to meet the needs of expanded, more sophisticated programs. Public relations is increasingly involved in identifying new target audiences, establishing and maintaining key relationships, refining messages, building trust, and more. The Digital Age and

When I began working as a young man the government had just started Social Security.

Part of every worker's paycheck would be matched by the boss and sent to the government. When we retired, we'd get enough of our money back to help us get by.

It was sort of a contract between working people and the government.

Now the administration wants to cut out some of the benefits you'd get at 65. And at 62 they want to cut your benefits . . . from 80% to 55%.

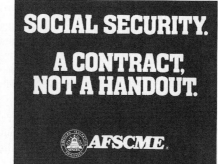

SOCIAL SECURITY.
A CONTRACT, NOT A HANDOUT.

AFSCME.

FIGURE 17.9

Afscme Television Spot, "Social Security"

Courtesy American Federation of State, County, and Municipal Employees.

globalization are forcing unions to better utilize public relations to mobilize members, tell their story, and gain public support. Public affairs management teams are now using research and the Internet along with the traditional means such as media relations, upgraded newsletters, and public service announcements (see Figure 17.9).

In labor unions, as in all other organizational settings, public relations will play a central role as organizations reinvent themselves and their relationships with publics. Change, in the final analysis, drives the public relations management function in all organizations.

Notes

[1] Eikenberry, Angela M. "Creating Social Equity: What Role for Nonprofit Organizations?" Unpublished manuscript presented to the National Academy of Public Administration Standing Panel on Social Equity in Governance's Social Equity Leadership Conference, 2 February 2006, page 4. 10 April 2008, www.napawash.org/aa_social_equity/Omaha-Aeikenberry.pdf.

[2] Lester M. Salamon and Helmet K. Anheier, *The Emerging Nonprofit Sector: An Overview* (Manchester, UK: Manchester University Press, 1996), 33–42.

[3] National Center for Charitable Statistics, "How Many Nonprofit Organizations Are There in the United States?" 10 April 2008, http://nccs.urban.org/resources/faq.cfm.

[4] Peter Dobkin Hall, *Inventing the Nonprofit Sector and Other Essays on Philanthropy, Voluntarism, and Nonprofit Organizations* (Baltimore, MD: Johns Hopkins University Press, 1992), 13, 14, and 82.

[5] Points of Light & Hands On Network, Commentary and Speeches, "Former President Bush Addresses Volunteer Leaders at the 2004 National Conference," 2004. 15 January 2008, http://nonprofit.about.com.

[6] Eikenberry, "Creating Social Equity," p. 2.

[7] United States Department of Labor, Bureau of Labor Statistics, "Volunteering in the United States 2007." 17 January 2008, http://www.bls.gov/news.release/union2.nr0.htm.

[8] Giving USA Foundation, "U.S. Charitable Giving Reaches $295.02 Billion in 2006." News release, 25 June 2007. Available at http://www.givingusa.org/press_releases/gusa.cfm.

[9] Ibid.

[10] Public Agenda Report, *The Charitable Impulse*, "New Study Shows Givers See Nation's Charities as Crucially Important But Wary of Slick, Pushy Marketing." News release, 24 October 2005. Available at http://nonprofit.about.com/od/trendsissuesstatistics/a/realitycheck.htm.

[11] Sharyl Attkisson, three-part series: "Disaster Strikes in the Red Cross Backyard," "Red Faces at the Red Cross," "The Battle Inside the Red Cross," July 2002. 8 January 2008. http://www.cbsnews.com.

[12] Ibid.

[13] Dana Priest and Anne Hull, "Soldiers Face Neglect, Frustration at Army's Top Facility," *Washington Post*, 18 February 2007: A01. Online at http://www.washingtonpost.com/wp-dyn/content/article/2007/02/17/AR2007021701172.html?referrer=emailarticle.

[14] Steve Vogel and William Branigan, "Army Fires Commander of Walter Reed; Former Chief, Also Criticized in Troop-Care Scandal, Temporarily Takes Over," *Washington Post*, 2 March 2007: A01. Online at http://www.washingtonpost.com/wp-dyn/content/article/2007/03/01/AR2007030100999.html.

[15] "Quality Counts 2008: Tapping into Teaching," *Education Week* (January 11, 2008). April 4, 2008, http://www.edweek.org/chat/transcript_01_11_08.html?qs = Quality+Counts+2008.

[16] Salamon and Anheier, *The Emerging Nonprofit Sector: An Overview*, 66.

[17] The Foundation Center, "Frequently Asked Questions/What Is a Foundation?" 10 April 2008 http://foundationcenter.org/getstarted/faqs/html/foundfun.html.

[18] Ibid.

[19] The Foundation Center, "*Foundation Giving Trends*, 2008 Edition, February 28, 2008, press release. Available at http://foundationcenter.org/media/news/pr_0802b.html.

[20] FedEx Corporation, "FedEx and the American Red Cross," 9 February 2008, http://www.fedex.com/us/about/responsibility/community/redcross.html

[21] Joanne Fritz, "Cause-Related Marketing: What You Need to Know," About.com, Nonprofit Charitable Organizations. 15 February 2008, http://nonprofit.about.com/od/fundraising/a/causemarketing.htm.

[22] Product (RED), "What (RED) Is." 7 March 2008, http://www.joinred.com/red.

[23] Sherry Glied, Ph.D., "Healthcare Crisis: Who's At Risk" (Division of Health Policy and Management, Columbia University, not dated). Posted at http://www.pbs.org/healthcarecrisis/Exprts_intrvw/s_glied.htm#Top.

[24] U.S. Census Bureau, Health Insurance Coverage in the United States, contained in the "Income, Poverty, and Health Insurance Coverage in the United States 2006 Report" (August 2007). Available at http://www.census.gov/prod/2007pubs/p60-233.pdf.

[25] Peter Harbage and Len M. Nichols, PhD, "A Premium Price: The Hidden Costs All Californians Pay in Our Fragmented Health Care System," Issue Brief #3. New American Foundation (December 2006). Available at http://www.newamerica.net/files/HealthIBNo3.pdf.

[26] Kaiser Family Foundation, "Health Care Priorities for the President and Congress, Health Poll Report, April 2005." 16 February 2008, http://www.kff.org/healthpollreport/apr_2005/care/3.cfm.

[27] Quoted by David Kirk in "Briefings: Hospital Research Targets 'Key Leaders,'" *Public Relations Journal* 49, no. 3 (March 1993): 12.

[28] Steven V. Seekins, "Forecast 1993: System Reform Looms," *Public Relations Journal* 49, no. 1 (January 1993): 21.

[29] John F. Seffrin, "United States Nongovernmental Organizations" (Encyclopedia of Public Health, undated). 11

April 2008, http://www.answers.com/nongovernmental%20organization.

[30] Ibid.

[31] Emily Bazar, "Iraq's Violence Tests Limits of Humanitarian Groups' Resolve." *USA Today,* 27 January 2007: A-9. 2 March 2008, http://proquest.umi.com/pqdweb?did=1203541701&Fmt=3&clientId=17862&RQT=309&VName=PQD.

[32] Hassan M. Fattah, "Rights Group Accuses Hezbollah of Indiscriminate Attacks on Civilians; Lebanon: Hezbollah Attacks on Haifa Designed to Kill Civilians," New York, July 18, 2006. 2 March 2008, http://www.hrw.org/english/docs/2006/07/18/lebano13760.htm.

[33] Farah Stockman, Michael Kranish, Peter S. Canellos, and Kevin Baron, "Bush Brings Faith to Foreign Aid," *Boston Globe*, Oct 8, 2006, p. A1. Online at http://proquest.umi.com/pqdweb?did=1142894051&Fmt=3&clientId=17862&RQT=309&VName=PQD.

[34] U.S. Census Bureau 2005, School Enrollment, "Table 1. Enrollment Status of the Population 3 Years Old and Over, by Sex, Age, Race, Hispanic Origin, Foreign-Born Parentage: October 2005." 19 February 2008, http://www.census.gov/population/www/socdemo/school/cps2005.html.

[35] U.S. Census Bureau, Newsroom, "Facts for Features, Back to School: 2006-2007," August 16, 2006 (reissued), 15 April 2008, http://www.census.gov/Press-Release/www/releases/archives/facts_for_features_special_editions/007108.html.

[36] U.S. Census Bureau, "Public Education Finances, Table 1. Summary of Public School Finances for Elementary-Secondary Education by State: 2004–2005," May 24, 2007, 19 February 2008, http://www.census.gov/govs/www/school05.html.

[37] William Bedsworth, Susan Colby, and Joe Doctor, "Reclaiming the American Dream, Executive Summary," The Bridgespan Group, October 2006. 9 February 2008, http://www.bridgespan.org/kno_articles_americandream.html.

[38] Richard D. Bagin, "What's Right with Our Schools," School PR Articles, National Public Relations Association, Copyright 2008, 31 March 2008. http://www.nspra.org.

[39] U.S. Census Bureau, American Fact Finder, American Community Survey, "School Enrollment by Level of School by Type of School for the Population 3 Years and Over," 2006. 14 February 2008, http://factfinder.census.gov/servlet/DTTable?_bm=y&-geo_id=01000US&-ds_name+ACS.

[40] U.S. Census Bureau, Fact Finder/People/Education, "One in Four U.S. Residents Attends School," Oct. 16, 2003. 18 February 2008, http://factfinder.census.gov/jsp/saff/SAFFInfo.jsp?_pageId=tp5_ education.

[41] Personal conversation with Jack Beresford, marketing communication director, San Diego State University, San Diego, CA, July 2004.

[42] Judith R. Phair, "1992 Education Report Card," *Public Relations Journal* 48, no. 2 (February 1992): 23.

[43] Christopher Simpson and Teresa V. Parrot, "University Communications Offices—How Will They Look in 2012?" *University Business* (January 2008). 27 March 2008, http://www.universitybusiness.com/viewarticle.aspx?articleid=990&p=2#0.

[44] "'In' Box," *The Chronicle of Higher Education* 37, no. 47 (August 7, 1991): A9. For the complete report, see Commission on Institutional Relations, Survey of College and University Presidents' Perceptions of the Public Relations Function (Washington, DC: Council for Advancement and Support of Education, 1991).

[45] Michael J. Worth and James W. Asp II, *The Development Officer in Higher Education: Toward an Understanding of the Role*. ASHE-ERIC Higher Education Report No. 4 (Washington, DC: George Washington University, Graduate School of Education and Human Development, 1994), 54.

[46] Pew Research Center for People and the Press, "Trends in Attitudes Toward Religion and Social Issues," March 22, 2007. 28 February 2008, http://pewresearch.org/pubs/614/religion-social-issues.

[47] Ibid.

[48] Pew Research Center for the People & the Press, "Survey Reports 'The Diminishing Divide . . . American Churches, American Politics,'" June 25, 1996.

[49] National Council of Churches, "National Council of Churches, Other Religious Groups Join 100 Organizations Urging Overhaul of Nation's Healthcare System," July 20, 2004. 21 January 2008, http://www.ncccusa.org/news/newshome.html.

[50] Sandi Dolbee, "Hunting for a Healer, San Diego Episcopal Diocese Must Carefully Choose a New Bishop at a Divisive Time for the Denomination," *San Diego Union Tribune*, March 25, 2004.

[51] "Episcopal Leaders Oust Conservative Bishop," *USA Today,* March 12, 2008. Available online at http://www.usatoday.com/news/religion/2008-03-12-episcopal-secession_N.htm (downloaded April 8, 2008).

[52] "Associations Matter: Associations by the Numbers," American Society of Association Executives, Washington D.C. (October 2007), page 12. 11 April 2008, http://www.asaecenter.org/AdvocacyOutreach/content.cfm?ItemNumber=17519&navItemNumber=17537.

[53] *Encyclopedia of Associations* (Farmington, MI: Thomson Gale, January 2006). 11 April 2008, http://library.dialog.com/bluesheets/html/610114.html.

[54] Chris Vest, "Association Jobs Top 1 Million—ASAE & The Center's New Research Looks at Associations by the Numbers," News release, Nov. 15, 2007, American Society

of Association Executives (ASAE), Washington D.C., 2008. 31 March 2008, http://www.asaecenter.org/About Us/newsreldetail.cfm?ItemNumber=29219.

[55] AFL-CIO, "Union Facts, 2008." 31 March 2008. http://www.aflcio.org/aboutus/faq.

[56] YMCA of the USA, "About the YMCA of the USA/2006 Statistics." 29 March 2008, http://www.ymca.net/about_the_ymca.

[57] Letter from Bill Novelli, chief executive officer, *AARP 2006 Annual Report*, p. 4.21, February 2008, http://assets.aarp.org/www.aarp.org_/build/common/pdf/aarp_2006_annual_report.pdf.

[58] "About the American Bar Association," American Bar Association. 9 April 2008, http://www.abanet.org/about.

[59] Personal interview with Bill Trumpfheller, president and CEO, Nuffer, Smith, Tucker, Inc., San Diego, CA, 11 March 2008.

[60] From "Wisconsin Milk Marketing Board 'Middle Nickel,'" unpublished 1993 case study, Morgan and Myers (public relations firm), Waukesha, WI.

[61] Helen Frank Bensimon and Patricia A. Walker, "Associations Gain Prestige and Visibility by Serving as Expert Resources for Media," *Public Relations Journal* 48, no. 2 (February 1992): 16.

[62] U.S. Department of Labor, Washington, D.C. Bureau of Labor Statistics, news release, "Union Members in 2007," Jan. 25, 2008. 1 April 2008, http://www.bls.gov/news.release/union2.nr0.htm.

[63] John J. Sweeney, "Out Front with John Sweeney: America Needs a Raise," March 24, 2006. 1 April 2008, http://www.aflcio.org/aboutus/thisistheaflcio/outfront/america_raise.cfm.

[64] Ted McKenna, "Teamsters Battle DOT over Cross-Border Trade," *PR News*, Feb. 14, 2008. 2 April 2008, http://www.prweekus.com/Teamsters-battle-DOT-over-cross-border-trade/article/105330/.

[65] David Washburn, "Lessons from Grocery Dispute Here Sink in Elsewhere," *San Diego Union Tribune*, July 11, 2004.

[66] David Moberg, "Organize, Strategize, Revitalize; Unions Debate Best Ways to Revive Labor's Fortunes," *In These Times*, 16 January 2004. 19 March 2008, http://www.inthesetimes.com/article/681/.

[67] American Rights at Work (Online), Resources/Fact Sheets/Fact Sheet: "A Profile of High Road Companies," May 23, 2004, http://www.araw.org/resources/facts/highroad.cfm.

[68] David Pearce Snyder, "The Revolution in the Workplace: What's Happening to Our Jobs?" *The Futurist* 30, no. 2 (March–April 1996): 13.

Additional Sources

Alliance for Health Reform, *Covering Health Issues 2006: A Sourcebook for Journalists* (Washington, D.C., 2006). 11 April 2008, http://www.allhealth.org/sourcebook2006/toc.asp.

Andreasen, Alan, and Philip Kotler, *Strategic Marketing for Nonprofit Organizations*, 7th ed. Upper Saddle River, NJ: Prentice Hall, 2008. Outlines application of marketing principles and practices to churches, government agencies, schools, health-care organizations, and fine and performing arts groups.

"Association Public Relations," special issue of *Public Relations Quarterly* 37, no. 1 (Spring 1992). Features a collection of articles on professional, ethical, legal, and management issues in association public relations.

Ballot, Michael. *Labor-Management Relations in a Changing Environment*, 2nd ed. New York: John Wiley and Sons, 1995. Covers the broad field of industrial relations, including the changing relationship between unions and employers, the future of organized labor, and public-sector unionization.

Cutlip, Scott M. *Fundraising in the United States*. New Brunswick, NJ: Transaction Publishers, 1990. Reprint of 1965 classic history of how fund-raising evolved to become big business, its early pioneers, and campaigns that had a major impact on society.

Dunlop, John T. *Industrial Relations Systems*, rev. ed. Boston: Harvard Business School Press, 1993. Former U.S. secretary of labor presents a general theory of industrial relations, outlining the formal and informal ways management organizations, workers, and government agencies are organized.

Godfried, Nathan. *WCFL: Chicago's Voice of Labor, 1926–78*. Champaign: University of Illinois Press, 1997. Traces Chicago Federation of Labor's attempt to create a "voice of labor" by establishing Chicago radio station WCFL.

Heckscher, Charles C. *The New Unionism*, rev. ed. Ithaca, NY: ILR Press, 1996. Argues that the displacement of manufacturing and production line jobs by white-collar and service-sector jobs is eroding the influence of traditional unions slow to change from their nineteenth-century origins.

Kelly, Kathleen S. *Effective Fund-Raising Management*. Mahwah, NJ: Lawrence Erlbaum Associates, 1997. First textbook to cover history, principles, theory, and process of contemporary fund-raising as a specialized public relations practice.

Masters, Marick F. *Unions at the Crossroads: Strategic Membership, Financial, and Political Perspectives*. Westport, CT: Quorum Books, 1997. Analyzes "institutional health" of the 28 unions in the United States with 80 percent of all union members and control over two-thirds of all union wealth.

Robinson, Archie. *George Meany and His Times: A Biography*. New York: Simon & Schuster, 1981. Details the life and personality of the man who shaped the American labor movement and the political events and social changes during his 63 years in labor unions.

INDEX